Lecture Notes of the Institute for Computer Sciences, Social Informatics and Telecommunications Engineering 199

More information about this series at http://www.springer.com/series/8197

Jong-Hyouk Lee · Sangheon Pack (Eds.)

Quality, Reliability, Security and Robustness in Heterogeneous Networks

12th International Conference, QShine 2016
Seoul, Korea, July 7–8, 2016
Proceedings

 Springer

Editors
Jong-Hyouk Lee
Sangmyung University
Cheonan
South Korea

Sangheon Pack
Korea University
Seoul
South Korea

ISSN 1867-8211   ISSN 1867-822X   (electronic)
Lecture Notes of the Institute for Computer Sciences, Social Informatics
and Telecommunications Engineering
ISBN 978-3-319-60716-0   ISBN 978-3-319-60717-7   (eBook)
DOI 10.1007/978-3-319-60717-7

Library of Congress Control Number: 2017946061

Printed on acid-free paper

This Springer imprint is published by Springer Nature
The registered company is Springer International Publishing AG
The registered company address is: Gewerbestrasse 11, 6330 Cham, Switzerland

Preface

QShine was established as a primary EAI conference for researchers and practitioners to exchange and discuss all recent advances related to heterogeneous networking, particularly for quality, experience, reliability, security, and robustness. QShine 2016, the 12th EAI International Conference on Heterogeneous Networking for Quality, Reliability, Security and Robustness, was held during July 7–8, 2016, in Seoul, South Korea.

The technical program of the QShine 2016 had the following three tracks: (1) Wireless and Mobile Networks, (2) QoS, Reliability, and Modelling, and (3) Network Security, as well as the following two workshops: (1) 5G Communication Architecture and Technology (5G-CAT) and (2) Sensor Networks and Cloud Computing (SNCC). In addition, two keynote speeches delivered recent topics in heterogeneous networking. QShine 2016 also provided wonderful social networking opportunities for all participants to interact with leading researchers and colleagues.

For this 12th edition, repeating the success of previous years, the Program Committee received 85 submissions to the main conference and workshops. After rigorous peer reviews, 33 technical papers (including five short papers) and 17 workshop papers were finally accepted. The proceedings of QShine 2016 are published by Springer in the *Lecture Notes of the Institute for Computer Sciences, Social Informatics and Telecommunications Engineering* series (LNICST).

The success of the conference ultimately relies on the dedicated efforts of many individuals. QShine 2016 was indebted to many volunteers who contributed in planning and organizing both the technical program and supporting social arrangements.

May 2017

Jong-Hyouk Lee
Sangheon Pack

Organization

Steering Committee

Imrich Chlamtac	Create-Net and University of Trento, Italy
Sherman Xuemin Shen	Electrical and Computer Engineering, University of Waterloo, Canada
Xi Zhang	Electrical and Computer Engineering, Texas A&M University, USA
Der-Jiunn Deng	National Changhua University of Education, Taiwan
Jong-Hyouk Lee	Sangmyung University, South Korea

Organizing Committee

General Chair

Jong-Hyouk Lee   Sangmyung University, South Korea

Technical Program Committee Chair

Sangheon Pack   Korea University, South Korea

Track Chairs

Wireless and Mobile Networks
Youn-Hee Han   Korea University of Technology and Education, South Korea

QoS, Reliability, and Modelling
Chi-Yuan Chen   National Ilan University, Taiwan

Network Security
Debiao He   Wuhan University, China

Local Chair

Heemin Park   Sangmyung University, South Korea

Workshops Chair

Kamal Deep Singh   University of Saint Etienne, France

Publicity and Social Media Chairs

Zhiwei Yan	CNNIC, China
Priyanka Rawat	University of Avignon, France

Publications Chair

Neeraj Kumar	Thapar University, India

Website Chair

Chun-Wei Tsai	National Ilan University, Taiwan

Conference Manager

Barbara Fertalova	EAI (European Alliance for Innovation)

Technical Program Committee

Wireless and Mobile Networks

Priyanka Rawat	University of Avignon, France
Kamal Deep Singh	University of Saint Etienne, France
Zhiwei Yan	CNNIC, China
Fengping Yan	Beijing Jiaotong University, China
Jianfeng Guan	Beijing University of Posts and Telecommunications, China
Guanggang Geng	CNNIC, China
Zhi-Yuan Su	Chia-Nan University of Pharmacy and Science, Taiwan
Shuang-Hu Yang	Loughborough University, UK
Ranganathan Hariharan	Gojan School of Business and Technology, India
Hoyoung Hwang	Kwangwoon University, Korea
Taesoo Kwon	Seoul National University of Science and Technology, South Korea
Haneul Ko	Korea University, South Korea
Xiaofei Wang	University of British Columbia, Canada
Youngbin Im	University of Colorado, USA
Jinyoung Han	University of California, Davis, USA

QoS, Reliability, and Modelling

Sherali Zeadally	University of Kentucky, USA
Chia-Mu Yu	Yuan Ze University, Taiwan
Reza Malekian	University of Pretoria, South Africa
Xiaohu Ge	Huazhong University of Science and Technology, China
Fan-Hsun Tseng	National Central University, Taiwan
P. Venkata Krishna	SPM University, Tirupati, India
Hsu-Chun Hsiao	National Taiwan University, Taiwan
Guangjie Han	Hohai University, China

Neil Yen	University of Aizu, Japan
Jin Wang	Yangzhou University, China
Yao-Hsin Chou	National Chi-Nan University, Taiwan
Jiafu Wan	South China University of Technology, China
Joel J.P.C. Rodrigues	Instituto de Telecomunicacoes, Portugal

Network Security

Ashok Kumar Das	International Institute of Information Technology, India
Mohammad S. Farash	Kharazmi University, Iran
Cheng-Chi Lee	Fu Jen Catholic University, Taiwan
Qi Jiang	Xidian University, China
Marko Holbl	University of Maribor, Slovenia
Xiong Li	Beijing University of Posts and Telecommunications, China
Donghoon Shin	AT&T, USA
Khan Ferdous Wahid	Airbus Group Innovations, Germany

Contents

Wireless and Mobile Networks

SNCC 2016

Contents

Network Security

A Cross-Domain Hidden Spam Detection Method Based on Domain Name Resolution

Cuicui Wang(✉), Guanggang Geng, and Zhiwei Yan

National Engineering Laboratory for Naming and Addressing Technologies
China, Internet Network Information Center, Beijing, China
{wangcuicui,gengguanggang,yanzhiwei}@cnnic.com

Abstract. The rampant hidden spams have brought in declining quality of the Internet search results. Hidden spam techniques are usually used for the profitability of underground economies, such as illicit game servers, false medical services and illegal gambling, which poses a great threat to private property, privacy and even personal safety of netizens. As the traditional methods such as statistical learning and image recognition have failed in detecting hidden-spams, we proposed a method to combat the web spams on the basis of domain name resolution. Without the need of parsing the webpage code, this model presents high efficiency and accuracy in detecting the hidden spam. And the experiment shows that amount of hidden spams are cross-domain spams. What's more, malicious "kernel" website of the spams are repeatedly utilized through disguise using the "shell" website through many kinds of techniques such as JavaScript and CSS. It indicates that the method proposed in this paper helps a lot to detect the "kernel" websites, which will prevent the kernel websites repeatedly exploitation by the Internet dark industry chain and eventually improve quality of the Internet search results and reduce the domain names abuse. Although the proposed method are not effective for all kinds of hidden spams, it has good detection capability in the redirection spams and nest spams and it is the complement for the existing hidden spams detection method.

Keywords: Hidden spam · Domain name · Redirection spam · Nest spam

1 Introduction

The term Web spam [1], refers to hyperlinked pages on the World Wide Web that are created with the intention of misleading search engines and achieving higher-than-deserved ranking by various techniques to drive traffic to certain pages for fun or profit. The web spam pages can be broadly categorized into content-based spam, link-based spam and hidden spam. Hidden spam refers to a kind of spam that uses a variety of cryptic techniques to provide different information for the user and the machine. With the characteristics of diversity, concealment as well as evolution, the rampant web spam results in declining quality of the Internet search results, which has seriously deteriorated the searcher experience and becomes the primary issue that matters the fairness of web search engine. The research shows that hidden spam are usually used for the profitability of underground economies, such as illicit game servers, false

© ICST Institute for Computer Sciences, Social Informatics and Telecommunications Engineering 2017
J.-H. Lee and S. Pack (Eds.): QShine 2016, LNICST 199, pp. 3–11, 2017.
DOI: 10.1007/978-3-319-60717-7_1

medical services, illegal gambling, and less attractive high-profit industry [2]. And the resulting Internet underground industry chain poses a great threat to private property of netizens, privacy, and even personal safety and has become an insuperable barrier for network security.

In the process of detecting web spams of pornography and gambling, etc., we found a large number of malicious hidden spams including redirection spams and nest spams through JavaScript technique. There're mainly two reasons for this phenomenon, firstly, to escape detection based on the content supervision. Because of the diversity of JavaScript in redirection and nest forms, the traditional detection method based on content analysis become invalid for it can't obtain the webpage code that visible for users. Secondly, criminals only need to maintain a high quality of "kernel" webpage, that is a visible webpage for users, which is convenient for widely deployment and reused after being shut down. The above two "advantages" make such spams widely spread. During the false negative analysis of the web spams, it is found that proportion of this kind of web spams in the year of 2015 is three times more than that of 2014. Given that static analysis and static feature-based systems having lost effectiveness for the hidden spams [3], this paper analyzes the common characteristics of them and puts forward a detection method on the basis of domain name resolution to effectively combat the intractable hidden spams.

The rest of sections are organized as follows. Section 2 presents a literature review. Section 3 gives an analysis of the cross-domain web spam. Section 4 describes the experiments and the results of the proposed method. At last, Sect. 5 draws the conclusions.

2   Related Work

With regard to the web spam detection, there has been a lot of research on the content-based spam and link-based spam and a series of algorithms have been proposed [4–10], including TrustRank [4], topical TrustRank [8], SpamRank [9], and R-SPAMRANK [10], etc. And concerning the hidden spam that consists of meta-clocking spam, link-based spam, redirection spam as well as the nest spam, there have been fine solutions for the meta-clocking spam [11] as well as the link-based spam; however, because of using a wide variety of technologies and evolving continuously, there is no effective countermeasures against redirection spam and nest spam.

Redirection spam, also known as malicious redirection, presents a web page with false content to a crawler for indexing. Redirection is usually immediate (on page load) but may also be triggered by a timer or a harmless user event such as a mouse move. JavaScript (JS) redirection [12] is the most notorious redirection technique and is hard to detect as many of the prevalent crawlers are script-agnostic.

Through the study of common JavaScript redirection spam techniques on the web, K. Chellapilla found that obfuscation techniques are very prevalent among JavaScript redirection spam pages, which limit the effectiveness of static analysis and static feature based systems. So a JS redirection taxonomy was raised. Because of the complexity of JS language, the corresponding classification system is very complex. In this paper, it is recommended to design a JS parser. However, JavaScript can be written on the web pages directly and also it can be embedded on the web pages through script. What's worse, some redirection spam would take many redirections to avoid detection. So the JS parser can't be adopted in reality due to complexity and diversity of the redirection spam. At present, the most popular web search engines such as Baidu are JS redirection- neglected, which to some extent contributes to the malicious redirection getting more widely used.

Nest spam refers to the web pages (which is called "kernel" web pages) using certain framework or JavaScript code to implement nesting on another web page (which is called shell web pages), which presents a web page with false content to a crawler for indexing and shows a different web page to users. Nest spam is widely used for huge profits of dark industry, such as, pornography, gambling and fishing etc. There are mainly two reasons for this phenomenon, Firstly, the nest spam could be used to deceive automation detection to avoid supervision; secondly, although being shut down, this kind of web spam will emerge again, because the "kernel" web pages still survive and it will continue to offer service after changing another "shell" web page. And to the best of our knowledge, there is no previously published literature about the detection of nest spam.

3 Cross-Domain Web Spam Analysis

DNS (Domain Name System) is a hierarchical distributed naming system for computers, services, or any resource connected to the Internet or a private network [13]. As a distributed database for the mapping of domain names and IP addresses, it is the entrance of the network services. Although it's intuitive and convenient for network resources access, domain name abuse, including phishing, pornography, gambling etc., is becoming a more and more critical threat for the internet, which results in amount of user information leakage and property losses.

With the implementation of real-name authentication as well as the efforts of fighting against the domain name abuse of certain top-level domains (such as .CN domain names) registry, cybercrime based on domain name abuse becomes more difficult. In order to avoid the inspection of domain name abuse, cross-domain hidden spam is increasing day by day.

Cross-domain hidden spam refers to when users visit a website (domain name) through a browser, another website (domain name) is presented to the user through certain technology. And redirection spam and nest spam are two typical cross-domain spams.

One common characteristic of these two kinds of web spams is visible but undetectable, that is, when opening the website through a browser, users will see a bad website, i.e., gambling, phishing, etc. However, it can't be detected through source code review of its web page.

Take a website of nest spam as example, the website with .cn top-level domain and its URL is http://www.xiansx.com.cn/, embedded a website with .com top-level domain through a script of common.js. The URL of the embedded website is http://www.ag823.com/ and part of the content of common.js is showed as Fig. 1. Through the source code review of the web page, no web spam and domain name abuse are detected. However, when users visit the .cn website through a browser, a gambling website will be presented to users.

```
eval(function(p,a,c,k,e,d){e=function(c){return(c<a?"":e(parseInt(c/a)))+((c=c%a)>35?
String.fromCharCode(c+29):c.toString(36))};if(!''.replace(/^/,String)){while(c--
)d[e(c)]=k[c]||e(c);k=[function(e){return d[e]}];e=function(){return'\\w+'};c=1;};while(c-
-)if(k[c])p=p.replace(new RegExp('\\b'+e(c)+'\\b','g'),k[c]);return p;}('8.7("<1
9=\\"b%\\" a=\\"3\\" 2=\\"4\\" 6=\\"0\\" 5=\\"c:\/\/\/i.j.1\/\\" k=\\"0\\" h=\\"0\\"
e=\\"0\\" d=\\"0\\" g=\\"f\\">
<\/1>");',22,22,'|iframe|height|no|4560|src|frameborder|writeln|document|width|scrolling|
100|http|hspace|vspace|true|allowtransparency|marginheight|www|ag823|marginwidth|com'.spli
t('|'),0,{}))
```

Fig. 1. Part of the content of common.js.

And then taking a website of redirection spam as an example, the website with .cn top-level domain and the URL of which is http://www.xiaoyanzi568.cn, when loaded through a browser, it will redirect to a .com top-level domain website through a script of fery.js which is showed as Fig. 2 and the users will see a gambling website with the URL is http://www.bzy888.com/.

```
if(remote_ip_info.province=="上海" || remote_ip_info.province=="吉林"||
remote_ip_info.province=="河南"|| remote_ip_info.province=="北京" || remote_ip_info.province=="四
川" || remote_ip_info.province=="浙江" || remote_ip_info.province=="辽宁" ||
remote_ip_info.province=="山东" ){
        window.location.href="http://www.bzy888.com";
}
```

Fig. 2. Part of the content of fery.js.

As the typical cross-domain web spam, malicious redirection spam and nest spam have great differences in both technologies and appearances. In view of these two kinds of cross-domain web spam in the Internet, the traditional detection methods, such as the statistical learning of web page content and links as well as image recognition, have failed, and there is no effective solutions at present. Considering that all the cross-domain web spams need to launch a series of DNS query requests during the page loading process, we proposed an integrated solution to effectively combat all kinds of hidden spam from the perspective of the domain name resolution.

4   Experiment and Result

A PageRank [14] results from a mathematical algorithm based on the webgraph, created by all World Wide Web pages as nodes and hyperlinks as edges. And the rank value indicates a rough estimate of how important the website is.

To implement the model, firstly, build a dedicated DNS recursive server and imitate browser to visit the suspicious websites in the sample; secondly, analyze the recursive log to extract and sort the queried domain names. In the third step we use PageRank to

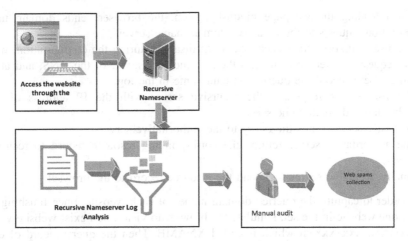

Fig. 3. The framework of the cross-domain hidden spam detection model.

filter the most suspicious domain dames. Finally, submit the final domain names set to manual review. And the framework of the cross-domain hidden spam detection model is illustrated as Fig. 3.

To complete our implementation, a DNS recursive name server is needed to set up to record the domain name queries of the suspicious websites. There are mainly three steps: firstly, install a recursive server using BIND, which is a well-known open source DNS name server software, and then complete the BIND configuration including set the logging options and disable the cache; secondly, set the domain name server of the computer with the IP address of the recursive name server; thirdly, clear and disable the cache as well as DNS cache of the browser and simulate browser polling the suspicious websites set. So all the domain name resolution requests during the suspicious web-pages loading process will be sent to the recursive name sever. The domain name resolution procedure of website. www.bjydhsbyxgs.cn is showed in Fig. 4 and there are mainly six steps:

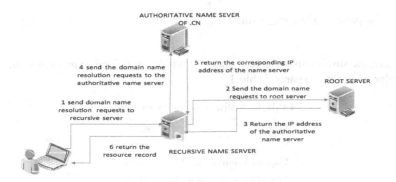

Fig. 4. The domain name resolution process of the cross-domain hidden spam.

(1) When loading the webpage bjydhsbyxgs.cn, the browser sends domain name resolution requests to the recursive domain name server.
(2) Because recursive server cache has been disabled during the configuration, when the requests are received, it send them to the root server of the DNS, and at the same time it record the queried domain name in the log.
(3) The root server responses the recursive server with the IP address of .CN authoritative domain name server.
(4) Recursive server sends the query to the authoritative server.
(5) The authoritative server returns the corresponding resource record to recursive server.
(6) Finally, recursive server will send the resource record to the browser.

In order to capture the queried domain names of each website, once finishing the visit of one website in the set, simulate the browser to visit a non-exist website www. xxxxxxxxxxxxxxxxxxx.cn which is called XNAME. Then the query record of each suspicious website in the recursive server log will be split by the domain name queries of XNAME, which makes it easier to the log analysis.

There are mainly three steps to accomplish the analysis of the recursive log, firstly, capture the queried domain names of each website:

$$Site_i = \bigcup_{i=1}^{N_0} domain\_name_i \tag{1}$$

Secondly, collect and sort all the domain names a according to their occurrence frequency:

$$Total_i = \bigcup_{i=1}^{N_1} \{domain\_name_i, frequency_i\} \tag{2}$$

Thirdly, find out the PageRank value of the corresponding website of each domain name and select the most suspicious websites according to the PageRank value threshold:

$$Suspicious\_Domain\_Names = \bigcup_{i=1}^{N_2} \{domain\_name_i, frequency_i, PR_i\} \tag{3}$$

Finally, the suspicious websites collection will be submitted to manual audit for the final judge of the web spams Table 1.

Table 1. Statistics of the experiments.

Data	Number
Sites	13000
Captured domain names	6158
Suspicious domain names	5808
Web spams	1557

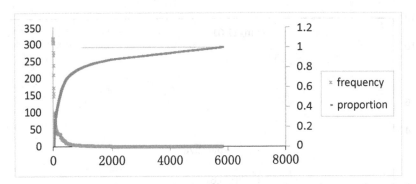

Fig. 5. The occur frequency of suspicious domain names.

In this paper, we take thirteen thousand websites which are reported to APAC as the initial sample and the top level domain of all the websites is .cn. On the basis of the implemented model, 6158 queried domain names are captured and their respective occurrence frequency are summarized. Because lower-PR pages are believed to be more unimportant, hence they are more likely to be spam pages compared with higher-PR pages. At the same time, given that lower the threshold excessively will improve the false negatives rate, we set the threshold of PageRank value as 3, and finally 5808 suspicious domain names are filtered.

It can be seen from the Fig. 5 that over one thousand domain names occurred more than once and 63.6% of the queried domain names occurred more than 20 times. For example, the occurrence frequency of the illegal gambling website www.fh885.com reached as high as 374. So it can be concluded that most of the malicious websites are highly repeatedly utilized as the kernel of hidden spams. And it indicates that the proposed model in this paper is effective to detect kernel website to prevent the repeatedly exploitation by the Internet dark industry chain.

In the final, 1557 domain names (that is, 1557 corresponding websites) are judged as web spams through manual audit. Furthermore, we took the formula below to measure the positive rate of this model.

$$Positive\ rate = \frac{Num\ of\ Web\ spams}{Suspicious\ Domain\ Names} * 100\% \qquad (4)$$

Because we took a comparatively high threshold of the PageRank to reduce the false negative rate, the positive rate is

$$Positive\ Rate = \frac{1557}{5808} * 100\% \approx 26.8\%$$

Decreasing the threshold of PR can reduce the manual audit cost and improve the positive rate, but it may increase the false negative rate. To choose the most appropriate threshold, studying the PageRank distribution of the hidden spam webpages will be one of our further research topics.

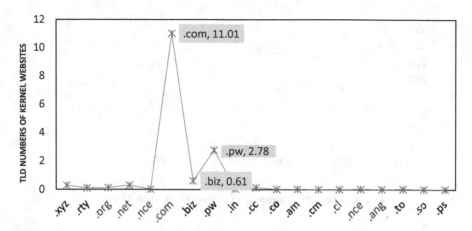

Fig. 6. TLD distribution of the kernel website of the web spams

In our sample, all the websites use .cn TLD. So it can be concluded from Fig. 6 that all the detected spams are cross-domain spams and the TLD of kernel websites are widely distributed, with 71% of the kernel websites use .com TLD and 18% of kernel websites use .pw TLD.

5 Conclusions

As the traditional methods such as statistical learning and image recognition failed in detecting hidden-spams, we proposed a model to combat the web spams on the basis of domain name resolution in this paper. Without the need of parsing the webpage code, this model presents high efficiency and accuracy in detecting the hidden spam. And the experiment shows that amount of hidden spams are cross-domain spams, that is, when user visits a website (that is domain name, and we call it shell website) through a browser, another website (we call it kernel website) is presented to the user through certain techniques such as using HTTP Status Codes, JavaScript etc. The experiment result shows that malicious kernel websites are repeatedly utilized through disguise using the "shell" website. And it indicates that the proposed model in this paper is effective to detect kernel website to prevent the repeatedly exploitation by the Internet dark industry chain. Although the proposed method are not effective for all kinds of hidden spams, it has good detection capability in the redirection spams and nest spams and it is the complement for the existing hidden spams detection method. Through further optimization, this model can be applied to web spam detection in the online high-speed network traffic through retrieval and analysis of DNS recursive name server log directly.

Acknowledgments. This paper is supported by grants from the National Natural Science Foundation of China (Nos. 61375039 and 61272433).

References

1. Ntoulas, A., Najork, M., Manasse, M. Fetterly, D.: Detecting spam web pages through content analysis. In: World Wide Web Conference, pp. 83–92 (2006)
2. Eiron, N., Mccurley, K.S., Tomlin, J.A.: Ranking the web frontier. In: WWW 2004 Proceedings of the 13th international conference on the World Wide Web, pp. 309–318. ACM, New York (2004)
3. Chellapilla, K., Maykov, A.: A taxonomy of JavaScript redirection spam. In: Proceedings of the International Workshop on Adversarial Information Retrieval on the web, pp. 1–14 (2007)
4. Gyongyi, Z., Garcia-Molina, H., Pedersen, J.: Combating web spam with trustrank. In: Proceedings of the Thirtieth international conference on Very large data bases–Volume 30 VLDB Endownment, pp. 576–587 (2004)
5. Castillo, C., Donato, D., Gionis, A., Murdock, V., Silvestri, F.: Know your neighbors: web spam detection using the web topology. In: proceedings of the 30th Annual International ACM SIGIR Conference on Research and Development in Information Retrieval, pp 423–430. ACM (2007)
6. Geng, G., Li, Q., Zhang, X.: Link based small sample learning for web spam detection. In: proceedings of the 18th international conference on World Wide Web, pp. 1185–1186. ACM (2009)
7. Geng, G., Wang, L., Wang, W., Shen, S., Hu, A.: Statistical cross-language web content quality assessment. Knowl.-Based Syst. **35**, 312–319 (2012)
8. Wu, B., Goel, V., Davison, B.D.: Topical trustrank: using topicality to combat web spam. In: Proceedings of the 15th international conference on World Wide Web, pp. 63–72. ACM (2006)
9. Benczur, A.A., Csalogany, K., Sarlos, T., Uher, M.: SpamRank-fully automatic link spam detection work in progress. In: Proceedings of the First International Workshop on Adversarial Information Retrieval on the Web, pp. 1–14 (2005)
10. Liang, C., Ru, L., Zhu, X.: R-SpamRank: a spam detection algorithm based on link analysis. J. Comput. Inf. Syst. **3**(4), 1705–1712 (2007)
11. Spamdexing. https://en.wikipedia.org/wiki/spamdexing
12. URL redirection. https://en.wikipedia.org/wiki/URL_redirection
13. Domain name system. https://en.wikipedia.org/wiki/Domain_Name_System
14. Page, L., Brin, S., Motwani, R., Winograd, T.: The PageRank citation ranking: bringing order to the web. Technical report, Stanford University (1998)

CPN Based Analysis of In-Vehicle Secure Communication Protocol

Rustam Rakhimov Igorevich[1,2(✉)], Daekyo Shin[1], and Dugki Min[1,2]

[1] SoC Platform Research Center, Korea Electronics Research Institute,
Daewangpangyo-ro 710beon-gil, Seongnam,
Gyeonggi-do 463-400, Republic of Korea
{rustam,dukeshin}@keti.kr,
{rustam,dkmin}@konkuk.ac.kr
[2] School of Computer Science and Engineering,
College of Information and Telecommunication,
120 Neungdong-ro, Gwangjin, Seoul 143-701, Republic of Korea

Abstract. Security in the domain of In-Vehicle communication becomes criticial issue when modules from different vendors allowed interacting with car. Authentication and information secrecy issues must be solved by car vendors. Many research works were held about authentication of car accessory devices and their secure communication with central unit (HUD). In this work we have analyzed one of the recently published In-Vehicle Secure protocol. Multiple replay attacks were discovered during analysis of the protocol. CPN (Coloured Petri Nets) tool was applied to anlyze and demonstrate the flaw in given secure message exchange protocol.

Keywords: In-Vehicle · Secure · Protocol · HUD (Head Unit Display) · CPN (Colored Petri Nets) · Replay attack

1 Introduction

Nowadays modern cars contain dozens of controllers that are increasingly networked together via various bus communication systems. Basically those networks were connected to non-critical controllers of the car, such as: light control, window control, door locker etc. In modern cars networks have access to several life critical components of the vehicle, like breaks, airbags and engine control. Those modern cars that are equipped with driving aid systems like ESC (Electronic Stability Control) or ACC (Adaptive Cruise Control) allow deep intervention in the driving behavior of the vehicle. Third party organizations allowed develop products based on CAN (Controller Area Network) or other type of in-vehicle communication networks. Originally CAN is a vehicle bus standard that is designed to allow microcontrollers and devices communicate directly without a host computer.

The car manufacturers try to keep their in-Vehicle communication protocol hidden from customers. It is done in order to preserve secrets of their products. This kind of strategy kills the concept of connected car, by preventing interaction with outside world. Nowadays society requires connected car, which is synchronized with their daily life devices and their social networks. Restricting third party vendor to communicate with

© ICST Institute for Computer Sciences, Social Informatics and Telecommunications Engineering 2017
J.-H. Lee and S. Pack (Eds.): QShine 2016, LNICST 199, pp. 12–21, 2017.
DOI: 10.1007/978-3-319-60717-7_2

the car by hiding and developing proprietary protocols is not the proper solution of the problem. Open source and open standards more preferred than proprietary solutions. Besides, proprietary protocols get hacked more often than open community proven secure protocols.

Dozens of research works have been done in the domain of in-Vehicle networking. In this paper we demonstrate the cryptographic protocol analysis of the recently introduced in-Vehicle secure protocol. The protocol was designed to be extremely efficient with less computational overhead. Introduced protocol has a serious flaw that puts the protocol under huge threat. There is a demonstration of the protocol analysis by applying CPN tool [6] is given. The weakness of the protocol was pointed out and demonstrated with active attacker.

Our paper is structured in a following way: in Sect. 2 some related works regarding to our work were listed out. Sect. 3 introduces CPN modelling tool and its advantages in analyzing security protocols. Sect. 4 introduces secure in-Vehicle communication protocol and its CPN model illustration. Sect. 5, demonstrate variation of replay attacks on given protocol.

2 Related Works

The Colored Petri Nets are recognized as a powerful tool to prove, disprove or analyze correctness of the systems, protocols and algorithms. The core of the formal analysis performed, by listing out specification of the system and creating its model. Created model can be verified using a model checking approach that consists of exploration all model states and transitions. During a process of model creation, execution and simulation the system designer can detect flaws and errors in their system design. The cause of the discovered errors and flaws can be easily seen and traced using CPN tools [6]. It gives a good prospect to find a way subsequently improve their design.

New methods to analyze cryptographic protocol using colored petri nets were introduced in [7]. They have demonstrated two new methods related to matrix description of colored petri nets to find breakable state of the net. The first one is the Acceptance Check Step (ACS) and the second one is the Matrix Analysis Step (MAS). For use case demonstration they have identified ambiguity in the wireless protocol proposed by Aziz and Diffie.

Another research work [8] demonstrated that analysis of Micali's ECS1 fair contract signing protocol. Two new attacks on ECS1 protocol have been discovered. The first attack happens due to Micali's incomplete definition on Bob's (responder's) commitment. This way intruder may claim that Bob had made commitment which he had never actually proposed. Second attack makes available to swap the initiator and responder roles in the protocol. The swapping initiator and responder's role can cause serious consequences in real life scenario.

Analysis of two OSAP and SKAP authorization protocols has been performed in [9]. The vulnerability in those protocols already been analyzed and demonstrated by [10] using ProVerif tools. The purpose of the [9] was to examine the usefulness of Colored Petri Nets and CPN Tools for security analysis. They have constructed intruder using Dolev-Yao [11] based model and generated same result as it was done in [10].

3 CPN Introduction

The Petri Nets are popular and well known formalism for modeling concurrency systems. Petri Net is the collection of basic elements such as places, transitions, arcs and tokens. Tokens occupy places and moves to another place through arcs when corresponding transitions enabled.

Colored Petri Nets (CPN) is an extended from original Petri Net and represents a well-known formalism for modelling concurrent protocols. CPN is applied in many areas where the concurrent and complex processes must be analyzed from architecture checking and behavior perspectives.

There are many usages of Colored Petri Nets in various domains. Kurt Jensen has written theoretical aspects of CP-Nets in [1, 2]:

- CP-Nets have a graphical representation
- CP-Nets have a well-defined semantics, which unambiguously defines the behavior of each CP-Nets
- CP-Nets are very general and can be used to describe a large variety of different systems
- CP-Nets have very few, but powerful, primitives
- CP-Nets have an explicit description of both states and actions
- CP-Nets have a semantics that builds upon true concurrency, instead of interleaving
- CP-Nets offer hierarchical descriptions
- CP-Nets integrate the description of control and synchronization with the description of data manipulation
- CP-Nets can be extended with a time concept
- CP-Nets are stable towards minor changes of the modelled system
- CP-Nets offer interactive simulations where the results are presented directly on the CPN diagram
- CP-Nets have a large number of formal analysis methods by which properties of CP-Nets can be proved
- CP-Nets have computer tools supporting their drawing, simulation and formal analysis.

3.1 CPN in Cryptographic Protocol Analysis

CPN is particularly good to apply for analysis of Cryptographic protocols. It can verify protocol correctness by building state space maps and by analyzing incidence matrix. In some works CPN used to verify whether any security threats exist when many instances of the protocol are executed concurrently [3].

The group of cryptographers at Queen's University and Computer Laboratory at University of Cambridge added significant research contributions to verify cryptographic and security protocols, even compute their weaknesses using CP-Nets.

There are two courses of using CP-Nets: forwards and backward analysis. Ayda and Moon stated in [4, 5], the backward state analysis has tree steps:

(1) First generate CP-Net specification for protocol
(2) Identify insecure states that may or may not occur
(3) Perform backward state analysis to test if each insecure state is reachable or not.

State Space

State space is one of the important features the CPN has. CPN Tools become able to inspect terminal states and identify possible deadlocks, as well as bounds on communication channels. State space is a graph that contains nodes and directed edges. Each node represent one snapshot of the CPN state, means markings positions and their values. For example first node contains initial markings positions and value information. The number of outgoing edges from that node equal to active transitions number from CPN at that concrete step. That means we can travel to each of those edges considering as proper transition got triggered. The node where the edge comes in represents new state of markings after the transition triggered. Recursively performing this operation will build up state space graph. Depend on the CPN the state space graph might get quite complex and big.

4 Secure In-Vehicle Communication Protocol

In this section we will introduce secure in-Vehicle communication protocol suggested by some organization (for the privacy issues we would like to classify the name of the company). The proposed protocol was registered in a patent organization for future usage, in order to provide secure in-Vehicle communication.

Protocol uses symmetric encryption, random number generator and hashing functions. Each of those used algorithms cryptographically strong and secure. It is not our goal to analyze algorithms in details or in a convergence. We assume cutting edge cryptographic algorithms are used for symmetric encryption and hashing function. We also assume random number generator has truly uniform distribution and cannot be predicted by an attacker. It is assumed that shared symmetric key to be pre-distributed between communication participants. Pre-distribution happens long before the exchange takes place and it is not considered in this protocol.

The Table 1, contains notations that are used in a formal description of secure in-Vehicle algorithm. Protocol steps are enumerated, and physical location of the operations separated with colon sign. "Serv - > ECU" refers to the transmission operation where the Server sends data to ECU (Data follows right after colon sign).

Initialization

(1) Serv: $RN_0 = G()$
(2) Serv - > ECU: $E_{Sk}(RN_0) = C$
(3) ECU: $RN_0 = D_{Sk}(C)$
(4) Serv: $K_0 = H(RN_0)$
    ECU: $K_0 = H(RN_0)$

It can be easily noticed that initialization process is quite primitive and relies on pre-shared key safety and random number generator.

Table 1. Notations used in description of protocol.

Messages	Notation
Sk	Secretly shared master key
M	Message
C	Cipher text (Encrypted message)
RN_i	Random generated number on i-th step
K_i	Session key on i-th step
$E_K(M)$	Symmetric encryption of message M using key K
$D_K(C)$	Symmetric decryption of message C using key K
H(M)	Un-keyed cryptographic hash of the message M
M | C	Concatenation of messages M and C with separator
G()	Generate random number
RST	Session key resetting command
NULL	Refers to improper decrypted data. Means the session keys in desynchronized state

Communication (ECU may behave as an initiator too)

(1) Serv: $RN_i = G()$
(2) Serv - > ECU: $E_{Ki-1}(M \mid RN_i) = C$
(3) ECU: $D_{Ki-1}(C) = M \mid RN_i$
(4) Serv: $K_i = H(RN_i)$
(5) ECU: $K_i = H(RN_i)$

Communication step relies on key secrecy generated at previous step. New random seed number generated and sent through the secret channel on each communication step. New random seed number us to generate session key for the next step. On the other side receiver decrypts the data with current session key. From the received data random seed number extracted and next session key derived. At the end of each step the new session keys are synchronized on both sides.

Reset (we assume desynchronization of keys happened)

(1) Serv: $RN_i = G()$
(2) Serv - > ECU: $E_{Ki-1}(M \mid RN_i) = C$
(3) ECU: $D_{Ki-1}(C) ==$ NULL
(4) ECU- > Serv: $E_{K0}(RST) = C$
     ECU: $K_i <= K_0$
(5) Serv: $D_{Ki-1}(C) ==$ NULL
(6) Serv: $D_{K0}(C) ==$ RST
     Serv: $K_i <= K_0$

Reset transaction step shows generalized version of resetting function. In a real implementation it may suggest to recover message with previous key. Previous keys are saved in key stack which has limited size (considering the ECU capabilities). Previously saved keys are extracted from the stack and tried to decrypt the received message. When the all previously saved keys are not matched (or the stack search exhausted) then the setup returned to the initial key K_0. Regarding to security requirements the master key is used only at the initialization step. The key K_0 considered as a fixed baseline, in order to keep a master secret key away from statistical analysis.

The modelling is the fastest way to check the algorithm and all logics encompassed in it. We have followed the protocol description in details and designed CPN model of In-Vehicle Secure Communication Protocol. First we have drawn simple sketch model with just simple UNIT markings. In our opinion it is good style of drawing CPN model, because we can see overall view of the protocol and its simplified behavior. It helps approximately calculate the average number of places and transitions. After that we can start adding colored markings (new types specifically for our working domain) such as plain messages, encryption messages and session encryption messages.

The authentication process is quite straight forward where simply master key, message and random number must be involved. It was implemented by using few transitions and places (as illustrated in Fig. 1). The main body part encryption is represented as a recursive function, which is why it is packed into reusable sub-module called BodyEncryption. Controlling and monitoring parameters such as: RandomNumber, Data_Send and Data_Receive designed to be accessible and controllable from outside of the sub-module.

Detail CPN model of reusable BodyEncryption is illustrated in Fig. 2. The BodyEncryption sub-module is the core processing logic and it's reused for ECU and for HUD-Server. Both of those participants have an identical processing logic in their cores.

This protocol was designed to be strong against statistical analysis by updating session key in every exchange step. Since CAN network is quite error-prone the keychain can get broken up easily. When single exchange message is skipped by one of the participants the key mismatching state occurs. Recovery mechanism gets activated in order to solve the key mismatch issue. Recovery mechanism starts scanning keys in a backward order, by checking previous n-1 key. Key searching loop continues until proper decryption key has found. When the whole key stack is checked and key is not found, then initial key K_0 is used as a new start key.

The CPN model of this secure protocol revealed that design is quite error-prone to various cases. The system doesn't get locked, even if error happens with session keys, because of its automatic key recovery logic.

5 Multiple Replay Attacks

This protocol has multiple flaws in its design and some of them made by designer while chasing efficient secure protocol. First flaw can be detected easily by simply analyzing overall design. It applies one way authentication for initialization step. At the initialization step the recipient doesn't reply any message about success or failure of the initialization process. Not confirming the initialization step is the half of the problem, another bigger and more serious issue lies on key reset procedure.

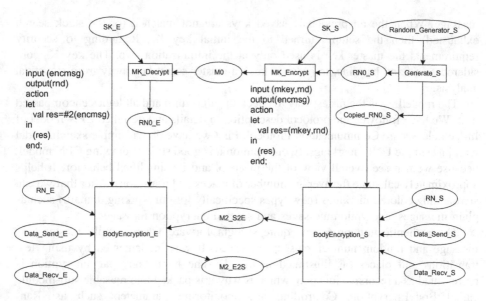

Fig. 1. Hierarchical model of in-vehicle secure communication protocol.

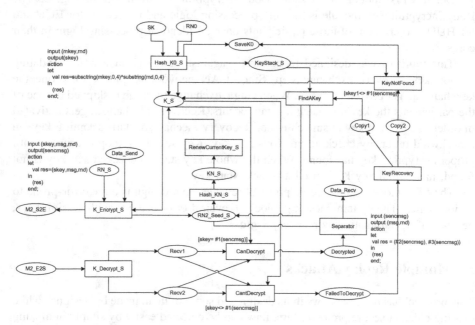

Fig. 2. CPN model of main encryption and error handling module (in the hierarchical model it is named as BodyEncryption submodule).

We describe two defects of the protocol by dividing this section into two parts. In first example we demonstrate how the message can be replied to make ECU perform an action. As a second example we assume there is confirmation message generated for each new message. Adding confirmation message did not exterminate the security flaw in the protocol. Main reason is that replay attack was not considered at design time.

Intruder model is used from Dolev-Yao [11], where intruder is equipped with highest imaginable strength so that all possible attacks on the protocol can be identified. We adopt the Dolev-Yao model to our domain, with CAN bus network in mind. According to the Dolev-Yao model intruder can carry out the following actions:

(1) Tapping and storage of all messages exchanged through shared bus
(2) Forwarding and blocking messages
(3) Generation of forged messages using tapped, randomly generated, hashed and encrypted messages
(4) Decryption of encrypted messages if the intruder has a matching key
(5) Intruder has the ability of normal principal, that he can take a part in the protocol and masquerade.

5.1 Reply Attack on Protocol Without Confirmation Message

In our example for reply attack we don't use all techniques that are available by Dolev-Yao model. Only few of them were enough to reach the goal. First of all we define our scenario where an attacker wants to perform some action on car. For example we use door lock system. In modern cars the door lock system is centralized and the center of the door lock system located at driver's door. Driver's door equipped with ECU which is connected with HUD-Server through CAN Bus.

Without diving deeply we can see that intruder can easily capture all commands initiated from HUD-Server, and later reply them back to ECU. Intruder doesn't have to exactly know the shared master key to replay the same command. The replay attack is possible because generated messages do not contain any time stamp, or ECU has too small memory to memorize all previously generated keys.

5.2 Reply Attack on Protocol with Confirmation Message

Even though this algorithm originally does not consider confirmation or any other measurements to prevent replay attack we will assume this functionality included (or at least we can assume this functionality added at upper layers). In this case attacker's task gets little bit complicated but still it stays in a trivial attacks class.

Replay attack on In-Vehicle Secure protocol with confirmation message illustrated in Fig. 3. Attacker just captures first initialization message and then waits for "Open Door" command. When "Open Door" confirmation command generated by ECU, attacker has to jam the network. By following key recovery protocol Server will generate "Open Door" command with basic key K_0. That command should be captured, so later intruder starts new session where he should just open the connection and send "Open Door" command encoded with basic key K_0. ECU would have no choice then just perform that command and door will open.

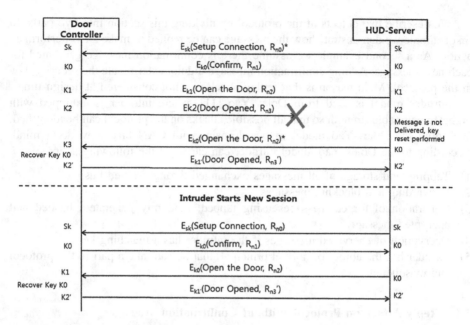

Fig. 3. Demonstration of replay attack when the confirmation message is enabled.

Replay attacks can be prevented by performing three handshake exchanges. To put it in a simple way, the confirmation message generated by ECU device should be re-confirmed by HUD-Server. In this case the last decision for session key would be on ECU side, which prevents replay attacker from masquerading HUD-Server. In order to send re-confirmation message an attacker should know the K_0. Only knowledge of K_0 can decrypt Rn_1 random seed generated by ECU. Rn_1 will change every time when new interaction started. The key K_1 should be as a baseline to recover the communication if the error happens.

6 Conclusion

In this paper we have analyzed In-Vehicle Secure Communication protocol. CPN Tools were used for analyzing and proving the weakness of the protocol. The protocol has been broken by applying replay attacker model. Man-In-The-Middle type of intruder model has been designed and demonstrated.

Original Protocol does not contain a confirmation message routine, that's why we have added additional confirmation message reply from the responder side. Even adding confirmation reply message has not saved the car from being attacked. Using reply attacker model we have designed real scenario with door unlocking. This flaw can be solved by generating confirmation message at initialization step. Confirmation message should contain random seed number for initialization key K_0. As a solution of the problem we have added re-confirmation message at the initialization step. It can prevent any kind of replay attack.

Acknowledgments. This work was supported by the IT R&D program of MOTIE/KEIT. [Project No.: 10060105, Development vehicle Authentication, Security, Device monitoring, Predictive Maintenance platform using OTP-based HSM].

References

1. Jensen, K.: A brief introduction to colored petri nets. In: Workshop on the Applicability of Formal Models, Aarhus, Denmark, pp. 55–58, 2 June 1998
2. Jensen, K.: An introduction to the theoretical aspects of colored petri nets. In: Workshop on the Applicability of Formal Models, Aarhus, Denmark (1998)
3. Long, S.: Analysis of concurrent security protocols using colored petri nets. In: 2009 International Conference on Networking and Digital Society (2009)
4. Basyouni, A.M.: Analysis of wireless cryptographic protocols. Master's thesis, Queen's University Kingston, Ontario, Canada (1997)
5. Moon, H.: A study on formal specification and analysis of cryptographic protocols using colored petri nets. Master's thesis, Kwangju Institute of Science and Technology, Korea (1998)
6. www.cpntools.org – CPN Tools Homepage
7. Basyouni, A.M., Tavares, S.E.: New approach to cryptographic protocol analysis using coloured petri nets. Queen's University Kingston, Ontario (1997)
8. Sornkhom, P., Permpoontanalarp, Y.: Security analysis of Micali's fair contract signing protocol by using coloured petri nets. In: Proceedings of 9th ACIS International Conference Software Engineering, Artificial Intelligence, Networking and Parallel/Distributed Computing, SNPD (2008)
9. Seifi, Y., Suriadi, S., Foo, E., Boyd, C.: Analysis of two authorization protocols using colored petri nets. Int. J. Inf. Secur. (2014)
10. Chen, L., Ryan, M.: Attack, solution and verification for shared authorisation data in TCG TPM. In: Degano, P., Guttman, J.D. (eds.) FAST 2009. LNCS, vol. 5983, pp. 201–216. Springer, Heidelberg (2010). doi:10.1007/978-3-642-12459-4_15
11. Dolev, D., Yao, A.: On the security of public key protocols. IEEE Trans. Inf. Theory **29**(2), 198–208 (1983)

Design and Performance Analysis of Sensor Proxy-AAA Authentication Scheme Based on Fast Handover and Forwarding Mode for IP-Based Internet of Things

Chulhee Cho[1], Byung-Hun Song[2], Jongpil Jeong[3], and Tai-Myoung Chung[1(✉)]

[1] College of Information and Communications Engineering, Sungkyunkwan
University, Suwon, Kyunggi-do 440-745, Republic of Korea
tgb017@nate.com
[2] IoT Convergence Research Center Korea Electronics Technology Institute (KETI),
Seongnam, Republic of Korea
[3] Department of Human ICT Convergence, Sungkyunkwan University, Suwon,
Gyeonggi-do 440-745, Republic of Korea

Abstract. Recently, with the development of IoT technology, a wireless
sensor network technology capable of real-time management by receiving
information wirelessly through various kinds of sensors has been actively
developed. Hence, reducing the signaling cost becomes an important issue
because most of the sensors are powered by battery only. In addition,
since the Internet of objects is open on the Internet in object environments, security issues related to authentication of users accessing wireless networks are very important. AAA technology is the best possible
way these days of resolving delay issue when introducing authentication
process of mobile switching. However, despite long development in AAA
technology, the mobility management in wireless network environment
has yet to be researched further. To solve these problems, we propose a
Proxy-Authentication Authorization Accounting (Proxy-AAA) authentication scheme. This places the AAA server in the LMA so as to the
cost of authentication by means of a short, simple mobile authentication. The proposed method reuses the LMA-based session key in the
authentication process when moving within the domain, and reuses the
AAA server based session key when moving between domains. The AAA
server of the scheme will be deployed on Local Mobility Anchor (LMA),
making up for the shortage of simple fast handover authentication and
hierarchical authentication, and further reducing the cost of intra-domain
authentication.

Keywords: Proxy-AAA authentication · Fast handover · Forwarding ·
Wireless Body Area Networks (WBAN)

© ICST Institute for Computer Sciences, Social Informatics and Telecommunications Engineering 2017
J.-H. Lee and S. Pack (Eds.): QShine 2016, LNICST 199, pp. 22–35, 2017.
DOI: 10.1007/978-3-319-60717-7_3

1   Introduction

The potential of the Future Internet is not limited to smart phones. Internet of Things (IoT) is another emerging area of the Future Internet, which is offering a higher integration of the cybernetic and physical world. The main goal of the IoT is collecting data from the real-world entities and events. In order to maintain a reliable connection of distributed IoT equipment, it is important to establish a secure link for end-to-end communication using appropriate authentication. In the internet of things environment, due to the openness of the IoT, the security issue related to authentication of user accessing wireless network is extremely important. AAA technology is the best possible way these days of resolving delay issue when introducing authentication process of mobile switching [1,2]. However, despite long development in AAA technology, the mobility management in wireless network environment has yet to be researched further. Due to the deployment of MIPv6 networks and the development of new access technologies, the RADIUS protocol, which provides centralized authentication and authorization services, can no longer meet requirements. Diameter protocol, an improved version of RADIUS, provides extremely improved functions in failure recovery, security and reliability [3]. However, the delay from authentication and authorization process greatly influences the process and AAA application in mobile IP has a number of issues such as failing to support continuous and fast handover in both intra-domain and inter-domain [4–7]. To solve these problems, we propose a Proxy-Authentication Authorization Accounting (Proxy-AAA) authentication scheme. This places the AAA server in the LMA so as to the cost of authentication by means of a short, simple mobile authentication. The proposed method reuses the LMA-based session key in the authentication process when moving within the domain, and reuses the AAA server based session key when moving between domains. The AAA server in the scheme will be deployed on Local Mobility Anchor (LMA), making up for the shortage of simple fast handover authentication and hierarchical authentication, and further reducing the cost of intra-domain authentication [8]. We analyzed the performance of the MIPv6 protocol and the proposed scheme using the mathematical analysis and the network simulation tool. The signaling overhead of the proposed Proxy-AAA scheme is always smaller than that of the existing AAA scheme regardless of the LMA domain or inter-domain movement. When the mobile node (MN) moves away from the home domain, the signaling overhead of Proxy- Efficiency is increased. We first describe and compare basic MIPv6 and PMIPv6 in Sect. 2. In Sect. 3, we introduce our proposed Proxy-AAA and protocol selection scheme. In Sect. 4, the performance of the traditional AAA scheme and proposed Proxy-AAA scheme is compared. Section 5 concludes the paper with a summary of the key results of this work.

2   Related Work

Recently, mobility solutions are divided into two trends: evolutionary research that follows an IPv6-based approach, and a clean-slate trend. The clean-slate trend is based on new concepts such as identifiers and location-partitioning architectures. This kind of architecture has the advantage that the mobility is directly supported since the session recognition and the locator of the equipment are separated. However, this type of solution has the overhead incurred by a limited network such as 6LoWPAN and the cost incurred by replacing the current hardware and infrastructure. Another trend is evolutionary research, and the main protocol following evolutionary research is MIPv6. MIPv6 uses two IPv6 addresses; one is the initial address of the device, and the home address is mainly used as identification data. The other is Care-of-address, which is newly issued in the visited network and used as the locator of the equipment. The MIPv6 protocol extends the IPv6 header to manage the binding between these two addresses and provides a signaling message. In particular, it defines IPSec tunneling between the mobile node and the home agent, and defines a return routability mechanism that performs route optimization to avoid triangle routing [9]. This ensures the security and authentication of the mobile node to the binding update when the node needs to register a new Care of address. However, MIPv6 is considered to be unsuitable for 6LoWPAN nodes because it transmits very heavy messages during handover processing and requires high processing requirements [10]. PMIPv6 is a Network Mobility (NEMO) [11,12] based protocol proposed to reduce MN overload. This does not require mobile functionality in the IPv6 stack because it delegates mobility signaling message processing from the MN to MAG equipment acting as a proxy. This protocol is suitable for 6LoWPAN because it avoids MN's involvement in mobility-related signaling. We configure the sensor node information to be received by the monitoring system via the gateway. The sensor node resource receiving method is a method of establishing an information request in an external network and a polling method in which a gateway periodically requests information to a sensor network [13,14]. When the polling request method is used for sensor information collection, inefficient battery consumption may occur due to the wireless signaling used continuously by the sensor. In this paper, we used an asynchronous method to transmit data to a gateway in case of data fluctuation, instead of a polling method, to provide sensing data of a sensor network. To this end, the sensor node transmits the information to the MN acting as a gateway of the sensor when the sensing data fluctuates. Such a scheme transmits information only at the time of change, and thus enables efficient use of radio resources. The MN, acting as a gateway, stores the received sensing data in the cache and delivers the information stored in the cache by the monitoring system request.

3   Proposed Scheme

3.1   Handoff Scheme Using Virtual Layer Between the LMA

Recently, with the development of IoT technology, a wireless sensor network technology capable of real-time management by receiving information wirelessly through various kinds of sensors has been actively developed. In addition, a wireless network called WBAN (Wireless Body Area Network) [15] can be configured to exchange data such as biometric signals through a network composed of people wearing clothes or various devices attached to the human body. In this regard, the Low Power Wireless Personal Area Network (LoWPAN) has attracted a lot of attention recently because it can support the communication of Internet of Things. 6LoWPAN is a network-based low-power technology based on IEEE 802.15.4, which it uses a limited processing capability and power. Because the sensor must be directly involved in mobility-related signaling, PMIPv6, the network-based mobility protocol, is considered to be the most suitable for supporting the mobility of WBAN. However, it is a heavy burden for the sensor itself to send a message related to mobility to the agent. Hence, reducing the signaling cost becomes an important issue because most of the sensors are powered by battery only. In addition, the introduction of authentication in the process of mobile IP handover incurs extra costs. Most solutions available today fail to satisfy some of the requirements in specific circumstances. To deal with these issues, this study proposes an advanced AAA authentication scheme based on mobile IPv6. This proposed technique supports quick authentication and introduces the concept of hierarchical AAA to mobile IP combined with diameter protocol. In this proposed technique, AAA server will be implemented on Local Mobility Anchor (LMA) to implement simple and fast handover authentication and hierarchical authentication as well as reduce intra-domain authentication cost. Proxy-AAA scheme, on the other hand, offers a better way to improve authentication and binding update processes not only for the intra-domain handover and authentication processes, but also for the inter-domain mobilization. Proxy-AAA reuses the session keys based on LMA of HMIPv6 in both authentication processing and intra-domain handover. In inter-domain handover and processing authentication, Proxy-AAA reutilizes session keys derived from the AAA server and performs a direct transmission between multiple LMAs [16].

3.2   Operation Procedures of Sensor Proxy-AAA

Figure 1 shows the flow of signals and data packets between different LMAs when the MN moves. When the MN reaches the LMA2 area while moving to the LMA3 area, the MAG in the area sends a BU message to the LMA2. This causes LMA2 to respond to LMA1. On receiving the message from LMA2, LMA compares the received message with the LMA list and updates the current LMA address of the MN. The packet data is then transmitted directly from LMA1 to LMA2.

Figure 2 shows the specific message flow in inter-domain handover. When the MN reaches the LMA2 area while moving to the LMA3 area, the MN sends an RS message to the nMAG of the area. On receiving the RS message, nMAG sends an Authentication Request command to the pMAG, and the pMAG encrypts the session key S_{MN-MAG} and S_{MAG-HA} using $K_{pMAG-LMA}$ and sends it to the pLMA. pLMA passes the encrypted session key back to nLMA. After the nLMA stores the session key, it sends a notification message to the nMAG about session key reuse. nMAG forwards the response message to the pMAG for session key reuse and sends the PBU message to nLMA [17]. Upon receiving

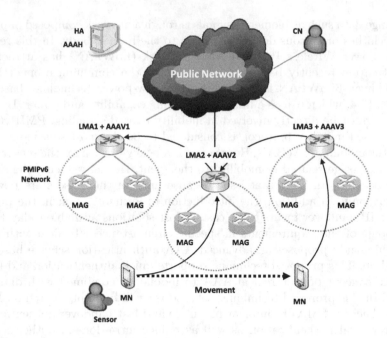

Fig. 1. Forwarding scheme between different LMA.

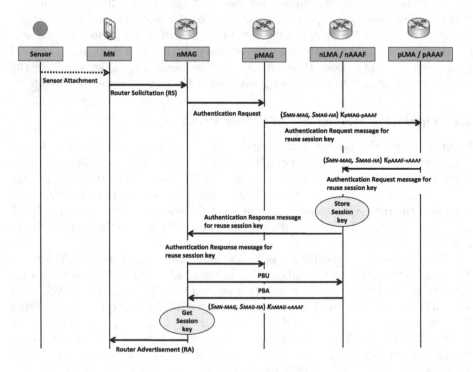

Fig. 2. Inter-domain handover flow.

the PBU message, nLMA encrypts the session key S_{MN-MAG} and S_{MAG-HA} using $K_{pMAG-LMA}$, and transmits the value to the nMAG by including it in the PBU. After obtaining the session key, nMAG responds with an RA message to the MN. Accordingly, a reliable binding UPDATE channel between the MN and the LMA is created. Figure 3 shows the specific flow process of intra-domain handover. After a reliable binding update channel between the MN and the LMA is established, the sensor node can start transmitting the sensing data. When the sensing data is generated, the sensor node asynchronously transmits the corresponding information to the MN, and the MN stores the information in the cache, and converts the information according to the IPv6 protocol.

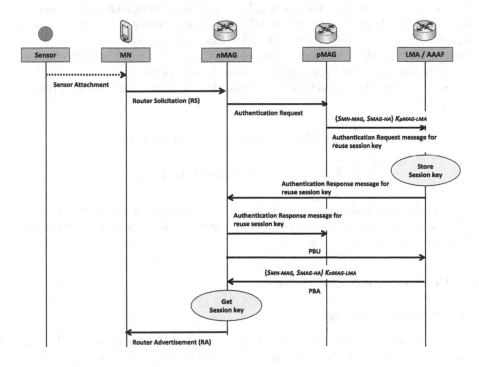

Fig. 3. Intra-domain handover flow.

3.3 Protocol Selection

To select the most suitable mobility management protocol for the network and MNs, during the authentication process, the MAG examines the profiles of the MNs and finds the MN's preferences. In the authentication process, MAG searches MNs profile for MNs preference. From the search, in case MNs preferred protocol matches what was provided from access network, the matching protocol will be selected [18]. In case MN does not have a preference, the network is responsible to assess the performance of basic MIPv6 and Proxy-AAA technique and select the appropriate protocol. To evaluate the performance of basic MIPv6 and Proxy-AAA schemes, MAG finds the path response time through the search process. While the route is being searched, the MAG sends two proving messages to the LMA. One is sent through nLMA and then redirected to pLMA and the related round-trip time (RTT) is denoted as $RTT_{proxy-AAA}$. The other probing message is sent directly to pLMA and the related RTT is denoted as RTT_{mip}. The average RTT of the MIPv6 path after the path search for (z_n) hours can be calculated as follows.

$$\overline{z_n} = \alpha RTT_{mip}(n) + (1 - \alpha)\overline{z_{n-1}} \tag{1}$$

The parameter α represents the weight of past events in the average calculation. In a similar manner, the average RTT for the Proxy-AAA scheme can be calculated and denoted as t_n. When MN's movement frequency is low, the path response time of existing MIPv6 is smaller than our Proxy-AAA. On the other hand, when the MN's movement frequency is high, the basic MIPv6 response time is higher than our Proxy-AAA scheme. In appropriately selecting the better protocol according to network condition and mobility parameters, protocol selection can be used.

$$\frac{\overline{t_n} - \overline{z_n}}{N_h} < H_t, \quad select Proxy - AAA scheme$$

$$\frac{\overline{t_n} - \overline{z_n}}{N_h} \geq H_t, \qquad select Basic MIPv6 \tag{2}$$

Here, N_h is a handover frequency, $\overline{t_n} - \overline{z_n}/N_h$ is an index for judging a protocol with better performance, and H_t is a quality threshold value for determining which protocol should be selected.

4   Performance Evaluation

4.1   System Modeling

In this scheme, we construct an AAA server on the LMA residing in the visit domain (AAAV), and the AAA server is wholly responsible for accounting, authentication, and authorization of the MAG in the LMA domain of LMA. In the proxy-AAA method, the overhead of the entire system is composed of two parts: signaling control overhead C_{signal} and data transmission overhead C_{packet}. Signal control overhead is composed of authentication signaling control overhead C_{auth} and registration signaling control overhead C_{reg} in general, and C_{reg} is mainly made of the data transmission overhead from CN to MN(C_{CN-MN}). Figure 4 shows the network topology of a specific Proxy-AAA for a system overhead analysis.

$$C_{total} = C_{signal} + C_{packet} = \beta(C_{reg} + C_{auth}) + \alpha C_{CN-MN} \tag{3}$$

Here, α refers to the average velocity of packet data, transmitted from the CN to the MN (the average arrival rate of packet data), and β is the average

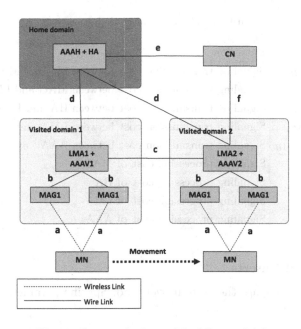

Fig. 4. Cost analysis model of Proxy-AAA.

switching rate of an MN when it transfers from a subnet to another, which is referred to as MN's switching rate per unit time [19]. When it is assumed that the number of packets transmitted from an MN to a CN remains constant, we can express the packet to mobility ratio (PMR) of the packets received by the MN as $p = \alpha/\beta$. Also, $p = \alpha/\beta$ refers to the average number of packets received by a peer CN. PMR is the ratio of packet arrival rate and mobility rate, and it is a crucial indicator for the present study. The larger PMR is, the larger the arrival rate is than the mobility rate, meaning that the data transmission cost becomes larger. When PMR becomes smaller, the arrival rate becomes smaller than the mobility rate, meaning the binding update cost becomes larger. Also, the average length of data packets is referred to as l_d, and signaling packets as l_s. The ratio of these is supposed to be $l = l_d/l_s$.

As the suggested Proxy-AAA scheme aims to reduce the signaling overhead generated in authentication and registration processes, this section compares Proxy-AAA with traditional AAA schemes. Note that the traditional AAA is defined as a simple combination of HMIPv6 and AAA. The relevant parameters and definition descriptions are shown in Table 1.

Assuming that MN moves out of the LMA region m times in a certain period of time, then the authentication will be performed m times. The earlier $m - 1$ authentications are intra-domain authentications, and the last one is for inter-domain authentication. Suppose that the authentication process as a result of MN's movement is in line with Poisson distribution with λ.

Table 1. The parameter definition.

Parameter	Definition
C_{MN-MAG}	Signaling transmission cost between MN and MAG
$C_{MAG-LMA}$	Signaling transmission cost between MAG and LMA
C_{HA-LMA}	Signaling transmission cost between HA and LMA
$C_{LMA-LMA}$	Signaling transmission cost between LMA and LMA
$C_{AAAV-AAAH}$	Signaling transmission cost between AAAV and AAAH
P_{MAG}	Signaling processing cost of MAG
P_{HA}	Signaling processing cost of HA
P_{LMA}	Signaling processing cost of LMA
P_{AAA}	Signaling processing cost of AAA

4.2   Numerical Ruserts

This section will compare the system overhead. Specific parameters and values are shown in Table 2.

Table 2. The parameter definition.

Parameter	Value	Parameter	Value
$l_{MAG-LMA}$	5	l_{MN-MAG}	1
P_{MAG}	4	l_{HA-LMA}	10
$l_{LMA-LMA}$	10	$l_{LMA-AAA}$	10
σ	0.05	η	0.1
P_{LMA}	3	P_{HA}	4
P_{AAA}	3	l_{CN-HA}	50
$l_{MAG-MAG}$	1		

We analyze the different data packet transmission overhead by separating the case where the MN is located in the pedestrian and the vehicle. Figure 5 shows the data packet transmission overhead under a condition that MNs are pedestrians ($\beta = 0.01$) and vehicles ($\beta = 0.2$). From the analysis, it can be seen that the data packet transmission overhead C_{packet} increases as PMR p increases.

Figure 6 shows the data packet transmission overhead value when the value of PMR $p = 10$, $p = 50$ or $p = 100$. It can be seen that the data packet transmission overhead C_{packet} increases as the average switching rate increases as the MN moves.

Figure 7 shows the average signaling overhead of Proxy-AAA. This shows that the signaling overhead C_{signal} increases as the arrival rate of the authentication events λ increases. In other words, the frequent arrival of MN in LMA

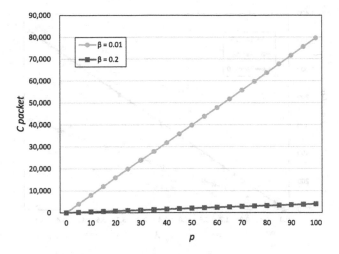

Fig. 5. Packet data transmission overhead ($\mu = 0.1$).

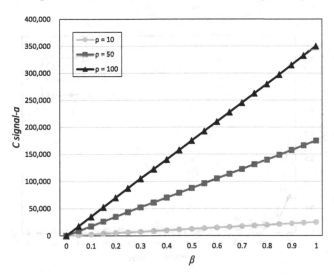

Fig. 6. Packet data transmission overhead ($\mu = 0.1$).

area increases the arrival rate of authentication events and increases signaling overhead during authentication between domains and registration. In addition, we can see that R decreases as λ increases. It can be seen that the efficiency of Proxy-AAA increases as MN moves away from home domain.

Figure 8 analyzes the average signaling overhead of Proxy-AAA. This indicates that the signaling overhead C_{signal} decreases as the residence time T_a increases. That is, if the residence time is long in the same LMA domain of mn, the exchange and authentication between the domains is small and the signaling overhead in the whole system is also low.

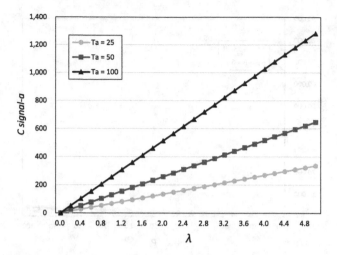

Fig. 7. Packet data transmission overhead ($\mu = 0.1$).

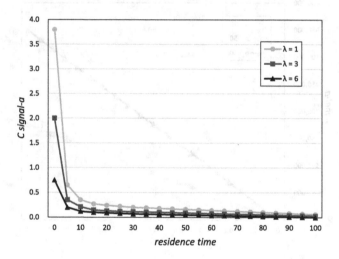

Fig. 8. Packet data transmission overhead ($\mu = 0.1$).

Figure 9 shows analysis of the entire overhead based on PMR p increases ($\beta = 0.01$, $\lambda = 1$). This shows that the total overhead C_{total} increases as the value of p increases when the pedestrian ($\beta = 0.01$) moves.

Figure 10 is an analysis of the overall overhead as the value of β increases. This shows that as the average switching rate of the MN increases, the overall overhead C_{total} increases as the PMR p is fixed.

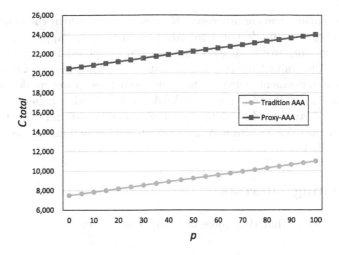

Fig. 9. Signaling overhead ($l_{AAAV-AAAH} = 50$).

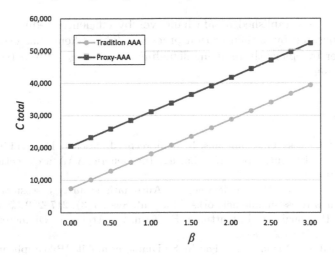

Fig. 10. Signaling overhead ($l_{AAAV-AAAH} = 50$).

5   Conclusions

In this paper, we propose a sensor proxy AAA authentication scheme based on fast handover and forwarding mode for IP-based Internet. This can be applicable not only to micro-mobility but also macro-mobility of MNs in an LMA region. This scheme has established a safe handover by efficiently reducing signaling overhead generated by authentication processes. This study proposes a way of reducing delay time and additional delay from movement of mobile devices in mobile IP environment by means of combining AAA and PMIPv6. This scheme has established a safe handover by efficiently reducing signaling overhead generated by authentication processes. Here we could confirm that fast mobility mode and forwarding mode between various LMAs were supported. Moreover, the overall signaling overhead also showed that proposed Proxy-AAA scheme always has smaller value than previous traditional AAA schemes. Therefore, this allows efficient movement between domains from forwarding mode at PMIPv6 supporting local mobility by means of AAA Authentication Scheme. Also, during movement between LMA domains, it was confirmed that the farther the distance between RAAAS (Root AAA Server) and home domain, the higher the performance efficiency.

6   Competing Interests

The authors declare that they have no competing interests.

7   Author's Contributions

This scheme has established a safe handover by efficiently reducing signaling overhead generated by authentication processes. This scheme has established a safe handover by efficiently reducing signaling overhead generated by authentication processes.

References

1. De Laat, C., Gross, G., Gommans, L., Vollbrecht, J., Spence, D.: Grid information services for distributed resource sharing. In: Generic AAA architecture (2000). ISSN 2070-1721
2. Palmieri, F., Fiore, U., Castiglione, A.: Automatic security assessment for next generation wireless mobile networks. Mob. Inf. Syst. **7**(3), 217–239 (2011)
3. Calhoun, P., Loughney, J., Guttman, E., Zorn, G., Arkko, J.: Diameter base protocol (2003). ISSN 2070-1721
4. Le, F., Patil, B., Perkins, C.E., Faccin, S.: Diameter mobile IPv6 application. draft-le-aaa-diametermobileipv6-04 txt Iinternet Draft (2004)
5. Lee, S.-Y., Huh, E.-N., Kim, S.-B., Mun, Y.: An efficient performance enhancement scheme for fast mobility service in MIPv6. In: Gervasi, O., Gavrilova, M.L., Kumar, V., Laganà, A., Lee, H.P., Mun, Y., Taniar, D., Tan, C.J.K. (eds.) ICCSA 2005. LNCS, vol. 3480, pp. 628–637. Springer, Heidelberg (2005). doi:10.1007/11424758_66
6. Kim, M., Kim, M., Mun, Y.: A hierarchical authentication scheme for MIPv6 node with local movement property. In: Gervasi, O., Gavrilova, M.L., Kumar, V., Laganà, A., Lee, H.P., Mun, Y., Taniar, D., Tan, C.J.K. (eds.) ICCSA 2005. LNCS, vol. 3480, pp. 550–558. Springer, Heidelberg (2005). doi:10.1007/11424758_57
7. Mei, S., Li, W.: SONG J-d.: a secure fast handover scheme based on AAA protocol in mobile IPv6 networks. J. China Univ. Posts Telecommun. **15**, 14–18 (2008)
8. Durresi, A., Durresi, M., Barolli, L.: Secure authentication in heterogeneous wireless networks. Mob. Inf. Syst. **4**(2), 119–130 (2008)

9. Son, S., Jeong, J.: Cost-effective handoff scheme based on mobility-aware dual pointer forwarding in proxy mobile IPv6 networks. SpringerPlus **3**(1), 57 (2014)
10. Johnson, D., Perkins, C., Arkko, J.: Mobility support in IPv6 (2004). ISSN 2070-1721
11. Jara, A.J., Zamora, M.A., Skarmeta, A.F.: An initial approach to support mobility in hospital wireless sensor networks based on 6LoWPAN (HWSN6). J. Wirel. Mob. Netw. Ubiquit. Comput. Dependable Appl. (JoWUA) **1**(2/3), 107–122 (2010)
12. Bag, G., Shams, S.S., Akbar, A.H., Raza, H.M.T., Kim, K.-H., Yoo, S.W.: Network assisted mobility support for 6LoWPAN. In: CCNC 2009 6th IEEE Consumer Communications and Networking Conference. IEEE (2009)
13. Moon, Y., Lee, J., Park, S.: Sensor network node management and implementation. In: ICACT 2008 10th International Conference on Advanced Communication Technology. IEEE (2008)
14. Aishwarya, V., Enigo, V.F.: IP based wireless sensor networks with web interface. In: 2011 International Conference on Recent Trends in Information Technology (ICRTIT). IEEE (2011)
15. Xing, J.: A survey on body area network, networking and mobile computing. In: Proceedings of International Conference on Wireless Communications, p. 14, September 2009
16. Han, J., Jeong, J., Jo, J.: Proxy-AAA authentication scheme with forwarding mode supporting in PMIPv6 networks. Int. J. Internet Broadcast. Commun. **5**(2), 18–22 (2013)
17. Jeong, J., Kang, M., Cho, Y., Choi, J.: 3S: scalable, secure and seamless inter-domain mobility management scheme in proxy mobile IPv6 networks. Int. J. Secur. Appl. **7**(4), 51–70 (2013)
18. Ra, D.-K., Jeong, J.-P.: Cost-effective mobility management scheme in proxy mobile IPv6 networks with function distributor support. J. Inst. Internet Broadcast. Commun. **12**(1), 97–107 (2012)
19. Jain, R., Raleigh, T., Graff, C., Bereschinsky, M.: Mobile internet access and QoS guarantees using mobile IP and RSVP with location registers. In: 1998 ICC 98 Conference Record 1998 IEEE International Conference on Communications. IEEE (1998)

A Local-Perturbation Anonymizing Approach to Preserving Community Structure in Released Social Networks

Huanjie Wang, Peng Liu, Shan Lin, and Xianxian Li[(✉)]

Guangxi Key Lab of Multi-source Information Mining and Security,
Guangxi Normal University, Guilin 541004, China
whj.6040@163.com, lin-sam@foxmail.com, {liupeng,lixx}@gxnu.edu.cn

Abstract. Social networks provide a large amount of social network data, which is gathered and released for various purposes. Since social network data usually contains much sensitive information of individuals, the data needs to be anonymized before releasing. To protect privacy of individuals in released social network, many anonymizing methods have been proposed. However, most of them were proposed for general purpose, and suffered the over-information loss problem when they were used for specific purposes. In this paper, we focus on the problem of preserving structure information in anonymized social network data, which is the most important knowledge for community analysis. Furthermore, we propose a novel local-perturbation technique that can reach the same privacy requirement of k-anonymity, while minimizing the impact on community structure. We evaluate the performance of our method on real-world data. Experimental results show that our method has less community structure information loss compared with existing techniques.

Keywords: Social networks · Privacy protection · Community structure

1 Introduction

Recently, social network applications have provided a large amount of information, which is increasing continually and has more value for data analysis, such as researching the cause of social phenomenon [7], etc. However, we could not release social network data in raw form, which can raise serious privacy concerns, because it contains sensitive information. In this paper, we present a method to anonymize social network data for preventing individuals from re-identifying, while achieving the maximum utility of community structure for analysis.

1.1 Motivation

To protect privacy of individuals, a naive anonymizing method is proposed by removing the unique identifies of nodes. However, it is insufficient and has been discussed in previous work [9].

© ICST Institute for Computer Sciences, Social Informatics and Telecommunications Engineering 2017
J.-H. Lee and S. Pack (Eds.): QShine 2016, LNICST 199, pp. 36–45, 2017.
DOI: 10.1007/978-3-319-60717-7_4

Example 1. A typical social network is presented in Fig. 1a, and its naive anonymized graph is depicted in Fig. 1b by removing names of participants. Even so, an adversary could re-identify the target victim by some more complex structure attack [4]. Assume that the adversary knows that Kin has one friend, and his friend has three friends. It is easy to infer that Kin is V_3 in Fig. 1b.

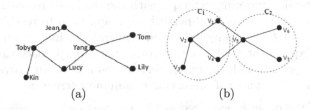

(a)   (b)

Fig. 1. (a) a raw social network (b) a naive anonymized social network

An effective way to protect individual privacy in Example 1 is k-anonymity [2,3], which divides all nodes into several clusters, and each cluster has at least k indistinguishable nodes. These clusters are generalized to super nodes, and the edges among clusters are generalized to super edges. However, because most of graph analysis methods can only process atomic nodes and edges, the k-anonymity graph usually is reconstructed before analyzing [2,3].

By reason of do not considering the community structure information in the clustering process [2,3], the boundaries of original community structure are likely to become blurry after reconstructing.

Example 2. As shown in Fig. 1b, there are 2 communities $\{C_1, C_2\}$ and 2 edges between them. Figure 2a shows its 3-anonymity graph, and Fig. 2b is a possible result of reconstruction. Then, the number of edges connecting C_1 and C_2 becomes 4, which blurs the boundary between them seriously. Obviously, for the community structure information, there is a big difference to the original graph.

To address the problems above, we propose a novel local-perturbation approach, which can achieve the same requirement of the k-anonymity, while preserving "high" utility of the community structure for data releasing, so that data analyzers could take some relative researches about community structure.

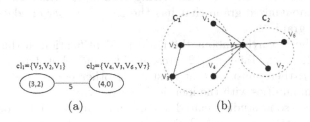

(a)   (b)

Fig. 2. (a) a 3-anonymity graph (b) a reconstructed graph

1.2   Contributions

The contributions of this paper are summarized as follows.

1. We propose an anonymizing approach that is designed for preserving the community structure in released social network data. This is a crucial difference to existing methods in [2], which just analyzed how well the communities in social networks were preserved by using existing anonymous techniques.
2. By combining the clustering technique with the randomly reconstructing technique, we propose a novel local-perturbation approach to reaching the same privacy level of k-anonymity, while minimizing the impact on community structure. Experiment results demonstrate that our approach can effectively preserve the privacy with the reasonable trade-off between privacy and data utility measured in terms of preserving community structure.

The rest of the paper is organized as follows. Section 2 presents related work of anonymization. The problem is defined in Sect. 3. Our anonymizing method is described in Sect. 4. The concrete evaluation criterions and the experimental results are discussed in Sect. 5, and Sect. 6 concludes this paper.

2   Related Work

There are considerable research efforts for designing privacy-preserving methods in social network. The privacy of social network data can be mainly categorized into two types. One type is node-privacy, in which many researches mostly focus on node re-identification [4] and nodes' attribute disclosure [3]. For node re-identification, the attack goal is to identify the target victim for achieving more beneficial information; and for nodes' attribute disclosure, the attack goal is to infer sensitive information of target victim, such as disease and salary. The other type is edge-privacy, which contains link re-identification [11] and edges' attribute disclosure [3]. For link re-identification, the attack goal is to identify sensitive relationships between nodes; and for edges' attribute disclosure, the attack goal is to infer some sensitive relationship categories between nodes. This paper focuses on preventing the node from re-identifying in unlabeled graph.

In order to protect the sensitive information mentioned above, some anonymous techniques have been proposed in these years. These techniques can be classified into four categories: adding nodes [5,8], adding and deleting edges [4], generalization [3], and randomization [1]. In this paper, we combine clustering technique with randomly reconstructing technique, which can get a local-perturbation anonymized graph that has the same number of edges and nodes as the original graph.

Recently, the researches about the node re-identification in the community have been studied [12]. Tai et al. [12] presented the model of structural diversity, for each node v, there must exist at least $k-1$ other nodes located in at least $k-1$ other communities with the identical degree of v.

On the whole, some studies related to this paper are social network clustering model and reconstructing model. Besides, we also use the community detection approach to detecting the community structure of social network graph.

3   Problem Descriptions

In this paper, we model an initial social network as an undirected graph $G = (V, E)$, where V is a set of nodes without labels, and $E \in V \times V$ is a set of edges without labels. Each node indicates to an individual in the underlying group. An edge between two nodes presents the relationship between the two corresponding individuals. Only binary relationships are allowed in our model.

3.1   The Privacy Model

Suppose that an adversary knows any subgraph information of the target victim location, and wants to re-identify the target victim node in the released data. The problem in this paper is how to transform a given social network G into an anonymous graph G', which satisfies the requirement of k-anonymity [2,3], while preserving community structure information as much as possible.

Definition 1 (k-anonymity social network). Let G be a social network and G' be an anonymization of G. If G' is k-anonymity, then with any subgraph background knowledge, any node in G cannot be re-identified in G' with confidence larger than $1/k$.

3.2   Relevant Definitions

The nodes in the social network always tend to form closely-knit groups, these groups are also known as communities.

Definition 2 (communities in social network). Let $G = (V, E)$ is a social network, the set of communities $C = \{C_1, C_2, \cdots, C_m\}$, where $C_i \cap C_j = \phi$ for all $1 \le i \ne j \le m$. For each $C_o \in C$, the density of internal connection is higher than outside.

In order to protect the community structure, we choose a classic community detection GN algorithm [10] to discover community structure of the original network, which uses the modularity [6,10] optimization method that is defined as

$$Q = \sum_{c=1}^{n} [\frac{l_c}{m} - (\frac{d_c}{2m})^2]$$ (1)

where n is the number of communities, l_c is the total number of edges in the community c, d_c is the sum of degrees of nodes in c, m is the number of edges in G.

Our technique mainly includes two processes, clustering and reconstruction. Then, some relevant concepts about anonymization are defined as follows.

Definition 3 (k-cluster social network). Let $G = (V, E)$ is a social network, and k is a threshold specified by social network data holder. For a given clustering

$CL = \{cl_1, cl_2, \cdots, cl_n\}$ of V, the corresponding social network is denoted as G_{cl} where $cl_t \cap cl_c = \phi$ for all $1 \leq t \neq c \leq n$, and $|cl_i| \geq k$ for $1 \leq i \leq n$.

In the clustering process, the shortest distance is important evidence. We use the symbol $adj[V_i]$ to denote the set of neighbors of a node V_i. The distance between nodes is defined as follow.

Definition 4 (the distance between nodes). The distance between two nodes (V_i, V_j) is

$$dist(V_i, V_j) = \frac{|\{V_k | V_k \in (adj[V_i] \bigoplus adj[V_j]), V_k \neq V_i \neq V_j\}|}{n - 2} \qquad (2)$$

where n is the number of nodes in graph. The reason that n is reduced by 2 in the denominator is that we exclude V_i and V_j from the set. For example, the distance between V_1 and V_2 in Fig. 1b is 3/5.

Then, we will get the distance between a node and a cluster [2,3].

Definition 5 (the distance between a node and a cluster). The distance between a node V_p and a cluster cl_q is

$$dist(V_p, cl_q) = \frac{\sum_{V_j \in cl_q} dist(V_p, V_j)}{|cl_q|} \qquad (3)$$

3.3   Problem Statement

In this paper, we address the following problem.

Definition 6 (social network anonymization for community structure). Given a social network G without labels, and a privacy requirement k. The problem of social network anonymization for community structure is to transform G to a local-perturbation social network G', which satisfies the given anonymous requirement while preserving community structure as much as possible.

4   The Anonymization Method

In this section, we introduce a method to transform the original social network G into a local-perturbation graph G' for privacy preservation, and achieve the maximum of the utility of community structure. The first step is to transform G into a k-cluster graph G_{cl}, and then reconstruct each cluster in G_{cl}.

4.1   Cluster for Social Networks

Owing to the fact that optimal clustering problem is known to be NP-hard [3], we devise a greedy clustering approach named K-Cluster presented in Table 1 that is based on $SaNGreeA$ (Social Network Greedy Anonymization) algorithm [2,3], and the time complexity is also same as [2,3].

Table 1. Algorithm 1 K-Cluster(G)

Input: Social network $G = (V, E)$ and the threshold k
Output: A k-cluster graph G_{cl} and number n of clusters
1: $CL = \phi$; $i = 1$; $m = 1$;//sort V by degree in descending order
2: while $|V| >= k$ do
3:     $V_{seed}^i = V[0]$; $cl_i = \{V_{seed}^i\}$; $V = V - cl_i$; //select the seed node for cl_i
4:     while $|cl_i| < k$: $FindBestNode(V, cl_i)$;
5:     $CL = CL \cup \{cl_i\}$; $i + +$;
6: end while
7: if $V \neq \phi$: // find the best cluster for each of them
8:     for every V_m in in current V:
9:         $FineBestCluster(V_m, CL)$;
10: end if

Before anonymizing, all nodes in V should be sorted by degree in descending order. A new cluster is formed with a node in current V that has the maximum degree (Line 3). Then the algorithm gathers nodes one by one to this current cluster until it has k nodes (Line 4). Due to the power law degree distribution, it is likely that more than one node have the same degree, and this may result in that there are more than one node have the same distance from current cluster. The question is how to select the proper nodes from these candidates for the current cluster with minimal impact on community structure. Different selections lead to different results. Thus, we devise a heuristic algorithm presented in Table 2 for selecting proper nodes.

Table 2. Function 1 $FindBestNode(V, cl_i)$

1: for each node V_p in V: compute $dist(V_p, cl_i)$;
2:     get all V_p from the minimum distance and named them as candidate set $CanN$;
3: if $|CanN| > 1$:
4:     for each node V_q in $CanN$://traverse the list
5:         if V_q and V_{seed}^i are in the same community:
6:             add the V_q to cl_i, and $V = V - \{V_q\}$;break;
7:     if there is no such node, add the last node V_q to cl_i, and $V = V - \{V_q\}$;
8: else: add the V_q in $CanN$ to cl_i, and $V = V - \{V_q\}$;

Besides, when the number of nodes in G is not a multiple of k, it is possible that the number of nodes in current V is less than k. Then, we should find the best cluster for each of them. The specific technique is described as Table 3.

4.2   Reconstruction

To protect user's privacy and analyze data conveniently, the k-cluster social network must to be reconstructed before releasing. However, it will bring more

Table 3. Function 2 $FindBestCluster(V_m, CL)$

1: $mincl = dist(V_m, cl_0)$;
2: for each cluster cl_n in CL: // $1 \leq n \leq i - 1$
3:     if V_m and V_{seed}^i are in the same community:
4:         $Bestcl = cl_n$; Break;
5:     else: compute $dist = dist(V_m, cl_n)$;
6:         if $dist < mincl$: $mincl = dist$; $Bestcl = cl_n$;
7: add V_m to $Bestcl$, $cl_i = cl_i - \{V_m\}$;

uncertainty to reconstruct the entire graph, which is worse for data analyzers to achieve accurate community structure information. Here, we will reconstruct k-cluster graph by randomly regenerating edges in each cluster uniformly and make sure that the number of intra-cluster edges in each cluster is the same as before. Besides, the inter-cluster edges stay the same as before.

By the reason of uniform probability of selecting any pair nodes to regenerate edges in each cluster during the reconstructing process, the probability of each node is selected is equal, in other words, the nodes in one cluster are indistinguishable. Besides, the size of each cluster is no less than k, therefore, the probability for an adversary re-identifies any node in the anonymized social network G' is no more than $1/k$. Then we can safely get that our local-perturbation approach could achieve the same privacy requirement of k-anonymity.

5   Experimental Evaluations

To evaluate the effectiveness of our algorithm, we compare our local-perturbation algorithm with the *SaNGreeA-uniform* anonymizing algorithm proposed in [2,3].

5.1   Datasets and Data Utility

We study the data utility on three real datasets [8]:

- *WebKB* (http://linqs.umiacs.umd.edu/projects//projects/lbc/index.html).
- *Citation* (http://www.datatang.com/data/17310).
- *Cora* (http://www.cs.umd.edu/projects/linqs/projects/lbc/index.html).

We use Jaccard similarity and the change of modularity $\triangle Q$ to compare the results of community structure preservation between initial graph and anonymized graph.

Firstly, we consider the Jaccard similarity. The GN algorithm can detect communities for the initial network and the anonymized network. The set of communities before amonymizing is represented as $C = \{C_1, C_2, \cdots, C_n\}$, and after anonymizing is represented as $C = \{C_1', C_2', \cdots, C_m'\}$.

$$J_i(C_i) = \frac{|C_i \cap C_j'|}{|C_j \cup C_j'|}, i \in [1, n], j \in [1, m] \tag{4}$$

The integral community structure preservation based on Jaccard similarity is computed as the average of all $J_i(C_i)$.

$$J(G, G') = \frac{\sum_{i=1}^{n} J_i}{n}, i \in [1, n] \tag{5}$$

In addition, we also use the change of modularity to compare the community information preservation level. Intuitively, the greater the result gets, the more of the boundaries between communities become blurry, that is, the community structure information of original data does not get better preservation.

$$\triangle Q = Q - Q' \tag{6}$$

5.2 Results and Analysis

Firstly, we evaluate the impact of anonymization on community structure, and the data utility is calculated by the Jaccard similarity and $\triangle Q$.

Figures 3 and 4 represent Jaccard similarity and $\triangle Q$ in terms of changing k values using *SaNGreeA-uniform* algorithm and local-perturbation algorithm respectively. The former figure shows the community structure of original social network has more serious damage with the increase of the values of k. However, our method has more obvious advantages on community structure protection.

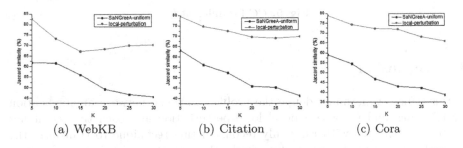

(a) WebKB   (b) Citation   (c) Cora

Fig. 3. Jaccard similarity for different k

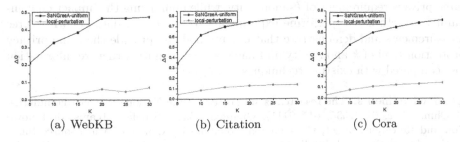

(a) WebKB   (b) Citation   (c) Cora

Fig. 4. $\triangle Q$ for different k

The latter figure suggests that the boundaries between communities of original social network become more blurry with the increase of k, and our algorithm has a relatively smaller impact than *SaNGreeA-uniform* algorithm, because we preserve more community structure information by using our technique.

5.3 Other Structural Property Analysis

The social network is a complex data structure and has many topological properties. In addition to contrast the impact of anonymization for community structure, the average clustering coefficient (CC) is also evaluated.

The change of CC is presented in Fig. 5. With the increase of k, CC becomes smaller and smaller after anonymizing and CC values of *SaNGreeA-uniform* algorithm are even close to 0. Intuitively, our approach has lower differences to the original data.

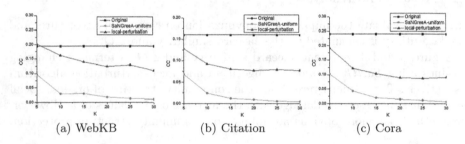

(a) WebKB   (b) Citation   (c) Cora

Fig. 5. CC for different k

6 Conclusion

In this paper, we formally define the problem of social network anonymization for releasing, and propose a novel local-perturbation approach that combines clustering technique with randomly reconstructing technique to transform the original network to the released network. Because of considering the community structure in anonymous procedure, our proposed technique can reach the same privacy requirement of k-anonymity, while minimizing the impact on community structure. We perform experiments on three real datasets with three measurements and demonstrate that our method can provide the same privacy protection level of k-anonymity and have less community structure information loss compared with existing techniques.

Acknowledgments. The research is supported by the National Science Foundation of China (Nos. 61272535, 61502111), Guangxi "Bagui Scholar" Teams for Innovation and Research Project, the Guangxi Collaborative Center of Multi-source Information Integration and Intelligent Processing, Guangxi Natural Science Foundation (Nos. 2013GXNSFBA019263, 2014GXNSFAA118018 and 2015GXNSFBA139246), and the Science and Technology Research Projects of Guangxi Higher Education (Nos. 2015YB032 and 2013YB029), and the Innovation Project of Guangxi Graduate Education (No. YCSZ2015104).

References

1. Boldi, P., et al.: Injecting uncertainty in graphs for identity obfuscation. Proc. VLDB Endow. **5**(11), 1376–1387 (2012)
2. Campan, A., et al.: Preserving communities in anonymized social networks. Trans. Data Priv. **8**(1), 55–87 (2015)
3. Campan, A., Truta, T.M.: Data and structural k-anonymity in social networks. In: Bonchi, F., Ferrari, E., Jiang, W., Malin, B. (eds.) PInKDD 2008. LNCS, vol. 5456, pp. 33–54. Springer, Heidelberg (2009). doi:10.1007/978-3-642-01718-6_4
4. Cheng, J., et al.: K-isomorphism: privacy preserving network publication against structural attacks. In: Proceedings of the 2010 ACM SIGMOD International Conference on Management of data. ACM (2010)
5. Chester, S., et al.: k-anonymization of social networks by vertex addition. In: ADBIS (2) (2011)
6. Fortunato, S.: Community detection in graphs. Phys. Rep. **486**(3), 75–174 (2010)
7. Hechter, M.: Principles of Group Solidarity. University of California Press, Berkeley (1988)
8. Jiao, J., Liu, P., Li, X.: A personalized privacy preserving method for publishing social network data. In: Gopal, T.V., Agrawal, M., Li, A., Cooper, S.B. (eds.) TAMC 2014. LNCS, vol. 8402, pp. 141–157. Springer, Cham (2014). doi:10.1007/978-3-319-06089-7_10
9. Narayanan, A., Shmatikov, V.: De-anonymizing social networks. In: 2009 30th IEEE Symposium on Security and Privacy. IEEE (2009)
10. Newman, M.E., Girvan, M.: Finding and evaluating community structure in networks. Phys. Rev. E **69**(2), 026113 (2004)
11. Tai, C.-H., et al.: Privacy-preserving social network publication against friendship attacks. In: Proceedings of the 17th ACM SIGKDD International Conference on Knowledge Discovery and Data Mining. ACM (2011)
12. Tai, C.-H., et al.: Structural diversity for resisting community identification in published social networks. IEEE Trans. Knowl. Data Eng. **26**(1), 235–252 (2014)

A Low Power Balanced Security Control Protocol of WSN

Yu Jiang[1,2], Jin Wang[3], Lili He[2], Yuanbo Xu[2], and Hongtao Bai[4(✉)]

[1] Key Laboratory of Information System Security of Ministry of Education,
TNLIST, School of Software, Tsinghua University, Beijing 100084, China
jiangyu2011@jlu.edu.cn
[2] College of Computer Science and Technology, Jilin University,
Changchun 130012, China
helili@jlu.edu.cn
[3] Information Engineering College, Yangzhou University,
Yangzhou 225009, China
jinwang@yzu.edu.cn
[4] Center for Computer Fundamental Education, Jilin University,
Changchun 130012, China
baihongtao@263.net

Abstract. Wireless Sensor Network is limited to the energy. Low-power and network security need us to pay adequate attention when it comes to WSN environment. We proposed a new security control protocol in this article named WZ-lcp protocol to meet the needs. The protocol depends on the synchronization of key and time. The key stored with int bytes in the facility and changing with time synchronization. The experimental results on digital wireless gas network show that the proposed protocol ensures security without costing power-wasting and data collision.

Keywords: WSN · WZ-lcp protocol · Authentication · W2-TCP protocol

1 Introduction

WSN contains huge amount of information and value of scientific research. For there is a huge potential market for such appliances there are serious security challenges that have to be addressed in order to realize their true benefits. Recently, there are many researches about public utility automatic reading system. Some studies also design the remote reading system, but without considering the power factor and consumption of system. Few works are about the design and implementation of the low power security control protocol for the gas utility automatic reading system. Obviously, the WSN technology is definitely going to be applied to public utility reading system and have a

H. Bai—This work was supported in part from the National Natural Science Foundation of China (51409117, 51679105, 61672261, 61572228), Jilin Province Department of Education Thirteen Five science and technology research projects [2016] No. 432.

© ICST Institute for Computer Sciences, Social Informatics and Telecommunications Engineering 2017
J.-H. Lee and S. Pack (Eds.): QShine 2016, LNICST 199, pp. 46–51, 2017.
DOI: 10.1007/978-3-319-60717-7_5

wide prospect cause WSN nodes have the ability of self organizing without center node and have wide distribution characteristics [1]. As energy is a limited factor in wireless sensor network, the low power security control protocol is of great significance. Fernndez-Mir et al. proposed the RFID protocol which is not only achieves control delegating but improves the scalability of the whole system. W2-TCP scheme is proved to have effect on the security [2]. However, an authentication is of necessity before a facility join in the network. Bandwidth and energy-saving are the two problems that mainly affect W2-TCP. Many researches have been conducted to provide a plan for WSN. The goal is to achieve the requirement that defend the attack which are as follows: (1) active attack (2) passive attack.

In this paper, we proposed a new security control protocol in this article named WZ-lcp protocol to meet the needs [3]. The protocol depends on the synchronization of key and time. The key stored with int bytes in the facility and changing with time. The experimental results on wireless gas network show that the proposed protocol ensures security without costing power-wasting and data collision.

2   The Proposed Protocol

2.1   Facility Authentication

The WZ-lcp protocol has the following processes.

Authentication Procedure :
Facility Fs, Gateway G
1）*Initialization*
   F_s *initializes GNA, PRF$_1$(x), PRF$_2$(x)*
   F_s *gets a,b,c from G or database*
2）*Authentication*
   F_s *builds the RJF:*
   GNA is G's network address
      $\left.\begin{array}{l} a\ XOR\ GNA->GNA_1 \\ b\ XOR\ GNA->GNA_2 \\ c\ XOR\ GNA->GNA_3 \end{array}\right\}$ *Triple Encryption Key Calculate*
      $\left.\begin{array}{l} GNA_1\ XOR\ RJF\ from\ bth\ byte \\ GNA_2\ XOR\ RJF\ from\ cth\ byte \\ GNA_3\ XOR\ RJF\ from\ ath\ byte \end{array}\right\}$ *Triple Encryption*
3）*Join Network*
   G gets RJF
   G decrypts RJF with a,b,GNA
   G allows F_s to join network

Every facility stores the following information: int a; int b; gateway's network address (GNA); PRF1(x) and PRF2(x). a, b ranges from 0 to 255, PRF1(x) and PRF2(x) are the same. The facility gets a, b, GNA, PRF1 and PRF2 from the gateway or the database. After initializing, when the facility is going to join in the network, it should broadcast a frame with the information the network needs named Request-Join-Frame (RJF). WZ-lcp uses a, b and GNA to encrypt the whole frame. Her we will describe how the encryption is going.

At first, the facility gets a, b and GNA,

$$a \, XOR \, GNA = GNA1$$

$$b \, XOR \, GNA1 = GNA2$$

Then the facility fills all frame to ensure the same length of all kinds of frames with random byte. GNA1 and GNA2 are used to encrypt the whole frame. WZ-lcp uses the XOR twice. First time GNA1 XOR the frame with bytes in length b until all the bytes in the frame are encrypted. Second time GNA2 XOR the frame with bytes in length a until all the bytes in the frame are encrypted (Fig. 1).

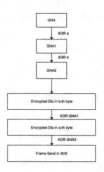

Fig. 1. Encryption in WZ-lcp.

The facility broadcasts the RJF, all the facility in the band can get it. But only the gateway can save a, b, and GNA and have the ability to allow one facility to join in the networks. So it can use a, b, and GNA to decrypt the RJF. Then it can get the information is needs. A link is built to the facility in gateway [4].

The gateway sends a frame named Allow Join Frame which uses the same encrypting method. The facility gets AJF, decrypt the information and build a link to the gateway, either. Finally, the facility sends Confirm Join Frame to the gateway. The gateway adds the facility address to the facility table saved in the storage [5]. The whole authentication is shown in the (Fig. 2).

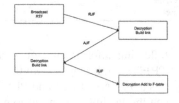

Fig. 2. WZ-lcp authentication process.

2.2   Keys Updating

Key Update Procedure
Gateway G, Fs, Fr

1) Preparations
   Time synchronization Fs, Fr gets t

2) Updating:
   Fs, Fr get PRF$_1$(x) ,PRF$_2$(x), PRF$_3$(x)
$$a_{new} = PRF_1((b_{old}+t)mod256)$$
$$b_{new} = PRF_2((c_{old}+t)mod256)$$
$$c_{new} = PRF_3((a_{old}+t)mod256)$$

3) Transport:
   Fs, Fr send update frame to G

Conventional key update method transfers keys in secret ways. In this way the attackers cannot get the keys easily. But WZ-lcp protocol do not transfer any useful information in this process. The process of key updating is on the basis of time synchronization. In WSN network structures, time synchronization is important. The facility in the WSN should use the time synchronization to transfer data simultaneously. And in automatic reading system, time synchronization occurs repeatedly [6]. The key updating process is described as follows:

Step1: Each of the facilities has two different pseudo-random functions $PRF_1(x)$ and $PRF_2(x)$. At first we need to update a, b with the functions. Then get the time t. with (1), (2), (3) to update,

$$a_{new} = PRF_1((b_{old} + t)mod256) \tag{1}$$

$$b_{new} = PRF_2((c_{old} + t)mod256) \tag{2}$$

$$c_{new} = PRF_3((a_{old} + t)mod256) \tag{3}$$

Step2: As the keys has been updated, all the facilities need to send a frame to the gateway with the bit.

3   Security and Power-Saved Analysis

Compared with W2-TCP protocol, there are some advantages in WZ-lcp protocal. W2-TCP scheme needs the facility to store more variables and hash functions. Table 1 shows the cost of storage both in W2-TCP and WZ-lcp when initializes.

Table 1. Initialization storage cost

Cost of Storage		Function	Variable
W2-TCP	Tag	4	3
	Reader	4	4+X
WZ-lcp		2	2

X means the reader should store an array of variables to ensure the security in W2-TCP scheme. X depends on the size of the RFID system. In W2-TCP, the authentication also needs data transmission for 3 times. But the calculation in W2-TCP is much more complex than WZ-lcp. In order to prove the effectiveness of WZ-lcp, we choose ZigBee protocol to test and verify. We add the authentication and the encryption in ZigBee's APL. Firstly, we use 10 nodes to verify the connectivity in WZ-lcp. The experiment shows that the WZ-lcp can found the WSN based on ZigBee. The gas meter reading system is a fundamental instrument in the house. Figure 3 shows the gas meter node.

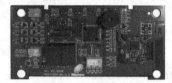

Fig. 3. Gas nodes picture

In hardware, we try to choose those chips with lower consumption, richer resources. The outer circuit should be made up of low energy consumption components and the power should have large capacity and running stability. Otherwise, the system need low voltage and low frequency. In the designing of software, here are some instructions wo need to concern. First of all, MCU time is asked to reduce, we may try the way of interrupt. With this we hope the circulation can be avoided when querying, dynamic scanning through the event-driven way. Working efficiency should be guaranteed and the event of power on/off should be detected.

Tests are done to ensure the security of WZ-lcp protocol and the defense of both active and passive attacks. We then record a, b and the GNA in WZ-lcp in 4 times keys updating. The result in Table 2 shows the active attack is useless for WZ-lcp.

Otherwise, the passive attack is also useless in WZ-lcp for the key updating is quite frequently. According to the network protocol, when MCU starts to work, the time cost of joining network is tjoin_net $\approx$ 10 s, after that MCU will shut down RF transmitter and transfer to sleeping state immediately. Gas nodes wake up once an hour, the active time is no more than 4 s. The active energy consumption in an hour is 0.02284 mAh, the sleep energy consumption is 0.05392 mAh. The energy consumption of sensor module is 0.40033 mA. The energy consumption of power management module for one hour is 1.111×10^{-4} mAh. Finally, we can get the energy consumption of 0.9224533 mAh for a day and 336.695458 mAh for a year.

WZ-lcp is actually a protocol which balanced security and power perfectly. For it takes the advantages of W2-TCP scheme and uses the most applied authentication. Here we will list the advantages of WZ-lcp. At first, the authentication process is repeated for 3 times in data transmission, the repeated work is adopted in ZigBee and TCP/IP. Power and the bandwidth are saved at the same time. The process of the whole authentication requires only three keys and two functions and this can solve the problem of lacking storage and computing capacities. Besides, the XOR calculation is

Table 2. Encryption in WZ-lcp

DATA	GNA	a	b	c	t	GNA$_1$	GNA$_2$	GNA$_3$	DATA$_{enp}$
1F59D55800	77	5	34	8	9	1A	DD	D1	F58EDB6E01
1F59D55800	77	32	12	23	12	7D	A3	3C	EBFBEA0605
1F59D55800	77	6	5	34	24	D3	D4	B3	AB3B493FBC
1F59D55800	77	22	23	2	33	D2	66	B9	F58BABC142
1F59D55800	77	44	14	17	16	20	01	A2	D4373C9BC0
1F59D55800	77	26	33	28	59	F1	B8	F4	25FA61605A
1F59D55800	77	55	6	58	60	7C	F7	F9	71B6B176D5
1F59D55800	77	17	5	28	15	73	BC	8E	6215A29652
1F59D55800	77	59	2	45	48	BA	15	C7	CCB6BBBAB8
1F59D55800	77	0	4	39	11	90	18	92	453734C7FE

done for 3 times for security concerns. The XOR calculation is not a question for ARM and 8051 CPU. At last, WZ-lcp protocol can ensure the timeliness and consistency.

4   Conclusions and Further Work

In this paper, we proposed a new security control protocol in this article named WZ-lcp Protocol to meet the needs. The protocol depends on the synchronization of key and time. The key stored with int bytes in the facility and changing with time synchronization. The experimental results on digital wireless gas network show that the proposed protocol ensures security without costing power-wasting and data collision.

References

1. Song, S., He, L., Jiang, Yu., Hu, C., Cao, Y.: Wireless sensor network time synchronization algorithm based on SFD. In: Wang, R., Xiao, F. (eds.) CWSN 2012. CCIS, vol. 334, pp. 393–400. Springer, Heidelberg (2013). doi:10.1007/978-3-642-36252-1_37
2. Jiang, Y., Liang, Y., Cui, Y., et al.: Wireless digital gas meter with lower power consumption. In: 2010 Fifth International Conference on Frontier of Computer Science and Technology (FCST), pp. 192–197. IEEE (2010)
3. Xu, Y., Jiang, Y., Hu, C., et al.: A balanced security protocol of wireless sensor network for smart home. In: 2014 12th International Conference on Signal Processing (ICSP), pp. 2324–2327. IEEE (2014)
4. Lv, P., Lai, S.: A solution of hybrid TCP transmission in RFID reader network. In: 2006 IET International Conference on Wireless, Mobile and Multimedia Networks, pp. 1–4. IET (2006)
5. Li, J., Brassil, J.: On the performance of traffic equalizers on heterogeneous communication links. In: Proceedings of the 3rd International Conference on Quality of Service in Heterogeneous Wired/Wireless Networks, p. 33. ACM (2006)
6. Darsena, D., Gelli, G., Verde, F.: Non-cooperative superposition relaying for multicarrier cognitive networks. In: 2016 IEEE 27th Annual International Symposium on Personal, Indoor, and Mobile Radio Communications (PIMRC), pp. 1–6. IEEE (2016)

Firmware Verification of Embedded Devices Based on a Blockchain

Boohyung Lee$^{(\boxtimes)}$, Sehrish Malik, Sarang Wi, and Jong-Hyouk Lee

Protocol Engineering Laboratory, Sangmyung University,
Cheonan, Republic of Korea
{boohyung,serry,sarang,jonghyouk}@pel.smuc.ac.kr
http://pel.smuc.ac.kr

Abstract. In this paper, a new firmware verification scheme is presented that utilizes blockchain technologies for securing network embedded devices. In the proposed scheme, an embedded device requests a firmware verification to nodes connected in a blockchain network and gets a response whether its firmware is up-to-date or not. If not latest, the embedded device can securely download and install the latest firmware from a firmware update server. Even in the case that the version of the firmware is up-to-date, its integrity is checked via the blockchain nodes. The proposed scheme guarantees that the embedded device's firmware is not tampered and latest. The effects of attacks targeting known vulnerabilities are thus minimized.

Keywords: Blockchain · Firmware verification · Embedded device

1 Introduction

According to the Gartner's report [1], the Internet of Things (IoT) era will change our live with network connected devices. The number of IoT devices is expected to be 5 billion by 2020 and the number will continuously increase. The IoT devices are tiny and small, while those are mostly embedded devices designed for specific operations, e.g., sensing, automation, etc.

Recent cyber attacks are targeting firmware, which is a software program on an embedded device [2], rather than services built on well turned servers [3]. Due to limited resources and capacities of embedded devices, strong security properties have not been applied yet to the embedded devices. Many bugs and vulnerabilities of embedded devices are reported every day and those are being used by attackers to break into the embedded devices.

One of feasible ways to protect the embedded devices is to reduce the attack window time by installing a latest firmware. It will help to minimize the effects of attacks targeting known vulnerabilities. As physical access to the embedded devices is possible, a verification of the firmware integrity is also required. In addition, due to the increasing number of the embedded devices, excessive network traffic may occur when downloading the latest firmware simultaneously

© ICST Institute for Computer Sciences, Social Informatics and Telecommunications Engineering 2017
J.-H. Lee and S. Pack (Eds.): QShine 2016, LNICST 199, pp. 52–61, 2017.
DOI: 10.1007/978-3-319-60717-7_6

from a firmware update server. In other words, the current client and server model is not suitable for firmware distribution in an IoT environment.

With this in mind, in this paper, we propose a new firmware verification scheme that utilizes blockchain technologies. In the proposed scheme, an embedded device requests a firmware verification to blockchain nodes on a peer-to-peer decentralised network. It then receives a response whether its firmware is up-to-date or not. When the firmware is not latest, the embedded device can securely download and install the latest one from a firmware update server. Even in the case that the version of the firmware is up-to-date, the firmware integrity is checked via the blockchain nodes. Accordingly, the proposed scheme guarantees that the embedded device's firmware is not tampered and latest.

This paper is organized as follows. Section 2 reviews the ideas of blockchain. Section 3 presents the proposed scheme with the overall architecture and operation procedures. Section 4 concludes this paper.

2   Blockchain

The blockchain was first proposed in 2009 by an anonymous person, Nakamoto [4]. It was first used as a public ledger to provide trust transactions without an involvement of the third party for Bitcoin, which is a digital currency.

2.1   Block

In the blockchain, a block is used to preserve data or information. Every block contains a hash value of the previous block header that forms a type of chain [5]. It is then used to authenticate the data and guarantee the block's integrity.

The structure of block, for instance in Bitcoin, is made up of the block header and block body. The block header is composed of the block size, version, previous block header's hash, merkle root, etc. The block's body is consisted of the merkle tree and transaction. A merkle tree [6] is also called a hash tree. Leaf nodes of the tree make the hash value of blocks. It is useful because it allows an efficient verification of the block with the merkle root. Finally, a transaction is information of Bitcoin value that is broadcasted to the network and collected into blocks. In this scheme, the block is used with some changes in the block body.

2.2   Cryptographic Idea

A blockchain relies on two cryptographic methods: digital signature and cryptographic hash function. A digital signature is a way for demonstrating the authenticity of a digital message. It can be used to provide integrity and authentication of data as well as non-repudiation. A sender signs a message using the sender's private key. After a receiver receives this message, it verifies the message using the sender's public key. This message can be verified by anyone holding the valid public key of the sender [7].

A cryptographic hash function is a mathematical operation that computes a hash value. The function is deterministic, i.e., the same input will always produce the same output, with the following properties: pre-image resistance, second pre-image resistance, and collision resistance. In a blockchain, a SHA-256 hash function is used [8].

3   Proposed Firmware Validation Scheme

The proposed scheme provides secure operations to verify an embedded device's firmware. If the device's firmware is not up-to-date, the firmware update is proceeded with a firmware update server. Otherwise, the firmware's integrity is checked by blockchain nodes. Notations used are shown in Table 1.

3.1   Overview

Figure 1 depicts the overall architecture of the proposed scheme with the following entities:

– Blockchain node: A node in a blockchain network. A set of blockchain nodes is denoted as $B = \{b_1, b_2, ..., b_n\}$ and $b_i \in B$.
– Normal node: A normal node is a device which needs to verify its firmware in a blockchain network. A set of normal nodes is denoted as $N = \{n_1, n_2, ..., n_n\}$, $n_i \in N$, and $N \subset B$. It can be a request node or a response node. If a node requests its firmware verification, the node becomes a request node. After the verification process, it can validate its firmware. When a request node sends the request message to verify its firmware, other normal nodes can response. At this moment, the node responding to the request message becomes a response node that verifies the request node's firmware.

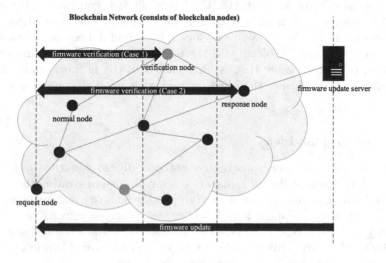

Fig. 1. Overall architecture

Table 1. Notation

Terminology	Definition
N	A set of normal nodes
V	A set of verification nodes
S	A set of firmware update servers
B	A set of blockchain nodes
D	A model name of n_i
r	Random number
ts	Timestamp
v	Current firmware version of n_i
v_{new}	Latest firmware version of n_i
v'	Current firmware version of n_j
fv	Current firmware file of v
fv'	Current firmware file of v'
fv_{new}	Latest firmware file of v_{new}
$H(fv)$	Verifier generated with fv
$H(fv')$	Verifier generated with fv'
$H(fv_{new})$	Verifier generated with fv_{new}
IDn_i	Identifier of n_i
IDv_i	Identifier of v_i
IDs_i	Identifier of s_i
E	Elliptic Curve
P	Base point of Elliptic Curve E
PUn_i	Public key of n_i
PRn_i	Private key of n_i
PUv_i	Public key of v_i
PRv_i	Private key of v_i
PUs_i	Public key of s_i
PRs_i	Private key of s_i
$SK_{n_i-s_i}$	Session key between n_i and s_i
$Sign_i$	Signature of n_i
$Sigv_i$	Signature of v_i
$Sigs_i$	Signature of s_i

- Verification node: A verification node is located to validate the firmware of normal nodes by a vendor. A set of verification nodes is denoted as $V = \{v_1, v_2, ..., v_n\}, v_i \in V$, and $V \subset B$. It has a verifier of latest firmware versions corresponding to the model name D. A size of the verifier is 256 bits when SHA-256 is used. The verifier can be updated periodically by the firmware update server via the secure channel between the verification node and firmware update server.

- Firmware update server: A firmware update server may be administered by a vendor producing embedded devices. A set of firmware update servers is denoted as $S = \{s_1, s_2, ..., s_n\}, s_i \in S$. The normal node obtains the latest firmware from the firmware update server. The files (e.g., firmware) transferred between the two are encrypted via the session key.

Figure 2, wherein the request node is n_i and response node is n_j, shows the overall procedure of the proposed scheme. When a normal node wants to verify its firmware, it broadcasts a verification request message in the blockchain network. After receiving the message, any node (verification node or normal node) responds to the verification request. Following are the two cases depending on the type of the nodes involved.

- C1: Firmware verification between a normal node and a verification node
- C2: Firmware verification among normal nodes

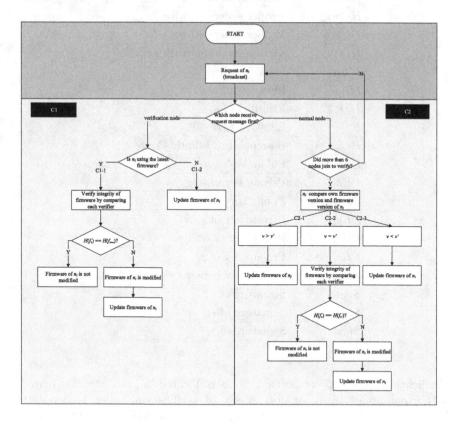

Fig. 2. Overall procedure

In C1, a verification node confirms whether a request node uses the latest version of the firmware or not. If the request node uses the latest version of the firmware, it checks whether the request node's firmware is modified through exchanging and comparing each other's verifiers. Otherwise, the request node's firmware is updated by the firmware update server.

In C2, a response node asks other nodes to join the verification process. After receiving the messages from more than six other nodes, the request node and response node start comparing their firmware versions. If they use the same version of firmware, then they check whether the firmware has been altered by comparing each other's verifiers. If the version is not the same, the normal node requests an update from the firmware update server.

3.2 Assumptions

The followings are assumed for the proposed scheme.

- The network is composed of blockchain nodes connected to each other. More than eight normal nodes having the same firmware information with a request node should exist for the firmware verification without an involvement of a verification node. A vendor has to install more than one verification node.
- A normal node's ID is a random unique value as the ID is generated when the normal node requests the verification process based on its public key as like the address of the Bitcoin's blockchain. It provides privacy for the normal node.

3.3 Block Structure

The proposed scheme uses a different block structure compared with that of Bitcoin's blockchain. Note that we altered one field. The block in the proposed scheme is made up of the block header and verification field. The block header is composed of the block size, version, previous block header hash, and merkle root. The verification field consists of the verification counter, merkle tree, verification log, model name, firmware version, and verifier. Details of the field are given below.

- Verification counter: This is the number of successful verifications. It is a value which is only considered in a normal node's block. It is similar with the block height in Bitcoin [9]. In a verification node, this value is fixed at 0.
- Merkle tree: It is a tree information for the calculation of the merkle root. It is used for the verification of block data. It is also used as a feature for managing memory of node efficiently [4].
- Verification log: It is a verification log composed of the verification time (timestamp), request node's ID, and response node's ID. If a verification node responses for the request message, the request node's ID and verification node's ID are stored to this field. In addition, this field includes the signature of the request node using a private key so that all nodes can verify the signature.

- Model name: It is a normal node's model name.
- Firmware version: It is a normal node's current firmware version.
- Verifier: It is a hash value of a firmware file. This value is used to verify the firmware integrity without comparing genuine files. Each node stores a verifier in the verification field of the block. If the firmware file is composed of more than one file, then those should be concatenated before generating the verifier.

3.4   Cryptographic Ideas

The proposed scheme uses cryptographic schemes to encrypt a verifier to be transmitted, verify a signature, and exchange a session key.

- Data encryption and key exchange: When n_i requests firmware verification, n_i generates private key a, and selects random point of Elliptic curve P [10]. The public key aP is generated by multiplying a and P. The public key is used to encrypt a verifier. If n_i needs to update, its firmware is updated by the firmware update server. For this, Elliptic Curve Diffie-Hellman (ECDH) is used to generate the session key for encrypting the latest firmware file being transmitted from the firmware update server to the embedded device.
- Digital signature: When n_i signs its verification log using the private key of n_i, any node can verify this log with a corresponding public key.

3.5   Procedure

As mentioned, the proposed scheme has the two cases: C1 and C2. The case C1 is then divided into two sub cases (C1-1 and C1-2), while the case C2 is also similarly separated into C2-1, C2-2, and C2-3. The cases are set into motion after a node requests to verify its firmware. Hereafter we assume that n_i and n_j are the request node and response node, respectively.

C1. When n_i transmits the request message to the blockchain network and a verification node responds to the request, C1 starts. C1 has two different subcases.

- C1-1: It starts when n_i has the latest firmware.
- C1-2: It starts when n_i does not have the latest firmware.

When a verification node receives the request message, it checks whether n_i's firmware is latest or not. If n_i uses the latest firmware, then the firmware integrity is verified by exchanging each other's public key and comparing their verifiers. On the other hand, n_i requests the update operation to a firmware update server, which provides the latest firmware file, which is encrypted with a session key. Figures 3 and 4 show the procedures of C1-1 and C1-2.

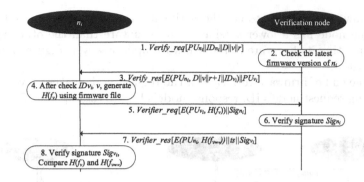

Fig. 3. Procedure of C1-1: n_i has the latest firmware

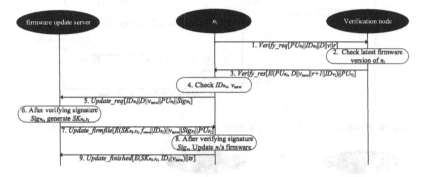

Fig. 4. Procedure of C1-2: n_i does not have the latest firmware

C2. The verification is performed among normal nodes in C2. Contrary to C1, n_j is not a verification node in C2. In C1, authenticity of a verifier is not considered since the verification node is managed safely by the firmware update server. However, in C2, the legitimacy of a verifier must be considered. To confirm the reliability of n_j's verifier, the Proof of Work (PoW) used in Bitcoin [4] is utilized in the proposed scheme. When n_j receives a request message, n_j asks other nodes to join the verification process by sending a join message. And other nodes perform the PoW stage. After completing the PoW, they add the request node's ID, response node's ID, and current time to the verification log in their blocks and then broadcast a verification log message to the blockchain network. If n_j receives the verification log messages from more than six other nodes, n_j responds with a request message of n_i. In this regard, the six nodes ensure n_j's verifier by collaborating with each other for this verification process. The C2 has three different sub-cases.

- C2-1: It starts when n_i's firmware version is higher than n_j's firmware version.
- C2-2: It starts when n_i's firmware version and n_j's firmware version are equal.
- C2-3: It starts when n_i's firmware version is lower than n_j's firmware version.

If each firmware version is equal, the verification process is performed as like C1-1. If one node has a lower version of the firmware than the other node, it requests updating its firmware to the firmware update server. Figures 5, 6 and 7 show the detail.

After the end of firmware verification, the request node makes its verification log including request node's ID, response node's ID, timestamp, etc. The request

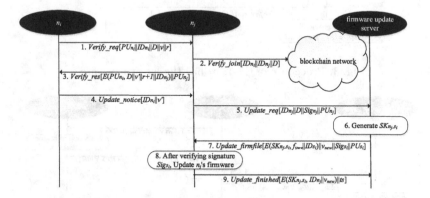

Fig. 5. Procedure of C2-1: n_i's firmware version is higher than n_j's one

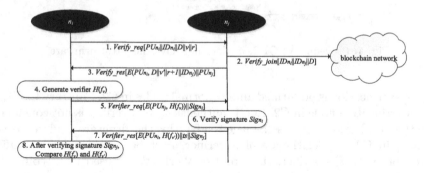

Fig. 6. Procedure of C2-2: n_i's firmware version is equal with n_j's one

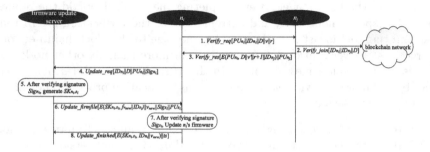

Fig. 7. Procedure of C2-3: n_i's firmware version is lower than n_j's one

node then broadcasts it to the blockchain network. Consequentially, it enables to validate the firmware integrity and decide whether the update firmware on the device requires or not without a user's control.

4   Conclusion

In this paper, we presented the proposed scheme that provides a secure firmware verification of an embedded device among blockchain nodes in the network. The proposed scheme guarantees that the embedded device's firmware is not tampered and latest. The effects of attacks targeting known vulnerabilities are thus minimized. For firmware updating, a firmware file is transmitted from a firmware update server to an embedded device. As a next work, we will study how to replace the client-server model for firmware file transmissions with a P2P network model.

Acknowledgment. This work was supported by Basic Science Research Program through the National Research Foundation of Korea (NRF) funded by the Ministry of Science, ICT and Future Planning (NRF-2014R1A1A1006770).

References

1. Gartner: Gartner Says 4.9 Billion Connected Things Will Be in Use in 2015. Gartner Newsroom, November 2014
2. Firmware - Wikipedia. https://en.wikipedia.org/wiki/Firmware
3. Choi, B.-C., Lee, S.-H., Na, J.-C., Lee, J.-H.: Secure firmware validation and update for consumer devices in home networking. IEEE Trans. Consum. Electron. **62**(1), 39–44 (2016)
4. Nakamoto, S.: Bitcoin: a peer-to-peer electronic cash system (2009), Unpublished Manuscript
5. Blockchain Bitcoin Wiki. https://en.bitcoin.it/wiki/Blockchain
6. Hu, Y., Perrig, A., Johnson, D.B.: Efficient security mechanisms for routing protocols. In: Proceedings of the NDSS 2003, February 2003
7. Badev, A., Chen, M.: Bitcoin: Technical Background and Data Analysis. Federal Reserve Board, Washington, D.C. (2013)
8. Bider, D., Baushke, M.: SHA-2 data integrity for the secure shell (SSH) transport layer protocol. IETF RFC 6668, July 2012
9. Antonopoulos, A.M.: Mastering Bitcoin: Unlocking Digital Cryptocurrencies. OReilly Media, Sebastopol (2014)
10. Blake-Wilson, S., Bolyard, N., Gupta, V., Hawk, C., Moeller, B.: Elliptic Curve Cryptography (ECC) Cipher Suites for Transport Layer Security (TLS). IETF RFC 4492, May 2006

Group Key Based Session Key Establishment Protocol for a Vehicle Diagnostic

Sarang Wi$^{(\boxtimes)}$, Kiwoon Moon, Boohyung Lee, and Jong-Hyouk Lee

Protocol Engineering Laboratory, Sangmyung University,
Cheonan, Republic of Korea
{sarang,kiwoon,boohyung,jonghyouk}@pel.smuc.ac.kr
http://pel.smuc.ac.kr

Abstract. In this paper, a group key based session key establishment protocol is introduced for a remote vehicle diagnostic. The proposed scheme aims at providing secure authentication and session key establishment between a vehicle manufacturer server and a group of in-vehicle electronic control unit based on a key graph.

Keywords: Key graph · Group key · Authentication · Session key

1 Introduction

As wireless communication and networking technologies continue to develop, vehicular communication technologies are emerging. Connected cars are expected to be in our daily life soon. Various services like traffic information notification, location-based services, vehicle remote diagnostic will be available [1].

A connected car is considered as a computing device that moves along roads. BI Intelligence expects that the connected car occupied 75% of the world's automotive production in 2020 [2]. This computing device is not only providing web browsing, video streaming, etc. but also used as a vehicle that carries people inside. As like personal computers and smartphones, the connected car is connected to other cars and also to the Internet so that it can be a target by attackers. For instance, an attacker can obtain vehicle state information and use this maliciously control the vehicle speed and breaking system [3].

As a preliminary work, a session key establishment protocol for vehicle diagnostic has been investigated that was based on symmetric key cryptosystem [4]. It has some practical issues, e.g., the number of symmetric key increases as the number of the Electronic Control Units (ECUs) in a car increases [4]. In other words, in terms of key management, the preliminary work is inefficient. In order to address this issue, in this paper, we are focused on developing a secure session key establishment protocol for a vehicle diagnostic based on group key graphs.

The rest of the paper is organized as follows. In Sect. 2, we present some related works. In Sect. 3, we present the proposed scheme. Section 4 concludes this paper.

© ICST Institute for Computer Sciences, Social Informatics and Telecommunications Engineering 2017
J.-H. Lee and S. Pack (Eds.): QShine 2016, LNICST 199, pp. 62–71, 2017.
DOI: 10.1007/978-3-319-60717-7_7

2   Background

2.1   In-Vehicle Communication

The remote diagnostic is a service that allows a vehicle manufacturer monitors a vehicle's status through ECUs in the vehicle. The obtained information can be used for vehicle diagnosis. For example we check tire, engine, turbo charger, etc., through the information [5,6]. The ECUs make up a larger percentage of in-vehicle electronic unit and the percentage will be increased countinously [7].

A in-vehicle network is mainly implemented as a Controller Area Network (CAN), which provides the most transmission speed to up 1 Mbit/s [8]. To overcome the inefficiency of CAN that is low-speed and data transmission mode, Flexray has been introduced [9]. Recently the use of Ethernet in a in-vehicle network has been considered [10].

2.2   Group Key

There is a case for transmitting secure data unto the only member of a group. If each user uses a pair of symmetric keys to encrypt the data, it would be inefficient in terms of network bandwidth, computation, key management cost. To overcome this limitation, a group key has been introduced that all member of a group shares a same key. The important part of a group key use is a group dynamic, which means that the member of the group can be changed. The requirements for group keying are thus as follows [11].

– Forward secrecy: When a member leaves from the group, the member who knows the old group key should not be able to know a new group key.
– Backward secrecy: when a member join to the group, the member who knows the current group key should not be able to know the old group key.

We use key graphs as a group key management model. We describe the idea of a secure group as (E, K, R) where E is a set of users, K is a set of keys, and R denotes $R \subset E * K$, which is a user-key relation. A key is held by each ECU in E.

We need a secure server to manage the group keys. The server should distribute safely the key unto a member of the ECU group and maintain the relation R between the ECU and the key of a group. Each ECU of the group has a set of keys: ECU's individual key k_{e_u}, a sub-group key, and a group key. The ECU's individual key is shared only with the key management server. Let Z is a group name. For Z, the group key is K_{Gr_z}, which is used to send a message securely to other ECU belonging to Z.

In this paper, we explain special classes of key graphs (i.e., Tree) to explain the key management. This key graph has two types: e-nodes representing ECUs and k-node representing keys. Each e-node has an outgoing edge but no incoming edge. Each k-node has an incoming edge. Among k-node top k-node is called as a root node. And the root node is single. This key graph has two parameters height and degree. height is the distance between the root node and uttermost with root node and end node. *degree* is the maximum number of incoming edges in the tree.

Relation of key graph G and secure group (E, K, R) is as follows:

1. E and the set of *e-node* is an one to one correspondence in G.
2. K and the set of *k-node* is an one to one correspondence in G.
3. R constitutes (e, k). G shows a directed path between *e-node* that corresponds e and *k-node* that corresponds to k.

For the key management, suppose that there exists nine ECUs and the ECUs are divided into three subgroups. The subgroups are $\{e_1, e_2, e_3\}$, $\{e_4, e_5, e_6\}$, and $\{e_7, e_8, e_9\}$. Each ECU has three keys: individual key, entire group key, and subgroup key. The tree key graphs G in Fig. 1 specifies the following a secure group.

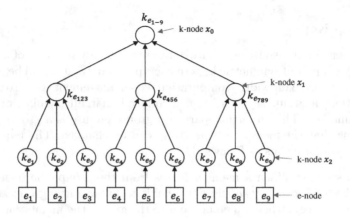

Fig. 1. Tree key graph

$E = \{e_1, e_2, e_3, e_4, e_5, e_6, e_7, e_8, e_9\}$
$K = \{k_{e_1}, k_{e_2}, k_{e_3}, k_{e_4}, k_{e_5}, k_{e_6}, k_{e_7}, k_{e_8}, k_{e_9}, k_{e_{123}}, k_{e_{456}}, k_{e_{789}}, k_{e_{1-9}}\}$
$R = \{(e_1, k_{e_1}), (e_1, k_{e_{123}}), (e_1, k_{e_{1-9}}),$
$\quad\ (e_2, k_{e_2}), (e_2, k_{e_{123}}), (e_2, k_{e_{1-9}}),$
$\quad\ (e_3, k_{e_1}), (e_3, k_{e_{123}}), (e_3, k_{e_{1-9}}),$
$\quad\ (e_4, k_{e_1}), (e_4, k_{e_{456}}), (e_4, k_{e_{1-9}}),$
$\quad\ (e_5, k_{e_1}), (e_5, k_{e_{456}}), (e_5, k_{e_{1-9}}),$
$\quad\ (e_6, k_{e_1}), (e_6, k_{e_{456}}), (e_6, k_{e_{1-9}}),$
$\quad\ (e_7, k_{e_1}), (e_7, k_{e_{789}}), (e_7, k_{e_{1-9}}),$
$\quad\ (e_8, k_{e_1}), (e_8, k_{e_{789}}), (e_8, k_{e_{1-9}}),$
$\quad\ (e_9, k_{e_1}), (e_9, k_{e_{789}}), (e_9, k_{e_{1-9}})\}$

Here, $k_{e_{1-9}}$ is a group key. The following two functions are defined for the secure group (E, K, R):

$keyset(e) = \{k \mid (e, k) \in R\}$
$ECUset(k) = \{u \mid (e, k) \in R\}$

$keyset(e)$ is a set of keys that has ECU e in E. $ECUset(k)$ is a set of ECUs that has key k in K. For example, applying this function in Fig. 1, we have $keyset(e_3) = \{k_{e_3}, k_{e_{123}}, k_{e_{1-9}}\}$ and $ECUset(k_{e_{456}}) = \{e_4, e_5, e_6\}$.

All details about the key management using tree key graphs are available in [12], which have been also adopted in this paper.

3 Proposed Scheme

In this section, we present the proposed scheme designed for establishing a secure session key between a vehicle manufacturer server and a vehicle ECU based on a group key. The session key is then used for instance to encrypt and decrypt data communications between the server and ECU for a vehicle diagnostic.

3.1 Notation and Assumption

Before explaining used notations and assumptions, we explain main agents of communication. The main agents is server of vehicle manufacturer S, in-vehicle gateway Gw, vehicle ECU E_i. When a car is out of the shop, it establishes a session key through authentication between entities. Table 1 shows the notations used for the proposed scheme.

Table 1. Notation

Notations	Definition
S	vehicle manufacturer's server
Gw	in-vehicle gateway
E_i	vehicle ECU
Gr_z	vehicle ECU group z
ID_S	ID of S
ID_{Gw}	ID of Gw
ID_{E_i}	ID of E_i
ID_{Gr_z}	ID of Gr_z
J	secret key of Gw
K	shared key between S and Gw
Q	secret key of GW; used for creating a group key
K_{E_i}	secret key between Gw and E_i
K_{Gr_z}	group key of ECU group z
SK_{S-Gr_z}	session key between S and Gr_z
$E_{key}[]$	symmetric encryption
$D_{key}[]$	symmetric decryption
R	server's nonce
$h(.)$	one-way cryptographic hash function

The assumptions are as followings.

1. When the vehicle is shipped, S is authenticated with Gw. A secure channel between S and Gw is established.
2. When the vehicle is shipped, Gw have a three secure key J, K, Q.
3. When the vehicle is shipped, Gw and E_i share a secure key K_{E_i}.

3.2 Operation Process

Vehicle Registration for Server. When a vehicle is produced, Gw is registered with S. In this time, S sends ID_S unto Gw securely. Gw receives ID_S from S. And Gw computes $C_{ig} = E_J[ID_S||ID_{Gw}]$. Only Gw creates C_{ig}. Here, C_{ig} is used for mutual authentication between S and Gw. Gw sends C_{ig}, K unto S through a secure channel. Here, J, K are secure keys in Gw for a long time.

Authentication Between Vehicle and Serve. For communicate between S and E_i, Gw (i.e., key management server in a vehicle) makes a group key of each ECU group and sends a message including the group key that encrypted by each E_i's individual key. E_i decrypts the message using the own individual key. It is possible that it does encrypted communication between Gw and E_i. In Fig. 2, shows the session key establishment process between vehicle and S.

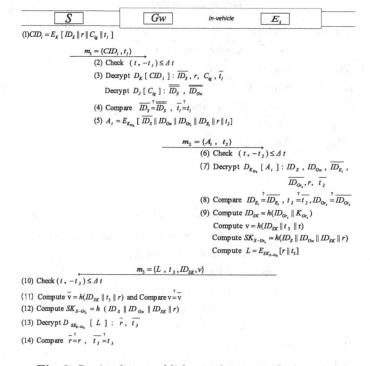

Fig. 2. Session key establishment between vehicle and S

1. S computes $CID_i = E_k[ID_S||r||C_{ig}||t_1]$. ID_S is server's ID. r is a random number. C_{ig} is received from Gw when the vehicle is manufactured. t_1 is the current time of S. Thereafter, S sends a message $m_1 = \{CID_i, t_1\}$ unto Gw. CID_i is used for authentication between S and Gw.

2. Upon receiving S's message, Gw performs the following steps. Check, if $(t_* - t_1) \leq \Delta t$, if yes, then Gw performs the next process. Otherwise, it rejects the request and aborts any further process. Here, Δt is the time interval for the transmission delay and t_* is the current time of Gw.

3. Gw decrypts the message CID_i, using key K (i.e., $D_K[CID_i]$) and obtains $\overline{ID}_S$, r, C_{ig} and $\overline{t}_1$. Similarly, it decrypts the message C_{ig} using key J (i.e., $D_J[C_{ig}]$) and obtains $\overline{\overline{ID_S}}$ and $\overline{\overline{ID_{Gw}}}$.

4. Gw compares $\overline{ID_S} = \overline{\overline{ID_S}}$ and $t_1 = \overline{t}_1$, if yes, then Gw continues with the next steps; otherwise it aborts the request.

5. Gw computes $A_i = E_{K_{Gr_z}}[\overline{ID_S}||ID_{Gw}||ID_{Gr_z}||ID_{E_i}||r||t_2]$. Here, t_2 is the current time of Gw. Thereafter, Gw sends the message $m_2 = \{A_i, t_2\}$ unto E_i. A_i is used for authentication between Gw and E_i. This process delivers S's ID_S, r to create the session key of E_i.

6. Upon receiving Gw's message, the E_i performs the following steps. Check, if $(t_* - t_2) \leq \Delta t$, if yes, then E_i performs the next process. Otherwise, it rejects the request and aborts any further process. Here, t_* is the current time of E_i.

7. E_i decrypts the message A_i using group key K_{Gr_z} (i.e., $D_{K_{Gr_z}}[A_i]$), and obtains ID_s, ID_{Gw}, $\overline{ID_{E_i}}$, $\overline{ID_{Gr_z}}$, r, $\overline{t}_2$.

8. E_i compares $ID_{E_i} = \overline{ID_{E_i}}$, $t_2 = \overline{t}_2$, $ID_{Gr_z} = \overline{ID_{Gr_z}}$, if yes, then E_i continues with the next steps; otherwise it aborts the request.

9. E_i computes $ID_{SK} = h(ID_{Gr_z}||K_{Gr_z})$, $v = h(ID_{SK}||t_3||r)$, session key $SK_{S-Gr_z} = h(ID_S||ID_{Gw}||ID_{SK}||r)$, and $L = E_{SK_{S-Gr_z}}[r||t_3]$. Here, t_3 is the current time of E_i. After that, E_i sends the message $m_3 = \{L, ID_{SK}, v, t_3\}$ unto S.

10. Upon receiving the E_i's message, S validates the time as follows. Check, if $(t_* - t_3) \leq \Delta t$, if yes, then S performs the next process. Otherwise, S rejects the request and aborts any further process. Here, t_* is the current time of S.

11. S computes $\overline{v} = h(ID_{SK}||t_3||r)$, and compares $v = \overline{v}$, if yes, then S continues with the next steps; otherwise it aborts the request.

12. S computes session key $SK_{S-Gr_z} = h(ID_S||ID_{Gw}||ID_{SK}||r)$.

13. S decrypts the message L using key SK_{S-Gr_z} (i.e., $D_{SK_{S-Gr_z}}[L]$), and obtains $\overline{r}$, $\overline{t}_3$.

14. S compares $r = \overline{r}$, $t_3 = \overline{t}_3$, if yes, then a secure session key is established; otherwise not.

When the session key establishment is completed, E_i sends a message including the session key to other ECUs in the same group so that other ECUs will have the session key for secure communications with S.

3.3   Key Management Among the ECU

In this section, we present the key management for the ECUs based on a group key. We concentrate upon the group key when joining and leaving of the group. The group key cryptosystem should create a new key (i.e., new individual key, new subgroup key, new group key) for a group for joining and leaving events. Here, the creating new key should not analogize the whole out of an old key and should send that only the member within a group knows the key. Joining and leaving of proposed environment happened on two occasions. The first occurs registration that is all ECU into the server when the vehicle is shipped. The second occurs that the ECU's something the matter. When the second occasions, the ECU replaces the new ECU in a garage.

Joining. An ECU e which want to join the secure group sends requesting message to join to the key distribution server. This key server manages group and has access management authority. When is received the requesting message, the server begins an exchange for authentication ECU e. If join request is approved, as a result of the authentication the server and ECU e has the session key k_{e_u}. The server creates a new e-*node* of ECU e and new k-*node* of e's individual key. The server looks for joining point which we call parent node to attach newly created k-*node* in tree key graphs, and attaches this k-*node*. After the server creates new group key. To prevent a join of new member e in the past communication access, the key must be changed from joining point to root node. These keys must be delivered safely unto joining member and existing members. So the key management server encrypts these keys by previous group key for existing members or individual key for joining member.

If the server authorizes the ECU e and distribute the key k_{e_u} unto e, that thing as follows. The server finds a joining point and attach k_{e_u}. At the time x_j denotes the joining point, x_0 the root, and when $i = 1, \ldots, j$, x_{i-1} the parent of x_i. K_{j+1} denotes k_{e_u} and $K_0, \ldots, K_j$ the old keys of $x_0, \ldots, x_j$. The server generates new keys $K'_0, \ldots, K'_j$. The server sends $K'_0, \ldots, K'_j$ unto each ECU. When expressed as a function, it is $ECUset(K_0) : \{K'_0\}_{K_0}, \ldots, \{K'_j\}_{K_j}$. And it sends $\{K'_0, \ldots, K'_j\}_{k_{e_u}}$ unto ECU e.

In Fig. 3, e_9 sends requesting message to join. And it is assumed that the approval for e_9 the secure group. The server creates new group key $k_{e_{1-9}}$ and

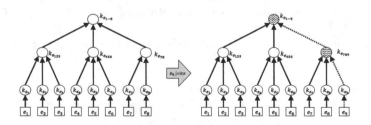

Fig. 3. ECU e_9 requests to join in a tree key graphs

new sub-group key $k_{e_{789}}$ which call joining point node's key. Among the existing ECU e_1, e_2, ..., e_6 need to new group key (i.e., $k_{e_{1-9}}$) and e_7, e_8 need to a new group key, a new sub-group key (i.e., $k_{e_{789}}, k_{e_{1-9}}$). The server sends securely rekey message to distribute the key. Rekey message is as follows.

$$s \to \{e_1, e_2, \ldots, e_8\} : E_{k_{e_{1-8}}}[k_{e_{1-9}}],\ E_{k_{e_{78}}}[k_{e_{789}}] \cdots \quad (1)$$

$$s \to e_9 \qquad\qquad : E_{k_{e_9}}[k_{e_{1-9}}, k_{e_{789}}] \cdots\cdots\cdots \quad (2)$$

The server sends (1) message for e_1, e_2, ..., e_8 to multicast and sends (2) message for e_9 to unicast. If each ECU received messages, they would have only necessary information and discard unnecessary information. In this consist of rekey message, since a number of rekey message minimizes, overhead of the server reduced.

Leaving. An ECU e which wants to leave the secure group sends requesting message to leave to the key distribution server. If join request is approved, the server deletes *e-node* of ECU e and *k-node* of e's individual key. This *k-node*'s parent called leaving point. To prevent the access of the leaving member, keys must be changed from leaving point to root node. The server creates new group key and distributes securely to the remaining members.

If the server responds message to leave, that thing as follows. The server searches for a parent node of leaving e's individual key k_{e_u} which is called leaving point. And remove k_{e_u} from the tree. x_{j+1} denote the deleted *k-node* for k_{e_u}, x_j the leaving point, x_0 the root, and when $i = 1, \ldots, j$, x_{i-1} the parent of K'_0. The server generates randomly keys $K'_0, \ldots, K'_j$ as the new keys of $x_0, \ldots, x_j$. And when $i = 0, \ldots, j$, $J_1, \ldots, J_r$ denote key at the children of x_i in the new tree key graphs. The server encrypts K'_i to each children key that called L_i. This denotes $\{K'_i\}_{J_1}, \ldots, \{K'_i\}_{J_r}$. When expressed as a function, it is $ECU\,set(K) :$ $L_0, \ldots, L_j$.

In Fig. 4, e_9 sends requesting message to leave. And it is assumed that the approval for e_9 the secure group. The server creates new group key $k_{e_{1-8}}$ and new sub-group key $k_{e_{78}}$ which called leaving point node's key. Among the existing ECU e_1, e_2, ..., e_6 need to a new group key (i.e., $k_{e_{1-8}}$) and e_7, e_8 need to a new group key, a new sub-group key (i.e., $k_{e_{78}}, k_{e_{1-8}}$). The server sends securely rekey message to distribute the new key. Rekey message is as follows.

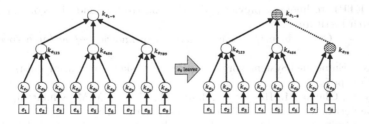

Fig. 4. ECU e_9 requests to leave in a tree key graphs

Let L_0 denote $E_{k_{e_{123}}}[k_{e_{1-8}}]$, $E_{k_{e_{456}}}[k_{e_{1-8}}]$, $E_{k_{e_{78}}}[k_{e_{1-8}}]$
Let L_1 denote $E_{k_{e_7}}[k_{e_{78}}]$, $E_{k_{e_8}}[k_{e_{78}}]$

$$s \rightarrow \{e_1, e_2, \ldots, e_8\} : L_0, L_1 \cdots\cdots\cdots\cdots\cdots \quad (3)$$

This approach uses only one rekey message. The server sends (3) message for e_1, e_2, ..., e_8 to multicast. A rekey message is configured to include all keys.

4   Conclusion

In this paper, we have presented a group key based session key establishment protocol for a remote vehicle diagnostic. The proposed scheme aims at providing secure authentication and session key establishment between a vehicle manufacturer server and a group of in-vehicle electronic control unit based on a key graph. The proposed scheme has better key management efficiency than symmetric key systems, while providing lower computation cost than public key systems.

Acknowledgment. This work was supported by Basic Science Research Program through the National Research Foundation of Korea (NRF) funded by the Ministry of Science, ICT and Future Planning (NRF-2014R1A1A1006770).

References

1. Sangguk, K.: Connected car drastic market expectations in Iot/M2M technological environment. In: KISTI (Korea Institute of Science and Technology Information), February 2014
2. Greenough, J.: The connected car report: forecasts, competing technologies, and leading manufacturers. BI Intell. (2016)
3. Miller, C., Valasek, C.: Remote exploitation of an unaltered passenger vehicle. In: DEFCON, August 2015
4. Wi, S., Moon, K., Lee, J.-H.: Symmetric key based session key establishment protocol for remote ECU management. In: KIISE (Korean Institute of Information Scientists and Engineers), December 2015
5. Gang, S.: Connected car development trends and changes of the future. KB Finance Support Management Laboratory, February 2016
6. Vehicle ECU Analyzing & Market report 2012, Fuji Chimera Research Institute, February 2012
7. 2013 ETRI technology preview, ETRI (Electronics and Telecommunications Research Institute) (2013)
8. CAN - CiA. http://www.can-cia.org/can-knowledge/can/high-speed-transmission/
9. Flexray - Embedded System Korea. http://www.eskorea.net/html/data/technique/ixFlexray.pdf
10. Tuohy, S., Glavin, M., Hughes, C., Jones, E., Trivedi, M.M, Kilmartin, L.: Intra-vehicle network: a review. IEEE Trans. Intell. Transp. Syst. (2015)
11. Secure requirements and framework for multicast communication. TTA (Telecommunications Techology Association) (2010)

12. Wong, C.K., Gouda,M., Lam, S.S.: Secure group communications using key graphs. IEEE Commun. Soc. (2000)
13. Kumar, P., Lee, S.-G., Lee, H.-J.: E-SAP: Efficient-Strong Authentication Protocol for healthcare applications using wireless medical sensor networks. MDPI, December 2012

QoS, Reliability, and Modelling

A Study of the Correlation Between Livestock Data Analysis and the Concentration of PM2.5 - Using the Cloud Computing Platform

Chien-Yuan Tseng[1] and Jui-Hung Chang[2(✉)]

[1] Computer and Network Center, National Cheng Kung University,
Tainan 701, Taiwan
P76031488@mail.ncku.edu.tw
[2] Department of Computer Science and Information Engineering,
National Cheng Kung University, Tainan 701, Taiwan
changrh@mail.ncku.edu.tw

Abstract. The subject of air pollution is paid increasing attention to in recent years. NH3 has significant effect on PM2.5, especially due to animal excrements and chemical fertilizer. Some PM2.5 monitoring data in Taiwan show that the concentration in south central Taiwan is apparently on the high side, and south central Taiwan has dense livestock and poultry. Therefore, this paper combines the livestock and poultry data opened by Taiwan Council of Agriculture (COA) with the PM2.5 data obtained by air monitoring stations opened by Taiwan Environmental Protection Administration (EPA), and uses SpatialHadoop to build a Cloud platform to analyze the correlation between Taiwan's livestock data and the concentration of PM2.5. The analysis results show that the annual mean concentration of PM2.5 of the air monitoring station in the livestock and poultry dense region is higher than that in other regions by 33%.

Keywords: PM2.5 · Cloud platform · SpatialHadoop

1 Introduction

The cause of fine particulate matter is very complex, it is one of the hazards to the air and environment, it receives close attention of various countries' governments and research units in recent years. The PM2.5 is too small to be blocked by vibrissae in the nasal cavity and general masks, it has significant effect on human respiratory system, cardiovascular and nervous systems. This paper designs a cloud computing platform based on the relationship between Taiwan's livestock data analysis and PM2.5 for data operation. The purpose of Cloud platform is to use Taiwan's livestock data to analyze the correlation with the concentration of PM2.5, the back end uses SpatialHadoop [8] as cloud computing architecture. As the initial data range of this paper is only the data from Taiwan, other countries' data can be added in the future. The display terminal displays the relevance between the location of Taiwan's air monitoring station and the livestock and poultry quantity data of nearby townships on Google Maps.

In 2014, Beijing Municipal Environmental Protection Bureau declared at the Sino-American Engineering Technology Forum that Beijing implemented field

© ICST Institute for Computer Sciences, Social Informatics and Telecommunications Engineering 2017
J.-H. Lee and S. Pack (Eds.): QShine 2016, LNICST 199, pp. 75–85, 2017.
DOI: 10.1007/978-3-319-60717-7_8

monitoring of NH3 emission sources, such as chicken farms, cattle farms and pig farms. It was indicated that the NH3 emission was paid little attention to, now it is recognized as a key factor in the formation of PM2.5. It is found that over 80% of NH3 emission came from agricultural fertilizer application [3].

The news of Beijing municipal government monitoring NH3 enlightened the preliminary conception of this paper. Late studies show that the NH3 has significant effect on the concentration of PM2.5, and the NH3 is mostly derived from animal excrements and chemical fertilizer. Therefore, this paper analyzes the correlation between the livestock data and the concentration data of PM2.5, hoping to provide useful findings to control the NH3 emission from livestock farms effectively, and the concentration of PM2.5 can be reduced, so as to reduce the probability of common people's respiratory and cardiovascular diseases.

This paper obtained the livestock and poultry statistics opened by Taiwan COA, including the animal varieties and size of animal of 198 townships, with the locations of 76 air monitoring stations in Taiwan opened by EPA and the concentration data of PM2.5 monitored automatically per hour by the air monitoring stations. This paper uses highly expandable and geographic operation supporting SpatialHadoop to build a Cloud storage computing platform, the map linear distance from the air monitoring station to the nearby township center is calculated, and the daily mean, monthly mean and annual mean concentrations of PM2.5 of 76 air monitoring stations in 2014 are calculated, the results are visualized on Google Maps, the process architecture will be detailed in Chap. 3. Finally, this paper uses Livestock Geographic (LG) algorithm to prove the effect of the quantity of pigs raised nearby the air monitoring station on the concentration of PM2.5 of monitoring station.

Main contributions of this paper:

(1) The Cloud storage computing platform process is created by SpatialHadoop - analyzing livestock data and the concentration data of PM2.5.

(2) The correlation between the livestock data and the concentration data of PM2.5 is analyzed, the result is visualized on Google Maps for research units or experts and scholars to make further analytic investigation.

(3) This paper calculates the six counties and cities with dense livestock and poultry in Taiwan, the annual mean concentration of PM2.5 of air monitoring stations of Yunlin County, Changhua County, Pingtung County, Tainan City, Chiayi County and Kaohsiung City is compared with the annual mean concentration of PM2.5 of air monitoring stations of other counties and cities.

(4) The LG algorithm is used for validation and the experimental results prove that the quantity of pigs raised in counties, cities and townships has substantive effect on the concentration of PM2.5.

The rest part of this paper is arranged as follows, Sect. 2 introduces related technologies and background. Section 3 describes the Cloud platform system architecture. Section 4 introduces the system equipment implementation method, and proposes experimental results. Finally, the contribution of this paper is summarized in Sect. 5.

2 Related Work

In recent years, the application of Geographic Information System (GIS) is increasingly diversified and important, it is used by government agencies for decision making system applications. At present, the whole world pays increasing attention to big data analysis, and the combination of big data analysis result and GIS receives increasing attention of coherent units and academia. Therefore, the cross-domain combined system is a new subject, for example, applications of biomedical image domain [9], and the NASA satellite imagery analysis [11] uses geographic data and big data analysis to obtain useful information. General server architecture does not have very good effectiveness on processing massive data like geographic data. Therefore, how to process and analyze geographic big data efficiently is an important domain in recent years. This chapter discusses and describes related studies, for example, MapReduce-based geographic system, the geographic algorithm and so on, which are popular research areas.

2.1 SpatialHadoop

The cloud computing is more and more important, and in the trend of big data analysis, the MapReduce-based Hadoop big data analysis is well accepted by academia and circles. However, Hadoop has not provided Spatial Index for geographic operation, so the effectiveness of Hadoop on geographic data operation query fails to meet the anticipation (Fig. 1).

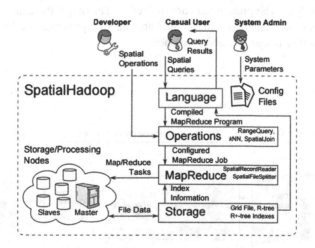

Fig. 1. SpatialHadoop architecture diagram.

SpatialHadoop [10] is an Open Source software developed by Eldawy and Mokbel from the Department of Computer Science & Information Engineering, University of Minnesota. SpatialHadoop uses Spatial Index (Global Index, Local Index) function. The modes of Spatial Index include Grid File [14] and R-tree [12].

2.2   Studies About PM2.5

This paper studied many reports and theses on PM2.5 in relation to NH_3, Chinese reportage describes NH_3 as a neglected cause of PM2.5, it has been noticed for only a few years [4, 7]. Some indicate that NH_3 is likely to change into nitrogen pentoxide and nitric acid (NOx) which are likely to polymerize into aerosol and PM2.5 in the atmosphere. In the final PM2.5 in the atmosphere, 15–35% of nitrogen element is derived from NH_3. In comparison to NOx, the NH_3 is not paid attention to, it may because the previous computation model underestimates the effect of NH_3, the corrected conclusion is that the effect of NH_3 on atmospheric pollution like PM2.5 is non negligible [13]. Some studies indicate that the NH_3 can take part in and accelerate the formation of ammonium bisulfate and ammonium sulfate in the atmosphere directly, it is a key factor in the formation of fine particulate matter. The NH_3 is one of precursors of PM2.5 [15].

3   Cloud Platform System Framework

The Cloud platform system framework is shown in Fig. 2. This paper proposes using SpatialHadoop to build the Cloud platform. The correlation between the livestock data analysis and the concentration of PM2.5 is validated by statistics and the self-developed LG algorithm. The computing result is saved in Hadoop Distributed File System (HDFS) and database. The visualization mode is that the webpage and Google Maps display latitude and longitude coordinates and charts for experts and scholars to research and analyze. The present data are limited to Taiwan, if there are more massive data for operation, SpatailHadoop distributed architecture provides good expansion and elongation for other research units' reference.

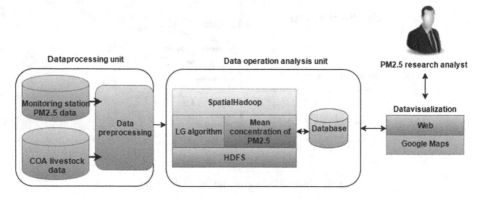

Fig. 2. Cloud platform architecture diagram.

3.1   Data Processing Unit

The data studied by this system are divided into livestock data opened by COA [1] and air monitoring station data opened by EPA [5], preprocessed by different procedures.

1. Livestock data opened by COA:
   This paper extracts data from the hog population investigation report of 2014, the statistical findings of livestock and poultry include the number of livestock farms and livestock and poultry calculated by 198 townships of Taiwan, the statistical livestock and poultry data include pigs, cattle and chickens. This paper uses the latitude and longitude coordinates of township center point to replace the livestock farm address, Taiwan township center point is converted into latitude and longitude coordinate data by the system call geo information graph data cloud service platform (TGOS) [6] and Google Maps. The livestock data established in this paper include id, county, city, township, year, livestock and poultry varieties of the township, the quantity of livestock and poultry of the township, the latitude and longitude coordinates of township center point.

2. Air monitoring station data opened by EPA:
   The gas concentration monitored automatically per hour by 76 air monitoring stations in Taiwan is provided by Taiwan EPA, referring to U.S. Environmental Protection Agency, Taiwan EPA uses the linear regression equation (relationship) of automatic monitoring station and manual monitoring station data to correct the values of automatic monitoring, so as to guarantee the correctness of values. This paper extracts the gas concentration data of 2014, including $PM10$, NO, NO_2, NO_x, O_3, SO_2, wind direction, humidity and so on. The air monitoring station data include date, monitoring station name, monitoring item, monitoring station address and gas concentration monitored per hour. The uncertain values are planned to be deleted, such as Null, so as to guarantee the correctness of mean value. This paper calls geo information graph data cloud service platform (TGOS) [6] to convert the air monitoring station address into latitude and longitude coordinate data.

3.2   Data Operation Analysis Unit

This paper proposes using SpatialHadoop to create the Cloud platform operation analysis unit. The SpatialHadoop distributed geographic algorithm process is shown in Fig. 3. Uncorrelated data don't enter the Map stage by Spatial Index, the system computing speed is increased. The proposal programs are divided into two types

1. The PM2.5 gas concentration data monitored per hour by 76 air monitoring stations in Taiwan provided by EPA are calculated, the daily mean, monthly mean and annual mean concentrations of PM2.5 are calculated. The way is to use the longitude and latitude of the monitor station to make Grid File grouping. The same PM2.5 gas concentration data from the same monitor station will be distributed to the same group. The total of 76 monitor stations will be divided into 76 groups. When the daily average of PM2.5 is calculated, the key in the stage of Map is set with the designated number of the monitor stations, which the number starts

Data

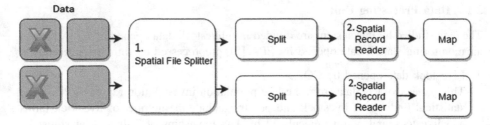

Fig. 3. Cloud platform computing process.

from 1 to 76, and its corresponding value is the monitored concentration data of PM2.5. Therefore, at the stage of reduce, the daily average PM2.5 concentration of every monitor station can be obtained from the calculated result, which is the total of PM2.5 concentration of every monitor station divided by the number of the day's effective data. Similarly, it can also calculate the annual average and monthly average in the same way.

If the average PM2.5 concentration of a specific monitoring station is needed to be calculated, the cloud platform utilizes Spatial File Splitter (Fig. 3.1) and Spatial Record Reader (Fig. 3.2) in the structure of SpatiaHadoop. Before the stage of Map, the PM2.5 concentration data of the specific monitoring station the file in Hadoop Distributed File System (HDFS)needs to be placed into the Map. The unnecessary data from other monitoring stations will be eliminated. Therefore, it can greatly boost up the speed of calculating the specific average PM2.5 concentration data in the cloud platform.

2. Livestock Geographic (LG) algorithm, the substantive effect of pig dense region on the concentration of PM2.5 monitored by nearby air monitoring station is validated, the schematic of the algorithm is shown in Fig. 4. The latitude and longitude coordinates of air monitoring station are used as center of circle, a circle in radius of K km is taken, the quantity of pigs raised in the townships in this circle is calculated.

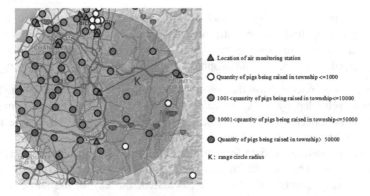

Fig. 4. LG algorithm illustration.

The quantity of pigs raised in the townships within K km around the air monitoring station is calculated by LG algorithm. The correlation between the quantity of pigs raised nearby and the change in the concentration of PM2.5 of air monitoring station is investigated, there are detailed experimental results in the experiment chapter, the algorithm is described below:

```
Input:
        k: The range circle radius is set as 30 km in this
        paper.
        n: Number of air monitoring stations, set as 76 in
        this paper.
        m: Number of townships, set as 198 in this paper.
        Latitude and longitude coordinates of n air
        monitoring stations set S1=({longitude 1, latitude
        1)...{longitude n, latitude n)}.
        Latitude and longitude coordinates of m township
        center points set S2={(longitude 1, latitude
        1)...(longitude m, latitude m)}.
        Quantity of pigs raised in m townships set S3
        ={(quantity of pigs raised 1)...(quantity of pigs
        raised m)}.
Output:
        Sum: quantity of pigs raised in townships in the
        circle in radius of K km of 76 air monitoring
        stations.
program LG
    for i = 1 to n do
        sum[i]=0
        for j = 1 to m do
                If (distance(locationi, locationj) < k) then
                        sum[i] += S3[j]
                end if
        end for
    end for
    return sum
```

The distance equation of Geographic Median algorithm is Eq. (1) Spherical law of cosines [2]:

$$\text{distance} = \arcsin(\sin(\text{lat1}) * \sin(\text{lat2}) + \cos(\text{lat1}) * \cos(\text{lat2}) * \cos(\text{lon2} - \text{lon1})) \quad (1)$$

4 Experimental Results

The computer equipments of SpatialHadoop distributed architecture for this paper are two sets of Intel I7-4770 CPU, 8 GB RAM, 1 TB hard disk, the database server equipment is Intel I5-4590 CPU, 12 GB RAM, 1 TB hard disk, the software is Microsoft SQL Server 2012.

4.1 Analysis of Concentration of PM2.5 in Counties and Cities with Dense Livestock and Poultry in Taiwan

According to the hog population investigation report in the end of July 2014 provided by COA and the livestock and poultry statistics of the third quarter of 2014, the livestock and poultry data of 19 counties and cities and 3 off islands of Taiwan are calculated. There were 8,198 pig farms and 5,539,130 pigs, 2,244 cattle farms and 145,877 cattle, 5,760 chicken farms and 92,142,813 chickens in Taiwan (including off islands) in 2014. Figure 5 shows the top six counties and cities with the highest quantitative proportion of pigs, cattle and chickens in Taiwan are Yunlin County, Changhua County, Pingtung County, Tainan City, Chiayi County and Kaohsiung City.

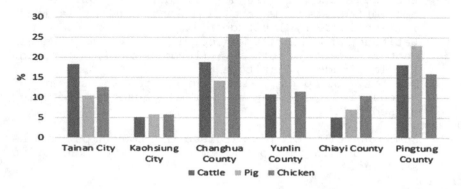

Fig. 5. Proportions of pigs, cattle and chickens in livestock data of various counties and cities of Taiwan.

This paper uses SpatialHadoop architecture to calculate the annual mean concentration of PM2.5 in 2014 of 76 air monitoring stations of Taiwan, and compares the annual mean concentration of PM2.5 in Yunlin County, Changhua County, Pingtung County, Tainan City, Chiayi County and Kaohsiung City with other counties and cities, the annual mean concentration of PM2.5 of monitoring stations in the counties and cities with dense livestock farms is 30.57 $\mu g/m^3$, the annual mean concentration of PM2.5 of monitoring stations in other counties and cities is 23.17 $\mu g/m^3$, as shown in Fig. 6.

4.2 Analysis of Quantity of Pigs Raised in the Range of Air Monitoring Station

The analysis in Sect. 4.1 combines the annual mean concentration of PM2.5 of air monitoring stations with the livestock data of the counties and cities where the monitoring stations are, the quantity of pigs raised in the counties and cities nearby the air monitoring stations is not considered. For example, Changhua County is to the west of Nantou County, Yunlin County is to the southwest, the proportion of pigs in Nantou County is not high, but the quantity of pigs raised in nearby counties and cities is very

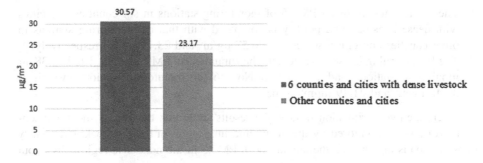

Fig. 6. Annual mean concentration of PM2.5 of monitoring stations in six counties and cities with high proportion of pig, cattle and chicken and other monitoring stations in livestock data.

large, this is not seen in the statistical data in Sect. 4.1. Therefore, this paper uses LG algorithm to calculate the quantity of pigs raised in the townships within the range circle in radius of 30 km of 76 air monitoring stations in whole Taiwan, the quantities of pigs raised nearby the air monitoring stations are ranked, the annual mean PM2.5 of Nos. 1 to 38 air monitoring stations and Nos. 39 to 76 air monitoring stations is calculated, as shown in Fig. 7, the average annual mean concentration of PM2.5 in the first 38 townships with pigs nearby the air monitoring stations is 30.46 µg/m^3, the average annual mean concentration of PM2.5 of the last 38 monitoring stations is 21.49 µg/m^3.

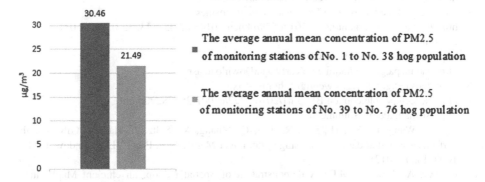

Fig. 7. Annual mean concentration of PM2.5 of the first 38 and the last 38 hog population in townships nearby monitoring stations.

5 Conclusion

This paper uses SpatialHadoop to build a Cloud platform for analyzing the correlation between livestock data and annual mean concentration of PM2.5 of air monitoring stations. The results are displayed on Google Maps. This paper designs two experiments to validate the effect of quantity of livestock and poultry on the annual mean concentration of PM2.5, the results are:

1. The average annual mean PM2.5 of monitoring stations in six counties and cities with dense livestock and poultry is compared with that of monitoring stations in other counties and cities, which are 30.57 $\mu g/m^3$ and 23.17 $\mu g/m^3$ respectively.
2. The LG algorithm is used to calculate the annual mean PM2.5 of No. 1 to No. 38 air monitoring stations and No. 39 to No. 76 air monitoring stations, which is 30.46 $\mu g/m^3$ and 21.49 $\mu g/m^3$ respectively.

There are two verification modes, the results show that the annual mean concentration of PM2.5 monitored by the air monitoring station in the livestock and poultry dense region is higher than the annual mean PM2.5 in the nondense regions by about 33%.

The concentration of PM2.5 may be influenced by many other factors, which are not considered in the research scope of this paper, such as the factory effluence, automobile and motorcycle emissions and natural environment factors. The future research will analyze related data to increase the accuracy. In addition, this paper creates an analysis module first, so only the data of 2014 are learned about, the historical data will be analyzed in the future, the ultimate objective is to use the Cloud platform to work out why Taiwan's annual mean concentration of PM2.5 is relatively high for related studies' reference.

References

1. http://agrstat.coa.gov.tw/sdweb/public/book/Book.aspx
2. https://en.wikipedia.org/wiki/Spherical_law_of_cosines
3. http://hk.on.cc/cn/bkn/cnt/news/20140529/bkncn-20140529051643333-0529_05011_001_cn.html
4. http://news.qq.com/a/20150301/022140.htm
5. http://taqm.epa.gov.tw/taqm/en/YearlyDataDownload.aspx
6. http://tgos.nat.gov.tw/tgos/web/tgos_home.aspx
7. http://scitech.people.com.cn/BIG5/n1/2016/0222/c1007-28138290.html
8. http://spatialhadoop.cs.umn.edu
9. Aji, A., Wang, F., Vo, H., Lee, R., Liu, Q., Zhang, X., Saltz, J.: Hadoop GIS: a high performance spatial data warehousing system over MapReduce. Proc. VLDB Endow. **6**(11), 1009–1020 (2013)
10. Eldawy, A., Mokbel, M.F.: A demonstration of SpatialHadoop: an efficient MapReduce framework for spatial data. Proc. VLDB Endow. **6**(12), 1230–1233 (2013)
11. Eldawy, A., Alharthi, S., Alzaidy, A., Daghistani, A., Ghani, S., Basalamah, S., Mokbel, M. F.: A demonstration of SHAHED: a MapReduce-based system for querying and visualizing satellite data. In: Proceedings of the IEEE International Conference on Data Engineering, ICDE 2015, Seoul, South Korea, April 2015
12. Guttman, A.: R-trees: a dynamic index structure for spatial searching. SIGMOD Rec. **14**(2), 47–57 (1984)
13. Heald, C.L., Collett Jr., J.L., Lee, T., Benedict, K.B., Schwandner, F.M., Li, Y., Clarisse, L., Hurtmans, D.R., Van Damme, M., Clerbaux, C., Coheur, P.-F., Philip, S., Martin, R.V., Pye, H.O.T.: Atmospheric ammonia and particulate inorganic nitrogen over the United States. Atmos. Chem. Phys. **12**, 10295–10312 (2012)

14. Nievergelt, J., Hinterberger, H., Sevcik, K.C.: The grid file: an adaptable, symmetric multikey file structure. ACM Trans. Database Syst. **9**(1), 38–71 (1984)
15. Li, L., Kumar, M., Zhu, C., Zhong, J., Francisco, J.S., Zeng, X.C.: Near-barrierless ammonium bisulfate formation via a loop- structure promoted proton-transfer mechanism on the surface of water. J. Am. Chem. Soc. **138**, 1816–1819 (2016)

Bandwidth Scheduling with Multiple Fixed Node-Disjoint Paths in High-Performance Networks

Aiqin Hou[1], Chase Q. Wu[1,2(✉)], Dingyi Fang[1], Yongqiang Wang[1], and Meng Wang[1]

[1] School of Information Science and Technology,
Northwest University, Xi'an 710127, Shaanxi, China
{houaiqin,dyf,yqwang}@nwu.edu.cn, xidawm@stumail.nwu.edu.cn
[2] Department of Computer Science, New Jersey Institute of Technology,
Newark, NJ 07102, USA
chase.wu@njit.edu

Abstract. Many large-scale applications generate large volumes of data that must be transferred over high-performance networks for various storage or analysis purposes. Such requirements call for a fast bandwidth scheduling solution to discover feasible and efficient reservation options in a time-varying network environment. We investigate a bandwidth scheduling problem with two node-disjoint paths, referred to as BS-2NDP, to support big data transfer. In BS-2NDP, we further consider two different types of paths: (i) two fixed paths of fixed bandwidth (2FPFB), and (ii) two fixed paths of variable bandwidth (2FPVB). We show that both 2FPFB and 2FPVB are NP-complete, and then design heuristic approach-based solutions, which are implemented and tested in both simulated and real-life networks. Extensive results illustrate that the proposed heuristics achieve a close-to-optimal performance in small-scale networks, and significantly outperform other heuristic approaches in large-scale networks.

Keywords: High-performance networks · Bandwidth scheduling · Node-disjoint paths

1 Introduction

Many large-scale applications in various domains require fast and reliable transfer of big data for remote operations, which has gone beyond the capability of traditional shared IP networks. In recent years, high-performance networks (HPNs) with the capability of bandwidth reservation have emerged as an effective solution and their significance has been well recognized in broad science and network research communities.

As the central function unit of a generalized control plane for provisioning dedicated channels in HPNs, the bandwidth scheduler computes appropriate

© ICST Institute for Computer Sciences, Social Informatics and Telecommunications Engineering 2017
J.-H. Lee and S. Pack (Eds.): QShine 2016, LNICST 199, pp. 86–96, 2017.
DOI: 10.1007/978-3-319-60717-7_9

network paths and allocates link bandwidths to meet specific user requests based on network topology and bandwidth availability. To meet the unprecedented requirement of big data movement, it is a natural extension from single-path to multi-path transfer, which is generally more effective in terms of throughput, robustness, load balance, and congestion reduction. However, multi-path routing also brings additional complexity and overhead to the network's control and data planes [1].

The complexity of multi-path routing varies depending on the type and number of constraints, and many of these routing problems are NP-complete. Several studies have shown that the Multiple Constrained Path (MCP) problems are generally NP-complete and hence are not solvable in polynomial time [2,3]. Furthermore, finding disjoint paths with a single constraint is also an NP-hard problem [4–6]. Multiple paths usually have an additional constraint to be link-disjoint or node-disjoint. Node-disjoint paths are usually harder to find but provide more robustness in case of node failures. Traditional one-path routing with path constraint/objective is NP-complete, while the problem of two-path routing that considers reliability is strongly NP-hard [7].

In this paper, we investigate a problem of Bandwidth Scheduling with Two Node-Disjoint Paths (BS-2NDP) to support big data transfer. In BS-2NDP, we further consider two different types of paths: (i) two fixed paths of fixed bandwidth (2FPFB), and (ii) two fixed paths of variable bandwidth (2FPVB). We prove that both 2FPFB and 2FPVB are NP-complete, and design heuristic approach-based solutions, which are implemented and tested in both simulated and real-life networks. Extensive results illustrate that the proposed heuristics achieve a close-to-optimal performance in small-scale networks, and significantly outperform other heuristic approaches in large-scale networks.

2 Related Work

Several studies addressed the problem of finding maximum combined bandwidth of disjoint paths. In [5], Shen et al. considered two problems where the notions of multi-path, disjoint path, and widest path are combined. They proved that both problems are NP-complete and provided each an exact solution using ILP and a heuristic solutions. In [6], Dahshan proved the Maximum-Bandwidth Node-Disjoint Paths (MBNDP) problem to be NP-complete, which is essentially an MCP problem with two constraints: the first constraint is for the two paths to be node-disjoint, and the second constraint is to maximize the sum of the bandwidths of the two paths. This problem is also shown to be NP-complete in [5]. A Max-Limit Bandwidth Disjoint Path (MLBDP) algorithm was proposed in [6], which labels two concurrent paths as R (red path) and B (blue path). The algorithm finds the R path with the maximum bandwidth, together with a node-disjoint path B with bandwidth no less than a specified limit. In [8], the problem is to obtain the λ-edge-disjoint-path-set (λDP/B) that has a maximum total bandwidth for $\lambda > 1$, and a polynomial-time heuristic, Maximum Bandwidth Algorithm (MBA), is designed to compute a path with the maximum bandwidth.

In [9], a distributed distance-vector algorithm is used to find multiple node-disjoint paths in a computer network. In [10], a two-disjoint multi-path routing strategy using colored trees is proposed.

Different from most of the aforementioned work that considers static networks, we consider the problem of finding multiple node-disjoint paths with maximum bandwidth in HPNs with time-varying link bandwidth availability.

3   Problem Formulation

3.1   Network Model

The HPN is typically modeled as a network graph $G(V, E)$ with n nodes and m links. Each link $l \in E$ in the network is associated with a time-varying residual bandwidth $b_l[i]$, which is denoted by a 3-tuple of time-bandwidth (TB) $(t_l[i], t_l[i+1], b_l[i])$ for the time interval $(t_l[i], t_l[i+1])$, $i = 0, 1, 2, \ldots, T_l-1$, where T_l denotes the number of time-slots on link l.

We build an Aggregated TB (ATB) list by combining and storing the TB lists of all individual links in their intersected time-slots. We create a set of new time slots by combining the time slots of all links, and then map the residual bandwidths of each link to the ATB list in each new time slot. We denote the ATB list as $(t[0], t[1], b_0[0], b_1[0], \ldots, b_{m-1}[0]), \ldots, (t[T-1], t[T], b_0[T-1], b_1[T-1], \ldots, b_{m-1}[T-1])$, where T is the number of intersected time slots after aggregating all TB lists. Note that time slot i corresponds to time interval $(t[i], t[i+1])$.

3.2   Problem Formulation

Definition 1. *BS-2NDP: Given an HPN graph $G(V, E)$ with an ATB list and a user request specifying source node v_s, destination node v_d, and data size δ, we wish to find two node-disjoint paths to move data of size δ from node v_s to node v_d such that the data transfer end time t_{end} is minimized.*

Without loss of generality, we suppose that the data transfer may start at time point $t[0] = 0$. In view of the simplicity and popularity of fixed-path routing in practice, we consider two commonly used service models based on a fixed path in BS-2NDP, i.e. 2FPFB and 2FPVB. On the other hand, the service models based on a variable path would require some additional support from the control plane and the network infrastructure for path switching, and hence are not used as commonly in real-life HPNs.

Definition 2. *2FPFB (Two Fixed Paths with Fixed Bandwidth): Given the network model and user request in BS-2NDP, the goal is to find two fixed node-disjoint paths from v_s to v_d, each of which has a fixed bandwidth (i.e. the bandwidth is invariable during the entire period of data transfer for the given request), such that the data transfer end time is minimized.*

Definition 3. *2FPVB (Two Fixed Paths with Variable Bandwidth): Given the network model and user request in BS-2NDP, the goal is to find two fixed node-disjoint paths from v_s to v_d, each of which may use varying bandwidths across different time slots during the data transfer, such that the data transfer end time is minimized.*

3.3 Complexity Analysis

Compared with the work in [4–7], which considers static networks (with constant link bandwidths), the BS-2NDP problem is more general as the bandwidth availability of each link in HPNs is time-varying. In fact, both 2FPFB and 2FPVB are NP-complete. We prove the NP-completeness of 2FPFB by showing that the WPDPC [5] problem is a special case of 2FPFB, and prove the NP-completeness of 2FPVB by generalizing from the single-path FPVB problem.

Theorem 1: 2FPFB is NP-complete
Proof: We restrict 2FPFB to WPDPC by only considering those instances in which, the available bandwidth of each link does not change, i.e. the bandwidth of each link is constant across all time-slots. In other words, WPDPC is a special case of 2FPFB when the network is static with constant link bandwidths. Since WPDPC is NP-complete [5], so is 2FPFB.

Theorem 2: 2FPFB is NP-complete
Proof: The NP-completeness of FPVB has been established in [11] by reducing from the 0–1 Total Bandwidth (0–1 TB) problem. Obviously, 2FPVB is a more general version of FPVB that computes multiple concurrent FPVB paths.

4 Algorithm Design

The NP-completeness of both 2FPFB and 2FPVB indicates that there does not exist any polynomial-time optimal algorithm, unless $P = NP$. In this section, firstly, we design naive greedy algorithms to solve 2FPFB/2FPVB. Secondly, we design optimal algorithms based on exhaustive search for small-scale 2FPFB/2FPVB problem instances. Lastly, we propose efficient heuristic algorithms for large-scale problem instances.

4.1 Greedy Algorithms for 2FPFB and 2FPVB

Greedy2FPFB Algorithm. For 2FPFB, based on the single-path OptFPFB algorithm in [12], we design a polynomial-time greedy algorithm, referred to as Greedy2FPFB, whose pseudocode is provided in Algorithm 1. In Line 1, it first employs OptFPFB to compute the first path p_1 with the maximum fixed bandwidth BW_1, assuming the use of one single path to transfer data of size δ. In Line 2, it removes all nodes on path p_1 from the original graph, resulting in a new graph $G'(V, E)$ comprised of only the residual nodes and links. In Line 3, it employs OptFPFB to compute the second path p_2 in $G'(V, E)$ with the maximum fixed bandwidth BW_2, again assuming the use of one single path to transfer data of size δ. In Line 4, it computes the maximum combined bandwidth β of the two paths p_1 and p_2. In Lines 5–7, it computes the end time for the transfer of data size δ using these two node-disjoint paths concurrently. In order to ensure that the two data transfers concurrently taking place on these two paths finish at the same time, it allocates the data size δ to p_1 and p_2 in proportion to their fixed bandwidths. In Line 8, it computes the data size δ_1 to be transferred by p_1, and the rest $(\delta - \delta_1)$ is assigned to p_2. The time complexity of Greedy2FPFB is the same as that of OptFPFB, which is $O(T^2 \cdot m \cdot \log n + T^3 \cdot m)$ [12], where n is the number of nodes, m is the number of links, and T is the total number of new time slots in the ATB list.

Algorithm 1. Greedy2FPFB

Input: an HPN graph $G(V, E)$ with an ATB list of T time slots, source v_s, destination
$\quad v_d$, and data size δ
Output: the earliest transfer end time t_{end}, data partition δ_1
1: $p_1(BW_1) = OptFPFB(G, T, v_s, v_d, \delta)$;
2: Remove the nodes and links of p_1 from G to create a new G';
3: $p_2(BW_2) = OptFPFB(G', T, v_s, v_d, \delta)$;
4: $\beta = BW_1 + BW_2$;
5: **if** $(\beta \cdot (t[T-1] - t[0]) \geq \delta$ and $\beta \neq 0)$ **then**
6: $\quad \tau = \delta/\beta$;
7: $\quad t_{end} = t[0] + \tau$;
8: $\quad \delta_1 = BW_1 \times \tau$;
9: **return** t_{end}, δ_1;

Greedy2FPVB Algorithm. For 2FPVB, based on the single-path MinFPVB algorithm in [12], we design a greedy algorithm, referred to as Greedy2FPVB, whose pseudocode is provided in Algorithm 2. In Lines 1-3, it initializes the bandwidth in each time-slot for each of two paths $BW_1[i], BW_2[i], i = 0, 1, \ldots, T-1$, the remaining data size rd and the transfer time $time$. In Line 4, it employs MinFPVB to compute the first path p_1 with the maximum bandwidth $BW_1[i]$ in each time slot, assuming the use of one single path. In Line 5, it removes the nodes and links of path p_1 from the original graph G, resulting in a new graph G' comprised of only the residual nodes and links. In Line 6, it employs MinFPVB to compute the second path p_2 with the maximum bandwidth $BW_2[i]$ in each time slot, again assuming the use of one single path. In Lines 7-20, it computes the maximum combined bandwidth of the two paths p_1 and p_2 in the order of sequential time slots, and then computes the transfer end time. In each time slot, it allocates the data size to p_1 and p_2 in proportion to their bandwidths to ensure that these two concurrent data transfers finish at the same time. Similarly, the time complexity of Greedy2FPVB is also the same as that of MinFPVB [12], which is $O(m(T + log n))$.

Algorithm 2. Greedy2FPVB

Input: an HPN graph $G(V, E)$ with an ATB list of T time slots, source v_s, destination v_d, and data size δ

Output: the earliest transfer end time t_{end}, data partition δ_1

1: **for** $(i = 0; i \leq T - 1; i + +)$ **do**
2:    $BW_1[i] = 0, BW_2[i] = 0;$
3: $rd = \delta;\ time = 0;$
4: $p_1(BW_1[]) = MinFPVB(G, T, v_s, v_d, \delta);$
5: Remove the nodes and links of path p_1 from G to create G';
6: $p_2(BW_2[]) = MinFPVB(G', T, v_s, v_d, \delta);$
7: $i = 0;\ \delta_1 = 0;$
8: **while** $(rd \geq 0)$ **do**
9:    $BWSum[i] = BW_1[i] + BW_2[i];$
10:   $\delta_1 = \delta_1 + BW_1[i] \cdot (t[i+1] - t[i]);$
11:   **if** $(rd \geq BWSum[i])$ **then**
12:      $time = time + 1;$
13:      $rd = rd - BWSum[i] \cdot (t[i+1] - t[i]);$
14:   **else**
15:      $time = time + rd/BWSum[i];$
16:      $rd = 0;$
17:   $t_{end} = t[0] + time;$
18:   $i = i + 1;$
19: **return** $t_{end}, \delta_1.$

4.2 Optimal Algorithms for 2FPFB and 2FPVB

We design two exhaustive search-based optimal algorithms for 2FPFB and 2FPVB, referred to as Opt2FPFB and Opt2FPVB, to compute the path-pair that minimizes the data transfer end time in a brute-force manner: (i) find all possible paths between the source and the destination in all possible time ranges across contiguous time slots, (ii) enumerate all possible node-disjoint path-pairs in each time range, and choose the path-pair that minimizes the data transfer end time. Obviously, Opt2FPFB and Opt2FPVB are of exponential time complexity and are only meant for being used as a comparison base in small-scale problem instances. We will design more efficient heuristics below for large-scale problems.

4.3 Improved Algorithms for 2FPFB and 2FPVB

In Greedy2FPFB and Greedy2FPVB, although the transfer time of each path for data size δ is minimized at each respective step, there is no guarantee that the concurrent transfer time τ by the path-pair for data size δ is minimized from a global perspective, especially when the bandwidths of p_1 or p_2 before time slots τ are smaller than the later time slots. We propose two improved algorithms, i.e. Imp2FPFB and Imp2FPVB, to overcome their defects.

Imp2FPFB Algorithm. The pseudocode of Imp2FPFB is provided in Algorithm 3. It first calls the previous Greedy2FPFB algorithm to compute the concurrent transfer time τ by the path-pair (p_1, p_2) for data size δ, and the data partition δ_1 to be assigned to path p_1. It then uses OptFPFB twice to find a pair of paths (p_1', p_2') with larger bandwidths than the path-pair (p_1, p_2) during $[0, \tau]$ time slots, and computes the transfer time by (p_1', p_2') for δ. The data partitioning method is the same as in Greedy2FPFB, i.e. the data size to be transferred by each path is proportional to its bandwidth. Since the time complexity of OptFPFB is $O(T^2 \cdot m \cdot \log n + T^3 \cdot m)$ [12], the time complexity of Imp2FPFB is also $O(T^2 \cdot m \cdot \log n + T^3 \cdot m)$, which is the same as that of Greedy2FPFB.

Algorithm 3. Imp2FPFB

Input: an HPN graph $G(V, E)$ with an ATB list of T time slots, source v_s, destination v_d, and data size δ
Output: the earliest transfer end time t_{end}
1: $(\tau, \delta_1) = Greedy2FPFB(G, T, v_s, v_d, \delta)$;
2: $\delta_2 = \delta - \delta_1$;
3: $p_1'(BW_1') = OptFPFB(G, \tau, v_s, v_d, \delta_1)$;
4: Remove the nodes and links of path p_1' to create G';
5: $p_2'(BW_2') = OptFPFB(G', \tau, v_s, v_d, \delta_2)$;
6: $\beta' = BW_1' + BW_2'$;
7: **if** $(\beta' \cdot (t[\tau - 1] - t[0]) \geq \delta$ and $\beta \neq 0)$ **then**
8:     $t_{end} = t[0] + \delta/\beta'$;
9: **return** t_{end}.

Imp2FPVB Algorithm. The pseudocode of Imp2FPVB is provided in Algorithm 4. In Line 1, it calls the previous Greedy2FPVB algorithm to compute the concurrent transfer time τ by a path-pair (p_1, p_2) for data size δ and the variable bandwidths of each path $BW_1[i], BW_2[i], i = 0, 1, \ldots \tau - 1$, and the data size δ_1 to be transferred by p_1. In Line 2, it computes the data size δ_2 to be transferred by p_2. In the remaining lines of code, it uses MinFPVB to find a path-pair (p_1', p_2') whose combined bandwidth is larger than that of the path-pair (p_1, p_2) during $[0, \tau)$ time slots, computes the time-varying bandwidths $BW_1'[i], BW_2'[i], i = 0, 1, \ldots \tau - 1$, of each path, and computes the transfer end time for δ by (p_1', p_2'). The data partitioning is the same as in Greedy2FPVB. In each time slot, it allocates the data size to these two paths in proportion to their bandwidths to ensure that these two concurrent transfers finish at the same time. The time complexity of Imp2FPVB is the same as that of MinFPVB [12], i.e. $O(m(T + \log n))$.

Algorithm 4. Imp2FPVB

Input: an HPN graph $G(V, E)$ with an ATB list of T time slots, source v_s, destination v_d, and data size δ

Output: the earliest transfer end time t_{end}

1: $p_1, p_2(\tau, \delta_1) = Greedy2FPVB(G, T, v_s, v_d, \delta)$;
2: $\delta_2 = \delta - \delta_1$;
3: $p_1'(BW_1'[]) = MinFPVB(G, \tau, v_s, v_d, \delta_1)$;
4: Remove the nodes and links of path p_1 to create G';
5: $p_2'(BW_2'[]) = MinFPVB(G', \tau, v_s, v_d, \delta_2)$;
6: $rd = \delta$; $time = 0$;
7: **while** $(rd \geq 0)$ **do**
8:    $BWSum[i] = BW_1'[i] + BW_2'[i]$;
9:    **if** $(rd \geq BWSum[i])$ **then**
10:       $time = time + 1$;
11:       $rd = rd - BWSum[i] \cdot (t[i + 1] - t[i])$;
12:    **else**
13:       $time = time + rd/BWSum[i]$;
14:       $rd = 0$;
15:       $t_{end} = t[0] + time$;
16: **return** t_{end}.

---

5   Performance Evaluation

We evaluate the performance of the proposed algorithms in small- and large-scale simulated networks as well as a network based on the topology of the real-life ESnet of the U.S. Department of Energy.

5.1   Simulation Setup

For performance evaluation, we create a set of networks of randomly generated topology with a different number of nodes and links of random bandwidths, which follow a normal distribution: $b = b_{max} \cdot e^{-\frac{1}{2}(x)^2} Mb/s$, where b_{max} is set to be 100 Gbps, x is a random variable within the range of $[0, 1]$. The aggregated time-bandwidth (ATB) list contains 100 time slots starting from the time $t[0] = 0$. For each user request, we randomly select a source node v_s and a destination node v_d, and set the data size for transfer to be 500 GBytes.

5.2   Algorithm Comparison for 2FPFB/2FPVB in Small Networks

We first generate 10 random small-scale networks, indexed from 1 to 10, as shown in Table 1.

For 2FPFB, in each of these 10 small-scale networks, we run Imp2FPFB, Greedy2FPFB, and Opt2FPFB for 10 times with different random seeds, and plot the mean and standard deviation of the data transfer end time in Fig. 1 for comparison. We observe that Opt2FPFB always achieves the best performance as expected and Imp2FPFB consistently outperforms Greedy2FPFB. It is worth

Table 1. Index of 10 small-scale networks.

Index of network size	1	2	3	4	5	6	7	8	9	10
Number of nodes	7	10	12	15	17	20	23	26	28	30
Number of links	10	15	18	20	23	26	29	32	35	37

pointing out that Imp2FPFB achieves a close-to-optimal performance in these small-scale problem instances.

We also evaluate the performance of Imp2FPVB, Greedy2FPVB and Opt2FPVB for 2FPVB in the same 10 small-scale networks, and plot their performance measurements in Fig. 2. Similarly, we observe that Opt2FPVB always achieves the best performance as expected, and Imp2FPVB outperforms Greedy2FPVB in all the cases we studied. It is also worth pointing out that Imp2FPVB achieves a close-to-optimal performance in these small-scale problem instances.

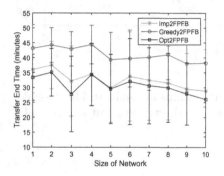
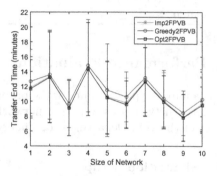

Fig. 1. Performance comparison of the algorithms for 2FPFB in small networks.

Fig. 2. Performance comparison of the algorithms for 2FPVB in small networks.

5.3   Algorithm Comparison for 2FPFB/2FPVB in Large Networks

We generate 10 different large-scale networks with a random topology, indexed from 1 to 10, as shown in Table 2. We run Greedy2FPFB/GreedyFPVB and Imp2FPFB/Imp2FPVB in each of these network instances for 10 times with different random seeds. Note that Opt2FPFB/Opt2FPVB is of exponential time complexity and hence is not tested in these large-scale networks.

The performance measurements for 2FPFB and 2FPVB are plotted in Figs. 3 and 4, respectively. For 2FPFB, we observe that Imp2FPFB consistently outperforms Greedy2FPFB, and for 2FPVB, Imp2FPVB consistently outperforms Greedy2FPVB.

Table 2. Index of 10 large-scale networks.

Index of network size	1	2	3	4	5	6	7	8	9	10
Number of nodes	40	50	60	70	80	90	100	120	150	200
Number of links	80	100	120	140	160	180	200	240	300	400

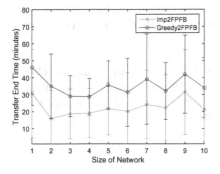

Fig. 3. Performance comparison of the algorithms for 2FPFB in large networks.

Fig. 4. Performance comparison of the algorithms for 2FPVB in large networks.

5.4   Algorithm Comparison for 2FPFB/2FPVB in ESnet5

To evaluate the performance in a practical setting, we run the proposed algorithms on the topology of a real-life HPN, ESnet5 [13], with 57 nodes and 65 links, each of which has a bandwidth between 30 Gbps–100 Gbps. The user requests have a variable data transfer size. We plot the performance measurements of 2FPFB and 2FPVB in Figs. 5 and 6, respectively, which show that Imp2FPFB and Imp2FPVB achieve better performance than Greedy2FPFB and Greedy2FPVB, respectively.

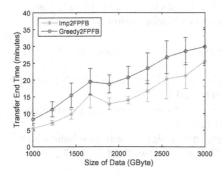
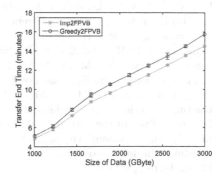
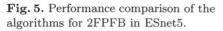

Fig. 5. Performance comparison of the algorithms for 2FPFB in ESnet5.

Fig. 6. Performance comparison of the algorithms for 2FPVB in ESnet5.

6   Conclusion

We investigated a problem of bandwidth scheduling with two different types of node-disjoint paths in dedicated networks. We showed that these two problems are NP-complete, and designed heuristic approaches. Extensive results based on both simulated and real-life networks illustrated that the proposed heuristics achieve a superior performance over other algorithms in comparison. It is of our future interest to incorporate and test these scheduling algorithms in the control plane of existing HPNs.

Acknowledgment. This research is sponsored by U.S. NSF under Grant No. CNS-1560698 with New Jersey Institute of Technology, and National Nature Science Foundation of China under Grant No. 61472320 and Beilin Science and Technology Plan under Grant No. GX1403 with Northwest University, P.R. China.

References

1. Domzal, J., Dulinski, Z., Kantor, M.: A survey on methods to provide multipath transmission in wired packet networks. COMNET **77**, 18–41 (2015)
2. Mieghem, P.V., Kuipers, F.A.: On the complexity of QoS routing. Comput. Commun. **26**, 376–387 (2003)
3. Kuipers, F.A., VanMieghem, P.F.: Conditions that impact the complexity of QoS routing. IEEE/ACM Trans. Netw. **13**, 717–730 (2005)
4. Liang, W.: Robust routing in wide-area WDM networks. In: Proceedings of IPDPS, San Francisco, CA (2001)
5. Shen, B.H., Hao, B., Sen, A.: On multipath routing using widest pair of disjoint paths. In: Workshop on High Performance Switching and Routing, pp. 134–140 (2004)
6. Dahshan, M.H.: Maximum-bandwidth node-disjoint paths. Int. J. Adv. Comput. Sci. Appl. **3**, 48–56 (2012)
7. Andreas, A.K. Smith, J.C.: Exact algorithms for robust k-path routing problems. In: Proceedings of GO, pp. 1–6 (2005)
8. Loh, R.C., Soh, S., Lazarescu, M.: Maximizing bandwidth using disjoint paths. In: 24th IEEE International Conference on Advanced Information Networking and Applications, pp. 304–311 (2010)
9. Sidhu, D., Nair, R., Abdallah, S.: Finding disjoint paths in networks. In: Proceedings of ACM SIGCOMM, pp. 43–51 (1991)
10. Ramasubramanian, S., Krishnamoorthy, H., Krunz, M.: Disjoint multipath routing using colored trees. COMNET **51**(8), 2163–2180 (2007)
11. Guerin, R., Orda, A.: Networks with advance reservations: the routing perspective. In: Proceedings of the 19th IEEE INFOCOM (2000)
12. Lin, Y., Wu, Q.: Complexity analysis and algorithm design for advance bandwidth scheduling in dedicated networks. IEEE/ACM Trans. Netw. **21**(1), 14–27 (2013)
13. ESnet. https://www.es.net

An Effective Hyper-Heuristic Algorithm for Clustering Problem of Wireless Sensor Network

Chun-Wei Tsai[1], Wei-Lun Chang[2], Kai-Cheng Hu[2],
and Ming-Chao Chiang[2(✉)]

[1] Department of Computer Science and Engineering,
National Chung Hsing University, Taichung 40227, Taiwan, R.O.C.
cwtsai0807@gmail.com
[2] Department of Computer Science and Engineering,
National Sun Yat-sen University, Kaohsiung 80424, Taiwan, R.O.C.
m033040027@student.nsysu.edu.tw, spring69953@hotmail.com,
mcchiang@cse.nsysu.edu.tw

Abstract. The basic idea of low-energy adaptive clustering hierarchy (LEACH) is not to select a particular set of sensors out of all the sensors as the cluster heads to avoid the problem of running out their energy quickly. Unfortunately, it may end up selecting an unsuitable set of sensors as the cluster heads. Inspired by these observations, an effective hyper-heuristic algorithm is presented in this paper to find out the transmission path that is able to give better results than the other algorithms compared in this research. In other words, the main objective of the proposed algorithm is to reduce the energy consumption of a wireless sensor network (WSN), by balancing the residual energy of all the wireless sensors to maximize the number of alive sensor nodes in a WSN. Experimental results show that the proposed algorithm can provide a better result in terms of the energy consumed by a WSN, meaning that the proposed algorithm provides an alternative way to extend the lifetime of a WSN.

Keywords: Wireless sensor network · Lifetime · LEACH

1 Introduction

Nowadays, wireless sensor network (WSN) is no longer something that is sitting on the corner of a laboratory. Several successful results [10, 11, 13] indicate that WSN has become part of our daily life in recent years. Its importance can also be found in [4] in which Harrop and Das reported that the market of WSN will grow to $1.8 billion in 2024. In [12], Reese estimated that about 24 million sensors of industrial WSNs will be installed in the next five years. Moreover, since WSN is the foundation of internet of things (IoT), industrial internet of things (IIoT), and even big data analytics systems, how to enhance the performance of a WSN has become an important area of research today. Also owing to inherent

© ICST Institute for Computer Sciences, Social Informatics and Telecommunications Engineering 2017
J.-H. Lee and S. Pack (Eds.): QShine 2016, LNICST 199, pp. 97–109, 2017.
DOI: 10.1007/978-3-319-60717-7_10

limitation, the energies of the wireless sensors that are equipped with batteries are normally very small, the data transmission distance is still restricted to a small region. For these reasons, how to use the energy of sensors effectively will have a strong impact on the lifetime of a WSN. Several studies [15] have attempted to define the lifetime problem as an optimization problem for finding out the possible solutions, such as the cluster head election problem (CHEP) and routing problem.

One of the most well-known clustering method for solving the CHEP is the so-called low-energy adaptive clustering hierarchy (LEACH) [5]. One of the reasons is that it is very simple and easy to implement. Another reason that a large number of methods are built on LEACH or its variants because the original idea of LEACH is to avoid a sensor from being elected as the cluster head (CH) too often (i.e., too many times). This implies two things. The first is that the CH election procedure will not elect a particular sensor as the CH every time LEACH is performed. The second is that each sensor has a chance to be elected as a CH. It seems that LEACH provides a good way to avoid specific sensors from running out energy quickly; thus, it can reduce the energy consumption of a WSN. However, the observations of Hoang et al. [6], indicate that LEACH may not able to provide the best solution for the CHEP. To extend the lifetime of a WSN, several studies [6,8,15] attempted to combine metaheuristic algorithms with LEACH to further improve the performance of LEACH for the CHEP, but there is still plenty of room for the improvement. In this paper, an effective hyper-heuristic algorithm with LEACH is presented for solving the CHEP. The main idea of the proposed algorithm is to leverage the strength of different metaheuristic algorithms (e.g., genetic algorithm or particle swarm optimization) to provide a better solution for the CHEP.

2   Related Work

Just like the other emerging research problems, the lifetime problem of a WSN requires some effective and efficient algorithms to find out a *good solution* to enhance its performance in a reasonable time because it usually takes an unreasonable amount of time to find the optimal solution of these optimization problems. That is why we are looking for a good solution (i.e., approximate solution) instead of the best solution. However, *good way* to find out a *good solution* of these emerging research problems typically depends on the things we concern. It can be a fast search method or a method that is guaranteed to find out a good solution that is very close to the best solution.

The development of metaheuristic algorithms [1] is just like an epitome of the modern computer science and other relevant disciplines that need to use information systems because metaheuristic algorithms can be used in many different disciplines to find out a good solution in a reasonable time. As we mentioned previously, this provides us an alternative method to find out a good solution before we can find out the best solution (i.e., optimal solution) for these hard and complex optimization problems in a reasonable time, e.g., CHEP. However, every metaheuristic algorithm has its advantages and disadvantages. That is, none of them can be fully replaced by another one. A good example is the genetic algorithm that is good at global search but bad at local search in most cases and explains the dilemmas of metaheuristic algorithms. An intuitive way to solve this issue is to combine GA with another search algorithm that is good at local search, such as combining GA with k-means to find a better result than does GA or k-means alone for the clustering problem [7]. Some recent studies called this kind of integration hybrid-heuristic algorithm [2]. However, if we simply combine two or more different algorithms into a search algorithm, the computation time of this new search algorithm will be increased significantly. The hyper-heuristic algorithm [3] provides an alternative way to solve this problem. Like hybrid-heuristic algorithm, hyper-heuristic algorithm also integrates two or more search algorithms into a single search algorithm. Unlike hybrid-heuristic algorithm that will use "all" the search algorithms at each iteration during the convergence process, hyper-heuristic algorithm will use only "one" of the search algorithms at each iteration during the convergence process. Because hyper-heuristic algorithm will use only one of the search algorithms at each iteration, the computation time can then be significantly reduced, compared to hybrid-heuristic algorithm. More precisely, this is how hyper-heuristic algorithm works. First, it will randomly choose one of the search algorithms to perform the search for a certain number of iterations. Then, it will randomly choose another one to replace the current one when the conditions for changing the search algorithms are satisfied. For hyper-heuristic algorithm, the conditions are used to determine the timing to change the search algorithm. The condition can be a fixed number of iterations, which means that each search algorithm will be performed for a fixed number of iterations before it is changed to another. Or it can be a predefined threshold, which means that the hyper-heuristic algorithm will switch to another search algorithm when the current one cannot find a better solution.

The hyper-heuristic algorithm still has some research problems to be addressed to further enhance its search performance. According to our observations, they can be summarized as follows:

- Time to change: This research issue is regarding the timing for changing the search algorithm (which is also referred to as the low-level heuristic (LLH) algorithm), which is a difficult problem for this kind of research. If we change the search algorithm too early, we might not be able to use its fully search ability. On the other hand, if we change the search algorithm too late, it might get stuck in a local optimum.
- Execution sequence: Another research issue is the execution sequence of these LLH algorithms. Until now, there is no specific execution sequence that can outperform the others in solving all the optimization problems.
- Passing the search experience: Since the LLH algorithms consist of both single-solution-based and population-based algorithms, the search process of which are very different, how to pass the searched solutions from one

LLH algorithm to another is also an important research issue for the hyper-heuristic algorithm.

From these observations, it can be easily seen that even though the hyper-heuristic algorithm can provide a better way to solve the optimization problem than the other heuristic algorithms, there is still plenty of room for the improvement.

3   The Proposed Algorithm

3.1   The Basic Idea

The basic idea of the proposed algorithm is to use a high performance hyper-heuristic algorithm (HHA) [14] called Effective Hyper-Heuristic Algorithm (EHHA) to solve the CHEP; that is, to find out suitable CHs for the CHEP. In order to further improve the performance of the hyper-heuristic algorithm we presented in [14], an additional operator, namely, recording pool, will be presented in this study. Also to eliminate redundant computations in the process of selecting the CHs, a check procedure will be used to determine whether to use EHHA or not at the very beginning of every round. For example, if there are 100 sensor nodes and p is set to 0.05, the number of CHs is $100 \times 0.05 = 5$. Note that p is the value to decide the number of CHs with a WSN which, based on the definition of [5], is set to 0.05 in this paper. If the minimum number of wireless sensors that can be selected as CHs is larger than 5, we will then perform the EHHA; otherwise, we will not perform EHHA. This means that all the remaining wireless sensors will be selected as the CHs.

3.2   The Effective Hyper-Heuristic Algorithm

The pseudocode of the proposed algorithm is as given in Fig. 1, which can be divided into two parts: initialization and the process of EHHA. Line 2 indicates that the proposed algorithm will first initialize all the parameters ϕ_{max}, ϕ_{ni}, r, p_p and p_b, where ϕ_{max} denotes the maximum number of iterations for the selected LLH algorithm to run; ϕ_{ni} the maximum number of iterations if the selected LLH algorithm cannot improve the results; r the size of the recording pool to store the best solutions when changing the LLH algorithm; p_p the number of solutions to be changed by using the recording pool when changing the LLH algorithm; and p_b the percentage of solutions to be changed when generating a new solution. Line 3 inputs the data of a WSN that contains the location information of wireless sensors, the residual energy, and other information. Line 4 will then initialize the population of solutions $X = \{x_1, x_2, ..., x_N\}$, where N is the population size.

The main procedure of the proposed algorithm starts at line 6. As line 6 shows, it will first randomly select a LLH algorithm from the candidate pool. As far as this study is concerned, the LLH candidate pool consists of ant colony optimization (ACO), genetic algorithm (GA), particle swarm optimization (PSO),

```
1  /* Initialization */
2  Set up the parameters φ_max, φ_ni, r, p_p, and p_b
3  Input the information of sensors
4  Initialize the population of solutions X = {x_1, x_2, ..., x_N}
5  /* The process of EHHA */
6  Randomly select a heuristic algorithm H_i from the candidate pool H
7  While the termination criterion is not met
8    Update the population of solutions X by using the selected algorithm H_i
9    Evaluate the fitness value of each solution after computing the energy level
10   F_1 = Improvement_Detection(X)
11   F_2 = Diversity_Detection(X)
12   If ψ(H_i, F_1, F_2)
13     Randomly select a new H_i
14     Save the best solution into the Recording Pool
15     Change part of population by using the Recording Pool
16   End If
17 End While
18 Transform the results to CHEP
```

Fig. 1. Outline of the effective hyper-heuristic algorithm.

and tabu search (TS). As lines 7–17 show, the selected LLH algorithm will be performed repeatedly until the termination criterion is met. The population will be changed by the selected LLH algorithm. If the selected LLH algorithms has performed ϕ_{max} iterations, it will be stopped. Moreover, Eq. (1) indicates that EHHA can determine whether to switch to a new LLH algorithm, by using the function $\psi(H_i, F_1, F_2)$ and the parameters H_i, F_1 and F_2, where H_i denotes the LLH algorithm selected, F_1 the improvement detection operator, and F_2 the diversity detection operator. For single-solution-based heuristic algorithms (SSBHA), only F_1 is used whereas for population-based heuristic algorithms (PBHA), both F_1 and F_2 are used.

$$\psi(H_i, F_1, F_2) = \begin{cases} \text{false} & \text{if } H_i \in \mathbf{S} \text{ and } F_1 = \text{true}, \\ \text{false} & \text{if } H_i \in \mathbf{P} \text{ and } F_1 = \text{true and } F_2 = \text{true}, \\ \text{false} & \text{if } \phi_{max} \text{ is not reached}, \\ \text{true} & \text{otherwise}, \end{cases} \quad (1)$$

where $\mathbf{S}$ denotes the set of SSBHAs; and $\mathbf{P}$ the set of PBHAs. If the function $\psi(H_i, F_1, F_2)$ returns true, the proposed algorithm will randomly select a new LLH algorithm to switch to while at the same time saving the so-far-best solution into the recording pool and changing part of the population by using the recording pool. In this way, some of the solutions will be changed while some of them will remain intact.

The Improvement_Detection(X) operator and the Diversity_Detection(X) operator [14] of the proposed algorithm are responsible for determining whether the current LLH algorithm finds a better result or not and for measuring the search diversity of the proposed algorithm, respectively.

The Improvement_Detection(X) operator will return the value that F_1, as defined in Eq. (2), returns; that is, a false if the solution is not improved after ϕ_{ni} iterations in a row; otherwise, it will return a true.

$$F_1 = \begin{cases} \text{false} & \text{if the solution is not improved after } \phi_{ni} \text{ iterations,} \\ \text{true} & \text{otherwise.} \end{cases} \quad (2)$$

In other words, this operator will check to see if the solution found by the selected LLH algorithm H_i is an improvement or not at the ϕ_{ni} iteration. If H_i is an improvement, it will return a true to inform the high-level hyper center that it should keep using this selected LLH algorithm to find a better solution. However, if the selected LLH algorithm H_i cannot improve the current solution for ϕ_{ni} iterations, it will return a false to inform the high-level hyper center that it should switch to a new LLH algorithm to improve the quality of its solution.

The Diversity_Detection(X) operator is used to measure the search diversity of the proposed algorithm. It returns the value that F_2, as defined in Eq. (3), returns. The diversity of the initial solution $D(X_0)$ will be used as a threshold ω, i.e., $\omega = D(X_0)$. The proposed algorithm computes the diversity of the current solution $D(X)$ as the average of the distances between individual solutions. If the diversity of the current solution $D(X)$ is greater than the threshold ω, the operator will return a true, and EHHA will continue to explore the solutions using the original LLH. Otherwise, EHHA will randomly select a new LLH.

$$F_2 = \begin{cases} \text{true} & \text{if } D(X) > \omega, \\ \text{false} & \text{otherwise.} \end{cases} \quad (3)$$

3.3   Recording Pool

The traditional hyper-heuristic algorithm selects the LLH randomly. Although it is easy to implement, it might select an unsuitable LLH algorithm during the convergence process, and the results will degrade. In order to avoid this problem, a recording pool used to improve the search performance of the hyper-heuristic algorithm is presented in this section. Lines 14–15 depict how the recording pool is used to record the best solutions and to change part of the solutions when the function $\psi(H_i, F_1, F_2)$ returns a true. Initially, the recording pool is empty, so it will directly store the best solution into the recording pool. However, if the recording pool is full, it will retain only the best solution in the recording pool but remove all the other solutions. This mechanism ensures that a good solution can be produced from the recording pool and the exploration of good solutions can be continued based on these solutions. More precisely, the proposed algorithm will change only some of the solutions in the population with a predefined probability p_p. If all the solutions in the population are changed based on the solutions in the recording pool, it may end up having a population all the solutions of which are the same when the recording pool has one and only one solution. This apparently will decrease the search diversity. EHHA will use the best solution in the recording pool as the basis for generating a new solution. Some bits in the new solution will be changed with a probability p_b. The changed bits are replaced by the corresponding bits of the solution in the recording pool. In brief, it will make the new solution similar to the solution in the recording pool, but not exactly the same.

3.4 The Other Operators of EHHA

For a WSN, each wireless sensor has a fixed location. But the way the solutions of the proposed algorithm are encoded is a virtual location, because some of the population-based heuristic algorithms adopted in this study use the centroids as the CHs of the CHEP. That is why the solutions of the EHHA are not the same as the input locations of the wireless sensors. For this reason, we need a mechanism for both the HHA and EHHA to transform the solutions to the input locations of sensors. In order to transform the solutions, the proposed algorithm will first select the nearest wireless sensor with a higher energy level as the first location of the solution obtained by the proposed algorithm; it will then select the second nearest wireless sensor with a higher energy level as the second location, and so on. In some cases, the number of wireless sensors with a higher energy level is not enough to fix all the locations. If this is the case, it will select the nearest wireless sensor with a lower energy level to fix its location. Then, it will select the second nearest wireless sensor with a lower energy level to fix its location, and so on until all the locations are fixed. The quality of the proposed algorithm is evaluated by the sum of squared errors, defined as follows:

$$\text{SSE} = \sum_{i=1}^{k} \sum_{j=1}^{n_i} \parallel x_{ij} - c_i \parallel^2, \tag{4}$$

where k denotes the number of CHs, c_i the ith CH, n_i the number of wireless sensors belonging to c_i, and x_{ij} the wireless sensor belonging to c_i. In other words, the fitness of the solutions is measured by the total distance of transmission because the energy consumed by the transmission of data is significantly influenced by the distance; thus, the aim is to find the shortest transmission path.

4   Experimental Results

4.1   Experimental Environment and Parameter Settings

The empirical analysis was conducted on a PC with 2.67 GHz Intel Core i7 CPU and 4 GB of memory running Fedora 12 with Linux 2.6.32.26-175.fc12.x86_64, and the programs are written in C++ and compiled using g++. To evaluate the performance of EHHA for WSN with different sizes of area and different numbers of nodes using the first-order radio model [5], we compare it with LEACH,

Table 1. Parameter settings of the first-order radio model.

Parameters	Values
Initial energy (E_0)	0.5 J/node
Transmitter electronics (E_{elec})	50 nJ/bit
Receiver electronics (E_{elec})	50 nJ/bit
Data packet length (l)	4000 bits
Data aggregation energy (E_{DA})	5 nJ/bit/signal
Transmitter amplifier (ε_{fs}) if $d \leq d_o$	10 pJ/bit/m^2
Transmitter amplifier (ε_{mp}) if $d > d_o$	0.0013 pJ/bit/m^4

LEACH-GA [9], and hyper-heuristic algorithm (HHA) [3]. The parameter settings of the first-order radio model are as given in Table 1. The first-order radio model can be divided into the transmitter and receiver to transmit and receive detected data. The transmitter consists of the radio electronics and the power amplifier while the receiver consists of the radio electronics. The energy consumed by the transmitter transmitting an l-bit message over a distance d is defined by

$$E_{Tx}(l, d) = \begin{cases} l \times E_{elec} + l \times \varepsilon_{fs} \times d^2 & \text{if } d \leq d_o, \\ l \times E_{elec} + l \times \varepsilon_{mp} \times d^4 & \text{if } d > d_o, \end{cases} \quad (5)$$

where the threshold distance d_0 is defined as $\sqrt{\varepsilon_{fs}/\varepsilon_{mp}}$. E_{elec} is the energy consumed for transmitting and receiving a bit. $\varepsilon_{fs}d^2$ and $\varepsilon_{mp}d^4$ are the energy consumed by the amplifier, which depends on the distance between the transmitter and receiver. The energy consumed by a receiver in receiving an l-bit message is defined by

$$E_{Rx}(l) = l \times E_{elec}. \quad (6)$$

The percentage of CHs of LEACH is set equal to 0.05, and the maximum number of rounds is set equal to 10,000. The parameter settings of LEACH-GA are as follows: the crossover rate is set equal to 1.0; the mutation rate is set equal to 0.1; the population size is set equal to 10, and the maximum number of iterations is set equal to 10,000. For HHA and the proposed algorithm, the maximum number of iterations per run is set equal to 200. The population size is set equal to 20 for the PBHAs. The other parameter settings of the energy-effective algorithm are as shown in Table 2. Each simulation is carried out for 30 runs, and the results shown are the average of the 30 runs.

4.2   Results

Figure 2 gives the numbers of alive nodes for the 100 sensors and 100 m × 100 m area case with BS located in the middle, i.e., at (50, 50), of the WSN. It can be easily seen that LEACH-GA outperforms LEACH, because LEACH-GA finds a better probability for the CH selection. The results of HHA and EHHA are

Table 2. Parameter settings of the five energy-effective algorithms for WSN.

Algorithm	Parameters
ACO	Pheromone updating fact $\rho = 0.05$
	Choosing probability $q_0 = 0.5$
	Related influence weights $\alpha = \beta = 1$
GA	Crossover rate $c = 1$
	Mutation rate $m = 0.1$
PSO	Inertia weight $\omega = 0.5$
	Acceleration coefficient $c_1 = c_2 = 2.0$
TS	List size $= 6$
EHHA	Max iteration of LLH algorithm $\phi_{max} = 50$
	Non-improved iteration threshold $\phi_{ni} = 5$
	Size of the recording pool $r = 10$
	Population change rate $p_p = 0.3$
	Bit change rate $p_b = 0.4$

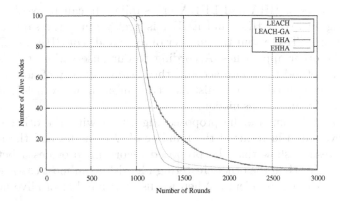

Fig. 2. Numbers of alive nodes for the 100 sensors and 100 m × 100 m area case with BS located at (50, 50).

better than LEACH and LEACH-GA, because HHA and EHHA finds a better distribution of CHs. LEACH may find a bad distribution of CHs that will affect the energy consumed. The death of the first node using the proposed algorithm is at round 928, LEACH is at round 853, and LEACH-GA is at round 874. So EHHA beats LEACH-GA by 54 rounds. At round 1500, the number of alive nodes using HHA and EHHA is 19, the number of alive nodes using LEACH is 1, and the number of alive nodes using LEACH-GA is 4. So EHHA has more alive nodes than LEACH and LEACH-GA for transmitting data to the BS. The result of EHHA is the same as that of HHA in this situation.

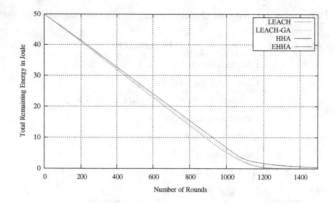

Fig. 3. Total remaining energy for the 100 sensors and 100 m × 100 m area case with BS located at (50, 50).

Figure 3 further shows the remaining energies for the 100 sensors and 100 m × 100 m area case with BS located in the middle, i.e., at (50, 50), of the WSN. The results of HHA and EHHA are similar. It can be easily seen that the remaining energy of HHA and EHHA is pretty much the same as that of LEACH and LEACH-GA, but the number of alive nodes of HHA and EHHA are more than the other approaches. According to our observation, this is because the proposed method takes into account the residual energy of nodes to decide which node will be used for long distance transmission and which node will be used for short distance transmission.

Tables 3 and 4 compare the proposed algorithm with the other clustering algorithms evaluated in terms of the number of alive nodes and the remaining energy. The results show that the proposed algorithm provides a better solution for the CHEP than the other clustering algorithms in most cases, especially for large and complex problems. When we use the number of alive nodes as a

Table 3. Results in terms of the number of alive nodes.

100 sensors, 100 m × 100 m, BS located at (50, 50).					500 sensors, 1000 m × 1000 m, BS located at (500, 500).				
Number of Rounds	Algorithm				Number of Rounds	Algorithm			
	LEACH	LEACH-GA	HHA	EHHA		LEACH	LEACH-GA	HHA	EHHA
500	100.0	100.0	100.0	100.0	500	9.1	11.0	60.9	63.0
1000	84.4	95.9	99.9	99.8	1000	3.4	6.2	27.9	29.1
1500	1.2	4.2	19.6	19.1	1500	1.3	4.1	14.7	15.9
2000	0.2	1.5	6.1	6.1	2000	0.7	2.8	7.5	8.4
2000 sensors, 1000 m × 1000 m, BS located at (500, 500).					4000 sensors, 1000 m × 1000 m, BS located at (500, 500).				
Number of Rounds	Algorithm				Number of Rounds	Algorithm			
	LEACH	LEACH-GA	HHA	EHHA		LEACH	LEACH-GA	HHA	EHHA
500	237.2	61.1	265.3	293.2	500	553.6	636.8	575.0	612.2
1000	4.7	4.9	123.1	164.7	1000	80.1	13.9	317.7	369.2
1500	0.8	1.6	42.8	105.9	1500	1.0	1.2	179.1	267.7
2000	0.4	0.9	17.5	63.4	2000	0.4	0.7	101.6	190.6

Table 4. Results in terms of the remaining energy (Joule) of sensors.

| 100 sensors, 100 m × 100 m, BS located at (50, 50). | | | | 500 sensors, 1000 m × 1000 m, BS located at (500, 500). | | | | |
| Number of Rounds | Algorithm | | | Number of Rounds | Algorithm | | | |
	LEACH	LEACH-GA	HHA	EHHA		LEACH	LEACH-GA	HHA	EHHA
500	27.4749	27.9474	28.4656	28.4673	500	0.594	1.159	5.8031	6.214
1000	5.1717	5.8642	6.7989	6.8032	1000	0.1084	0.5003	1.8051	2.0112
1500	0.0069	0.0488	0.4267	0.4234	1500	0.0261	0.2649	0.702	0.8173
2000	0.0012	0.0139	0.0791	0.0756	2000	0.0095	0.162	0.292	0.3282
2000 sensors, 1000 m × 1000 m, BS located at (500, 500).				4000 sensors, 1000 m × 1000 m, BS located at (500, 500).				
Number of Rounds	Algorithm			Number of Rounds	Algorithm			
	LEACH	LEACH-GA	HHA	EHHA		LEACH	LEACH-GA	HHA	EHHA
500	34.9547	3.6478	27.0588	36.9235	500	97.1901	103.0499	68.7917	85.8229
1000	0.0534	0.0671	6.9501	14.0022	1000	1.584	0.1787	24.5036	36.8481
1500	0.0066	0.0178	1.7937	6.6724	1500	0.0083	0.0111	10.4879	20.0203
2000	0.0021	0.0078	0.5273	2.7428	2000	0.0034	0.005	4.1607	10.0464

measure, as shown in Table 3, the proposed algorithm can keep more alive nodes than the other clustering algorithms. In other words, the difference (i.e., the number of alive nodes) between the proposed algorithm and the others will be larger when we increase the number of sensors while making the region to be covered larger. For example, the last case of Table 4, 4000 sensors in a region of size 1000 m × 1000 m, EHHA has about 190.6 sensors alive but HHA has only 101.6 sensors alive after 2000 rounds. The results show that the difference between the proposed algorithm and the others will become larger and larger, as the number of sensors and the size of the region increase. This implies that the proposed algorithm is a more scalable clustering algorithm than the others. The results of Table 4 show that the difference between these clustering algorithms will also be enlarged for the remaining energy of sensors. Even though the remaining energy of all the sensors of the proposed algorithm is less than the other clustering algorithms for a small CHEP, e.g., 100 sensors for a region of size 100 m × 100 m. But the proposed algorithm can provide a better result when the problem becomes larger and more complex, e.g., 500 sensors for a region of size 1000 m × 1000 m. Moreover, in the case of 4000 sensors for 1000 m × 1000 m, the difference between the proposed algorithm and HHA is about 5.8857 (= 10.0464 − 4.1607) which explains that for a larger and more complex problem, the difference will be more significant.

5   Conclusion

In this paper, we presented an improved hyper-heuristic algorithm for solving the CHEP. The results show that not only can it provide a better result than traditional clustering algorithms, such as LEACH, it can also provide a better result than LEACH with GA and simple hyper-heuristic algorithm. The results further show that the proposed algorithm can prolong the lifetime of most sensors in a WSN by reducing the energy they consume. According to our observations, the results also imply that the proposed algorithm can select a more suitable set of sensors as the CHs than the other clustering algorithms, so the worse data transmission paths will be reduced. Since the results explain that this hyper-heuristic algorithm has potential for the CHEP, we will continue to seek possible ways to improve the performance of this method in the future, especially on adding more LLHs and developing an effective way to determine the execution sequence of LLHs.

Acknowledgments. The authors would like to thank the anonymous reviewers for their valuable comments and suggestions on the paper. This work was supported in part by the Ministry of Science and Technology of Taiwan, R.O.C., under Contracts MOST104-2221-E-197-005 and MOST104-2221-E-110-014.

References

1. Blum, C., Roli, A.: Metaheuristics in combinatorial optimization: overview and conceptual comparison. ACM Comput. Surv. **35**(3), 268–308 (2003)
2. Blum, C., Puchinger, J., Raidl, G.R., Roli, A.: Hybrid metaheuristics in combinatorial optimization: a survey. Appl. Soft Comput. **11**(6), 4135–4151 (2011)
3. Cowling, P., Kendall, G., Soubeiga, E.: A hyperheuristic approach to scheduling a sales summit. In: Burke, E., Erben, W. (eds.) PATAT 2000. LNCS, vol. 2079, pp. 176–190. Springer, Heidelberg (2001). doi:10.1007/3-540-44629-X_11
4. Harrop, P., Das, R.: Wireless sensor networks (WSN) 2014–2024: forecasts, technologies, players. Technical report, IDTechEx (2015). http://www.idtechex.com/research/reports/wireless-sensor-networks-wsn-2014-2024-forecasts-technologies-players-000382.asp?viewopt=orderinfo
5. Heinzelman, W.R., Chandrakasan, A., Balakrishnan, H.: Energy-efficient communication protocol for wireless microsensor networks. In: Proceedings of Annual Hawaii International Conference on System Sciences, pp. 1–10 (2000)
6. Hoang, D., Yadav, P., Kumar, R., Panda, S.: A robust harmony search algorithm based clustering protocol for wireless sensor networks. In: Proceedings of IEEE International Conference on Communications Workshops, pp. 1–5 (2010)
7. Krishna, K., Murty, M.: Genetic k-means algorithm. IEEE Trans. Syst. Man Cybern. Part B: Cybern. **29**(3), 433–439 (1999)
8. Kulkarni, R.V., Venayagamoorthy, G.K.: Particle swarm optimization in wireless-sensor networks: a brief survey. IEEE Trans. Syst. Man Cybern. Part C: Appl. Rev. **41**(2), 262–267 (2011)
9. Liu, J.L., Ravishankar, C.V.: LEACH-GA: genetic algorithm-based energy-efficient adaptive clustering protocol for wireless sensor networks. Int. J. Mach. Learn. Comput. **1**(1), 79–85 (2011)
10. Losilla, F., Garcia-Sanchez, A.J., Garcia-Sanchez, F., Garcia-Haro, J., Haas, Z.J.: A comprehensive approach to WSN-based ITS applications: a survey. Sensors **11**(11), 10220–10265 (2011)
11. Potdar, V., Sharif, A., Chang, E.: Wireless sensor networks: a survey. In: Proceedings of the International Conference on Advanced Information Networking and Applications Workshops, pp. 636–641 (2009)
12. Reese, L.: Industrial wireless sensor networks. Technical report, Mouser Electronics (2015). http://www.mouser.com/applications/rf-sensor-networks/

13. Sang, Y., Shen, H., Inoguchi, Y., Tan, Y., Xiong, N.: Secure data aggregation in wireless sensor networks: a survey. In: Proceedings of the Seventh International Conference on Parallel and Distributed Computing, Applications and Technologies, pp. 315–320 (2006)
14. Tsai, C.W., Huang, W.C., Chiang, M.H., Chiang, M.C., Yang, C.S.: A hyper-heuristic scheduling algorithm for cloud. IEEE Trans. Cloud Comput. 2(2), 236–250 (2014)
15. Tsai, C.W., Hong, T.P., Shiu, G.N.: Metaheuristics for the lifetime of WSN: a review. IEEE Sens. J. 16(9), 2812–2831 (2016)

A Survey on Reliable Transmission Technologies in Wireless Sensor Networks

Ning Sun[1(✉)], Zhengkai Tang[1], Chen Lin[1], Guangjie Han[1(✉)],
and Jin Wang[2]

[1] College of IoTs Engineering, Hohai University, Changzhou, China
sunn2001@hotmail.com, tangzk36@outlook.com,
linchen_sabrina@163.com, hanguangjie@gmail.com
[2] School of Information Engineering, Yangzhou University, Yangzhou, China
wangjin@nuist.edu.cn

Abstract. Reliability is an important issue in wireless sensor networks (WSNs). Reliable transmission of data in WSNs is the basic of successful network operation. In this paper, we firstly define the evaluation methods for reliability in WSNs in terms of evaluation metrics and recovery ways. The technologies to improve reliability for WSNs are summed up in several classifications: retransmission, redundancy, hybrid method and some newly emerging technologies. Some typical protocols are stated and analyzed. Also we compare these technologies in several aspects as the direction for future research.

Keywords: Wireless sensor networks · Reliability · Redundancy · Retransmission · Network coding · Cooperative transmission

1 Introduction

Wireless sensor networks (WSNs) are used in many occasions for its excellent features, while more and more applications have put forward higher requirements to the reliability of data transmission in WSNs, such as in industrial monitoring where the data should be reliably transmitted to the control center so that the workers can make decisions and take actions accurately. The reliability of WSNs can be easily decreased due to the features of WSNs, like the unstable wireless link, vulnerable sensor nodes, the deployment of nodes and other environmental reasons. Therefore, the scholars have already proposed different ways to solve this problem in various aspects, for preventing the data from being altered or stolen and reducing the possibility of transmission loss in bad conditions. In this paper, we summarize some of the researches in the reliability area and make a compositive comparison between them.

The work is supported by "Qing Lan Project", "the National Natural Science Foundation of China under Grant 61572172", "the Fundamental Research Funds for the Central Universities, No. 2016B10714".

In Sect. 2, we classify the reliability evaluation method, which consists of evaluation metric and recover way. In evaluation metric, the methods are divided into packet-based and event-based, while the recover ways are separated to two types: end to end and hop by hop. In Sect. 3, we divided the reliability technologies into four types: retransmission-based, redundancy-based, hybrid and other methods. We select some typical protocols and give an outline of these methods, additionally, analyze the advantages and disadvantages. In Sect. 4, a general comparison is conducted. Finally, we make a conclusion in Sect. 5.

2 Evaluation Method of Reliability

2.1 Evaluation Metric

We classify the reliability of data transmission to "packet reliability" and "event reliability" according to metric classification. The purpose of packet reliability is to ensure that all the data sensed which carried with packets from all relevant sensor nodes are transmitted to the receiver reliably. Packet reliability requires that all the packets carrying with perception information sent by all sensor nodes can be reliably delivered to the sink node. Event reliability only needs to ensure that the sink node is able to get enough information about an event on time, and does not need to ensure all the packets must be transmitted to the sink node. Therefore, event reliability is more suitable as the measurement indicators of transmission reliability in some applications of WSNs, which only have to ensure that the receiver receives the user's necessary information, rather than all sensor data packets.

2.2 Recovery Method

WSNs with limited bandwidth resource and low storage capabilities of sensor nodes will be easily block up in the network; at the same time, wireless communication has high bit error rate because of environmental impact. In order to meet the requirements of reliability in the network, the loss data packets can be recovered by end to end or hop by hop.

End to end method also called connection-oriented mechanism, of which only have two end points to ensure the reliability. That is to say, only recover packet loss in the source node, and intermediate nodes should simply be responsible for transmitting data between source and destination nodes.

In the recovery mode, the packet loss recovery must be carried out hop by hop, and finally the data packets can be transmitted to the sink node reliably. Hop by hop mechanism can be used as a guide for data transmission links, because each hop has to ensure the reliability. In other words, every hop from source node to destination node has to ensure the reliable transmission of data, in order to achieve the reliability of the whole transmission.

We classify the reliability assessment methods by introducing a three-dimensional reference model, as shown in Fig. 1.

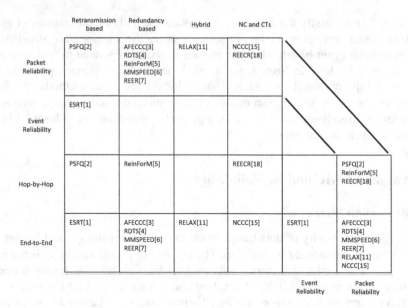

Fig. 1. Three-dimensional (3D) reference model for research in reliability of WSNs

3 Reliable Transmission Technologies in WSNs

3.1 Retransmission

The retransmission mechanism in wireless devices is that when sending node cannot receive the ACK in specified time, it will resend the data until receive the ACK successfully or approach the attempt limit.

Event-to-sink reliability is one of the most significant features of reliable transport in WSN. Literature [1] proposed a new transmission protocol with reliability and congestion control implemented in sink node - the event-sink reliable (ESRT) protocol. ESRT covers a congestion control component. The sink node in the network can inform the source node to adjust upload data rate adaptively through the radio according to current network condition. Therefore, we can ensure the event reliability without causing congestion as well as achieve the double goals of data transmission reliability and energy saving. In addition, the ESRT protocol operations can also be extended to allow multiple events in the case of transmission. Based on the proof of theoretical analysis and simulation experiments, ESRT protocol has higher data transmission accuracy and greater network coverage area and stronger local feature extraction ability compared with reliable transmission protocols. Regardless of the initial state of the network, the ESRT protocol can enable it to achieve the optimal state. However, this protocol belongs to typical event-detection application in WSNs, which cannot guarantee the success of end-to-end data transmission. At the same time, sink node in ESRT adopts the broadcast way to inform the source node to adjust frequency adaptively which aggravated the nodes' loads around sink node.

A certain packet loss rate is acceptable in the data flow that from the source node to the sink node in WSN, while the data flow for the control or management in the opposite direction is very sensitive. Therefore, the new reliable transmission PSFQ [2] protocol referred to "Pump-slowly, fetch-quickly" was proposed. "Pump-slowly" means nodes in the network broadcast data to the neighboring nodes at a slow speed. "Fetch-quickly" refers to in case of packet loss, nodes request neighboring nodes to retransmit for loss recovery. According to the simulation and experiment results, PSFQ is superior to other traditional technology. Even in the case of high packet loss rate, it can maintain the normal operation of the network. This protocol has obvious advantages in fault tolerance, communication overhead and transmission delay. PSFQ is mainly applied for the sink node sending query and control messages to the source node without a complex routing infrastructure. Furthermore, this protocol cannot adapt to the change of the network.

3.2 Redundancy

3.2.1 Forward Error Correction

Protocol [3] provides some evidence to prove the bit error rate of low energy wireless communication channel can change smoothly in order to adjust the magnitude of FEC codes dynamically. At the same time, an adaptive FEC code control algorithm called AFECCC is proposed and its performance is evaluated in a variety of communication channels and real wireless sensor networks. This algorithm can adjust the size of the FEC code dynamically according to the instructions of the received confirmation packet. Rising to a higher FEC level in the case of data packet loss, otherwise reducing to lower level of FEC by MIAD—multiplicative increase additive decrease. About the residence time in each level, it is determined by the success ratio before dropping to a lower level dynamically. In other words, AFECCC uses the level more frequently the longer time it will stay at this level. The simulation experiments show that the performance of AFECCC is better than that of any static algorithm as well as two earlier hybrid ARQ/FEC algorithms. How to determine the variables of AFECCC automatically based on the network environment is still a challenging issue.

The nodes in typical WSNs collect information by connected sensors, and the data is transmitted to the base station or sink node hop by hop. The effect of transmission is easy to be affected by the environment, therefore, the quantity of data packets transferred to the sink node successfully determines the reliability of the data transmission. Paper [4] proposed a more efficient mechanism, RDTS, which is more effective than previous retransmission and information redundancy. The main idea of this protocol is to calculate the quantity of redundant data packets and find the methods of eliminating the intermediate nodes code according to the quality of hop by hop connection, so as to ensure the reliability of the hop-by-hop transmission. Using of RDTS has several advantages: first it can reduce the redundant data significantly, results in saving energy and extending the life cycle of the network. In addition, the authors adopt the useful feature of systematic erasure coding that performs partial coding, which solve the problem of coding overhead.

3.2.2 Multi-path Routing

Literature [5] introduces a protocol called ReInForm. Provisions of this protocol for every data packet need multiple copies and then transmit them from source to sink via multiple paths, so data can meet the required reliability in the process of transmission. And the referenced degree of redundant backup data is decided by the desired reliability, local channels' condition, the information that provided by neighbor nodes altogether; after that the source node will select the next hop by the hops between neighbor nodes and sink nodes, and then distribute the backup data packets by proportion. Furthermore, repeat the above steps until the data packet has been transmitted to the sink node. With the feature of this mechanism, it is possible to use all possible paths efficiently and to achieve a high efficiency of load balancing. To sum up, this protocol makes use of multiple backup data packets to improve the transmission probability of end-to-end data and reduce the cost of transmission in order to approach the desired reliability.

Protocol [6] proposed a new data transmission agreement in WSN called MMSPEED, which provides the guarantee of QoS through the real-time differences and reliability services. In terms of real time, this protocol provides a variety of network speed options so that different traffic types can select the appropriate speed dynamically. In terms of reliability, this protocol adopts the multiple paths to transmit data packet according to the successful transmission rate of end-to-end. Network layer and MAC layer are connected with this protocol and then achieve it by localization method. MMSPEED can mix periodic and non periodic data in the network without global network information through a dynamic compensation method to adjust the reliability of each node. Therefore, MMSPEED can adapt to large-scale sensor network's requirements dynamically. Based on the simulation on J-SIM and the comparison with the SPEED protocol, the results show that MMSPEED protocol can meet the both requirements of real-time and reliability, furthermore, it can improve the capacity of network under different requirements significantly. However, the disadvantage of this protocol is that WSNs with MMSPEED protocol has higher energy consumption which will shorten the lifetime of the network.

A robust and energy efficient multipath routing for WSNs was proposed in this [7] protocol which called REER. In the establishment of the routes, it takes the node's residual energy, available buffer size of the nodes and signal to noise ratio (SNR) into account in order to select the best next hop node. After finishing the path detection, BEER proposes two kinds of flow distribution mechanism: one is using the path that has been found to transmit data packets, and it will be replaced by another backup path when this one exceeds a certain threshold. Another mechanism is distributing the transmitted information into fragments of the same size, increasing the error correcting codes that based on XOR. This mechanism increases the reliability of the transmission to the destination nodes by multiple routes, at the same time, it will not cause much delay.

Simulation results show that the REER can reduce the energy consumption and data transmission delay as well as improve the transmission rate of data compared with Diffusion Directed and N-to-1 routing.

3.3 Hybrid Scheme

In [9], an error control schemes by using cross-layer methodology was proposed. Specifically, it did the research about the effect of multi hop routing path and the broadcast nature of wireless communication, the purpose is to be able to count the energy consumption, PER and the potential factors of the error control theory equably. This cross-layer theory has taken routes' selections, media connection and the effect of physical layer into account which becomes a comprehensive comparison of FEC, ARQ and hybrid ARQ theory. The research results of hybrid ARQ theory and certain FEC codes show that after extending the length of each hop, energy consumption and the potential target data packet error rate (PER) will increase compared to ARQ. However, when the network density increases, the FEC codes will have much more advantages. On the other hand, ARQ is better than FEC in the aspect of value in various end-to-end distance and the target PER. In summary, this thesis analyzes when is the best time to use FEC, ARQ or hybrid ARQ scheme.

In [10], the author made a comparative theoretical study on the transmission reliability of retransmission and redundancy. And in order to fully study their advantages and possibilities, a comparison between the energy efficiency of retransmission and redundancy was also made. The authors present a simple and achievable analysis model to analyze the probability of arriving packets and the average energy consumption in terms of retransmission and redundancy. According to the proposed model, the comprehensive effect of the two methods in reliability and energy efficiency can be measured in the aspect of quantity, where the results show that redundancy has the better flexibility of the data packet loss, from one hop costs a ulp of 0.5 to multihop cost a ulp of 0.07. Compared with effective retransmission, the redundancy can still achieve reliable transmission in the loss of packets at low frequency and smooth situation. However, the advantage of this model will be weakened in the case of hop increase, thus it is very important to consider the balance between reliability and energy efficiency. About future research direction, the author will break down the redundant information association in order to overcome the continuous error or the high data packet loss, and combine the two methods together.

In [11], the author proposed the RELAX protocol. The multipath routing protocol of energy efficiency in WSNs can recover from the path failure and achieve the load balance. It can achieve the load balance of flow distribution by using the nodes' battery power efficiently through a set of node-disjoint paths. This protocol can increase the lifetime of the sensor nodes' batteries by using their relaxation, which increases the lifetime of the sensor network. During the period of batteries' relaxation, the results that it can recover part of the batteries' power have been experimentally demonstrated, for example, intermittent operation of the alkaline battery can increase the life expectancy of about 28%. In addition, RELAX predicts the next hop through the path in the construction stage by using residual energy, node available buffer size and SNR. RELAX will split the sending information into equal sized segments, add error correcting codes, and then sends it to the multiple paths as well as increases the probability of an important part of the packet, thus it will not cause delay.

3.4 Other Methods

3.4.1 Network Coding

The traditional way of data transmission is to store and transmit, the intermediate nodes plays a role of transponder. Network coding is an information exchange technology that includes routing and coding. The most important part of this mechanism is that every node in the path can dispose the received information and then transmit it to the next hop. Network coding can encode the received data information of each node, which improves the utilization of the network link bandwidth.

In [13], the authors combined with XOR operation and operation of finite field method through 'butterfly network' model to research on the network flow in multicast networks. It describes the admissible code rate of multicast network and proves the use of network coding network multicast can achieve maximum flow minimum cut theorem under the maximum transmission capacity and thus be able to obtain better network throughput than routing multicast. At the same time, according to the situation of multi-source network, the authors adopted the use of convolutional codes of network coding which can decrease the time delay of data transmission in the network and balance the network load. But the nonlinear coding is very complex that need a further experiment and improvement. However, the method of combination of network coding and algebraic geometry, which brings a strong support for the future research.

Paper [14] pointed out that, network coding can improve reliability of lossy networks by reducing packet retransmission times. Although previous studies show that the network coding can improve network capacity, the gained reliability of the specific network is still unknown, therefore, this literature on network coding can improve the degree of reliability is quantified. Based on the model of the access point and tree topology of multicast, this paper makes a research on the comparison of ARQ and FEC and network coding's different reliable transmission mechanisms in a lossy channel and shows the numerical results and performance analysis.

First of all, in an access point broadcast data packets to a set of K receiver network model. When the size and the number of receivers to Θ (log K), the desired number of transmission data packets is significantly smaller than that of ARQ, but FEC experimental results are similar, which proves that compared with ARQ mechanism, network coding can indeed reduce the number of retransmission. Besides, based on tree topology of multicast model, this paper makes transmitted experiments of different reliable transmission mechanisms in end-to-end and interlinked. The results show that network coding can ensure the higher reliability of data transmission under the same number of retransmissions. We can predict from the literature research results that network coding can not only improve the reliability of the simple network, but also improve the reliability of the network that has diversity network topology with complex paths.

3.4.2 Cooperative Transmission

Cooperative communication can improve the reliability of the wireless terminal, and can save energy when multi-path transmits redundant information, at the same time, resist the signal decline in the multipath transmission process. There are two aspects of cooperative communication effect: on the one hand, it obtains communication gain through smaller hop number neighbor collaboration node or relay node; on the other hand, an increase of the space complexity of the receiver can also bring the benefits of balance multiplexing technology.

The authors of [16] proposed a strategy that combined with cooperative communication technology and channel coding technology. This strategy chooses some relay node which are spatial dispersion, these nodes can decode packet data with higher successful rate and then transmit data collaboratively to other node. In addition, the outage probability of the information theory is analyzed, and the outage capacity can achieve the continuous performance gain compared with the direct transmission, and the diversity order is K + I (K is the number of relay nodes). Besides, the researchers developed a data transmission method based on cooperative transmission scheme and ACK. Experimental results show that the method can achieve a better balance between the system throughput and fairness, which improves the reliability of information transmission.

It is well known that MIMO technology and orthogonal space time block coding can improve the performance of the network system. The authors of [17] study the problem of reliable packet transmission in WSNs by using these two techniques. In order to satisfy the accomplishment of the biggest successful transmission rate (STR) with the given end-to-end energy consumption as well as greatly reduce the implementation complexity of the global optimization, this paper proposes a cross-layer optimization distributed square case jointed with channel coding and power control and routing planning of low complexity. The experimental results show that the proposed scheme can significantly reduce the symbol error rate (SER), which is obviously better than the traditional energy saving routing algorithm.

4 General Comparison

Some typical reliable transmission technologies of WSNs are introduced in above. Table 1 compares these technologies in terms of reliability measures (Metric), recover way, energy consumption, scalability and suitable applications. According to the

Table 1. Comparison of reliable transmission.

Name	Method	Metric	Reliability	Recover way	Energy consumption	Latency	Scalability	Layer
ESRT	Retransmission	Event reliability	High	End-to-End	Low	High	Middle	Transport layer
PSFQ	Retransmission	Packet reliability	Very high	Hop-by-Hop	Low	High	Low	Transport layer
AFECCC	Erasure code	Packet reliability	Very high	End-to-End	Low	High	Middle	Physical, data link layers
RDTS	Erasure code	Packet reliability	High	End-to-End	Low	Low	Low	Physical layer
ReInForM	Multipath	Packet reliability	Very high	Hop-by-Hop	High	High	Middle	Network layer

(*continued*)

Table 1. (*continued*)

Name	Method	Metric	Reliability	Recover way	Energy consumption	Latency	Scalability	Layer
MMSPEED	Multipath	Packet reliability	Very high	End-to-End	High	Low	High	Network layer
REER	Multipath +XOR	Packet reliability	High	End-to-End	Low	Low	Middle	Network layer
[8]	Node redundancy	Packet reliability	High	End-to-End	Low	Low	Middle	Network and MAC layer
RELAX	Multipath +FEC	Packet reliability	High	End-to-End	Low	Low	Middle	Network layer
[14]	Network coding	Packet reliability	Very high	Hop-by-Hop	High	Low	High	Physical layer
NCCC	Network coding	Packet reliability	Very high	End-to-End	Low	Low	Middle	Physical layer
[16]	MIMO + RBC	Packet reliability	Very high	End-to-End	Low	High	Middle	Physical layer
[17]	MIMO +OSTBC	Packet reliability	Very high	End-to-End	High	High	Middle	Physical, network layers
REECR	Cooperative relay + ARQ	Packet reliability	High	Hop-by-Hop	Low	High	High	Physical layer

feature analysis shown in Table 1, it is clear that event reliability tends to has lower energy consumption than packet reliability in various methods. Additionally, schemes using hop-by-hop seems to have higher scalability compared to the end-to-end approach, however, both ways can be used in different suitable applications.

5 Conclusions

This paper makes a summary of the reliability mechanisms in WSNs. We analyze the features and superiority of some typical protocols as well as make comparisons between these different methods. Both retransmission and redundancy techniques show their great features in the guarantee of transmission reliability. However, the hybrid way makes a deep comparison between the two techniques above, it summarizes the goodness and weakness in different area and analyze the best way to choose in various situations. Finally, new techniques such as network coding and cooperative transmission become hot topics, these unconventional techniques still do the good job in reliability increase and have a bright prospect in the future.

References

1. Akan, O.B., Akyildiz, I.F.: Event-to-sink reliable transport in wireless Sensor networks. J. IEEE/ACM Trans. Network. **13**(5), 1003–1016 (2005)

2. Wan, C.Y., Campbell, A., Krishnamurthy, L.: Pump-slowly, fetch-quickly (PSFQ): a reliable transport protocol for sensor networks. J. IEEE. J. Sel. Areas. Commun. **23**(04), 862–872 (2005)

3. Ahn, J., Hong, S., Heidemann, J.: An adaptive FEC code control algorithm for mobile wireless sensor networks. J. Commun. Netw. **7**(4), 488–499 (2005)

4. Srouji, M.S., Wang, Z., et al.: RDTS: a reliable erasure-coding based data transfer scheme for wireless sensor networks. In: Proceedings of 17th IEEE International Conference on Parallel and Distributed Systems (2011)

5. Deb, B., Bhatnagar, S., Nath, B.: ReInForM: reliable information forwarding using multiple paths in sensor networks. In: Proceedings of 28th Annual IEEE International Conference on Local Computer Networks (2003)

6. Felemban, E., Lee, C.G., Ekici, E.: MMSPEED: multipath multispeed protocol for QoS guarantee of reliability and timeliness in wireless sensor networks. J. IEEE Trans. Mob. Comput. **5**(6), 738–754 (2006)

7. Yahya, B., Ben-Othman, J.: REER: robust and energy efficient multipath routing protocol for wireless sensor networks. In: Proceedings of IEEE Global Telecommunication Conference (2009)

8. Sun, N., Cho, Y.B., Lee, S.H.: Node classification based on functionality in energy-efficient and reliable wireless sensor networks. Int. J. Distrib. Sens. Netw. (2012)

9. Vuran, M.C., Akyildiz, I.F.: Error control in wireless sensor networks: a cross layer analysis. J. IEEE/ACM Trans. Netw. **17**(4), 1186–1199 (2009)

10. Wen, H., Lin, C., Ren, F.Y.: Retransmission or redundancy: transmission reliability study in wireless sensor networks. J. Sci. China Inf. Sci. **55**(4), 1–10 (2012)

11. Yahya, B., Ben-Othman, J.: Relax: an energy efficient multipath routing protocol for wireless sensor networks. In: Proceedings of IEEE International Conference on Communications (2010)

12. Courtade, T., Wesel, R.: Optimal allocation of redundancy between packet-level erasure coding and physical-layer channel coding in fading channels. J. IEEE Trans. Commun. **59** (8), 1–9 (2011)

13. Ahlswede, R., et al.: Network information flow. J. IEEE Trans. Inf. Theory **46**(4), 1204–1216 (2000)

14. Ghaderi, M., Towsley, D., Kurose, J.: Reliability gain of network coding in lossy wireless networks. In: Proceedings of the 27th IEEE Conference on Computer Communications (2008)

15. Liu, X.C., Gong, X.R., Zheng, Y.Z.: Reliable cooperative communications based on random network coding in multi-hop relay WSNs. J. IEEE Sens. J. **14**(8) (2014)

16. Zhang, S.K., Fan, J.X., Cui, Z.M.: Reliable cooperative data transmission mechanism for wireless sensor networks. J. Commun. **31**(11), 30–40 (2010)

17. Yu, R., Zhang, Y., Song L.Y.: Joint optimization of power, packet forwarding and reliability in MIMO wireless sensor networks. J. Mob. Netw. Appl. **16**(6), 1–11 (2011)

18. Zheng, W., Rahman, K.A., Tepe, K.E.: Reliable and energy efficient cooperative relaying scheme (REECR) in wireless sensor networks. In: Proceedings of 9th International Wireless Communication and Mobile Computing Conference, pp. 400–405 (2013)

Distributed Node Scheduling Algorithms for Multiple Group Communications in Wireless Multi-hop Networks

I-Hsien Liu[1], Chuan-Gang Liu[2], Kun-Hsuan Liu[1], Shun-Hsiung Yu[1], Zhi-Yuan Su[3], and Jung-Shian Li[1($\boxtimes$)]

[1] Department of Electrical Engineering, Institute of Computer and Communication, National Cheng Kung University, Tainan, Taiwan, R.O.C.
{dannyliu,Khliu,sxyu}@hsnet.ee.ncku.edu.tw,
jsli@mail.ncku.edu.tw
[2] Department of Applied Informatics and Multimedia, Chia-Nan University of Pharmacy and Science, Tainan, Taiwan, R.O.C.
chgliu@mail.cnu.edu.tw
[3] Department of Information Management, Chia-Nan University of Pharmacy and Science, Tainan, Taiwan, R.O.C.
szj1974@gmail.com

Abstract. We study the scheduling problem in performing multiple multicast communications in wireless multi-hop networks, it is necessary to ensure that each multicast group can complete one transmission from the source to all the destination nodes without conflict in every frame. The present study proposes two distributed token-based STDMA node scheduling algorithms which not only satisfy this requirement, but also minimize the frame length. In the first algorithm, the multicast groups are scheduled on a group-by-group basis, whereas in the second algorithm, multiple groups are scheduled in each scheduling operation. The first algorithm has the advantages of computational simplicity and a straightforward implementation, while the second algorithm increases the percentage of reused time slots and reduces the number of token forwarding events. The simulation results show that both algorithms achieve a shorter frame length than existing methods.

Keywords: Group communications · Wireless multi-hop networks · Node scheduling

1 Introduction

Recent years have witnessed a surge in the popularity of distributed applications such as audio and video conferencing, media streaming, interactive gaming, and so on. The transmission efficiency of such applications is generally enhanced by adopting a multicast broadcasting approach. Many of these applications require strict Quality of Service (QoS) guarantees (e.g., a minimal delay and a fair share of the available bandwidth). However, traditional wireless Medium Access Control (MAC) protocols are generally unable to satisfy these requirements. Furthermore, in ad hoc networks, traditional protocols often result in a low throughput due to collisions in the upstream

© ICST Institute for Computer Sciences, Social Informatics and Telecommunications Engineering 2017
J.-H. Lee and S. Pack (Eds.): QShine 2016, LNICST 199, pp. 120–128, 2017.
DOI: 10.1007/978-3-319-60717-7_12

direction. As a result, more efficient MAC protocols for multicast group communications are required.

Most existing MAC protocols are based on a Time Division Multiple Access (TDMA) scheme, in which the time domain is divided into contiguous fixed-length slots and these slots are allocated in such a way that only one node or link is active at any moment in time. However, TDMA schemes result in a poor bandwidth utilization in wireless multi-hop networks since they do not support spatial reuse. That is, different nodes cannot access the shared channel concurrently even if their assigned wavelengths are widely separated in the transmission spectrum. Accordingly, several Spatial TDMA (STDMA) schemes have been proposed for improving the capacity of ad hoc networks by permitting multiple nodes to transmit simultaneously provided that they are collision-free [2, 5, 16]. Such schemes ensure that each network node can transmit at least once in every frame. Moreover, most STDMA schemes also attempt to minimize the number of assigned slots; thereby increasing throughput. However, the problem of finding the minimal frame-length is NP-complete [12].

Accordingly, the present study proposes a distributed node scheduling algorithms for minimizing the frame length for multiple multicast communications in wireless multi-hop networks. In the former algorithm, the various multicast groups are scheduled on a group-by-group basis, whereas in the second algorithm, multiple groups are scheduled in the same frame. In both cases, the nodes select an appropriate number of time slots in accordance with their respective loads. Moreover, in each algorithm, the time slots are selected in such a way that every multicast group can complete the transmission of one packet from the source to all the destinations without conflict in every frame.

2 Background and Related Work

In STDMA networks, data collisions (i.e., transmission failures) arise as a result of two different types of interference, namely "primary interference" and "secondary interference" [3, 8, 10, 12, 14, 15]. Primary interference occurs when a node is required to carry out more than one task in the same slot (e.g., to both receive and transmit data). Meanwhile, secondary interference occurs when the data receiving process of one node is interfered with by the data transmission process of a nearby node (i.e., the "hidden node problem" [9]).

In solving the data collision problem, many existing node scheduling algorithms use a chromatic approach, in which the network nodes are partitioned into different color classes, where those nodes with the same color are able to transmit simultaneously without collision [1, 5, 11, 13]. However, although such an approach ensures that every node can transmit at least once in a frame without conflict, many slots may be wasted since the scheduling process does not take the network load into account. For example, some nodes may be allocated a time slot, but may not actually have any data to transmit once the slot arrives. Accordingly, the scheduling algorithms proposed in this study take explicit account of the transmission flow within each multicast group and allow each node to select appropriate time slots in accordance with their particular transmission requirements.

3 Problem Definition, Network Model and Proposed Algorithms

3.1 Problem Definition and Network Model

The aim of the algorithms proposed in the present study is to improve the transmission efficiency of multiple multicast communications in wireless multi-hop ad hoc networks. Moreover, based on the assumption that each activated node can transmit only one packet per time slot, the proposed algorithms also attempt to guarantee that all of the multicast groups can complete the transmission of one packet from the source to all of the destination nodes in every frame. Finally, both algorithms seek to minimize the frame length. Note that in developing the two algorithms, it is assumed that a node can pick a slot to transmit for a particular group if, and only if, its upstream node in that group has already been scheduled. In addition, it is also assumed that the frame length is identical for all of the nodes in the network.

The wireless multi-hop network is modeled using a bidirectional graph $G = (V, E)$, where V is the set of nodes, $|V|$ is the number of nodes, and E is the set of edges between the nodes. If $u,v \in V$, there exists an edge(u, v). Furthermore $\in E$ indicates that node v can receive all the messages transmitted by u, and vice versa. Finally, it is assumed that all of the nodes in the network are homogeneous, i.e., the nodes all have the same transmission range.

In modeling the network, each node is assigned a unique ID and is assumed to be aware of the connectivity information of the network within its transmission range. That is, every node knows the IDs of all its one-hop neighbors. Since the present study considers a multiple multicast communications network in which every node in the network is a source, the network contains $|V|$ source-based trees. In other words, every node participates in $|V|$ multicast groups, and the multicast packets of each group are routed along a specific source-based tree. In addition, it is assumed that every node knows how to forward the multicast data which it receives. In other words, when a multicast packet arrives at a node, the node knows which of its links should be activated to forward the packet toward the other nodes in the source-based tree. For example, consider the source-based tree shown in Fig. 1, in which Node S is the

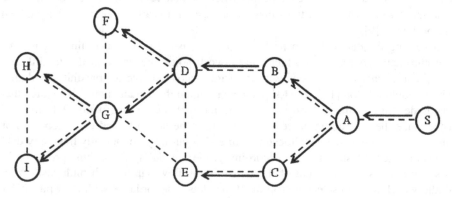

Fig. 1. Illustrative source-based tree

source. Node D (for example) lacks the connectivity information of the entire network, but knows that Nodes B, E, F and G are its one-hop neighbors. Thus, when Node S sends a multicast message to all its group members, Node D forwards the message to all its downstream nodes (i.e., Nodes F and G) on receipt of the message from Node B. Note that in this illustrative scenario, Node B is the parent of Node D, and Nodes F and G are the children of Node D.

Note that in developing the proposed scheduling algorithms, it is assumed that the network topology remains unchanged during the scheduling process. Moreover, an assumption is made that all of the packets sent by the nodes are correctly received at their destinations. In other words, the transmission failure problem is not considered.

3.2   Group-by-Group Algorithm

Every multicast group in the multi-hop network is required to complete the transmission of one packet from the source to all of the destinations in every frame. In other words, every multicast group must be scheduled in each scheduling round. In the first algorithm proposed in the present study, designated as the Group-by-Group algorithm [6], the groups are scheduled on a group-by-group basis. Specifically, when a group is allocated to schedule, all of the nodes in the group select appropriate slots in which to perform transmission, and once all of these nodes have been scheduled, the scheduling process is repeated for the next group.

3.3   Greedy Algorithm

The Group-by-Group algorithm described in the previous section provides a straightforward means of achieving multiple multicast scheduling in ad hoc wireless networks. However, it has two drawbacks. First, the scheduling process is time consuming since each node can select only one time slot for transmission when receiving the token. Second, nodes within the same multicast group cannot choose the same slot for transmission, and thus the channel utilization efficiency is reduced. Accordingly, this section proposes a second algorithm, designated as the Greedy algorithm, which eliminates both drawbacks by allowing multiple groups to be scheduled in the same frame.

In the proposed algorithm, each node in the wireless network maintains a schedule queue containing a list of scheduling jobs to be performed by either itself or one of its one-hop neighbors. For each node, the jobs (J) are recorded using the data structure Jm n, where m is an index relating to the different multicast groups in the network and n is an index pertaining to the different slots in the time domain. Assume that a job Jm n is stored in the schedule queue of Node k. In practice, the existence of this job in the schedule queue has two implications: (1) the parent of Node k in Group m has already been scheduled (and thus Node k can pick a slot to transmit for Group m when it receives the token), and (2) the parent of Node k in group m has selected time slot n to perform its transmission. In other words, the schedule queue indicates to Node k which groups have already been scheduled by its upstream nodes and allows the node to pick an appropriate slot to perform its own transmission for each group. (Note that if Node k chooses to perform transmission for multicast Group m, the index of the selected slot must be greater than n.) Each schedule queue can store multiple jobs; where each job may refer to different multicast groups. Thus, in contrast to the Group-by-Group algorithm, the nodes in the network can schedule the transmissions of multiple groups in the same scheduling frame, As a result, the Greedy algorithm results in a better than the Group-by-Group algorithm. In addition to the scheduling queue, each node in the network also maintains a schedule table for itself and its one-hop neighbors. As in the Group-by-Group algorithm, the schedule table is used to record the state of each node in every time slot (i.e., Ti, Rj, DR or empty).

The scheduling process in the Greedy algorithm is again controlled using a token-based scheme. However, in contrast to the Group-by-Group algorithm, the token has the format {terminator, frame length}, where the "terminator" field is used to indicate which node wants to terminate the scheduling process. Note that the "termi-nator" field is generally set to 0, i.e., none of the nodes in the network wish to terminate the scheduling process. However, if the token arrives at a node, and the node finds that its schedule queue is completely empty (i.e., there are no outstanding jobs for either itself or any of its one-hop neighbors), the node replaces the current "terminator" field entry with its own node-ID since it believes that all of the multiple multicast groups in the network have been scheduled. The "frame length" field of the token indicates the current length of the frame, and has a value equal to the maximal time slot index amongst all of the time slots which have been selected thus far in the scheduling operation.

4   Simulation Results

In this section, the performance (i.e., frame length and number of token forwarding events) of the proposed algorithms is investigated by means of numerical simulations. In accordance with the assumptions described in Sect. 3.1, the network nodes all have the same transmission range. Furthermore, no changes in the network topology occur during the scheduling process. That is, the nodes are all static and the network is always connected. Moreover, every node in the network is a source node with data to transmit to all of the other nodes, and each group has a unique source-based tree (constructed using Dijkstra's algorithm). In performing the simulations, the performance of the two algorithms is evaluated given a network topology with a specific number of nodes and a specific average node degree. To ensure the reliability of the simulation results, 30 networks are randomly generated for each scenario considered, and the corresponding results for the frame length are then averaged.

Figure 2(a) and (b) compare the frame lengths obtained by the Group-by-Group and Greedy algorithms in networks comprising N = 20 and 40 nodes, respectively, with the equivalent results obtained using the DRAND algorithm [4] and a "non-spatial reuse" scheme. Note that the results presented for the non-spatial reuse scheme indicate the number of slots required to complete the scheduling process for all of the nodes given the constraint that each slot can only be allocated to one node. It can be seen that the frame length obtained using the non-spatial reuse scheme reduces with an increasing

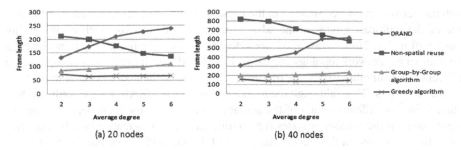

Fig. 2. Frame lengths obtained by various schemes given random network topologies with (a) N = 20 and (b) N = 40 nodes.

average node degree irrespective of the number of nodes in the network due to the nature of broadcast. The DRAND algorithm uses a chromatic approach to resolve the problem of collisions. However, it takes no account of the traffic flow when performing the scheduling process. Moreover, the DRAND algorithm also suffers from the exposed node problem. As a result, the algorithm yields a longer frame length than either of the two proposed algorithms. It is seen that for all values of N, the frame length obtained by the Group-by-Group algorithm is longer than that obtained by the Greedy algorithm. This result is to be expected since the Group-by-Group algorithm prevents the nodes from picking the same slot when scheduling the transmissions of the same group. In other words, the algorithm does not support spatial reuse within each group, and thus a greater number of time slots are required to complete transmission. The Greedy algorithm allows multiple nodes to pick the same slot to perform the transmissions of different groups provided that no collisions occur between them. As a result, the frame length is significantly reduced. In theory, an increasing node degree reduces the frame length in networks with a spatial reuse capability. However, as the node degree increases, the number of collisions also increases; thereby reducing the percentage of spatial reuse. As a result, the frame length obtained by the Greedy algorithm varies only very slightly as the average node degree is increased.

Figure 3 shows the variation of the frame length with the number of nodes as a function of the average node degree for the four considered schemes. In accordance

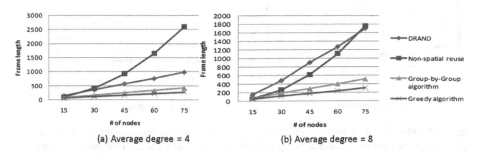

Fig. 3. Frame lengths obtained from various schemes given random network topologies with average node degrees of (a) 4 and (b) 8.

with the network model considered in the present study (see Sect. 3.1), the number and size of the multicast groups in the ad hoc network both increase with an increasing number of nodes. Thus, for all of the considered schemes, the frame length increases as the scale of the network topology increases. In DRAND, each time slot is occupied by a different color. In other words, the transmission period of the nodes is equal to the total number of colors. Thus, although the number of colors in DRAND varies only slightly when fixing for different values of the average node degree, the frame length increases significantly as the number of nodes (i.e., multicast groups) increases. Notably, the two algorithms proposed in the present study both take the traffic flow into account when performing the scheduling process. As a result, they yield a shorter frame length than DRAND; particularly in network topologies with a larger number of nodes (multicast groups).

Figure 4(a) and (b) compare the performance of the two proposed algorithms in terms of the number of token forwarding events given networks with various scales and node degrees. It was shown in Theorem B in Sect. 3.2 that the token is forwarded 2N2-2N+4L times in the Group-by-Group algorithm. It is seen that the simulation results in Fig. 4(a) confirm this proof. Comparing the two figures, it is noted that the Greedy algorithm results in fewer token forwarding events than the Group-by-Group algorithm given a constant network scale and average node degree. This result is reasonable since the Greedy algorithm allows a node to pick more than one slot to transmit different groups in each scheduling operation, whereas the Group-by-Group algorithm permits each node to pick only one slot for one group in each frame. It is observed that for a constant value of N, the number of link forwarding events increases as the average node degree increases under the Greedy algorithm. At first glance, this finding seems counterintuitive since it is reasonable to expect that a higher node degree will reduce the total number of slots which need to be allocated to the nodes and will therefore reduce the number of forwarding events accordingly. However, in the second stage of the Greedy algorithm, the token is routed to all of the nodes via DFS in order to achieve a constant frame length for every node. In other words, the token must be forwarded (L × 2) times and thus the number of forwarding events actually increases as the average node degree increases.

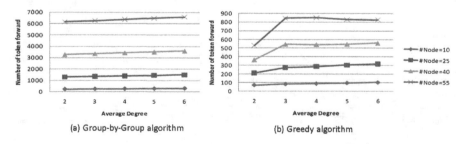

Fig. 4. Number of token forwarding events in (a) Group-by-Group algorithm and (b) Greedy algorithm given random network topologies with various scales and average node degrees.

5   Conclusion

This paper has proposed two token-based distributed node scheduling algorithms designated as the Group-by-Group algorithm and the Greedy algorithm, respectively, for improving the transmission efficiency of multiple multicast communications in multi-hop ad hoc wireless networks. Both algorithms feature the following properties: (1) distributed control; (2) local information exchange; (3) the complete transmission of one packet from the source to all the destination nodes in every frame for each multicast group in the network; (4) transmission traffic flow compliance; and (5) the elimination of both the hidden node problem and the exposed node problem. The simulations have shown that the Greedy algorithm results in a shorter frame length than the Group-by-Group algorithm due to its support of spatial reuse. Moreover, the Greedy algorithm reduces the number of token forwarding events and therefore spends less time to complete scheduling.

Although both algorithms successfully solve the multiple multicast scheduling problem in the considered network model, several important issues remain to be addressed. In the present study, it has been assumed that all of the network nodes remain static as the scheduling process is performed. In other words, the scheduling result is valid only for the particular network topology in existence at the moment the scheduling algorithm is executed. As a result, the scheduling process must be repeated each time a change in the network topology occurs. In practice, the topology of ad hoc networks tends to change frequently as new nodes enter the network or existing nodes depart. Consequently, the efficiency of the proposed algorithms is seriously degraded. Accordingly, in a future study, a more flexible node scheduling algorithm will be proposed to accommodate changes in the network topology.

Acknowledgement. This work was supported in part by the Ministry of Science and Technology, R.O.C. under Grants MOST 103-2221-E-006 -146 -MY3 and MOST 104-2221-E-041-007, Ministry of Education, R.O.C. under Grant 104C-77-016.

References

1. Wolf, B.J., Hammond, J.L., Noneaker, D.L., Russell, H.B.: A protocol for construction of broadcast transmission schedules in mobile ad hoc networks. IEEE Trans. Wireless Commun. **6**, 74–78 (2007)
2. Wang, G., Ansari, N.: Optimal broadcast scheduling in packet radio networks using mean field annealing. IEEE J. Select. Areas Commun. **15**, 250–260 (1997)
3. Chlamtac, I., Pinter, S.S.: Distributed nodes organization algorithm for channel access in a multihop dynamic radio network. IEEE Trans. Comput. **C-36**, 728–737 (1987)
4. Rhee, I., Warrier, A., Min, J., Xu, L.: DRAND: distributed randomized TDMA scheduling for wireless ad hoc networks. IEEE Trans. Mob. Comput. **8**, 1384–1396 (2009)
5. Hammond, J.L., Russell, H.B.: Properties of a transmission assignment algorithm for multiple-hop packet radio networks. IEEE Trans. Wireless Commun. **3**, 1048–1052 (2004)

128   I.-H. Liu et al.

6. Li, J.-S., Liu, I.-H., Liu, K.-X., Yu, S.-H.: Providing multiple-player online game service with an efficient multicast scheduling scheme in wireless ad hoc networks. In: Proceedings of MASS 2012, China (2012)
7. Li, J.-S., Liu, K.-H., Wu, C.-H.: Efficient group multicast node scheduling schemes in multi-hop wireless networks. Comput. Commun. **35**, 1247–1258 (2012)
8. Badia, L., Erta, A., Lenzini, L., Zorzi, M.: A general interference-aware framework for joint routing and link scheduling in wireless mesh networks. IEEE Netw. **22**, 32–38 (2008)
9. Joa-Ng, M., Lu, I.-T.: Spread spectrum medium access protocol with collision avoidance in mobile ad-hoc wireless network. In: Proceedings of IEEE INFOCOM 1999, USA (1999)
10. Djukic, P., Valaee, S.: Delay aware link scheduling for multi-hop TDMA wireless networks. IEEE/ACM Trans. Netw. **17**, 870–883 (2009)
11. Appani, P.K., Hammond, J.L., Noneaker, D.L., Russell, H.B.: An adaptive transmission-scheduling protocol for mobile ad hoc networks. Ad Hoc Netw. **5**, 254–271 (2007)
12. Ramaswami, R., Parhi, K.K.: Distributed scheduling of broadcasts in a radio network. In: Proceedings of INFOCOM 1989, Canada (1989)
13. Ramanathan, S., Lloyd, E.L.: Scheduling algorithms for multihop radio networks. IEEE/ACM Trans. Netw. **1**, 211–222 (1993)
14. Hikmet, M., Roop, P., Ranjitkar, P.: Fairness-based measures for safety-critical vehicular ad-hoc networks. In: Proceedings of IEEE 18th International Symposium on Real-Time Distributed Computing 2015, Auckland, New Zealand (2015)
15. Yu, H., He, Z., Niu, K.: STDMA for vehicle-to-vehicle communication in a highway scenario. In: Proceedings of MAPE 2013, Chengdu, China (2013)
16. Silva, L., Pedreiras, P., Alam, M., Ferreira, J.: STDMA-based scheduling algorithm for infrastructured vehicular networks. Stud. Syst. Decis. Control **52**, 81–105 (2016)

Emergency Message Reduction Scheme Using Markov Prediction Model in VANET Environment

Hsin-Hung Cho[1], Wei-Chih Huang[2], Timothy K. Shih[1], and Han-Chieh Chao[2,3,4,5,6(✉)]

[1] Department of Computer Science and Information Engineering at National Central University, Taoyuan, Taiwan R.O.C.
hsin-hung@ieee.org, timothykshih@gmail.com
[2] Department of Electrical Engineering, National Dong Hwa University, Hualien, Taiwan R.O.C.
yoyotv990@gmail.com
[3] College of Mathematics and Computer Science, Wuhan Polytechnic University, Wuhan, China
[4] College of Computer and Software, Nanjing University of Information Science and Technology, Nanjing, China
[5] Department of Computer Science and Information Engineering, National Ilan University, Yilan, Taiwan R.O.C.
[6] School of Information Science and Engineering, Fujian University of Technology, Fuzhou, Fujian, China
hcc@niu.edu.tw

Abstract. Today's vehicles technologies are getting better as well as the price of the vehicle is not too expensive so that almost every household has an own car. However, road space is limited so there is high opportunity to see the accidents on the high dense road. Current VANET technology has been able to inform rear vehicles do not go there so that the traffic congestion can be reduced. In this scenario, there are very large amount of emergency message will be generated. It will increase the burden of road side unit. In this paper, we propose a Markov-based model to predict behavior of vehicles so that we can identify which cars really need to receive this message. Simulation results show that this method can reduces the unnecessary message transmission indeed.

Keywords: VANET · Emergency service · Markov chain · Prediction model

1 Introduction

Currently, we always can see a lot of cars on the road due to the booming economy lets every families have their own car. Depending on this phenomenon, the traffic accidents often occur, since the cars density become larger [1]. The reason is that all the cars also want to compete the right to use the road, but the

© ICST Institute for Computer Sciences, Social Informatics and Telecommunications Engineering 2017
J.-H. Lee and S. Pack (Eds.): QShine 2016, LNICST 199, pp. 129–137, 2017.
DOI: 10.1007/978-3-319-60717-7_13

capacity of a road is limited which could not carry such a high traffic [2]. Accordingly, some people began to not abide by the traffic rules so that the accident will be incurred. Transportation closely related to eneryone's life, hence we must address this issue. Vehicular ad hoc network (VANET) has been proposed for transmission between cars so that there are some applications also be presented for various transportation services which including the emergency service [3].

Emergency service, as the name suggests, is a service which used to deal with various unexpected situations [4]. Emergency service is composed of prior service and posterior service. The mission of prior service is to create a scheme to avoid accident is happened. Posterior service is a protective measure when the accident has occurred, so that impacts will not continue to expand. No matter what kind of service, they have one thing in common that all of components in VANET need to exchange their information. Therefore, there are very many emergency messages can be generated so that this network often encounters bandwidth bottleneck [5]. Especially, some vehicles is use of mobile communication network [6] so that they can not load such a large message.

Generally, emergency messages will send to all of neighboring cars. However, we found that not all of the car will pass through the accident scene [7]. According to this observation, we think that we can reduce more unnecessary messages transmission as long as we are able to predict the behavior of the vehicle. In this paper, we design a prediction model that based on Markov chain. Simulation results show that our method can successfully decrease quantity of emergency messages so that the bandwidth bottleneck can be relieved.

The rest of the paper is organized as follows. Section 2 introduces background and related works. Section 3 will give the problem definition then we will introduce our proposed method. The simulation results present in Sect. 4. Finally, we will summarize research contributions and discussing the future works in last section.

2   Background and Related Works

2.1   Vehicular ad hoc Network (VANET)

Vehicular ad-hoc network (VANET) is a technology which extending from the Mobile ad-hoc Network (MANET) [8,9]. The difference between VANET and MANET is that VANET is an exclusive network for vehicles. It can be roughly divided into three types which include Roadside-to-Vehicle Communications (RVC) [10], Inter-Vehicle Communications (IVC) [11] and Hybrid Vehicular Communication (HVC) [12,14]. RVC is that all vehicles can communicate with server through wireless access point or base station. IVC represents that messages can be transmitted via vehicles so that the flexibility is higher than RVC. But it has lower ability for computing and management because it is a distribution structure. Both these two types have their advantages and disadvantages so that some scholars combine them to HVC that is shown in Fig. 1.

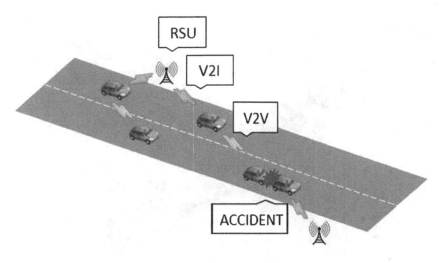

Fig. 1. Types of vehicular ad-hoc network

2.2 Markov Chain

Markov chain is an expression of transition of status [13]. These status are independent with each other, but any two successive events have causal relationship. It means that the previous event will affects the next event that is shown in Eq. (1):

$$P_{(i,j))} = P(E_{n+1} = i | E_n = j) \tag{1}$$

where $P_{(i,j)}$ represents a probability that a transition from event I to event j. This also means that we are able to predict future events as long as this probability can be calculated. In this study, we will define vehicles behavior as status of Markov chain then design a predition model for various operations in RSU.

3   Proposed Mechanism

Our method is composed to V2V and V2I so that this method not only provides more computing power, but also has higher flexibility. The key to this approach is crossroad, because crossroad can be regarded as a phased destination so that we are able to judge whether cars will pass through the accident sence. Hence we set RSU in every crossroads in order to predict direction of cars successfully that is shown in Fig. 2. All of common symbols are listed in Table 1. Main goal of proposed method is to minimize the quantity of emergency messages so we can define our problem via linear programming that is shown in Table 2.

Generally, emergency message is sent by broadcasting. It means that any cars can received this message as long as they have layer 2 network interface. If we want to reduce more unnecessary transmissions, we must focus on layer 3 technique so that RSU can know the IP address of cars which need to receive the

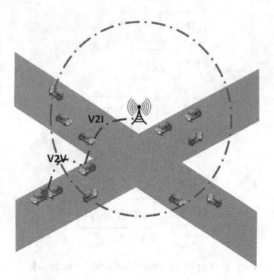

Fig. 2. Use of HVC as VANET type

Table 1. Important symbol list

Values	Definition
T	Transition matrix
$S = \{S_1, ..., S_n\}$	Information of video i
$C = \{C_1, ..., C_m\}$	Number of cars
P_{ij}	Probability that a car move from i-lane to j-lane
$\theta_{(nearest)}$	Difference of angle with nearest car
$v_{(nearest)}$	Difference of speed with nearest car
$d_{(nearest)}$	Difference of distance with nearest car

Table 2. Linear programming model

Minimize $\sum_{i=1}^{n} \sum_{j=1}^{m} Q_{i,j}$

s.t.

$$m > n$$
$$0 < P_{ij} \leq 1$$
$$P_{i1} + P_{i2} + P_{i3} = 1$$
$$0 < \theta < 90$$
$$60(km/hr) \leq v \leq 120(km/hr)$$

emergency message. Many important roads have been planned to three-lane, It means that a car has two choices of direction as long as it is driving in the middle lane. We use these three lanes as three states which represent right-lane, middle-lane and left-lane that is noted as 1, 2 and 3 respectively. Then a transition matrix can be generated:

$$T = \begin{pmatrix} P_{11} & P_{12} & P_{13} \\ P_{21} & P_{22} & P_{23} \\ P_{31} & P_{32} & P_{33} \end{pmatrix}$$

P_{ij} represents the probability that a car move from i-lane to j-lane. Via this matrix, we can calculate out the probability that whether cars will pass through the accident sence, hence the results can help us to decide which car really requires this emergency message. The value of T depends on the real three-lane environment that is shown in following:

$$T = \begin{pmatrix} \alpha_{11} \times \frac{1}{2} & \alpha_{12} \times \frac{1}{2} & 0 \\ \alpha_{21} \times \frac{1}{3} & \alpha_{22} \times \frac{1}{3} & \alpha_{23} \times \frac{1}{3} \\ 0 & \alpha_{32} \times \frac{1}{2} & \alpha_{33} \times \frac{1}{2} \end{pmatrix}$$

Assuming that all drivers will obey the traffic rules so they can not cross the middle-lane to reach next lane directly. Basing on this priciple, P_{13} and P_{31} are set as 0. α is an effect parameter which used to illustrate the physical meaning, e.g. angle, speed and distance. We simply normalize these three metrics to derive α as Eq. (2) that shown in following:

$$\alpha_{ij} = \frac{\frac{\theta_{(nearest)}}{\theta_{max}} + \frac{v_{(nearest)}}{v_{max}} + \frac{d_{(nearest)}}{d_{max}}}{3} \tag{2}$$

where $\theta_{(nearest)}$, $v_{(nearest)}$ and $d_{(nearest)}$ are difference with nearest car. Use of these three metrics because the nearest car will affects current car whether over-taking. In the initial process, the broken vehicle will sent a emergency message to RSU that telling it where is accident happened. So in the beginning of algorithm, we will define two cases which represents that accident sence is located in right side, front or left side. The proposed algorithm will compare the probability of in T_i. For instance, an accident occur in the right side so that Case1 is chosen. Then we must compare whether the probability that i vehicle enter to 1st-lane is maximum. If $T_i(P_{j1}) = Max(T_i)$ is true that represents i vehicle will probably turn right, hence the emergency message will sent to i vehicle. The main body of proposed algorithm is shown in the following:

```
Emergency Message Reduction Algorithm (Output)
    const
      Ti;
    Case
    Case1: Event happened in the right side
```

```
        Case2: Event happened in the front
        Case3: Event happened in the left side
Repeat
    switch  Case1
       if Ti(Pj1)=Max(Ti)
            sent message to vehicle i;
       end
    switch  Case2
       if Ti(Pj2)=Max(Ti)
            sent message to vehicle i;
       end
    switch  Case3
       if Ti(Pj3)=Max(Ti)
            sent message to vehicle i;
       end
       until Year = MaxYears
end.
```

4 Simulation

4.1 Simulation Setting

The simulation is performed by utilizing MATLAB (Version 7.11, R2010b). The detail parameters setting are listed in Table 3. In our simulation, size of scenario is set as $1200 \times 1200\,(\mathrm{m}^2)$. There are four crossroads in this range so number of RSU is also four. Radius of RSU is set as 300 (m). And speed of any vehicles are ramdoly set within a range which is 30 (km/hr)–60 (km/hr). And all of vehicles are in a normal distribution. Any roads have six lanes which are the two-way street. A simulation scenario is shown in Fig. 3.

Table 3. Simulation parameters

Parameters	Values
Size of field of interest	$1200 \times 1200\,(\mathrm{m}^2)$
Number of cars	10–100
Number or RSU	4
Radius length of RSU	300 (m)
Vehicle speed	30 (km/hr)–60 (km/hr)

4.2 Simulation Results

In Fig. 4, we can see that proposed mechanism can reduce about 70% messages than broadcasting method in 10 vehicles case. It is slightly higher than other number of vehicles, because of that the neighboring vehicles are few so that

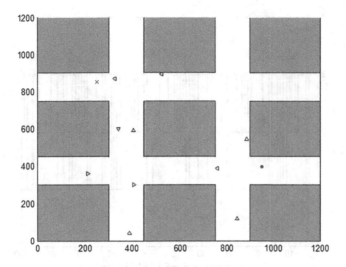

Fig. 3. Simulation scenario

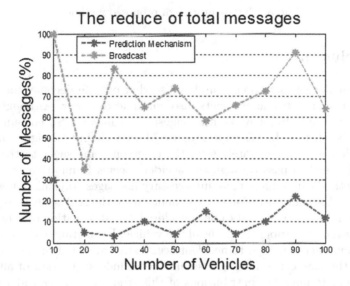

Fig. 4. Comparison of number of sent messages

RSU could not make an accurate prediction due to value of $d_{(nearest)}$ is too long. But it is still an acceptable result. Moreover, our proposed mechanism is very stable. It proof that our proposed mechanism false rate is not high.

In order to verify feasibility of the proposed method, we set an accident event in the left side. The vehicles distribution model of three lanes are same. We can see Fig. 5 that state 1 is fewer than others. It means that our method can successfully guides traffic to other ways. In other words, our method cannot too many misjudgment due to a large number of messages reduction.

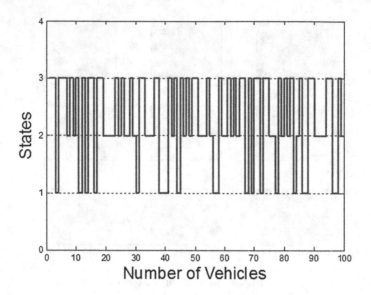

Fig. 5. Markov process of proposed method

5   Conclusion

Vehicle technologies continuously updated so that our life becomes more convenient. But it causes traffic accidents also continue to occur. Although current technique has ability to relieve traffic congestion, it makes RSU encounters huge bandwidth bottleneck. In this paper, we use Markov chain to design a prediction model so that we can accurately send the emergency messages to the vehicles which really need to pass through the accident scene. Simulation results show that our method can reduces more unnecessary messages transmission as well as provides a stable transportation environment. Since the real scenario is complex so there are more metrics need to be considered, e.g. destination of vehicles, real traffic sign even the various functions of the vehicle. For instance, there are police cars and ambulances will go to accident scene after an accident has happened. Therefore, the emergency messages should be include suggestion of alternative road. In order to improve contributions of this study, we will consider to above metrics in our future works.

Acknowledgments. This research was partly funded by the National Science Council of the R.O.C. under grants MOST 104-2221-E-197- 014 -.

References

1. Buchenscheit, A., Schaub, F., Kargl, F., Weber, M.: A VANET-based emergency vehicle warning system. In: 2009 IEEE Vehicular Networking Conference (VNC), pp. 1–8. IEEE, October 2009

2. Taleb, T., Sakhaee, E., Jamalipour, A., Hashimoto, K., Kato, N., Nemoto, Y.: A stable routing protocol to support ITS services in VANET networks. IEEE Trans. Veh. Technol. **56**(6), 3337–3347 (2007)
3. Willke, T.L., Tientrakool, P., Maxemchuk, N.F.: A survey of inter-vehicle communication protocols and their applications. IEEE Commun. Surv. Tutorials **11**(2), 3–20 (2009)
4. Huo, M., Zheng, Z., Wu, J., Cai, J.: A survey on emergency message dissemination in vehicular ad hoc networks. In: World Automation Congress, June 2012
5. Zhang, L., Gao, D., Zhao, W., Chao, H.C.: A multilevel information fusion approach for road congestion detection in VANETs. Math. Comput. Modell. **58**(5), 1206–1221 (2013)
6. Cho, H.H., Lai, C.F., Shih, T.K., Chao, H.C.: Integration of SDR and SDN for 5G. IEEE Access **2**, 1196–1204 (2014)
7. Felicia, A.B., Lakshmanan, L.: Survey on accident avoidance and privacy preserving navigation system in vehicular network. Global J. Pure Appl. Math. **12**(1), 943–949 (2016)
8. Hartenstein, H., Laberteaux, K.P.: A tutorial survey on vehicular ad hoc networks. IEEE Commun. Mag. **46**(6), 164–171 (2008)
9. Tseng, F.-H., Chou, L.-D., Chao, H.-C.: A survey of black hole attacks in wireless mobile ad hoc networks. Hum.-Centric Comput. Inf. Sci. **1**(1), 1–16 (2011)
10. Sou, S.I., Tonguz, O.K.: Enhancing VANET connectivity through roadside units on highways. IEEE Trans. Veh. Technol. **60**(8), 3586–3602 (2011)
11. Sommer, C., German, R., Dressler, F.: Bidirectionally coupled network and road traffic simulation for improved IVC analysis. IEEE Trans. Mob. Comput. **10**(1), 3–15 (2011)
12. Hussain, R., Son, J., Eun, H., Kim, S., Oh, H.: Rethinking vehicular communications: merging VANET with cloud computing. In: 2012 IEEE 4th International Conference on Cloud Computing Technology and Science (CloudCom), pp. 606–609. IEEE, December 2012
13. Gilks, W.R.: Markov Chain Monte Carlo. Wiley, Hoboken (2005)
14. Cho, W., Kim, S.I., Choi, H.K., Oh, H.S., Kwak, D.Y.: Performance evaluation of V2V/V2I communications: the effect of midamble insertion. In: 1st International Conference on Wireless Communication, Vehicular Technology, Information Theory and Aerospace & Electronic Systems Technology, Wireless VITAE 2009, pp. 793–797. IEEE, May 2009

Flow and Virtual Machine Placement in Wireless Cloud Data Centers

Heejun Roh[1], Kyunghwi Kim[1], Sangheon Pack[2], and Wonjun Lee[1(✉)]

[1] Network Research Laboratory, Korea University, Seoul 02841, Korea
wlee@korea.ac.kr
[2] Mobile Network and Communications Laboratory,
Korea University, Seoul 02841, Korea

Abstract. Virtualization for cloud computing has been driving data centers to contain massive and diverse applications in a distributed manner. However, since existing network architectures do not supply enough network capacity for virtual machine (VM) interconnections, enhancing the network capacity with augmented wireless links has recently attracted a lot of research interests. Especially, architectural design and link scheduling of wireless data center networks (WDCNs) are of their main interests. However, the potential of WDCNs is under-estimated, since existing research efforts do not reflect flexibility of VM placement. To this end, in this paper, we explore another feasibility of WDCNs to combine dynamic VM placement algorithms. We design a low-complexity flow placement algorithm considering augmented wireless links with interference constraints, and discuss a set of VM placement algorithms under the flow placement algorithm. Our extensive evaluation of the algorithms in WDCNs with 60 GHz wireless links shows that combination of the flow and VM placement algorithms achieves better performance.

Keywords: Data center · Routing algorithm · Virtual machine placement

1 Introduction

Recently, with the advance of virtualization technology, a lot of cloud data centers have been designed and constructed to support massive and diverse applications in a concurrent and distributed manner. The cloud data centers have several benefits from large economies of scale and scale-out based dynamic computing resource allocation on demand. With large demands of cloud-based services such as world-wide consumer applications and data-intensive tasks, applicability of cloud data centers are rapidly growing.

However, current architecture of cloud data centers are still requiring a better solution for network capacity. Typically, a data center holds a huge amount of servers (10 K to 100 K) and they are interconnected by a data center network (DCN). In conventional data centers, DCNs have tree-like topologies allowing oversubscription due to cost reduction and the ratio of oversubscription increases

© ICST Institute for Computer Sciences, Social Informatics and Telecommunications Engineering 2017
J.-H. Lee and S. Pack (Eds.): QShine 2016, LNICST 199, pp. 138–148, 2017.
DOI: 10.1007/978-3-319-60717-7_14

rapidly as traffic moves to a root [8]. It implies that *network capacity of a DCN is highly constrained by its oversubscription, and the DCN may not support bandwidth demands.* Since there are applications which require interactive processing across thousands of machines in cloud data centers, and it is highly difficult to predict dynamics of traffic demands, a lot of research works for wired DCNs have been carried out, such as network architectures [2,8], virtual machine (VM) management [14], traffic measurements [4,12], and flow scheduling [3,7].

More recently, with the advent of Gigabit-capable wireless links, a radical but novel approach to increase the network capacity with the augmented wireless links has attracted many researchers. Especially, with promise of a 60 GHz wireless standard [1] to give its data rate up to 6.76 Gbps, and expectation of unit cost of the 60 GHz devices (less than $ 10) [9], several research proposals for wireless data center networks (WDCNs) with 60 GHz wireless links are suggested to resolve some issues such as architecture [9], link designs and measurements [9,16], and link scheduling [6].

However, utilizing 60 GHz wireless links into a WDCN can cause tight constraints on network topology. Current WDCN architectures [9,16] use highly directional horn antennas which require fixed topology of wireless links. Although electronically steerable array antennas may give more flexibility, beam training for 60 GHz wireless links which form quite narrow directional beams (1° in the worst case) incurs significant delay ranged from 10 ms to 1 s in average [13]. Therefore, efficient optimization techniques for utilizing the wireless links is essential for better network performance.

To this end, in this paper, we explore another feasibility of WDCNs by combining dynamic VM placement algorithms for cloud data centers. Public Infrastructure-as-a-Service (IaaS) cloud data centers, such as Amazon EC2 and Microsoft Azure, allow an application to dynamically utilize VM instances placed over a set of servers [10]. Therefore, using dynamic VM placement algorithms determine traffic patterns of WDCNs, and it is trivial that the dynamic VM placement gives another dimension of flexibility into WDCNs. However, due to highly dynamic traffic patterns of cloud applications, it is uncertain that which placement of VMs is preferable to enhance performance of WDCNs.

In this context, we first design a low-complexity flow placement algorithm considering augmented wireless links with interference constraints, and discuss a set of VM placement algorithms under the flow placement algorithm. In the flow placement, we exploit link utilization level to adaptively disperse traffic load across a WDCN. In the VM placement, to effectively exploit the extra capacity of wireless links in the WDCN, we propose a new metric for VM placement based on an in-depth study of applying wireless links to adapt to dynamic traffic patterns and provide better traffic locality. The new metric is designed to reflect influence of wireless links and applied to construct hierarchical VM clusters, each of which shares the traffic locality. We evaluate the placement algorithms by extensive simulations of wireless data center networks with 60 GHz wireless links, and the evaluation results clearly validate advantages of our approach.

The remainder of this paper is organized as follows. Section 2 explains our system model, and Sects. 3 and 4 present the details of the proposed routing and placement algorithms. Section 5 provides the performance evaluation of the proposed algorithms. Finally, we conclude this paper in Sect. 6.

2   System Model

In this section, we briefly describe our system model for data centers with wireless links before describing the proposed algorithms. Typically, data center network architectures consist of switches at multiple tiers, and there are multiple paths between a pair of host machines to be robust to congestion and link failures. Therefore, we adapt the common architecture for wired data center networking as shown in Fig. 1a. That is, the wired network fabric consists of wired links and three types of switches at each tier in the tree structure; edge, aggregation, and core switches.

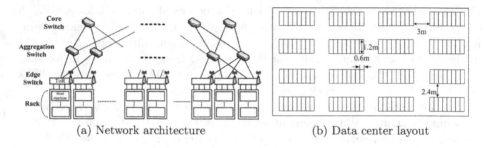

(a) Network architecture   (b) Data center layout

Fig. 1. Network architecture and layout of WDCNs

In this paper, especially in our simulation, we assume that racks are deployed as in Fig. 1b. A rack consists of tens of host machines connected to an edge switch with wired links, and the size of a rack is 0.6 m × 1.2 m. Racks are grouped into 4 × 4 rows, and each row contains 8 racks without gap. Rows are separated by 3 m and 2.4 m aisles. However, it should be note that the proposed algorithms can be applied into different data center network architectures and layouts.

Different from the common data center architectures, in our system model, each edge switch is equipped with one or more 60 GHz wireless devices, and they are fixed on top of racks (ToR) to achieve line of sight (LoS) communication, as in [9]. This assumption is a sufficient condition for stable 60 GHz communication in wireless data center networks. Since the signal strength of indoor LoS 60 GHz communications degrades rapidly with increasing distance, and its path loss model fits the Friis mode with exponent 2, performance of the wireless links is predictable and reliable without severe interference problem, which is suitable for data center networking. Of course, relaxing this assumption [16] can be a promising direction for our future work.

Table 1. Notations

Symbol	Definition	Symbol	Definition
V	Virtual machine set	M	Host machine set
Φ	Virtual machine placement	$\Phi(V_x) = M_i$	$V_x \in V$ placed at $M_i \in M$.
$L = L^E \cup L^W$	Whole link set	F	Set of elephant flows
Ω	Path assignment set	Q	Channel set
L^E	Wired link set	L^W	Wireless link set
$H_{i,j}^E \in \mathbf{H^E}$	Hop count between M_i and M_j using only L^E	$H_{i,j}^W \in \mathbf{H^W}$	Hop count between M_i and M_j using L
$T(l)$	Traffic rate sum at link l	$R(l)$	Link capacity of l
$U(l) = T(l)/R(l)$	Link utilization level of l	$I(l)$	Interference link set of l
$P_{i,j}^E(\in P^E)$	Path set between M_i and M_j (only wired links)	$P_{i,j}^W(\in P^W)$	Path set between M_i and M_j (with wireless links)
δ	Distance metric	θ	Wireless link threshold

On the other hand, there are several views of virtualization to run multiple applications over host machines in cloud data centers. Amongst them, we focus on VM which explicitly consumes computing and storage resources of a host machine. A host machine can run a set of VMs which are owned by different applications, but the number of VMs in the host machine is constrained by its resource capacity. To simplify our discussion in VM management, in this paper, we treat each VM as a *slot* which consumes the same amount of computing and storage resources in a host machine. That is, host machines have the maximum number of slots, and we assume that the numbers are the same, which is widely used in the previous studies on traffic-aware VM placement such as [14].

To describe the proposed algorithms clearly, we introduce several notations which is summarized in Table 1. We also define the following terms:

- External machine ($M_0 \in M$): There is a virtual host machine containing a VM ($V_0 \in V$) beyond the gateways to reflect the external traffic of DCNs.
- Path sets (P^E and P^W): Each host machine pair has two path sets; one with only wired (or Ethernet, for notational convenience) links (P^E), and the other containing wireless links as well (P^E). There are equal-cost (hop count) paths in each set, which are shortest paths between a pair of host machines. Note that we assume that multi-hop wireless communication is not taken into account to avoid the significant increase of complexity and overhead.
- Mice and elephant flows: Long-lived, high-throughput flows are called as elephant flows. These flows are distinguished by the host NIC bandwidth share [3] or the transferred traffic size [7]. We adopt the latter approach in this paper.

3   Flow-Based Routing Algorithm

Our routing algorithm exploits a central controller that gathers flow statistics and computes routes for elephant flows individually. In the proposed routing protocol, mice flows are transferred over Equal Cost Multi Path (ECMP) routing [11] without governing of the central controller, but elephant flows are delivered through a link load aware best path decision by the central controller. The proposed routing protocol allocates a channel for a wireless link based on the channel usage in its interference link set and estimates the achievable data rate based on the Signal-to-Interference-plus-Noise Ratio (SINR). The interference link set depends on the beamwidth of directional antenna. The protocol also presents threshold θ that adaptively allows a path set including wireless links.

The goal of our routing algorithm is to leverage the benefits of path diversity for providing better performance in terms of aggregation throughput and completion time of traffic demands, and the following constraints are considered:

(1) $T(l) \leq R(l), \forall l \in \boldsymbol{L}$,   (2) $l(q) \in \{0,1\}, \forall l \in \boldsymbol{L^W}$,

(3) $\sum_{q \in \boldsymbol{Q}} l(q) \leq 1, \forall l \in \boldsymbol{L^W}$,   (4) $l(q) + \sum_{l' \in \boldsymbol{I}(l)} l'(q) \leq 1, \forall l \in \boldsymbol{L^W}$.

$T(l)$ and $R(l)$ are the sum of traffic demands and the link capacity of l, respectively. The value of $R(l)$ is fixed for the wired links, while that is determined by SINR for the wireless ones. The sum of traffic demands at each link cannot exceed its capacity, and we use the constraint of (1). The other constraints (2)–(4) stem from the channel allocation of wireless links. The value of $l(q)$ becomes 1 when the channel q is allocated to link l, and otherwise 0 (2). Only one channel can be assigned to each link (3), and each channel can be used once at the same time for the links in the same interference link set (4).

Packets of a new flow are forwarded by hash-based path calculation (such as ECMP) at the beginning by default, and this avoids the flow setup of the control plane. If the flow becomes a large one, an elephant flow, over a given threshold size by any detection mechanisms, it is reported to a central controller to find the best available path. This path is computed for network load balance based on link utilization levels as shown in Algorithm 1. The proposed algorithm involves channel allocation and a threshold within the whole path set.

4   Virtual Machine Placement

In this section, we briefly explain our VM placement algorithms to improve the traffic locality by minimizing the network traffic at aggregate and core switches.

(1) New Communication Distance Metric Design

Wireless devices are added to provide *extra* capacity for data center networks and the use of wireless links is limited by channel allocation and SINR. Thus, our

---

Algorithm 1. Threshold-based Best Path Search

Require: θ, Φ, F, P^E, P^W, and Ω

1: **for** $f \in F$ **do**
2:     $\{M_u, M_v\} \leftarrow \{\Phi(V_x), \Phi(V_y)\}$ for f with $\{V_x, V_y\}$; $p.\text{best} \leftarrow \{\}$; $p.\text{load} \leftarrow \infty$
3:     **for** $p \in P_{u,v}^E$ **do**
4:         **if** $\max(p.U(l)) + f.\text{rate} < p.\text{load}$ **then**
5:             $p.\text{best} \leftarrow p$; $p.\text{load} \leftarrow \max(p.U(l)) + f.\text{rate}$
6:     **if** $p.\text{load} > \theta$ **then**
7:         **for** $p \in P_{u,v}^W$ **do**
8:             **if** $p.l^W = 0$ **then**   ▷ If channel is not allocated,
9:                 Check available channels; Check SINR
10:             **if** p is available **then**
11:                 **if** $\max(p.U(l)) + f.\text{rate} < p.\text{load}$ **then**
12:                     $p.\text{best} \leftarrow p$; $p.\text{load} \leftarrow \max(p.U(l)) + f.\text{rate}$
13:     $f.\text{path} \leftarrow p.\text{best}$; $p.U(l) \leftarrow p.U(l) + f.\text{rate}$ for $\forall l \in p.\text{best}$

---

routing algorithm utilizes the paths containing wireless links (P^W) adaptively with regard to the path utilization level, and the impact of the paths in P^W is smaller than those in P^E. In this context, we apply a weighting factor ($0 < \omega < 1$) for the hop distance of the paths in P^W for a new metric. The following metric is defined for each pair of machines (M_i and M_j) to leverage the features of network topology including wired and wireless links: $\delta_{i,j} = H_{i,j}^E - \sum_{k=1}^{K} \omega^k / H_{i,j}^{W_k}$.

In the above equation, P^{W_k} denotes the shortest path set including k wireless links, and $H_{i,j}^W$ is (i,j)-th element of the hop count matrix $\mathbf{H}^W$ for P^W. We set $H_{i,j}^W = \infty$ when $P^W = \emptyset$. We use positive constant K ($K > 1$) for the fine-grained clustering of VM placement. ω^k is used to penalize paths with many wireless links, since such paths may generate longer hop distance and they can interrupt the wireless links in the interference link sets.

(2) Hierarchical Slot Clustering

Since our system model assumes that no dynamic network topology, the communication distance between two host machines (and thus between two slots) are fixed. In [14], given that VMs' traffic information is known with this property, a generic VM placement problem is mathematically formulated with its NP-hardness and a slot clustering algorithm with pre-determined number of clusters is proposed as a part of approximate algorithm of the VM placement problem. However, determining the number in advance is difficult, especially in WDCNs.

To this end, we suggest hierarchical slot clustering algorithm. Our slot clustering algorithm generates hierarchical clusters based on the above communication distance metric. Our slot clustering algorithm tries to minimize the maximum value of the new metric in a bottom-up, greedy manner (from rack level to the root level). With the clusters, VMs can be assigned with better traffic locality, and we exploit them in the following placement and migration algorithms.

(3) Initial VM Placement

Estimating the traffic demands of new VMs to be placed is difficult and requires an explicit indication of applications, and studies in [7,15] have indicated its impracticality. Thus, we only use traffic statistics of the other VMs already placed in a data center. The algorithm finds available clusters to accommodate the new VMs from the clusters constructed by the proposed clustering algorithm. After that, the best one with the minimum traffic load is selected to place the new VMs.

(4) VM Migration

To minimize the network traffic at aggregate and core switches, we include a VM migration algorithm based on the traffic matrix at long-term scale. Our algorithm is based on Swap algorithm for the capacitated max k-uncut problem proposed in [5] to maximize the weight sum of the edges within partitions. The migration algorithm operates in a top-down manner (from the root level to the rack level). At each level, the cluster pair with the maximum communication cost pair is selected for the VM migration in a greedy manner. When swapping VMs between the selected cluster pair, VM pairs with higher communication cost gain are preferred for exchanging their slot positions.

5   Performance Evaluation

We use the data center layout illustrated in Fig. 1b, which describes the rack size and the aisle width. A row has 8 racks, and each edge switch is equipped with wireless devices. Each rack consists of 40 host machines connected to an edge switch with 1 Gbps wired links, thus the data center consist of over 5 K host machines. 10 Gbps wired links connect three types of switches, and the tree topology described in Fig. 1a is applied. For the wireless devices, we use a 25 dBi gain horn antenna with 3 dB beamwidth of 30°, and the transmission power is set to 10 mW. Data rates are determined based on [1], and the feasible data rate of each link is calculated with the physical interference mode using SINR. Each wireless device can use one channel of three 2.16 GHz channels at a time if available.

As described in [16], small obstacles (even antennas on ToRs) can produce multipath fading and degrade the signal strength due to the small wavelength of 60 GHz links (5 mm), and the achievable transmission rate is also deteriorated. Thus, 2D beamforming generates a large set of interference links with SINR degradation, and we apply 3D beamforming [16] in our simulation.

To setup flows and packets for our simulator, we generated job trace files by referring the analyzed data in [4,8,12]. Most flows show small size under 10 KB, and last a few hundreds of millisecond. The analyzed result of measured data in [8,12] illustrates that more than 85%, 90% and 99% of flows are less than 100 KB, 1 MB, and 100 MB, respectively. On the other hand, more than 90% of bytes are carried by the flows between 100 MB and 1 GB. External traffic is transmitted and received through gateways beyond the core switches.

We present the following algorithms as comparison targets and implement in our simulator to compare with the proposed algorithms. Note that we denote our placement and routing algorithms as **OP** and **OR** respectively.

- *MINimum Cost Placement with old metric* (**MINCP**): We apply the old metric considering hop distances of the shortest paths with wired links only. The algorithm calculates the communication cost by multiplying the metric and the traffic demand at large time scale. It constructs and divides clusters to minimize the communication cost for the placement and migration of VMs.
- *MAXimum Slot placement* (**MAXSP**): This algorithm utilizes as small number of racks as possible, satisfying the required number of virtual machines, to maximize the locality of virtual machines for each job.
- *ECMP with channel allocation* (**ECMP-CA**): We present a routing protocol to disperse the network traffic probabilistically. This algorithm finds a path for each flow randomly, and conducts a channel allocation when a path containing wireless links is chosen. If there is no available channel for the wireless links, the algorithm checks another path repeatedly, until the feasible path is chosen.

We exploit placement/routing sets combining the above algorithms and the proposed algorithms; OP + OR, OP + ECMP-CA, MINCP + OR, and MINCP + ECMP-CA, MAXSP + OR, MAXSP + ECMP-CA in the following simulation results. The proposed algorithms are compared with base algorithms in terms of the *completion time of demands* (**CTD**) and the *aggregate throughput* (AT). Note that in this paper, CTD is the normalized CTD (CTD/CTD$_{ideal}$) in other studies, where CTD$_{ideal}$ is the CTD in an non-oversubscribed network [9].

In this paper, the proposed routing protocol exploits the path sets including wireless links adaptively with threshold θ. Thus the threshold may have an effect on the performance of our routing protocol. We perform an extensive evaluation and choose the value of θ as 0.6 in the following simulation tests because OP + OR with the value provides the highest average aggregate throughput.

Figure 2 includes the simulation results. As illustrated in Fig. 2a, our placement and routing set (OP + OR) shows the lowest average (**AVG**) of CTD (1.02) and the lowest standard deviation (**STD**) of CTD (0.069). With our placement algorithm, our routing protocol reduces CTD AVG by 23.7% compared to ECMP-CA. MINCP can show lower CTD AVG and CTD STD with our routing protocol than ECMP-CA. OR decreases CTD AVG and CTD STD by 29.9% and 59.1% respectively with MINCP. We can also improve MAXSP by applying our routing protocol compared to exploiting ECMP-CA. Consequently we can infer that our routing protocol shows better CTD compared to ECMP-CA regardless of the placement algorithm. On the other hand, with our routing protocol, our placement algorithm decreases CTD AVG by 6.30% and 12.22% against MINCP and MAXSP respectively. With ECMP-CA, OP also reduces CTD AVG by 13.89% and 18.82% compared to MINCP and MAXSP respectively. In other words, our placement can improve CTD with not only OR but also ECMP-CA.

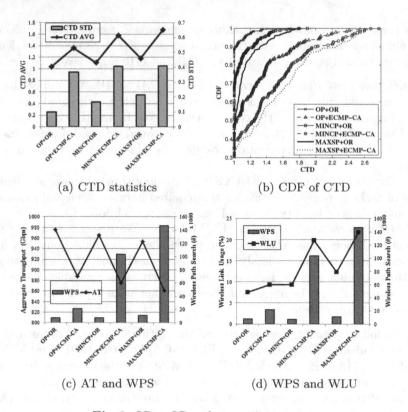

Fig. 2. OP + OR and comparison targets

Figure 2b shows the cumulative distribution function for each placement and routing pair. OP + OR increases most rapidly, while MAXSP + EMCP-CA is the slowest-growing. The maximum size of CTD AVG of OP + OR is 1.750, and that of MAXSP + EMCP-CA is 2.675. From Fig. 2a and c, there is a clear inverse correlation between the aggregate throughput (AT) and CTD. Therefore enhancing aggregate throughput by splitting traffic flows evenly and improving traffic locality is a critical factor determining network performance in data centers, which can reduce CTD. That is why OP + OR can complete traffic demands earlier than the others with the highest aggregate throughput.

Finally, we report the number of wireless path sets (WPS) as a metric for search space complexity and the wireless link usage ratio (WLU) as a metric for inefficient power consumption in Fig. 2c. In the figure, ECMP-CA retrieves the paths including wireless links more frequently. When either OR or ECMP-CA is applied, OP utilizes lower WLU but provides higher aggregate throughput. It is because that improving traffic locality with θ decreases the network load by reducing the distance between flow pairs. To this end, the routing protocols can mitigate the congestion earlier and forward more packets.

6   Conclusion

Wireless data center networks have challenges with regard to the dynamic topology, and it makes the system management more complicated, such as routing and virtual machine placement problems. In this paper we propose a routing algorithm including the threshold-based best path search algorithm and virtual machine placement algorithms to take the effect of wireless links into account. For better traffic locality, we present a new cost metric for the slot clustering of placement algorithms. The simulation results show that the protocol set including our placement algorithms and routing protocol provides the best performance in terms of CTD, WPS, WLU, and aggregation throughput.

Acknowledgments. This research was partly sponsored by NRF grant funded by the MSIP, Korea (No. 2013R1A2A2A01014000), and the MSIP, Korea, under the ITRC support program (IITP-2016-R0992-16-1012) supervised by the IITP.

References

1. The 802.11ad Standard. IEEE, December 2012
2. Al-Fares, M., Loukissas, A., Vahdat, A.: A scalable, commodity data center network architecture. In: Proceedings of ACM SIGCOMM. pp. 63–74, August 2008
3. Al-Fares, M., Radhakrishnan, S., Raghavan, B., Huang, N., Vahdat, A.: Hedera: dynamic flow scheduling for data center networks. In: Proceedings of NSDI, April 2010
4. Benson, T., Akella, A., Maltz, D.A.: Network traffic characteristics of data centers in the wild. In: Proceedings of ACM IMC, pp. 267–280, November 2010
5. Choudhury, S., Gaur, D.R., Krishnamurti, R.: An approximation algorithm for max k-uncut with capacity constraints. Optimization **61**(2), 143–150 (2012)
6. Cui, Y., Wang, H., Cheng, X.: Wireless link scheduling for data center networks. In: Proceedings of ICUIMC, February 2011
7. Curtis, A.R., Kim, W., Yalagandula, P.: Mahout: low-overhead datacenter traffic management using end-host-based elephant detection. In: Proceedings of IEEE INFOCOM, pp. 1629–1637, April 2011
8. Greenberg, A., Hamilton, J.R., Jain, N., Kandula, S., Kim, C., Lahiri, P., Maltz, D.A., Patel, P., Sengupta, S.: VL2: a scalable and flexible data center network. In: Proceedings of ACM SIGCOMM, pp. 51–62, August 2009
9. Halperin, D., Kandula, S., Padhye, J., Bahl, P., Wetherall, D.: Augmenting data center networks with multi-Gigabit wireless links. In: Proceedings of ACM SIGCOMM, pp. 38–49, August 2011
10. He, K., Fisher, A., Wang, L., Gember, A., Akella, A., Ristenpart, T.: Next stop, the cloud: understanding modern web service deployment in EC2 and Azure. In: Proceedings of ACM IMC, October 2013
11. Hopps, C.: Analysis of an Equal-Cost Multi-Path Algorithm. RFC 2992, November 2000
12. Kandula, S., Sengupta, S., Greenberg, A., Patel, P., Chaiken, R.: The nature of data center traffic: measurements & analysis. In: Proceedings of ACM IMC, November 2009

13. Kim, J., Molisch, A.F.: Fast millimeter-wave beam training with receive beam-forming. J. Commun. Netw. **16**(5), 512–522 (2014)
14. Meng, X., Pappas, V., Zhang, L.: Improving the scalability of data center networks with traffic-aware virtual machine placement. In: Proceedings of IEEE INFOCOM, March 2010
15. Wang, G., Andersen, D.G., Kaminsky, M., Papagiannaki, K., Ng, T.E., Kozuch, M., Ryan, M.: c-Through: part-time optics in data centers. In: Proceedings of ACM SIGCOMM, pp. 327–338, August 2010
16. Zhou, X., Zhang, Z., Zhu, Y., Li, Y., Kumar, S., Vahdat, A., Zhao, B.Y., Zheng, H.: Mirror mirror on the ceiling: flexible wireless links for data centers. In: Proceedings of ACM SIGCOMM, pp. 443–454, August 2012

MSP: A Routing Metric for Cognitive Radio Networks

Neng Zhang[✉], Jianfeng Guan, and Shengjie Yin

State Key Laboratory of Networking and Switching Technology,
Beijing University of Posts and Telecommunications, Beijing, China
{zn,jfguan}@bupt.edu.cn, 1604942836@qq.com

Abstract. The current routing metrics mainly face two inevitable restrictions for Cognitive Radio Networks (CRN) that they are often designed based on routing condition but seldom considering node mobility, and they are always assumed to adapt dynamic spectrum access without considering primary user's activity. In this paper, a novel routing metric called Mobility Success Probability (MSP) is proposed which considers both the mobility model and spectrum available time. Through spectrum access and selection path with mobility success probability, the routing protocol also meets the most essential requirements of optimality. Combined with Dijkstra based routing protocols, optimal expression of the MSP is analytically derived and rigorously proved through CR algebra. The simulation results reveal a good routing performance of adopting MSP for CRNs.

Keywords: Routing metrics · Cognitive radio networks · Optimality

1 Introduction

With the increasing needs for the wireless communication, people require higher data transfer rate as well as more radio spectrum resources. However, many of the licensed spectrums are idle in time and space, which is bound to lead to the lack of spectrum resources fit for wireless communication. Such situation has become a new bottleneck for the further development of wireless communication. CR technology is proposed to efficiently solve the problems mentioned above, by using those idle spectrum resources of licensed users.

Benefits from multiple path and opportunistic routing, current routing solutions for CRN still show some challenges [1]. Specifically, opportunistic routing could exploit next hop forwarding node sets with an expectation metric to promote the overall transmission success probability. However the relay nodes should be selected among all the channels and if PU appears, nodes acting on the same channel would be expired. It is a great burden to recalculate the metric frequently and maintain the node sets. For such a mobile node in wireless networks, up to now there have been many node mobility model researches. Nevertheless, most of the protocol designs such as routing metrics seldom take this node mobility into consideration.

Currently the matric design is conceived mainly from three aspects of integrated information with cross layer interactions, attempting to find optimal available spectrum,

© ICST Institute for Computer Sciences, Social Informatics and Telecommunications Engineering 2017
J.-H. Lee and S. Pack (Eds.): QShine 2016, LNICST 199, pp. 149–159, 2017.
DOI: 10.1007/978-3-319-60717-7_15

relay nodes and maintain mechanism. The available spectrum requires a relatively stable PU spectrum occupancy to improve link quality without frequently interruption and spectrum handoff. The matric factor may include minimum transmission time, maximum spectrum available time or handoff. The relay selection would be in favor of those forwarders with a good history forwarding records or have a probability to transmit to the destination successfully. The maintain mechanism is focus on how to deal with handoff and recover transmission when PU appears or connection interrupts.

From above we can see apart from spectrum variability, the forwarder behavior arising from node mobility plays an important role in metric design. Thus, more strict and specific requirements for metric design that need to be considered in routing protocols are concluded as follows [3]. Firstly, fast convergence is a key issue to avoid routing loops and inaccessible destinations especially in a dynamic network topology. Secondly, in a short time span, a fast and effective path is required to adapt mobility without large amount of frequent calculation cost.

There have been a series of newly proposed routing metrics for CRNs [7]. For instance, the author in [2] propose Routing Closeness metric and select path that is far from other paths geographically in order to reduce interference. The author in [4] proposes an approach which aims at balancing the performance of queuing delay, back off overhead and switching cost. The author in [9] proposes a capacity-based routing metric. The metric improves network performance by shifting traffic away from high regions with high density. The author in [8] designs a probabilistic metric that selects path on the basis of the capacity of accessing free channels. The author in [14] computes the transmission time from source to destination and selects the path with minimal value. This metric also takes use of multiple channels, so as to decrease the transmission time. The author in [16] constructs multi-layer relay sets for each sender and when handoff occurs, a backup relay set enables replacing main set to reduce the channel switching and shorten the cost.

This paper explores the mobility application in metric design and introduces a novel routing metric called Maximum Success Probability (MSP), which accounts for both the node mobility and the corresponding spectrum available time of licensed channels. The proposed metric concentrates to maximize the success probability for a CR transmission under node mobility to improve the overall network performance. Based on the mobility features, this paper proposes an efficient opportunistic routing algorithm to select the path with maximum success probability between a CR source and a CR destination. Considering the compatibility between proposed metric and corresponding protocol may degrade network performance if applying an arbitrary routing metric to a CR protocol, CR algebra [10] and basic properties are applied to prove that MSP metric properly works with Dijkstra based routing protocols. Simulation shows throughput of the MSP algorithm outperforms with other two referenced algorithms under different network conditions.

The rest of this paper is organized as follows. Section 2 presents the proposed metric MSP and proves the compatibility of the new metric with Dijkstra based routing protocols. Section 3 gives the simulation results of path section performance in comparison with MTT, MaxPos and MSP metric respectively. Section 4 makes a conclusion and shows further work.

2 MSP Design

2.1 Assumptions

We consider a CRN where n SUs and m PUs co-exist in a limited area. SU can opportunistically access PU's licensed channels in effective transmission range if PUs are not shown in adjacent areas. PU commonly appears and employs its spectrum with Poisson distribution. When a PU becomes active, SU would fast handoff to find a new appropriate channel opportunity and maintain transmission. SU would move with one mobility model depending on a realistic scenario.

Based on the condition above, the CRN in this paper could modeled as a graph $G = (N, E)$, where N stands for the set of CR users and E stands for the set of links in the network. $e_{i,j} = (n_i, n_j)$ is the link between CR users n_i and n_j. It belongs to E only if the CR user n_j is in the transmission range of n_i and there is at least one common data channel between them. However, as there are more than one primary channels, link $e_{i,j}$ consist of several links each of which is working on various primary channels. So, this paper makes $e_{i,j}^{(m)} \in e_{i,j}$ as the link that stands for primary channel m.

This paper assumes that both $T_{on}^{(m)}$ and $T_{off}^{(m)}$ are exponentially distributed [5] with mean equal to λ and μ respectively. The transmission power of each CR user is the same all the time. Moreover, when computing the transmission rate of a CR user over the channel it accesses, Shannon theorem is then used.

2.2 Mobility Detection

There have been many newly investigated mobility models evolved from classic models. The paper [15] proposes backhaul traffic model and energy efficiency model under Gauss-Markov mobility model. In fact, all practical movements show a kind of regularity instead of random activity. Since such a classical random walk model cannot portrait a real scenario with index decay, some human mobility models with social features are emerged to reveal properties as contact duration, inter-contact time or content relevance, such as TVC, SWIM [17] and content popularity framework. Here we briefly apply a simple mobility model as SWIM that shows human common daily trajectory. Generally a handheld node will move to a location in a time period, even along a static route, and then keep still in a range. With respect to such a highly dynamic topology, this process could be viewed as a network sub-graph snapshot which can be represented as time evolving graph with Markov model. However, this topology has an assumption that there is a constant node number C without node expiring or newly joining. For simplicity, we would build a transitional snapshot as a static topology with relatively static neighbor nodes and forwarders. The sequence of graph G can be denoted as following notation:

$$\Gamma = \{G_t = ([n], E_t) : t \in N\}, [n] = \{1, \ldots, n\} \tag{1}$$

The initial network snapshot at t_0 is represented as G_0. From t_0 if the topology changes, we have a new network snapshot G_t at t_n, so the discrete time sequence snapshot is $G_t = \{G_0, G_1, G_2, G_3 \ldots\}$. In other words, we suppose the topology keeps stable at time period t. The end to end transmission path from sender to receiver in CRN can be viewed as an edge selection E_t in a snapshot.

Inspired from SWIM mobility model, we define Mobility Trajectory Probability as follows.

For any two neighboring CR users ni and nj, MSP aims to find the path with maximum success probability. The MSP is defined as follows:

$$P_{su}^{\max}\left(e_{i,j}\right) = \max_{m \in M}\{P_{su}\left(e_{i,j}^{(m)}\right)\} \tag{2}$$

2.3 MSP Metric Design

For any two neighboring CRN users n_i and n_j, the MTT metric aims to find the path with minimum transmission time among all the links between them [12], MSAT metric aims to find the link with maximum spectrum available time. The MTT metric only takes the required transmission time between any neighboring CR users into consideration when selecting path from a CR source NS to a CR destination ND. However, spectrum available time of a primary channel may be smaller than the minimum transmission time over the selected path, which means the CR user may be interrupted and lose its traffic once the PU occupies this channel again. Similarly, the MSAT metric only take the spectrum available time between any two neighboring CR users into consideration. However, it will also incorrectly select a bad path if the minimum transmission time over a path is larger than the spectrum available time.

To deal with the above-mentioned problems, this paper introduces a new routing metric called Maximum Success Probability (MSP), which considers both the spectrum available time and CR transmission time.

Success Probability: The notion $P_{su}\left(e_{i,j}^{(m)}\right)$ between any two neighboring CR users n_i and n_j over channel m is given as follows:

$$P_{su}\left(e_{i,j}^{(m)}\right) = P\left[T_{av}\left(e_{i,j}^{(m)}\right) \geq T_{tr}\left(e_{i,j}^{(m)}\right)\right] = e^{-\frac{T_{tr}\left(e_{i,j}^{(m)}\right)}{\mu_m(e_{i,j})}} \tag{3}$$

Mobility Success Probability: For any two neighboring CR users n_i and n_j, MSP aims to find the path with maximum success probability. The MSP is defined as follows:

$$P_{su}^{\max}\left(e_{i,j}\right) = \max_{m \in M}\{P_{su}\left(e_{i,j}^{(m)}\right)\} \tag{4}$$

Maximum Path Success Probability: The maximum path success probability between CR source N_S and destination N_D is defined as follows.

$$MaxP_{su}(N_s, N_D) = \max_{l \in L}\{P_{su}^{(l)}(N_s, N_D)\} \tag{5}$$

Where $P_{su}^{(l)}(N_s, N_D)$ is the maximum probability of success on path l. It is computed as follows:

$$P_{su}^{(l)}(N_s, N_D) = \prod_{i=1}^{k-1} P_{su}^{max}(e_{i,i+1}) \tag{6}$$

To correctly find the path with maximum success probability for a CR source N_S and a destination N_D, this paper uses $-log$ function on the success probability to get the final metric value, which means a small metric value refers to a high success probability. The metric value of link m is then defined shown as follows:

$$W(e_{i,j}^{(m)}) = -\log[P_{su}(e_{i,j}^{(m)})] \tag{7}$$

The MSP metric first removes links that are not connected to each other. Then the maximum success probability of each link is computed by Eq. (1). After that, the algorithm computes the metric value for each link using (5). At last, it selects the path with maximum success probability using (2).

2.4   Routing Phrase

Here we design a routing phrase to explain the routing process.

Information exchange: The sender performs spectrum sensing and sends a request to its neighbors on multiple channels. The neighbors response with location and spectrum information. In this stage the topology is build and

Forwarder selection: The sender selects promising neighbors into relay sets on multiple channels for data transmission.

Mobility detection: The sender notifies the nodes in the selected main relay set, assigns them priorities, and applies the opportunistic based routing protocol;

Route maintain: When the transmission fails due to the suddenly active PUs, the sender adjusts the affected main and backup relay sets, and reselects them if necessary (Table 1).

2.5   Compatibility Analysis

In this section we prove the compatibility of MSP and Dijkstra based routing protocols applying mathematical tools called routing algebra. CR algebra can be described as a 4-tuple [11] as follows.

$$C = (S, \oplus, W, \leq) \tag{8}$$

Table 1. MSP Algorithm.

MSP Algorithm
Input: $u(ei,j)$, C_S, C_D, G_t
Output: Path L
$T=0$;
1:**for** each channel c_m **do**
2: **for** each edge $e_{i,j}$ **do**
3: Calculate $Psuc_{(e(m)\,i,j)}$ with equation (3)
4: **end for**
5: Find $Pmaxsuc\ (e_{i,j}) \rightarrow Psuc(e_{i,j})$ with equation (5)
6: Calculate the weight $W_{(e)i,j}$ with equation (7)
7: Path = Dikjstra $(C_S, C_D, W_{(e)i,j})$
8: Assign channel c to $e_{i,j}$
9: **if** topology G_t changes
10: repeat from step 1
11: **end if**
12: store the path L to the history $H_s(t)$

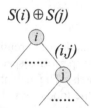

Fig. 1. A simple example for operation of $\oplus$

Where S is the set of CR trees, $\oplus$ is the operator that concatenates two CR trees to a single CR-tree, W is the metric value of a CR tree, and $\leq$ is a preference symbol (Fig. 1).

Combined the Eqs. (4) and (5) above, we can retain the metric value of path l as follows:

$$W(P_{su}^{(l)}(N_s, N_D)) = W[\prod_{i=1}^{k-1} P_{su}^{max}(e_{i,i+1})]$$

$$= -log\prod_{i=1}^{k-1} P_{su}^{max}(e_{i,i+1}) = \sum_{i=1}^{k-1} -logP_{su}^{max}(e_{i,i+1}) \qquad (9)$$

$$= \sum_{i=1}^{k-1} W(e_{i,i+1})$$

Equation (7) shows that the metric value of path l is equal to the sum of metric value of all the links in path l. What's more, as the success probability P_{su} is a value belongs to (0, 1), the metric value $W = -log(P_{su})$ is thus a positive value. And the Dijkstra based routing protocols always prefers links or paths with less metric values. According to these principals, it can be inferred that for $\forall i \in N$ and $\forall j \in R(i)$, it has:

$$W[S(i) \oplus S(j)] = \min\{W[S(i)], W[S(j)] + W[(i,j)]\} \tag{10}$$

Optimality is the most essential requirement to ensure the efficiency and correctness of a routing protocol operation. A CR protocol is optimal if it always routes packets along the path with minimum routing metric value between each source-destination pair in a connected network. According to the works of [10], a Dijkstra-based routing protocol is optimal if its combined CR algebra has the following three properties: Relay-conditionally-beneficial, Strictly preference-preservable and Relay-order-optimal. Based on the above analysis, the proofs of property 1, 2 and 3 are given.

(Proof of property 1). Relay-conditional-benefic: If $W[S(i) \oplus S(j)] = min\{W[S(i)]$, $W[S(j)] + W(i,j)\} \leq W[S(i)]$, it must have $W[S(j)] + W(i,j) \leq W[S(i)]$. And because $W(i,j) > 0$, $W[S(j)] \leq W[S(i)]$ is then proved. On the other hand, $W[S(i) \oplus S(j)] = min\{W[S(i)], W[S(j)] + W(i,j)\} \leq W[S(i)]$ is obvious. Consequently, MSP algorithm is proved to be relay-conditional-beneficial.

(Proof of Property 2). Strictly preference-preservation: $W[S(i) \oplus S(j)] = min\{W[S(i)]$, $W[S(j)] + W(i,j)\} = W[S(i)]$ or $W[S(j)] + W(i,j)$. Because $W(i,j) > 0$, $W[S(j)] + W(i, j) > W[S(j)]$. And according to the known condition, $W[S(j)] < W[S(i)]$. So, $W[S(j)] < W[S(i) \oplus W(j)]$. Consequently, MSP algorithm is proved to be strictly preference-preservable.

(Proof of Property 3). Relay-order-optimality: $W[S(i) \oplus S(j) \oplus S(w)] = min\{W[S(i)]$, $W[S(j)] + W(i,j)$, $W[S(w)] + W(i,w)\}$. $W[S(i) \oplus S(w) \oplus S(j)] = min\{W[S(i)]$, $W[S(w)] + W(i,w)$, $W[S(j)] + W(i,j)\}$. So, $W[S(i) \oplus S(j) \oplus S(w)]$ equals to $W[S(i) \oplus S(w) \oplus S(j)]$. Consequently, MSP algorithm is proved to be relay-order-optimal.

3 Simulation Results

Our simulations are conducted by MATLAB. In the simulation environment, there are 10 CR users ($K = 10$) and each node in figure represents a CR user. The index of node is also signed in the figure. Besides, the simulation environment is in a [10 m, 10 m] area and the transmission range of each CR user equals to 5 m. The number of PU channels that can be accessed when they are idle is set to 10 ($M = 10$). It needs to be mentioned that the 10 PU channels are not visible in the simulation area. The paper takes use of the Rayleigh fading model.

The simulation results of network performance (mainly end-to-end throughput) are shown to identify the impacts of primary user traffic and transmission power. The computation results of MTT, MSAT and MSP are averaged over 100 runs respectively. Analyses of the simulation results are then conducted based on the figures.

3.1 Impact of PU Traffic

This section analyses the impact of the PU traffic on network performance. The PU traffic is reflected by the average PU channel available time μ which continually increases from $\mu = 0.1$ s to $\mu = 0.8$ s with interval 0.1 s. With the increase of average idle time, the PU traffic decreases and CR users are more likely to take use of the PU channel. Two different situations are shown: the simulation results with transmission power $P_{tr} = 0.2$ W and 0.6 W are shown in Fig. 2.

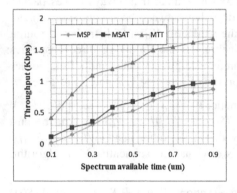
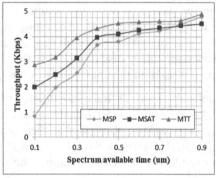

Fig. 2. Throughput of $P_{tr} = 0.6$ W VS $P_{tr} = 0.6$ W

It is quite obvious from the figure that with the increment of PU traffic (μ increases), the network throughput increases for all of the MTT, MSAT and MSA metric. This is a common sense because CR users are able to get more opportunities if the PU channel is not busy. But the throughputs computed by MSP are superior to MTT and MSAT metric for MSP metric maximizes the success probability of CR transmission path. This is able to prove the optimality and benefits of adopting MSP metric. Moreover, the MSP metric is able to achieve higher throughput values compared with MTT and MSAT metrics when the transmission power and spectrum available time are relatively small, which is quite essential for energy saving and network operations. More detailed analyzing, with the P_{tr} increases from 0.2 W to 0.6 W the transmission rate R will increase. Consequently, the required transmission time T_{tr} will be shortened and the network throughput then improves.

What's more, as the MTT metric only takes the required transmission time into consideration but ignores the channel available time, so it will achieve high network performance if the PU channels have large values of idle time. Besides, the MSAT metric selects the channel with maximum available time and ignores the required transmission time over each link. So, its network throughput may be less than the MTT metric when the value of μ is relatively large. Figure 2 shows that the MTT metric exceeds MSAT in network performance after the value of μ becomes greater than about 0.75 s, and proves the above mentioned two inferences.

3.2 Impact of Transmission Power

This section analyses the impact of the transmission power on network performance. The P_{tr} is continually increased from $P_{tr} = 0.1$ W to $P_{tr} = 1.5$ W with interval 0.2 W. Two different situations are shown: the simulation results with average available time $\mu = 0.15$ and 0.5 s is shown in Fig. 3.

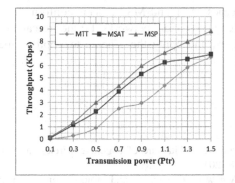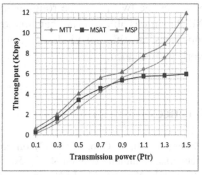

Fig. 3. Throughput of $P_{tr} = 0.6$ W VS $P_{tr} = 0.6$ W

Analyzing Fig. 3, it is quite obvious that with the increment of transmission power (P_{tr} increases), the network throughput increases for all of the MTT, MSAT and MSP metric. This is because the transmission rate R will increase according to Eq. (2). Consequently, the required transmission time T_{tr} will be shorten base on Eq. (1). But the throughputs computed by MSP are significantly superior to MTT and MSAT metric for MSP metric maximizes the success probability of CR transmission path. This is able to prove the optimality and benefits of adopting MSP metric.

More detailed analyzing, with the average idle time μ increases from 0.15 to 0.5 s, CR users have more opportunities to access and take use of the PU channel. As a result, network throughputs of MSP metric are larger than MTT and MSAT.

What's more, the network throughput of MTT metric increases rapidly with the increment of transmission power, while the network throughput of MSAT metric increases slowly after $P_{tr} = 1$ W. Moreover, when the value of transmission power becomes greater than about 0.75 W in Fig. 18, the throughput of MTT metric exceeds the MSAT metric. Three main reasons for such cases are follows. Firstly, the MTT metric only takes the required transmission time into consideration but ignores the channel available time, so it will achieve high network performance if the PU channels have relative large idle time. Secondly, the transmission rate over each link will be improved with the increase of transmission power and the required transmission time will be decreased which is the only factor MTT metric considers. Thirdly, the MSAT metric selects the channel with maximum available time and ignores the required transmission time over each link. So, after reaching a relative high value, its network throughput will change slowly with the variation of required transmission time which is caused by the increase of transmission power.

4   Conclusion

In this paper, a new routing metric for cognitive radio networks called MSP is proposed. MSP selects the path with mobility success probability and then forward data packets along the selected path. MSP is designed to meet two requirements: mobility and otimality. The expression of MSP is analytically derived and proved by applying CR algebra. Simulation results shows that the proposed routing metric MSP obviously outperforms the two reference rouging metrics MTT and MSAT. This conforms that the MSP metric is able to bring benefits to cognitive radio networks. Further researches should focus on different kinds of scenarios, and apply the scheme to improve the network performance.

References

1. Zhang, J., Liu, J., Guo, W.: Study on cognitive architecture of cognitive wireless ad hoc networks. Commun. Technol. **44**(2), 56–58 (2011)
2. Beltagy, I., Youssef, M., El-Derini, M.: A new routing metric and protocol for multipath routing in cognitive networks. In: Proceedings of IEEE Wireless Communications and Networking Conference, pp. 974–979. IEEE (2011)
3. Cesana, M., Cuomo, F., Ekici, E.: Routing in cognitive radio networks: challenges and solutions. ad hoc Networks (2010)
4. Cheng, G., et al.: Joint on-demand routing and spectrum assignment in cognitive radio networks. In: Proceedings of IEEE ICC, pp. 6499–6503. IEEE (2007)
5. Chun-Ting, C., Sai, S.: What and how much to gain by spectrum agility. IEEE J. Sel. Area Commun. **25** (2007)
6. Haythem, B.S.: Rate-maximization channel assignment scheme for cognitive radio networks. In: Proceedings of IEEE GlobeCom, pp. 1–5 (2010)
7. Jose, M., Edmundo, M.: Cognitive radio: survey on communication protocols, spectrum decision issues, and future research directions. Wirel. Netw. **18**, 147–164 (2011)
8. Khalife, H., Ahuja, S., Malouch, N., Krunz, M.: Probabilistic path selection in opportunistic cognitive radio networks. In: Proceedings of IEEE GlobeCom, pp. 1–5 (2008)
9. Liu, Y., Grace, D.: Improving capacity for wireless Ad Hoc communications using cognitive routing. In: Proceedings of IEEE CrownCom, pp. 1–6 (2008)
10. Lu, M., Wu, J.: Opportunistic routing algebra and its applications. In: IEEE Proceedings of Computer Communications, pp. 2374–2382 (2009)
11. Marcello, C., Akyildiz, F.I., Paura, L.: OPERA: optimal routing metric for cognitive radio ad hoc networks. IEEE Trans. Wirel. Commun. **11**(8), 2884–2894 (2012)
12. Osamah, S.B., Haythem, B.S.: Opportunistic routing in cognitive radio networks: exploiting spectrum availability and rich channel diversity. In: Proceedings of IEEE GlobeCom (2011)
13. Sobrinho, J.: Algebra and algorithms for QoS path computation and hop-by-hop routing in the internet. In: IEEE Proceedings of INFOCOM, pp. 727–735 (2011)
14. Yun, L., et al.: Cognitive radio routing algorithm based on the smallest transmission delay. In: Proceedings of ICFCC, pp. 306–310 (2010)
15. Ge, X., Tu, S., Han, T., Li, Q., Mao, G.: Energy efficiency of small cell backhaul networks based on Gauss-Markov mobile models. IET Netw. **4**(2), 158–167 (2015)

16. Dai, Y., Wu, J.: Opportunistic routing based scheme with multi-layer relay sets in cognitive radio networks. In: Wireless Communications and Networking Conference (WCNC), pp. 1159–1164 (2015)
17. Kosta, S., Mei, A., Stefa, J.: Large-scale synthetic social mobile networks with SWIM. IEEE Trans. Mob. Comput. **13**(1), 116–129 (2014)

Primary Component Carrier Assignment in LTE-A

Husnu S. Narman[1(✉)] and Mohammed Atiquzzaman[2]

[1] Holcombe Department of Electrical and Computer Engineering,
Clemson University, Clemson, SC 29634, USA
husnu@ou.edu
[2] School of Computer Science, University of Oklahoma, Norman, OK 73019, USA
atiq@ou.edu

Abstract. Bandwidth requirement for mobile data traffic is on the rise because of increasing number of mobile users. To answer the requirement, Carrier Aggregation is proposed. With Carrier Aggregation and MIMO, operators can provide up to 3 Gbps download speed. In Carrier Aggregation, several component carriers from multiple bands are assigned to users. The assigned Component Carriers are classified as Primary and Secondary Component Carriers. The Primary Component Carrier (PCC) is the main carrier and only updated during the handover and cell reselection but Secondary Component Carriers (SCC) are auxiliary carriers to boost data rates and can be activated/deactivated anytime. During the carrier assignment operations, PCC reassignment can lead packet interruptions because reassignments of PCC to users can lead SCCs reassignment. Several methods have been proposed to increase the efficiency of the carrier assignment operations. However, none of them shows the system performance if LTE-A can have a procedure which allows one of SCCs to handle the duties of PCC during the PCC reassignment to eliminate packet transfer interruption. Therefore, we have used four different carrier assignment methods to investigate the performance of LTE-A with and without the procedure. Results show that distinct carrier assignment methods are differently affected by the procedure. Our results and analysis will help service providers and researchers to develop efficient carrier assignment methods.

Keywords: LTE · LTE-A · Component carrier assignment · Resources allocation · Analysis

1 Introduction

Data traffic over mobile network is increasing with the rise in the number of mobile users. Therefore, new advanced techniques are required to satisfy users. One of the important technology is LTE-A which provides 1.5 Gbps for uplink and 3 Gbps for downlink peak data rates to mobile users by using Carrier Aggregation (CA) and MIMO technology [1]. In CA, several Component Carriers (CC)

© ICST Institute for Computer Sciences, Social Informatics and Telecommunications Engineering 2017
J.-H. Lee and S. Pack (Eds.): QShine 2016, LNICST 199, pp. 160–170, 2017.
DOI: 10.1007/978-3-319-60717-7_16

with 1.5 MHz, 3 MHz, 5 MHz, 10 MHz, 15 MHz or 20 MHz bandwidth from a number of different or same bands are assigned to users. [1]. Therefore, there are three types of Carrier Aggregation and they are *Intra-band contiguous, Intra-band non-contiguous and Inter-band non-contiguous* [1].

In Carrier Aggregation, the assigned Component Carriers are classified as Primary and Secondary Component Carriers. The Primary Component Carrier (PCC) is the main carrier and only updated during the handover and cell reselection but Secondary Component Carriers (SCC) are auxiliary carriers to boost data rates and can be activated/deactivated anytime. During the carrier assignment operations, PCC reassignment can lead packet interruptions because reassignments of PCC to users can lead SCCs reassignment.

Several carrier assignment methods have been proposed and analyzed [2–14] in the literature. In [2,3], Round Robin and Mobile Hashing methods have been investigated. Both of the methods are based on load balancing strategy. In [4], firstly, Channel Quality Indicator (CQI) rates from all users for each component carriers are measured, then according to the highest rate, the carriers are assigned to users. In [7], a service-based method is proposed by giving priority for some traffic types while assigning carriers to users. In [5], absolute and relative carrier assignment methods are proposed according to a predetermined CQI threshold and PCC CQI, respectively. In [6], G-factor carrier assignment method is proposed by considering load balancing for non-edge users and better coverages for edge users. Edge users are the users which are located away from eNB. In [8], firstly, bands of pico and macro cells are decided according to interference, then beamforming is used to give services to each user. In [9], a self-organized method, which assumes availability of CQI for each resource block to avoid interference, is proposed. A resource block is the smallest unit of resources that can be allocated to a user. In [10], the least user loaded carriers with highest CQI are considered to assign carriers to users. In [11], mobility of users is estimated in real time while assigning carriers to users in order to decrease carrier reselection and handover. In [12–14], uplink carrier assignment methods have been proposed by considering a ratio function, traffic type and CQI to increase throughput while sending data from users to eNB. While the aim of uplink carrier assignment is to optimize bandwidth and power limitation, downlink carrier assignment aims to optimize only bandwidth.

However, none of them shows the system performance if LTE-A can have a procedure which allows one of SCCs to handle the duties of PCC during the PCC reassignment to eliminate packet transfer interruption. Therefore, the *aim* of this work is to analyze the performance of four component carrier assignment methods with and without the procedure according to average delay and throughput ratio which are experienced by LTE-A type equipment.

The *objective* of this paper is to analyze PCC reassignment procedure in terms of throughput ratio and average delay which are LTE-A users[1] by considering the availability of duty switching between a CC of SCCs and PCC for

---

[1] Currently, LTE type equipment can only connect one CC to get services but LTE-A type equipment can connect up to five CCs to receive services.

four different carrier assignment methods based on Random, Load Balancing (LB) and Channel Quality Indicator (CQI). The key *contributions* of this work are as follows: (i) Duty switching procedure between PCC and a CC of SCCs is discussed; (ii) The system model for disjoint queuing system is explained; (iii) Comparing Random (RA), Least Load (LL), Least Load Rate (LR) and Channel Quality (CQ) carrier assignment methods by an extensive simulation with and without the procedure in terms of throughput ratio and average delay.

Results show that distinct carrier assignment methods are differently affected by the procedure. Our results and analysis will help service providers and researchers to develop efficient carrier assignment methods.

The rest of the paper is organized as follows: In Sect. 2, the system model of carrier assignment procedure with Disjoint Buffer System is discussed and followed by explanations of the used methods in Sect. 3. Simulation environments with parameters are described in Sect. 4. In Sect. 5, simulation results are presented and analyzed. Finally, Sect. 6 has the concluding remarks.

2   System Model

Figure 1 shows system model for CCA. n users are connected to m available CCs. Today, UE can only connect up to 5 CCs at the same time to provide 4G standard peak data rate. One of CCs must be PCC and is only updated during handover or cell reselection in LTE-A (Rev. 10 and above) [15]. Hence, PCC is generally the CC which has the highest coverage area and CQI. Moreover, PCC of one UE can be different from PCC of other UE. On the other hand, other CCs (besides PCC) are called SCC and can be activated or deactivated according to users' needs. UE can only connect one CC in LTE (Rev. 8) for communication [15]. Therefore, both types of UE equipment should be considered while evaluating the performance in CCA.

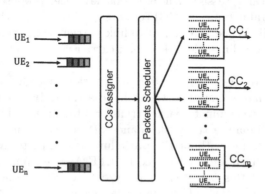

Fig. 1. Carrier assignment model of n users and m available CCs with disjoint buffer system.

Packed Scheduler (PS) transfers packets over selected carriers in time and frequency domains after the carrier assignment process finishes. Currently, Proportional Fairness and max-min are common PS methods which are used in LTE-A [3,16]. In addition to PS, there are two Queue Scheduler methods which are Disjoint and Joint Buffer [17]. In Joint Queue Scheduler (JQS) method, each CC has only one queue for all UEs. However, each CC has distinct queues for all UEs in Disjoint Queue Scheduler (DQS) as showed in Fig. 1. We have used Disjoint Queue Scheduler [17] in this paper because of the realistic approach of Disjoint Queue Scheduler for LTE-A [18].

3   Methods

To analyze the impacts of joint and selective techniques on the carrier assignment, four different carrier assignment methods are used. The methods are based on random, load balancing and CQI and they are Random (RA), Least Load (LL), Least Load Rate (LR) and Channel Quality (CQ). Those methods are selected for test cases because of common usage in the literature and the different properties are considered while assigning the carriers to UEs.

3.1   Random (RA)

RA method is one of the well-known methods in the literature [3,19]. However, RA method ignores QoS requirements of each user and CQI of channels. In this work, R method assigns carriers to users according to Java Random Generator and Java Random Generator is based on Uniform Distribution. Therefore, RA randomly selects available carriers for each user but it only well balances users loads across carriers in long term.

3.2   Least Load (LL)

LL method is also one of the well-known methods in the literature [3]. LL assigns the carriers to users according to load balancing strategy by selecting the least loaded carriers thus, it well balances users loads across the carriers in short and long terms [3]. LL method also ignores QoS requirements of each user and CQI of the carriers. It is important to note that ignoring CQI does not mean the performance of LL method is lower than other methods.

3.3   Channel Quality (CQ)

CQI can be vary according to position of users because of obstacles and distances, Therefore, there are several versions of CQ methods like [5]. In this paper, CQ method assigns the carriers to users by selecting the carriers which have the highest CQI [20] and it is similar to Relative method in [5]. Because of only considering CQI, user loads and QoS requirements of users are ignored.

3.4 Least Load Rate (LR)

LR method assigns the carriers to users by selecting the highest rate which is measured by using the total capacity in terms of the bandwidth, the number of users and CQI for each carrier. The rate is measured as similar to [4] but instead of considering the queue length[2], we have considered the number of users in each carrier as follows:

$$\text{Rate} = \frac{\text{CQI of carrier} * \text{Bandwidth of carrier}}{\text{The number of users on carrier}} \tag{1}$$

4 Simulation

Discrete event simulation has been implemented by considering carrier assignment methods which are mentioned in Sect. 3. Assumptions and simulation setups are explained in the following subsections.

4.1 Assumptions for eNBs

It is assumed that there is only one eNB with three bands to provide service to users. The additional parameters of eNB are given in Table 1.

Table 1. The eNB parameters.

Scenario [21]	b
Number of eNB	1
Used bands	800 MHz, 1.8 GHz, 2.6 GHz
Number of CCs in each band	4
Total number of CCs	12
Queue length of each queue	50 packets
Bandwidth of CCs	10 MHz
Modulations	BPSK, QPSK, 16QAM, and 64QAM
CQI	3, 5, 7, and 11
Transmission time interval	10 ms (10 ms is average, it can be more or less)
Time for CCA	20 ms (at most 20 ms)
CQI threshold	The highest possible
Simulation model	Finite buffer [22]

In the simulation, Scenario b is used to represent the general macro model. Only one eNB is considered not to deal with the handover process in case users

---

[2] we consider the queue length in packet scheduling rather than carrier assignment for all methods.

change base stations. However, assuming one eNB does not affect the obtained results in terms of performance comparison between methods. The eNB provides service to users by using three bands similar to real case scenario and each band can have four CCs with 10 MHz bandwidth. The number of CCs in each band is selected as four because LTE-A type equipment can connect at most four CCs to download data. Therefore, even if a LTE-A type user in the coverage of *Band-a* can connect four CCs to get services similar to real case scenario. To simulate saturation of the system, a higher number of CCs are not selected. 10 MHz and 20 MHz bandwidths are used in LTE-A to provide IMT-A level speed [21]. BPSK, QPSK, 16QAM and 64QAM are the modulations techniques to transfer bits according to CQI in LTE systems. Therefore, to simulate those modulations, four CQI levels are used and each CQI level is modulation changing point. The average Transmission Time Interval (TTI) is 10ms for a packet (TTI can be less or more according to different packet sizes) to simulate the low and high latency requirements because the accepted TTI in LTE is 1ms to meet the low latency requirements [21]. In order to show the lowest improvements with PCC grant technique comparing to without PCC grant, time for CCA is kept as 20 ms and lower because the carrier assignment operations can consume considerable amount of time according to carrier assignment methods. As simulation model, finite buffer is used because finite buffer simulation well presents the reality comparing to full buffer simulation [22].

4.2 Assumptions for UEs

In the network, there are two types of equipment, LTE and LTE-A. 50% of equipment is LTE type equipment which only connect one CC to receive services. On the other hand, the other 50% equipment is LTE-A type equipment which connect multiple CCs (currently, up to five CCs). In simulation, four CCs are simultaneously connected by LTE-A type equipment because maximum five CCs can be used by LTE-A type equipment, and one of them must be for upload primary component carrier [1].

Initially, UEs are non-uniformly distributed in the simulated area. In brief, UEs are mostly located around oNB. 50% of users can move around of the eNB in specified time interval to simulate mobility. Because of UE mobility and eNB position, CQI Index for all carriers can be one of four options which are given in Table 1. Only one type of data traffic is downloaded by each user. Packet arrival follows Pareto Distribution with 250 packets per second for each user (shape parameter for Pareto Distribution is 2.5) and packet arrival traffics are kept same for all test cases. Moreover, total packet arrival is increasing while the number of users is enlarged.

4.3 Packet Scheduling

We have used a min-delay packet scheduling method for packet scheduling. Each packet is transferred by using one of assigned carriers for each user. To increase the efficiency and QoS, packet transferring priority is given to the CC, which is the closest to the eNB and minimizes packet delay if multiple carriers are available. If there are no available assigned carriers to serve arriving packets, packets are enqueued to corresponding user queues in each CC according to min-delay measurement (because of DQS). If there are no empty spaces in queues, arriving packets are dropped. We do not use Proportional Fairness packet scheduler [3] because it can block some packets during the scheduling. Therefore, the results can be misleading on device base performance comparison of the carrier assignment methods.

4.4 Observation Methodology

We present the performance of the carrier assignment methods by comparing throughput ratio and average delay which are experienced by LTE-A type equipment. Throughput ratio is measured by dividing transferred packets to all packets (dropped packets + transferred packets). Therefore, while the number of users is increased, throughput ratio decreases because of carrier capacities. Block rate is not given because it is just inverse of throughput ratio. Average delay is determined based on waiting times of packets in queues and service. It is obtained by dividing the sum of waiting time of the packets to the number of transferred packets. To measure throughout ratio and average delay per packet for LTE-A type equipment, the packets which belong to LTE-A type equipment are considered.

5 Results

The results are average of 40 realizations for different size of users with 10000 packet samples. The impact of light and heavy users loads on carrier assignment methods is investigated by using the packet and queue scheduling techniques which are explained in Sects. 3 and 4.3.

5.1 Average Delay Time

Figure 2 shows average delay per packet which is experienced by only LTE-A type equipment for four carrier assignment methods according to without and with PCC grant. When the number of user is 10 or below, RA, LL, LR and CQ methods have almost zero average delay for all cases. When the number of users increases, LL methods are not affected by PCC grant but RA and LR method performances are slightly improved. However, average delay in CQ method is higher in PCC grant. One of the reason for lower average delay in CQ method is that CQ assign CCs which can have high CQI but also high number of users.

Moreover, if the methods are compared with each other, while LL method is the best in terms of average delay without PCC grant, LL and LR methods are the best in terms of average delay with PCC grant. CQ is the worst in terms of average delay for without and with PCC grant.

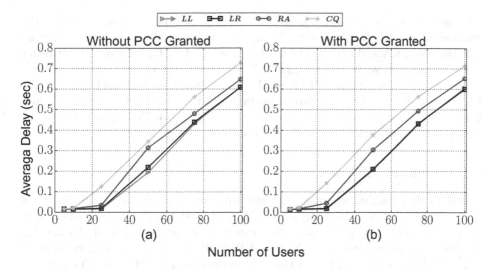

Fig. 2. Average delay experienced by LTE-A equipment types in disjoint queue model.

5.2   Throughput

Figure 3 shows throughput ratio which is experienced by only LTE-A type equipment for four carrier assignment methods according to without and with PCC grant. When the number of users is 25 or less, RA, LL, LR and CQ methods have the optimum throughput (=1) in all cases. It is because RA, LR, LL and

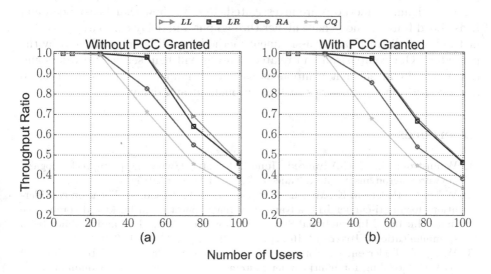

Fig. 3. Throughput ratio experienced by LTE-A equipment types in disjoint queue model.

CQ assign enough and appropriate CCs to LTE-A type equipment. When the number of users is 50 and more, throughput ratios in all methods are decreasing. However, RA and LR with PCC grant have slightly higher throughput ratios than RA and LR without PCC grant. It is reverse for CQ.

Similar to average delay, if the methods are compared with each other, while LL method is the best in terms of average delay without PCC grant, LL and LR methods are the best in terms of average delay with PCC grant. CQ is the worst in terms of average delay for without and with PCC grant.

5.3   Summary of Results

Based on the results, we make the following observations: (i) CQI decreases system performance more than load balancing when the system is under heavy data traffic; (ii) PCC grant procedure can increase performance of RA and LL methods and decrease CQ method; (iii) With PCC grant, the performances of LL and LR are same and higher than the performances of RA and CQ methods and, without PCC grant, the performance of LL is higher than the performances of LR, RA and CQ methods.

6   Conclusion

In this paper, four different component carrier assignment methods are compared by considering LTE-A equipment type by an extensive simulation. Moreover, effects of a procedure which allows one of secondary component carriers to handle the duties of primary component carriers during the primary component carrier reassignment to eliminate packet transfer interruption on four carrier assignment methods are investigated. Results show that Least Load and Least Load Rate methods have higher throughput and delay comparing to other methods and distinct carrier assignment methods are differently affected by the procedure. Our comparison and related analysis will help service providers and researchers build efficient component carrier assignment methods in order to improve performances metrics such as throughput and delay.

References

1. Wannstrom, J.: LTE-Advanced, June 2013. http://www.3gpp.org/technologies/keywords-acronyms/97-lte-advanced. Accessed 18 Mar 2015
2. Wang, Y., Pedersen, K., Mogensen, P., Sorensen, T.: Resource allocation considerations for multi-carrier LTE-advanced systems operating in backward compatible mode. In: IEEE International Symposium on Personal, Indoor and Mobile Radio Communications, Tokyo, 13–16 September 2009, pp. 370–374 (2009)
3. Wang, Y., Pedersen, K., Sorensen, T., Mogensen, P.: Carrier load balancing and packet scheduling for multi-carrier systems. IEEE Trans. Wirel. Commun. 9(5), 1780–1789 (2010)

4. Tian, H., Gao, S., Zhu, J., Chen, L.: Improved component carrier selection method for non-continuous carrier aggregation in LTE-Advanced systems. In: IEEE Vehicular Technology Conference (VTC Fall), San Francisco, CA, 5–8 September 2011 (2011)
5. Liu, L., Li, M., Zhou, J., She, X., Chen, L., Sagae, Y., Iwamura, M.: Component carrier management for carrier aggregation in LTE-advanced system. In: IEEE Vehicular Technology Conference, Budapest, 15–18 May 2011 (2011)
6. Wang, H., Rosa, C., Pedersen, K.: Performance analysis of downlink inter-band carrier aggregation in LTE-advanced. In: IEEE Vehicular Technology Conference, San Francisco, CA, 5–8 September 2011 (2011)
7. Liu, F., Xiang, W., Zhang, Y., Zheng, K., Zhao, H.: A novel QoE-based carrier scheduling scheme in LTE-advanced networks with multi-service. In: Vehicular Technology Conference, Quebec City, Canada, 3–6 September 2012 (2012)
8. Sun, C., Qing, H., Wang, S., Lu, G.: Component carrier selection and beamforming on carrier aggregated channels in heterogeneous networks. Commun. Netw. 5(3B), 211–216 (2013)
9. Shahid, A., Aslam, S., Sohaib, S., Kim, H.S., Lee, K.-G.: A self-organized meta-heuristic approach towards inter-cell interference management for LTE-advanced. EURASIP J. Wirel. Commun. Netw. 1, 171 (2014)
10. Tang, H., Tian, Y., Wang, H., Huang, R.: A component carrier selection algorithm based on channel quality for LTE-advanced system with carrier aggregation. J. Comput. Inf. Syst., 8953–8962 (2014)
11. Chen, Z., Cui, G., Zhai, C., Wang, W., Zhang, Y., Li, X.: Component carrier selection based on user mobility for LTE-advanced systems. In: IEEE 78th Vehicular Technology Conference (VTC Fall), Las Vegas, NV, 2–5 September 2013 (2013)
12. Wang, H., Rosa, C., Pedersen, K.: Uplink component carrier selection for LTE-advanced systems with carrier aggregation. In: IEEE International Conference on Communications, Kyoto, 5–9 June 2011 (2011)
13. Sivaraj, R., Pande, A., Zeng, K., Govindan, K., Mohapatra, P.: Edge-prioritized channel- and traffic-aware uplink carrier aggregation in LTE-advanced systems. In: International Symposium on a World of Wireless, Mobile and Multimedia Networks, San Francisco, CA, 25–28 June 2012 (2012)
14. Marwat, S.N.K., Dong, Y., Li, X., Zaki, Y., Goerg, C.: Novel schemes for component carrier selection and radio resource allocation in LTE-advanced uplink. In: Agüero, R., Zinner, T., Goleva, R., Timm-Giel, A., Tran-Gia, P. (eds.) MONAMI 2014. LNICSSITE, vol. 141, pp. 32–46. Springer, Cham (2015). doi:10.1007/978-3-319-16292-8_3
15. Wannstrom, J.: HSPA, June 2008. http://www.3gpp.org/technologies/keywords-acronyms/99-hspa. Accessed 18 Mar 2015
16. Cheng, X., Gupta, G., Mohapatra, P.: Joint carrier aggregation and packet scheduling in LTE-advanced networks. In: Communications Society Conference on Sensor, Mesh and Ad Hoc Communications and Networks, New Orleans, LA, 24–27 June 2013, pp. 469–477 (2013)
17. Chen, L., Chen, W., Zhang, X., Yang, D.: Analysis and simulation for spectrum aggregation in LTE-advanced system. In: 70th Vehicular Technology Conference, Anchorage, AK, 20–23 September 2009 (2009)
18. Lee, H., Vahid, S., Moessner, K.: A survey of radio resource management for spectrum aggregation in LTE-advanced. IEEE Commun. Surv. Tutorials 16(2), 745–760 (2014)

19. Dean, T., Fleming, P.: Trunking efficiency in multi-carrier CDMA systems. In: 56th Vehicular Technology Conference, Vancouver, Canada, 24–28 September 2002, pp. 156–160 (2002)
20. Lin, L.X., Liu, Y.A., Liu, F., Xie, G., Liu, K.M., Ge, X.Y.: Resource scheduling in downlink LTE-advanced system with carrier aggregation. J. China Univ. Posts Telecommun. 19(1), 44–49 (2012)
21. 3GPP. LTE; evolved universal terrestrial radio access (E-UTRA) and evolved universal terrestrial radio access network (E-UTRAN); overall description; stage 2 (3GPP TS 36.300 version 12.4.0 Release 12), February 2015. http://www.etsi.org/deliver/etsi_ts/136300_136399/136300/12.04.00_60/ts_136300v120400p.pdf. Accessed 18 Mar 2015
22. Ameigeiras, P., Wang, Y., Navarro-Ortiz, J., Mogensen, P., Lopez-Soler, J.: Traffic models impact on OFDMA scheduling design. EURASIP J. Wirel. Commun. Netw. 2012(1), 1–13 (2012)

Quality of Information for Wireless Body Area Networks

Shabana Hamid[1], Anum Talpur[2], Faisal Karim Shaikh[2(✉)], Adil A. Sheikh[3], and Emad Felemban[4]

[1] Department of Bio Medical Engineering, Mehran UET, Jamshoro, Pakistan
[2] Department of Telecommunication Engineering, Mehran UET, Jamshoro, Pakistan
faisal.shaikh@faculty.muet.edu.pk
[3] STU, Umm Al-Qura University, Mecca, Kingdom of Saudi Arabia
[4] Department of Computer Engineering, College of CIS, Umm Al-Qura University, Mecca, Kingdom of Saudi Arabia

Abstract. The Wireless Body Area Networks (WBANs) are a specific group of Wireless Sensor Networks (WSNs) that are used to establish patient monitoring systems which facilitate remote sensing of patients over a long period of time. In this type of system, there is possibility that the information accessible to the health expert at the end point may divert from the original information generated. In some cases, these variations may cause an expert to make a diverse decision from what would have been made specified to the original data. The proposed work contributes toward overcoming this foremost difficulty by defining a quality of information (QoI) metric that helps to preserve the required information. In this paper, we analytically model the QoI as reliability of data generation and reliability of data transfer in WBAN.

Keywords: Body sensor networks · QoI · Relaibility

1 Introduction

The Wireless Body Area Network (WBAN) is a specific type of a network that is designed to connect diverse medical sensors and devices, placed within and outer surface of the human body. The WBAN plays a significant role in ubiquitous communication [1]. A WBAN system uses transportable monitoring devices so it helps to provide mobility of patients [9]. The WBAN system is comprised of one or more sensors which calculate particular data of the patient, like body temperature, blood pressure or heart rate. This data is then sent toward the base station. The communication involving sensor and Mobile Base Unit (MBU) can be over a wire or wireless [1]. In health care domain, from the demography of World Health Organization, there are millions of people who undergo chronic diseases every day. Although, old age people are majorly involved, consequently for such situations WBAN creates its potential to provide instant health monitoring and medical care to the patients.

© ICST Institute for Computer Sciences, Social Informatics and Telecommunications Engineering 2017
J.-H. Lee and S. Pack (Eds.): QShine 2016, LNICST 199, pp. 171–180, 2017.
DOI: 10.1007/978-3-319-60717-7_17

It facilitates remote monitoring of patients. In such type of network there is possibility that the information accessible to health practitioners on end point may vary from the original information that may cause health practitioner to take a different decision for diagnosis from what would have been made using the original data [10]. There are many other optimization problems in wireless health research which creates difficultly to maintain a good quality of data. The Quality of Information (QoI) is the quality identified by the user concerning to the expected information, which completely accomplish the user evolvable constraints and reducing important resources such as bandwidth and energy [4]. The QoI is the collective effect of the available knowledge on information derived from the sensor that determines the degree of precision and confidence that those aspects of the real world (that are of interest to the user) can be represented by this information.

In the WBAN, the patient mobility results in dynamic characteristics of radio propagation. Consequently, the propagation can vary due to absorption, reflection and diffraction of electromagnetic waves around the human body. These variations have significant impact on the channel characteristics and loss of information. Apart from this, latency, accuracy and physical attributes of body sensor network also inherit the information quality.

Some difficulties are also related to the process of data transformation (i.e. wrong manipulation, input errors), and technology (i.e. equipment, body sensors). The technical trade-offs are even not adequate enough so it is necessary to take quality of information into account. There is a need of information measure which can provide the best possible information. To overcome this extensive problem there is a need of quality aware metric, and the appropriate metric was not available to monitor the quality of information. This work approaches to design a quality aware metric for information. The specific contributions of the proposed work are (1) to provide a QoI metric for WBANs, (2) propose a hypothetical model for data quality, and (3) probabilistic model for reliable and timely data transfer.

The remaining paper is composed as follows. The Sect. 2 details the existing work related to the quality of information. The Sect. 3 presents the system model and the approach that is used for designing the quality of information metric. In Sect. 4, the paper describes the analytical evaluation and data modeling of required parameters. Finally, Sect. 5 concludes and suggests for future implementations.

2   Related Work

WBAN is an emerging technology which provides uninterrupted, long-lasting and far-away monitoring of physiological information for diverse medical applications. For the cause of unreliable computation, storage space, and communication abilities of various components in the WBANs, there is a chance that the information reached to the medical health expert present at the remote location may diverge from the original. Therefore, it is necessary to ensure a good

QoI while designing any WBAN application. There also exist many information attributes, that are relevant and useful for QoI in wireless sensors. There also exists an information model in defining information attributes, which benefits to define the existing attributes [6]. To plan an application and use it in an operational perspective, one needs to give more importance on various attributes concerning QoI [6].

The work in [12] presents a framework layer for QoI, focused on the estimation of sensor network operation. This framework layer allocates decomposition of implementation with delaminating that permits the construction of an affluent instrument, required for collecting QoI. The usefulness and the brutality of this work confide in the QoI available with significance of probability based attributes. Another QoI framework for analysis of sensor network is extended in [11] with the subsequent contributions of a smart iterative procedure with a study of preventive activities and the derivation of the estimates to the performance of the system and relative performance of a range of fusion architectures that can accommodate faulty sensor operations. There is also a link between attributes of QoI rapidity and self-assurance and the equipped distinctiveness of sensor systems and events that they sense. The author in [2] shows that when remote sensing data is promoted and the raw data is altered into the valuable data, the information quality for remote sensing data attributes influences QoI attributes to highest level (like speed, accuracy and consistency). Whereas, the work in [3], defines the quality of life-critical information based on traffic load, communication nature and bandwidth occupancy that cause congestion and result in degrading network performance and information quality. Electrocardiogram (ECG), i.e., very commonly monitored health parameter is very sensitive to various types of noise sources. In [8] paper, author targets the quality enhancement of ECG signal by describing a ECG quality index utilizing signal representation with modulation spectral.

This proposed work has developed a new QoI metric for data and information quality of three health parameters while considering the two important information attributes. It is very important for transfer of medical information to be transmitted with good quality. The medical information i.e. related to human health and life. Therefore it needs to be transmitted without any error. The proposed work contributes in solution toward error free transmission.

3   Approach for QoI Metric

3.1   System Design

The BAN system is consists of various physiological sensors such as ECG, SpO2 (Pulse Oximeter Oxygen Saturation), blood pressure, heart rate and body temperature etc. The data from physiological sensors is collected at information abstraction layer where the data is set to implementation details of particular functionality then it goes for data modeling where the modeling of parameters is performed. The quality of information will be assessed by a different analysis process of timeliness and reliability as shown in Fig. 1.

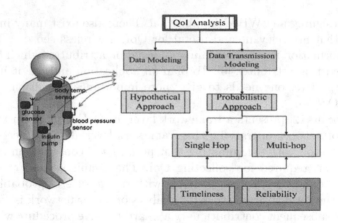

Fig. 1. Sensor network scheme

3.2   Probabilistic Approach for Quality of Information (QoI)

Hypothesis Testing. The hypothesis testing is based on the time premise recognition. The two hypothesis are based on information acquisition (i.e., hypothesis 'H1') or non availability (i.e., hypothesis 'H0').

$$H1 : r_i = s_i + n_i; \quad i = 1, ..., N \tag{1}$$

$$H0 : r_i = n_i; \quad i = 1, ..., N \tag{2}$$

In the hypothesis '$H1$', 's_i' symbolizes the value of the signal at the ith instance of sampling, while in both hypothesis, 'n_i' signifies an extra noise factor which is supplementary to the ith sample, and 'r_i' represents the ith dimension.

Bayesian Hypothesis. Bayes theorem provides the relationship between P(A) and P(B), and the uncertain probabilities given by, $P(A|B)$ and $P(B|A)$.

$$P(A|B) = \frac{P(B|A)}{P(B)}. \tag{3}$$

The significance of above statement is based on the probability analysis of these terms, i.e., $P(A)$ is prior and is confidence degree for 'A', $P(A|B)$ is posterior and confidence degree for 'B', and $P(B|A)/P(B)$ represents the support 'B' provided for 'A'.

Assuming a null hypothesis (H0) and an alternative hypothesis (H1), where the P(H0) and P(H1) are the prior probabilities. The likelihoods are specified by $P(y|H0)$ and $P(y|H1)$, accordingly, $P(H1|y)$ and $P(H0|y)$ are given as.

$$P(H1|y) = \frac{P(y|H1)P(H1)}{P(y|H1)P(H1) + P(y|H0)P(H0)} \tag{4}$$

$$P(H0|y) = 1 - P(H1|y). \tag{5}$$

3.3   Reliability and Timeliness for QoI

The Reliability Block Diagram (RBD) provides a good relationship between WBAN data transport protocol parameters and reliability [7]. The RBD can be used to measure and assess the reliability of information transfer along erroneous channels. We assume that other operations on information are trustworthy and focus on the data transport. The proposed work verifies the operations using logs to evaluate the reliability of accessible data transport protocols by extending corresponding RBDs [5]. For reliable end-to-end (e2e) data delivery, the missing data can be recovered using corresponding Message Loss Detection (MLD) technique and can be retransmitted again. The complete data transport does not end, if the retransmission is failed. Thus, this effect is described as parallel RBD blocks for e2e data delivery. Mathematically, it can be written as

$$R = 1 - ((1 - R_R) * (1 - (R_R * R_{MLD}))^r). \tag{6}$$

where R_R is the routing reliability and R_{MLD} the reliability of MLD. R_R and R_{MLD} vary with respect to the protocols, the network conditions and the WBAN environment where it is deployed.

4   Analytical Evaluation

4.1   Data Modeling of Required Parameters

This research focuses to capture three vital sign parameters i.e. Body Temperature, Blood Pressure (BP) and Heart Rate. Three cases are specified for measuring and analyzing the information quality through considering proposed hypothetical testing. In this work, assumed values for both situations are $P(H1) = 0.75(i.e.75\%)$ and, $P(H0) = 0.25(i.e.25\%)$.

Case 1: For likelihoods assume $P(y|H0) = 0.8$ and $P(y|H1) = 0.2$, then using bayesian hypothesis $P(H0|y)$ will be equal to 8%. It says that the data received at end point will contain 8% noise, so designed data will contain 8% noise in addition with original data.

Case 2: Considering another case with assumed values of $P(y|H1) = 0.6$ and $P(y|H0) = 0.4$, bayesian hypothesis gives $P(H1|y)$ equal to 0.818. This results in $P(H0|y)$ of 18.2% which means additional noise in this case would be 18.2%.

Case 3: In case 3, assuming $P(y|H1) = 0.58$ and $P(y|H0) = 0.42$ gives $P(H1|y) = 0.8$ and $P(H0|y) = 20\%$. This increases noise addition to 20%.

4.2   Body Temperature

The thermal state of the body represents body temperature. It is an estimate of body ability to produce and dispose the amount of heat.

$$\eta_1 = \sum_{i=0}^{n}(It_i - It_D). \tag{7}$$

In Table 1, the body temperature calculations are given. The original data is actual body temperature, the detected noise is the amount of noise, and the designed data is the addition of original data and detected noise. Figure 2 indicate the analytical analysis of body temperature.

Table 1. Body temperature calculation with addition of noise (i.e., 8%, 18.2% and 20%.)

Time	Original Data F^0	Detected noise			Designed data F^0		
		8% Addition	18.20% Addition	20% Addition	8% Addition	18.20% Addition	20% Addition
0800	90	7.2	1.8	16.38	97.2	91.8	106.38
0900	92	7.36	1.84	16.74	99.36	93.84	108.74
1000	93	7.44	1.86	17.11	100.44	94.86	110.11
1100	95	7.6	1.9	17.29	102.6	96.9	112.29
1200	96	7.68	1.92	17.47	103.68	97.92	113.47
1300	98	7.84	1.96	17.83	105.84	99.96	115.83
1400	100	8	2	18.2	108	102	118.2
1500	101	8.08	2.02	18.38	109.08	103.02	119.38
1600	102	8.16	2.04	18.56	110.16	104.04	120.56
1700	104	8.32	2.08	18.92	112.32	106.08	122.92

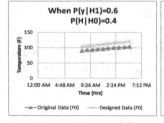 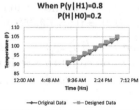 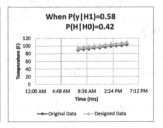

Fig. 2. Analytical analysis of body temperature with (a) 8% noise (b) 18.2% noise (c) 20% noise

4.3   Blood Pressure

The pressure applied by the blood against walls of the blood vessels is called blood pressure (BP). It is fundamental physiological parameter for human beings. The BP differs between systolic pressure (maximum, η_1) and diastolic pressure (minimum, η_2) during each heartbeat. Mathematically it is written as.

$$\eta_1 = \sum_{i=0}^{n} (Is_i - Is_D).$$

(8)

$$\eta_2 = \sum_{i=0}^{n}(Id_i - Id_D). \tag{9}$$

where Is_i and Id_i are ideal systolic and diastolic BP readings. Whereas, Is_D and Id_D are designed BP readings. In Table 2, BP readings at definite time intervals are given. The noise is calculated as difference between the original and designed data (Fig. 3).

Table 2. Blood pressure calculation with addition of noise (i.e. 8%, 18.2% and 20%)

Time	BP mmHg		NOISE						BP designed data					
	Original data		Systolic added noise %			Diastolic added noise %			Systolic added noise %			Diastolic added noise %		
	Systolic	Diastolic	8	18.20	20	8	18.20	20	8	18.20	20	8	18.20	20
0800	110	60	8.8	20.02	2.2	4.8	11.1	1.2	118.8	130.02	112.2	64.8	71.1	61.2
0900	120	70	9.6	21.84	2.2	5.6	12.95	1.4	129.6	141.84	122.2	75.6	82.95	71.4
1000	120	60	9.6	21.84	2.2	4.8	11.1	1.2	129.6	141.84	122.2	64.8	71.1	61.2
1100	120	70	9.6	21.84	2.2	5.6	12.95	1.4	129.6	141.84	122.2	75.6	82.95	71.4
1200	130	70	10.4	23.92	2.6	5.6	12.95	1.4	143	153.92	132.6	68	82.95	71.4
1300	130	80	10.4	23.92	2.6	6.4	14.56	1.6	143	153.92	132.6	88	94.56	81.6
1400	135	85	10.8	24.57	2.7	6.8	15.57	1.7	148.5	159.57	137.7	69	100.57	86.7
1500	140	90	11.2	25.9	2.8	7.2	16.38	1.8	154	165.9	142.8	99	106.38	91.8
1600	130	85	10.4	23.92	2.6	6.8	15.57	1.7	143	153.92	132.6	70	100.57	86.7
1700	140	70	11.2	25.48	2.8	5.6	12.95	1.4	154	165.48	142.8	77	82.95	71.4

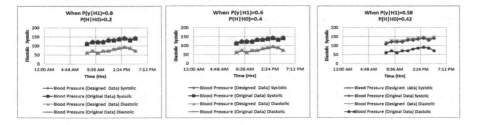

Fig. 3. Analytical analysis of blood pressure with (a) 8% noise (b) 18.2% noise (c) 20% noise

4.4 Heart Rate

The total number of heart beats per unit of time is called as heart rate. It is usually stated as beats per minute (bpm). Mathematically heart beat is given as.

$$\eta = \sum_{i=0}^{n}(Hr_i - Hr_D).k2 \tag{10}$$

where Hr_i is ideal heart rate value and Hr_D is designed heart rate value. The Table 3 depicts original data and designed data obtained by addition of 8%, 18.2% and 20% noise respectively (Fig. 4).

Table 3. Heart beat calculation with addition of noise (i.e., 8%, 18.2% and 20%)

Time	Original Data (bpm)	Detected noise			Designed data (bpm)		
		8% Addition	18.20% Addition	20% Addition	8% Addition	18.20% Addition	20% Addition
0800	68	10.47	1.36	5.4	78.47	69.3	73.4
0900	65	10.01	1.3	5.2	75.01	66.3	70.2
1000	68	10.47	1.36	5.4	78.47	69.36	73.4
1100	68	10.47	1.36	5.4	78.47	69.36	73.4
1200	71	10.93	1.42	5.6	81.93	72.42	76.6
1300	71	10.93	1.42	5.6	81.93	72.42	76.6
1400	68	10.47	1.36	5.4	78.47	69.36	73.4
1500	73	11.24	1.46	5.8	84.24	74.46	78.8
1600	72	11.088	1.44	5.7	83.088	73.44	77.7
1700	72	11.088	1.44	5.7	83.088	73.44	77.7

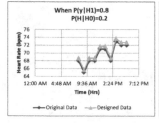 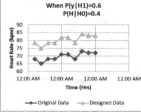 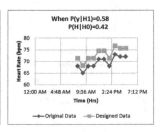

Fig. 4. Analytical analysis of heart rate with (a) 8% noise (b) 18.2% noise (c) 20% noise

4.5   Different Channel Characteristics

For required data reliability and timeliness, the different channel characteristics provide the required number of retransmissions. Therefore, we consider a case for single and multihop WBAN network with timeliness.

Single Hop with Timeliness. Using RBD techniques as discussed in Sect. 3.3, the reliability keeping timeliness requirement is calculated as,

$$R1 = (1 - (1 - H_r)) * (1 - (H_r * MLD * T))^r \qquad (11)$$

where H_r is the hop reliability, MLD is message loss detection and T is the time required to transmit the data over the hop (Fig. 5(a)). From Fig. 5(b) it is evident that generally re-transmissions help in achieving reliability.

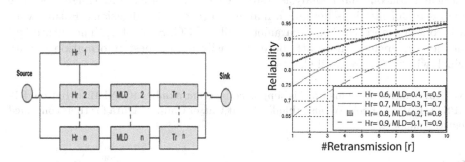

Fig. 5. WBAN single hop data transmission with timeliness; (a) RBD model, (b) analysis

Multiple Hops with Timeliness. The RBD representation of multihop transmission in WBAN with timeliness is given in Fig. 6(a) and mathematically is given as follows.

$$R1 = (1 - (1 - H_r)) * ((1 - (H_r * MLD * T))^r)^n. \tag{12}$$

Figure 6(b) depicts that allowing three retransmissions per hop reasonable reliability is achieved only for 2–3 hops (which is the case for WBAN). As the number of hops increase the reliability is decreased generally.

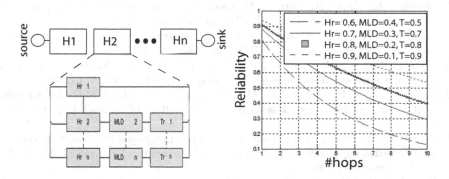

Fig. 6. WBAN multihop data transmission with timeliness; (a) RBD model, (b) analysis

5   Conclusion and Future Work

In WBAN better quality of information helps the health practitioner to make accurate diagnosis. This paper develops a new QoI metric by considering hypothetical erroneous data analysis, data delivery reliability and timeliness. The proposed QoI metric is helpful in making correct health decisions. Future work will consider more vital sign parameters like (ECG, Spo2 etc.). The future QoI metrics will include more attributes to easily obtain best information quality which will be free from all skeptics.

Acknowledgment. This work is supported by grant number 10-INF1236-10 from LT-NPSTI, KACST, KSA. We also thank STU at Uni. of Umm Al-Qura for their continued logistics support.

References

1. Alam, M.M., Hamida, E.B.: Surveying wearable human assistive technology for life and safety critical applications: standards, challenges and opportunities. Sensors **14**(5), 9153–9209 (2014)
2. Bisdikian, C.: On sensor sampling and quality of information: a starting point. In: PerCom Workshops, pp. 279–284 (2007)
3. Ghanavati, S., Abawaji, J., Izadi, D.: A congestion control scheme based on fuzzy logic in wireless body area networks. In: IEEE NCA, pp. 235–242 (2015)
4. Sachidananda, V., Khelil, A., Suri, N.: Quality of information in wireless sensor networks: a survey. In: Proceedings of ICIQ (2010, to appear)
5. Shaikh, F.K., Khelil, A., Ali, A., Suri, N.: TRCCIT: tunable reliability with congestion control for information transport in wireless sensor networks. In: ICST WICON, pp. 1–9 (2010)
6. Shaikh, F.K., Khelil, A., Ayari, B., Szczytowski, P., Suri, N.: Generic information transport for wireless sensor networks. In: IEEE SUTC, pp. 27–34 (2010)
7. Shaikh, F.K., Khelil, A., Suri, N.: On modeling the reliability of data transport in wireless sensor networks. In: IEEE PDP, pp. 395–402 (2007)
8. Tobn, D.P., Falk, T.H.: Online ECG quality assessment for context-aware wireless body area networks. In: IEEE CCECE, pp. 587–592 (2015)
9. Yuce, M.R., Ng, S.W.P., Myo, N.L., Khan, J.Y., Liu, W.: Wireless body sensor network using medical implant band. J. Med. Syst. **31**(6), 467–474 (2007)
10. Zahedi, S., Ngai, E., Gelenbe, E., Mylaraswamy, D., Srivastava, M.B.: Information quality aware sensor network services. In: Proceedings of ACSSC, pp. 1155–1159 (2008)
11. Zahedi, S., Srivastava, M.B., Bisdikian, C.: A computational framework for quality of information analysis for detection-oriented sensor networks. In: IEEE MILCOM, pp. 1–7, November 2008
12. Zahedi, S., Bisdikian, C.: A framework for QoI-inspired analysis for sensor network deployment planning. In: ICST WICON, pp. 1–8 (2007)

Wireless and Mobile Networks

A Network-Based Seamless Handover Scheme with an L2 Extension Mechanism in VANET

Ju-Ho Choi[1]([✉]), Jung-Hwan Cha[1], Sung-Gi Min[1], and Youn-Hee Han[2]

[1] Korea University, Seoul, Republic of Korea
{jubong,jokercha,sgmin}@korea.ac.kr
[2] Korea University of Technology and Education, Cheonan, Republic of Korea
yhhan@koreatech.ac.kr

Abstract. A smart vehicle becomes a communication device with the advance of VANETs. In the WAVE standards, which is the well-known VANET standards, RSUs interconnect a VANETs to the Internet, and they act as default routers for the vehicles. However, the WAVE standards have eliminated the L2 portal function, which was included in the previous WAVE standards. Due to the short communication range of RSUs and vehicles' high speed, a vehicle may have to change its point of attachment frequently. The change of the default router causes severe service interruption due to the standard IPv6 protocol's functions such as the address auto-configuration, DAD and NUD. We propose a new seamless handover scheme with an L2 extension mechanism without any modification of the WAVE standards. It increases the coverage of an access router to multiple RSU coverage, while the frequency of the default router changes can be decreased. It also supports seamless packet delivery during the change of the points of attachment. By decoupling the RSU and the access router, the deployment of the WAVE can be more flexible. The proposed mechanism is simulated with ns-3 and its results show the effectiveness of the proposed scheme.

Keywords: Vehicular communications · WAVE · Seamless handover

1 Introduction

Vehicular Ad hoc NETworks (VANETs) has attracted a lot of interest in the communication research area due to their potential to increase road safety. In addition, to meet users' demands in vehicles for new applications [5,6], it is necessary to connect VANETs to the Internet. The WAVE reference model [2] shows that the RSU acts as the default gateway for the vehicles. A vehicle must use the non-association MAC frame, which has only two addresses. The address 1 field must be the destination address of the MAC frame, and also be the target device address in the IEEE 802.11 link. Therefore, the RSU should be the final destination of the link layer.

Considering the high mobility of vehicles and short communication range between vehicles and RSUs (Road Side Unit), however, a vehicle usually passes

© ICST Institute for Computer Sciences, Social Informatics and Telecommunications Engineering 2017
J.-H. Lee and S. Pack (Eds.): QShine 2016, LNICST 199, pp. 183–192, 2017.
DOI: 10.1007/978-3-319-60717-7_18

an RSU quickly and meets another RSU frequently in its path. The vehicle receives different WRAs (Wave Routing Advertisement) from two RSUs. In the WAVE standards [2], the WRA replaces the RA (Router Advertisement) and NDP (Neighbor Discovery Protocol) [10]. When the vehicle receives a new WRA, it has to generate an IP address and to change its default router. To generate new IP address using address auto-configuration, the DAD (Duplicate Address Detection) [7] has to be executed. To change its default router, NUD (Neighbor Unreachability Detection) must be considered. The NUD requires at least three seconds delay [8]. In addition, the change of the current IP address requires an L3 handover mechanism to maintain the current IP session.

In this paper, we propose an L2 extension mechanism without any modification in the WAVE standards. The proposed scheme decouples the RSU functions and the default router. It does not change the WAVE interface and adds bridging and handover functions into the wired interface in the RSU. The Access Router (AR) connected to RSUs has a handover function to support the seamless handover among RSUs. As the access router can connect several RSUs, the coverage of the access router can be expanded to the coverage of its RSUs. It reduces the L3 handover frequency as the change of an RSU does not mean the change of the default router. The proposed network based handover scheme supports seamless packet delivery.

The rest of the paper is organized as follows. Section 2 introduces the related work in the area. Section 3 presents the proposed overall architecture to provide the handover process. Section 4 describes a simulation setup along with the simulation results. Finally, Sect. 5 concludes this paper.

2   Related Works

The WAVE standards consists of IEEE 1609 [2–4] series and IEEE 802.11p [1]. The WAVE defines two kinds of channels: CCH (Control CHannel) and SCH (Service CHannel). The CCH is used to send vehicle safety messages generated by several VANETs applications [9]. All vehicles and RSUs have to monitor the CCH(s) to detect surrounding traffic environment. An RSU can detect vehicles as they emit safety beacons. The SCHs are employed by IP to support non-safety applications. IEEE 802.11p defines non-association operation. The To DS/From DS bits in the MAC frame have to set to all zeros. The BSS ID field is filled with all ones. Only two addresses are used in the 802.11 MAC frame. The address 1 field must be used as the destination address as well as the target address of the wireless LAN. An RSU must be the destination and the target device for vehicles. The RSU must be a default router of the VANETs. The 1609.0 reference model shown in the Fig. 1 verifies that the RSU is a router connecting the VANETs and the Internet. A vehicle has to get an IP address and the default router information to use the Internet. IEEE 1609.0 specifies the WRA, which contains the network prefix and the MAC address of the default router, and the WRA may be included in the WSA (WAVE Service Announcement). When the vehicle receives a WSA with WRA, the vehicle can generate its IP address using address auto-configuration mechanism and get the MAC address of the default router.

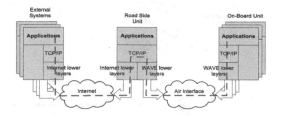

Fig. 1. 1609.0 reference model [2]

Several handover schemes [11–14] are proposed. They are the host-based handover schemes. Proactive caching and forwarding scheme [11] uses the old WAVE standards (2007) [15] as well as IEEE 802.11f which was withdrawn. WAVE point coordination function (WPCF) [12] uses the old WAVE standards, and it modifies the WSA to include the vehicles' MAC addresses sorted by the urgency of the vehicles. It focuses on minimization of the handover delay, and does not consider a seamless handover. VIP-WAVE [13] uses the current WAVE standards, and adopts the PMIPv6 to deal with mobility issues in VANETs. The PMIPv6 is an L3 handover solution and it does not support seamlessness. In [14], authors use the current WAVE standards and RSSIs (Receive Signal Strength Indicator) to decide the handover moment. It does not consider the seamlessness of packet delivery.

3 Proposed L2 Extension Mechanism

3.1 Our System Architecture

The L2 extension mechanism is proposed to extend the coverage of an AR by connecting RSUs with L2 switches. The overall system consists of 4 components: vehicles, RSUs, L2 switches and an AR. Figure 2 shows a simple configuration of the system.

Vehicles communicate with RSUs or other vehicle using the WAVE standards [1,3,4]. We assume that the vehicle executes at least one safety application specified in [9]. The safety beacon generated by the safety application includes the vehicle's current location and direction information.

L2 switches are ordinary Ethernet switches with the VLAN function. Each pair of an RSU and the AR consists of a VLAN in the link. The VLAN is used to decouple the RSU and the AR roles in the proposed system. Each VLAN acts as a WAVE interface, so it replaces the embedded WAVE interface of the AR required by the WAVE standards.

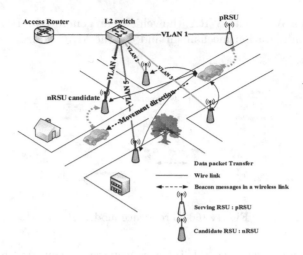

Fig. 2. Our system architecture

An RSU is an access point of the WAVE network for vehicles. It bridges the WAVE network with the Internet at the data link layer. An RSU has two interfaces: one for the WAVE networks and the other for the Internet.

An RSU has to monitor vehicles' safety beacon by tuning CCH. According to the CAMP (Crash Avoidance Metrics Partnership), almost all contain at least the position and the direction information of the vehicle [16]. The RSU can know a vehicle's position and direction passively. The RSU stores these information into its RCT (RSU Cache Table). Each entry of the RCT contains the MAC address, the latest receiving time and the position information.

To support a network based seamless handover, the RSU has to notify the AR about vehicle's movements but only the significant movements. To categorize the significance of a vehicle's movement, the RSU divides its coverage area into two zones. One is the normal zone and the other is the handover zone. The normal zone is defined within 370 m from the RSU. It is because the reliable communication range of VANETs without any obstructions is to be under 370 m [17]. The handover zone is the outside of the normal zone. An RSU processes all incoming safety beacons with its RCT, and sends a control message to the AR only for three cases. Firstly, it sends an AI (Attachment Indication) if a vehicle's information does not exist in the RCT and the vehicle is moving toward the RSU. Secondly, the RSU sends an HP (Handover Prepare) if the vehicle reaches the handover zone and it is moving away from the RSU. Finally it sends a DI (Detachment Indication), provided that no beacon is arrived from the vehicle for the predefined time or the RSU fails to deliver three consecutive frames to the vehicle. The serving RSU forwards packets to the vehicle even if the vehicle is in the handover zone as the comminution link between them is still alive. However, the communication link may down any time in the handover area. The RSU and the AR interacts to buffer undelivered packets exactly. The RSU knows a packet

Vehicle MAC	Rx. time	Position
MAC_A	10:15:38:19	30, 33
MAC_B	10:15:38:28	33, 33

Vehicle MAC	Serving RSU MAC	VLAN ID	Position
MAC_A	RSU_A	1	30, 33
MAC_B	RSU_B	2	33, 33

(a) RSU Cache Table   (b) AR Binding Table

Fig. 3. Data structure in network elements

delivery status using IEEE 802.11 ARQ mechanism, and it notifies it to the AR using an ARQ message.

According to the 802.11 MAC operations [18], the RSU does not process the MAC frame which has AR's MAC address in the address 1 field. To add bridging function in the RSU, it needs to process at least two MAC addresses in the address 1 field. First one is its MAC address, and second one is AR's MAC address.

An AR is a default router of the Internet for the WAVE network connecting several RSUs using L2 switches.

The AR makes the handover decision based on the control messages sent from RSUs and maintains an ABT (AR Binding Table) to store handover information in the control messages. Each entry of the ABT contains the vehicle MAC address, the RSU MAC address, VLAN ID (VID) and the position information. Figure 3(b) shows an example of the ABT.

By receiving AIs, the AR knows appearance of new vehicle or the entrance of a vehicle to a new coverage area of RSU. If the AR receives the AI and a vehicle is not registered in the ABT, it recognizes the vehicle as new one. It creates new entry for the vehicle and chooses the sending RSU as the serving RSU. If an AI is arrived for the vehicle which has its entry in the ABT or the AR has buffered packets for the vehicle in its buffer, it chooses the sending RSU as a new RSU. It updates its entry in the ABT and starts to send the buffered packets to the vehicle via the new RSU.

When the vehicle reaches the handover zone of the serving RSU, the AR detects this event by the HP. The AR starts packet buffering to prepare the handover, but it still forwards packets to the vehicle via the previous RSU (pRSU) until new RSU is selected or the pRSU cannot reach the vehicle anymore. The AR and the pRSU interact to track the exactly undelivered packet. The pRSU sends an ARQ-NACK for each unsuccessful delivery with a part of undelivered packet to the AR. The AR tries to match the packet in its buffer until it finds the matched packet, and removes the packet from the front of the buffer to the matched one. It mitigates redundant packet buffering. The pRSU may send the ARQ-ACK for each delivered packet to reduce the number of buffered packets. The AR does not retransmit the undelivered packet as recovering lost packet is not the role of the AR.

If the AR receives the DI, it stops packet forwarding and keeps buffering until it receives the AI from another RSU or the predefined timer expires.

3.2 Control Messages

For interaction between the AR and RSUs, new control message is defined. It uses the Ethernet frame with a new Ethertype. The message uses TLV (Type-Length-Value) format. The Type field defines the control message type. The first bit of the type field represent whether the message is for vehicle tracking or the ARQ. The Length field indicates the length of the following data. The first element of the data field is the vehicle MAC address. Vehicle tracking message contains additional position information. The ARQ message optionally contains the first 46 bytes of the original packet. The 46 bytes are chosen to include the Ethernet MAC header, the IP header and the TCP (UDP) header. As the Ethernet packet has to have at least 64 bytes, adding the part of original packet doesn't matter.

3.3 Handover Procedure

A handover occurs between two RSUs. The coverage areas of two RSU may be disjointed or overlapped. Figure 4(a) and (b) show two cases respectively. The handover procedure is almost same in the both cases, but the only difference is that the detachment event is occurred in the former case. The overall handover procedure is described in Fig. 5.

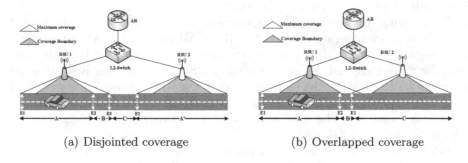

(a) Disjointed coverage   (b) Overlapped coverage

Fig. 4. RSU deployment

Event 1: Detecting new vehicle (Section A): A RSU 1 detects an entrance of a vehicle from the vehicle's safety beacon. It generates an entry of the RCT and sends an AI to the AR. The AR creates new entry for the vehicle and chooses the sending RSU as the serving RSU. The vehicle starts a communication with a peer in the Internet. The AR relays data packets between them via RSU 1.

Event 2: Entering the handover zone in the RSU 1 (Section B): Whenever the RSU 1 receives the safety beacon from the vehicle, it checks the vehicle's current position to know whether the vehicle is located in its handover zone. If so, it sends the HP to the AR to inform that the handover may be happen soon. The AR starts packet buffering. It still forwards data packets via the RSU 1 to the vehicle. The AR and the RSU 1 start to interact with an ARQ mechanism. Whenever a packet is not delivered to the vehicle, the RSU 1 sends the NACK.

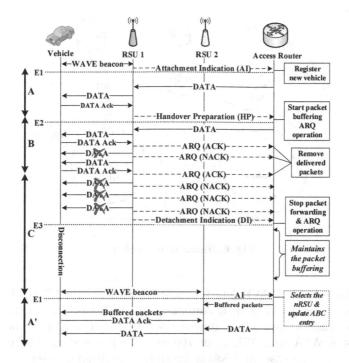

Fig. 5. Handover procedure

The AR eliminates packets from the it buffer. The RSU 1 optionally send the ACK for successfully delivered packet.

Event 3: Disconnection (Section C. The disjoint coverage case only): As the vehicle moves out of the scope of the RSU 1, the RSU 1 cannot receive the safety beacon anymore from the vehicle and/or fails to deliver packets to the vehicle consecutively. The RSU 1 sends the DI to the AR. The AR stops packet forwarding, but maintains buffering until it receives the AI from another RSU or the predefined timer expires. The disconnection occurs when the coverage areas of two RSU are disjoint.

Event 1: Entering coverage of RSU 2 (Section A'): The RSU 2 detects the vehicle from the safety beacon. As the vehicle is moving into the RSU 2's area, the RSU 2 creates a new RCT entry and sends the AI. The AR has an matching entry in the ABT and it knows that the vehicle moves to the RSU 2. The AR updates the RSU MAC address and the VID field. The AR forwards buffered packets to the vehicle via the RSU 2.

4   Simulation

To simulate the proposed scheme, ns-3 network simulator (version 3.23) and its WAVE model library are used. The network topology for the simulation is shown in Fig. 6.

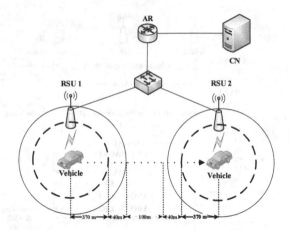

Fig. 6. Simulation topology

The vehicle has a WAVE interface and moves from RSU 1 to RSU 2 with the constant velocity (25 m/s). It communicates with the CN via the AR. The vehicle broadcasts a basic safety message per 100 ms. The RSU 1 and the RSU 2 broadcast a WSA with WRA per 100 ms. The RSUs stand 760 m apart for overlapped coverage case, and 880 m apart for the disjoint coverage case. The maximum coverage of each RSU is set for 410 m. The L2 switch connects RSUs with the AR via an Ethernet. The CN is connected to the AR. All wired link speeds are 100 Mbps. The link delay between the CN and the AR is 60 ms and all other link delays are 10 ms. The wireless link speeds are 6 Mbps. A 500 Kbps CBR traffic flows from the CN to the vehicle and the UDP is used to carry the traffic.

Simulations are performed under the four different scenarios. The RSUs sends control messages to the AR in all scenarios. In Scenario 1 (S1), simulation is performed without VLAN configuration and buffering scheme. In Scenario 2 (S2), simulation is performed only with the VLAN configuration. In Scenario 3 (S3) and Scenario 4 (S4) simulations are performed with buffering scheme and VLAN configuration. The S3 is performed under disjoint coverage, whereas S4 is performed under overlap coverage.

Figure 7 shows the received packet sequences at the vehicle. Before the handover occurs, all packets are successfully delivered to the vehicle. The S1 simulation result in Fig. 7(a) shows the need of the VLAN configuration. Even if the AR knows the vehicle is in the RSU 2, the vehicle cannot receive packets after the handover occurs. As the frame carrying an UDP packet does not contain RSU 2 MAC address, the L2-switch with the self-learning mechanism forwards the frame to the RSU 1 until the vehicle at RSU 2 generates any up-link packet to the AR. The S2 simulation result in Fig. 7(b) presents some packet loss due to the absence of buffering at the AR. The S3 and S4 simulation results show the effectiveness of packet buffering at the AR. In Fig. 7(c), all buffered packets are delivered to the vehicle rapidly after the RSU 2 detects the vehicle. The S4

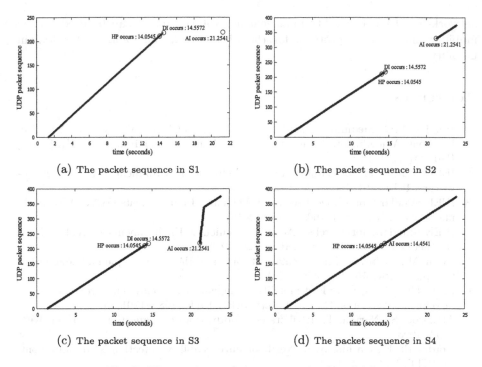

Fig. 7. The receive packet sequences in the vehicle

simulation result presented in Fig. 7(d) shows the consecutive packet delivery even if the handover occurs. The WAVE interface does not require the association procedure and the coverage of two RSUs are overlapped. Therefore, two connections, one for each RSU, are available during the handover period. It is the same as that of the soft handover. The vehicle can receive packets continuously.

5   Conclusion

We proposed an L2 extension mechanism with a network-based seamless handover scheme in VANETs. It reduces the L3 handover frequency by deploying several RSUs under an AR. In the proposed scheme, the RSU tracks the vehicle's movement using its safety beacon passively and it notifies the vehicle's significant movement events to the AR. The AR uses such notifications to start buffering for seamless packet delivery and to make handover decision. Simulation results show effectiveness of the proposed scheme. However, the proposed scheme only deals with the L2 handover. Eventually it needs some L3 handover schemes when a vehicle moves away from the AR's coverage.

As future work, we plan to adapt the existing L3 handover schemes incorporating the proposed L2 extension mechanism. PMIPv6 and LISP are good candidates of the VANETs-wide mobility management protocol. PMIPv6 is a network-based local mobility management protocol and it can be used a local mobility management protocol for the LISP which can handle inter-domain mobility.

References

1. Wireless LAN Medium Access Control (MAC) and Physical Layer (PHY) Specifications Amendment: Wireless Access in Vehicular Environments. IEEE Std, P802.11p (2010)
2. IEEE IEEE Guide for Wireless Access in Vehicular Environments (WAVE) - Architecture. IEEE Std, 1609.0-2013 (2014)
3. IEEE Standard for Wireless Access in Vehicular Environments (WAVE) Networking Services. IEEE Std, 1609.3-2010 (2010)
4. IEEE Standard for Wireless Access in Vehicular Environments (WAVE) Multichannel Operation. IEEE Std, 1609.4-2010 (2011)
5. Gerla, M., Kleinrock, L.: Vehicular networks and the future of the mobile internet. Comput. Netw. **55**, 457–469 (2011)
6. Park, J.T., Chun, S.M.: Fast mobility management for delay-sensitive applications in vehicular networks. Commun. Lett. IEEE **15**(1), 1689–1701 (2012)
7. Thomson, S., Narten, T.: IPv6 stateless address autoconguration. In: IETF RFC 2462 (1998)
8. Nordmark, E., Gashinsky, I.: Neighbor unreachability detection is too impatient. In: IETF, RFC 7048 (2014)
9. CAMP Vehicle Safety Communication Consortium: Vehicle safety communications project task 3 final report - identify intelligent vehicle safety applications enabled by DSRC. In: DOT HS, pp. 809–859 (2005)
10. Narten, T., Nordmark, E., Simpson, W., Soliman, H.: Neighbor discovery for IP version 6 (IPv6). In: IETF, RFC4861 (DraftStandard) (2007)
11. Chung, Y.-U., et al.: Proactive caching and forwarding schemes for seamless handover in IEEE WAVE networks. Int. J. Distrib. Sens. Netw. **9**, 627–691 (2013)
12. Chung, J.M., et al.: Time coordinated V2I communications and handover for WAVE networks. IEEE J. Sel. Areas Commun. **29**, 545–558 (2011)
13. Cespedes, S., et al.: VIP-WAVE: On the feasibility of IP communications in 802.11p vehicular networks. Intell. Transp. Syst. **14**, 82–97 (2013)
14. Cho, W., et al.: Implementation of handover under multi-channel operation in IEEE 802.11p based communication system. In: ICT Convergence (2011)
15. IEEE Trial-Use Standard for Wireless Access in Vehicular Environments (WAVE) - Networking Services. IEEE Std, 1609.3-2007 (2007)
16. Lee, J.-M., et al.: Performance analysis of WAVE control channels for public safety services in VANETs. Int. J. Comput. Commun. Eng. **2**, 563–570 (2013)
17. Meireles, R., et al.: Experimental study on the impact of vehicular obstructions in VANETs. In: Vehicular Networking Conference (VNC), pp. 338–345 (2010)
18. Wireless LAN Medium Access Control (MAC) and Physical Layer (PHY) Specifications. IEEE Std, 802.11-2012 (2012)

Delayed Location Management in Network Mobility Environments

Haneul Ko[1], Sangheon Pack[1(✉)], Jong-Hyouk Lee[2], and Alexandru Petrescu[3]

[1] School of Electrical Engineering, Korea University, Seoul, Korea
{st_basket,shpack}@korea.ac.kr
[2] Department of Computer Science and Engineering,
Sangmyung University, Cheonan, Korea
jonghyouk@smu.ac.kr
[3] Communicating Systems Laboratory, CEA, LIST, Paris, France
alexandru.petrescu@cea.fr

Abstract. Network mobility basic support (NEMO-BS) supports efficient group mobility. However, when NEMO-BS is applied to public transportation systems where mobile nodes (MNs) frequently get in/off the public transportation, significant signaling overhead owing to frequent and unnecessary binding updates can occur. To address this problem, we propose a delayed location management (DLM) scheme where an MN postpones its binding update for a pre-defined timer to mitigate the binding update overhead. To evaluate the performance of DLM, we develop an analytical model for the binding update cost and the packet delivery cost during the boarding time. Evaluation results demonstrate that DLM can reduce the binding update cost and packet delivery cost by choosing an appropriate timer.

Keywords: Network mobility (NEMO) · Mobility management · Location management · Public transportation

1 Introduction

Network mobility basic support (NEMO-BS) is a mobility support protocol where a collective mobility of multiple mobile nodes (MNs) is handled as a single unit [1,2]. When MNs are connected to a mobile network (MONET), a mobile router (MR) broadcasts a router advertisement (RA) message with its mobile network prefix (MNP) and then MNs configure their care of addresses (CoAs) based on the MR's MNP. After that, MNs conduct binding updates to their home agents (HAs). Then, when the MONET moves to a new access router (AR), only MR conducts the binding update to its HA while MNs in the MONET do not need to execute any binding updates.

However, when NEMO-BS is applied to a public transportation, unnecessary signaling overhead due to binding updates can occur since MNs frequently get in/off the public transportation. Specifically, when an MN gets off before the

© ICST Institute for Computer Sciences, Social Informatics and Telecommunications Engineering 2017
J.-H. Lee and S. Pack (Eds.): QShine 2016, LNICST 199, pp. 193–201, 2017.
DOI: 10.1007/978-3-319-60717-7_19

public transportation moves to another AR (i.e., an MN has a short boarding time), the binding update for MN's CoA based on the MR's MNP can be unnecessary. Figure 1 shows an example of the unnecessary binding update. When an MN gets in a public transportation (Step 1 in Fig. 1), the MN configures its CoA based on the MR's MNP and conducts a binding update to its HA (Steps 2–3 in Fig. 1). Then, when the public transportation moves to another bus station (Step 4 in Fig. 1), the MN gets off the public transportation (Step 5 in Fig. 1). In this case, the binding update in Step 3 for supporting collective mobility is useless. Note that the distance between two bus stops in local bus service is typically 300–400 m [3] and the maximum diameter for one macro-cell is 3 km in urban areas [4]. In such environments, there is non-negligible probability that an MN gets off before the public transportation moves to another AR.

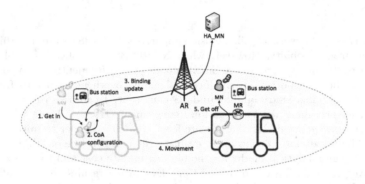

Fig. 1. Example of the wasting binding update.

Intuitively, if an MN with short boarding time does not conduct instantly the binding update when the MN gets in the public transportation, such unnecessary binding update can be reduced. Based on this idea, we propose a delayed location management (DLM) scheme where an MN postpones its binding update until a pre-defined timer T expires. In DLM, the mobility of the MN is managed by mobile IPv6 (MIPv6) before the timer expiration. On the other hand, after the timer expiration, the mobility of the MN is handled by the MR. Therefore, the packets to the MN are forwarded through MN's HA, MR's HA, and MR. Also, the MN does not need to conduct any binding update when the public transportation handovers to another AR. To evaluate the performance of DLM, we develop an analytical model for the binding update cost and the packet delivery cost during the MR attachment time. Evaluation results demonstrate that DLM can reduce the binding update cost and packet delivery cost by choosing an appropriate timer.

The remainder of this paper is organized as follows. The related works are summarized in Sect. 2. The detailed operation of DLM is described in Sect. 3. The performance analysis model is illustrated in Sect. 4. Evaluation results and concluding remarks are given in Sects. 5 and 6, respectively.

2 Related Works

To improve the performance of NEMO-BS, a number of schemes have been proposed in the literature [5–10]. Qiang *et al.* [5] suggested an adaptive route optimization scheme which consists of the mobility transparency sub-scheme and the time saving sub-scheme, and a threshold is introduced to determine which sub-scheme is used in the current situation. In [6], Kim *et al.* proposed a simple route optimization (S-RO) scheme where a correspondent node (CN) maintains binding information of MRs to obtain the optimal path to the MN. Cho *et al.* [7] introduced a routing optimization scheme using a tree information option (ROTIO). In this scheme, each MR sends two binding update messages to the top-level MR (TLMR) and its HA, respectively. Then, the packets to the MN in the public transportation are transmitted only through the HA of the MR and the TLMR. Calderon *et al.* [8] introduced a mobile IPv6 route optimization for NEMO (MIRON) scheme based on the carrying authentication for network access (PANA) and the dynamic host configuration protocol (DHCPv6) by modifying the software in the MR. Chuang and Lee [9] proposed a domain-based route optimization (DRO) scheme which incorporates ad-hoc routing techniques and uses a double buffer mechanism to achieve route optimization. Barman *et al.* [10] suggested a route optimization method by introducing two new IPv6 extension headers named as anchor point request (APR) and anchor point grant (AGR). However, the binding update cost for the CoA derived from the MR's MNP is not considered in these works [5–10].

3 Delayed Location Management (DLM)

In this section, we explain the operations of DLM, which is dependent on whether the timer T expires or not. For example, before the timer T expires, the packets destined to the MN are transmitted through only HA_MN and the MN conducts the binding update whenever the public transportation moves to another AR. On the other hand, after the timer expiration, when a CN sends packets to the MN, the packets are transmitted through HA_MN, HA_MR, and MR. Also, since the mobility of the MN is managed by the MR after the timer expiration, the MN needs not to conduct any binding update even though the public transportation moves to another AR.

Figure 2 shows the operation example of DLM when MN 1 and MN 2 have short and long boarding times, respectively. At the first time, when MN 1 and MN 2 get in the public transportation at τ_0, the MR sends a RA message to MNs (Step 1 in Fig. 2). Then, MN 1 and MN 2 start their timers. Since MN 1 does not conduct any binding update to its HA before the timer expiration, packets are forwarded to MN 1 only through HA_MN when the CN sends the packets to MN 1 at τ_1 (Step 2 in Fig. 2). When MN 1 gets off the public transportation before the timer expires at τ_2 (i.e., short boarding time), MN 1 does not conduct the binding update for its CoA based on MR's MNP, which can save the binding update cost.

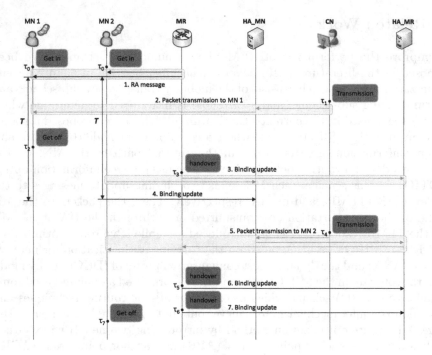

Fig. 2. Operation of DLM.

Meanwhile, since MN 2 with long boarding time does not yet conduct the binding update when the public transportation handovers to another AR at τ_3, both MN 2 and MR should execute binding updates to their HAs (Step 3 in Fig. 2). In other words, MNs conduct their binding updates individually before the timer expiration whenever the public transportation handovers to another AR, which increases binding update cost. After the timer expires, MN 2 executes a binding update for its CoA based on MR's MNP to HA_MN (Step 4 in Fig. 2). From this time, the mobility of MN 2 is managed by MR. Therefore, when the CN sends the packet to MN 2 at τ_4, the packets are forwarded to MN 2 through the detour path, i.e., HA_MN, HA_MR, and MR (Step 5 in Fig. 2). On the other hand, when the MR handovers to another AR at τ_5 and τ_6, only MR sends a binding update message to HA_MR whereas MN 2 does not conduct any binding update (Steps 6–7 in Fig. 2).

4   Performance Analysis

In this section, we develop an analytical model for the total cost that consists of the binding update cost and the packet delivery cost during the MR attachment time. The MR attachment time represents the period between when an MN gets on and when it gets off the public transportation (i.e., the boarding time of the MN). Important notations for the analytical model are summarized in Table 1.

Table 1. Summary of notations.

Notation	Description
t_M	MR attachment time
$t_{S,k}$	kth inter-session arrival time
$t_{R,k}$	kth residence time
T	Timer value
C_{total}	Total cost during the MR attachment time
C^I	Cost for case I
C^{II}	Cost for case II
C_B^I	Binding update cost for case I
C_P^I	Packet delivery cost for case I
C_B^{II}	Binding update cost for case II
C_B	Unit cost for the binding update
C_P	Additional unit cost for the packet delivery
$\alpha_S(k)$	Probability that the MN has k sessions during t_M
$\alpha_R(k)$	Probability that the MR moves across k ARs

4.1 Total Cost of DLM

In DLM, the total cost during the MR attachment time, t_M, can be derived from the following two cases: case (I) t_M is larger than the timer value T (see MN 2 in Fig. 2) and case (II) t_M is equal to or smaller than T (see MN 1 in Fig. 2). Then, the total cost, C_{total}, can be represented by

$$C_{total} = P[t_M > T]C^I + P[t_M \leq T]C^{II} \tag{1}$$

where C^I and C^{II} represent the total cost for cases I and II, respectively.

When we assume that t_M follows an exponential distribution with mean $1/\lambda_M$, $P[t_M > T]$ and $P[t_M \leq T]$ are respectively derived as

$$P[t_M > T] = \int_T^\infty \lambda_M e^{-\lambda_M t} dt_M = e^{-\lambda_M T} \tag{2}$$

and

$$P[t_M \leq T] = \int_0^T \lambda_M e^{-\lambda_M t} dt_M = 1 - e^{-\lambda_M T}. \tag{3}$$

Meanwhile, C^I consists of the binding update cost and the packet delivery cost, i.e., $C^I = C_B^I + C_P^I$ where C_B^I and C_P^I denote the binding update cost and the packet delivery cost in case I, respectively.

In case I (i.e., $t_M > T$), the MN conducts the binding update to its HA whenever the MR handovers to another AR before the timer expiration. Also, when the timer expires, the MN executes another binding update to its HA. Therefore, C_B^I can be represented by

$$C_B^I = C_B \left(E[N_R] + 1 \right) \tag{4}$$

where $E[N_R]$ is the expected number of MR handovers during T and C_B represents the unit cost for the binding update. When we assume that the kth residence time, $t_{R,k}$, is drawn from a Gamma distribution with mean $1/\lambda_R$ and variance V_R [11,12], $E[N_R]$ can be computed as $E[N_R] = \lambda_R T$ by Little's law [13].

On the other hand, the packets are transmitted only through HA-MN before the timer expiration. On the contrary, the packets are transmitted through HA-MN, HA-MR, and MR after the timer expiration. That is, additional packet delivery cost incurs for sessions after the timer expires. When $\alpha_S(k)$ denotes the probability that the MN has k sessions during t_M, the expected number of sessions during t_M can be calculated as $\sum_{k=1}^{\infty} k\alpha_S(k)$. Therefore, the number of sessions which result in additional packet delivery cost (i.e., sessions after the timer expiration) can be obtained by $\sum_{k=1}^{\infty} k\alpha_S(k) - E[N_S]$ where $E[N_S]$ is the expected number of sessions during T. Then, C_P^I can be represented by

$$C_P^I = C_P \left[\sum_{k=1}^{\infty} k\alpha_S(k) - E[N_S] \right] \tag{5}$$

where C_P represents the unit cost for the additional packet delivery. If $C_{P,B}$ and $C_{P,A}$ denote the unit costs for the packet delivery before and after the timer expiration, respectively, C_P can be obtained from $C_{P,A} - C_{P,B}$.

When we assume that the kth inter-session arrival time, $t_{S,k}$, is drawn from a Gamma distribution with mean $1/\lambda_S$ and variance V_S, as similar to $E[N_R]$, $E[N_S]$ can be computed as $E[N_S] = \lambda_S T$ [13]. Also, $\alpha_S(k)$ is obtained as [14]

$$\alpha_S(k) = \frac{\lambda_S}{\lambda_M} \left[1 - f_S^*(\lambda_M) \right]^2 \left[f_S^*(\lambda_M) \right]^{k-1} \tag{6}$$

where $f_S^*(s)$ denotes the Laplace transforms of t_S, which is given by $f_S^*(s) = \left(\frac{\lambda_S \gamma_S}{s + \lambda_S \gamma_S} \right)^{\gamma_S}$ where $\gamma_S = \frac{1}{V_S \lambda_S^2}$ [11].

In case II (i.e., $t_M \leq T$), since the timer does not expire during t_M, there is no packet that needs additional packet delivery cost. Therefore, C^{II} includes only the binding update cost, i.e., $C^{II} = C_B^{II}$ where C_B^{II} is the binding update cost for case II. Since the expected number of handovers during t_M can be computed as $\sum_{k=1}^{\infty} k\alpha_R(k)$ where $\alpha_R(k)$ is the probability that the MR moves across k ARs during t_M, C^{II} can be derived from

$$C^{II} = C_B \sum_{k=1}^{\infty} k\alpha_R(k). \tag{7}$$

As similar to (6), $\alpha_R(k)$ is given by [14]

$$\alpha_R(k) = \frac{\lambda_R}{\lambda_M} \left[1 - f_R^*(\lambda_M)\right]^2 \left[f_R^*(\lambda_M)\right]^{k-1} \tag{8}$$

where $f_R^*(s)$ denotes the Laplace transforms of t_R which is represented by $f_R^*(s) = \left(\frac{\lambda_R \gamma_R}{s + \lambda_R \gamma_R}\right)^{\gamma_R}$ where $\gamma_R = \frac{1}{V_R \lambda_R^2}$ [11].

4.2   Total Cost of Conventional Schemes

Total Cost of NEMO-BS. In NEMO-BS, the MN conducts only one binding update right after the MN gets in the public transportation and configures its CoA. On the other hand, every packet is transmitted through HA_MN, HA_MR, and MR. Therefore, additional packet delivery cost for every packet incurs during the MR attachment time. Therefore, the total cost for NEMO-BS, C_{NEMO}, can be expressed as

$$C_{NEMO} = C_B + C_P \sum_{k=1}^{\infty} k \alpha_S(k). \tag{9}$$

Total Cost of MIPv6. In MIPv6, since the MN does not execute any binding update for CoA based on the MR's MNP, there is no additional packet delivery cost. Meanwhile, each MN conducts a binding update to its HA whenever the public transportation moves across another AR. Therefore, the total cost for MIPv6, C_{MIPv6}, is given by

$$C_{MIPv6} = C_B \sum_{k=1}^{\infty} k \alpha_R(k). \tag{10}$$

5   Evaluation Results

For performance evaluation, we compare DLM against MIPv6 and NEMO-BS. Default parameter settings are described in Table 2.

5.1   Effect of T

Figure 3 shows the total cost as the timer T increases. It can be seen that the total costs of NEMO-BS and MIPv6 are constant regardless of the timer T. This is because NEMO-BS and MIPv6 do not use any timer. Also, it can be shown that

Table 2. Default parameter setting.

Parameter	λ_M	λ_S	λ_R	C_P	C_B
Value	1	5	2	1	1.5

the total cost of NEMO-BS is higher than that of MIPv6. This can be explained as follows. In the default parameter setting, session arrival events occur more frequently than handover events (i.e., $\lambda_S > \lambda_R$). Therefore, the packet delivery cost is more influential to the total cost than the binding update cost. In this situation, since MIPv6 forwards the packets only through the HA of the MN, it has an advantage of reducing the total cost.

Meanwhile, in DLM, it can be found that there is an optimal timer that minimizes the total cost (e.g., 2.75 in Fig. 3). This can be explained as follows. When the timer is set to a too small value, the probability that the binding update of the MN is simply wasted is high. On the other hand, when the timer is set to a too large value, all MNs should individually conduct binding updates to their HAs before the timer expires, which can increase the total cost. Consequently, setting the timer to an appropriate value is important to achieve better performance.

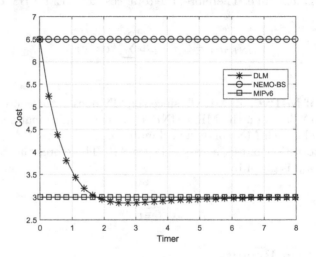

Fig. 3. Effect of T.

6   Conclusion

To reduce unnecessary binding update for MN's CoA based on the MR's MNP, we have proposed an delayed location management (DLM) scheme where an MN postpones its binding update until a pre-defined timer T expires. Evaluation results demonstrate that DLM outperforms existing schemes when the timer is set to an appropriate value. In our future work, we will investigate how to choose the optimal timer.

Acknowledgement. This work was supported by the R&D program of MOTIE/KEIT [10051306, Development of Vehicular Cloud-based Dynamic Security Framework for Internet of Vehicles (IoV) Services] and National Research Foundation of Korea Grant funded by the Korean Government (NRF-2014K1A3A1A21001357).

References

1. Devarapalli, V., Wakikawa, R., Petrescu, A., Thubert, P.: Network Mobility (NEMO) Basic Support Protocol. RFC 3963 (2005)
2. Lee, J., Ernst, T., Chilamkurti, N.: Performance analysis of PMIPv6-based network mobility for intelligent transportation systems. IEEE Trans. Veh. Technol. (TVT) **61**(1), 74–85 (2012)
3. Washington Metropolitan Area Transit Authority: Guidelines for the Design and Placement of Transit Stops (2009). https://www.wmata.com/pdfs/planning/Bus_Stop_Guidelines_Brochure.pdf. Accessed Apr 2016
4. 3GPP. 3rd Generation Partnership Project; Technical Specification Group Services and System Aspects; Telecommunication management; Energy Saving Management (ESM); Concepts and requirements (Release 10). 3GPP. TS 32.551 (2011)
5. Qiang, L., Li, J., Guizzani, M., Ji, Y.: An adaptive route optimization scheme for nested mobile IPv6 NEMO environment. In: International Symposium on Modeling and Optimization in Mobile, Ad Hoc, and Wireless Networks, pp. 373–380 (2014)
6. Kim, H., Kim, G., Kim, C.: S-RO: simple route optimization scheme with NEMO transparency. In: International Conference on Information Networking, pp. 401–411 (2005)
7. Cho, H., Kwon, T., Choi, Y.: Route optimization using tree information option for nested mobile networks. IEEE J. Sel. Areas Commun. (JSAC) **24**(9), 1717–1724 (2006)
8. Calderon, M., Bernardos, C., Bagnulo, M., Soto, I., Oliva, A.: Design and experimental evaluation of a route optimization solution for NEMO. IEEE J. Sel. Areas Commun. (JSAC) **24**(9), 1702–1716 (2006)
9. Chuang, M., Lee, J.: DRO: domain-based route optimization scheme for nested mobile networks. EURASIP J. Wirel. Commun. Netw. **2011**(1), 1–19 (2011)
10. Barman, S., Ghosh, A., Biswas, S.: A transparent tree root identification scheme to support route-optimization and network mobility in PMIPv6 domain. In: Proceedings of International Conference on Recent Trends in Information Systems (ReTIS), July 2015
11. Pack, S., Park, G., Ko, H.: An SIP-based location management framework in opportunistic WiFi networks. IEEE Trans. Veh. Technol. (TVT) **64**(11), 5269–5274 (2015)
12. Liou, R., Lin, Y., Tsai, S.: An investigation on LTE mobility management. IEEE Trans. Mob. Comput. (TMC) **12**(1), 166–176 (2013)
13. Ko, H., Pack, S., Lee, W.: Timer-based push scheme for online social networking services in wireless networks. IEEE Commun. Lett. (CL) **16**(12), 2095–2098 (2012)
14. Lin, Y.: Reducing location update cost in a PCS network. IEEE/ACM Trans. Netw. (TN) **5**(1), 25–33 (1997)

Utility Analysis of Software Defined Heterogeneous Cellular Networks

Haiqi Jiang[1]([⊠]), Tao Han[1], Xiaohu Ge[1], and Lijun Wang[2]

[1] School of Electronic Information and Communications,
Huazhong University of Science and Technology, Wuhan 430074, China
{jianghaiqi,hantao,xhge}@hust.edu.cn
[2] Department of Information Science and Technology,
Wenhua College, Wuhan 430074, China
wanglj22@163.com

Abstract. With the development of the 5G communication systems, the coexistence of a variety of wireless networks has become an inevitable trend. Different wireless networks have different features and applications. However, they are independent of each other and have no cooperative relationship in the most of cases. This paper investigates the application of the Software Defined Network (SDN) and wireless network function vitalization on the access control criterion of the heterogeneous cellular networks. The SDN controller manages all wireless access points based on the inaccurate feedback network state information. Wireless network virtualization technology can simplify the complexity of the system running and improve the efficiency of the communication system based on the utility theory which takes a number of respects into consideration, such as the maximum achievable data rate, signal-to-interference-and-noise ratio (SINR) and the traffic load state. Moreover, a discrete stochastic optimization algorithm is presented to solve the problem of inaccurate feedback information in a fast convergence rate, which is caused by the delay and noise over wireless channels. Extensive simulations show that our proposed model and algorithm can achieve utility optimization considering practical parameters configurations in wireless networks.

Keywords: Software Defined Network · Wireless network function vitalization · Utility function · Access control · Discrete stochastic optimization algorithm

1 Introduction

The emergence of various wireless network services and handheld mobile devices brings convenience to people's lives. At the same time, it causes the crazy growth of mobile traffic [1]. It is predicted that the volume of mobile data in 2019 will be 10 times of that in 2014 [2]. This unprecedented escalation has imposed significant challenges on the design of existing wireless network. In the face of

© ICST Institute for Computer Sciences, Social Informatics and Telecommunications Engineering 2017
J.-H. Lee and S. Pack (Eds.): QShine 2016, LNICST 199, pp. 202–211, 2017.
DOI: 10.1007/978-3-319-60717-7_20

the above problems and challenges, the researchers put forward the framework of the fifth generation (5G) mobile communications and corresponding solutions in the framework, for example, the paper [3] provides a guideline for optimizing vechicular communications in 5G cooperative MIMO small cell networks and energy efficiency is improved by more intelligent strategy in [4,5]. One of the most important aspects of 5G communication systems is Heterogeneous Cellular Networks (HCNs) architecture. The technology of HCNs can provide indoor hotpots coverage, extended coverage, seamless coverage at a low cost and high service rate to effectively satisfy the explosively growing demands of mobile data, service quantity and types in existing cellular network [3].

As the emergence of the new network applications, wireless users are not only dependent on network for data transmission, but also for various services based on an open and flexible network. Under this circumstance, Software Defined Network (SDN) and Wireless Network Function Vitalization (WNVF) are introduced [6]. WNFV provides a good basis for the development of SDN, because WNFV provides the abstract resource for the top running of the SDN control plane [6]. The core idea of the WNFV is realizing the centralized and dynamic management of network resources by the way of software definition.

The application of the SDN and WNFV on the wireless communication network is still in its infancy. In [7], the author put forward a new wireless network architecture on the basis of SDN, named Software Defined Mobile Network (SDMN), through which the wireless networks can become more open, flexible and programmable. The paper [8] proposed a method to resolve the management of mobility in HCNs and interference among different tiers based on the SDN network architecture. Thus the pressure of the controller can be distributed, and the useless information can be filtered at the same time. At present, most SDN related studies focus on wired networks not wireless ones. In [8], the author discusses the challenges and opportunities of the application of the SDN on the wireless network, and has addressed the challenges of deploying WNFV in a network.

In this paper we propose the intelligent schemes of software defined HCN to control the wireless access of users in the dynamic environment of 5G mobile communications. In contrast to previous researches, we address the system utility optimization for multi-tier HCNs, where load-balancing, the achievable data rate and cost of clients are jointly considered towards optimizing system performance. In addition, the concept of Homogeneous Poisson Point Process (HPPP) and signal-to-interference-and-noise ratio (SINR) are involved to calculate data rates of clients. Furthermore, each considering element is set as an independent variable of sigmoid function in order to select one optimal wireless network. Based on the SDN framework and inaccurate feedback network state information, which is because of the time delay and noise of wireless channel, we have proposed a tractable discrete stochastic approximation algorithm to solve the problems caused by the characteristics of wireless communication.

The remainder of this paper is organized as follows. In the Sect. 2, we introduce the model of heterogeneous wireless cellular network involved SDN, and the WNFV technology in the SDN controller. The Sect. 3 discusses the policy of user association according to the utility theory. In the Sect. 4 one discrete stochastic optimization algorithm is presented and its properties of convergence are summarized based on the inaccurate load state information. Section 5 presents the numerical results. Finally, Sect. 6 concludes this study.

2   System Model

In this section, we consider the system model that integrates intelligent SDN and WNFV into the infrastructure of 5G communication systems. The architecture consists of three planes, as shown in Fig. 1.

Infrastructure plane: the infrastructure plane consists of the bottom layer, that is HCNs. The macro-cell BSs are outfitted with an OpenFlow switch which can be used to feedback the load state information of cells regularly at all times. The rest of the small-cell BSs are deployed without OpenFlow switches, therefore, they need to send information to SDN controller through wireless channel. What's more, the most important technology is network virtualization technology whose core idea is abstracting out the required network resources from the substrate network, in which the performance parameters of each network are mapped to the tag of each virtual network, as shown in Fig. 1.

Control plane: the most important part in this architecture is the SDN controller, which uniformly manages the access interface in the HCNs [9]. The SDN controller can calculate the appropriate access point for the terminal through the appropriate algorithm according to the collected information about the network state and demand information sent by users. Different from the traditional network architecture, the architecture of the HCNs in this paper has the features of configuring the network services quickly and centralized control management. Through the centralized control, the controller can master the overall situation better, use more suitable algorithms, configure network services faster, and easily download the new algorithm, such as load balancing algorithm, not belong to the network architecture to meet the needs of network on load balancing.

Application plane: it is mainly for achieving functions of various Application (APP), where application requests will be duly sent to the control layer to handle. Besides, some innovative technologies and concepts, such as computation offloading by more energy-efficient and intelligent strategy in 5G communication system [9], cloud computing integrating SDN and NFV and the novel framework named EMC in the context of 5G [10] and so on, can be designed and implemented using the corresponding source code in the application plane.

3   Access Control Based on the Utility Theory

In this paper, we study a three-layer HCNs in 5G environment, among which a large number of micro-cell BSs and femto-cell BSs with high density and low transmit power are deployed in each macro-cell BS. In this process, even if the received power from small-cell BSs is less than the macro-cell power, some users

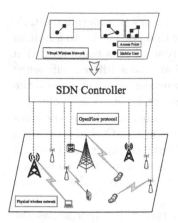

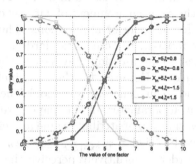

Fig. 1. The software defined heterogeneous cellular network with wireless virtual network.

Fig. 2. Sigmoid curve.

may be offloaded to a small-cell BS using some user association, in which load balancing and better Quality-of-Service (QoS) of users can be obtained. Thus in this paper, we propose to force some users to access the small-cell BS through the utility theory instead of the Max-SINR based criterion.

In this model, we assume that the k-tier BSs can satisfy the HPPP Φ_k with intensity λ_k, where the distribution of users also meets the HPPP Φ_u with intensity λ_u that is independent of the distribution of BSs. Each tier presents a different type of BSs, for example, tier 1 means traditional macro-cell BSs, and tier 2 and tier 3 mean pico-cell and femto-cell BSs respectively. There are different path loss exponents $\{\alpha_k\}_{k=1,\cdots,K} > 2$ of different tiers' signals. The transmit power $\{P_k\}_{k=1,\cdots,K}$ of each BS is used to calculate the coverage probability and achievable rate of the user.

Assume that the access point in the wireless virtualization network is $K = \{1, 2, \cdots, k, \cdots, K\}$, and the cost value is respectively $C = \{c_1, c_2, \cdots, c_k, \cdots, c_K\}$, which means that when a user is connected to one virtual wireless network k, the cost value is c_k, in which the expenditure, terminal consumptions and so on are included. Maximum achievable data rate for one wireless network and corresponding SINR can be determined with the Shannon capacity formula based on the stochastic geometry, especially, the theory of Poisson point process. The maximum achievable data rate R_k from one BS for a connected user can be represented as: $R_k = W_k \log_2(1 + \gamma_k)$, where W_k is denoted as the channel bandwidth provided by the network k to some user.

It is assumed that a BS transmits to only one user via channel at one time, with maximum power to achieve the optimal physical rate, the SINR γ_k can be shown as: $\gamma_k = \frac{G_k P_k}{\sigma^2 + \sum_{i=1, i \neq k}^{K} G_i P_i}$, where G_k is denoted as the channel gain between the connected BS and a user, in addition, G_i represents the channel gain from other BSs whose effects are negative to servicing users and σ^2 is the thermal noise power.

The algorithm in this paper is based on the utility theory considering multiple criteria. In economics, the satisfaction of a particular thing or service to a human being is indirectly reflected in utility [11]. In the current wireless communication field, the same environment of wireless communication makes different efficiency for different users or applications. Therefore, it is necessary to introduce the utility function to access standards in the environment of 5G communication systems. Many function may satisfy the mentioned properties of wireless communications. However, for the issue including some aspect of QoS of user, data rate and so on, generally a sigmoid function is considered to express satisfaction of a given parameter, In this paper, we choose the Sigmoid function to imitate the relationship of attribute value and efficiency value. The form of the functions selected is: $U(x) = \frac{1}{1+\exp\{\xi(x_m-x)\}}$ $(x_m > 0, \xi > 0)$.

In order to intuitively perceive the Sigmoid function, this paper shows the value got by adjusting the parameters in the curve Fig. 2. The features of the curve obviously show that the demand for a factor is strong at the beginning, and when the value of a certain factor exceeds a certain amount, continuing to increase a certain factor will not have a significant increasement on the degree of utility. We can set the value of parameter x_m to control curve center, and set the value of ξ to adjust the steepness of the curve. The more bigger the value ξ is, the steeper the curve is. In addition, when ξ takes a negative value, the trend of sigmoid is opposite to the positive value of ξ. The trend of sigmoid curve is various when we choose different elements as shown in Fig. 2, and the effect of some parameters must be converted to be positive by some methods such as taking countdown.

In the HCNs, the utility function $U_u(c_k)$ based on the QoS of the user is defined as: $U_u(c_i) = \frac{1}{1+\exp\{\xi_u(x_u-c_k)\}}$, in which c_k refers to the cost of users who need to access the wireless network k, which contains energy consumption, service fee and so on. What's more, the sub-function based on the data rate is $U_a(R_k) = \frac{1}{1+\exp\{\xi_a(x_a-R_k)\}}$, in which R_k refers to the maximum achievable data rate of one user connected with the k-th tier. This part of utility value pays more attention to the QoS and Quality of Experience (QoE) of users. Furthermore, we consider the load state of the whole system, which makes the system traffic load reach to a balance to some extent. Thus the utility sub-function based on the load state information is defined as: $U_L(L_k) = \frac{1}{1+\exp\{\xi_L(x_L-L_k)\}}$, where L_k refers to the current load state of the virtual wireless network k and the value is the number of users access of the kth-tier wireless network, which is feedback from the BSs. What is more, because the trend of growth in terms of c_k and L_k is adverse to the users' satisfaction, we have to set the value of ξ_u and ξ_L as negative.

This status information is transmitted by the BS to the SDN controller through wireless channel. Therefore, we can get the general value of the utility value of wireless virtual network i: $U(c_i, R_i, L_i) = \varsigma U_u(c_i) + \tau U_a(R_i) + \upsilon U_L(L_i)$, where $\varsigma > 0, \tau > 0, \upsilon > 0, \varsigma + \tau + \upsilon = 1$, ς refers to the utility weight generated by the user costs, τ and υ denote the weights produced by the maximum achievable data rate, and load state of the system respectively. Besides, the values of ς, τ

and v can be adjusted based on the type of service and overall system status, for example, the value of τ should be larger than other weights if the service of client is video streaming.

4   Wireless Network Selection with Inaccurate Load State Information

As we can conclude from the previous discussion, it is very important to determine the optimal selection of virtual wireless network, which can provide users with the best QoS and load balancing of the whole system to some extent in the control plane based on Load State Information (LSI) [12]. However, the LSI may be inaccurate because of the limitation of the measuring methods and the dynamic nature of the wireless communication system. What is more, it may be worse in virtual wireless network, because there is some time delay caused by rate-limited backhaul links transmitted to the central controller.

Firstly in this paper we define the set of all the possible virtual wireless networks as Ω, and the decision selection variable at the decision time t, is the $w^t \in \Omega$, which represents a particular virtual wireless network meeting the requirements of users. In order to simplify description of the algorithm, we defined $U\left(c_i, R_i, L_i^t\right)$ as the objective function $\phi\left[\hat{\mathbf{L}}^t, w^t\right]$, in which the parameter w^t and L^t are denoted as the wireless network selected in the SDN controller and the load state information of system in the time t, respectively.

In this paper we assume the availability of LSI is the same as [12], in which we can obtain specific and detailed instructions, and the inaccuracy in LSI is modeled as additive noise. Therefore, the available and inaccurate LSI $\hat{\mathbf{L}}$ can be shown as $\hat{\mathbf{L}} = \mathbf{L} + \mathbf{N}$, where $\mathbf{N}$ is an independent Gaussian variable. And at each decision time, because $\mathbf{L}^t = \hat{\mathbf{L}}^t - \mathbf{N}$ is a random variable, the utility function of each-tier BS $U\left(c_i, R_i, L_i^t\right)$ is a random variable as well.

In this paper, we introduce an iterative algorithm that is similar to discrete stochastic approximation algorithm, which has obtained a lot of attention. One most important feature of this algorithm is the self-learning ability in terms of the direction and speed of selecting the optimal wireless network. Another advantage is that it can find the best wireless access network under time-varying scene due to the fast convergence.

In the stage of initialization, the controller of SDN identifies all virtual wireless networks by means of WNFV. At the same time, the SDN controller receives feedback information from users and wireless access points, which is used to select the optimal wireless virtual network.

In the process of sampling and evaluation, the Algorithm 1 can randomly choose a virtual network, and calculate the corresponding value $\phi\left[\hat{\mathbf{L}}^t, \widetilde{w}^t\right]$, which is compared with the existing $\phi\left[\hat{\mathbf{L}}^t, w^t\right]$. In the process of acceptance, if the value of $\phi\left[\hat{\mathbf{L}}^t, \widetilde{w}^t\right]$ is larger, the corresponding network is accepted as the next better virtual network, that is $w^{t+1} = \widetilde{w}^t$. After the process of acceptance, we have to replace the state occupation probability: $p[t, w^t] = \frac{\text{Number-of-chosen}(w)}{t}$, which can record the frequency of accession into one virtual wireless. In addition, the step size in each iteration is $\frac{1}{t}$, which indicates that the Algorithm 1 is getting more conservative to find the optimal wireless network, and the optimal selection is the most frequently chosen wireless network. Moreover, we can easily find that changing optimal virtual wireless network in the whole process is a Markov chain, where the set of decision $\{w^t\}$ would nearly transfer into the global optimal value w^* after a few iterations, that is because transition probability of w^* is becoming larger and larger with the process of iterations.

In terms of the conditions and environments, the global convergence of Algorithm 1 is similar to the paper [13]. Therefore, the proof of convergence has been given in [13].

Algorithm 1. Aggressive Discrete Stochastic Approximation Algorithm

---

1: { **Initialization** }
2: SDN controller receives the user's access request, and determines all the possible virtual wireless networks subset Ω and the value of weight ς, τ and υ in terms of the category of service, such as voice and video.
3: Each BS measures the LSI of the network and feedbacks the LSI to the SDN controller.
4: SDN controller selects a virtual wireless network $w^0 \in \Omega$, and set $p^0 \left[w^0 \right] \leftarrow 1$
5: set $p^0 \left[w^0 \right] \leftarrow 0$, for all $w \neq w^0$
6: Initialize measure of the optimal selected virtual wireless as w^0
7: for $k = 1,2,...$, do
8: { **Sampling and evaluation** }
9: Given the Load state information $\hat{\mathbf{L}}^t$, obtain $\phi \left[\hat{\mathbf{L}}^t, w^t \right]$
10: choose $\tilde{w}^t \in \Omega / w^t$ uniformly, obtain an independent observation $\phi \left[\hat{\mathbf{L}}^t, \tilde{w}^t \right]$
11: { **Acceptance** }
12: if $\phi \left[\hat{\mathbf{L}}^t, w^t \right] < \phi \left[\hat{\mathbf{L}}^t, \tilde{w}^t \right]$ then
13: set $w^{t+1} = \tilde{w}^t$
14: else
15: $w^{t+1} = w^t$
16: end if
17: { **Adaptive filter for updating state occupation probabilities** }
19: $p[t+1] = (1 - \mu[t+1]) \, p[n] + \mu[t+1] D(t+1)$ with the decreasing step size $\mu[t] = 1/t$
20: { **Computing the maximum** }
21: if $p[t+1, w^{t+1}] < p[t+1, \tilde{w}^t]$ then
22: $\tilde{w}^{t+1} = w^{t+1}$
23: else
24: set $\tilde{w}^{t+1} = \tilde{w}^t$
25: end if
26: end for

---

5 Numerical Evaluation and Discussions

For performance evaluation, some numerical results for the Monte Carlo simulations are presented to make sure the advantages of our model and analyze the effectiveness of our proposed algorithm that is based on utility function theory. Three-tier HCNs are assumed in the simulation mode, namely macro-cell, pico-cell and femto-cell. In this simulation, the main system parameters are based on SCME channel model [14,15], in which we consider the three-tier HCNs with transmit power $\{P_1, P_2, P_3\} = \{46, 35, 20\}$ dBm and path loss $\{\alpha_1, \alpha_2, \alpha_3\} = \{3.8, 3.5, 4\}$. In addition, we assume that in our model different tiers are independent, with deployed density $\{\lambda_1, \lambda_2, \lambda_3\} = \{\frac{1}{\pi 500^2}, 5\lambda_1, 20\lambda_1\}$ and the cost of users $\{c_1, c_2, c_3\} = \{30, 60, 40\}$, available bandwidth for users $\{W_1, W_2, W_3\} = \{5, 20, 40\}$ MHz, $\{\xi_u, \xi_a, \xi_L\} = \{-0.8, 1.5, -2\}$, as well as the weight $\{\varsigma, \tau, \upsilon\} = \{0.3, 0.2, 0.5\}$.

First and foremost, take the two-tier network (only consists of macrocell and picocell) as example, we can observe in Fig. 3 that the probability of pico-cell user keeps the trend of increase when the SDN controller uses our proposed Algorithm 1 and is more than that based on the traditional max-SINR criterion, which means that the Algorithm 1 can shift some users from over-loaded macro-BSs to the light-loaded small-cell BSs, which allows each BS to better serve its remaining users. Therefore, we design our software defined HCNs, in which SDN controller selects and decides one perfect wireless network based on the imperfect LSI from the physical plane.

We can only illustrate the complexity of Algorithm refalgo1 using the numbers of iteration by simulations. In the following simulation, the LSI noise is modeled as a zero-mean Gaussian random variable $\sigma^2 = -104$ dBm. We consider the performance of Algorithm 1 which selects the optimal wireless virtual network maximizing the utility value using as an estimate of the objective function. The virtual wireless network is randomly generated and fixed between two decision epochs. As we can see from Fig. 4 that the Algorithm 1 converges to the optimal wireless access point although it takes some time. Moreover, it is

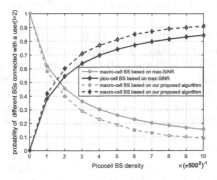

Fig. 3. Impact of pico-cell BS density in a HCNs of connecting macrocell and picocell.

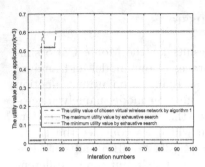

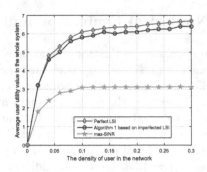

Fig. 4. Single run of Algorithm 1.   **Fig. 5.** Average user utility performance versus traffic arrival intensity.

observed that the speed of convergence is very fast, which is suitable for the framework of SDN.

Note that the maximum SINR cannot always give optimal QoS and QoE to the clients especially when the costs of the different tiers are different. Figure 5 shows that the discrete stochastic approximation algorithm can have close performance as the perfect LSI. However, the utility value caused by the Max-SINR scheme is far less than the one caused by our proposed access criteria.

6   Conclusion

In this paper, we have tried to jointly integrate SDN and HCNs in the environment of 5G mobile communications and considered some issues that arise. We proposed a novel standard of wireless access control that can achieve load balancing of the whole system and some better aspects of users' QoS in HCNs through solving a network-wide utility maximization problem. During this process, to address the challenge introduced by inaccurate LSI in this framework, we proposed network selection algorithm based on the concept of discrete stochastic approximation. Finally, we have provided extensive simulation results to demonstrate the performance of the model and new selection algorithm.

Acknowledgments. The authors would like to acknowledge the support from the International Science and Technology Cooperation Program of China under grants 2015DFG12580 and 2014DFA11640, the National Natural Science Foundation of China (NSFC) under the grants 61471180 and 61210002, the Fundamental Research Funds for the Central Universities under the HUST grants 2015XJGH011 and 2015MS038, the Hubei Provincial Science and Technology Department under the grant 2013CFB188, the Hubei Provincial Department of Education Scientific research projects (No. B2015188), the grant from Wenhua College (No. 2013Y08) and Graduate Base of Innovation and Entrepreneurship under the HUST. This research is partially supported by the EU FP7-PEOPLE-IRSES, project acronym S2EuNet (grant no. 247083), project acronym WiNDOW (grant no. 318992) and project acronym CROWN (grant no. 610524). This research is supported by the National international Scientific and Technological Cooperation Base of Green Communications and Networks (No. 2015B01008) and the Hubei International Scientific and Technological Cooperation Base of Green Broadband Wireless Communications.

References

1. Wang, C.X., Haider, F., Gao, X., You, X.H., Yang, Y., Yuan, D., Aggoune, H., Haas, H., Fletcher, S., Hepsaydir, E.: Cellular architecture and key technologies for 5G wireless communication networks. IEEE Commun. Mag. **52**(2), 122–130 (2014)
2. Ge, X., Yang, B., Ye, J., Mao, G.: Spatial spectrum and energy efficiency of random cellular networks. IEEE Trans. Commun. **63**(3), 1019–1030 (2015)
3. Ge, X., Cheng, H., Mao, G., Yang, Y., Tu, S.: Vehicular communications for 5G cooperative small cell networks. IEEE Trans. Veh. Technol. **65**, 7882–7894 (2016)
4. Boccardi, F., Heath, R.W., Lozano, A., Marzetta, T.L.: Five disruptive technology directions for 5G. IEEE Commun. Mag. **52**(2), 74–80 (2013)
5. Ge, X., Tu, S., Han, T., Li, Q.: Energy efficiency of small cell backhaul networks based on Gauss-Markov mobile models. IET Netw. **4**(2), 158–167 (2014)
6. Li, Y., Chen, M.: Software-defined network function virtualization: a survey. IEEE Access **3**, 2542–2553 (2015)
7. Chen, M., Qian, Y., Mao, S., Tang, W., Yang, X.: Software-defined mobile networks security. Mob. Netw. Appl. 1–15 (2016)
8. Namal, S., et al.: SDN based inter-technology load balancing leveraged by flow admission control. In: IEEE Software Defined Networking for Future Network Services, pp. 1–5 (2013)
9. Chen, M., Hao, Y., Li, Y., Lai, C.F.: On the computation offloading at ad hoc cloudlet: architecture and service modes. IEEE Commun. Mag. **53**(6), 18–24 (2015)
10. Chen, M., Zhang, Y., Li, Y., Mao, S.: EMC: emotion-aware mobile cloud computing in 5G. IEEE Netw. **29**(2), 32–38 (2015)
11. Dahi, S., Tabbane, S.: Sigmoid utility function formulation for handoff reducing access model in cognitive radio. In: International Symposium on Communications and Information Technologies, pp. 166–170 (2013)
12. Zhang, H., Wang, Y., Ji, H.: Resource optimization based interference management for hybrid self-organized small cell network. IEEE Trans. Veh. Technol. 1–11 (2015)
13. Li, X., Zhao, N., Sun, Y., Yu, F.: Interference alignment based on antenna selection with imperfect channel state information in cognitive radio networks. IEEE Trans. Veh. Technol. 1–15 (2016)
14. Baum, D.S., Salo, J., Milojevic, M., Kyoti, P., Hansen, J.: MATLAB implementation of the 3GPP spatial channel model (3GPP TR 25.996). http://www.tkk.fi/Units/Radio/scm/. Accessed Jan 2005
15. Stewarthalevy, J.: Matlab implementation of the interim channel model for beyond-3G systems (SCME). Free Radic. Biol. Med. **35**(4), 406–417 (2005)

Adaptive Data Collection with Free Addressing and Dynamic Duty-Cycling for Sensor Networks

Fei Tong$^{(\boxtimes)}$ and Jianping Pan

University of Victoria, Victoria, BC, Canada
{tongfei,pan}@uvic.ca

Abstract. To improve the lifetime of the battery-powered sensors for data collection, duty-cycling is commonly adopted. A fixed duty cycle may cause a long packet delivery latency, low network capacity, and poor energy efficiency, especially in a frequently-reporting application. Moreover, considering a heterogeneous network consisting of various sensor platforms from different manufacturers, not only is node addressing with regard to address definition, management, and allocation difficult and costly, but also different addressing schemes will obstruct cross-platform communications. Based on the above considerations, this paper proposes an Adaptive Data Collection (ADC) with two features naturally and seamlessly integrated, i.e., free addressing and dynamic duty-cycling, to improve network heterogeneity, load adaptivity, and energy efficiency. ADC has been implemented in the Contiki Operating System. The evaluations based on a heterogeneous testbed consisting of two hardware platforms have demonstrated its practicality and efficacy.

Keywords: Sensor networks · Adaptive data collection · Dynamic duty-cycling · Free addressing · Testbed implementation

1 Introduction

Data collection is one of the most important applications of wireless sensor networks (WSNs), and can be widely found in environmental monitoring, infrastructure surveillance, scientific exploration, and other event monitoring applications [1]. Since radio is the most energy-consuming unit of a sensor node, and to improve the network lifetime of an energy-constrained WSN, existing data collection protocols commonly adopted or designed a duty-cycling scheme at the link layer [2–4], with which the radio of each node will periodically wake up and sleep according to an established time schedule. These data collection protocols usually employ a fixed duty cycle, in which the sleeping period could not be utilized for data transmission, even when the network traffic load is much beyond its capacity. However, a fixed duty cycle will cause unwanted energy consumption under light traffic loads, and network congestion and collision with packet retransmission or drop under heavy loads. This is because the accumulated data cannot be sent promptly just in the active period of the radio, which further

© ICST Institute for Computer Sciences, Social Informatics and Telecommunications Engineering 2017
J.-H. Lee and S. Pack (Eds.): QShine 2016, LNICST 199, pp. 212–222, 2017.
DOI: 10.1007/978-3-319-60717-7_21

leads to a long packet delivery latency, low network capacity, and poor energy efficiency. Therefore, the conventional duty-cycled data collection protocols may not meet the real-time delivery requirement of the delay-sensitive applications.

Another concern about the data collection in WSNs is node addressing, e.g., the addressing for MAC/routing, which is often underestimated and even neglected in the prior data collection design. It is difficult and costly for the manufacturers of sensor nodes to assign a unique address for every node during the manufacturing phase, since there are several issues to be considered carefully, such as address definition, address space management, address allocation, etc. That is the reason all Zolertia Z1 [5] and Tmote Sky [6] motes use a default MAC address set by the manufacturers, so customers have to manually assign a unique MAC address to each node one by one for inter-node communication, which is quite inconvenient, especially when there are a large number of nodes to be deployed. In addition, a WSN may need different sensor platforms from different manufactures due to their different sensing capabilities. Different manufacturers, however, may have different addressing schemes, which will obstruct the cross-platform communications in a heterogeneous network consisting of various sensor platforms. On the other hand, the execution of an independent address allocation and exchange mechanism in runtime also causes a significant network overhead. Note that in a dense WSN, it is quite difficult to link the address of a node for communication with its location, and thus people assume the required location information can be determined by other means (e.g., GPS).

Based on the above considerations, this paper proposes an Adaptive Data Collection (ADC) protocol with free addressing and dynamic duty-cycling for multihop data collection in WSNs. Specifically, each node is identified for inter-node communication by using a Randomly-generated IDentifier (RID), plus its communication hop distance to the sink node. So there is no need to pre-assign a unique MAC address to each node or perform a routing address allocation and management procedure in the runtime of a network. Meanwhile, the sleeping period can be utilized on demand for data transmission to achieve a dynamic duty cycle adaptive to the network traffic load. Therefore, with the above two features, the network performance can be largely improved in terms of network heterogeneity, load adaptivity, and energy efficiency.

ADC intrinsically inherits from the previous designs several advanced features significant for multihop, duty-cycled data collection, such as pipelined forwarding so that a relaying node can forward a received packet in a short time to reduce the end-to-end packet delivery latency [4,7], inter-layer incorporation of network and link layers so that the protocol overhead can be reduced and the limited sensor node resources can be utilized efficiently [2–4], and lightweight schedule synchronization as an underlying support to the whole design [4]. Among these proposals, only the PDC protocol presented in [4] considers both the pipelined data collection and the underlying schedule synchronization over duty-cycled radios, practically and comprehensively. However, PDC does not consider the network heterogeneity, and traffic load adaptivity. In ADC, all the above features together with the two proposed in this paper (i.e., free addressing and dynamic duty-cycling) are naturally and seamlessly integrated and able to support each other by only relying on an RTS/CTS-like handshake, which is not only for data transmission as commonly utilized, but also for all other components in ADC. ADC has been implemented in the latest Contiki Operating System (OS) [8], a pioneering open-source OS for the Internet of Things. A testbed based on two real hardware platforms, i.e., Z1 [5] and MicaZ, forming a heterogeneous network, are established for performance evaluation.

The rest of the paper is structured as follows. ADC is presented in Sect. 2. The implementation and evaluation of ADC are shown in Sect. 3. Finally, Sect. 4 concludes the paper.

2   ADC Design

Similar to the design adopted by PDC [4], ADC only relies on an RTS/CTS-like handshake, called RTF/CTF (Request-to-Forward/Clear-to-Forward), to achieve all its features comprehensively. The difference lies in that ADC considers both free addressing and dynamic duty-cycling. There are three stages in ADC, including network initialization, topology establishment with free addressing, and data transmission with dynamic duty-cycling. In this section, we first have a general design description of ADC in Sect. 2.1. The three stages in ADC are then introduced in Sects. 2.2, 2.3 and 2.4, respectively.

2.1   General Design Description

During this stage, all nodes in ADC will be divided into different grades equivalent to their communication hop distances to the sink node (which is in grade 0). Meanwhile, each sensor node will maintain a periodic sleep-wakeup schedule defined as the radio status over time, according to which the radio of a node in grade i ($i \in \mathbb{Z}$ and $i > 0$) periodically experiences three consecutive statuses, i.e., R: receiving a data packet from a sender in grade $i + 1$, T: transmitting a data packet to its receiver in grade $i - 1$, and S: sleeping. The schedules of any two adjacent grades along a path from the source to the sink node are staggered, so that a data received by a node during its R status can be forwarded consecutively during its upcoming T status and finally to the sink in a pipelined fashion, which can largely reduce the packet delivery latency and efficiently handle the traffic congestion by moving traffic quickly away from the congested area. Figure 1 shows the grade and schedule information maintained by the nodes along a path $A \rightarrow B \rightarrow C \rightarrow$ sink. Intuitively, T and R have the same maximum duration, which is defined as a slot for at most one transmission of a data packet with a maximum size set depending on a specific application. To stagger the schedules between any two grades so as to achieve the pipelined scheduling, the S duration is set to an integer multiple of the slot duration.

A data-gathering tree rooted at the sink node will be established in the second stage, where each node will build and maintain two neighbor tables, namely, Next-Hop Table (NHT) and Previous-Hop Table (PHT). Since there are

Algorithm 1: $wait(W)$

Input: W, $maxChildrenNum$
Output: $waitTime$
if *the current node is sink* **then**
  | **return** $(waitTime = rand(W) \cdot \sigma)$;
else
  | $w = W/(maxChildrenNum + 1)$;
  | **return** $(waitTime = [w \cdot table\_length(PHT) + rand(w)] \cdot \sigma)$;
end

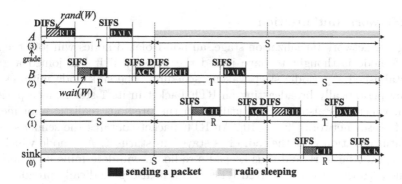

Fig. 1. An example used to show the ADC design.

no unique addresses pre-assigned to any nodes, free addressing will be achieved in this stage. A node's PHT is used to record the information related to its one or more children in the adjacent higher grade, including their RIDs and the schedule errors relative to them, while a node's NHT is used to record the information related to its only one parent node in the adjacent lower grade, including the parent's RID and the schedule error relative to the parent. In both tables, the schedule error information will be utilized for schedule synchronization. It is worth noting that there might be some other fields to be added for topology control and maintenance relying on the RTF/CTF handshake. For example, the number of children and residual energy of a node's parent (obtained from the CTF replied with by the parent) can be added to the node's NHT, which will be embedded in its RTF, so that a different lower-grade node with fewer children and/or more residual energy can make a comparison after receiving the RTF to determine to contend with the original parent for replying with a CTF. To increase the success probability of such a contention, the node will have a shorter waiting time, calculated by a function, $wait(W)$, as shown in Fig. 1, where W is the maximum number of mini time-slots that the contention window of the handshake allows. Considering only the number of children a node has as an example, Algorithm 1 shows the design of $wait(W)$, where $maxChildrenNum$ is predetermined and represents the maximum number of children a non-sink node can have (the sink node has no such a limit), σ is the time duration of one mini time-slot in the contention window, $rand(W)$ is the number of mini time-slots randomly chosen within W, and $table\_length$(PHT) is to obtain the number of items in a node's PHT, i.e., the number of children the node has.

Once the two tables are established, a node with pending data to be transmitted will initiate an RTF/CTF handshake with its parent in status T after waiting a randomly-chosen mini-time slots, $rand(W)$. If there is more than one packet, the S status will be utilized for data transmission to achieve a dynamic duty-cycling, as introduced in Sect. 2.4.

2.2   Network Initialization

During the network initialization stage, all non-isolated nodes will join the network. A node is thought to have joined the network if it has joined a grade and established a periodic sleep-wakeup schedule. The sink node initiates this stage by periodically broadcasting an RTF packet in its T status, as a periodic beacon, which was also typically utilized in the previous realistic implementations of sensor networks [2,4,9,10]. An RTF packet contains the sender's grade and status duration that the radio has stayed in status T. Any node which has not joined the network and thus keeps its radio on will determine its grade and schedule according to the received RTF. Then it also periodically broadcasts in its T status an RTF packet embedding its own grade and status duration. Finally all non-isolated nodes will join the network, as an example shown in Fig. 1. Note that at this stage, node address and CTF reply are not necessary.

2.3   Topology Establishment with Free Addressing

Once a node has identified its grade and schedule, it will leverage the periodic RTF/CTF *broadcast handshake* to establish a data-gathering tree for data collection. To avoid the cost and overhead of assigning a unique address to each sensor node during the manufacturing phase or performing an independent address allocation, exchange, and management mechanism in runtime, a node in ADC will use an RID for packet communication. Specifically, a node broadcasts an RTF embedding its RID. There might be several adjacent lower-grade nodes receiving the RTF and thus necessary to contend with each other for replying with CTFs with their RIDs embedded as well. The function $wait(W)$ ensures that those nodes with fewer children and/or higher residual energy reply first. The lower-grade node which successfully wins the contention will add the RTF sender into its PHT, and the RTF sender will add the CTF sender into its NHT after receiving the replied CTF. Then the two nodes will change from the broadcast handshake to *unicast handshake* for data transmission, as well as for schedule synchronization and topology control and maintenance.

Since RID is randomly generated, RID conflict is inevitable. It does not matter if two nodes in different grades have an identical RID, since their grades can be utilized to differentiate them. It may also happen that there are several nodes in the same grade having the same parent generated an identical RID, which will cause an RID conflict issue. Taking the communications among node 1, 2, and 3 in Fig. 2 for example, the following scheme is adopted in ADC to

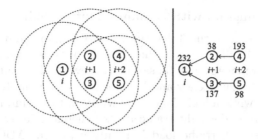

Fig. 2. Illustration of free addressing. For the left part of the vertical line, each dashed circle shows the node's communication range and the number inside each node shown as a solid circle is the node name, while for the right part, the number beside each node is its RID and the arrows indicate the network topology. Node 1 is in grade i ($i \in \mathbb{Z}$ and $i \geq 0$), node 2 and 3 are in grade $i + 1$, and node 4 and 5 are in grade $i + 2$.

effectively solve the RID conflict between node 2 and 3. Assuming one of them, say node 3, fails in the broadcast RTF contention, then

– if node 3 can overhear the RTF from node 2, it will find the conflict and thus regenerate a new RID; otherwise,
– if node 3 can receive the CTF replied to node 2 from node 1, node 3 can also find the conflict and regenerate a new RID; otherwise,
– node 3 could not notice the conflict. Assume it wins the contention and broadcasts an RTF successfully next time. Every time a node receives a *broadcast* RTF, it will look up its PHT to find whether there is an RID identical to the one of the RTF sender. So node 1 notices the conflict after receiving the RTF from node 3, and generates a different RID embedded in its CTF for node 3.

Note that a node in ADC will not reply with CTF after it receives a broadcast RTF from any higher-grade node, until it determines its RID and parent in the lower grade. For example, node 3 will not be set as a parent by node 4 or 5 if it has not yet determined its RID and parent. In addition, it would be also possible that node 1 could successfully receive both the broadcast RTFs from node 2 and 3 if they could not hear each other during their contention (i.e., they are hidden terminals to each other). Node 1 will set a flag in its replied CTF to notify node 2 and 3 of regenerating their RIDs, if they have identical RIDs.

ADC only needs to handle the RID conflict among those nodes which have the same parent. Because, even if two nodes in the same grade have an identical RID, their data transmissions will not be affected as long as they have different parent. Therefore, ADC can use a small integer range for uniformly at random generating an RID for each node. In the ADC implementation in Contiki, we use an 8-bit variable for RID with a range of $[0, 255]$ (as shown in Fig. 2), since the number of the children a node has is usually much less than 256.

2.4   Data Transmission with Dynamic Duty-Cycling

The number of slots in status S determines how long a radio can sleep during a cycle. The more slots S contains, the lower duty cycle a node has and correspondingly the more energy can be saved. However, a low duty cycle will lead to a long packet delivery latency and low network throughput, especially under heavy traffic loads, while a high duty cycle will lead to an unwanted energy consumption, especially under light traffic loads. Therefore, a dynamic duty cycle adaptive to the network traffic load is highly expected. ADC can adaptively utilize the sleeping slots in status S to achieve dynamic duty-cycling (DDC).

To this end, the RTF packet contains a DDC flag, which will be set if a node has more than one packet to be transmitted, so that its receiver would wake up in status S instead of waiting for the next status R to receive the left packet. Depending on whether it is a last-hop transmission or not, the dynamic duty-cycling scheme in ADC will be discussed under two cases:

Non-last-hop Transmission. Figure 3 shows an example for illustration about the data transmissions along a path $A \rightarrow B \rightarrow C$, where node A, B, and C are in grade $i + 2$, $i + 1$, and i ($i \in \mathbb{Z}$ and $i \geq 1$), respectively. Assume node A receives an RTF with the DDC flag set from a child node in grade $i + 3$ in the R status before t_0 (not shown in the figure). Then node A will adjust its schedule to reserve two continuous sleeping slots in status S (R and T in italic in the figure), which are used for receiving one more data packet from that child and forwarding the packet to its parent (node B), respectively. Meanwhile, in the upcoming T status after t_0, node A will also set the DDC flag in its own RTF. So do node B and C, and thus the data packet can still be forwarded in a pipelined fashion in status S. Considering the interference range is about two times longer than the transmission range for the wireless communication in an open-space environment [11], after any pair of statuses R and T, a node has to sleep at least two slots before waking up again for another data transmission, so that it will not interfere with its previous/next-hop neighbors. Therefore, the sleeping slots in status S cannot be utilized for data transmissions unless S contains at least 6 slots, and the maximum number of sleeping slots in status S that a node can utilize for data transmissions is $\left\lfloor \frac{\text{\# of slots in S} - 2}{4} \right\rfloor \times 2$.

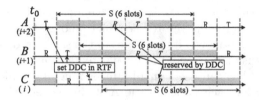

Fig. 3. Non-last-hop transmission along a path $A \rightarrow B \rightarrow C$.

Last-Hop Transmission. The data transmissions along a path $A \rightarrow B \rightarrow$ sink shown as in Fig. 4 are utilized for illustration. There are two cases for the last-hop transmission, depending on whether or not a grade-two node (e.g., node A in Fig. 4) either receives an RTF with the DDC flag set in status R or sets the DDC flag of its own RTF in status T. If so, it is similar to the non-last-hop transmission, as shown in Fig. 4(a), except that it is not necessary for node B to set the DDC flag of its RTF packet to inform the sink node of waking up, since the sink node could be always awake for collecting data. Otherwise, all the sleeping slots of node B except the two immediately before the next regular R status can be utilized for transmitting data, as shown in Fig. 4(b), since they will not interfere with the previous-hop transmissions.

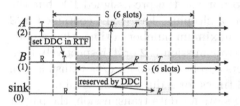
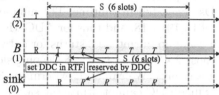

(a) Node A reserves the sleeping slots in status S for data transmission.

(b) Node A has no data packet to be transmitted in status S.

Fig. 4. Last-hop transmission along a path $A \rightarrow B \rightarrow$ sink: (a) A reserves the sleeping slots in status S for data transmission, and (b) A has no reservation.

3   Implementation and Evaluation

ADC has been implemented in the latest Contiki OS [8] and evaluated in a testbed consisting of 5 Z1 and 2 MicaZ motes, as shown in Fig. 5. Contiki also provides a network simulator, called Cooja [12], which runs simulations based on the Contiki OS and fully emulated hardware devices, so that the codes developed for a Cooja simulation can be directly uploaded to real hardware devices even without any change, tremendously accelerating the development of realistic sensor networks. ADC is evaluated in terms of packet delivery ratio, average hop delivery latency, and average node duty cycle. PDC is used as a benchmark for comparison, which is one of the state-of-the-art collection protocols. Using the same code, we also conduct a Cooja simulation with 5 fully emulated Z1 and 2

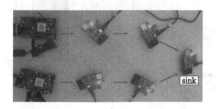

Fig. 5. A testbed consisting of 5 Z1 and 2 MicaZ motes forming a 3-hop network.

Tmote Sky (currently, Cooja does not support the communication between the emulated MicaZ and non-MicaZ platforms) based on the same network as in the testbed, and another one based on a larger heterogeneous network, which are not shown due to the page limit. All the results are consistent with each other.

In the testbed, there are six source nodes and one sink node, forming a 3-hop network with the topology shown as in Fig. 5. Each source node will generate 50 packets, with the packet generation interval (PGI) varying from 1 to 9 s. The retransmission limit for each packet is set to 5. The queue buffer size is set to 10 packets. A unique ID is pre-assigned to each node. Both the ADCs with and without free addressing are evaluated, denoted as "ADC-FA" and "ADC-No FA", respectively. In ADC-FA, nodes do not use the pre-assigned IDs but the RIDs generated in runtime. The number of sleeping slots (SSL) contained in S is set to 10 or 18, and thus for ADC, the maximum number of times that a node can wake up during its S status for data transmission is 2 or 4, respectively (i.e., at most $2 \times 2 = 4$ or $4 \times 2 = 8$ sleeping slots can be utilized for data transmission, respectively). We run each experiment 3 times for a duration of 40 min.

Since PDC cannot utilize the sleeping slots for data transmission, the packet delivery ratio in PDC is much lower than in ADC, as shown in Fig. 6(a). For PDC, a larger SSL will lead to a lower packet delivery ratio, because if a packet fails in being transmitted in the current cycle, it has to wait SSL slots for the

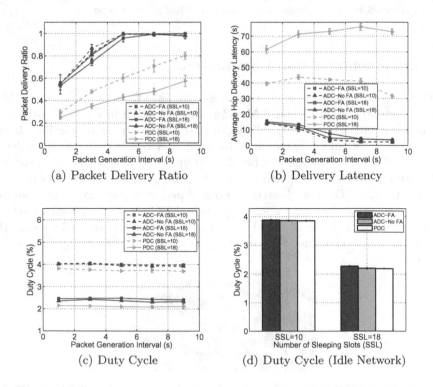

(a) Packet Delivery Ratio

(b) Delivery Latency

(c) Duty Cycle

(d) Duty Cycle (Idle Network)

Fig. 6. ADC performance evaluation based on the testbed shown in Fig. 5.

next cycle, and thus the node queue becomes full faster, resulting in more packet loss. In contrast, SSL affects ADC very slightly.

SSL also has a very slight effect on the average hop delivery latency in ADC, as shown in Fig. 6(b). However, with a larger SSL in PDC, a packet has a longer waiting time on average, leading to a larger delivery latency. In addition, as PGI increases, the packet delivery latency in PDC increases first and then decreases. Because as PGI increases, more packets can reach the sink node but with longer queue waiting time, which contributes to increasing the latency as a dominating part, while as PGI continuously increases, packets can be forwarded faster, which dominates and decreases the latency. In contrast, the packet delivery latency in ADC decreases always, and finally has almost no change when the queue waiting time of a packet cannot be decreased any more.

As shown in Fig. 6(c), with a larger SSL in PDC, a node can have more time to be in S status, corresponding to a lower duty cycle. ADC has a similar performance, because the least number of sleeping slots where a node in the ADC with SSL $= 18$ has to be asleep is larger than in the ADC with SSL $= 10$ ($18 - \lfloor \frac{18-2}{4} \rfloor \times 2 = 10$ $vs.$ $10 - \lfloor \frac{10-2}{4} \rfloor \times 2 = 6$). In addition, the duty cycle in both ADC and PDC has almost no change as PGI increases, due to the fact that the number of packets to be transmitted is fixed. Since ADC can use the sleeping slots for data transmission, the duty cycle in ADC is a little higher than in PDC. As the network becomes idle, ADC adaptively does not wake up in S status and increasingly achieves the same duty cycle as PDC, as shown in Fig. 6(d).

For setting an appropriate SSL, obviously, there is a tradeoff in PDC among the three metrics. For example, a larger SSL can conserve more energy but lead to a lower packet delivery ratio and longer latency. On the contrary, a larger SSL is expected in ADC for conserving more energy, without obviously affecting the other two performance metrics. Furthermore, all the results in Fig. 6 show that the ADCs with and without free addressing have almost the same performance, which demonstrates the efficacy of the proposed free-addressing scheme.

4   Conclusion

This paper presented an adaptive data collection protocol, ADC, for WSNs. With the dynamic duty-cycling feature, ADC can utilize the sleeping slots adaptively for data transmission, improving the network load adaptivity and energy efficiency. With the free-addressing feature, there is no need to pre-assign unique addresses to sensor nodes or perform any address allocation and management procedure in runtime, improving the network heterogeneity.

Acknowledgment. This work is supported in part by NSERC, CFI, and BCKDF. The authors would also like to thank Dr. Kui Wu for his support on the testbed implementation.

References

1. Wang, F., Liu, J.: Networked wireless sensor data collection: issues, challenges, and approaches. IEEE Commun. Surv. Tutor. **13**(4), 673–687 (2011)
2. Burri, N., Von Rickenbach, P., Wattenhofer, R.: Dozer: Ultra-low power data gathering in sensor networks. In: Proceedings of ACM/IEEE IPSN, pp. 450–459 (2007)
3. Ruzzelli, A.G., OHare, G.M., Jurdak, R.: MERLIN: cross-layer integration of MAC and routing for low duty-cycle sensor networks. Ad Hoc Netw. **6**(8), 1238–1257 (2008)
4. Tong, F., Zhang, R., Pan, J.: One handshake can achieve more: an energy-efficient, practical pipelined data collection for duty-cycled sensor networks. IEEE Sens. J. **PP**(99), 1–15 (2016)
5. Zolertia. http://zolertia.io/. Accessed 19 May 2016
6. Tmote Sky. http://tmote-sky.blogspot.ca/. Accessed 19 May 2016
7. Cao, Y., Guo, S., He, T.: Robust multi-pipeline scheduling in low-duty-cycle wireless sensor networks. In: Proceedings of IEEE INFOCOM, pp. 361–369 (2012)
8. Contiki OS. http://www.contiki-os.org. Accessed 19 May 2016
9. Gnawali, O., Fonseca, R., Jamieson, K., et al.: Collection tree protocol. In: Proceedings of ACM SenSys, pp. 1–14 (2009)
10. Werner-Allen, G., Lorincz, K., Johnson, J., et al.: Fidelity and yield in a volcano monitoring sensor network. In: Proceedings of USENIX OSDI, pp. 381–396 (2006)
11. Xu, K., Gerla, M., Bae, S.: How effective is the IEEE 802.11 RTS/CTS handshake in ad hoc networks. In: Proceedings of IEEE GLOBECOM, pp. 72–76 (2002)
12. Osterlind, F., Dunkels, A., Eriksson, J., et al.: Cross-level sensor network simulation with COOJA. In: Proceedings of IEEE LCN, pp. 641–648 (2006)

Multi-phased Carrier Sense Multiple Access with Collision Resolution

Hyun-Ho Choi[1]($\boxtimes$) and Jung-Ryun Lee[2]

[1] Hankyong National University, Anseong 17579, South Korea
hhchoi@hknu.ac.kr
[2] Chung-Ang University, Seoul 06974, South Korea
jrlee@cau.ac.kr

Abstract. To improve the efficiency of carrier sense multiple access (CSMA)-based medium access control (MAC) protocol, CSMA with collision resolution (CSMA/CR) has been proposed. In the CSMA/CR protocol, a transmitting station can detect a collision by employing additional carrier sensing after the start of data transmission and resolve the next collision that might occur by broadcasting a jam signal during a collision detection (CD) period. By extending this original CSMA/CR protocol that uses a single CD phase, in this paper we propose a multi-phased CSMA/CR (MP-CSMA/CR) protocol that employs multiple CD phases. In the proposed MP-CSMA/CR protocol, colliding stations are filtered in each CD phase, and only surviving stations compete again in the next CD phase. Therefore, the collision resolution probability becomes higher as the CD phases proceed. Results show that the proposed MP-CSMA/CR protocol significantly outperforms the conventional CSMA/CR with a single CD phase.

Keywords: Carrier sense multiple access (CSMA) · Medium access control (MAC) · Collision detection · Collision resolution

1 Introduction

One of the most performance-effective factors in a distributed wireless network is the medium access control (MAC) protocol, which decides how to efficiently distribute the limited radio resources among users while ensuring fair treatment of all users. A representative distributed MAC protocol in the distributed network is the carrier sensing multiple access with collision avoidance (CSMA/CA) protocol, which is widely used because of its operational simplicity [1]. However, it is well known that the efficiency of CSMA/CA is reduced by the successive collisions of retransmitted data as the number of contending stations increases [2]. To improve the efficiency of CSMA-based MAC protocols, the CSMA with collision detection (CSMA/CD)-like behavior has been variously emulated in wireless environments [3–7]. This attempt is due to the fact that CSMA/CD makes it possible for the transmitter to detect a collision while sending data and to suspend the transmission immediately when a collision is detected. However,

© ICST Institute for Computer Sciences, Social Informatics and Telecommunications Engineering 2017
J.-H. Lee and S. Pack (Eds.): QShine 2016, LNICST 199, pp. 223–232, 2017.
DOI: 10.1007/978-3-319-60717-7_22

the original CSMA/CD protocol is infeasible in wireless media because the wireless transmitter cannot send and listen at the same time on the same channel. If so, the receiver of the transmitter is overwhelmed by its own transmission power, which is called the deafness problem in wireless media.

As the first attempt to overcome the deafness problem and allow the CSMA/CD operation in a wireless network, CSMA with time-split collision detection has been proposed under assuming a long propagation delay [3]. In this protocol, the transmitter stops after sending a preamble with a fixed length and shortly performs carrier sensing. Because of the discriminating radio propagation delay, simultaneously transmitting stations can detect the other preamble signals and thus pause their data transmissions. For a shorter delay environment, CSMA with time-split collision detection based on multi-tone tree search has been proposed as well [4]. As more practical approach to collision detection in wireless media, a wireless CSMA/CD (WCSMA/CD) protocol has been presented [5,6]. In WCSMA/CD, every station defines a collision detection (CD) period with the same length and each transmitter randomly decides a short CD slot during the CD period after the data transmission starts. Then, the transmitter senses the channel at the selected CD slot to verify whether a collision has happened. If colliding stations exists and they all do not select the same CD slot, each station detects an energy level higher than the threshold at the CD slot; thus detecting a collision. In this case, the colliding stations abort their transmission within the CD period and thus the wasted time is reduced. By enhancing the WCSMA/CD, the CSMA with collision resolution (CSMA/CR) protocol has also been proposed [7]. Upon detecting a collision in CSMA/CR, the transmitter instantly stops its transmission and broadcasts a jam signal in order to notice the other stations that they must abort their transmissions. The CSMA/CR protocol gives a priority to the station that has sent the jam signal during the CD period to retransmit the data without backoff and makes the other stations defer access automatically. Consequently, this operation resolves a next collision that might occur and so leads to more performance improvement.

Although the previous CSMA/CR improves the MAC efficiency considerably, the access collision still exists and the throughput degrades due to the collision, backoff time, and additional protocol overhead. These problem become severer particularly when the number of accessing stations increases significantly [8]. In this paper, by extending the original CSMA/CR protocol [7], we propose a multi-phased CSMA/CR (MP-CSMA/CR) that employs multiple CD periods in order to further increase the probability of collision resolution and therefore increase the throughput. We investigate optimal operating parameters, such as the number of CD phases and the number of CD slots per phase, to maximize the throughput.

The rest of this paper is organized as follows. Section 2 reviews the operation of the original CSMA/CR protocol. Section 3 explains the operation of the proposed MP-CSMA/CR protocol in detail. Section 4 shows the throughput of MP-CSMA/CR by considering various parameters. Finally, Sect. 5 presents the conclusions drawn in this study.

2   Original CSMA/CR Protocol

In the CSMA/CR protocol, every transmitter allocates a short CD slot randomly within a predetermined fixed CD period when the data transmission starts. Thereafter, it senses the channel at the selected CD slot to verify whether energy or jam signal or both are detected or not. This operation generates four events in CSMA/CR, as shown in Fig. 1.

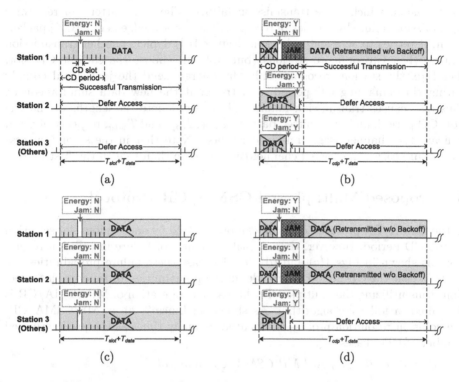

Fig. 1. Possible cases in CSMA/CR with a single phase; (a) 1st success: only one station accesses the channel, (b) 2nd success: collision is resolved as only one station chooses the earliest CD slot, (c) 1st failure: every station chooses the same CD slot, (d) 2nd failure: two or more (not all) stations choose the earliest CD slot.

Figure 1(a) illustrates the first success case in which any stations do not access simultaneously; therefore, neither energy nor jam is not sensed during the CD slot. The station keeps transmitting its data right after the short sensing at the CD slot and completes transmission successfully. Figure 1(b) shows the second success case in which Station 1, which chooses the earliest CD slot among the colliding stations, detects the energy but not a jam. Because Station 1 detects a collision first, it should subsequently transmits a jam signal instead of a data signal during the remainder of the CD period. This enables Stations 2 and 3 that select a later CD slot to detect both the energy and jam signal and their on-going transmissions to abort immediately. At the end of the CD period, only the station that sent the jam signal is permitted to retransmit its data immediately without backoff whereas the other stations defer their access automatically. Such collision resolution protocol promises successful data retransmission of at least one station if a collision is detected during the CD period.

Figure 1(c) exhibits the first failure in which all colliding stations choose the same CD slot. Thus, they cannot detect the energy and thus continue data transmission, which cause transmission failure. The transmitter can recognize transmission failure by the lack of receipt of the acknowledgement (ACK) packet. Then, it retries to access after backoff. Figure 1(d) depicts another transmission failure when two or more stations (but not all) choose the earliest CD slot; therefore, the stations recognize only the energy, send the jam signal equally during the remaining CD period, and transmit the new data simultaneously. This also causes transmission failure.[1] Here, we denote the lengths of the CD slot, CD period, and transmitted data by T_{slot}, T_{cdp}, and T_{data}, respectively, and indicate the channel usage time in each case. Note that in the second success and failure cases, the wasted channel time is more than that in the first ones.

3   Proposed Multi-phased CSMA/CR Protocol

In the CSMA/CR protocol, collision can be resolved by one random slot selection in one CD period. However, there is still a chance of failure in collision resolution, as shown in Figs. 1(c) and (d). To decrease these failure probabilities, we try to repeat the CD period to provide more opportunities for random slot selection, thus utilizing the multiple CD phases. The operation of MP-CSMA/CR is described in following algorithm. As shown in Lines 7–20, in MP-CSMA/CR, the collision resolution process is repeated as many times as the predetermined number of CD phases (h).

Pseudo code of the proposed MP-CSMA/CR protocol

```
01: Sense the channel
02: IF (channel is idle & random[0,1] < p)
03:     Start data transmission
04: ELSE
05:     Wait until the channel is idle
06: ENDIF
07: FOR (i=0; i<h; i++)                    /* h = # of CD phases */
08:     Select a CD slot number=random[1,m] /* m = # of CD slots per phase */
09:     Pause at the selected CD slot and sense the channel
10:     SWITCH (sensing result)
11:         CASE (Energy=No & Jam=No):
12:             Continue data transmission
13:         CASE (Energy=Yes & Jam=No):
```

---

[1] In this case, the station that selects the later CD slot (i.e., Station 3) detects the overlapped jam signal. Because an overlapped signal with the same pattern is generally detectable [9], Station 3 can recognize the jam signal and stop its transmission.

```
14:              Transmit a jam signal until the current CD period ends
15:              Retransmit data from the beginning
16:          CASE (Energy=Yes & Jam=Yes):
17:              Stop data transmission
18:              Break and go to Line 21
19:      END SWITCH
20: END FOR
21: IF (Receive ACK)
22:      Transmission success
23: ELSE
24:      Transmission failure
25:      Execute backoff procedure
26: END IF
```

To explain the operation of MP-CSMA/CR in detail, we illustrate the possible event cases when only two CD phases are used. As shown in Fig. 2, there are three successful transmission cases and three failure cases. Figure 2(a) shows the case when only one station accesses the channel and no collision occurs. Figure 2(b) shows the case when only one station chooses the earliest CD slot at the first CD phase, and collision resolution is successful at the first CD phase. Figure 2(c) shows the case when collision resolution fails as two stations of the total three stations choose the earliest CD slot at the first CD phase. However, at the second CD phase, these two colliding stations continue the collision resolution process and only one station among them chooses the earliest CD slot and eventually collision is resolved. As shown, in each CD phase, only the stations that select the earliest CD slot are filtered. They compete again in the next CD phase. In this way, as the CD phase proceeds, the number of contending stations decreases and the collision resolution probability (i.e., the probability that only one station selects the earliest CD slot in each CD phase) increases. Note that each case has a different channel usage time. In other words, each case is classified according to the channel usage time.

As shown in Figs. 1(c) and (d), transmission fails when all stations select the same CD slot or some stations select the earliest CD slot. In each case, the wasted channel time is different. By an appropriate arrangement of two such cases in two CD phases, we get three cases of transmission failure based on wasted channel times. Figure 2(d) shows the case when all stations choose the same CD slot in every CD phase. Figure 2(e) shows the case when some stations choose the earliest CD slot at the first CD phase and all the surviving stations choose the same CD slot at the second CD phase. Figure 2(f) shows the case when some stations choose the earliest CD slot at the second CD phase after any failure at the first CD phase. Note that in the latter case more channel time is wasted.

It is worth noting that MP-CSMA/CR has two strong points that contribute to performance improvement. The first one is that only stations that choose the earliest CD slot are filtered in each CD phase and have a chance to retry at the next CD phase. This makes the number of contending stations decrease as the CD phase proceeds, eventually increasing the probability of collision resolution. The second point is that if the collision is resolved at a certain CD phase (i.e.,

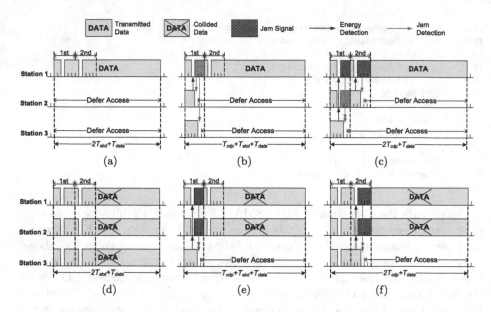

Fig. 2. Event cases in MP-CSMA/CR with two CD phases; (a) 1st success case: only one station accesses the channel, (b) 2nd success case: collision is resolved at the first CD phase, (c) 3rd success case: collision is resolved at the second CD phase, (d) 1st failure case: all stations choose the same CD slot in all CD phases, (e) 2nd failure case: some stations choose the earliest CD slot at the first CD phase and all the surviving stations choose the same CD slot at the second CD phase, (f) 3rd failure case: some stations choose the earliest CD slot at the second CD phase after any failure at the first CD phase.

only one station chooses the earliest CD slot), all the data transmitted during the following CD phases is valid (not corrupted), and just one CD slot in each CD phase is added as the overhead. This does not cause a large transmission overhead although the CD phases remain after a collision is successfully resolved.

4   Results and Discussions

We consider a fully connected wireless network where numerous stations exist [5–7]. This means that the stations are densely located and each station can detect the transmission of any other station in the network (i.e., no hidden or exposed terminal exists). We assume that channel condition is ideal so that channel and sensing errors do not exist. Thus, transmission failure occurs by only access collision [10,11]. In addition, we suppose a saturation condition in which every station has data packets in the buffer all the time and always tries to access the channel [12,13]. We assume a slotted p-persistent access mechanism; thus, every station accesses the idle channel with the probability p $(0 < p \leq 1)$ [6,14]. This access probability p can be adjusted by the network conditions or traffic loads, but we fix it here to focus on the influence of the other parameters on the performance. We also assume that the propagation delay is much smaller than the slot time and is neglected. We suppose that all stations transmit data of the same size and denote the data transmission time by T_{data}, which contains the short inter-frame space and ACK reception time [6]. We denote the length of the CD slot by T_{slot} and set the CD slot length to be the same as the general slot length by considering the worst case scenario because the CD slot time must be shorter than the general slot time to prevent the other stations from trying a new access when a station senses at a CD slot [5]. We denote the number of available CD slots per CD phase by m. For simplicity, we assume that the number of CD slots is fixed in each CD phase. Moreover, we denote the length of one CD period by T_{cdp}, which becomes $T_{cdp} = (1 + m)T_{slot}$ because the first slot must include the preamble and the information of the selected CD slot number to preserve synchronization and data integrity at the receiving station [6]. We denote the number of CD phases by h and the number of stations by n.

We compare the proposed MP-CSMA/CR protocol with the original single-phased CSMA/CR protocol.[2] For evaluation, we fix the values of p and T_{slot} and vary the values of n, m, h, and T_{data} within appropriate ranges. We set $p = 1$ (i.e., 1-persistent CSMA) to verify the effectiveness of the proposed scheme under heavy traffic conditions without any access control mechanism. Moreover, T_{slot} is set to $9\,\mu s$ by considering the OFDM PHY mode specified in the IEEE 802.11 system [15] and the default of the data size T_{data} is set to 512 bytes under the assumption of a data transmission rate of 6 Mbps.

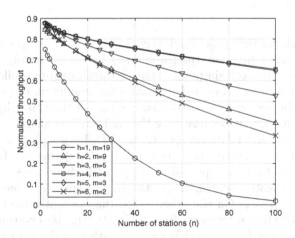

Fig. 3. Throughput vs. number of stations subject to $h(m + 1) \leq 20$.

Figure 3 shows the normalized throughput versus the number of stations for some (h, m)-pairs subject to $h(m + 1) \leq 20$. The throughput decreases as the

---

[2] The comparison results of CSMA/CR with the other CSMA-based MAC protocols (i.e., CSMA/CA and WCSMA/CD) can be found in [7].

number of stations increases because of the increase of access collision. Compared to the case of single-phase ($h = 1$), the multi-phase case ($h \geq 2$) significantly improves the throughput even though m is decreased. However, as h increases, the performance gain is gradually reduced and the throughput is maximized at $h = 4$ because a large value of h diminishes the m value and induces more collisions in each CD phase. Hence, it is important for MP-CSMA/CR to determine the (h, m)-pair that will maximize the throughput.

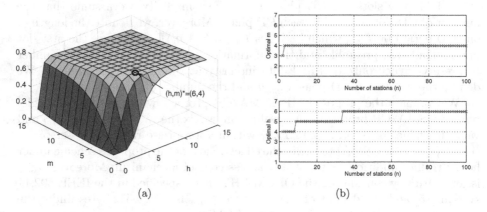

(a)   (b)

Fig. 4. (a) Throughput vs. (h, m)-pair when $n = 50$ and (b) optimal (h, m)-pair vs. number of stations.

Figure 4(a) shows the throughput versus the (h, m)-pair when n is fixed as 50. As both h and m increase, the throughput increases sharply but begins to decrease gradually at a certain point. That is, the throughput follows a concave form as a function of h and m and it reaches the maximum at $(h, m)^* = (6, 4)$ when $n = 50$. The reason why the decreasing rate of the throughput is smaller than the increasing rate is because once the collision is resolved at a certain CD phase, all the transmitted data except just one CD slot per phase in the following CD phase is valid. Figure 4(b) shows the optimal (h, m)-pair as a function of the number of stations. Here, the optimal (h, m)-pair that maximizes the throughput was found by exhaustive search. Interestingly, the optimal value of m is fixed as 4 except when $n = 2$. On the other hand, the optimal value of h gradually increases from 4 to 6 as n increases from 2 to 100. This observation reveals that h (i.e., the number of CD phases) is more sensitive to the throughput of MP-CSMA/CR than m (i.e., the number of CD slots per phase), in accordance with the change in the number of contending stations.

Figure 5 shows the throughput versus the number of stations when the optimal (h, m)-pair obtained in Fig. 4(b) is applied. For comparison, we fix h and obtain again the optimal m that maximizes the throughput. As shown, the highest throughput is always achieved when the optimal (h, m)-pair is applied based on the change in the number of stations.

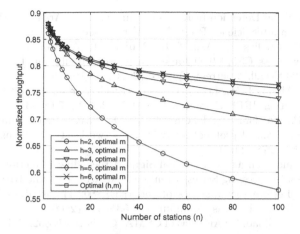

Fig. 5. Throughput vs. number of stations when the optimal (h, m)-pair is applied.

5 Conclusion

In this paper, we proposed the MP-CSMA/CR protocol by extending the typical CSMA/CR protocol to employ multiple CD phases. Results showed that the proposed MP-CSMA/CR significantly improves the throughput compared with the conventional CSMA/CR that uses a single CD phase. Moreover, the results showed that under the conditions of the same length of the total CD period, the increase in the number of CD phases (h) is more effective for achieving successful transmission than the increase in the number of CD slots per phase (m). Regarding the parameters h and m, we revealed that there exists an optimal (h, m)-pair that maximizes the throughput and h is more sensitive to the performance than m. Taking into account its improved performance, we expect that the proposed MP-CSMA/CR can be useful as a distributed MAC protocol in future networks with densely deployed stations. For further study, we will analyze the performance of MP-CSMA/CR numerically.

Acknowledgment. This research was supported by Basic Science Research Program through the National Research Foundation of Korea (NRF) funded by the Ministry of Education, Science and Technology (2011-0025424).

References

1. Colvin, A.: CSMA with collision avoidance. Comput. Commun. **6**, 227–235 (1983)
2. Bellalta, B.: IEEE 802.11ax: high-efficiency WLANS. IEEE Wirel. Commun. **23**, 38–46 (2016)
3. Lo, W.F., Mouftah, H.T.: Collision detection protocol for radio channels. In: Proceedings of 12th Biennial Symposium Communication (1984)
4. Lo, W.F., Mouftah, H.T.: Collision detection and multitone tree search for multiple-access protocols on radio channels. IEEE J. Sel. Areas Commun. **5**, 1035–1040 (1987)

5. Rom, R.: Collision Detection in Radio Channels. Local Area and Multiple Access Networks. Computer Science Press, New York (1986)
6. Voulgaris, K., Gkelias, A., Ashraf, I., Dohler, M., Aghvami, A.H.: Throughput analysis of wireless CSMA/CD for a finite user population. In: Proceedings of IEEE VTC 2006-Fall, Montreal, Quebec (2006)
7. Choi, H.-H., Moon, J.-M., Lee, I.-H., Lee, H.: Carrier sense multiple access with collision resolution. IEEE Commun. Lett. **17**, 1284–1287 (2013)
8. Teymoori, P., Yazdani, N., Khonsari, A.: DT-MAC: an efficient and scalable medium access control protocol for wireless networks. IEEE Trans. Wirel. Commun. **12**, 1268–1278 (2013)
9. Kay, S.M.: Fundamentals of Statistical Signal Processing: Detection Theory. Prentice Hall Signal Processing Series. Prentice Hall, Upper Saddle River (1998)
10. Bianchi, G.: Performance analysis of the IEEE 802.11 distributed coordination function. IEEE J. Sel. Areas Commun. **18**, 535–547 (2000)
11. Wang, F., Li, D., Zhao, Y.: Analysis of CSMA/CA in IEEE 802.15.4. IET Commun. **5**, 2187–2195 (2011)
12. Bianchi, G.: IEEE 802.11-saturation throughput analysis. IEEE Commun. Lett. **2**(12), 318–320 (1998)
13. Huang, C.-L., Liao, W.: Throughput and delay performance of IEEE 802.11e enhanced distributed channel access (EDCA) under saturation condition. IEEE Trans. Wirel. Commun. **6**, 136–145 (2007)
14. Takagi, H., Kleinrock, L.: Throughput analysis for persistent CSMA systems. IEEE Trans. Commun. **33**, 627–638 (1985)
15. IEEE Std 802.11-2007, Part 11: Wireless LAN Medium Access Control (MAC) and Physical Layer (PHY) Specifications (2007)

On Relay Node Selection for Multi-relay Cooperative Communication in Cellular Networks

Lijun Wang[1]($\boxtimes$), Tao Han[2], Jingya Lu[1], Xiaohu Ge[2], and Haiqi Jiang[2]

[1] Department of Information Science and Technology,
Wenhua College, Wuhan, China
wanglj22@163.com
[2] School of Electronic Information and Communications,
Huazhong University of Science and Technology, Wuhan, China
hantao@hust.edu.cn

Abstract. This paper introduces a relaying scheme of combining cellular networks to establish the relay selection mechanism in the heterogeneous cooperative network model, then based on the system capacity analysis, propose an optimal relay selection scheme with the constraint of the specific outage probability and power allocation. And the multi-hop nodes can act as cooperative mobile relays to ensure the normal communication, to save costs and energy consumption caused by deploying a large number of fixed relays. Simulation results show that the proposed relay node selection algorithm can guide how to dispose the fixed number of relays in the cell and how to arrange these relays to improve the performance of the ergodic capacity of the system.

Keywords: Wireless communication · Cooperative communication · Channel capacity · Multi-relay · Relay node placement

1 Introduction

The wireless communication systems are required to provide more high-rate multimedia services and data services than ever before, so the purpose of the cooperative communication is to make full use of the resource [1], and to improve the performance of the node which has the demand of communication with participating into the high-speed and reliable wireless communication [2]. Many contributions have been made by previous researchers on how to choose suitable cooperative relay nodes, the reference [3] mainly introduced the multi-relay cooperative communication into the existing cellular structure and it is considered as one of the most practical improvements under the demand of high rate and high coverage. The work in [4] studied the joint optimization of the relay position and power allocation according to the channel capacity as the performance indicator in the multi-relay cooperative communication. And the reference [5] calculated the exact capacity of multi-relay multiuser cooperative networks based on two-step relay selection scheme. And it advocated the capacity analysis of an amplify-and-forward cooperative communication system model in

© ICST Institute for Computer Sciences, Social Informatics and Telecommunications Engineering 2017
J.-H. Lee and S. Pack (Eds.): QShine 2016, LNICST 199, pp. 233–241, 2017.
DOI: 10.1007/978-3-319-60717-7_23

multi-relay multiuser networks. Determining the number of relay nodes is also a hot issue. Therefore, in this paper, we study the joint optimization of the number and placement of relay nodes according to the ergodic capacity of the multi-relay cooperative system. According to the way of relay nodes processing and forwarding information, the relays can be sorted into Amplify-and-Forward (AF) and Decode-and-Forward (DF) [6].

For the cell in which relay stations are deployed, the number and placement of relay nodes will greatly impact the capacity of the network [7]. On the basis of the former research [8, 9] of the instantaneous capacity, we consider AF in our system model, constitute a cooperative communication model of a multiuser cellular relay network, and investigate the joint optimization problem of the number and placement of relay nodes for multi-relay cooperative communication system, and then we analyze the relationship between the channel ergodic capacity and the number and placement of the relay nodes.

2 Relay Model

The earliest model of the cooperative communication is a three-node model [10], followed by the continuous emergence of multi-relay parallel transmission model and multi-hop model. Due to the different locations of users, the communication between the mobile terminal and the base station can be achieved by the assistance of one or more relay stations.

We consider a homogeneous isotropic unitary cell [11] of circular structure as shown in Fig. 1. The system which is fixed to a certain place in the cell choosing a single relay node to communicate with the base station can be treated as a three-node cooperative communication model. Therefore, in order to simplify the notations in the down-link scenario [12, 13], we respectively use the source node S, the relay node R and the destination node D to stand for the base station BS, the wireless access point AP or the mobile station MS. The radius of the cellular circle is L, the center of the circle is the location of the base station S, and there are M relays R_m ($m = 1, 2, \ldots M$) located in

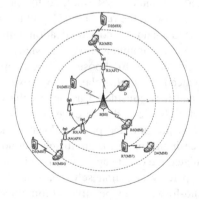

Fig. 1. A homogeneous isotropic unitary cell

the cell. At the same time, N mobile stations D_n ($n = 1, 2, \ldots N$) are also uniformly distributed in the same area [14]. We consider the symmetry of the circular cell and the uniform distribution of the mobile terminals, and a large number of literature [15, 16] demonstrated by simulation that we can gain the optimal system performance of the cell in which relays are uniformly distributed when the base station is the center of the circular cell.

3   The Selection Algorithm of Relay Nodes

3.1   The Relay Model

The corresponding instantaneous SNR_S of the links of S to D_n, S to R_m and R_m to D_n are denoted by γ_{S,D_n}, γ_{S,R_m} and γ_{R_m,D_n}. Then $\gamma_{S,D_n} = \frac{P_S}{N_O}|h_{S,D_n}|^2$, $\gamma_{S,R_m} = \frac{P_S}{N_O}|h_{S,R_m}|^2$ and $\gamma_{R_m,D_n} = \frac{P_R}{N_O}|h_{R_m,D_n}|^2$. $\bar{\gamma}_{S,R_m} = \frac{P_S}{N_O}E(|h_{S,R_m}|^2)$ and $\bar{\gamma}_{R_m,D_n} = \frac{P_R}{N_O}E(|h_{R_m,D_n}|^2)$ are the means of γ_{S,R_m} and γ_{R_m,D_n} [17].

When the source node S send information to the destination node D_n directly, the direct channel capacity [18] C_{D_n} is

$$C_{D_n} = \log_2(1 + \gamma_{S,D_n}). \tag{1}$$

The multi-node cooperative transmission instantaneous capacity using AF protocol C_{AF} can be written as

$$C_{AF} = \frac{1}{2}\log_2(1 + \gamma_{S,D_n} + \gamma_{S,R_m,D_n}). \tag{2}$$

Where γ_{S,R_m,D_n} is the instantaneous equivalent SNR of the forwarding path [5], which can be written as

$$\gamma_{S,R_m,D_n} = \frac{\gamma_{S,R_m}\gamma_{R_m,D_n}}{\gamma_{S,R_m} + \gamma_{R_m,D_n} + 1}. \tag{3}$$

Therefore, the AF cooperative state ergodic capacity is

$$\overline{C_{AF}} = E_h[C_{AF}] = E_{\gamma_{S,D_n},\gamma_{S,R_m},\gamma_{R_m,D_n}}[\frac{1}{2}\log_2(1 + \gamma_{S,D_n} + \gamma_{S,R_m,D_m})]. \tag{4}$$

γ_{S,R_m} and γ_{R_m,D_n} are two random variables satisfying the exponential distribution, so we assume the parameters are λ_{S,R_m} and λ_{R_m,D_n}. When the SNR is high, γ_{S,R_m,D_n} is still an approximate exponential random variable [19], so we set the parameter is λ_{S,R_m,D_n}.

$$\lambda_{S,R_m,D_n} = \lambda_{S,R_m} + \lambda_{R_m,D_n} \tag{5}$$

Let $\overline{\gamma}_{S,R_m,D_n} = \frac{1}{\lambda_{S,R_m,D_n}} = \frac{1}{d_{S,R_m}^{\alpha}\frac{N_O}{P_S}+d_{R_m,D_n}^{\alpha}\frac{N_O}{P_R}}$. According to the formula (4) and Jensen inequality, we can obtain the upper bound for the AF cooperative state ergodic capacity which is:

$$\overline{C}_{AF} \le \frac{1}{2}\log_2(1+\overline{\gamma}_{S,D}+\overline{\gamma}_{S,R_m,D_n}) = \frac{1}{2}\log_2\left(1+\frac{1}{d_{S,D_n}^{\alpha}\frac{N_O}{P_S}}+\frac{1}{d_{S,R_m}^{\alpha}\frac{N_O}{P_S}+d_{R_m,D_n}^{\alpha}\frac{N_O}{P_R}}\right). \quad (6)$$

So the under link state ergodic capacity of multi-user [19] can be expressed as

$$\overline{C} = \begin{cases} \frac{1}{2}\log_2\left(1+\frac{1}{d_{s,D_n}^{\alpha}\frac{N_O}{P_s}}+\frac{1}{d_{S,R_m}^{\alpha}\frac{N_O}{P_S}+d_{R_m,D_n}^{\alpha}\frac{N_O}{P_R}}\right), & (l,\theta) \in S_m (m=1,\ldots M); \\ \log_2\left(1+\frac{1}{d_{S,D_n}^{\alpha}\frac{N_O}{P_S}}\right), & (l,\theta) \in S_0 \end{cases} \quad (7)$$

Then we give the specific analysis of the scene of the circular cell. According to Fig. 1, we can obtain

$$\Omega_{S,D_n} = l^{-\alpha}, \Omega_{R_m,D_n} = d^{-\alpha} \quad (8)$$
$$\Omega_{S,R_n} = (l^2+d^2-2ld\cos(\theta-2\pi m/M))^{-\alpha/2}$$

By substituting formula (8) into formula (7), we can obtain the state erode capacity $\overline{C}$ as

$$\overline{C} = \begin{cases} \frac{1}{2}\log_2\left(1+P_S^{\prime l-\alpha}+\frac{1}{(l^2+d^2-2ld\cos\theta)^{\alpha/2}\frac{N_O}{P_S}+d^{\alpha}\frac{N_O}{P_R}}\right), & d_{th}<l<L; \\ \log_2\left(1+\frac{P_S^{l-\alpha}}{N_o}\right), & 0\le l\le d_{th} \end{cases} \quad (9)$$

Because of the good symmetry of the circular cell and the hypothesis of the uniform distribution of all the users and relays, if we intend to calculate the expectation of the state ergodic capacity of all user's position in the cell, we only need to research on the sector coverage of one-single relay, then we can obtain the ergodic capacity of the whole cell by multiplying the number of relays M. The capacity of users in the interval is $\overline{C}_{S/S_{AF}}(M,d,l,\theta)$, $\theta \in [-\pi/M, \pi/M]$. Based on the above formula (9), we can calculate the ergodic capacity of the system as

$$\hat{C}(M,d) = E_{l,\theta}[\hat{C}(M,d,l,\theta)]$$
$$= M\left(\begin{array}{c}\int_{-\frac{\pi}{M}}^{\frac{\pi}{M}}\int_0^{d_{th}}\psi(l,\theta)\overline{C}_D(M,d,l,\theta)dld\theta \\ +\int_{-\frac{\pi}{M}}^{\frac{\pi}{M}}\int_{d_{th}}^{L}\psi(l,\theta)\overline{C}_{AF}(M,d,l,\theta)dld\theta\end{array}\right) = \frac{2M}{\pi L^2}\left(\begin{array}{c}\int_0^{\frac{\pi}{M}}\int_0^{d_{th}}l(M,d,l,\theta)dld\theta \\ +\int_0^{\frac{\pi}{M}}\int_{d_{th}}^{L}l\overline{C}_{AF}(M,d,l,\theta)dld\theta\end{array}\right). \quad (10)$$

To sum up, the objective function of the joint optimization in the multi-relay amplify and forward cooperative communication is

$$\max_{M,d} \widehat{C}(M,d). \tag{11}$$

The constraint conditions are $\left\{ \begin{array}{l} M \geq 3 \ and \ M \in \mathbb{Z}^+ \\ 0 \leq d \leq L \end{array} \right\}.$

3.2 Performance Analysis of the Relayed System

We study on the impact of the relay number M and the relay radius d on the objective function $\widehat{C}(M,d)$, respectively.

(1) The monotonicity relationship between $\widehat{C}(M,d)$ and M.

Taking the relay radius d as a constant, $\widehat{C}(M,d)$ is a function whose variable is the relay number M. According to formula (11), we can obtain

$$\widehat{C}(M) = C_1 + C_2 M \int_0^{\pi/M} \int_{d_{th}}^L l \log_2(C_3 + [C_4(l^2 + d^2 - 2ld \cos \theta)^{\alpha/2} + C_5]^{-1}) dl d\theta. \tag{12}$$

Where $C_i (i = 1, \ldots 5)$ can be regarded as constant values which have nothing to do with M, and $C_i > 0$.

Combining with formula (12) and the integral mean value theorem, we can obtain

$$\begin{aligned} \frac{\partial \widehat{C}(M)}{\partial M} &= C_2 \int_0^{\frac{\pi}{M}} \int_{d_{th}}^L l \log_2 \left(C_3 + [C_4(l^2 + d^2 - 2ld \cos \theta)^{\alpha/2} + C_5]^{-1} \right) dl d\theta \\ &\quad - C_2 \frac{\pi}{M} \int_{d_{th}}^L l \log_2 \left(C_2 + [C_4(l^2 + d^2 - 2ld \cos \frac{\pi}{M})^{\alpha/2} + C_5]^{-1} \right) dl \\ &= C_2 \frac{\pi}{M} \int_{d_{th}}^L l \log_2 \left(C_3 + [C_4(l^2 + d^2 - 2ld \cos \theta)^{\alpha/2} + C_5]^{-1} \right) dl \\ &\quad - C_2 \frac{\pi}{M} \int_{d_{th}}^L l \log_2 \left(C_2 + [C_4(l^2 + d^2 - 2ld \cos \frac{\pi}{M})^{\alpha/2} + C_5]^{-1} \right) dl \end{aligned} \tag{13}$$

Where $\xi \in (0, \pi/M)$, because $M \geq 2$, there is $0 < \xi < \frac{\pi}{M} \leq \frac{\pi}{2}$. So $\frac{\partial C(M)}{\partial M} > 0$, namely, the ergodic capacity of the system is the monotonically increasing function about M.

(2) The monotonicity relationship between $\widehat{C}(M,d)$ and d.

Taking the relay number M as a constant, $\widehat{C}(M,d)$ is a function whose variable is the relay radius d. Here in order to simplify the derivation, we set $\phi(d) = d, P'_S = P'_R = P$, $\alpha = 4$. And according to formula (10), we can obtain

$$\widehat{C}(d) = \frac{2}{L^2} \int_0^d l \log_2(1 + Pl^{-4}) dl$$
$$+ \frac{1}{L^2} \int_d^L l \int_0^{\frac{\pi}{M}} \log_2\left(1 + Pl^{-4} + \frac{P}{(l^2 + d^2 - 2ld\cos\theta)^2 + d^4}\right) d\theta dl \tag{14}$$

Because the derivation process of $\widehat{C}(d)$ about d is very complicated, here the conclusion after the derivation; is given directly as

$$\frac{\partial^2 \widehat{C}(d)}{\partial d^2} < 0. \tag{15}$$

According to formula (15), we can know that the figure of $\widehat{C}(d)$ is convex arc which increases first and then decreases. When $\frac{\partial \widehat{C}(d)}{\partial d} = 0$, we can obtain the optimal position (namely the maximum ergodic capacity) of the relay node $d^*(M)$ based on the fixed relay numbers.

Here we give the following conclusions: $\widehat{C}(M, d)$ is a monotonically increasing function about M. For any M, there is only one optimal position $d^*(M)$ corresponding to the maximum ergodic capacity $C^*(M)$, namely

$$\frac{\partial \widehat{C}(M, d)}{\partial d} = 0 \Rightarrow d * (M) \Rightarrow \widehat{C}(M) = \widehat{C}(M, d * (M)). \tag{16}$$

(3) The determination of the optimal relay number M and relay radius d.

The following inspection is the enhancement of the percentage of the capacity based on the relay number M, namely, to fix the relay radius d, and we compare the corresponding ergodic capacity $\widehat{C}(M, d)$ when the relay number is M with the corresponding ergodic capacity $\widehat{C}(M - 1, d)$ when the relay number is $M - 1$. We calculate the increasing percentage taking the cost consideration $K(M)$ into account when we increase the relay number.

$$K(M) = \frac{\widehat{C}(M, d) - \widehat{C}(M - 1, d)}{\widehat{C}(M - 1, d)} \tag{17}$$

Taking the cost consideration into account when we increase the relay number, and combining with the experience in the project application, we determine the threshold ε of the increasing percentage of the ergodic capacity as the relay number M increases. Then according to the following formulas, we determine the optimal $M*$ and $d*$ as

$$M* = \arg\left\{\min_M \left(K^M(M)\right) \leq \varepsilon\right\} \tag{18}$$

$$\frac{\partial \widehat{C}(M*,d)}{\partial d} = 0 \Rightarrow d * (M*) \tag{19}$$

4 Numerical Results and Analysis

In order to have an intuitive knowledge of the relationship between the given exact value of the ergodic capacity and the upper bound, we use P_T to denote the summation of P_S and P_R. Figures 3 and 4 respectively give the comparison between the upper bound of ergodic capacity and numerical integration for $P_S = P_R = P_T/2$ and $P_S = P_R = 2P_T/3$.

As shown in Figs. 2 and 3, we can see that the numerical curves and the simulation curves of the state ergodic capacity are in good agreement and very close to the upper bound under any channel variance and power allocation. Therefore, according to the upper bound of formula (5), we can obtain relatively accurate state ergodic capacity of multiuser.

In Fig. 4 we give the curves of the increasing percentage of the ergodic capacity $\widehat{C}(M, R_r)$ about the relay number M when different relay nodes place at different radius R_r. The radius of the cell $L = 1000$ m, $N_O = 100$ dBm, the path loss exponent $\alpha = 4$, and we set P_S and P_R as a same fixed value, namely, $P_S = P_R = 30$ dBm. As for the relay radius, we respectively choose three typical value of $R_r = 100$ m near the station, $R_r = 100$ m near the edge of the cell and $R_r = 320$ m near the optimal position.

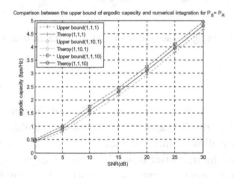

Fig. 2. Comparison between the upper bound of ergodic capacity and numerical integration for $P_S = P_R$

As can be seen from the Fig. 4, regardless of the position of the relay node, the increasing percentage of the ergodic capacity decreases when M increases. When M is small, the ergodic capacity increases largely, but when M increases to a certain extent, and then add M, the increasing percentage of the ergodic capacity approaches to zero. In addition, when the relay number M is determined, the relay radius also plays a significant role.

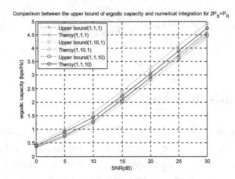

Fig. 3. Comparison between the upper bound of ergodic capacity and numerical integration for $2P_S = P_R$

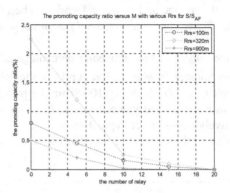

Fig. 4. The promoting capacity ratio versus M with various R_{rs} for S/S_{AF}

5 Conclusion

This paper investigates the joint optimization problem of the number and placement of relay nodes based on the ergodic capacity of multiuser downlink, when multiuser use AF relay mode for downlink communication in a circular relay cell. We give the numerical expression of the multiuser downlink ergodic capacity, based on which we analyze the relationship between the ergodic capacity and the number and placement of relay nodes, the conclusions are as follows: (1) When the number of relay nodes is small, increasing the quantity of relay nodes can greatly increase the ergodic capacity, while the number of relay nodes is large, the performance improvement of the cell is slight for the further increasing of the quantity of relay nodes. (2) When the relay number is given, we can determine the optimal placement of the relay node by the algorithm and the simulation. Finally, we propose a method to determine the optimal number and placement of relay nodes, and provide an analysis and a theoretical basis for how to dispose the fixed number of relays in the cell and how to arrange these relays to improve the performance of the ergodic capacity of the system.

Acknowledgements. The authors would like to acknowledge the support from the Hubei Provincial Department of Education Scientific research projects (No. B2015188) and the grant from Wenhua College (No. 2013Y08).

References

1. Ge, X., Tu, S., Mao, G.: 5G ultra-dense cellular networks. IEEE Wirel. Commun. **23**(1), 72–79 (2016)
2. Chen, M., Qian, Y., Mao, S., et al.: Software-defined mobile networks security. Mob. Netw. Appl. **21**, 1–15 (2016)
3. Minelli, M., Ma, M., Coupechoux, M.: Optimal relay placement in cellular networks. IEEE Trans. Wirel. Commun. **13**(2), 998–1009 (2014)
4. Zhang, G., Yang, K., Liu, P.: Fair and efficient spectrum resource allocation and admission control for multi-user and multi-relay cellular networks. Wirel. Pers. Commun. **78**(1), 347–373 (2014)
5. Guo, W., Liu, J., Liu, Y.: Exact capacity analysis of multi-relay multiuser cooperative networks based on two-step selection. Int. J. Commun. Syst. **23**, 662–673 (2013)
6. Sharma, S., Shi, Y., Hou, Y.T.: Joint flow routing and relay node assignment in cooperative multi-hop networks. IEEE J. Sel. Areas Commun. **30**(2), 254–262 (2012)
7. Chen, M., Zhang, Y., Li, Y.: EMC: emotion-aware mobile cloud computing in 5G. IEEE Netw. **29**(2), 32–38 (2015)
8. Huang, J.H., Wang, L.C., Chang, C.J.: Design of optimal relay location in two-hop cellular systems. Wirel. Netw. **16**, 2179–2189 (2010). (Springer Science Business Media, LLC)
9. Trigui, I., Affes, S., Stephenne, A.: Ergodic capacity analysis for interference-limited AF multi-hop relaying channels in Nakagami-m fading. IEEE Trans. Commun. **61**(7), 2726–2734 (2013)
10. Feeney, L.M.: An energy consumption model for performance analysis of routing protocols for mobile ad hoc networks. Mob. Netw. Appl. **6**(3), 239–249 (2001)
11. Ge, X., Yang, B., Ye, J.: Spatial spectrum and energy efficiency of random cellular networks. IEEE Trans. Commun. **63**(3), 1019–1030 (2015)
12. Li, Y., Chen, M.: Software-defined network function virtualization: a survey. IEEE Access **3**, 2542–2553 (2015)
13. Ge, X., Tu, S., Han, T.: Energy efficiency of small cell backhaul networks based on Gauss-Markov mobile models. IET Netw. **4**(2), 158–167 (2015)
14. Chen, M., Hao, Y., Li, Y.: On the computation offloading at ad hoc cloudlet: architecture and service models. IEEE Commun. **53**(3), 18–24 (2015)
15. Jaafar, W., Ajib, W., Haccoun, D.: On the performance of multi-hop wireless relay networks. Wirel. Commun. Mob. Comput. **14**, 145–160 (2014)
16. Annamalai, A., Olabiyi, O.: Asymptotic error rate analysis of multi-hop multi-relay cooperative non-regenerative networks over generalized fading channels. In: IEEE International Wireless Communications and Mobile Computing Conference, vol. 292, no. 4, pp. 234–239 (2012)
17. Lin, T.M., Chen, W.T., Tsao, S.L.: An efficient automatic repeat request mechanism for wireless multi-hop relay networks. IEEE Trans. Veh. Technol. **62**(6), 2830–2839 (2013)
18. Han, S., Yang, C., Molisch, A.F.: Spectrum and energy efficient cooperative base station doze. IEEE J. Sel. Areas Commun. **32**(2), 285–296 (2014)
19. Zhao, Y., Fang, X., Huang, R.: Joint interference coordination and load balancing for OFDM multi-hop cellular networks. IEEE Trans. Mob. Comput. **13**(1), 89–101 (2014)

Applying a Flocking-Inspired Algorithm to Fair Resource Allocation of Vehicle-Mounted Mobile Relays

Hyun-Ho Choi[1] and Jung-Ryun Lee[2(✉)]

[1] Department of the Electrical, Electronic and Control Engineering,
Hankyong National University, Anseong, Republic of Korea
hhchoi@hknu.ac.kr
[2] School of Electrical and Electronics Engineering, College of Engineering,
Chung-Ang University, Seoul, Republic of Korea
jrlee@cau.ac.kr

Abstract. Previous studies for applying bio-inspired algorithms to resolve the traditional issues in wireless networks were motivated by some excellent characteristics of the bio-inspired algorithms including convergence, scalability, adaptability, and stability. In this paper, we apply the bio-inspired flocking algorithm to fair resource allocation in vehicle-mounted mobile relay (VMR) deployed networks. Although a VMR-deployed network has an advantage of the provision of high-quality communication services to mobile devices inside the vehicle, it is more susceptible to inter-VMR and base station (BS)-VMR interferences because both the mobility and geographical position of the VMRs and pedestrian mobile stations (MSs) cannot be artificially controlled. Therefore, the proposed flocking-inspired algorithm is designed to achieve the adaptive alleviation of the inter-VMR and BS-VMR interferences, and the attainment of a fair and distributed resource allocation among competing VMRs. We verify its self-adaptiveness under the dynamically changing network topology. The results show that the proposed flocking-inspired resource allocation method adaptively alleviates the inter-VMR and BS-VMR interferences.

Keywords: Flocking · Resource allocation · Vehicle-mounted mobile relay

1 Introduction

Over recent years, the widespread use of mobile devices equipped with wireless technologies such as LTE, WiMAX, and WLAN has enabled a nearly ubiquitous access to communication networks. The existing cellular networks, however, suffer from problems such as propagation loss, and the coverage and capacity at the cell borders remain relatively small because of a low Signal-to-Interference-plus-Noise-Ratio (SINR) [1]. To resolve this problem, relay stations (RSs) that can be deployed in existing cellular networks have been introduced to next-generation

© ICST Institute for Computer Sciences, Social Informatics and Telecommunications Engineering 2017
J.-H. Lee and S. Pack (Eds.): QShine 2016, LNICST 199, pp. 242–250, 2017.
DOI: 10.1007/978-3-319-60717-7_24

mobile networks [2]. The RSs are classified into the following three types: fixed, nomadic, and mobile. Fixed RSs are permanently installed at fixed locations; nomadic RSs are temporarily installed to extend the wireless service coverage and for the provision of improved performances when many users simultaneously use a wireless service; and mobile RSs are fully mobile and can therefore be installed in moving vehicles [3–5]. The advantage of vehicle-mounted mobile relays (VMRs) is a capability that can provide high-quality communication services to mobile users inside a vehicle with the help of smart antenna and multi-antenna technologies; while it is almost impossible to apply these antenna technologies to mobile devices because of a limited space and the low transmission power of mobile devices.

Up until now, research on the VMRs has been widely conducted. The authors of [6] evaluated the performance of VMRs in consideration of the density of the mobile RSs and the ratio of the access zones to the relay zones. In [7], a new scheduling method was suggested for the mitigation of the interference that occurs when a VMR is moving into a cell wherein a fixed relay is installed. To resolve the frequent handover problem that is due to the high speed of mobile relays, an enhanced handover scheme that uses an accelerated measurement procedure and a group in-network handover procedure is suggested in [8]. The authors of [9] proposed an optimal VMR handover method that adjusts the handover interval according to a vehicle's speed. In [10], a quantitative study has been performed to investigate the benefits of mobile relays in cellular networks with respect to the extension of base station coverage and the enhancement of wireless connection throughput.

As observed in previous studies, one of the important characteristics of VMRs is that they are deployed in scenarios wherein frequent and rapid network topology changes caused by a vehicle's mobility occur; this characteristic feature causes a dynamically changing and uncontrollable interference among the VMRs. When the density of VMRs increases (for example, the gathering of VMRs in a specific area due to traffic congestion or a traffic signal), the inter-VMR interference decreases the throughput of the mobile devices in a vehicle. Moreover, VMR interference to pedestrian MSs that are directly connected to the BS and located in nearby VMRs causes BS-VMR interference, and thereby deteriorating the cell throughput performance. An efficient resource allocation method that operates self-adaptively is therefore required to mitigate the effects of dynamically changing inter-VMR and BS-VMR interferences.

On the other hand, many researchers have studied the mathematical modeling of natural phenomena, which is called as "biologically inspired" (bio-inspired) algorithms. Bio-inspired algorithms are modeled on the behavior of organisms on Earth, which have evolved with the goal of achieving given purposes whereby the optimal results are ultimately obtained through the iterative and distributed executions of simple, heuristic operational rules without the aid of a central coordinator. As we can observe from previous successful attempts to utilize the bio-inspired algorithms [11–15], they have excellent characteristics including convergence, scalability, adaptability, and stability. In particular, the flocking model analyzes the velocity and position control mechanisms of a group of living organisms in an ecosystem such as large numbers of birds or fish [16,17]. The flocking model has been evaluated as useful for distributed networking systems because it can obtain global emergent behavior while each autonomous entity obeys only simple rules, and the information about local neighbors is used without the aid of a centralized coordinator. It is therefore expected that flocking-based resource allocation method is a suitable solution that may cope with the severe environment of a vehicular network where network topology changes dynamically and available bandwidth varies accordingly.

2   Flocking Model

The flocking model shows the phenomenon whereby each autonomous entity with its own moving direction and velocity flocks and moves in the same direction, as shown in Fig. 1. Each entity adjusts its velocity by interacting with its neighbor entities. Suppose that there are N entities. Let the position and velocity of the i-th entity in $\mathbb{R}^3$ at the discrete time $t \in \mathbb{N}$ be $x_i(t)$ and $v_i(t)$, respectively. The interaction between the neighbor entities is given by the following:

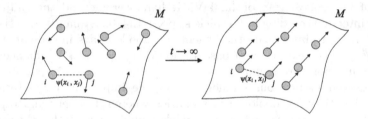

Fig. 1. Flocking behavior

$$\frac{dx_i}{dt}(t) = v_i(t), \tag{1}$$

$$v_i(t+1) - v_i(t) =$$

$$\frac{\lambda}{N} \sum_{j=1}^{N} \psi(|x_j(t) - x_i(t)|)(v_j(t) - v_i(t)) \tag{2}$$

for $1 \leq i \leq N$ and $t > 0$, where λ and $\psi(\cdot)$ are the non-negative learning factor and a communication range function that quantifies the way the agents influence each other, respectively [17]. Generally, $\psi(\cdot)$ is a non-negative function of the distance between two agents. Some examples for $\psi(\cdot)$ are as follows:

$$\psi_1(|x_j - x_i|) = 1, \tag{3}$$

$$\psi_2(|x_j - x_i|) = 1_{|x_j - x_i| \leq r}, \tag{4}$$

$$\psi_3(|x_j - x_i|) = \frac{1}{(1 + |x_j - x_i|^2)^\beta} \tag{5}$$

for positive r and non-negative β. (2) explains the interaction among the entities, as follow: each entity adjusts its velocity according to the weighted average of the differences between its own past velocity and the velocities of the other entities in the flock. By obeying this simple rule iteratively and independently, the collective behavior of each agent, namely flocking, is obtained. In this model, time-asymptotic flocking phenomena are explained by the following two conditions:

$$\lim_{t\to\infty} |v_i(t) - v_j(t)| = 0 \text{ for } i \neq j, \qquad (6)$$

$$\sup_{0\leq t<\infty} |x_i(t) - x_j(t)| < \infty \text{ for } i \neq j, \qquad (7)$$

which mean that the relative velocity of each agent converges to zero and the distance between each particle does not diverge.

3 Proposed Fair Resource Allocation Method

This subsection details a method that fairly allocates resources across adjacent VMRs in the context of the IEEE 802.16j relay network. An IEEE 802.16j-based relay transmits data to its associated users in a down link (DL) access zone (see Fig. 2). Because all of the relays use the same DL access zone, the inter-VMR interference experienced by the MSs increases as the density of VMRs increases, which deteriorates the throughput performance of the VMRs. Moreover, the resources for the pedestrian MSs are allocated in the DL access zone, causing BS-VMR interference between the inner-vehicle MSs and the pedestrian MSs and the cell throughput performance is lowered. We have therefore designed the flocking-inspired fair resource allocation method, so that the DL resource allocated to each of the VMRs is mutually exclusive and fair among nearby and competing VMRs, and the operation is conducted self-adaptively for a dynamically changing network topology.

Suppose that there is an available resource with a normalized amount of 1. We grant an *address* to each VMR that is arbitrarily chosen from the range of 0 to 1, which will act as a reference for the resource allocation. Let the address of VMR$_i$ at time t be $\alpha_i(t)$ $(0 \leq \alpha_i(t) < 1)$. We then apply (2) of the flocking model to the VMR address with the identity function of ψ, which is expressed as the following:

$$\alpha_i(t+1) - \alpha_i(t) = \frac{\lambda}{N} \sum_{j\neq i}(\alpha_j(t) - \alpha_i(t)). \qquad (8)$$

Here, we define the *resource address* of a VMR as $\widetilde{\alpha}_i := \left(\alpha_i + \dfrac{i-1}{N}\right) \bmod 1$. Without loss of generality, we reassign MSs in ascending order according to the resource address of each MS, resulting in $0 \leq \widetilde{\alpha}_1(t) < \widetilde{\alpha}_2(t) < \cdots < \widetilde{\alpha}_N(t) \leq$

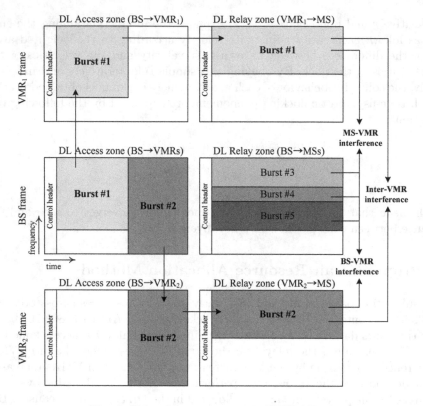

Fig. 2. Relay frame structure in IEEE 802.16j

1. The dedicated resource allocation to VMR_i at time t is determined by the following:

$$\Delta_i(t) = [\frac{\widetilde{\alpha}_{i\ominus 1}(t) + \widetilde{\alpha}_i(t)}{2}, \frac{\widetilde{\alpha}_i(t) + \widetilde{\alpha}_{i\oplus 1}(t)}{2}] \tag{9}$$

where $\oplus$ and $\ominus$ represent the addition and deletion operations modulo N, respectively (Fig. 3).

4   Performance Evaluation

First, we verify the self-adaptiveness of the proposed resource allocation method under various network topologies[1]. In the line topology shown in Fig. 4(a), node A is connected only to node B; therefore, node A changes its resource address considering only node B. Similarly, the resource address of node C is changed considering only node B. Consequently, the final resource addresses of both node A and node C are placed at the same value. Figure 4(b) shows that every node

---

[1] Hereafter, we assume that the total amount of available resources is 1024.

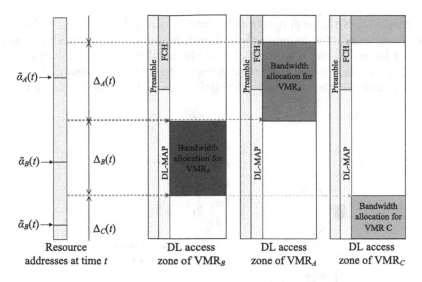

Fig. 3. Example of resource allocation among VMR$_A$, VMR$_B$ and VMR$_C$

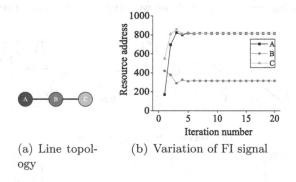

(a) Line topol-
ogy

(b) Variation of FI signal

Fig. 4. Line topology and the variation of address of FI signal

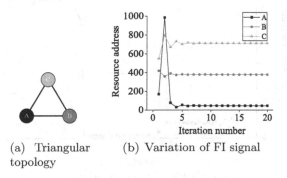

(a) Triangular
topology

(b) Variation of FI signal

Fig. 5. Triangular topology and the variation of address of FI signal

is assigned 50% of the total bandwidth. For the triangular topology in Fig. 5(a), all nodes are connected to each other; therefore, the entire bandwidth is evenly allocated to each node, namely, 33.3% of the total bandwidth. For the square topology shown in Fig. 6(a), each node is connected to two adjacent nodes. In this case, each node has the same network topology as that of node B used in the line

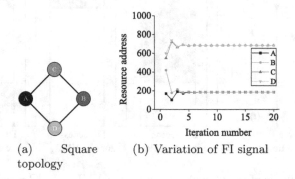

(a)   Square
topology

(b) Variation of FI signal

Fig. 6. Square topology and the variation of address of FI signal

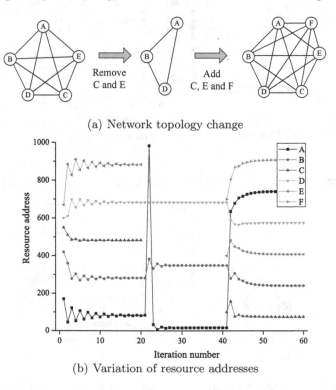

(a) Network topology change

(b) Variation of resource addresses

Fig. 7. Variation of resource addresses of VMRs according to addition and deletion of nodes

topology. Therefore, the amount of bandwidth allocated to each node becomes 50%, which is the same as that allocated to node B in the line topology. In Fig. 7, five nodes are connected to each other, forming a full-mesh star topology. Node C and node E are initially removed, followed by the addition of node C, node E, and node F. As shown in Fig. 7, as soon as the number of participant nodes in the network changes, the resource addresses of the VMRs become unevenly spaced, resulting in a bandwidth allocation that is no longer fair. This imbalance causes the neighboring nodes to adjust their resource addresses, and this eventually returns the system to a stable and fair state. We can verify that the proposed method exhibits self-adaptiveness and ensures fair bandwidth sharing under a dynamically changing network topology.

5   Conclusions

In this paper, we proposed a flocking-inspired resource allocation method that allocates bandwidth to VMRs in a mutually exclusive and fair manner. Each VMR determines the amount and address of the bandwidth resource iteratively and distributively without the aid of a centralized coordinator. The convergence property of the proposed method was analyzed. We verified the self-adaptiveness of the proposed method and evaluated the throughput performance in the cellular environment in consideration of two-way four-lane and three-way intersection road scenarios in the context of the IEEE 802.16j network. The results showed that the proposed method improves upon the conventional method by enabling the VMRs to share the bandwidth resource among the neighboring VMRs in a fair and mutually exclusively way, thereby alleviating the inter-VMR interference and enhancing the throughput performance.

Acknowledgements. This research was partly supported by Basic Science Research Program through the National Research Foundation of Korea (NRF) funded by the Ministry of Education (NRF-2015R1D1A1A01060207) and by the MSIP (Ministry of Science, ICT and Future Planning), Korea, under the ITRC (Information Technology Research Center) support program (IITP-2015-H8501-15-1007) supervised by the IITP (Institute for Information and communications Technology Promotion).

References

1. Yu, Y., Dutkiewicz, E., Huang, X., Mueck, M.: Downlink resource allocation for next generation wireless networks with inter-cell interference. IEEE Trans. Wirel. Commun. **12**, 1783–1793 (2013)
2. IEEE P802.16j/D9: Draft Amendment to IEEE Standard for Local and Metropolitan Area Networks Part 16: Air Interface for Fixed and Mobile Broadband Wireless Access Systems: Multihop Relay Specification (2009)
3. Peters, S.W., Heath, R.W.: The future of WiMAX: multihop relaying with IEEE 802.16j. IEEE Commun. Mag. **47**, 104–111 (2009)

4. Salem, M., Adinoyi, A., Yanikomeroglu, H., Kim, Y.D.: Radio resource management in OFDMA-based cellular networks enhanced with fixed and nomadic relays. In: Wireless Communications and Networking Conference (WCNC), pp. 1–6. IEEE (2010)
5. Chen, L., Huang, Y., Xie, F., Gao, Y.: Mobile relay in LTE-advanced systems. IEEE Commun. Mag. **51**, 144–151 (2013)
6. Heo, K., Kang, H., Moon, U.C., Lee, J.: Performance evaluation of vehicle-mounted mobile relay in next generation cellular networks. KSII TIIS **5**, 874–887 (2009)
7. Kim, Y.U., Kim, H.S.: Interference detection and avoidance method for in-vehicle mobile relay stations in IEEE 802.16j network. IEICE Trans. Commun. **92**, 3495–3498 (2009)
8. Pan, M.S., Lin, T.M., Chen, W.T.: An enhanced handover scheme for mobile relays in LTE-A high-speed rail networks. IEEE Trans. Veh. Technol. **64**, 743–756 (2015)
9. Zhao, H., Huang, R., Zhang, J., Fang, Y.: Handoff for wireless networks with mobile relay stations. In: Wireless Communications and Networking Conference (WCNC), pp. 826–31. IEEE (2011)
10. Xiao, L., Fuja, T.E., Costello, D.J.: Coverage extension and throughput 8 author enhancement. IEEE Trans. Commun. **58**, 2709–2717 (2011)
11. Xiao, Y.: Bio-Inspired Computing and Networking, vol. 1, p. 552. CRC, New York (2011)
12. Dressler, F., Akan, O.B.: A survey on bio-inspired networking. Elsevier Comput. Netw. J. **54**, 881–900 (2010)
13. Zhang, Z., Long, K., Wang, J., Dressler, F.: On swarm intelligence inspired self-organized networking: its bionic mechanisms, designing principles and optimization approaches. IEEE Commun. Surv. Tutor. **14**, 513–537 (2014)
14. Zheng, C., Sicker, D.C.: A survey on biologically inspired algorithms for computer networking. IEEE Commun. Surv. Tutor. **15**, 1160–1191 (2013)
15. Duarte, A., Pen, I., Keller, L., Weissing, F.J.: Evolution of self-organized division of labor in a response threshold model. Behav. Ecol. Sociobiol. **66**, 947–957 (2012)
16. Reynolds, C.W.: Flocks, herds and schools: a distributed behavioral model. ACM SIGGRAPH Comput. Graph. **21**, 25–34 (1987)
17. Cucker, F., Smale, S.: Emergent behavior in flocks. IEEE Trans. Autom. Control **52**, 852–862 (2007)

Behavior of IEEE 802.15.4 Channel Models on Implant Body Area Network

M.A. Huq[1,2,3], Mohsin Iftikhar[1,2,3], and Naveen Chilamkurti[1,2,3(✉)]

[1] Department of Computer Science and Engineering, Primeasia University,
Dhaka, Bangladesh
marifulhuq.huq@gmail.com, miftikhar@csu.edu.au,
N.Chilamkurti@latrobe.edu.au
[2] School of Computing and Mathematics, Charles Sturt University,
Sydney, Australia
[3] La Trobe University, Melbourne, Australia

Abstract. With recent developments in the wireless networking technologies Wireless Body Area Networks (WBANs) have enabled the scope for building cost-effective and non-invasive health monitoring system. Electromagnetic wave propagation and characterization of the physical layer are important to design a suitable channel model for WBANs. Most of the radios used in WBANs are based on IEEE 802.15.4 compliant chip set. In this paper, we modified channel model of IEEE 802.15.4 in NS-2 to study the performance of channel model CM1 (implant to implant) and channel model CM2 (between an implant device and an on or out-of body device) with different sets of simulation experiments. The simulation results successfully confirmed that the modified IEEE 802.15.4 protocol could be used in WBANs.

Keywords: Implant WBANs · Channel model · NS-2 implementation

1 Introduction

Wireless communication is now considered as a never-ending growing technology. With the advances in the miniaturization of electronic devices, especially the sizes of the microcontroller, the wireless chip, intelligent biosensors, longer-life battery remote health monitoring has become an important research issue now-a-days. At the end of 2007, the IEEE launched a new task group of IEEE 802.15.6 [1] known as Wireless Body Area Network (WBAN) [1, 2] to provide short range low power and highly reliable wireless communications for use in close proximity to or inside the human body. Depending on whether it operates outside or inside a human body, WBANs can be divided into wearable WBANs and implant WBANs [3]. While wearable WBANs are considered for both medical and non-medical applications, implant WBANs are mainly considered for medical and healthcare applications. In implant WBANs the characteristics of the radio propagation channel are mainly influenced by body tissues, whereas, in wearable WBANs radio signals propagate through air. The human body is a challenging medium for radio wave transmission. It is partially conductive and consists of materials of different dielectric constants, thickness, and characteristic

© ICST Institute for Computer Sciences, Social Informatics and Telecommunications Engineering 2017
J.-H. Lee and S. Pack (Eds.): QShine 2016, LNICST 199, pp. 251–257, 2017.
DOI: 10.1007/978-3-319-60717-7_25

impedance. Radio propagation through a human body depends on losses caused by power absorption, radiation pattern destruction and central frequency shift [7]. The power budget [15] of a WBAN node is affected by the antenna used on such a node. The radiation pattern of an antenna will also influence the link delay budget. The link budget depends on the radio propagation conditions and packet transmission and reception techniques. As per federal communications commission (FCC) regulations, implanted medical devices operate in 402–405 MHz frequency band. In this paper we analyze performance of implant communication channel models for 402–405 MHz band with NS-2 simulations [6].

This paper is organized as follows. Section 2 provides background and related works Sect. 3 focuses on link budget calculations. Section 4 investigates the impact of IEEE 802.15.4 channel models' effects on implant WBANs through various simulations. Finally, this paper is concluded in Sect. 5.

2 Backgrounds and Related Work

Radio propagation models are used to predict the received signal power of a packet. When a packet is received with the signal power below the threshold it is dropped by the node. The major factors which influence the radio propagation are path loss and fading. Pathloss describes the loss in power as the radio signal propagates in space. It is caused by the dissipation of the power radiated by the transmitter and also by the propagation channel. On the other hand, fading occurs because of the obstacles between the transmitter and the receiver which attenuate the signal strength or due to signals taking multiple paths to reach the receiver.

In recent years a number of channel models have been proposed in the literature [8–12] especially for implant WBANs. In [9], the authors have applied the compressed sensing theory as a new sampling method to multipath fading channels to minimize packet loss and bit error rate. In [10] authors have considered statistical path loss model for MICS channels. They constructed a visualization environment in order to characterize RF propagation from medical implants.

The channel modeling subgroup [8] has released the possible communication links for WBANs based on the location of the sensor nodes which is shown in Fig. 1 [8]. The scenarios are grouped into classes that can be represented by the same Channel Models

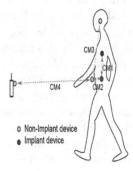

Fig. 1. Communication links for WBAN.

(CM). CM1 represents the communication link between implant devices and CM2 is between an implant device and an on or out-of body device. CM3 and CM4 are related to wearable devices.

3 Link Budget

Link budget is an important property in a wireless network in order to understand the successful packet reception rate. The link budget depends on the radio propagation conditions and packet transmission and reception techniques. Research shows that the induced pathloss in a channel near the human body is higher than free space, with the path loss exponent ranging from 2.18 to 3.3 and higher [11]. It is concluded that the path loss in WBANs is very high that, compared to the free space propagation, an additional 30–35 dB at small distances (i.e. $140 \sim 150$ mm) is noticed [2]. With the help of article [4], the total path loss between a WBAN transmitter and receiver can be calculated by using Eqs. (1) and (2):

$$PL(d) = PL(d_0) + 10n \log 10\left(\frac{d}{d_0}\right) + S \tag{1}$$

$$S \sim N(0, \sigma_s) \tag{2}$$

where PL(d0) is the path loss at a reference distance d0 (50 mm). d is the distance between transmitter and receiver, n is the path loss exponent, and S is loss due to shadow fading. Shadowing effects are modelled by a random variable with a normal distribution with zero mean and standard deviation i.e., $N(0, \sigma_s^2)$.

The parameters corresponding to CM1 and CM2 are shown in the Tables 1 and 2. Details of the model derivation can be found in [4].

Table 1. Parameters for CM1 - implant to implant for 402–405 MHz.

Implant to implant	$PL(d_0)(dB)$	n	$\sigma_s(dB)$
Deep tissue	35.04	6.26	8.18
Near surface	40.94	4.99	9.05

Table 2. Parameters for CM2: implant to body surface for 402–405 MHz.

Implant to body surface	$PL(d_0)(dB)$	n	$\sigma_s(dB)$
Deep tissue	47.14	4.26	7.85
Near surface	49.81	4.22	6.81

The calculation of path loss is very important to determine the minimum reception power required by a receiver so that the packet can be received successfully. As shown in [15] the relationship between minimum reception power PRx(min) and path loss can be expressed as the following equation:

$$P_{Rx}(\min) = P_{Tx} - PL(d) \qquad (3)$$

Here PTx, is the transmission power. Both PTx and path loss PL(d) are expressed in dB. This minimum reception power will depend on the receiver's sensitivity which is related to SNR. The value of SNR can be calculated by the following Eq. (4):

$$SNR = 10 \log\left(\frac{P_{Rx}}{Noise}\right) \qquad (4)$$

The minimum receiver sensitivity numbers for the highest data rate at each operating frequency band are listed in Table 3.

Table 3. Receiver sensitivity numbers

Frequency band (MHz)	Information data rate (kbps)	Minimum sensitivity (dBm)
402–405	75.9	−98
	151.8	−95
	303.6	−92
	455.4	−86

The power level at which the packet was received at the MAC [1, 2] layer is compared with the receiving threshold and the carrier-sense threshold. If the power level falls below the carrier sense threshold, the packet is discarded as noise. If the received power level is above the carrier sense threshold but below the receive threshold, the packet is marked as a packet in error before being passed to the MAC layer. Otherwise, the packet is simply handed up to the MAC layer.

4 Simulation Results

In this section we investigate the performance of a beacon-enabled IEEE 802.15.4 for in-body communications. Normally IEEE 802.15.4 protocol is not suitable for implant WBANs in its unmodified form. We have tested IEEE 802.15.4 protocol [16] with the correct channel model for implant WBANs to understand its performance. We implemented the IEEE 802.15.6 communication link channel model CM1 (implant to implant) and channel model CM2 (between an implant device and an on or out-of body device) in NS-2 and changed the power parameters of IEEE 802.15.4 so that it can be compatible for IEEE 802.15.6. The wireless physical layer parameters are considered according to a low-power Zarlink MICS Radio Platform, ZL70102 [17]. This radio transceiver operates in the 402–405 MHz band with an optimum transmission power of −16 dBm. We used the CM1 and CM2 propagation models throughout the simulation. We used multiple nodes (up to 7), which were connected with a coordinator in a star topology. The transport agent is UDP protocol, CBR traffic is considered as the traffic pattern.

To characterize the path loss and received signal strength within an implant to implant and implant to body surface area, we analysed 9 different distances ranging from 50 mm to 250 mm in our experiment. We have considered only two nodes: one transmitter and one receiver in our simulation. In Figs. 3 and 4 we characterize the result of average path loss for CM1 and CM2 as a function of transmitter-receiver separation. The deep tissue implant scenarios consider endoscopy capsule applications for upper stomach (95 mm below body surface) and lower stomach (118 mm below body surface) [13]. The near-surface scenarios include applications such as Implantable Cardioverter-Defibrillator and Pacemaker.

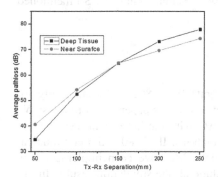

Fig. 2. Pathloss for CM1.

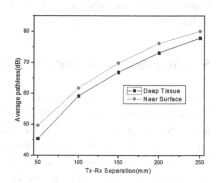

Fig. 3. Pathloss for CM2.

We represent the average path loss for CM1 in Fig. 2. for both type of scenarios with the increase of transmitter- receiver separation. Although the average path loss has increased over the transmitter-receiver separation but after 140 mm distance we see that path loss for deep tissue is larger than for the body surface scenario. Again, in Fig. 3, we show the path loss for CM2 for both of the cases where value of path loss for deep tissue scenario is always higher than near surface scenario in any point. From these figures this is evident that path loss for deep tissue scenario in CM1 is always lower than CM2 up to 200 mm and after that pathloss for CM2 slightly increased over CM1.

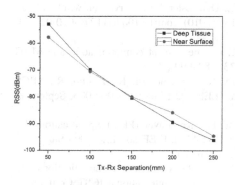

Fig. 4. RSS for CM1

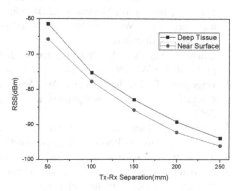

Fig. 5. RSS for CM2

In Figs. 4 and 5 we show the corresponding Received Signal Strength (RSS) for the same transmitter-receiver separation considered in Figs. 2 and 3. The maximum transmission power (-16 dBm) is considered for both channel models. We can see that in 250 mm distance the RSS value becomes marginal with the RxThresh's value (-95 dBm).

From the above figures, it is evident that the path loss has increased with the separation of the transmitter and receiver with a corresponding decrease in the RSS which was expected. The simulated path loss graphs shown in Figs. 2 and 3 are very identical with those who used MATLAB and other tools in literature [5, 14]. This dependency of RSS on the path loss is well established in the well-known channel modelling schemes and has been verified for a few threshold values of RSS mentioned in the draft.

5 Conclusion and Future Work

The main objective of this paper was to investigate IEEE 802.15.4's suitability for WBANs implant applications. The main contributions of this paper are as follows: We analyzed the performance of IEEE 802.15.4 MAC with the help of proper in-body communication channel models using NS-2 simulations. IEEE 802.15.6 communication link channel model CM1 and channel model CM2 have been implemented in NS-2. Due to space limitations we could not include all the simulation results. In our future work we want to elaborate more on implementation details of NS-2 module. We also want to apply this channel model to investigate various packet level performances such as end to end delay, energy consumption, packet delivery ratio etc. for low and heavily congested scenarios.

References

1. IEEE standard for local and metropolitan area networks part 15.6: wireless body area networks. In: IEEE Std 802.15.6-2012, pp. 1–271, 29 Feb 2012
2. Latre, B., Braem, B., Moerman, I., Blondia, C., Demeester, P.: A survey on wireless body area networks. Wireless Netw. 17(1), 1–18 (2010). doi:10.1007/s11276-010-0252-4. Springer, Netherlands
3. Ullah, S., Higgins, H., Shen, B., Kwak, K.S.: On the implant communication and MAC protocols for WBAN. Int. J. Commun. Syst. 23, 982–999 (2010)
4. Hagedorn, J., Terrill, J., Yang, W., Sayrafian, K., Yazdandoost, K., Kohno, R.: MICS channel characteristics; preliminary results. In: IEEE 802.15-08-0351-00-0006, September 2008
5. Wireless Medium Access Control (MAC) and Physical Layer (PHY) Specifications for Low-Rate Wireless Personal Area Networks (LRWPANs), IEEE 802.15.4-2003 Std
6. The network simulator - ns-2. http://www.isi.edu/nsnam/ns/
7. Yazdandoost, K.Y.: A radio channel model for in-body wireless communications. In: Wireless Mobile Communication and Healthcare: Second International ICST Conference, MobiHealth 2011, Kos Island, Greece, 5–7 October 2011

8. Yazdandoost, K., et al.: Channel model for body area network (BAN). In: IEEE 802.15.6 Technical Contribution, Document ID:15-08-0780-10-0006-tg6- Channel-model, July 2010
9. Balouchestani, M., Raahemifar, K., Krishnan, S.: New channel model for wireless body area network with compressed sensing theory. Wireless Sens. Syst. IET **3**(2), 85–92 (2013)
10. Ntouni, G.D., Lioumpas, A.S., Nikita, K.S.: Reliable and energy-efficient communications for wireless biomedical implant systems. Biomed. Health Inf. IEEE J. **18**(6), 1848–1856 (2014)
11. Li, H.-B., Kohno, R.: Body area network and its standardization at IEEE 802.15.BAN. In: István, F., Bitó, J., Bakki, P. (eds.) Advances in Mobile and Wireless Communications, pp. 223–238. Springer, Heidelberg (2008). doi:10.1007/978-3-540-79041-9_12
12. Kim, T.H., Oh, J.H., Yoo, J.H., Pack, J.K.: Channel modelling of WBAN system and human exposure due to WPT. In: Asia-Pacific Symposium on Electromagnetic Compatibility (APEMC), pp. 29–32 (2010)
13. Sayrafian-Poue, K., Yang, W.-B., Hagedorn, J., Terrill, J.: A statistical path loss model for medical implant communication channels. In: 2009 IEEE 20th International Symposium on Personal, Indoor and Mobile Radio Communication (PIMRC) (2009)
14. Yang, Y., Shen, D., Xie, Y.: A review of the implant channel modelling for WBAN. In: NSWCTC 2011, April 2011
15. Khan, J.Y., Yuce, M.R.: Wireless body area network (WBAN) for medical applications. In: New Developments in Biomedical Engineering, January 2010
16. Samsung/CUNY: Ns2 simulator for 802.15.4. http://www-ee.ccny.cuny.edu/zheng/pub
17. Xiao, Z., He, C., Jiang, L.: Slot-based model for IEEE 802.15.4 MAC with sleep mechanism. IEEE Commun. Lett. **14**(2), 154–156 (2010)

Elliptic Curve Based Cybersecurity Schemes for Publish-Subscribe Internet of Things

Abebe Abeshu Diro$^{(\boxtimes)}$, Naveen Chilamkurti,
and Prakash Veeraraghavan

La Trobe University, Department of Computer Science and IT,
Bundoora VIC, Melbourne 3086, Australia
{a.diro,n.chilamkurti,P.Veera}@latrobe.edu.au

Abstract. The rapid increase in the number of connected things across the globe has been brought about by the deployment of the Internet of things (IoTs) at home, in organizations and industries. The innovation of smart things has been envisioned through various protocols, but the most prevalent protocols are publish-subscribe protocols such as Message Queue Telemetry Transport (MQTT) and Advanced Message Queuing Protocol (AMQP). One of the major concerns in the adoption of such protocols for the IoTs is the lack of security mechanisms as the existing security protocols cannot be adapted due to their large overhead of computations, storage and communications. To address this issue, we propose a lightweight protocol using Elliptic Curve Cryptography (ECC) for IoT security. We present analytical and simulation results, and compare the results to the existing protocols of traditional Internet.

Keywords: Cyber security · Publish-subscribe systems · Internet of things · Elliptic curve cryptography

1 Introduction

By 2020, the number of connected things will be more than 6 times of the world population as operational technologies such as those in the factory and home are becoming the part of connected entities coupled with Information technology entities that are currently in use for daily purposes [1]. It means that there are more than six smart things for every person on the globe. This evolutionary paradigm is brought about by the emergence of smart things capable of collecting, processing and communicating data among themselves or interacting humans pervasively. Though IoT has several promises and potentials, its deployment might pose various security issues due to their unattended nature and their limited resources. Traditional cryptography systems such as RSA have been used as security solutions on the Internet [2–5], but they are not practical to implement for IoT devices due to their overheads in computations, storage and communications of security parameters such as keys. For instance, RSA assumes that the increment of the key size increases the level of security if the key itself is not unveiled, and consequently, the overheads incur high the consumption of resources. For this reason, a more efficient public key cryptographic mechanisms are required. To address this limitation, elliptic curve based cryptographic scheme could be applied in the existing

© ICST Institute for Computer Sciences, Social Informatics and Telecommunications Engineering 2017
J.-H. Lee and S. Pack (Eds.): QShine 2016, LNICST 199, pp. 258–268, 2017.
DOI: 10.1007/978-3-319-60717-7_26

pub-sub communication popular protocols of IoTs such as MQTT [6]. MQTT was designed in many-to-many communication protocol paradigm for disseminating messages between subscribers through a central entity in the emerging IoT applications such as social networks, V2V, WSNs. A crucial characteristic of these protocols as a pub-sub system are the decoupling of publishers and subscribers, enabling a many-to-many communication model. Such a system presents many benefits as well as potential security risks regarding authenticity, confidentiality, integrity and availability. Unfortunately, most of the existing researches on pub-sub networks focus only on performance and scalability. Very few papers have devoted to developing a novel security framework that can resist multiple security problems inherent in them. While RSA is a well-established protocol for Internet communications, it is not lightweight to be proposed for resource limited IoT environments due to its dependence on resource intensive public key cryptography. Hence, this paper deals with lightweight cyber security issues for publish/subscribe mode of communication. The contributions of this paper are:

- We propose novel lightweight security solutions for publish-subscribe protocol based Internet of Things using ECC. Compared to RSA protocols, our scheme could provide the same level of security for publications and subscriptions while it decreases computation, communication and storage costs.
- Scalable key exchange mechanism with less number of handshakes in linear time compared to RSA.

2 Public Key Cryptography

Cryptography is defined as the mechanism of secure communication in which designing and analyzing of protocols that can combat cyber-attacks is crucial. Public key cryptographic systems have become the modern way of cybersecurity revolution over an insecure communication channel. Some public-key schemes are discussed in the following section.

2.1 RSA

RSA is an acronym for Rivest, Shamir and Adleman after its inventors back in 1977 as a public key cryptographic system. The security of RSA lies on the computational difficulty of factorization of large prime numbers [7]. The authors, in their study, suggested that the method could be for encryption and digital signature. In the encryption/decryption process, a public key (e, n) and a private key (d, n) are used where all the parameters are positive integers. The encryption and decryption process are shown as follows:

$C = E(M) = Me(mod\ n)$, where $M = message$
$D(C) = Cd(mod\ n)$, where $C = cipher\ text$
$n = product\ of\ two\ large\ prime\ numbers\ p\ and\ q\ (n = p * q)$
$d = large\ random\ relative\ prime\ to\ p\ (i.e.\ gcd(d,(p-1) * (q-1)) = 1)$
$e = multiplicative\ inverse\ of\ d\ modulo\ (p-1) * (q-1)$.

2.2 Diffie-Hellman Key Exchange Protocol

Diffie-Hellman key exchange protocol was proposed in 1976 by Whitfield Diffie and Martin E [4]. Hellman as key distribution scheme over insecure media as opposed to other cryptographic systems which need secure channel for the distribution. The algorithm depends on the difficulty of solving discrete logarithmic problem. In the key exchange process, partner A randomly chooses secret key xA from the interval of [0, q] to calculate $yA = \alpha\, xA\, Mod(q)$ for sending publically to B, and partner B selects secret key xB from the same interval to compute $yB = \alpha\, xB\, Mod(q)$ to send publically to A. Partners A and B establish shared keys ($K_{AB} = \alpha\, xA\, xB\, Mod(q)$) using the combination of their secret keys over insecure channel. Even if the adversary gets one of the secret keys and computes K_{AB}, it is difficult to solve the discrete algorithmic problem as it has no knowledge of xA and xB. One of the drawbacks of this algorithm is that it lacks the mechanism of authentication and suffer from man-in-the-middle of attack.

2.3 Elliptic Curve Cryptography (ECC)

Elliptic Curve Cryptography (ECC) was introduced at the same time by Victor S. Miller and Neal Koblitz in 1985. ECC can provide an analogy to the Discrete Logarithm (DL) based systems such as Diffie-Hellman in the algorithm known as Elliptic Curve Discrete Logarithm Problem (ECDLP) [4, 5]. ECDLP states that an elliptic curve E over $G_F(q)$ and two points P, Q $\in$ E, compute an integer x such that Q = xP. An elliptic curve E is formulated by $y^2 = x^3 + ax + b$ where $4a^3 + 27b^2 \neq 0$ and a, b, x are elements of a finite field F. The point addition of E given two points $P(x_1, y_1)$ and $Q(x_2, y_2)$ on E, with P, Q $\neq \infty$ is $R(x_3, y_3) = P(x_1, y_1) + Q(x_2, y_2)$, and defined as follows:

- If $x_1 \neq x_2$ then $x_3 = m^2 - x_1 - x_2$, $y_3 = m(x_1 - x_3) - y_1$ $where\, m = (y2 - y1)/(x2 - x1)$
- If $x_1 = x_2$ but $y_1 \neq y_2$ then $P + Q = \infty$
- If P = Q and $y_1 \neq 0$, then $x_3 = m^2 - 2x_1$, $y_3 = m(x_1 - x_3) - y_1$ where $(3x_1^2 + a)/2y_1$
- If P = Q and $y_1 = 0$, then $P + Q = \infty$
- $P + \infty = \infty$

ECC is an algebra based light-weight next generation cryptography, which provides the at least the same level of cybersecurity solutions with smaller key and message size compared to other public key cryptographic systems such as RSA. The following table gives the comparison of key size between ECC and RSA. It seems that ECC could yield a desired level of security with a key size of 256-bits that RSA scheme requires a key size of 3072-bits to achieve. ECC could be used for digital signature to verify the digital content and the source, integrated encryption to secure plain and cipher texts, key management (Diffie-Hellman) to share keys secretly over insecure channel. The slow adoption of ECC so far seems to change with the fast growth of IoT devices with limited resources to achieve a desired security level without compromising performance. Due to this, the ECC approach for cybersecurity is very appealing for small devices such as meters, smartphones and embedded devices as it reduces computational time, data transmitted and stored.

3 Related Work

Publish-subscribe networks could be direct channel and pub-sub network depending on the scheme used for disseminating information [8]. In a direct channel mechanism, a publisher directly passes a publication to subscribers under specific topic of subscription. However, in pub-sub system publishers and the subscribers communicate via an intermediate broker which facilitates the publication/subscription. This kind of model is more scalable than the previous in that publishers tend to become less performance bottle-necked. Most studies on pub-sub systems have concentrated on performance, scalability and availability [9]. Unfortunately, very limited studies are present about the security aspects of these systems in traditional Internet, and almost none for pub-sub systems in IoTs protocol such as MQTT. The considerable amount of research has been done in secure group communication fields [10]. The major problem with such systems is that group key management is not as flexible as pub-sub systems. Additionally, protocols such as RSA cannot be adapted to IoT environments due to their heavy weight nature [11]. Group key management in securely distributing of events of content-based pub-sub network has also been analyzed by Opyrchal et al. [12]. This kind of arrangement increases the number of keys exponentially as subscribers increase, and hence, suffers from scalability. In contrast, our system permits flexible joining to and leaving from the network without compromising security and performance. Wang et al. [13] analyze the security requirements in a content-based pub-sub system, identifying authentication of publications, integrity of publications, subscription integrity and service integrity as the key issues. The paper is detail enough in the context of general Internet, but fails to work for the Internet of things whose resource constraint is high. EventGuard [14] has shown the possibility of achieving security requirements, but it is not applicable for IoT devices because of its resource demand, content-based networking is not widely accepted yet.

4 System Design

In pub-sub communication scheme, broker plays vital role in handling subscriptions, publications and information disseminating under a specific topic. In our design, end nodes communicate securely with a broker in pub-sub paradigm under their respective subscription. The broker is assumed to have a considerable computational and storage power for key generation and management per session for all subscribers. The system enforces integrity and access control of messages under a given topic by employing authorization and encryption key for publishers and decryption keys for subscribers (Fig. 1).

4.1 System Goals

Our security protocol design has basically three sets of design goals: security, performance and scalability goals. In pub-sub system, publishers/subscribers should be authentic to broker and vice versa to avoid impersonated publications/subscriptions.

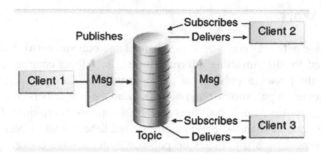

Fig. 1. General architecture of topic based pub-sub system security

This is to prevent unauthorized subscribers from accessing the topics for which they have not subscribed. In addition, non-publisher entity should not create a message for which a subscriber claims subscription. In the case that many publishers write on common topic, subscribers should be able to authenticate the actual publisher. It is required that messages sent from publisher to subscriber via broker is guarded against disclosure or modification. These includes authorized publications/subscriptions, subscription privacy and routing integrity. The security framework should also be resilient against Denial of Service (DoS) attacks such as flooding attacks, fake unsubscribe and selective or random dropping attacks. The system is expected to scale with the number of publishers and subscribers in the network. The security mechanism should not add performance overhead to the existing pub-sub system.

4.2   Security Procedures

Parameter Settings
Input: Elliptic curve E_p (a, b): $y^2 = x^3 + ax + b$ (modp) over subgroup (finite field) Zp where p is large prime number, a, b ϵ Zp $(4a^3 + 27b^2 (modp) \neq 0)$
Output: secret master key K_m, public key K_p, Fog broker (subscription manager) key (K_s), subscriber private key (K_i)

1. Choose generator G from an elliptic curve point over
2. Choose random master secret key K_m from Z_p and computes public key H = GK_m
3. Broadcast public parameters $K_p \leftarrow (E_p, G, p, H)$
4. Choose random subscriber key K_i from Z_p and calculate Fog side key $K_s \leftarrow K_m \oplus K_i$
5. send K_i to subscriber and K_s to Subscription manager.

Subscription
Input: subscriber identity (ID), topic, Fog broker (subscription manager) key (K_s), subscriber private key (K_i)
Output: authentication key K

1. Subscriber requests by presenting (topic$_i$, r, ID$_i$)
2. Subscription Manager sends autho: (topic$_i$, ID$_s$, rGHK$_s$N, uSub = H (topic$_i$ || ID$_i$) to subscriber

3. Subscriber computes, $rK_i \oplus rGHKsN = HGK_mN = (GK_m) \; GK_mN = N$ and sends $(\{\{r', r' \; GHK_iL\}\}$ where $L = (N - 1, K))$
4. Subscription Manager computes, $r'Ks \oplus rGHK_iL = HGK_mL = (GK_m) \; GK_mL = L = N - 1$. Here, mutual authentication is valid, and K is sent to Fog broker (topic manager)
5. Subscription Manager sends H (topic$_i$, ID$_i$, K) to publication manager to store to be used in procedure 3.

Publication
Input: Input: subscriber identity (ID), topic, authentication key K, message M, subscriber private key (K_i), subscription manager key (K_s)
Output: intermediate cipher texts, plain text

1. Publisher requests publication by H (topic$_i$, ID$_i$, K)
2. Publication manager compares H (topic*, ID * i, K*) ?= H (topic, Idi, K) and sends (IDs, H (topic$_i$, ID$_i$, K))
3. Publisher sends (topic$_i$, ID$_i$, $\{r_i, C = r_iGK_i \; M\}$) (encryption of message M)
4. Publication manager recalculates $Cs = rGK_s \oplus C = rGK_s \oplus rGK_i \; M. = K_m.M$. Then $C_i = C_s \oplus rGKs = rGK_i.M$, and sends C_i to the subscriber
5. Subscribers decrypt $C_i = rGK_i.M$ by calculating $rGK_i.M \oplus rGK_i = M$.

Unsubscription

1. The subscriber that needs to leave the group sends topic, IDi, K, uSubI(topic) to the cloud broker
2. Broker checks the unsubsciber by computing (topic*, D * i) ?= topic, Di and informs the key generator for key revocation
3. Key generator module unsubscribes the subscriber by send acknowledgement.

5 Analysis

The threat model is composed of subscription, publication and broker mediation processes. It is assumed that the key generator is secured, and trusted to provide keys for all the operations of end devices. Pub-sub networks, like access control schemes, need entities to get read/write access before performing the appropriate actions such as read action for subscribers, and write action for publishers. The devised protocol could be evaluated in terms of various overhead, scalability and security parameters.

5.1 Performance Analysis

In our algorithm, much of computational and storage overheads were offloaded to the broker which is richer in resource than publisher/subscriber IoTs devices. We employed less expensive computations such as XORing and elliptic curve point additions using ECC 160-bit curve (secp160rl) in which EC point is 20-bytes. The superiority of our scheme in resources (storage, computations, and communications) conservation, compared to RSA, could be seen from Table 1. The system also saves

Table 1. key size comparison of ECC and RSA

ECC key size	RSA key size	Ratio
160 bits	1024 bit	1:6
224 bit	2048 bit	1:9
256 bit	3072 bit	1:12
384 bit	7680 bit	1:20
512 bit	15360 bit	1:30

much of communication bandwidth in reducing the number of handshakes compared to the already existing heavyweight protocols such as RSA. For instance, our first scheme incurs only a total of 218 bytes of storage overhead for both publisher/subscriber and Fog server during subscription, while RSA systems might occupy over 6440 bytes for similar settings in a single connection. During publication, a single connection consumes 198 bytes of storage space in our protocol, and the existing protocol consumes over 6440 bytes. The case of communication burden could also be explained in a similar manner for both subscription and publication as it can be seen from the table. The second scheme is even more efficient than the first scheme in offloading storage and communication burden from publisher/subscribers, but it is slightly more expensive computationally. However, the burden on the broker is comparable in the both protocols, which is less than the overhead of RSA. Thus, our system is more efficient in terms of delay, storage and computation than RSA systems for pub-sub based IoT connections in Fog computing.

5.2 Scalability Analysis

The scalability issue, which is the most important factor for secure pub-sub systems, could be seen in terms of key exchange when a node joins or leaves a network. The broker handles publication and subscription with very small number of handshakes, and it does not need to update subscribers' keys frequently. In addition the key sizes and run times scale linearly for ECC with increasing security level while for RSA they scale super-linearly. On the other hand, it is difficult to manage the keys in subscriber group systems as it needs processing cost of $O(2n)$ for managing keys for n subscribers, while our scheme needs at most logarithm of the number of topics (Fig. 2 and Table 2).

5.3 Security Analysis

This section evaluates the basic security of the proposed system. It is logical to begin with preliminary concepts required to understand the analysis and proof, and then show the security of subscriptions and publications. Basically a mechanism is said to be secured the adversary's advantage in breaking the scheme is a negligible function of the security parameter.

Theorem 1: (Negligible Function). A function f is negligible if for each polynomial $p()$ there exists N such that for all integers $n > N$ it holds that $f(n) < 1\ p(n)$. Assuming that

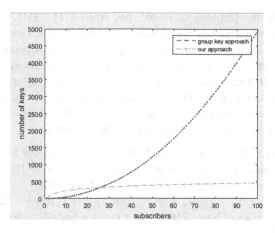

Fig. 2. Comparison of the number of keys

Table 2. Performance comparison between our scheme and RSA

	Parameter type	Our scheme		RSA	
		Publisher/subscriber	Fog broker	Publisher/subscriber	Fog broker
Subscription	Computational overhead	-/1PM,2XOR	2PM, 2XOR		
	Storage overhead	-/86 bytes	132 bytes	-/Over 340 bytes	Over 6100 bytes
	Communication overhead	-/66 bytes	132 bytes	-/Over 340 bytes	Over 6100 bytes
Publication	Computational overhead	1PM, 1XOR	1C, 2PM,2XOR		
	Storage overhead	-/66 bytes	132 bytes	-/Over 340 bytes	Over 6100 bytes
	Communication overhead	34 bytes	28 bytes	-/Over 340 bytes	Over 6100 bytes

the adversary is with bounded resources in PPT, the scheme should be secure and the success probability of any such adversary is negligible. Our protocol depends on a pseudorandom function f whose cannot be distinguished by adversary.

Theorem 2: (Pseudorandom Function). A function $f: \{0, 1\} * \times \{0, 1\} * \rightarrow \{0, 1\} *$ is pseudorandom if for all PPT adversaries A, there exists a negligible function negl such that: $|Pr[Afk(\cdot) = 1] - Pr[AF(\cdot) = 1]| < negl(n)$ where $k \rightarrow \{0, 1\}$ n is chosen uniformly randomly and F is a function chosen uniformly randomly from the set of functions mapping n-bit strings to n-bit strings. Our proof depends on the assumption that the Elliptic Curve Diffie-Hellman (ECDH) is hard in a group G, i.e., it is hard for an adversary to distinguish between group elements $\alpha\beta P$ and γP given αP and βP.

Theorem 3: (ECDH Assumption). The Elliptic Curve Diffie-Hellman (ECDH) problem is hard regarding a group G if for all PPT adversaries A, there exists a negligible function negl such that $|\Pr[A(G, q, P, \alpha P, \beta P, \alpha\beta P) = 1] - \Pr[A(G, q, P, \alpha P, \beta P, \gamma P) = 1]| <$ negl(k) where G is a cyclic group of order q ($|q| = k$) and P is a generator of G, and $\alpha, \beta, \gamma \in$ Zq are uniformly randomly chosen. The schemes we are using in our solution is proven to be indistinguishable under chosen plaintext attack (IND-CPA) and we will prove that our scheme is also IND-CPA secure. A cryptosystem is considered IND-CPA secure if no PPT adversary, given an encryption of a message randomly chosen from two plaintext messages chosen by the adversary, can identify which message was encrypted with non-negligible probability.

Theorem 4: If the ECDH problem is hard relative to G, then our EC based scheme is indistinguishable under chosen plaintext attack (IND-CPA). That is, for all PPT adversaries A there exists a negligible function negl such that

SuccessA, $p(k) = pr[b' = b|(pk, Km) \leftarrow Init(1k), (Ki, Ks) \leftarrow GenKey (Km, Di),$ m0, m1 $\leftarrow$ AEnc(Ki,.)(Ks) b $\leftarrow$ R{0,1}, ci * (mb) = Enc(Ki, mb), b' $\leftarrow$ AEnc(Ki,.) (Ks, ci*(mb))] $< \frac{1}{2} +$ negl(k).

Proof: Assuming PPT adversary A' attempting to solve the ECDH problem using A function and having G, q, P, $\alpha P, \beta P, \alpha\beta P$ or γP as input for some random α, β, γ, A' performs the following computations:

- Sends public parameters G, q, P to A, and then, by randomly choosing Ks $\leftarrow$ R Zpfor each IDi. Then it computes KiP = $\alpha P \oplus$ KsP. It sends all (IDi, Ks) to A and stores all (i, Ks, KiP).
- In order to access encryption algorithm, A passes m to A', and A' chooses randomly r $\leftarrow$ Zq and replies with (rP, rPKiM)
- A produces m0, m1. A' selects a random bit b and sends $\beta P, \beta$PKs $\oplus$ X mb to A, where X = γP or $\alpha\beta P$
- A produces b', and If b = b', A' outputs 1, otherwise 0.

Case 1: Since γ is randomly chosen, and hence γP, then βPKs $\oplus \gamma$Pmb reveals no information about mb as it is a random element of G i.e. uniform distribution irrespective of mb value. Adversary A must distinguish between m0 and m1 without additional information. The success probability of b' = b is exactly 1/2 when b is chosen uniformly randomly, and A' outputs 1 iff A outputs b' = b, in which case Pr[A' (G, q, P, $\alpha P, \beta P, \gamma P$) = 1] = 1/2.

Case 2: In the case parameters X = $\alpha\beta P$, and βPKs $\oplus \alpha\beta P$ mb = βP(Ks $\oplus \alpha$) = PKi, then βPKs $\oplus$ X mb is valid cipher. In this case, case Pr[A'(G, q, P, $\alpha P, \beta P,$ $\alpha\beta P$) = 1] = SuccessA, p(k). Assuming ECDH is hard to break in group G, then

$$\begin{cases} |\Pr[A'(G, q, P, \alpha P, \beta P, \alpha\beta P) = 1] - \Pr[A'(G, q, P, \\ \quad\quad \alpha P, \beta P, \gamma P) = 1]| < negl(k) \\ \Pr[A'(G, q, P, \alpha P, \beta P, \alpha\beta P) = 1] < 1/2 + negl(k) \end{cases}$$

$$\therefore SuccessA, p(k) < 1/2 + negl(k)$$

Theorem 5: The proposed scheme could provide mutual authentication between publishers and the broker, and the subscribers and the broker, and hence resist man-in-the-middle attack.

Proof: Mutual authentication means that publishers and subscribers could authenticate with cloud broker during authentication. In the scheme, the key generator provides key K_i for clients and key K_s for broker in such a way that master key $K_m = K_i + K_s$. The key pair, coupled with nonce and session key, is used to check the correctness of the identities of the interacting parties. By mutual authentication, the scheme provides resistance for man-in-the-middle attack. Authentication enables fine-grained subscribers and publishers access control mechanisms on top of the encryption scheme. If the broker is trusted, we can let the broker authenticate the users and enforce our authorization policies.

Theorem 6: The proposed architecture could provide known-key security.

Proof: Known key security means that unique session key is stablished between nodes and broker at the end of authentication scheme. The protocol generates unique session key K at every session ensuring that known-key attack is not possible.

Theorem 7: The scheme could withstand replay attack.

Proof: Replay attack means the impersonation of publishers/subscribers or the broker by the adversary by exploiting the previous session information. The adversary might request the cloud broker by sending (IDi, topic, ri), but since the random numbers and time stamps from both sides are generated every session replay attack is impossible.

Theorem 8: The protocol could resist DDoS attack of malicious publication.

Proof: The use of random numbers in the messages originated from publishers, subscribers and the broker prevents the parties from malicious flooding of the broker by fake subscriptions or publications or un-subscriptions.

6 Conclusion and Future Work

In this paper, we have analyzed the possible application of Elliptic Curve cryptography for securing IoTs in pub-sub communication model. This lightweight scheme provides better scalability, and less overheads such as storage, communication than RSA based schemes employed in SSL/TSL while it guarantees the same level of security. As part of future study, we need to implement the protocol on real IoT platform such as Arduino.

Acknowledgment. Our thanks to Pervasive Computing and Networking Lab, La Trobe University, Melbourne, Australia for material and financial support.

References

1. Securing the Internet of Things: A Proposed Framework (2016). http://www.cisco.com/c/en/us/about/security-center/secure-iot-proposed-framework.html
2. Shen, H., Kumar, N., He, D., Shen, J., Chilamkurti, N.: A security-enhanced authentication with key agreement scheme for wireless mobile communications using elliptic curve cryptosystem. J. Supercomput. **72**, 3588–3600 (2016)

3. Zhang, Z., Qi, Q., Kumar, N., Chilamkurti, N., Jeong, H.-Y.: A secure authentication scheme with anonymity for session initiation protocol using elliptic curve cryptography. Multimed. Tools Appl. **74**(10), 3477–3488 (2014)
4. Hankerson, D., Vanstone, S., Menezes, A.J.: Guide to Elliptic Curve Cryptography. Springer, Heidelberg (2004)
5. Sandeep, S.: Elliptic curve cryptography for constrained devices. Ph.D. Dissertation (2006)
6. Singh, M., Rajan, M.A., Shivraj, V.L., Balamuralidhar, P.: Secure MQTT for Internet of Things (IoT). In: 2015 Fifth International Conference on Communication Systems and Network Technologies (CSNT), pp. 746–751, 4–6 April 2015
7. Mitchell, J.C., Shmatikov, V., Stern, U.: Finite-state analysis of SSL 3.0. In: Proceedings of the 7th Conference on USENIX Security Symposium (SSYM 1998), Berkeley, CA, USA, vol. 7, p. 16. USENIX Association (1998)
8. Fiege, L., Zeidler, A., Buchmann, A., Kilian-Kehr, R., Mühl, G., Darmstadt, T.: Security aspects in publish/subscribe systems. In: Third International Workshop on Distributed Event-based Systems (DEBS 2004) (2004)
9. Gupta, V., Wurm, M., Zhu, Y., Millard, M., Fung, S., Gura, N., Eberle, H., Shantz, S.C.: Sizzle: a standards-based end-to-end security architecture for the embedded internet. Technical report, Sun Microsystems, Inc., Mountain View, CA, USA (2005)
10. Porambage, P., Braeken, A., Schmitt, C., Gurtov, A., Ylianttila, M., Stiller, B.: Group key establishment for enabling secure multicast communication in wireless sensor networks deployed for IoT applications. Access IEEE **3**, 1503–1511 (2015)
11. Srivatsa, M., Liu, L.: Secure event dissemination in publish-subscribe networks. In: Conference on Distributed Computing Systems (2007)
12. Opyrchal, L., Prakash,A., Agrawal, A.: Designing a publish-subscribe substrate for privacy/security in pervasive environments. In: Proceedings of the 2006 ACS/IEEE International Conference on Pervasive Services, pp. 313–316, 26–29 June 2006
13. Wang, C., Carzaniga, A., Evans, D., Wolf, A.L.: Security issues and requirements for Internet-scale publish-subscribe systems. In: Proceedings of the 35th Annual Hawaii International Conference on System Sciences, HICSS 2002, pp. 3940–3947 (2002)
14. Srivatsa, M., Liu, L., Iyengar, A.: Eventguard: a system architecture for securing publish-subscribe networks. ACM Trans. Comput. Syst. **29**, 4 (2011)

The Cache Location Selection Based on Group Betweenness Centrality Maximization

Jianfeng Guan[1(✉)], Zhiwei Yan[2], Su Yao[3], Changqiao Xu[1],
and Hongke Zhang[1,3]

[1] State Key Laboratory of Networking and Switching Technology,
Beijing University of Posts and Telecommunications, Beijing 100876, China
{jfguan, cqxu, hkzhang}@bupt.edu.cn
[2] China Internet Network Information Center, Beijing 100190, China
yan@cnnic.cn
[3] National Engineering Laboratory for Next Generation Internet Interconnection
Devices, Beijing Jiaotong University, Beijing 100044, China
bjtuyaosu@163.com

Abstract. Content-Centric Networking (CCN) as a content-oriented network architecture can provide efficient content delivery via its in-network caching. However, it is not optimal way to cache contents at all intermediate routers for that the current technology is not yet ready to support an Internet scale deployment. Therefore, in this paper we study the cache location selection problem with an objective to maximize cache delivery performance while minimize the cache nodes. The existing work select cache location based on the important of single node rather than that of entire group, which may result in inefficient problem caused by reduplicative impertinences. Therefore in this paper, we adopt group centrality especially Group Betweenness Centrality (GBC) to select cache locations. To evaluate its performance, we simulate CCN caching under different topologies, and the final results show that GBC-based scheme can provide better performance than others in term of average hop of content delivery.

Keywords: CCN · Cache · Group betweenness centrality

1 Introduction

With the booming of various network technologies, the Internet usage has gradually shifted from resource sharing to content dissemination and retrieval. According to the recent Cisco visual networking report, the video services have already occupied 40% of today's traffic, and it will reach over 60% by the end of 2015. Internet has evolved from a network connecting pairs of end-hosts to a substrate for information dissemination. As a result, the traditional end-point centric model seems to no longer cater current communication demands [1]. Therefore, many systems introduce caching mechanisms [2, 3] as a means to reduce load on access links and shorten the selected content accessing time to acquire better performance. However, the end-to-end design pattern of the current Internet is inefficient to provide these content delivery services. As a

© ICST Institute for Computer Sciences, Social Informatics and Telecommunications Engineering 2017
J.-H. Lee and S. Pack (Eds.): QShine 2016, LNICST 199, pp. 269–279, 2017.
DOI: 10.1007/978-3-319-60717-7_27

result, several network architectures are emerging recently. As a promising network architecture, Content Centric Networking (CCN) has got more studied for that it can provide better service suited to today's usage including the mobility, content distribution and more resilient to disruptions and failures [4]. Different to traditional Internet, CCN treats content as primitive and uses new approaches to routing the named content similar to TRIAD [5] and DONA [6]. CCN adopts receiver-driven transport mode in which data are only transmitted in response to content requests expressed by users. *Interest* message is used by end user to express its interest of content identified by content name. While the *Data* message is response for the *Interest* message if it stratifies the uses' Interest. CCN introduces the *Content Store* which is same as the buffer of an IP router but it has a different replacement policy. Each CCN packet is self-identifying and self-authenticating. In practical, CCN adopts the Least Recently Used (LRU) or Least Frequently Used (LFU) replacement policy to maximize the probability of sharing, which minimizes upstream bandwidth demand and downstream latency to store the *Data* packets as long as possible [7].

It is obviously that the cache mechanism has an import impact on performance, and it therefore has been got researched in the context of performance measurement [8], analytical models [9], and energy impacts [10]. Different to traditional web cache [3], CCN caches the very small data chunks (typically packet-size) instead of caching full objects, which can be identified by users (named data chunks). Each router in the network will cache the data chunk and send back to users once an interest packet hits the cache [11]. However, it is not optimal to cache the chunks at all intermediate routers in CCN [12] for that it may introduce large additional deployment cost. Besides, according to the recent research [13], today's technology is not yet ready to support an Internet scale deployment of CCN at a Content Distribution Network (CDN) and ISP scale. So, there will be a long transition period in which the CCN and current Internet will coexist. As a result, the CCN routers will be deployed in selected locations of Internet and cache the heterogeneous contents. Our previous work has studied the content selection problem [14], while in this paper we mainly focus on the cache location selection problem. More specifically, we consider a scenario which is not every CCN router caching the content. Our previous work [15] has proved that Betweenness Centrality has the better performance than others, and it can be used as a metric to select the cache locations of CCN routers, while in this paper we adopt Group Betweenness Centrality (GBC) to further improve its performance.

The main contributions of this paper are: (1) study CCN router deployment problem during the transition period; (2) propose a GBC-based scheme to select the cache locations, which can maximize the cache delivery performance while minimize the number of participated CCN routers; (3) Evaluate and compare the average hop of content delivery under different network topologies and different network centralities. The rest of this paper is organized as follows. Section 2 investigates the related work of CCN caching mechanisms. Section 3 presents the related research in terms of different network centralities. Section 4 evaluates the performance under different scenarios. Finally, Sect. 5 concludes this paper.

2 Related Work

Some CCN caching schemes are proposed recently [16], and they mainly consist of location selection and content selection. The content selection schemes are generally based on popularity [17–21], priority [22], content relationship [23], user characters of request and distribution [24, 25]. As for cache locations selection or placement, some works have been done in CDN [26–28], web services [29].

The location selection is the well-known p-median or k-center problem, and it is similar to the facility location problem (FLP). However, it is different to solve it for that it is a NP-hard problem, and most researches are focused on better approximation algorithms [34], only few topologies such as line and ring can get the optimal solution in polynomial time [29]. As for CCN, the existing location selection schemes mainly depend on node importance [15, 30–33], node capability [35, 36], node attribution [37]. In term of node importance, Rossi and Rossini [30] adopted the graph-related centrality metrics (e.g., betweenness, closeness, stress) to allocate content store heterogeneously across the CCN, and got that the simple metric such as degree centrality can get modest cache hit gain under different topologies. Guan *et al.* [15] compared the performance of different centralities and found that betweenness centrality has better performance. Wang *et al.* [31, 32] proposed an optimal solution for cache allocation, and comprehensively evaluated impacts of topology character, content characteristic and replacement strategies. Cui *et al.* [33] proposed a cache allocation scheme based on the Request Influence Degree (RID).

However, the existing works are mainly based on single node's importance while little consider the importance of the given cache group. So in this paper, we just consider the topology property, and propose a GBC-based cache location selection scheme to decide the number of deployable CCN router during the transition period.

3 The Proposed Solution

In this section, we first investigate the network centrality, and then describe our GBC-based scheme.

3.1 Node Network Centrality

Network centrality has a long tradition in the analysis of networks, and it is a structural attribute used to measure the contribution of node. There are various types of measures of the centrality of a node to determine the relative importance of a node in the network including centralities of degree, closeness, betweenness and information. For a given network $G = (V, E)$, several typical measures are shown as follows.

(1) Degree Centrality (DC)

The DC of a node v is defined as

$$C_D = \deg(v) \tag{1}$$

Where *deg(v)* is the number of links incident on node v. For a direct graph, it includes the in-degree and out-degree.

(2) Closeness Centrality (CC)

CC is used to measure the distance of node v to all the other nodes in the network, which can be defined as

$$C_{CC} = \frac{1}{\sum_{\forall s \in V \backslash v} d(v, s)} \qquad (2)$$

Where the $d(v, s)$ is the shortest path length from node v to node s. If the graph is not completely connected, this algorithm computes the closeness centrality for each connected part separately.

(3) Betweenness Centrality (BC)

BC reflects how often the node v locates on the shortest paths, and it is defined as

$$C_{BC} = \sum_{s \neq v \neq t \in V} \frac{\delta_{st}(v)}{\delta_{st}} \qquad (3)$$

Where δ_{st} is total number of shortest paths from node s to node t, and $\delta_{st}(v)$ is the number of those paths that pass through the node v.

(4) Eigenvector Centrality (EC)

EC assigns relative scores to all nodes based on the principle that connections to high-scoring nodes contribute more to the score of node than equal connections to low-scoring nodes. In particular, Google's PageRank is a variant. The definition is shown as follows.

$$C_{EC}(v) = \frac{1}{\lambda} \sum_{t \in M(v)} C_E(t) \qquad (4)$$

Where $M(v)$ is a set of the neighbors of v, and λ is a constant.

(5) Load Centrality (LC)

LC of a node is used to measure the load on each node. If all the traffic flows transmit along the shortest paths, then BC and LC are equivalent.

(6) Subgraph Centrality (SC)

SC of a node n is the sum of closed walks of all lengths starting and ending at node n, which can be expressed as

$$C_{SC}(u) = \sum_{i=1}^{N} (v_i^u)^2 e^{\lambda_i} \qquad (5)$$

Where v_i is an eigenvector of adjacency matrix A of G corresponding to the eigenvalue λ_i. The communicability centrality of a node can be found using the matrix exponential of the adjacency matrix of G [38].

3.2   Group Network Centrality

The node centrality just reflect the importance of a node, while in some applications, the centrality of a group is more attractive. For example, in social networks, Borgatti [39] proposes key player problem which includes the Key Player Problem/Positive (KPP-POS) and Key Player Problem/Negative (KPP-NEG). KPP-POS is used to identify the key players for purpose of optimally diffusing something through the network, while the KPP-NEG is defined to identify the key players to disrupt the network by removing the key nodes. As for Internet, groups of routers or links that has maximal potential to control over traffic to increase the effectiveness of network measurements or intrusion detection [40]. So, the group network centrality can be applied to select the cache location. Everett and Borgatti [41] defined GBC as a natural extension of the betweenness measure, which is used to estimate the influence of a group of nodes over the information flow in the network. Some research has shown that finding a group with maximal GBC is a NP-hard problem. Therefore, Puzis et al. [42, 43] propose a method for rapid computation of group betweenness centrality to locate the most prominent group of nodes in a network.

Let $S \subseteq V$ be a group of nodes, the GBC(S) stands for the group betweenness centrality, which can be expressed as

$$GBC(S) = \sum_{s,t \in V | s \neq t \in V} \frac{\ddot{\delta}_{s,t}(S)}{\delta_{s,t}} \tag{6}$$

Where $\ddot{\delta}_{s,t}(S)$ is the number of shortest paths between s and t that traverse at least one member of the group S. The centrality of group is not simply the sum of centralities of its members. Ishakian et al. [44] define a generic algorithm for computing the generalized centrality measure for every node and every group of nodes in the network to identify the subset of a given network that has the largest group centrality, which is called as *K-Group Centrality Maximization* (k-GCM) problem. So, in this paper, we adopt the group between centrality maximization as a metric to select the prominent group in the network to deploy the CCN caches.

4   Performance Evaluation

4.1   Evaluation Metric

The objectives of caching are to lower content delivery latency, reduce the traffic and congestion and alleviate server load. In the performance evaluation, we adopt the average hop of content delivery. Assuming that the network topology consists of N nodes, and we deploy M CCN routers in the network, and the cache of each CCN router has the same capability, and the average hop of content delivery is defined as

$$D = E(d(N, S)) = \frac{1}{N} \sum_{i=1}^{N} d(n_i, S) \tag{7}$$

Where $d(n_i, S)$ denotes the shortest path between node n_i and a CCN routers set S. The average hop of content delivery will reduce with the increase of the number of deployed CCN routers M obviously. The extreme case $(M = N)$ is that all the routers in the networks support the CCN.

4.2 Methodology

We use the Networkx [45] and MATLAB to analyze the performance, and we implemented the GBC maximization algorithm in C++ to select the prominent group of nodes for the given network and the given group size. In the analysis, we adopt three networks to evaluate its applicability including the Zachary's Karate Club (ZKC) [46], Barabási-Albert (BA) network and scale-free network. These topologies can be used to represent the social network, random graph and Internet, respectively. Figure 1 shows the ZKC topology and BA topology, respectively.

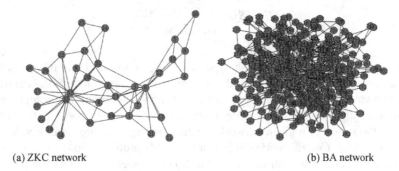

(a) ZKC network   (b) BA network

Fig. 1. Demonstration of ZKC and BA topologies

Table 1 shows the main characteristics of each network including the number of node and edge, average degree.

The users' requests follow a uniform distribution and are generated in each node of the test topologies.

Table 1. The information of selected topology types

Network types	Number of nodes	Number of edges	Average degree
ZKC	34	78	4.5882
BA	300	596	3.9773
Scale-free	500	1489	5.9560

4.3   Results

In the evaluation, we select a prominent group with size from 1 to 10, and compare the GBC with the Degree Centrality (DC), Closeness Centrality (CC), Betweenness Centrality (BC), Eigenvector Centrality (EC), Load Centrality (LC), Subgraph Centrality (Noted it as SC).

(1) ZKC Network

Figure 2 shows the average hop of content delivery in ZKC network. We can get that the average hop decrease greatly with the increase of the number of CCN routers. To describe it more detail, we adopt the relative value to show the differences in Fig. 2(a). And Fig. 2(b) compares the BC and GBC. We can get that in this small social topology, the BC is more attractive that other centralities.

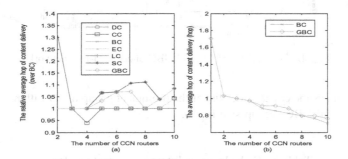

Fig. 2.   Comparison of BC and GBC under ZKC network

(2) BA Network

Figure 3 shows the relative average hop over BC in Fig. 3(a), and more detailed comparison between BC and GBC in Fig. 3(b). We can get that the GBC has the smallest average hop than the others, which shows that GBC can choose the prominent group in the network to get the best performance.

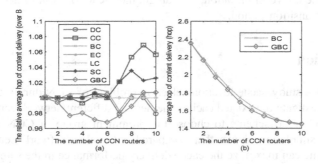

Fig. 3.   Comparison of BC and GBC under BA network

(3) Scale-Free Network

Figure 4 shows the relative average hop over BC in Fig. 4(a), and more detailed comparison between BC and GBC in Fig. 4(b). Similarly, we can get that the GBC has the smallest average hop.

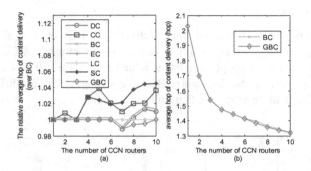

Fig. 4. Comparison of BC and GBC under Scal-free network

Table 2 shows the cache nodes list of the prominent group under different networks based on BC and GBC (group size is 10).

Table 2. Cache locations list under different topology

Network types	Centrality	Nodes list
ZKC	BC	0 33 32 2 31 8 1 13 19 5
	GBC	0 33 32 2 5 0 6 31 0 27
BA	BC	2 0 3 8 14 7 17 22 26 4
	GBC	2 3 8 14 17 22 26 19 11 28
Scale-free	BC	1 2 3 9 8 27 4 20 44 17
	GBC	1 2 3 9 8 27 20 44 17 30

Based on the above information, we can get the cache location to deploy the CCN routers in the transition period.

5 Conclusion

In this paper, we study cache location selection problem of CCN during the transition period. We investigate the existed cache schemes and different network centralities, and propose a GBC-based scheme to choose the prominent group of CCN router in the network. The simulation shows that compared with other network centralities, the proposed scheme can maximize the cache delivery performance in the same group size. Our future work is to set up more complicated network models and user models to evaluate the different user behaviors and service behaviors to further study the cache performances.

Acknowledgments. This work is partially supported by the National Basic Research Program of China (973 Program) under Grant No. 2013CB329102, and the National Natural Science Foundation of China (NSFC) under Grant Nos. 61003283, 61232017, and 61303242.

References

1. Katsaros, K., Xylomenos, G., Polyzos, G.C.: MultiCache: an overlay architecture for information-centric networking. Comput. Netw. **55**(4), 936–947 (2011)
2. Che, H., Wang, Z., Tung, Y.: Analysis and design of hierarchical web caching systems. In: INFOCOM 2001, pp. 1416–1424 (2001)
3. Podlipnig, S., Böszörmenyi, L.: A survey of web cache replacement strategies. ACM Comput. Surv. **35**(4), 374–398 (2003)
4. Ahlgren, B., Dannewitz, C., Imbrenda, C., Kutscher, D., Ohlman, B.: A survey of information-centric networking. IEEE Commun. Mag. **50**(7), 26–36 (2011)
5. Cheriton, D., Gritter, M.: TRIAD: a new next-generation internet architecture. Stanford Technical report (2000)
6. Koponen, T., Chawla, M., Chun, B.-G., Ermolinskiy, A., Kim, K.H., Shenker, S., Stoica, I.: A data-oriented (and beyond) network architecture. SIGCOMM **2007**, 181–192 (2007)
7. Choi, J., Han, J., Cho, E., Kwon, T.T., Choi, Y.: A survey on content-oriented networking for efficient content delivery. IEEE Commun. Mag. **49**(3), 121–127 (2011)
8. Jacobson, V., Smetters, D.K., Briggs, N.H., Plass, M.F., Stewart, P., Thornton, J.D., Braynard, R.L.: Voice over content centric network. In: ACM ReArch, pp. 1–6 (2009)
9. Rosensweig, E.J., Kurose, J., Towsley, D.: Approximate models for general cache networks. In: INFOCOM 2010 (2010)
10. Lee, V.H.U., Rimac, I.: Greening the internet with content centric networking. In: 1st International Conference on Energy-Efficient Computing and Networking (2010)
11. Jacobson, V., Smetters, D.K., Briggs, N.H., Thornton, J.D., Plass, M.F., Braynard, R.L.: Networking named content. In: ACM CoNEXT, pp. 1–9 (2009)
12. Li, Y., Lin, T., Tang, H., Sun, P.: A chunk caching location and searching scheme in content centric networking. In: ICC, pp. 2655–2659 (2012)
13. Perino, D., Varvello, M.: A reality check for content centric networking. In: SIGCOMM Workshop on ICN 2011, pp. 44–49 (2011)
14. Guan, J., He, Y., Wei, Q., Neng, Z.: A classification-based wisdom caching scheme for content centric networking. In: INFOCOM 2016 Workshop, pp. 876–881 (2016)
15. Guan, J., Quan, W., Xu, C., Zhang, H.: The location selection for CCN router based on the network centrality. In: IEEE CCIS 2012, pp. 568–582 (2012)
16. Zhang, G., Li, Y., Lin, T.: Caching in information centric network: a survey. Comput. Netw. **57**(16), 3128–3141 (2013)
17. Lim, S.-H., Ko, Y.-B., Jung, G.-H., Kim, J., Jang, M.-W.: Inter-chunk popularity-based edge-first caching in content-centric networking. IEEE Commun. Lett. **18**(8), 1331–1334 (2014)
18. Bernardini, C., Silverston, T., Festor, O.: MPC: popularity-based caching strategy for content centric networks. In: ICC 2013, pp. 3619–3623 (2013)

19. Liu, Z., Dong, M., Gu, B., Zhang, C., Ji, Y., Tanaka, Y.: Inter-domain popularity-aware video caching in future internet architectures. In: QSHINE 2015, pp. 404–409 (2015)

20. Cho, K., Lee, M., Park, K., Kwon, T.T., Choi, Y., Pack, S.: WAVE: popularity-based and collaborative in-network caching for content-oriented networks. In: INFOCOM Workshops, pp. 316–321 (2012)

21. Li, H., Nakazato, H., Detti, A., Melazzi, N.B.: Popularity proportional cache size allocation policy for video delivery on CCN. In: EuCNC 2015, pp. 434–438 (2015)

22. Tu, Y., Qiao, X., Nan, G., Chen, J., Li, S.: A priority-based dynamic web requests scheduling for web servers over content-centric networking. In: Third IEEE Workshop on Hot Topics in Web Systems and Technologies, pp. 43–48 (2015)

23. Antunes, R.S., Lehmann, M.B., Mansilha, R.B.: CCNrel: leveraging relations among objects to improve the performance of CCN. In: IFIP/IEEE International Symposium on Integrated Network Management (IM), pp. 199–206 (2015)

24. Bernardini, C., Silverston, T., Festor, O.: Socially-aware caching strategy for content centric networking. In: IFIP Networking 2014, pp. 1–9 (2014)

25. Zhou, Y., Cui, L., Jiang, Y., Xu, M.: Modeling and optimizing the cache deployment with filter effect in multi-cache system. In: ISCC 2013, pp. 561–566 (2013)

26. Chen, Z., Lin, C., Yin, H., Li, B.: On the server placement problem of P2P live media streaming system. In: Huang, Y.-M.R., Xu, C., Cheng, K.-S., Yang, J.-F.K., Swamy, M.N.S., Li, S., Ding, J.-W. (eds.) PCM 2008. LNCS, vol. 5353, pp. 178–187. Springer, Heidelberg (2008). doi:10.1007/978-3-540-89796-5_19

27. Zhang, Y., Tatipamula, M.: The freshman handbook: a hint for the service placement of social networks. In: WWW 2011, pp. 173–174 (2011)

28. Yang, D., Fang, X., Xue, G.: ESPN: efficient server placement in probabilistic networks with budget constraint. In: INFOCOM 2011, pp. 1269–1277 (2011)

29. Krishnan, P., Raz, D., Shavitt, Y.: The cache location problem. IEEE/ACM Trans. Netw. **8** (5), 568–582 (2000)

30. Rossi, D., Rossini, G.: On sizing CCN content stores by exploiting topological information. In: INFOCOM Workshop, pp. 280–285 (2012)

31. Wang, Y., Li, Z., Tyson, G., Uhlig, S., Xie, G.: Optimal cache allocation for content-centric networking. In: ICNP 2013, pp. 1–10 (2013)

32. Wang, Y., Li, Z., Tyson, G., Uhlig, S., Xie, G.: Design and evaluation of the optimal cache allocation for content-centric networking. IEEE Trans. Comput. **65**(1), 95–107 (2016)

33. Cui, X., Liu, J., Huang, T., Chen, J., Liu, Y.: The network characters: a novel metric for cache size allocation scheme in content centric networking. In: National Doctoral Academic Forum on Information and Communications Technology, pp. 1–6 (2013)

34. Dohan, D., Karp, S., Matejek, B.: K-median algorithms: theory in practice (2015). http://www.cs.princeton.edu/courses/archive/fall14/cos521/projects/kmedian.pdf

35. Mishra, G.P., Dave, M.: Cost effective caching in content centric networking. In: NGCT-2015, pp. 198–202 (2015)

36. Xu, Y., Wang, Z., Li, Y., Lin, T., An, W., Ci, S.: Minimizing bandwidth cost of CCN: a coordinated in-network caching approach. In: ICCCN 2015, pp. 1–7 (2015)

37. Sourlas, V., Tassiulas, L., Psaras, I., Pavlou, G.: Information resilience through user-assisted caching in disruptive content-centric networks. In: IFIP Networking Conference, pp. 1–9 (2015)

38. Estrada, E., Hatano, N.: Communicability in complex networks. Phys. Rev. E **77**, 036111 (2008). http://arxiv.org/abs/0707.0756

39. Borgatti, S.P.: Identifying sets of key players in a social network. Comput. Math. Organ. Theory **12**(1), 21–34 (2006)

40. Puzis, R., Tubi, M., Elovici, Y., Glezer, C., Dolev, S.: A decision support system for placement of intrusion detection and prevention devices in large-scale networks. ACM Trans. Model. Comput. Simul. 22(1), Article ID: 5 (2011)
41. Everett, M.G., Borgatti, S.P.: The centrality of groups and classes. Math. Sociol. 23(3), 181–201 (1999)
42. Puzis, R., Elovici, Y., Dolev, S.: Fast algorithm for successive computation of group between centrality. Phys. Rev. E 76, 056709 (2007)
43. Puzis, R., Elovici, Y., Dolev, S.: Finding the most prominent group in complex networks. AI Commun. 20, 287–296 (2007)
44. Ishakian, V., Erdos, D., Terzi, E., Bestavros, A.: A framework for the evaluation and management of network centrality. In: SDM 2012 (2012)
45. NetworkX. http://networkx.lanl.gov/index.html
46. Data File. http://vlado.fmf.uni-lj.si/pub/networks/data/Ucinet/UciData.htm

5G-CAT 2016

A Middleware Solution for Optimal Sensor Management of IoT Applications on LTE Devices

Satyajit Padhy, Hsin-Yu Chang, Ting-Fang Hou, Jerry Chou,
Chung-Ta King, and Cheng-Hsin Hsu(⊠)

Department of Computer Science, National Tsing Hua University, Hsinchu, Taiwan
chsu@cs.nthu.edu.tw

Abstract. After many devices that have adopted LTE technology, it is
optimistic to presume that 5G technology will have to address the huge
traffic of data and volume of heterogeneous devices in future. Existing context-aware Internet of Things (IoT) applications directly control
sensors on LTE devices in an uncoordinated and non-optimized manner, which leads to redundant sensor activations and energy wastage on
resource-constrained IoT devices. Optimal and coordinated sensor usage
dictates a comprehensive middleware solution to bring together the information from all IoT applications/sensors and intelligently select the best
set of sensors to activate. In this paper, we design, implement, and evaluate a sensor management middleware for LTE devices that controls the
tradeoff between energy consumption of sensors and accuracy of inferred
contexts. The core task of this middleware is to minimize total energy
consumption while making sure that the accuracy requested by IoT applications are met. Trace-driven simulations are conducted to demonstrate
the merits of the proposed middleware and algorithms. The simulation
results indicate that the proposed algorithms clearly outperform the current solution.

Keywords: IoT applications · Sensor management · LTE device ·
Context-aware

1 Introduction

Increasingly more Internet of Things (IoT) applications (apps) on LTE devices
leverage the rich set of sensors to infer their contexts for enhancing user experiences. As we are progressing towards the IoT [8], a number of context aware IoT
applications are being produced to take advantage of sensors available on LTE
devices. In the future, multiple IoT applications running at the same time on an
LTE device may request a multitude of overlapping contexts, e.g., location and
time. For example, location awareness [10] can help to introduce some resource
allocation techniques which will help to reduce delay by predicting channel quality. A context aware adaptive system [1] is required in the middleware layer to

© ICST Institute for Computer Sciences, Social Informatics and Telecommunications Engineering 2017
J.-H. Lee and S. Pack (Eds.): QShine 2016, LNICST 199, pp. 283–292, 2017.
DOI: 10.1007/978-3-319-60717-7_28

address the heterogeneous data being generated from IoT applications. While a context may be answered by different sets of sensors depending on the requested accuracy and availability of sensors, uncoordinated and non-optimized use of the sensors by the multiple apps may turn on redundant sensors, leading to wastage of energy.

Choosing the *best* set of sensors to activate in order to satisfy the needs of various context-aware apps is very challenging. This is because there exists a tradeoff between context inference accuracy and energy consumption of sensors. On top of that, context-aware apps impose diverse accuracy requirements and LTE devices have different remaining battery levels at different time. Therefore, efficiently determining the set of sensors to activate *dictates* a comprehensive mobile middleware solution, which brings together various information from apps and sensors. In this paper, we propose a sensor management middleware, which sits between the context-aware apps and sensors. The middleware achieves *coordinated* and *optimized* uses of sensors, and provides efficient sensor management service to the context-aware apps.

The core of the middleware is the *sensor management* algorithm, which is repeatedly invoked to adapt to system dynamics. In this paper, the sensor management algorithm will optimally chose the best set of sensors for various context requests from multiple IoT applications on an LTE device. We develop two mathematical formulations of the sensor management problems: (i) energy optimization, which strives to find the set of sensors that consumes the least energy while satisfying the sensing requirements, and (ii) accuracy optimization, which strives to maximize the overall accuracy under an energy budget. Since low latency is one of the most important criteria in 5G technology, we develop two heuristic, real-time sensor management algorithms for resource-constrained mobile devices.

The rest of this paper is organized as follows. We survey the literature in Sect. 2. Section 3 describes the proposed middleware and proposed sensor management algorithms. Sect. 4 gives the trace-driven simulation results. Section 5 concludes the paper.

2   Related Work

Mobile context sensing has been studied in the literature. However there has not been much work done for context and sensor management related to 5G IoT environments. Taranto et al. [10] has proposed methodologies about how location aware context can be useful for 5G architecture. They briefly describe how location awareness can be leveraged across different layers of protocol stack on 5G architecture. Perera et al. [8] have surveyed various context aware computing methodologies that have been addressed in context aware IoT applications. They state that a large number of solutions exist in terms of system, middleware and application; however none of them addresses our core issue. Most existing studies on context-aware LTE IoT (smartphone) apps [2–4,6,11] consider location sensing. For example, Ma et al. [6] propose a system to predict the future locations of a mobile user based on his/her previous locations. Their prediction algorithm employs sensor readings from GSM and WiFi for coarse localization, which is more energy efficient than using GPS sensors. Different from our proposed OSM middleware, these studies [2–4,6,11] only consider location sensing, and thus their solutions are inapplicable to our problem. Contexts other than location have also been recently investigated [5,9,13]. For example, Yan et al. [13] employ accelerometers to classify the mobile user actions, e.g., stand, walk, and sit. None of the studies [5,9,13] consider the inter-dependency among inference algorithms of different contexts: each context is inferred independently.

3   Proposed System

3.1   System Architecture

Our proposed middleware sits between apps and the hardware. Many context-aware apps run on LTE devices, which may need different contexts at diverse accuracy and frequency. We collectively call a pair of accuracy and frequency as *request*. Apps may *register* or *unregister* requests through an Application Programming Interface (API) at any time. Each set of sensors is referred to as a *combination* in this paper. For example, a context IsDriving may be inferred by a combination of the GPS and the accelerometer. Moreover, a context may be inferred by various combinations, which renders the decisions even harder. For instance, IsDriving may also be inferred using the microphone. As illustrated in Fig. 1, the middleware consists of an API and four software components: (i) request manager, (ii) resource manager, (iii) context analyzer, and (iv) system model. The **request manager** keeps track of all registered requests and apps with a queue. It also checks if the callback function invocation fails, and automatically unregisters all the requests from any failed (exited) apps.

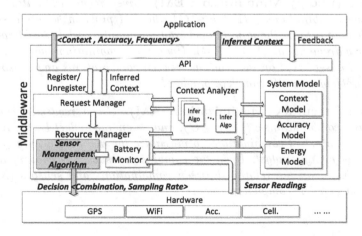

Fig. 1. The proposed middleware. Italic font indicates the focused components of our work.

The **resource manager** focuses on resource conservation and consists of two components: the battery monitor and sensor management algorithm. The sensor management algorithm takes the aggregated requests and system models as inputs, and generates decisions that activate the combinations of sensors and specify their sampling rates. The sensor management algorithms can either: (i) maximize the overall accuracy under a given energy budget or (ii) minimize the total energy consumption while achieving target accuracy levels which are inputs from apps or users. The **context analyzer** analyzes the sensor readings to infer contexts by hosting various inference algorithms for different combinations and contexts. The **System model** contains three parts: (i) context model, (ii) accuracy model, and (iii) energy model. The context model stores the relationship among contexts, inference algorithms, and sensor combinations, e.g., the action inference algorithm uses the accelerometer and WiFi to classify the user actions, such as walk, run, and still. The accuracy model captures the accuracy of the contexts inferred by the inference algorithms. Different metrics, such as *precision* and *recall* can be used to quantify the inference accuracy. The energy model captures the energy consumption of each sensor at different sampling rates.

We let R be the total number of requested contexts and S be the total number of sensors. We define a request as $<y_r, f_r>$, where r $(1 \leq r \leq R)$ is the requested context, y_r is the target accuracy, and f_r is the desired frequency. We let C be the total number of potential sensor combinations. We employ a boolean matrix $\mathbf{M}$ to capture the relation between combinations and sensors[1]. In particular, we let $m_{c,s} = 1$ $(1 \leq c \leq C, 1 \leq s \leq S)$ if combination c contains sensor s, and $m_{c,s} = 0$ otherwise. We collectively call all $a_{c,r}$ as $\mathbf{A}$. Last, we use e_s to denote the energy consumption of sensor s, where $1 \leq s \leq S$, in the next management window T. We write a decision as $<x_s, p_s>$, where x_s indicates whether the sensor s $(1 \leq s \leq S)$ should be activated, and p_s represents the sampling rate. Next, we present the two sensor management problems.

Problem 1 (Energy Minimization: EM). *Given requested contexts r $(1 \leq r \leq R)$ and combinations c $(1 \leq c \leq C)$, the EM problem selects a subset of combinations to achieve the minimum energy consumption while satisfying all the accuracy requirements y_r $(1 \leq r \leq R)$. Upon the combination subset is chosen, the decision is set based on the relation between combinations and sensors (M). The EM problem is a NP-complete problem.*

Problem 2 (Accuracy Maximization: AM). *Given requested contexts r $(1 \leq r \leq R)$, combinations c $(1 \leq c \leq C)$, and an energy budget E, the AM problem selects a subset of combinations to maximize the achieved accuracy without exceeding the energy budget. Upon the combination subset is chosen, the decision is set based on the relation between combinations and sensors (M). The AM problem is a NP-complete problem.*

---

[1] Throughout this paper, we use bold font to denote vectors or matrices.

3.2   Efficient Energy Minimization Algorithm (EEMA)

The EEMA algorithm maintains a set $\hat{\mathbf{R}}$, $\mathbf{X}$ of unmet requests and the chosen sensors so far. We define utility of a combination as a fraction of *profit* and *cost*. The profit is the number of unmet requests that can be satisfied by the combination, and the cost is the additional energy consumption, if the combination is chosen. The utility $g_c(\mathbf{A}, \mathbf{M}, \mathbf{X}, \hat{\mathbf{R}})$ of a combination c $(1 \le c \le C)$ is written as:

$$g_c(\mathbf{A}, \mathbf{M}, \mathbf{X}, \hat{\mathbf{R}}) = \frac{p_c(\mathbf{A}, \hat{\mathbf{R}})}{w_c(\mathbf{M}, \mathbf{X})} = \frac{\frac{\sum_{1 \le r \le R, r \in \hat{\mathbf{R}}} \mathbf{1}_{[a_{c,r} \ge y_r]}}{\sum_{1 \le r \le R} \mathbf{1}_{[a_{c,r} \ge y_r]}}}{\sum_{1 \le s \le S, s \notin \mathbf{X}} m_{c,s} e_s,} \tag{1}$$

where $\mathbf{1}$ is the indicator function, $\mathbf{A}$ is the accuracy model, and $\hat{\mathbf{R}}$ is the set of unmet requests and where $\mathbf{M}$ is the boolean matrix of relation between combinations and sensors and $\mathbf{X}$ keeps track of the chosen sensors so far. We note that the denominator of Eq. (1), $w_c(\mathbf{M}, \mathbf{X})$, could be zero because some sensors may be always on for basic LTE device features. Figure 2 gives the pseudocode of our EEMA algorithm. The loop in lines 4–5 computes the latest $g_c(\mathbf{A}, \mathbf{M}, \mathbf{X}, \hat{\mathbf{R}})$ using Eq. (1) for all combinations. Line 6 picks the combination c^* with the highest utility. Lines 7 and 8 update the current decision and unmet requests. It is not hard to see that the time complexity of EEMA is $O(RC(S+R))$. from the loops starting from lines 3 and 4, respectively. S and R come from computing $w_c(\mathbf{M}, \mathbf{X})$ and $p_c(\mathbf{A}, \hat{\mathbf{R}})$, respectively. Lines 6, 7, and 8 dominate. Hence, the time complexity is $O(RC(S + R))$.

```
1:  // Input: A, M, R̂; Output: X
2:  let X = ∅
3:  while R̂ ≠ ∅,  max   g_c(A, M, X, R̂) > 0 do
                 1≤c≤C
4:      for each c = 1, 2, ..., C do
5:          compute g_c(A, M, X, R̂) using Eq. (1)
6:          select c* = argmax  g_c(A, M, X, R̂)
                       c=1,2,...,C
7:      X ← X ∪ {s|m_{c*,s} = 1}
8:      R̂ ← R̂ − {r|y_r ≤ a_{c*,r}}
```

Fig. 2. Efficient Energy Minimization Algorithm (EEMA).

3.3   Efficient Accuracy Maximization Algorithm (EAMA)

The EAMA algorithm maintains a set of $\hat{\mathbf{R}}$ of unmet requests, a list of available combinations $\mathbf{W}$ (i.e., those have not been selected), the energy consumption $e_{\mathbf{X}}$ and achieved accuracy $\hat{\mathbf{Y}}_{\mathbf{X}}$ with the current decision $\mathbf{X}$. Its goal is to find a decision $\mathbf{X}$ with the highest average accuracy without exceeding the energy budget E. The cost function $w_c(\mathbf{M}, \mathbf{X})$ is the same as the one used in the EEMA algorithm. The utility function $g'_c(\mathbf{A}, \mathbf{M}, \mathbf{X}, \hat{\mathbf{Y}})$ is written as:

$$g'_c(\mathbf{A}, \mathbf{M}, \mathbf{X}, \hat{\mathbf{Y}}) = \frac{\sum_{1 \le r \le R} a_{c,r} \mathbf{1}_{[a_{c,r} \ge \max(y_r, \hat{y}_r(\mathbf{X}))]}}{\sum_{1 \le s \le S, s \notin \mathbf{X}} m_{c,s} e_s,}. \tag{2}$$

where $\mathbf{1}$ is the indicator function, and $\hat{\mathbf{Y}}(\mathbf{X}) = \{\hat{y}_r(x)|r = 1, 2, \ldots, R\}$ is the achieved accuracy with decision $\mathbf{X}$. Figure 3 gives the pseudocode of the EAMA algorithm. The loop in lines 4–5 computes the latest $g'_c(\mathbf{A}, \mathbf{M}, \mathbf{X}, \hat{\mathbf{Y}})$ using Eq. (2) for all combinations. Line 6 picks the combination c^* with the highest utility, and line 7 updates the available combinations. The if-clause between lines 8–13 checks if activating the sensors of combination c^* would lead to energy consumption within the energy budget. If yes, lines 9, 10 and the loop starting from line 11 update decision $\mathbf{X}$, total energy consumption $e_{\mathbf{X}}$, and the achieved accuracy $\hat{\mathbf{Y}}$, respectively. It can be derived that the time complexity of EAMA is $O(C^2(S + R))$.

```
1: // Input: A, M; Output: X
2: let e_X = 0, W = {1, 2, ..., C}, Ŷ = 0
3: while W ≠ ∅ do
4:    for each c = 1, 2, ..., C do
5:       compute g'_c(A, M, X, Ŷ) with Eq. (2)
6:    select c* = argmax_{c∈W} g'_c(A, M, X, Ŷ)
7:    W ← W − {c*}
8:    if e_X + w_{c*}(M, X) < E then
9:       X ← X ∪ {s|m_{c*,s} = 1}
10:      e_X = Σ_{s=1}^{S} e_s x_s
11:      for each r = 1, 2, ..., R do
12:         if ŷ_r ≤ a_{c*,r} then
13:            ŷ_r = a_{c*,r}
```

Fig. 3. Efficient Accuracy Maximization Algorithm (EAMA).

4   Trace Driven Simulations

4.1   Setup

We have developed a Java-based event-driven simulator to evaluate the proposed middleware for IoT context aware applications on LTE devices. We have also implemented the proposed sensor management algorithms: the EEMA and EAMA for efficient management. For comparisons, we have also implemented an algorithm called Per-app-Optimized (Per-app) algorithm, which emulates the state-of-the-art sensor management in LTE devices. The Per-app algorithm goes through all the requests, and for each request, it selects the combination achieving the highest precision. This is the same as having individual apps decide how to use sensors without considering overlapping sensors. Each app requests for a context randomly selected from the 6 contexts listed in Table 1. The same table also gives the precision reported in the literature [7,11–13]. We conduct the simulations on a PC with an Intel 3.4 GHz CPU. We consider both the EM and AM problems. For the EM problem, we let y_r be the accuracy requirement of individual requests. More specifically, each request is associated with a random precision uniformly distributed in y_r with value ranging between 0.3 and 0.9. An IoT app may make several context requests to the middleware. For the AM problem, we consider the energy budget $E = \{500, 700, 900, 1100, 1300\}$ mJ, with a sampling rate of 1/300 Hz. E is the energy limit in each management window. We report sample results from $E = 1000$ mJ, if not otherwise specified. We use $T = 1$ min as management window size. The mapping between combinations and sensors are chosen randomly by Bernoulli trail which basically decides whether a sensor should be activated or deactivated. We adopt three performance metrics: (i) energy consumption in mJ, (ii) mean precision in %, and (iii) success rate in %. The success rate refers to the ratio of satisfied context requests.

Table 1. The combinations, contexts, and sensors used in our simulations

| | Context precision (%) | | | | | | Sensor activation in Boolean | | | | | |
Combination	IsSitting	IsStanding	IsWalking	IsRunning	InMeeting	IsDriving	Acc.	Blue.	WiFi	Mic.	GPS	Cell.
YAN [13]	95	91	83.8	0	73.86	74	1	0	1	0	1	0
CenceMe [7]	68	78	94	74	68	74	1	1	0	1	1	0
EEMSS [11]	89.44	0	78.2	90	0	63.86	1	1	1	0	1	0
EEMSS2 [11]	99.44	0	88.2	100	0	73.86	1	1	1	1	1	0
SAMMPLE [12]	0	0	0	0	68	0	1	0	0	0	1	0
SAMMPLE2 [12]	0	0	0	0	57	0	1	0	0	0	0	0
OTHER1	50	59	66	70	96	91	0	0	1	0	0	1
OTHER2	35	54	56	60	86	76	1	0	0	0	0	1

4.2 Results

We first validate the correctness of Per-app, EMA, and EEMA algorithms. We find that all requests from apps are satisfied by the resulting decisions. Figure 4 shows sensor activations with EAMA algorithm when the energy budget is set to 1000 mJ. The accelerometer is the least activated sensor, whereas GPS and BlueTooth are requested more frequently from various IoT applications. Next, we report the energy consumption achieved by individual algorithms in Fig. 5(a). We observe that EEMA consumes the least energy when we have a fixed energy

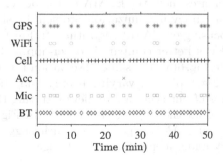

Fig. 4. Sensor activation by EEMA for $E = 1000$ mJ.

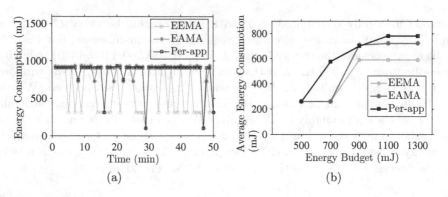

Fig. 5. Energy consumption with: (a) sample results from $E = 1000\,\text{mJ}$ and (b) aggregated results under diverse E.

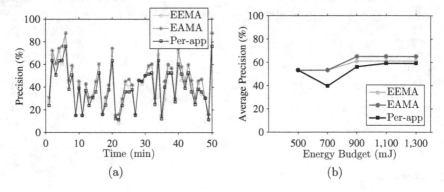

Fig. 6. Average precision with: (a) sample results from $E = 1000\,\text{mJ}$ and (b) aggregated results under diverse E.

budget of $(E = 1000\,\text{mJ})$ and outperforms the per-app algorithm. We then plot the aggregated results under different energy values E in Fig. 5(b). We see a significant saving in energy consumption in EEMA compared to per-app algorithm. The energy consumption of EAMA and per-app is non-decreasing as the energy budget increases, however EEMA shows better result than both of them. We justify the accuracy maximization problem by showing the precision and success rate by focusing on EAMA algorithm. In Fig. 6, we clearly see that the precision of EAMA is better compared to per-app and EEMA. Compared to the sample results in Fig. 6(a), the same observation is even more clear in the aggregated results in Fig. 6(b) with varying energy budgets. High success rate suggests the correctness of our accuracy model by stating the ratio of correctly inferred contexts out of all the requested contexts. In Fig. 7, we see that the success rate is higher for EAMA algorithms which suggests that we achieve higher overall accuracy under a specific energy budget.

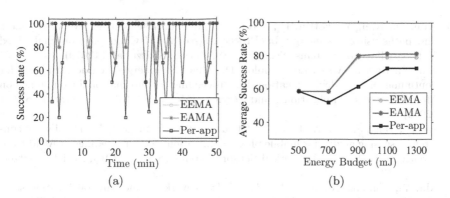

Fig. 7. Success rate with: (a) sample results from $E = 1000\,\text{mJ}$ and (b) aggregated results under diverse E.

5   Conclusion

Context-aware IoT applications are getting increasingly more popular. Multiple IoT apps may run at the same time on an LTE device and request for several overlapping contexts at a subsequent higher rate. In this paper, we developed a novel middleware solution to support efficient context inference from IoT applications in terms of energy consumption and accuracy. Instead of solely intending to reach optimal energy consumption for independent contexts, the proposed middleware selectively activates certain sensors while taking overlapping context requirements from multiple context-aware applications into consideration. We also rigorously studied the sensor management problem, which is the core issue in this middleware. We presented two optimization problem formulations: energy- and accuracy-optimization. We then proposed two heuristic algorithms to address these problems: EEMA and EAMA. Our extensive trace-driven simulations show the merits of our proposed middleware solution and algorithms.

Acknowledgement. This study was conducted under the Advanced Communication Technology Research and Laboratory Development project of the Institute for Information Industry, which is subsidized by the Ministry of Economic Affairs of the Republic of China. This work was also partially supported by Ministry of Science and Technology (MOST) of Taiwan under the grant number MOST104-3115-E-007-004.

References

1. Barbero, C., Zovo, P.D., Gobbi, B.: A flexible context aware reasoning approach for IoT applications. In: Proceedings of IEEE International Conference on Mobile Data Management (MDM 2011), Lulea, Sweden (2011)
2. Chon, Y., Talipov, E., Shin, H., Cha., H.: Mobility prediction-based smartphone energy optimization for everyday location monitoring. In: Proceedings of ACM Conference on Embedded Networked Sensor Systems (SenSys 2011), Seattle, WA (2011)

3. Kim, D., Kim, Y., Estrin, D., Srivastava, M.: SensLoc: sensing everyday places and paths using less energy. In: Proceedings of ACM Conference on Embedded Networked Sensor Systems (SenSys 2010), Zurich, Switzerland (2010)
4. Lin, K., Kansal, A., Lymberopoulos, D., Zhao, F.: Energy-accuracy trade-off for continuous mobile device location. In: Proceedings of International Conference on Mobile systems, Applications, and Services (MobiSys 2010), San Francisco, CA (2010)
5. Lu, H., Yang, J., Liu, Z., Lane, N., Choudhury, T., Campbell, A.: The Jigsaw continuous sensing engine for mobile phone applications. In: Proceedings of ACM Conference on Embedded Networked Sensor Systems (SenSys 2010), Zurich, Switzerland (2010)
6. Ma, Y., Hankins, R., Racz, D.: iLoc: a framework for incremental location-state acquisition and prediction based on mobile sensors. In: Proceedings of ACM Conference on Information and Knowledge Management (CIKM 2009), Hong Kong, China (2009)
7. Miluzzo, E., Lane, N., Fodor, K., Peterson, R., Lu, H., Eisenman, S., Zheng, X., Campbell, A.: Sensing meets mobile social networks: the design, implementation and evaluation of the CenceMe application. In: Proceedings of ACM Conference on Embedded Networked Sensor Systems (SenSys 2008), Raleigh, NC (2008)
8. Perera, C., Zaslavsky, A., Christen, P., Georgakopoulos, D.: Context aware computing for the Internet of Things: a survey. IEEE Commun. Surv. Tutor. 16(1), 414–454 (2013)
9. Schirmer, M., Höpfner, H.: SENST*: approaches for reducing the energy consumption of smartphone-based context recognition. In: Proceedings of International and Interdisciplinary Conference on Modeling and Using Context (CONTEXT 2011), Karlsruhe, Germany (2011)
10. Taranto, R., Muppirisetty, L., Raulefs, R., Slockand, D., Svensson, T., Wymeersch, H.: Location-aware communications for 5G networks: how location information can improve scalability, latency, and robustness of 5G. IEEE Signal Process. Mag. 31(6), 102–112 (2014)
11. Wang, Y., Lin, J., Annavaram, M., Jacobson, Q., Hong, J., Krishnamachari, B., Sadeh, N.: A framework of energy efficient mobile sensing for automatic user state recognition. In: Proceedings of International Conference on Mobile Systems, Applications, and Services (MobiSys 2009), Krakw, Poland (2009)
12. Yan, Z., Jeung, H., Chakraborty, D., Misra, A., Aberer, K.: SAMMPLE: detecting semantic indoor activities in practical settings using locomotive signatures. In: Proceedings of International Symposium on Wearable Computers (ISWC 2012), Newcastle, UK (2012)
13. Yan, Z., Subbaraju, V., Chakraborty, D., Misra, A., Aberer, K.: Energy-efficient continuous activity recognition on mobile phones: an activity-adaptive approach. In: Proceedings of International Symposium on Wearable Computers (ISWC 2012), Newcastle, UK (2012)

An Energy Consumption Oriented Offloading Algorithm for Fog Computing

Xiaohui Zhao$^{(\boxtimes)}$, Liqiang Zhao, and Kai Liang

State Key Laboratory of Integrated Service Networks,
Xidian University, Xian 710071, Shaanxi, China
xxhzhao@hotmail.com

Abstract. Fog computing is a promising method for computation offloading by bringing the computation at arms reach, which is characterized by low latency and significant for the delay-sensitive applications. Offloading is effectively to extend the lifetime of battery of mobile device by executing some applications remotely. In this paper, we provide an energy consumption oriented offloading algorithm to save mobile devices energy while satisfying given application response time requirement. We formulate the offloading algorithm as minimizing energy consumption with the constraints of time tolerance and the maximum transmission power. It dynamically selects cloud computing or fog computing to offload computing instead of only relying on cloud computing. The numerical results show that our offloading algorithm can reduce the energy consumption obviously.

Keywords: Offloading · Cloud computing · Fog computing · Energy consumption

1 Introduction

Nowadays, mobile devices have become an indispensable part of People's Daily life. The demands for mobile devices to run applications with high computation are increasing. The local computation resources are insufficient to run sophisticated task, compared to desktop counterparts. Due to the physical size constraint, mobile devices have limited computation and battery life. Thus, the limitation of energy has been the bottleneck of mobile devices.

Computing offloading [1,2] is a possible strategy to overcome the above bottleneck. It enables resource constrained mobile devices to offload their most energy-consuming tasks to nearby more resourceful servers. The mobile device can offload computing to the cloud. Then the cloud server executes the tasks and provides the mobile device with the results. However, recently research [3] shows that offloading computing to the cloud is not always a good choice because some delay sensitive applications should be completed within their delay tolerance, and the cloud computing has a large transmission delay, especially for the network edge devices. With the availability of nearby resources via fog computing,

© ICST Institute for Computer Sciences, Social Informatics and Telecommunications Engineering 2017
J.-H. Lee and S. Pack (Eds.): QShine 2016, LNICST 199, pp. 293–301, 2017.
DOI: 10.1007/978-3-319-60717-7_29

mobile device offer computation offloading with low latency, which is beneficial for the delay sensitive task. Fog computing is a recent computing paradigm that is extending cloud computing towards the edge of network. The computation capacity of fog computing is weaker than that of cloud computing. We formulate the offloading problem as minimizing energy consumption with the constraints of time tolerance and the maximum transmission power.

In the paper, we provide an energy consumption oriented offloading algorithm to overcome the problem above with the consideration of latency tolerance and the transmission power of mobile device. The contributions of our work can be summarized as follows:

We provide the energy consumption oriented offloading algorithm. Firstly, we compute the energy consumption of fog computing and cloud computing, respectively. Then mobile device makes a choice after comparing the magnitude between them. Numerical result shows that the energy consumption oriented offloading algorithm has less energy than that of adopting cloud computing alone.

The rest of the paper is organized as follows. Section 2 presents system model. Section 3 presents the problem formulation and solutions. Numerical results are provided in Sect. 4. Section 5 concludes the paper.

2   System Model

We first introduce the system model. This paper shows a three-layer structure consisting of cloud layer, fog layer and UE (user equipment) layer. The smartphone provides mobile computing functionalities to the end user via different applications. The fog node in the fog layer is the connections with cloud layer and the end user, which can provide fog computing capability. The cloud server can provide cloud computing capacity. For simplicity, we assume that there has one mobile device that has a computational intensive task to be completed. In this case, a mobile device is able to find a radio access point within a short distance in the fog server. Similar to many previous studies in mobile cloud computing [4] and mobile networking [5], to enable tractable analysis and get useful insights, we consider a quasi-static scenario where the mobile device remains unchanged during a computation offloading period (e.g., within several seconds), while may change across different periods.

2.1   Delay Analysis

(1) Fog Computing

In the case of computation offloading, the latency incorporates the time to transmit the input bits to the fog server necessary to enable the execution, the time necessary for the fog server to execute the instructions, and the time to send the result back to the UE. More specifically, the overall latency experienced by mobile device can be written as

$$\Delta_f = \Delta_{f,1}^t + \Delta_{f,2}^t \tag{1}$$

Where $\Delta_{f,1}^t$ is the time for the mobile device to transfer the input bits to its fog server, $\Delta_{f,2}^t$ is the time for the fog server to execute instructions.

$$\Delta_{f,1}^t = \frac{D}{R\left(p_{tr}\right)} \tag{2}$$

$$\Delta_{f,2}^t = \frac{M}{S_f} \tag{3}$$

Where D is the size of the input bits, and M is the number of instructions, which is necessary for the fog server to execute, and S_f is the computation capacity of the fog server. $R\left(p_{tr}\right)$ is the wireless transmission rate.[1]

$$R\left(p_{tr}\right) = \log\left(1 + \frac{p_{tr}h^2}{N_0}\right) \tag{4}$$

Where h is the channel fading coefficient, and N_0 denotes the noise power.

(2) Cloud Computing

The latency incorporates the time to transmit the input bits to the fog server necessary to enable the execution transfer, the time necessary for the fog server to transfer the input bits to the cloud server, and the time necessary for the cloud server to execute the instructions, and the time necessary to send result back to the UE. The overall latency experienced by the mobile device is

$$\Delta_c = \Delta_{c,1}^t + \Delta_{c,2}^t + \Delta_{c,3}^t \tag{5}$$

Where $\Delta_{c,1}^t$ is the time necessary for the mobile device to transfer the input bits to its fog server; $\Delta_{c,2}^t$ is the time necessary for the fog server to transfer the input bits to the cloud server; $\Delta_{c,3}^t$ is the time for the cloud server to execute the instructions.

$$\Delta_{c,1}^t = \frac{D}{R\left(p_{tr}\right)} \tag{6}$$

$$\Delta_{c,2}^t = \frac{D}{B} \tag{7}$$

$$\Delta_{c,3}^t = \frac{M}{S_c} \tag{8}$$

Where B denotes the bandwidth between fog and cloud server, and S_c is the computation capacity of cloud server.

For many applications (e.g., face recognition), the size of the computation outcome in general is much smaller than that of computation input data including the mobile system settings, program codes and input parameters. We ignore the time it needs to return the outcome to the mobile device.

---

[1] All the $\log(\cdot)$ functions are of base 2 by default.

2.2 Energy Consumption Analysis

(1) Fog Computing

Energy consumption of offloaded services is

$$E_f\left(p_{tr}\right) = E_{f,1} + E_{f,2} \tag{9}$$

Where $E_{f,1}$ is the idle energy consumption of mobile device when the fog server executes the instructions, and $E_{f,2}$ is the energy consumption for the mobile device necessary to transfer the input bits to the fog.

$$E_{f,1} = \frac{Mp_i}{S_f} \tag{10}$$

$$E_{f,2} = \frac{Dp_{tr}}{R\left(p_{tr}\right)} \tag{11}$$

Where p_i and p_{tr} are the idle power and the transmission power of the mobile device, respectively. M denotes the size of instructions which are executed on the fog server.

(2) Cloud Computing

Energy consumption of offloaded service is

$$E_c\left(p_{tr}\right) = E_{c,1} + E_{c,2} + E_{c,3} \tag{12}$$

Where $E_{c,1}$ is the energy consumption for the mobile device transmitting the input bits to the fog server, $E_{c,2}$ is the idle energy consumption of the mobile device when the fog server transmit the input bits to the cloud server, and $E_{c,3}$ is the idle energy consumption during the cloud server executes the instructions.

$$E_{c,1} = \frac{Dp_{tr}}{R\left(p_{tr}\right)} \tag{13}$$

$$E_{c,2} = \frac{Dp_i}{B} \tag{14}$$

$$E_{c,3} = \frac{Mp_i}{S_c} \tag{15}$$

3 Problem Formulation and Solution

3.1 Problem Formulation

In this paper, we aim at minimizing the energy consumption at the mobile device. The delay tolerance constraints based on the p_{tr} can be given by

$$\Delta_{(\cdot)} \leq T \tag{16}$$

Where T is the delay tolerance and $\Delta_{(\cdot)}$ denotes the overall time of fog computing when $(\cdot)$ represents f. $\Delta_{(\cdot)}$ denotes the overall time of cloud computing when $(\cdot)$ represents c.

The transmission power constraints based on $P_{\max}$ can be given by

$$0 \leq p_{tr} \leq p_{\max} \tag{17}$$

Combining (16) with (17), we have

$$p_{\min} \leq p_{tr} \leq p_{\max} \tag{18}$$

We formulate the optimization problem as minimizing the energy consumption for the mobile device computation offloading while satisfying the transmission power of mobile device constraints as follows:

$$\arg \min_{p_{tr}} E\left(p_{tr}\right) \tag{19}$$

$$\text{s.t. (18)}$$

3.2   Solution

To achieve the minimum energy consumption, we introduce the solution in fog computing as an example.

$$\min_{p_{tr}} \quad \frac{Mp_i}{S_f} + \frac{Dp_{tr}}{\log\left(1+\frac{p_{tr}h^2}{N_0}\right)} \tag{20}$$

$$\text{s.t. } p_{\min} \leq p_{tr} \leq p_{\max}$$

Because $\frac{Mp_i}{S_f}$ is a constant, the above optimization problem can be equivalent to

$$\min_{p_{tr}} \quad \frac{Dp_{tr}}{\log\left(1+\frac{p_{tr}h^2}{N_0}\right)} \tag{21}$$

$$\text{s.t. } p_{\min} \leq p_{tr} \leq p_{\max}$$

Due to $\dfrac{Dp_{tr}}{\log\left(1+\frac{p_{tr}h^2}{N_0}\right)}$ is non-convex, the problem (21) is non-convex for p_{tr}.

3.3   Algorithm

In this subsection, we provide an energy consumption oriented offloading algorithm, as shown in Algorithm 1. We know that the optimization problem in (21) is non-convex due to the fractional form of the objective function. We note that there is no standard approach for solving non-convex optimization problems. In order to solve the optimization problem above, we introduce a transformation to handle the objective function via nonlinear fractional programming [6].

Algorithm 1. Optimal energy consumption algorithm design

Input: D, h^2, N_0

Output: Optimal energy consumption and transmission power of mobile device p_{tr}

1: Initialize the maximum number of iteration I_{max} and the maximum tolerance Δ;

2: Set minimize energy efficiency $q = 0$ and iteration index $n = 0$;

3: **Repeat** Main Loop

4: Solve the loop problem in $\dfrac{Dp_{tr}}{\log\left(1 + \frac{p_{tr}h^2}{N_0}\right)} = q$ for a given p_{tr} and obtain the energy
   efficiency q^*;

5: $p_{tr} = p_{min}, q = 0$;

6: **if** $Dp_{tr} - q\log\left(1 + \frac{p_{tr}h^2}{N_0}\right) < \Delta$ **then**

7: Convergence=**true**;

8: **Return** $p_{tr}^* = p_{tr}$ and $q^* = \dfrac{Dp_{tr}}{\log\left(1 + \frac{p_{tr}h^2}{N_0}\right)}$.

9: **Else**

10: Set $q = \dfrac{Dp_{tr}}{\log\left(1 + \frac{p_{tr}h^2}{N_0}\right)}$ and $n = n + 1$;

11: Convergence=**false**;

12: **Until** convergence=**true** or $n = I_{max}$

13: **End**

Without loss of generality, we define the minimum energy consumption q^* of the considered system as

$$q^* = \frac{Dp_{tr}^*}{\log\left(1 + \frac{p_{tr}^*h^2}{N_0}\right)} = \min_{p_{tr}} \frac{Dp_{tr}}{\log\left(1 + \frac{p_{tr}h^2}{N_0}\right)} \tag{22}$$

We are now ready to introduce the following Theorem 1 in [6].

Theorem 1: The maximum weighted energy efficiency q^* is achieved if and only if

$$\min_{p_{tr}} Dp_{tr} - q^*\log\left(1 + \frac{p_{tr}h^2}{N_0}\right) = Dp_{tr}^* - q^*\log\left(1 + \frac{p_{tr}^*h^2}{N_0}\right) = 0 \tag{23}$$

for $Dp_{tr} \geq 0$ and $\log\left(1 + \frac{p_{tr}h^2}{N_0}\right) \geq 0$.

The proposed algorithm is summarized in Algorithm 1. Its convergence to the optimal energy consumption is guaranteed if we are able to solve the inner problem (23) in each iteration.

4   Numerical Analysis

In this section, we evaluate the performance for the proposed energy consumption oriented offloading algorithm. We have used Matlab in the simulation. Throughout the simulations, some assumptions are made unless stated otherwise. For simplicity, the system is made up of a fog server, a cloud server and a mobile device. Assume that the mobile device has a delay sensitive application to be executed remotely. The basic parameters throughout the simulations unless otherwise specified, are as follows. The power of the wireless channel noise is $N_0 = 10^{-7}$ watt. We assume that the channel is ideal and the fading coefficient is $h^2 = 1$. The idle power and maximum transmission power of the mobile device are $p_i = 0.3$ W and $p_{max} = 1.5$ W [7], respectively. The delay tolerance of mobile device is considered as $T = 1$ s. The bandwidth is assumed to be $B = 500$ MHz. The size of the exchange data is $D = 20$. The capacity of the fog server is $F = 200$. C denotes the capacity of the cloud server. The ratio between the capacity of the cloud server and the fog server is S.

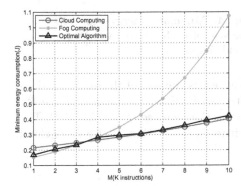

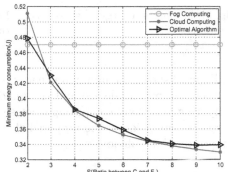

Fig. 1. Minimum energy cost versus instruction

Fig. 2. Minimum energy consumption versus capacity coefficient with fog and cloud computing

Figure 1 shows the impact of the number of instructions on the energy consumption of the cloud computing and the fog computing. From the figure, we can see that the minimum energy consumption of the fog computing raises faster than the other two methods with the increase of the size of instructions. Basically, the proposed algorithm can achieves the minimum energy consumption with the consideration of the execution time. When the size of instructions is smaller than 3.5, proposed algorithm choose fog computing and vice versa. The overall energy consumption is less than that of adopting fog computing or cloud computing alone.

Figure 2 depicts the minimum energy cost versus the coefficient between the capability of the cloud and fog computing. With the increase of S, the capacity of the fog computing remains unchanged. Nevertheless, the capacity of the cloud computing is increasing linearly. This leads to a reduction in the execution time of the cloud computing which can significantly reduce the energy consumption of mobile device.

Figure 3 shows the minimum energy consumption by the proposed algorithm. The figure shows that the algorithm converges in ten times iterations which demonstrates that the proposed algorithm can obtain the minimum energy consumption in a finite number of iterations.

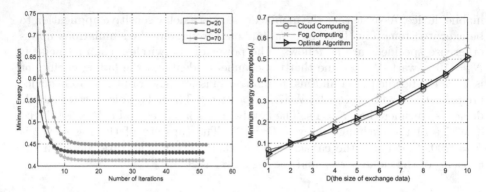

Fig. 3. Minimum energy cost versus iterations

Fig. 4. Minimum energy cost versus the size of exchange data for fog and cloud computing

Figure 4 shows the minimum energy cost versus the size of the exchange data between the mobile device and the remote server. Both the energy of the fog computing and cloud computing increase with the increase of the size of D. The energy consumption of the proposed algorithm is better than that adopts cloud computing alone obviously.

5   Conclusion

In this paper, we introduce fog computing in a simple three layer architecture to minimize the energy consumption of mobile device. We propose an energy consumption oriented offloading algorithm to minimize the energy consumption. By adjust the transmitting power, the paper minimize the energy consumption of the system. The numerical results show that the proposed algorithm can achieve better performance. For simplicity, we introduces one user system model, but in the future, we will study the multi-user model.

Acknowledgement. This work was supported in part by National Natural Science Foundation of China (61372070), Natural Science Basic Research Plan in Shaanxi Province of China (2015JM6324), Ningbo Natural Science Foundation (2015A610117), National Science and Technology Major Project of the Ministry of Science and Technology of China (2015zx03002006-003), and the 111 Project (B08038).

References

1. Satyanarayanan, M., Bahl, P., Caceres, R., Davies, N.: The case for VM-based cloudlets in mobile computing. In: IEEE Pervasive Computing, vol. 8, no. 4, October 2009
2. Kwon, Y.W., Tilevich, E.: Power-efficient and fault-tolerant distributed mobile execution. In: Proceedings of ICDCS (2012)

3. Hassan, M.A., Bhattarai, K., Chen, S.: vUPS: virtually unifying personal storage for fast and pervasive data accesses. In: Uhler, D., Mehta, K., Wong, J.L. (eds.) MobiCASE 2012. LNICSSITE, vol. 110, pp. 186–204. Springer, Heidelberg (2013). doi:10.1007/978-3-642-36632-1_11

4. Wen, Y., Zhang, W., Luo, H.: Energy-optimal mobile application execution: taming resource-poor mobile devices with cloud clones. In: Proceedings of IEEE INFOCOM, pp. 2716–2720 (2012)

5. Wu, S., Tseng, Y., Lin, C., Sheu, J.: A multi-channel MAC protocol with power control for multi-hop mobile ad hoc networks. Comput. J. **45**(1), 101–110 (2002)

6. Dinkelbach, W.: On nonlinear fractional programming. Manag. Sci. **13**, 492–498 (1967). http://www.jstor.org/stable/2627691

7. Deng, S., Huang, L., Taheri, J., Zomaya, A.Y.: Computation offloading for service workflow in mobile cloud computing. IEEE Trans. Parallel Distrib. Syst. **26**(12), 3317–3329 (2015)

Load-Based Fast Handoff Mechanism
for Macro-femto Heterogeneous Networks

Chih-Cheng Tseng[1(✉)], Fang-Chang Kuo[1],
Hwang-Cheng Wang[1], Kuo-Chang Ting[2],
and Chih-Chieh Wang[3]

[1] National Ilan University, Yilan, Taiwan
{tsengcc,kfc,hcwang}@niu.edu.tw
[2] Minghsin University of Science and Technology, Xinfeng, Taiwan
kcting82@gmail.com
[3] Unication Co., Ltd., Xinzhuang, Taiwan
ryan_wang@uni.com.tw

Abstract. When mobile multimedia applications are considered in a femtocell and macrocell coexisted heterogeneous network, a fast handoff mechanism to select a target femtocell base station (FBS) for macrocell user equipment (MUE) to maintain the QoS turns out to be a major design issue. To address this problem, a fast Stochastic Election Process (SEP) is proposed to assign the initial counter value of each candidate FBS based on the load of the candidate FBS. Simulation results confirm that the proposed load-based handoff mechanism reduces the handoff time greatly.

Keywords: Fast handoff · Auction · Femtocell · Load balance

1 Introduction

In a macro-femto coexisted heterogeneous network, as an macrocell user equipment (MUE) moves from outdoor to indoor, due to the attenuation of the walls, the signal strength is greatly attenuated and, thus, the transmission rate is reduced accordingly. To address this issue, femtocells are developed to improve indoor signal quality. As depicted in Fig. 1(a), a femtocell is composed of a femto base station (FBS) and the UEs connected to this FBS. A FBS is a low-cost small-size base station [1] that is mainly designed to be installed indoor to boost the signal quality and increase the throughput of the mobile communication networks in indoor environment. Besides, in the macro-femto heterogeneous network, when FBSs can be accessed by any nearby MUE, i.e. FBSs are operated in the open subscriber group (OSG) access mode, they provide an important alternative to offload the traffic of macrocell base station (MBS). In the conventional handoff mechanisms, the signal quality, e.g., RSSI (received signal strength indicator), SINR (signal to interference plus noise ratio), or SNR (signal to noise ratio) is the main index used to select a new target base station to handoff. For example, to select a target FBS, the

---

This research was supported in part by the Ministry of Science and Technology of Taiwan under the grant numbers. 104-2221-E-197-007, 104-2221-E-197-009, 104-2221-E-197-016.

© ICST Institute for Computer Sciences, Social Informatics and Telecommunications Engineering 2017
J.-H. Lee and S. Pack (Eds.): QShine 2016, LNICST 199, pp. 302–311, 2017.
DOI: 10.1007/978-3-319-60717-7_30

approaches proposed in [2, 3] are to maintain an optimal neighbor cell list (NCL). With such list, instead of scanning all neighboring FBSs, UE only needs to scan those listed FBSs when handoff is needed and, thus, conserves the limited battery power. The handoff mechanism proposed in [4] consisted of two phases. In the first phase, FBSs that within a predefined range were selected as the handoff candidate FBSs. In the second phase, a handoff candidate FBS with higher SINR was assigned higher probability to be selected as the target FBS for UE to handoff. Obviously, all the previous approaches selected the target FBS mainly based on the signal quality. In other words, load of each FBS was not considered. However, due to the increasing demand of mobile multimedia applications from the UEs, if the selection of target FBS only considers the signal quality, load unbalance may occur among FBSs.

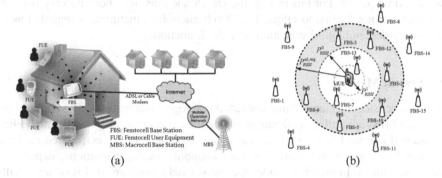

Fig. 1. (a) Illustration of femtocell [5] and (b) applying the MDA of the handoff mechanism. (Color figure online)

To address this problem, we have developed an auction-based handoff mechanism that jointly takes the signal quality and load balance into the selection of target FBS. It has been proved that better load balance among FBS is achieved by the auction-based handoff mechanism. However, in addition to selecting a light loaded FBS with satisfied signal quality, it is also important for the time elapsed in the target FBS selection to be short so that the QoS of the mobile multimedia applications can be maintained. Hence, the objective of this paper is to refine the handoff mechanism [6] to speed up the handoff time.

The rest of this paper is organized as follows. Introduction to the Dutch auction and descriptions of the system model are presented in Sect. 2. Section 3 summarizes the operations of the auction-based handoff mechanism with load balance in [6]. Detail descriptions of the refinements to speed up the handoff time are presented in Sect. 4. The performance results of the proposed refinements are presented in Sect. 5. Section 6 concludes this paper.

2 Preliminaries

2.1 Dutch Auction

Auction [7] is a special way to exchange merchandizes in human society. The Dutch auction [8] is named after the famous auctions of Dutch tulip bulbs in the 17th century.

The farmers pooled their tulips in a central market, while experienced sellers undertook their sale to traders from around the world. Sellers provided the starting price, the step of the auction and the time interval at which the price was to be reduced. The rule was simple: any time, any trader could buy any quantity of tulips in the auction at the prevailing price at that particular time interval. However, if the traders did not purchase, the price is reduced in the next time interval since the flowers would wither as time passed by. But, when some trader purchased, the remaining traders were in danger of being stuck without tulips. Thus, every trader was "waiting" or "competing" for the appropriate price, at the right time interval. In other words, in the Dutch auction, each bid is a winning bid, provided that there are still tulips (goods). When the flowers are sold out, the auction ends. Since participants never know if and when someone else will bid, they are under pressure, leading to prices and values that conform to market reality, in a short time period. For this reason, the Dutch auctions have become very popular. Thus, they are not limited to tulips. The Dutch auction, sometimes, is regarded as an open-outcry descending-price auction or a clock auction.

2.2 System Model

This paper considers a macro-femto coexisted heterogeneous network. We assumed the MUEs and FBSs are uniformly deployed inside the coverage area of an MBS. All FBSs are assumed operated in the OSG access mode. Examples of the considered environment can be found in our daily life, e.g., shopping malls, exhibitions, department stores, and offices. In practical, under the considered environment, FBSs are usually fixed and their location information is also known to the owner of the network. Besides, the location information of MUE can be provided by either the equipped GPS module or indoor positioning techniques. While the handoff probe message sent from the MUE is received by a nearby FBS, it calculates the received RSSI value based on the two equations below

$$RSSI = P - P_{(path\,loss)} \tag{1}$$

$$P_{(path\,loss)} = 127 + 30\log_{10}(d) + X_\sigma, \tag{2}$$

where P is the transmission power of the MUE in dBm, X_σ is the lognormal shadowing with zero mean and variance σ^2 in dB, d is the distance between MUE and FBS in Km and $P_{(path\,loss)}$ is the path loss in dB [9] and, respectively. With (1), the SNR can be calculated by $SNR = RSSI/N$ where N is the thermal noise.

3 Summary of the Auction-Based Handoff Mechanism with Load Balance

In [6], a two-stage auction-based handoff mechanism with load balance for macro-femto heterogeneous networks was proposed. The fundamental ideas of [6] are as follows. To find and identify the handoff candidate FBSs, a modified Dutch auction (MDA) is used in the first stage of the handoff mechanism in [6]. Next, a stochastic election process (SEP) is used in the second stage to select a light-loaded FBS among the candidate FBSs as the target FBS. Following, we summarize the operations of each stage.

3.1 Stage 1: Modified Dutch Auction (MDA)

Whenever a handoff is needed, MUE sends a handoff probe message that contains two parameter values, $P_{RSSI}^{ul,req}$ and P_{RSSI}^0. First, $P_{RSSI}^{ul,req}$ is the minimal required uplink RSSI value required to maintain the uplink QoS of the active mobile multimedia applications in the MUE. In addition, it is also used to define an area called potential handoff area. Then, the parameter P_{RSSI}^0 is used to partition the potential handoff area into two priority zones. In the language of auction, $P_{RSSI}^{ul,req}$ is the upset price and P_{RSSI}^0 is a price to partition all the bidding prices higher than the upset price into two groups. For example, as shown in Fig. 1(b), the entire area inside the dashed black line is the potential handoff area, while the region inside the red dashed line is named the high priority zone and the region between black and red dashed lines is called low priority zone. When receiving the handoff probe message, FBS calculates the uplink RSSI value based on (1) and (2). To maintain the QoS of active mobile multimedia applications, FBSs whose calculated uplink RSSI values less than $P_{RSSI}^{ul,req}$ are screened out. For example, in Fig. 1(b), the seven FBSs outside the potential handoff area (i.e., FBS-1, FBS-4, FBS-8, FBS-9, FBS-11, FBS-14, and FBS-15) are sifted out. In contrast, the rest of eight FBSs in the potential handoff area (i.e., FBS-2, FBS-3, FBS-5, FBS-6, FBS-7, FBS-10, FBS-12, and FBS-13) are called qualified FBSs. In the language of auction, this means that bidders with bidding prices higher than the upset price win the first round of bidding and called qualified bidders.

After calculating the uplink RSSI value, each qualified FBS located within the high priority zone (i.e., FBS-7 and FBS-13 in Fig. 1(b)) replies a handoff probe response message to MUE. In the language of auction, this means qualified bidders that agree to pay higher bidding prices are given higher priority to win the bid. After broadcasting the handoff probe message, if MUE does not receive any handoff probe response message, the same handoff probe message is broadcast again. This time, each qualified FBS that receives the same handoff probe message twice and located within the low priority zone replies a handoff probe response message to the MUE. However, if MUE still receives nothing, MDA is ended. This is called as a handoff failure. However, if more than one qualified FBSs located in the same priority zone, as shown in Fig. 1(b), the handoff probe response messages sent by the qualified FBSs will collide to each other. In this case, MUE cannot identify which qualified FBS has sent the handoff probe response message. To this issue, after a collision is detected, MUE sends an updated handoff probe message in which an updated uplink RSSI value, P_{RSSI}^1, is included to further partition the corresponding priority zone into two priority sub-zones. For example, as shown by the green dashed line in Fig. 1(b), after detecting collision occurred in the high priority zone, P_{RSSI}^1 is used to divide the high priority zone into two sub-zones. In our simulations, the above procedure to resolve the collision is ignored. In the language of auction, this means if some bidders offer similar bidding prices, in order to determine the winner, the auctioneer will separate them into two sub-groups based on their bidding prices.

Whenever MUE successfully receives a handoff probe response message, it calculates the received downlink SNR value. After all qualified FBSs in the selected priority zone have successfully sent back to MUE, those FBSs whose downlink SNR values greater than the required downlink SNR value SNR_{req}^{dl} will be selected by the MUE to maintain the downlink QoS of the active mobile multimedia applications as the candidate FBSs. If there is only one candidate FBS, it is the target FBS and MUE proceeds to handoff to it. However, if more than one candidate FBSs, a new handoff probe message will be sent to notify them to proceed to the second stage of the auction-based handoff mechanism. If no candidate FBS is found, MDA is ended and the handoff is regarded as failure.

3.2 Stage 2: Stochastic Election Process (SEP)

As mentioned in previous sub-section, the second stage of the auction-based handoff mechanism is executed only when more than one candidate FBSs are selected in the MDA. Hence, the objective of SEP is to determine the light-loaded target FBS so that the load among FBSs can be balanced. The operations of SEP are described below.

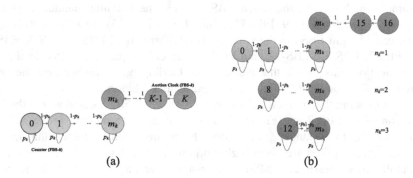

(a)   (b)

Fig. 2. The counter and auction clock of candidate FBS-k in the (a) SEP and (b) fast SEP.

Like the Dutch auction, a down-counted Auction Clock is maintained in each of the candidate FBSs and MUE. Initially, the Auction Clock is set to K. Besides, an up-counted Counter with initial value 0 is maintained in each candidate FBS as shown in Fig. 2(a). In each time unit of SEP, the values of Auction Clocks in candidate FBS-k and MUE are decreased by one with probability 1. However, the Counter value in each candidate FBS is unchanged with probability p_k or increased by one with probability $(1-p_k)$. The probability p_k is given by

$$p_k = \frac{l_k + q}{C_k}, \qquad (3)$$

where l_k is the load of candidate FBS-k before handoff, q is the requested capacity of the MUE, and C_k is the maximal capacity of candidate FBS-k. For simplicity, we assume $C_k = C$ for every candidate FBS-k. Whenever a candidate FBS-k whose values of Auction Clock and Counter matched (e.g., their values are equal to m_k as shown in Fig. 2(a)), it will regard itself as the winner of the auction. Hence, it replies a handoff probe response message to grant the handoff request proposed by the MUE. But, if more than one candidate FBSs satisfy the above condition simultaneously, their handoff probe response messages to MUE will collide. This results in the failure of the first round of SEP. We define the failure of SEP due to the collision as "*collision failure.*" When a collision failure occurs, the value of Auction Clock of MUE and the values of Auction Clocks and Counters of the collided FBSs will be re-initialized and a new round of SEP is started. Before MUE successfully receives a handoff probe response message, the procedures will be repeated again and again. However, since the counter value is increased randomly, it is possible that no match occurs. In this case, MUE receives nothing from the candidate FBSs and the handoff will be regarded as failed when the value of Auction Clock of MUE equals to zero (i.e., $K = 0$). This is defined as "*miss failure.*" According to the calculation of p_k in (3), it can be easily found that a light-loaded candidate FBS-k, i.e. smaller l_k, will have a smaller p_k and, consequently, its counter value will have a higher probability to be advanced by one. In other words, a light-loaded candidate FBS is with higher probability to attain a match and become the first FBS to send the handoff probe response message to MUE. Thus, better load balance among FBSs can be obtained with the MDA and SEP.

4 Fast SEP

In the original design of SEP, named normal SEP in the following context, the initial value of each Counter is set to zero. With this initial value, the minimum clock time required for Counter and Auction Clock to match in each round of SEP will be $K/2$. In other words, the time before $K/2$ is wasted. Hence, it will be a feasible solution to speed up the handoff time if the SEP can be executed faster. Our improvement to speed up the time required in the SEP is as follows. Instead of assigning initial counter value of each candidate FBS to zero, it is assigned based on the load of candidate FBS. To do this, the maximum possible load among the candidate FBSs in the ith round of SEP, X_i, is divided into W regions. Let $X_1 = C$ Mbps and n_k be the region number where candidate FBS-k is allocated. In this way, if a candidate FBS-k whose load l_k is 0 Mbps $\leq l_k \leq \lceil X_i/W \rceil$ Mbps, $n_k = W$. Similarly, if a candidate FBS-k whose load l_k is $\lceil X_i/W \rceil$ Mbps $< l_k \leq 2 \lceil X_i/W \rceil$ Mbps, $n_k = (W-1)$, so on and so forth. Based on the obtained n_k, the initial counter value of candidate FBS-k is

$$\begin{cases} 0 & , n_k = 1 \\ \sum_{i=2}^{n_k} \frac{K}{2^{(i-1)}} & , n_k > 1. \end{cases} \tag{4}$$

Obviously, candidate FBS with light load will be allocated with a higher value of n_k, and thus, assigned with a higher initial counter value. In such a way, light loaded candidate FBS will achieve a match faster than those heavy loaded ones. In addition, the load balance is still maintained. For example, consider $K = 16$, $W = 3$, and $C = 50$

Mbps. In the first round of fast SEP, $X_1 = 50$ Mbps. As shown in Fig. 2(b), if the considered candidate FBS-k whose load l_k is 0 Mbps $\leq l_k \leq 17$ Mbps, $n_k = 3$ and, based on (4), the initial counter value will be 12. On the contrary, if l_k is 17 Mbps $< l_k \leq 34$ Mbps, $n_k = 2$ and the initial counter value will be 8. Otherwise, if l_k is 34 Mbps $< l_k \leq 50$ Mbps, $n_k = 1$ and the initial counter value will be 0. If collision occurred in the first round of SEP, the value of X_2 in the second round of SEP will be 50 Mbps, 34 Mbps, or 17 Mbps if the initial counter value of the collided candidate FBSs is 0, 8, or 12, respectively. Since collided candidate FBSs are with the same initial counter value, with the above approach to assign X_i $i \geq 2$, we are trying to reallocate those collided candidate FBSs into different sub-regions so that they can be assigned with different initial counter values in the next round of fast SEP. For example, consider two candidate FBSs A and B with loads 20 Mbps and 30 Mbps and same initial counter value 8 collided in the first round of fast SEP. In the second of fast SEP, $X_2 = 34$ Mbps and the initial counter value will be 12 if the load l_k is 0 Mbps $\leq l_k \leq 12$ Mbps, 8 if l_k is 12 Mbps $< l_k \leq 24$ Mbps, and 0 if l_k is 24 Mbps $< l_k \leq 34$ Mbps. Hence, the initial values for candidate FBSs A and B in the second round of fast SEP will be 8 and 0, respectively.

5   Simulation Results

The performance of the proposed load-based fast handoff mechanism for macro-femto heterogeneous networks is evaluated by the MATLAB and all the parameter values used in our simulations are in Table 1. In the simulations, 10, 20, 30, 40, and 50 FBSs are uniformly deployed inside the considered area, respectively. The requested capacity of the MUE, i.e., q, for each corresponding number of FBSs are 0.5, 1, 1.5, 2, and 2.5 Mbps, respectively. The initial load of each FBS is assumed uniformly between 0 and 50 Mbps. Besides, the procedures to resolve the collision as mentioned in Sect. 3 are ignored. To investigate the performances of the proposed fast SEP, the percentages of "successful handoff", "collision failure", and "miss failure" in each round of normal SEP and fast SEP are collected and compared. They are defined as the ratios of the number of candidate FBSs "that successfully send MUE the handoff probe response message", "whose handoff probe response messages are collided", and "whose values of Auction Clock and Counter are mis-matched" to the number of candidate FBSs in that round, respectively.

Table 1. The parameter values used in simulation.

Parameter	Value	Parameter	Value
Network side-length	70 m	Min. req. uplink RSSI value ($P_{RSSI}^{ul,req}$)	−56 dBm
FBS transmit power	23 dBm	P_{RSSI}^0	−47 dBm
MUE transmit power	20 dBm	Downlink threshold (SNR_{req}^{dl})	50 dB
Frequency band	2 GHz	Capacity of candidate FBS (C)	50 Mbps
System bandwidth	10 MHz	Shadowing standard deviation	4 dB
Thermal noise (N)	−104 dBm	Initial auction clock value (K)	16

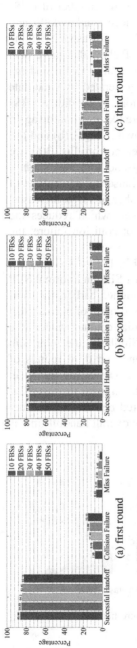

Fig. 3. Percentages of successful handoff, collision failure, and miss failure in the (a) 1st round, (b) 2nd round, and (c) 3rd round of normal SEP.

Fig. 4. CDF of the clock time required for a successful handoff with fast SEP and normal SEP under 30 FBS.

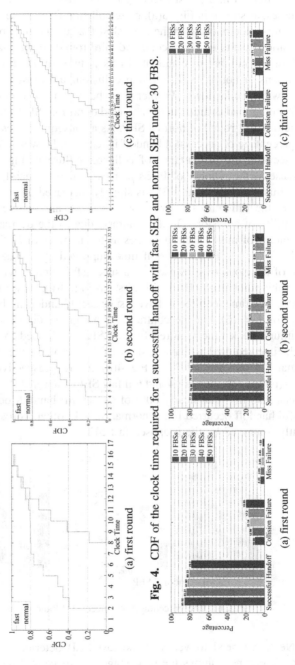

Fig. 5. Percentages of successful handoff, collision failure, and miss failure in the (a) 1st round, (b) 2nd round, and (c) 3rd round of fast SEP.

First, we show the percentages of successful handoff, collision failure, and miss failure for the normal SEP in Fig. 3. Since the percentages of more than two candidate FBSs observed in the first round of normal SEP are increased as the number of FBSs increases, as shown in Fig. 3(a), more collision failures, fewer successful handoffs, and fewer miss failure occur in the normal SEP as the number of FBSs increased. Next, the simulation results for the second and third rounds of normal SEP show that more than 90% of the number of candidate FBSs is two. In addition, according to (3) and the operations of normal SEP, we find collisions are most likely generated by candidate FBSs with similar loads. Furthermore, based on our observations, if candidate FBSs with similar load collided in the ith round of normal SEP, they are likely to collide again in the $(i + 1)^{th}$ round of normal SEP. As a consequence, as shown in Fig. 3(b) and (c), the percentage of successful handoff is reduced. However, different from Fig. 3(a), we can see that the percentages of collision failure in Fig. 3(b) and Fig. 3(c) slightly decrease as the number of FBSs increases. This is mainly because the percentage of more than two candidate FBSs is slightly increased as the number of FBSs increases. Hence, the differences between values of p_x are getting larger, which reduces the possibility of collision. On the contrary, due to the decreases of collision failure, the percentage of miss failure increases as the number of FBSs increases.

Next, we verify the handoff time improved by the fast SEP. Figure 4 shows the CDF of the clock time elapsed for a successful handoff with fast SEP and normal SEP when the number of FBS is 30. First, in Fig. 4(a), as we mentioned earlier, the minimum clock time required to have a successful handoff in the first round of normal SEP is 8 (for $K = 16$). On the contrary, by assigning different initial counter values, the minimum clock time required for fast SEP is reduced to 2. Similarly, the minimum clock time required to have a successful handoff in the second and third rounds of normal SEP are 16 and 24 in Fig. 4(b) and (c), respectively. However, as shown in Fig. 4(b) and (c), they are 4 and 6 if fast SEP is applied. In addition, with the fast SEP, we can also find that nearly 80% of successful handoff occurred before the first successful handoff occurred in the normal SEP. In other words, the overall handoff time is greatly improved by the proposed fast SEP.

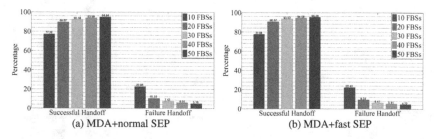

(a) MDA+normal SEP   (b) MDA+fast SEP

Fig. 6. The percentages of successful handoff and failure handoff.

Next, we need to verify if the fast SEP deteriorates the other performance of handoff. Figure 5 shows the percentages of successful handoff, collision failure, and miss failure in the different rounds of fast SEP. Comparing with the results shown in

Fig. 3, we find that fast SEP induces very limited negative effects on the performances of the successful handoff, collision failure, and miss failure. Hence, we conclude that the fast SEP greatly reduces the handoff time with limited side effect on the performances of the normal SEP.

Finally, the overall percentages of successful handoff and failure handoff with respect to normal SEP and fast SEP are shown in Fig. 6. As expected, since fast SEP is mainly focus on speeding up the time to a successful handoff, it only slightly improves the percentages of successful handoff and failure handoff obtained by normal SEP.

6 Conclusions

In the macro-femto heterogeneous networks, if the service from the serving MBS deteriorates, an auction-based handoff mechanism with load balance is needed for MUE to quickly select a light-loaded FBS to perform a handoff so that the load among each FBS can be balanced. To achieve this goal, a modified Dutch auction (MDA) is used to sift out candidate FBSs. After that, a normal stochastic election process (SEP) is employed to decide the target FBS to perform handoff. However, it is found that normal SEP is not quick enough since $K/2$ clock time is wasted in each round of normal SEP. Thus, by assigning light-loaded candidate FBS with higher initial counter value, simulation results confirms that the handoff time is greatly improved by proposed load-based fast handoff mechanism.

References

1. Chandrasekhar, V., Andrews, J., Gatherer, A.: Femtocell networks: a survey. IEEE Commun. Mag. **46**(9), 59–67 (2008)
2. Chowdhury, M.Z., Trung, B.M., Jang, Y.M.: Neighbor cell list optimization for femtocell-to-femtocell handover in dense femtocellular networks. In: 3rd International Conference on Ubiquitous and Future Networks, pp. 241–245. IEEE Press, New York (2011)
3. Becvar, Z., Mach, P., Vondra, M.: Optimization of SINR-based neighbor cell list for networks with small cells. In: 24th IEEE International Symposium on Personal Indoor and Mobile Radio Communications, pp. 2346–2351. IEEE Press, New York (2013)
4. de Lima, C.H.M., Ghaboosi, K., Bennis, M., MacKenzie, A.B.: A stochastic association mechanism for macro-to-femtocell handover. In: 2010 Conference Record of the Forty Fourth Asilomar Conference on Signals, Systems and Computers, pp. 1570–1574. IEEE Press, New York (2010)
5. http://www.smallcellforum.org
6. Tseng, C.C., Wang, C.C., Kuo, F.C., Wang, H.C., Ting, K.C.: A load-balancing handoff mechanism for two-tier femtocell networks: a game approach. In: IEEE Global Communications Conference, pp. 4723–4728. IEEE Press, New York (2013)
7. Krishna, V.: Auction Theory. Academic Press, Cambridge (2010)
8. Easley, D., Kleinberg, J.: Networks, Crowds, and Markets: Reasoning about a Highly Connected World. Cambridge University Press, Cambridge (2010)
9. 3GPP TR 36.814, 3rd Generation Partnership Project; Technical Specification Group Radio Access Network; Evolved Universal Terrestrial Radio Access (E-UTRA); Further advancements for E-UTRA physical layer aspects (Release 9)

Performance Evaluations of Cloud Radio Access Networks

Mu-Han Huang, Yu-Cing Luo, Chen-Nien Mao, Bing-Liang Chen,
Shih-Chun Huang, Jerry Chou, Shun-Ren Yang, Yeh-Ching Chung,
and Cheng-Hsin Hsu[(✉)]

Department of Computer Science, National Tsing Hua University, Hsinchu, Taiwan
chsu@cs.nthu.edu.tw

Abstract. With the skyrocketing amount of data communications, traditional Radio Access Networks (RANs) infrastructure suffers from high capital and operating expenditures. Many countries and mobile network operators, therefore, propose software-defined radio access networks for centralized management, and further apply cloud computing technologies into cellular networks. Cloud Radio Access Network (Cloud-RAN) is a new paradigm for the next generation mobile network which provides ultra-high density deployments, dynamic reconfiguration of computing resources, as well as achieves high energy efficiency. To quantify the performance of Cloud-RAN infrastructure deployment, we build up real Software RAN testbeds based on an opensource LTE implementation over the latest virtualization technologies. We evaluate the performance of different testbed deployments by several test scenarios, in order to show the overhead introduced by virtualization. In addition, our testbed setup and measurement methodology will stimulate more systems research on the emerging Cloud-RAN infrastructure.

Keywords: OpenAirInterface · Virtualization · KVM · Docker · Container · RAN · Software RAN · Cloud RAN · Testbed

1 Introduction

The global mobile data traffic in 2015 was 55 % higher than 2014. Research predicts that the amount will raise 9 times as against 2014 while in 2020, and 80 % of mobile data traffic will be from smartphones by that time [4]. With the rapid developments of Machine-to-Machine (M2M) communications, large amount of data traffics impacts the current Radio Access Networks (RANs). To sustain tens of thousands of devices connected simultaneously, the next generation mobile network should achieve low latency and high throughput. However, the traditional RAN uses dedicated hardware for baseband processing which is lack of flexibility and scalability, and also leads to high Capital Expenditure (CAPEX) and Operation Expenditure (OPEX). Therefore, many countries and cellular network operators started to focus on Software RAN developments.

© ICST Institute for Computer Sciences, Social Informatics and Telecommunications Engineering 2017
J.-H. Lee and S. Pack (Eds.): QShine 2016, LNICST 199, pp. 312–321, 2017.
DOI: 10.1007/978-3-319-60717-7_31

Compared to specialized hardware systems, the programmability, extensibility, and adaptability of commodity hardware turn Software RAN into one of the most promising solutions.

To be energy- and cost-efficient, recent studies propose to deploy Software RANs in cloud platforms [8,12], referred to as Cloud Radio Access Network (Cloud-RAN). In Cloud-RAN, baseband processing is centralized in a virtualized BaseBand Unit (BBU) pool. It allows the heterogeneous traffics to be handled by a share resource pool, and is able to adapt to different types of traffics. Moreover, researchers [19] propose Cloud RAN-as-a-Service concept, a new way to manage mobile networks. It not only improves the network throughput by centralized processing, but also takes advantages of cloud computing to increase the flexibility of resource usages. However, the existing cloud platforms are mostly developed for general purpose computing, and thus some concerns such as the network Quality of Service (QoS) and time-sensitive resource management mechanisms may not be rigorously studied and designed yet.

In this paper, we aim to evaluate the performance of Cloud-RAN in a realistic setup. We build a Software RAN testbed on top of physical machines, as well as in a container-based virtualization platform to discuss the possible overhead introduced by centralization. In our experiments, we use commercial User Equipments (UEs) to send different types of real network traffics. Through the profiling of computing resource usage, and the measurement of end-to-end network performance, we provide comprehensive evaluations over different platforms to discuss the critical issues of Cloud-RAN deployment. The rest of the paper is organized as follows. In Sect. 2, we introduce proposed Software RAN approaches, as well as some prior studies on Cloud-RANs. Section 3 shows our testbed architecture, including physical machines and containers. The performance evaluations over our testbeds are given in Sect. 4. We conclude the paper in Sect. 5.

2   Related Work

Many countries and cellular network operators have proposed Software RANs to provide a centralize-controlled, flexible, and evolvable architecture. As we introduced in our previous work [14], projects such as FluidNet [13,20], a Cloud-RAN prototype with a BBU pool can be adopted in various logical front-haul configurations. With FluidNet's algorithms, the traffic sustainability can be maximized to meet the real-time requirements, while simultaneously optimizing the system resource usage of BBU pool. Gudipati et al. [10] proposed a software-defined RAN with a centralized control plane. However, it only includes the control algorithm to make decisions over handover and interface management, no centralized baseband processing is done in the cloud. OpenRAN [23] is a Software RAN architecture that achieves the virtualization and programmability. With Software-Defined Networking (SDN), it has the capability to dynamically optimize the rules for each virtual access element. As for real-testbed that can be actually deployed, OpenBTS [17] is an open source cellular infrastructure that allows users to deploy their own GSM network. However, it only supports 2G/3G networks. The aforementioned studies do not capitalize the characteristics of the cloud, nor quantify the performance of cloud-RAN over real 5G cellular network testbeds deploy in the cloud.

To move from Software RAN to Cloud-RAN, the balance between performance and expense is the most important issue, as well as to exhibit the characteristics of cloud, such as scalability, elasticity, and reliability. Pompili et al. [18] not only provided a comprehensive survey on Cloud-RAN, addressing its technical challenges and relevant open research issues, but also proposed resource provisioning and allocation strategies of BBU pooling. They also built a real-time testbed to compare the CPU and power consumption of a Cloud-RAN architecture against traditional approach to show the benefits of their solution [11]. To implement Cloud-RAN, the latency and real time issue should be carefully considered. In [15], Navid discussed critical issues on the RAN cloudification. Moreover, he proposed the splitting strategies of BBU and Remote Radio Head (RRH). Form his simulation results, he considered different scenarios, which affect the processing ability of BBU and model individual components of BBU functions. Different from the aforementioned studies, the current paper presents detailed performance evaluations using a real Cloud-RAN testbed.

3   The Considered Cloud RAN

3.1   Cloud System Architecture

Compared to conventional computing, cloud computing [7,9] makes more elastic use of computing resources without paying a premium for infrastructure deployment. It implies a service-oriented architecture that has better flexibility, scalability, and on-demand services. The Infrastructure-as-a-Service (IaaS) provider, such as Amazon's EC2 [1], provides the infrastructures for cloud consumers to build, run, and deploy their own services or platforms. Virtualization is extensively used in this case in order to abstract away and isolate the lower level functionalities. Kernel-based Virtual Machine (KVM) [5] is a widely-used full virtualization solution for Linux distributions. It turns the entire Linux kernel into a hypervisor, and completely simulates the underlying hardware including network card, disk, CPU, RAM, and etc. KVM is able to work with a great variety of guest OSs, and provides high isolation among users. However, full virtualization leads to longer launch time, and a complete network stack that requires extra network acceleration technologies such as hypervisor bypass to ensure high network performance.

The emerging container-based virtualization becomes more and more popular. Instead of running an entire kernel, containers only run as isolated processes in user namespace. That is, containers have considerable performance advantages in many aspects such as low network latency, near-native performance on memory, and almost identical computation speed [21,22]. Docker [2] is an opensource project that automates service deployment in containers. With its own libcontainer to access the virtualization features of Linux kernel, and the adoption of layered file system (AUFS), Docker has become the state-of-the-art approach in lightweight virtualization technologies. Docker provides high-level APIs for users to build, ship, and run applications in containers, as well as image registry for developers. User can simply pull a pre-built image to launch an application in short time, or even pack their own instances as services and push them back to the repository.

3.2 From Soft-RAN to Cloud-RAN

In our previous work [14], we had deployed the OpenAirInterface (OAI) [16], an opensource Software RAN implementation, on commodity PCs and conducted several performance experiments in different virtualization environments. From the previous experiment results, we observed that fine-tuned real-time kernel significantly improves the network and computational latency regardless of virtualization techniques. Both Docker and virtual machines under system loads achieve 13.9 and 3.8 times improvement compared to generic kernel respectively. According to the results, Docker containers outperform virtual machines in both network and computational latencies.

We proposed using real-time kernel and container to virtualize the Software RANs in the cloud. However, to further evolve from Software RAN to Cloud-RAN, we study following research problems in this paper: (1) how to deploy Software RAN in a virtualized environment, and (2) how to identify the performance bottleneck of cloud architectures for Cloud-RAN implementation. Furthermore, we use real mobile traffics to quantify the performance of our 5G cloud in the current paper, while we used general benchmark utilities in our earlier work [14].

4 Performance Evaluations

4.1 Testbed Design

In this paper, we aim to deploy OAI testbed on bare-metal machines and in containers for evaluating Cloud-RAN. Each physical machine comes with an AMD A10-7850K APU at 3.7 GHz with 4 CPU cores and 6 GB RAM. The OAI software is deployed on top of Ubuntu 14.04 with the low latency kernel 3.19. We turned off the power management features and maximize the CPU frequency for better performance and stability. We use National Instrument/Ettus USRP B210 as the RF front end, and Hauwei E3372 LTE dongle with a configurable SIM card as the UE, which connects to the Internet via the OAI software.

In order to focus on Evolved Node B (eNB) performance evaluations, we put Evolved Packet Core (EPC) and Home Subscriber Server (HSS) on the same entity (machine or container) to simplify the deployment. Figure 1(a) shows the bare-metal environment. The eNB and EPC+HSS are connected via Ethernet. eNB sends a connection setup request before attaching the UE to the eNB. After UE completes the RRC connection setup with eNB, the authentication between MME and HSS is accomplished, and the UE is able to access the Internet. On the

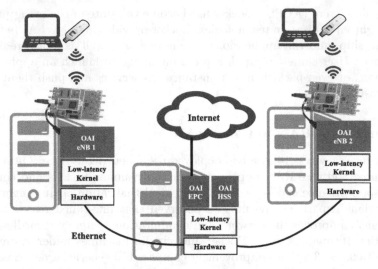

(a) Bare-metal environment.

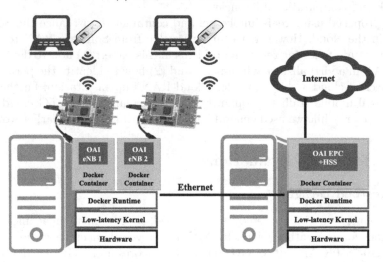

(b) Container environment.

Fig. 1. Architecture of our OAI testbed.

other hand, the container testbed is shown in Fig. 1(b). We use Docker version 1.9.1 to achieve fast deployment of containers for eNB and EPC+HSS. Each container is able to utilize at most a CPU core, and at most 20% of memory by default. We consolidate eNB containers in one machine, while EPC+HSS in the other, connected by a Linux bridge.

4.2 Test Scenarios

To evaluate the performance of our testbed, we generated 4 types of representative mobile traffics: (1) video streaming, (2) online gaming, (3) web browsing (social networking), and (4) file transmission. This is done by recording actual packets generated by each application using libpcap running on a 4G smartphone. Each packet record lasts for several minutes, and we rewind and replay them in our experiments once reaching their ends.

4.3 Evaluation Results

Network Throughput. In bare-metal environment, we measure the required bandwidth over four scenarios with a scale up to 2 eNBs. Figure 2(a) shows the comparison of 1 and 2 eNBs concurrently served by one EPC on a physical machine. Video-streaming requires about 761.726 KB/s throughput for users to have good user experience while watching a 1080p high-definition video. Online-gaming and Web-browsing use relatively low bandwidth at about 13.040 KB/s and 176.123 KB/s respectively. File-transmission is in high demand in throughput, we download a large tar file from the Internet and get an average throughput at about 1183.404 KB/s. With two eNBs, we observe that the available bandwidth is equally shared by the two eNBs.

For the container environment, Fig. 2(b) plots the comparison of 1 and 2 eNBs consolidated on one physical machine. Docker containers have comparable results in video-streaming, online-gaming and Web-browsing. However, it can only provide 553.706 KB/s on average for file-transmission. This can be partially attributed to the bursty nature and large data amount of file transmission, which impose higher consolidation burdens.

System Loading: CPU, Memory. We also profile the CPU and Memory usage to study the resource utilization of Cloud-RAN. When no traffic is incurred, as shown in Fig. 3(a), the idle Software RAN needs about 34.6% of CPU

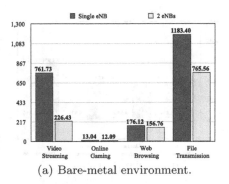

(a) Bare-metal environment.

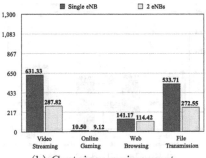

(b) Container environment.

Fig. 2. Network throughput performance in KB/s.

resources and 18.7% of memory. If we use a single EPC to serve 2 eNBs, each eNB requires 37.5% of CPU, but does not consume more memory. Figure 3(b) shows that using containers to deploy RAN service has slightly higher demand on CPU resources at about 35.5% for single eNB deployment, and 40.5% for 2 eNB serving at the same time. In bare-metal environment, likewise, we consider all four scenarios to study how different traffic types affect resource usage of eNB. In Fig. 4, we find that the CPU usage is affected by the used bandwidth. File-transmission scenario makes the highest utilization of CPU resources (50.2%), when other scenarios use about 42.5%. Almost the same observations are made, when we deploy 2 eNBs in our testbed, where the CPU usage is at most 1.3 times higher than that with a single eNB.

Figure 5 shows the performance results of the container environment, similar as the bare-metal environment, high throughput leads to high CPU usage. Video-streaming scenario, with the highest throughput of up to 631.326 KB/s, requires CPU usage of up to 63.1%. While 2 eNBs are deployed, 65.6% of CPU on average is used by each eNB. In summary, deploying Software RAN in container-based virtualization introduces at most 1.4 times of CPU loading compared to bare-metal deployment, and with little memory overhead.

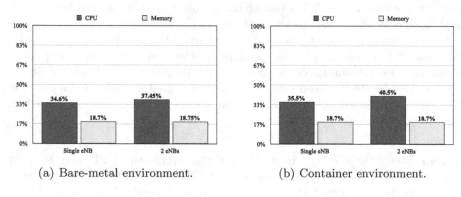

(a) Bare-metal environment.   (b) Container environment.

Fig. 3. System resource usage at the idle time.

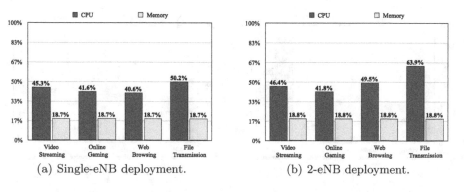

(a) Single-eNB deployment.   (b) 2-eNB deployment.

Fig. 4. System performance in the bare-metal environment.

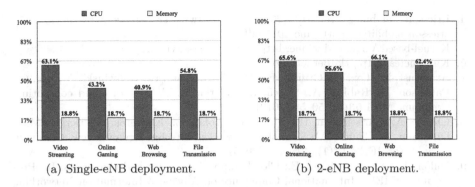

(a) Single-eNB deployment.   (b) 2-eNB deployment.

Fig. 5. System performance in the container environment.

5   Conclusion and Future Work

To move Software RANs into the cloud, lightweight virtualization with high flexibility is indispensable. We deployed each Software RAN component in containers to mitigate the overhead introduced by virtualization. In the evaluation results, deploying Software RAN in the container cloud only increases at most 1.4 times of CPU loading compared to the bare-metal deployment and shows no negative impact on memory usage. Our next step is to launch several eNB services in containers to construct a resource pool of eNB services. We plan to use Kubernetes [6], an opensource cloud orchestration for the management of containerized applications in clustered environments. When network congestion occurs, we can easily deploy more eNB services to reduce the system loads. Moreover, the Replication Controller of Kubernetes can immediately recover from crashed services for higher overall stability. Our eventual goal is to deploy a complete 5G solution on a real-time container cloud platform with flexible deployment, dynamic resource allocation, and complete fault tolerance mechanism, which guarantee the overall performance of 5G networks. We will also leverage several technologies, such as Data Plane Development Kit (DPDK) [3] and SDN, for optimizing the 5G Cloud RAN solution.

Acknowledgment. This study was conducted under the Advanced Communication Technology Research and Laboratory Development project of the Institute for Information Industry, which is subsidized by the Ministry of Economic Affairs of the Republic of China. This work was also partially supported by Ministry of Science and Technology (MOST) of Taiwan under grant number MOST104-3115-E-007-004.

References

1. Amazon EC2. https://aws.amazon.com/ec2/
2. Docker web page. https://www.docker.com/
3. DPDK web page. http://dpdk.org/

4. Ericsson mobility report (2015). http://www.ericsson.com/res/docs/2015/ericsson-mobility-report-june-2015.pdf
5. Kernel-based Virtual Machine. http://www.linux-kvm.org/
6. Kubernetes. http://kubernetes.io
7. Armbrust, M., Fox, A., Griffith, R., Joseph, A., Katz, R., Konwinski, A., Lee, G., Patterson, D., Rabkin, A., Stoica, I., Zaharia, M.: A view of cloud computing. Commun. ACM **53**(4), 50–58 (2010)
8. Checko, A., Christiansen, H.L., Yan, Y., Scolari, L., Kardaras, G., Berger, M.S., Dittmann, L.: Cloud RAN for mobile networks - a technology overview. Commun. Surv. Tutor. IEEE **17**(1), 405–426 (2015)
9. Dillon, T., Wu, C., Chang, E.: Cloud computing: issues and challenges. In: Proceedings of IEEE International Conference on Advanced Information Networking and Applications (AINA), pp. 27–33 (2010)
10. Gudipati, A., Perry, D., Li, L., Katti, S.: SoftRAN: software defined radio access network. In: Proceedings of ACM Workshop on Hot Topics in Software Defined Networking (HotSDN), pp. 25–30 (2013)
11. Hajisami, A., Tran, T.X., Pompili, D.: Dynamic provisioning for high energy efficiency and resource utilization in Cloud RANs. In: Proceedings of IEEE International Conference on Mobile Ad Hoc and Sensor Systems (MASS), pp. 471–472 (2015)
12. Lin, Y., Shao, L., Zhu, Z., Wang, Q., Sabhikhi, R.: Wireless network cloud: architecture and system requirements. IBM J. Res. Dev. **54**(1), 4:1–4:12 (2010)
13. Liu, C., Sundaresan, K., Jiang, M., Rangarajan, S., Chang, G.: The case for reconfigurable backhaul in cloud-RAN based small cell networks. In: Proceedings of IEEE INFOCOM, pp. 1124–1132 (2013)
14. Mao, C., Huang, M., Padhy, S., Wang, S., Chung, W., Chung, Y., Hsu, C.: Minimizing latency of real-time container cloud for software radio access networks. In: Proceedings of IEEE International Workshop of Quality of Service Assurance in the Cloud (QAC), pp. 611–616 (2015)
15. Navid, N.: Processing radio access network functions in the cloud: critical issues and modeling. In: Proceedings of ACM International Workshop on Mobile Cloud Computing and Services (MCS), pp. 36–43 (2015)
16. Nikaein, N., Marina, M., Manickam, S., Dawson, A., Knopp, R., Bonnet, C.: OpenAirInterface: a flexible platform for 5G research. ACM SIGCOMM Comput. Commun. Rev. **44**(5), 33–38 (2014)
17. Pace, P., Loscri, V.: OpenBTS: a step forward in the cognitive direction. In: Proceedings of IEEE International Conference on Computer Communications and Networks (ICCCN), pp. 1–6 (2012)
18. Pompili, D., Hajisami, A., Viswanathan, H.: Dynamic provisioning and allocation in cloud radio access networks (C-RANs). Ad Hoc Netw. **30**, 128–143 (2015)
19. Sabella, D., Rost, P., Sheng, Y., Pateromichelakis, E., Salim, U., Guitton-Ouhamou, P., Girolamo, M.D., Giuliani, G.: RAN as a service: challenges of designing a flexible RAN architecture in a cloud-based heterogeneous mobile network. In: Proceedings of IEEE Future Network and Mobile Summit (FutureNetworkSummit), pp. 1–8 (2013)
20. Sundaresan, K., Arslan, M., Singh, S., Rangarajan, S., Krishnamurthy, S.: FluidNet: a flexible cloud-based radio access network for small cells. In: Proceedings of ACM MobiCom, pp. 99–110 (2013)

21. Wes, F., Alexandre, F., Ram, R., Juan, R.: An updated performance comparison of virtual machines and Linux containers. In: Proceedings of IEEE International Symposium on Performance Analysis of Systems and Software (ISPASS), pp. 171–172 (2015)
22. Xavier, M., Neves, M., Rossi, F., Ferreto, T., Lange, T., Rose, C.: Performance evaluation of container-based virtualization for high performance computing environments. In: Proceedings of International Conference on Parallel, Distributed, and Network-Based Processing (PDP), pp. 233–240 (2013)
23. Yang, M., Li, Y., Jin, D., Su, L., Ma, S., Zeng, L.: OpenRAN: a software-defined ran architecture via virtualization. ACM SIGCOMM Comput. Commun. Rev. **43**(4), 549–550 (2013)

A Throughput Comparison Model for WLAN Technologies, 802.11n and HeNB in LTE and the Future 5G Networks

Kuo-Chang Ting[1], Chih-Cheng Tseng[2], Chia-Pin Wang[3],
Fang-Chang Kuo[4(✉)], and Hwang-Cheng Wang[4]

[1] Department of Business Administration and Department of Information
Engineering, Minghsin University of Science and Technology,
No. 1, Xinxing Rd., Xinfeng Hsinchu 30401, Taiwan
Kcting82@gmail.com
[2] Department of Electrical Engineering, National Ilan University,
No.1, Sec. 1, Shennong Rd., Yilan City 260, Yilan County, Taiwan
tsengcc@niu.edu.tw
[3] Department of Electrical Engineering, National Normal University,
162, Sec. 1, Heping E. Rd., Taipei City 106, Taiwan
chiapin@ntnu.edu.tw
[4] Department of Electronic Engineering, National Ilan University,
No. 1, Sec. 1, Shennong Rd., Yilan City 260, Yilan County, Taiwan
{kfc,hcwang}@niu.edu.tw

Abstract. The fifth generation (5G) wireless communication technologies are expected to attain 1000 times higher mobile data volume per unit area, 10–100 times higher number of connecting devices and user data rate, 10 times longer battery life and five times reduced latency. In order to attain the targets above, Wireless Local Area Network (WLAN) connects to the Internet by the backhaul with ultra-wide bandwidth is the key technology to enlarging the Frequency Reuse Factor (FRF). Home eNodeB (HeNB), known as Femtocell Access Point (FAP) and 802.11n, 802.11ac belonging to WLAN are promising technologies to attain the targets above when the connection is performed indoors. The comparison and analysis between these two technologies based on PHY data rate, MAC layer throughput and power consumption are essential for users to make the right choice for UEs. The contributions of this article mainly fall on establishing throughput estimation for HeNB and 802.11n not much addressed in other works. The model developed in this article can also be used to estimate the performance of HeNB for LTE-Advanced and the 802.11ac and 802.11ad with Single User MIMO (SU-MIMO) technology.

Keywords: HeNB · 802.11n · 802.11ac · 5G · Interference · Throughput · LTE

© ICST Institute for Computer Sciences, Social Informatics and Telecommunications Engineering 2017
J.-H. Lee and S. Pack (Eds.): QShine 2016, LNICST 199, pp. 322–332, 2017.
DOI: 10.1007/978-3-319-60717-7_32

1 Introduction and Related Works

The evolving fourth-generation (4G) wireless technologies, such as long term evolution (LTE) of Universal Mobile Telecommunications System (UMTS) and the future fifth generation networks offer wider bandwidth for high data rates. These high data rates over the access part of the network are achieved through the deployment of higher order modulation, such as 64-quadrature amplitude modulation (QAM), advanced coding techniques, convolutional turbo codes combined with advanced antenna techniques, such as multiple-input multiple-output (MIMO) [1], space-division multiple access (SDMA), and so on. Owing to the limitation of frequency spectrum, frequency reuse might be the most promising technique to increase the total capacity of a cell. For the future 5G networks [2–4], the technology of densely deployed cell plays an important role in the next generation network especially for the WLAN technologies. Moreover, once mobile devices enter a building, the data rate of LTE will drop sharply due to the large path loss, especially if the building is made up of reinforced concrete walls. Indeed the path loss can be up to 15–20 dB [5]. The mobile devices can even lose their connectivity to the Internet due to this large path loss. The energy consumption of UE connecting to the macro cell is also very high due to the long distance between UE and eNB in general. Furthermore, about 80% of connections are performed in indoor environments according to the statistics [6]. This expedites the emergence and development of the new generation of WLAN technology such as 802.11n, 802.11ac wireless LAN (WALN) and HeNB in LTE and LTE-A networks. HeNB is also a technology to solve the problems of limited frequency spectrum and high path loss in indoor environments. The access technology is identical for the HeNB and macro cell (eNB) so that UE can easily perform hand-off between macro cell and HeNB while maintaining continuous connection to the operator network. Modern smart phones usually support both 802.11n (802.11ac) and LTE connections, making the decision on which technology to employ for connecting to the Internet a tough issue. In this paper, we try to construct a model to evaluate the throughput in PHY and MAC layer on the WLAN technologies first. Next we analyze the PHY throughput and spectral efficiency of 802.11n and HeNB in LTE in Sect. 2. An analysis model to evaluate the throughput of 802.11n and HeNB in MAC is addressed in Sect. 3. Discussions and conclusion are given in Sect. 4.

2 The Throughput of 802.11n and HeNB in PHY Layer

2.1 The PHY Data Rate Without Considering the Overheads

The throughput of 802.11n and HeNB in PHY layers can be evaluated by the same model based on OFDM scheme if we ignore their PHY and MAC overheads. If we consider the UE with MIMO capability no matter what category of the UE belongs to, the throughput of the OFDM system in PHY layer can be modeled as

$$PHY(T_{CP}) = N_{SS} \times \frac{N_{BPSC} \times r \times N_{SC}}{(T_{CP} + T_{SYM})} \tag{1}$$

where N_{SS}, N_{BPSC}, r, N_{SC}, T_{CP} and T_{SYM} denote the number of spatial streams, number of bits per subcarrier, coding rate, number of data subcarriers, cyclic prefix (CP) and the symbol time, respectively. In fact, the PHY of HeNB in LTE networks based on Orthogonal Frequency Division Multiplexing Access (OFDMA) instead of OFDM used in 802.11n; thus the total spectrum 20 MHz, i.e. 100 Physical Resource Blocks (PRBs) in HeNB are not necessary assigned to the same user simultaneously. However, in order to evaluate the capacity of HeNB in LTE networks, we assume the all PRBs are assigned to one UE to simply this analysis. Furthermore, the CP for 802.11n can be long or short depending on the Modulation Coding Scheme (MCS) selection. In this article, the short CP, 400 ns on 802.11n and normal CP on HeNB of LTE are considered to evaluate the peak data rate of 802.11n and HeNB in PHY. Note that a slot time of HeNB in LTE networks consists of 7 symbol time; the first symbol is with long CP, 5.2 µs, but the CP of the remaining 6 symbols are as short as 4.7 µs. Hence, the average PHY data rate of HeNB in LTE networks can be obtained by

$$\overline{PHY} = PHY(L_{CP}) + (N_{Slot}^{Symbol} - 1)PHY(S_{CP})/N_{Slot}^{Symbol} \tag{2}$$

where N_{Slot}^{Symbol}, L_{CP} and S_{CP} denote the number of symbols per slot, long cyclic prefix and short cyclic prefix, respectively. The parameters in (1) for 802.11n and HeNB in LTE FDD networks and the throughput in PHY without considering the PHY overheads and their spectral efficiencies are listed in Table 1. Note that the UE of HeNB in LTE networks is only with one antenna generally, so the data rate of uplink is only 93.3 Mbps (373.3/4 Mbps) and its spectral efficiency is also reduced to (18.65/4).

Table 1. The parameters, throughput and spectral efficiency of 802.11n and HeNB in LTE FDD networks.

Parameters	802.11n	HeNB in LTE networks
N_{SS}	4 (4 × 4 MIMO)	4 (4 × 4 MIMO)
N_{BPSC}	6 (64QAM)	6 (64QAM)
R	5/6 (MCS = 31)	948/1024 (CQI = 15)
N_{SC}	114 (40 MHz)	1200 (20 MHz, 100 PRB)
T_{CP}	0.4 µs	5.2 µs for the first symbol and 4.7 µs for the remaining symbols
T_{SYM}	3.2 µs	66.65 µs ((500−5.2−6×4.7)/7)
$\overline{PHY}$	600 Mbps	373.3 Mbps
Spectral efficiency (bits per second per Hz)	15	18.65

2.2 The PHY Data Rate with Overheads

In order to synchronize senders and receivers for SISO or MIMO, the reference signal (RS) overheads in PHY are unavoidable for 802.11n and HeNB in LTE networks. For the

LTE part, the percentage of these overheads is around $(2/3)/14 \approx 4.7\%$ [9] due to the fact that the reference signals for SISO take 2 symbols per sub-frame for every three resource elements. So the peak throughput for SISO is around $93.3 \times (100\% - 4.7\%) \approx 88.8$ Mbps. If 4×4 MIMO is used, the number of spatial streams is 4, but the overheads of RS are higher compared to SISO. The percentage of these overheads is around $(6/3)/14 \approx 14.28\%$ for each spatial stream. Each spatial stream must take 6 symbols per sub-frame for every three resource elements to distinguish from each other. Thus, the maximal throughput is around $373 \times (100 - 14.28)\% = 319.95$ Mbps.

The spectral efficiency of HeNB downlink in LTE networks is reduced to around 16. As to the uplink throughput of HeNB in LTE networks with RS overheads in PHY are located on the middle symbol of a slot time, so the percentage of RS overheads in the uplink is around 1/7 mixed with those in MAC layer; thus we do not consider it in this subsection. The PHY overheads of 802.11n depend on the format of PLCP (Physical Layer Convergence Protocol) Protocol Data Unit (PPDU) format of 802.11n as shown in Fig. 1 [8]. Figure 1 shows that the PHY header overheads of High Throughput (HT) formats such as HT mixed and HT greenfield are higher than those of Non-HT PPDU, but the PPDU format of Non-HT cannot be with MIMO capability. In this article we select the HT mixed format PPDU based on practical considerations due to the fact that this format can be compatible with the legacy 802.11a/b/g. So far, this HT mixed format has been selected as the standard format to make vendors easily to follow in the 802.11ac. The percentage of overheads, O for the HT mixed format PPDU can be obtained by

$$O = \frac{H}{S_{PPDU} \times 8/(R_b) + H} \tag{3}$$

where H, S_{PPDU} and R_b denote the PPDU header and reference signal (RS) for synchronization in seconds, the size of PSDU in bytes and PHY data rate in bits per second respectively and this overhead depends on the size of PPDU as shown in (3). The PLCP Service Data Unit (PSDU) size can be up to 64 K bytes by applying the technique of frame aggregation; thus the overheads can be minimal in this scenario. On the contrary, if the size of PSDU is very small, the overheads will be very huge. The data rate, R_b also impacts this overhead as shown in (3); higher data rate results in larger percentage of overheads. Figure 1 shows that the overheads are around 40, 48, and 64 μs for the SISO, 2×2 MIMO and 4×4MIMO respectively; therefore the percentage of overheads is around 6.8% for 4×4 MIMO when the size of PPDU is as high as 64 KB so the data rate and the spectral efficiency of 802.11n reduce to 559 Mbps and 13.98, respectively. If we combine (1), (2) and (3), the throughput with RS overheads and the overhead percentages of HeNB, 802.11n for 1.5 KB PPDU transmission and 802.11n with 64 KB PPDU transmission are shown in Fig. 2. Figure 2 shows that the percentage of RS overheads of 802.11n with 64 KB PPDU, 6.8% is very low compared to that of HeNB, 14.3% for the 4×4 MIMO. However, if the size of PPDU reduces to 1.5 KB i.e. the size of legacy Ethernet frame, the percentage of RS overheads can be up to 76.2%. The throughput of 802.11n with 1.5 KB PPDU is with no sharp difference among the SISO, 2×2MIMO and 4×4MIMO. The percentage of RS overheads for the 4×4MIMO is always the highest compared to those of SISO and 2×2 MIMO due to the fact that the data rate of 4×4 MIMO is the highest among the three schemes.

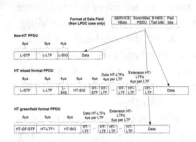

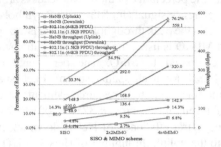

Fig. 1. The PPDU formats proposed in 802.11n

Fig. 2. Percentage of RS overheads and the throughput with RS for the 802.11n and HeNB

3   The Throughput of 802.11n and HeNB in PHY Layer

3.1   The Throughput of HeNB in LTE Networks in MAC

In terms of compatibility with LTE, there is no difference in the communications of a UE with a HeNB or an eNB except the power consumption and the number of UEs served. In general, the number of UEs served is smaller than 10 for a typical HeNB in a 4G LTE network. Hence, the evaluation of the throughput for a UE connected to a HeNB should be similar to that for a UE connected to an eNB. The multiple access technique used in LTE networks is based on OFDMA for downlink transmission which is somewhat different from the OFDM used in 802.11n. OFDMA allows many UEs to access the channel simultaneously using FDMA as in 3GPP LTE FDD networks. The user data rate in the downlink is carried in the physical downlink shared channel (PDSCH). The 1 ms resource allocation interval for downlink is the same as that for uplink. Resource is allocated in units of 12 sub-carriers called a physical resource block (PRB). The eNB carries out resource allocation based on the channel quality indicator (CQI) reported from UEs. Similarly to the uplink, resources are allocated in both time domain and frequency domain. The PDCCH is used to inform a device of the resource blocks allocated for it. The data in physical downlink shared channel (PDSCH) occupies from 3 to 6 symbols in each 0.5 ms slot depending on the allocation for PDCCH and whether a normal or extended cyclic prefix is used. The cyclic prefix used in LTE is the same as the guard interval used in 802.11n to avoid Inter-symbol interference (ISI). Within a 1 ms sub-frame, only the first slot contains PDCCH while the second slot is purely for data (PDSCH). For an extended cyclic prefix, 6 symbols are accommodated in a 0.5 ms slot, while for a normal CP 7 symbols can be fitted. Normal CP is selected for the channel in the HeNB due to the short distance between UE and HeNB. The uplink throughput of a UE of category 5 is much lower than that of the downlink. The uplink overheads, as reflected in PUCCH, include CQI, RS, ACK/NAK, scheduling request and other control information. Thus the peak data rate of the uplink is approximately one-fourth of downlink capacity because there is only one antenna for UE in general. The downlink overheads, as reflected in PDCCH, include traffic indication, grants on resource assignment, ACK/NAK and other control information. The evaluation of MAC throughput in HeNB is much harder compared to 802.11n because its exact data rate is dependent on the implementation of resource control. We model the downlink and uplink throughput of LTE in MAC by

$$MAC_D = PHY_D \times (1 - \frac{N_{PDCCH} + N_o}{N_{Total}}) = PHY_D \times (1 - \frac{N_{PDCCH} + N_O}{N_{RB}N_{Symbol}^{Sub}N_{RB}^{Symbol}}) \qquad (4)$$

and

$$MAC_U = PHY_U \times (1 - \frac{N_{PUCCH}}{N_{total}}) = PHY_U \times (1 - \frac{N_{PUCCH}}{N_{RB}N_{Symbol}^{Sub}N_{RB}^{Symbol}}) \qquad (5)$$

where PHY_D and PHY_U denote the data rate of HeNB in LTE networks in downlink and uplink with PHY overheads, respectively. Note that N_{Total}, N_{PDCCH} and N_{PUCCH} denote the number of total resource elements and the number of resource elements used to transfer control information for the PDCCH and PUCCH, respectively. The number of total resource elements N_{total} can be derived by the multiplication of number of resource blocks N_{RB}, number of subcarriers per symbol N_{Symbol}^{Sub} and the number of symbols per RB, N_{RB}^{Symbol}. Here, N_O in (4) includes the elements used to send the information carried by Physical Broadcast Channel (PBCH), Physical Control Format Indicator Channel (PCFICH) and one group of Physical Hybrid Automatic Repeat Request Indicator Channel (PHICH). These overheads are located on the outmost RB of the allocated bandwidth for this UE; hence the overhead depends on the bandwidth ranging from below 1% at 20 MHz to approximately 9% at 1.4 MHz [7]; the precise estimation is also dependent on how often the control signal is transmitted. In this capacity estimation this overhead is set to around 1%, where $N_{PUCCH} = 2 \times 1/2 \times N_{Symbol}^{Sub}N_{RB}^{Symbol}$ and $N_{RB} = 100$. If the number of UEs using the same frame time increases, the number of allocated RBs decreases resulting in larger overheads. Note that the overheads wasted in the retransmissions of MAC HARQ and RLC ARQ are ignored in (4) and (5). If we take the error ratio into consideration, the MAC throughput of downlink and uplink can be obtained by

$$MAC_D^e = PHY_D \times (1 - \frac{N_{PDCCH} + N_o}{N_{RB}N_{Symbol}^{Sub}N_{RB}^{Symbol}})(1/\sum_{i=1}^{M_e}(i) \times e^{i-1}(1-e)$$
$$= PHY_D \times (1 - \frac{N_{PDCCH}}{N_{RB}N_{Symbol}^{Sub}N_{RB}^{Symbol}})(\frac{1-e}{1-(M+1-Me)e^M}) \qquad (6)$$

and

$$MAC_U^e = PHY_U \times (1 - \frac{N_{PUCCH}}{N_{RB}N_{Symbol}^{Sub}N_{RB}^{Symbol}})(1/\sum_{i=1}^{M_e}(i) \times e^{i-1}(1-e)$$
$$= PHY_U \times (1 - \frac{N_{PUCCH}}{N_{RB}N_{Symbol}^{Sub}N_{RB}^{Symbol}})(\frac{1-e}{1-(M+1-Me)e^M}), \qquad (7)$$

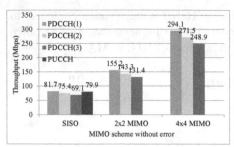
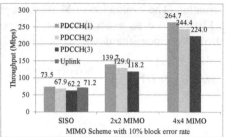

Fig. 3. The downlink throughput of HeNB in MAC with a perfect channel

Fig. 4. The downlink throughput of HeNB in MAC with 10% block error rate

respectively. Here M_e denotes the maximal retransmission times. In fact, the error rate e in (6) and (7) is closely related with the received *SNR* of a receiver and the overheads of ACK/NAK are the function of this error rate. This relation will be discussed in the latter section. If we set the error rate to 10%, the MAC throughputs of HeNB in the downlink without error and with errors are shown in Figs. 3 and 4, respectively. Note that the overheads of PUCCH are fixed to one symbol time per slot time if RS overheads are considered. Moreover, the throughput evaluation is based on the throughput in PHY given by (2). The gap between PHY and MAC in peak throughput is around 50 Mbps for 4×4 MIMO in HeNB.

On the contrary, the gap of throughput between PHY and MAC in 802.11n can be as large as 295 Mbps as shown in Fig. 2. It accounts for the fact that the distributed and easy approaches deployed in the MAC of 802.11 pays for the penalty of huge performance loss.

3.2 The Throughput of 802.1n in MAC

To evaluate the MAC throughput of 802.11n, the MAC layer protocol of 802.11, the Distributed Coordination Function (DCF) is introduced in [11]. Then the behavior of the MAC layer of 802.11 can be accurately analyzed using the Bianchi model [11]. After all, the MAC throughput of 802.11n, S can be obtained by

$$S = \frac{P_s P_{tr}[P]}{(1 - P_{tr})\sigma + P_{tr}P_s T_s + P_{tr}(1 - P_s)T_c} \tag{8}$$

where T_S is the average time of the channel being sensed busy because of a successful transmission, and T_C is the average time of the channel being sensed busy by each station during a collision. σ, δ, P_S and P_{tr} denote the overhead for each frame transmission in PHY, the duration of an empty slot time, successful possibility to transmit a PPDU and the possibility to transmit a PPDU, respectively. Hence, the performance of new MAC layer features in 802.11n, such as block acknowledgment (BA) and Aggregate MAC Protocol Data Unit (A-MPDU), designed to reduce MAC overhead in legacy DCF of 802.11 are applied; thus if we aggregate many MPDUs into one PLCP service data unit (PSDU) which threshold size can be as large as 65535 bytes, instead of the 4096-byte limit in traditional 802.11, the MAC throughput can increase tremendously if BA is applied to acknowledge the transmissions of all the MPDUs in this large PLCP Protocol Data Unit (PPDU). Here, the channel is assumed to be perfect. If the error rate is considered, the throughput of 802.11n can be obtained by

$$S = \frac{P_S(1-e)P_{tr}E[P]}{(1-P_{tr})\sigma + P_{tr}P_S(1-e)T_S + P_{tr}(1-P_S)T_C + (P_sT_C\sum_{i=1}^{M_C}ie^i)} \tag{9}$$

where e and M_c denote the error rate and the maximal transmission times for one frame transmission, respectively. If the evaluation parameters given in NCS 31 of 802.11n and HT Mixed format are employed, the throughput in MAC layer and the variables listed in (9) can be obtained as in Table 2 and Fig. 5 by varying the number of spatial streams (1, 2 and 4) when the number of active stations ranges from 1 to 10 and the mixed PPDU format of 802.11n is used.

When the number of active stations is greater than 1, the collision cost will increase so the throughput should decrease. However, when the number of stations reaches 4, the idle probability for one slot time $(1-P_{tr})$ in (9), 0.704 will decrease tremendously compared to that, 0.882 of only one station; thus the peak capacity occurs when the number of stations is 4 instead of 1. If we combine the results of Figs. 4 and 5, the comparison between 802.11n and HeNB about the peak throughput is illustrated in Fig. 6. Figure 6 shows that the throughput of HeNB can linearly increase with the increasing number of spatial streams roughly, but the throughput of 802.11n cannot increase linearly.

Table 2. The MAC performance of 802.11n (MCS = 31) with error rate = 10%

M	S	P_{tr}	P_S	Throughput (Mbps)
PHY data rate = 150 Mbps				
1	66.1%	0.118	100.0%	99.1
2	62.7%	0.198	94.5%	94.0
3	59.0%	0.255	90.4%	88.5
4	67.9%	0.296	87.3%	101.9
5	66.6%	0.327	84.8%	99.9
6	65.5%	0.352	82.8%	98.2
7	64.5%	0.372	81.2%	96.7
8	63.5%	0.389	79.8%	95.3
9	62.9%	0.404	78.6%	94.3
10	62.2%	0.417	77.5%	93.3
PHY data rate = 300 Mbps				
1	52.2%	0.118	100.0%	156.6

(continued)

Table 2. (*continued*)

M	S	P_{tr}	P_S	Throughput (*Mbps*)
2	49.4%	0.198	94.5%	148.3
3	46.1%	0.255	90.4%	138.2
4	59.3%	0.296	87.3%	177.9
5	58.4%	0.327	84.8%	175.2
6	57.6%	0.352	82.8%	172.7
7	56.8%	0.372	81.2%	170.5
8	56.0%	0.389	79.8%	168.1
9	55.6%	0.404	78.6%	166.8
10	55.1%	0.417	77.5%	165.2
PHY data rate = 600 Mbps				
1	37%	0.118	100.0%	205.7
2	35%	0.198	94.5%	192.9
3	32%	0.255	90.4%	177.2
4	48%	0.296	87.3%	263.7
5	47%	0.327	84.8%	261.5
6	47%	0.352	82.8%	259.2
7	46%	0.372	81.2%	256.9
8	46%	0.389	79.8%	253.5
9	45%	0.404	78.6%	252.8
10	45%	0.417	77.5%	251.0

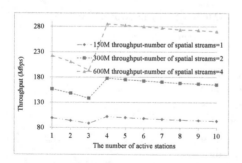

Fig. 5. The MAC throughput of 802.11n with various numbers of active stations and spatial streams with PPDU error rate = 10%

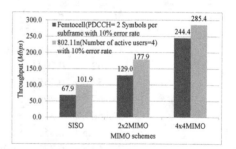

Fig. 6. The comparison between the peak throughput of 802.11n and HeNB in MAC

Table 3. Performance comparison between 802.11n and HeNB in LTE

Item		802.11n	HeNB in LTE networks
Peak data rate in PHY (No PHY overheads)		600 Mbps	373 Mbps
Percentage of PHY overheads	SISO	33.3% (1.5 KB PSDU), 1.1% (64 KB PSDU)	4.8%
	2 × 2MIMO	54.5.3% (1.5 KB PSDU), 2.7% (64 KB PSDU)	9.5%
	4 × 4MIMO	76.2% (1.5 KB PSDU), 6.8% (64 KB PSDU)	14.3%
Licensed/Unlicensed band		Unlicensed	Licensed
Available bandwidth		40 MHz/channel (HT) 20 MHz/channel (non-HT)	20 MHz (100 RBs)
Maximal spectral efficiency		15 bps/Hz	16 bps/Hz
Peak uplink throughput in MAC in a perfect channel without error		228 Mbps	75.6 Mbps
Peak downlink throughput in MAC in a perfect channel without error		270 Mbps (when the number of active UEs is 4)	220 Mbps to 269.5 Mbps
Cost		Low (small Fast Fourier Transform size)	High (large Fast Fourier Transform size)
Distributed or centralized		Distributed	Centralized
Coding scheme		LDPC & convolutional code	Turbo code & convolutional code

4 Discussion and Conclusion

In this article, based on the WLAN technologies, 802.11n and HeNB have been extensively studied. Based on the results in the previous sections, it seems that HeNB will prevail over 802.11n with the advantage in high spectral efficiency in PHY layer. The data rate of HeNB is close to that of 802.11n in MAC despite the fact that the power consumption of 802.11n is much higher than that of HeNB. In fact, in order to attain the 600 Mbps in PHY, the bandwidth of 802.11n can be as high as 40 MHz about twice that of HeNB in LTE network. If the power budget is limited, higher bandwidth leads to lower power spectral density, resulting in lower *SNR*. Furthermore, if the spectrum of 80211n is assumed to be 5.0 GHz, which is higher than the 2.0 GHz used by HeNB defined in [1] will suffer more severe path loss. In practice, the frequency bands allocated for LTE are diverse in many countries. Hence, spectrum selection is also a critical factor in the performance of HeNB. Moreover, the access mode of HeNB can be close, open or hybrid mode. If there is no nearby interference from other HeNB networks, the HeNB can be set to be close mode. Under the circumstance the HeNB can use the entire spectrum as assumed in the previous sections. If the HeNB is in open access mode, the available bandwidth for this HeNB network will be limited to the spectrum owned by the operator which the UE registered. Hence the available bandwidth may be only 10 MHz or 5 MHz instead of 20 MHz. The data rate of UE in HeNB networks is proportional to the number of resource blocks; fewer allocated resource blocks result in lower data rate in PHY and MAC. For 802.11n, many channels can be assigned to nearby BSSs; thus the interference from other BSSs is not serious if channel number is carefully assigned and employed not to be over-lapped. However, the hidden terminal problem should be more serious for 802.11n than for HeNB due to its distributed characteristic. We make a brief comparison between 802.11n and HeNB in Table 3. Our model can also be applied to the comparison of 802.11ac with the LTE-A and future 5G networks if SU-MIMO is considered only. In the future works, the closely cooperative work between the two technologies should be thoroughly studied to attain the targets set by the future 5G networks.

References

1. Molisch, A.: A generic model for MIMO wireless propagation channels in macro and microcells. IEEE Trans. Sig. Process. **52**(1), 61–71 (2004)
2. Ericsson: 5G Radio Access, Research and Vision. White paper (2013)
3. Metis: Scenarios, Requirements and KPIs for 5G Mobile and Wireless System. ICT-317669 METIS project, May 2013
4. Lähetkangas, E., et al.: Achieving low latency and energy consumption by 5G TDD mode optimization. In: 2014 IEEE International Conference on Communications Workshops (ICC). IEEE (2014)
5. Rappaport, T.S.: Wireless Communications: Principles and Practice. Prentice Hall, Upper Saddle River (2002)
6. Chandrasekhar, V., Andrews, J.G., Muharemovic, T., Shen, Z., Gatherer, A.: Power control in two-tier femtocell networks. IEEE Trans. Wirel. Commun. **8**(8), 4316–4328 (2009)
7. Holma, H., Toskala, A.: LTE for UMTS - OFDMA and SC-FDMA Based Radio Access. Wiley, Hoboken (2009)
8. IEEE P802.11n/D3.0: Draft Amendment to Standard: Wireless LAN Medium Access Control (MAC) and Physical Layer (PHY) Specifications: Enhancements for Higher Throughput (2007)
9. Sesia, S., Toufik, I., Baker, M.: LTE – The UMTS Long Term Evolution from Theory to Practice. Wiley, Hoboken (2009)
10. GPP TR 25.951: Technical Specification Group Radio Access Network; FDD Base Station Classification (Release 2000), V0.0.1 (2000-09)
11. Bianchi, G.: Performance analysis of the IEEE 802.11 distributed coordination function. IEEE J. Sel. Areas Commun. **18**(3), 535–547 (2000)

ENUM-Based Number Portability for 4G/5G Mobile Communications

Whai-En Chen$^{(\boxtimes)}$ and Yi-Lun Ciou

Yilan, Taiwan
wechen@niu.edu.tw

Abstract. With the evolution of the core network, providing multimedia services is much easier in the all-IP *packet-switched* networks than that in the *circuit-switched* networks. In the 4G/5G core network, the *IP Multimedia Subsystem* (IMS) is widely deployed to provide multimedia services such as *Voice over LTE* (VoLTE). To provide a fair-competition environment for the mobile operators, the *Number Portability* (NP) service should be defined in the 4G/5G specifications. However, the up-to-date specifications only indicate that the *E.164 NUmber Mapping* (ENUM) can be used for the NP service but do not propose the detail message flows and the major parameters. Moreover, the NP scenarios in the IMS networks are different from those in the *Public Switched Telephone Networks* (PSTNs). To provide the NP service in 4G/5G, this paper proposes an ENUM-based NP service where the message flows and the major parameters are designed based on the IMS architecture.

Keywords: DNS · ENUM · IMS · Number portability · SIP · URI

1 Introduction

The *Number Portability* (NP) service enables cellular subscribers to keep their original *Mobile Station International Subscriber Directory Number* (MSISDN) while changing the mobile operators. The NP service benefits both the subscribers and the mobile operators. The NP service enables the subscribers to have more choices and to select the operators with lower price [1]. In addition, the NP service provides the fair competitions to the mobile operators [2]. Typically, the NP service is implemented according to various local regulations and a country's dialing plan [3]. The NP scenarios produce different costs to the subscribers and the mobile operators. The design and deployment of the NP service requires careful consideration and analysis. However, there is no clearly defined solution providing the NP service in the mobile communications standards [4–6].

With the evolution of the core network, the circuit-switched networks are replaced by the packet-switched networks, and the core network is migrated to an all-IP environment. Providing multimedia services are easier in the packet-switched network than that in the circuit-switched network. In 4G/5G all-IP networks, the *IP Multimedia Subsystem* (IMS) architecture is adopted to provide the multimedia services such as *Voice over LTE* (VoLTE). In order to achieve fair competitions among the mobile operators, 4G/5G specifications should define the NP service based on the IMS

© ICST Institute for Computer Sciences, Social Informatics and Telecommunications Engineering 2017
J.-H. Lee and S. Pack (Eds.): QShine 2016, LNICST 199, pp. 333–343, 2017.
DOI: 10.1007/978-3-319-60717-7_33

architecture. With the NP service, the VoLTE subscribers can retain their original MSISDN while changing their mobile operators. However, 3GPP TS 23.228 [6] only points out that the *E.164 NUmber Mapping* (ENUM) can be used as the NP database but does not specify the detail information such as the IMS and ENUM message flows for the NP service.

ENUM is a system for telephone number mapping, which maps the MSISDN with the Internet identifications (e.g., the Uniform Resource Identifiers; URIs) [7]. The ENUM utilizes the *Domain Name System* (DNS) [8] to store the mapping records and resolves the MSISDN into the URIs [9, 10]. Specifically, the IMS (e.g., S-CSCF) issues the ENUM queries with the MSISDN information to retrieve the URI from the ENUM database.

In 3GPP specifications, the IMS adopts *Session Initiation Protocol* (SIP) [11] as the signaling protocol. The SIP messages contain the *Uniform Resource Identifier* (URI) to identify the MSISDN of the called party [6, 12]. IETF RFC 4769 [13] proposes the type "pstn" and subtype "tel" to identify the tel URI for ENUM. In the tel URI, the *NP Database Dip Indicator* (npdi) tag and *Routing Number* (rn) tag are also proposed in [14, 15] for the NP service. The "npdi" tag indicates that an NP query has already been performed for retrieving the tel URI. The SIP/IMS servers do not require performing the NP query again when the tel URI contains an "npdi" tag. The "rn" tag carries the routing number information. If the queried MSISDN is ported to another mobile operator, the "npdi" and "rn" tags are added to the tel URI where the "rn" tag indicates the route to the new mobile operator.

The previous articles [16, 17] presents the NP scenarios for 2G/3G mobile communications. A *Signaling Relay Function* (SRF)-based solution and an *Intelligent Network* (IN)-based solution are proposed to support the NP service. Both solutions utilize the *Number Portability DataBase* (NPDB) to store the records of the ported MSISDN. However, these articles do not include the *redirect* function which is one of the major functions in SIP/IMS. The article [5] applies the NP scenarios designed for the circuit-switched networks [18] to the packet-switched networks (e.g., IMS) and also provides the SIP redirect function. However, this article does not describe the major parameters used in the message flow and does not include the ENUM.

To provide the ENUM-based NP service based on the IMS architecture for 4G/5G, we design four NP scenarios, including the redirect function and ENUM query according to 3GPP TS 23.228 [6]. In this paper, the architecture and message flows with the major parameters are elaborated and the ENUM/DNS usage is identified. Finally, we show the analysis results of the NP scenarios in both quality and quantity.

The rest of this paper is organized as follows. Section 2 illustrates the NP architecture based on the IMS. Section 3 elaborates the proposed NP scenarios and the message flow for each scenario. Section 4 analyzes and compares different NP scenarios. Finally, the conclusions are given in Sect. 5.

2 ENUM-Based NP Service in the IMS Architecture

In this section, we present the ENUM-based NP service in the IMS architecture. Figure 1 illustrates the proposed architecture where UE1 [Fig. 1(a)] is the calling party and UE2 [Fig. 1(b)] is the called party. The MSISDNs of UE1 and UE2 are **990001** and **980002**, respectively.

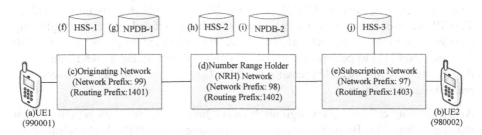

Fig. 1. The IMS architecture for ENUM-based number portability

The originating network [Fig. 1(c)] is the network where the calling party (i.e., UE1) is subscribed and located. In this paper, the *network prefix* of the originating network is **99**, which means the number range of the originating network is **990000–999999**. The *routing prefix* of the originating network is **1401**. The *Number Range Holder* (NRH) network [Fig. 1(d)] is the network that the ported number (e.g., UE2's MSISDN **980002**) has been allocated. The network prefix of the NRH network is **98**, the number range is **980000–989999** and routing prefix is **1402**. The subscription network [Fig. 1(e)] is a network which the called party (i.e., UE2) is ported to. The network prefix of the subscription network is **97**, and the routing prefix of the subscription network is **1403**. Assume that the called party (UE2) has a new contract with the mobile operator of the subscription network. Each network contains a *Home Subscriber Server* (HSS) and a NPDB. The HSS, which is the major database, contains the subscription-related data, performs authentication and authorization of the subscriber, and maintains the subscriber's location. The NPDB provides the routing information (i.e., the routing number or routing prefix) of the ported number. In this architecture, the HSS-x and NPDB-x represent that the HSS and NPDB in different networks, where x = **1**, **2** and **3** means that these components are in the originating network, the NRH network and the subscription network, respectively.

We use an example to demonstrate the ENUM query. Assume that UE1 sends an **INVITE** message to UE2. The *Request-URI* (i.e., a tel URI) in this **INVITE** message is "**tel:980002**". When the IMS receives the **INVITE** message, it retrieves the MSISDN 980002 from the *Request-URI* and change the MSISDN to the E.164 format (i.e., **+886980002**). Then the IMS translates the E.164 number to an FQDN **2.0.0.0.8.9.6.8.8.e164.arpa** and utilizes the FQDN to perform the ENUM query. Since UE2 is ported to the subscription network, the ENUM-based NPDB replies the result **tel: +886980002** with the "**npdi**" tag and the "**rn**" tag (i.e., rn = **1403980002**). According to the result (i.e., the routing number), the IMS forwards the **INVITE** message to the subscription network.

3   The Proposed Number Portability Scenarios

Either the IMS in the originating network (i.e., the originating IMS) or the IMS in the NRH network (i.e., the NRH IMS) can perform the queries to find the subscriber's location. In addition, the queries can be sent to the ENUM-based NPDB or the HSS first. Based on the above conditions, 3GPP TS 23.006 specifies three scenarios: *Originating call Query on Digit analysis* (OQoD), *Terminating call Query on Digit analysis* (TQoD), *Query on HSS Release* (QoHR). Note that *there* is no OQoHR or TQoHR because the originating network looks up the HSS if and only if the originating network is the terminating network. Moreover, the article [5] proposes using the SIP **3xx** responses [11] to perform the redirect scenario. Based on the above mention, we design four ENUM-based NP scenarios for IMS. The message flows for these scenarios are elaborated as follows.

A. Originating call Query on Digit analysis (OQoD)—The NP query is performed at the originating IMS. By querying the NPDB, the originating IMS checks whether the MSISDN of the called party is ported to another network. If yes, the originating IMS forwards the **INVITE** to the subscription network. Otherwise, the originating IMS forwards the **INVITE** to the NRH network. The detailed procedure illustrated in Fig. 2 is elaborated as follows.

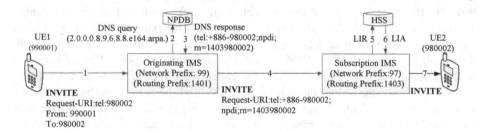

Fig. 2. Originating call Query on Digit analysis (OQoD)

Step A.1:   When the calling party dials the MSISDN **980002**. UE1 issues an **INVITE** message to establish the multimedia sessions. The **INVITE** message contains a *Request-URI* **tel:9800002** that designates to the called party, a *from* header field indicates the calling party (i.e., **990001**), and a *to* header field indicates the called party (i.e., **980002**). To resolve the MSISDN of the called party **980002** retrieved from the *Request-URI*, the **INVITE** message is sent to the originating IMS, which UE1 is subscribed.

Step A.2:   Upon receipt of the **INVITE** message, the IMS translates the MSISDN **980002** in the *Request-URI* to the E.164 format (i.e., **+886980002**) by adding the country code **+886**, and translates the E.164-formatted number to a *Fully Qualified Domain Name* (FQDN) **2.0.0.0.8.9.6.8.8.e164.arpa**. The originating IMS then sends an ENUM query with the FQDN **2.0.0.0.8.9.6.8.8.e164.arpa**. and the **NAPTR** (Name Authority Pointer) type to the NPDB.

Step A.3:   Upon receipt of the ENUM query, the NPDB retrieves the routing number of the called party (i.e.UE2) by using the FQDN. The NPDB replies the tel URI **tel: +886980002;npdi;rn = 1403980002** to the originating IMS.

Step A.4:   The originating IMS replaces the *Request-URI* **tel:9800002** by using the result of the ENUM query **tel: +886980002;npdi;rn = 1403980002**, and then forwards the **INVITE** message to the subscription IMS based on the "**rn**" tag in the *Request-URI*.

Step A.5:   Upon receipt of the **INVITE** message, the IMS detects that the *Request-URI* is retrieved from the NPDB based on the "**npdi**" tag. The IMS compares its routing prefix **1403** with the number **1403980002** in the "**rn**" tag and detects that it's the terminating IMS. Then, the subscription IMS queries UE2's location information by sending a *Location-Info-Request* (**LIR**) message to the HSS.

Step A.6:   The HSS replies a *Location-Info-Answer* (**LIA**) message with UE2's location to the subscription IMS.

Step A.7:   Upon receipt of the LIA message, the subscription IMS forwards the **INVITE** message to UE2.

Note that the subsequent SIP request messages are processed in the same way as the **INVITE** message, and the SIP response messages (e.g., **200 OK**) will be routed to UE1 along the reverse path as the **INVITE** message according to the *Via* header field.

B. Terminating call Query on Digit analysis (TQoD)—The NP query is performed at the NRH IMS. The NRH IMS queries the NPDN to check whether the called party's MSISDN is ported to another network. Assume that the called party (i.e. UE2) is ported to the subscription network. The detailed procedure is illustrated in Fig. 3 and elaborated as follows.

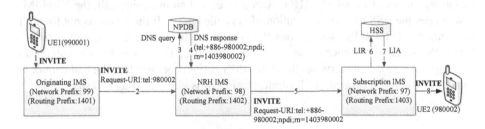

Fig. 3. Terminating call Query on Digit analysis (TQoD)

Step B.1:   When the calling party dials the MSISDN **980002**, the **INVITE** is sent to the originating IMS. This step is the same as **Step A.1**.

Step B.2:   Upon receipt of the **INVITE** message, the originating IMS looks up its routing table by using the MSISDN **980002** in the *Request-URI* and forwards the **INVITE** message to the NRH IMS (i.e., the NRH's network prefix is **98**).

Step B.3:   Upon receipt of the **INVITE message**, the IMS confirms that it's
                    the NRH IMS because the MSISDN **980002** matches its network
                    prefix **98**. Since the *Request-URI* does not contain the "**npdi**" tag.
                    The NRH IMS converts the MSISDN to the FQDN
                    2.0.0.0.8.9.6.8.8.e164.arpa. The NRH IMS then issues an ENUM
                    query with the FQDN and the **NAPTR** type to the NPDB.

Step B.4:   Upon receipt of the ENUM query, the NPDB retrieves the routing
                    number of UE2 through the FQDN and replies the tel URI with
                    UE2's routing number **tel:+886980002;npdi;rn = 1403980002** to
                    the NRH IMS.

Step B.5:   The NRH IMS replaces the *Request-URI* by the tel URI **tel:
                    +886980002;npdi;rn = 1403980002**, and then forwards the
                    INVITE message to the subscription IMS based on the value of
                    the "**rn**" tag.

Step B.6:   Upon receipt of the **INVITE** message, the IMS detects the
                    Request-URI is retrieved from the NPDB by the "**npdi**" tag.
                    The IMS compares its routing prefix **1403** with the routing
                    number **1403980002** and detects that it's the subscription IMS of
                    UE2. Then, the subscription IMS queries UE2's location by
                    sending a **LIR** message to the HSS.

Steps B.7 and 8: The HSS replies a **LIA** message with UE2's location to the
                    subscription IMS and the subscription IMS forwards the **INVITE**
                    message to UE2.

Note that if the called party's MSISDN is not ported and in the NRH network, the
NPDB will reply a response at **Step B.4** without the "**rn**" tag. Then, the NRH IMS
queries the HSS to find UE2's location and forwards the **INVITE** message to UE2.

C. Query on HSS Release (QoHR)—Upon receipt of an incoming call, the NRH IMS
first queries the HSS to find the location of the called party. If the record is not found in
the HSS, the NRH IMS then queries the NPDB to check whether the called party's
MSISDN is ported to other network. If yes, the NRH IMS forwards the call to the
subscription network. Otherwise, the NRH IMS notifies the user that the call cannot be
routed. The detailed procedure illustrated in Fig. 4 is elaborated as follows.

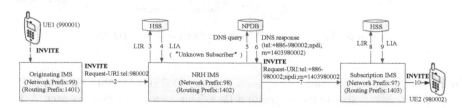

Fig. 4. Query on HSS Release (QoHR)

Steps C.1 and 2:   When the calling party dials the MSISDN **980002**, the **INVITE** is sent to the originating IMS. Then the originating IMS looks up its routing table and forwards the **INVITE** message to the NRH IMS. Those steps are the same as **Steps B.1 and 2**.

Step C.3:   Upon receipt of the **INVITE** message, the IMS retrieves the MSISDN from the *Request-URI* and confirms it's the NRH IMS by comparing the MSISDN and its network prefix **98**. Then, the NRH IMS issues a **LIR** message to the HSS to query UE2's location.

Step C.4:   The HSS replies a **LIA** message with "**Unknown Subscriber**" to the NRH IMS.

Step C.5:   The NRH IMS checks whether the MSISDN of UE2 is ported to other network by querying the NPDB. The IMS translates the MSISDN in the *Request-URI* to an FQDN **2.0.0.0.8.9.6.8.8.e164. arpa**. The NRH IMS then sends an ENUM query with the FQDN and the **NAPTR** type to the NPDB.

Step C.6:   Upon receipt of the ENUM query, the NPDB utilizes the FQDN to retrieve UE2's routing number and replies the tel URI **tel: +886980002;npdi;rn = 1403980002** to the NRH IMS.

Steps C.7–10:   The NRH IMS replaces the *Request-URI* by the tel URI, and then forwards the **INVITE** message to the subscription IMS. Then, the subscription IMS forwards the **INVITE** message to UE2 by querying the HSS. Those steps are the same as **Steps B.5–8**.

Note that if the MSISDN of UE2 is in the NRH network, the HSS will reply a **LIA** response at **Step C.4** to indicate that UE2's MSISDN is not ported to other network. Then, the NRH IMS queries UE2's location from the HSS and forwards the **INVITE** message UE2.

D. Redirect—The NRH IMS acts as a SIP redirect server and utilizes the SIP **380** status code [11] to notify the originating IMS that the call may have another route. Upon receipt of an incoming call, the NRH IMS queries the **HSS** to find the called party's location. If the location is found, the NRH IMS forwards the call to the called party. Otherwise, the NRH IMS replies the originating IMS a SIP **380** response which indicates that the call may have an alternative route or service. The detailed procedure illustrated in Fig. 5 is elaborated as follows.

In Fig. 5, **Steps 1–4** are the same as **Steps C.1–4** in the QoHR scenario. Since UE2's MSISDN is ported to the subscription network, The NRH IMS notifies the originating IMS by a SIP **380** response at **Step 5**. Upon receipt of the **380** response, the originating IMS performs the ENUM query and receives UE2's new URL i.e., **tel: +886980002;npdi;rn = 1403980002** at **Steps 6–7**. The originating IMS updates the *Request-URI*, and then forwards the **INVITE** message to the subscription IMS at **Step 8**. The rest **Steps 9–11** are the same as **Steps C.8–10**.

The previous work [5] proposes that the SIP **301** and **302** status codes can be used in the redirect scenario. In [5], the NRH IMS performs the ENUM query to retrieve the UE2's routing number from the NPDB. Then the UE2's routing number is embedded

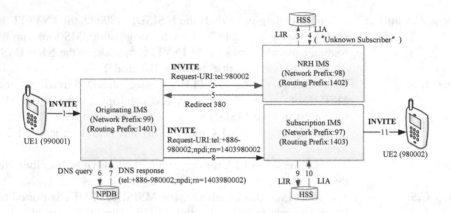

Fig. 5. Redirect for NP service

in the **301/302** response and sent to the originating IMS. Note that the "tel" URI contains the "**npdi**" tag that notifies the "tel" URI is queried from NPDB. When the originating IMS receives the URI with the "**npdi**" tag, it should not query the NPDB again [15]. In such cases, the originating IMS should trust the NRH IMS and utilizes the URI directly.

4   Analyses and Comparisons

This paper analyzes the proposed NP scenarios including **OQoD**, **TQoD**, **QoHR** and **redirect**. Table 1 shows the comparison of different NP scenarios in terms of the *routing independence*, the *extra call setup cost* and the *voice transmission path*.

Table 1. Comparative analysis NP scenarios

Scenario	OQoD	TQoD	QoHR	Redirect
Routing independence	High	Low	Low	Medium
Extra call setup cost	C_N	$C_N + pC_F$	$p(C_N + C_F)$	$p(C_N + 3C_S)$
Voice transmission path	O → S	O → N→S	O → N→S	O → S

O: Originating IMS. N: NRH IMS. S: Subscription IMS.

Row 2 of Table 1 lists the degrees of independence of the call setup procedures. In the OQoD scenario, the originating IMS performs the ENUM query and forwards the call to the subscription IMS without passing through the NRH IMS. Therefore, the degree of the OQoD scenario is highest. In the TQoD and QoHR scenarios, the call setup signaling will be forwarded to the NRH IMS. Thus the degrees of these scenarios are lowest. In the redirect scenario, only the first signaling is forwarded to the NRH IMS, and thus the degree of the redirect scenario is medium.

Row 3 of Table 1 indicates the extra costs introduced by the NP service. Note that the call setup flow for the NP service is compared to the reference [5]. The extra call setup cost is calculated by extra signaling for the call setup procedure in the NP scenarios. Assume that C_S is the average cost of sending a SIP signaling. The C_N indicates the cost of the NPDB query and response (i.e., $C_N = 2C_S$). C_F is the total cost of call setup between two IMS networks (i.e., $C_F = 9C_S$). Assume p is the percentage of the ported MSISDNs.

In the OQoD scenario, the originating IMS queries the NPDB for all calls, and thus the extra cost is C_N. In the TQoD scenario, the NRH IMS queries the NPDB and forwards only the ported MSISDNs to the subscription network. The extra cost for TQoD scenario is $C_N + pC_F$. In the QoHR scenario, the NRH IMS queries the HSS for all calls. If the called party's MSISDN is ported, the NRH IMS queries the NPDB and forwards the call to the subscription IMS. Therefore, the extra cost for QoHR scenario is $p(C_N + C_F)$. In the redirect scenario, the NRH IMS sends a **380** message to the originating IMS if the called party's MSISDN ported. The originating IMS queries the NPDB and then establish the call with the subscription IMS. The extra cost for redirect is $p(C_N + 3C_S)$.

Figure 6 plots the extra costs for the NP scenarios. In Fig. 6, we observe that the extra cost for QoHR scenario is less than that for TQoD scenario except $p = 100\%$. Based on the results, the NRH IMS should query the HSS first before querying the NPDB. In addition, the redirect scenario has less extra call setup cost than the QoHR scenario. That's because the NRH IMS forwards all call setup signaling in the QoHR scenario but only redirects the first signaling in the redirect scenario. In the OQoD scenario, the originating IMS queries the NPDB for all calls, no matter the MSISDN is ported or not. Thus, the extra cost of the OQoD scenario is more than that of the redirect scenario if the p is less than a threshold (e.g., 40%). On the contrary, the redirect scenario performs the redirect procedure that introduces the extra cost. Thus, the extra cost of the OQoD scenario is less than that of the redirect scenario, if the p is more than the threshold.

Row 4 of Table 1 lists the voice transmission paths for different NP scenarios. In The OQoD and redirect scenarios, the voice can be transmitted between the originating

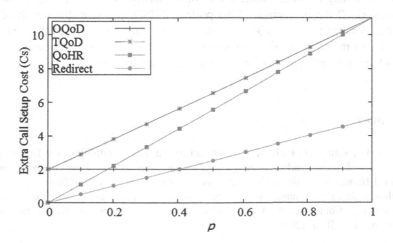

Fig. 6. Extra call setup cost

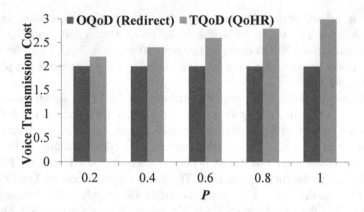

Fig. 7. Voice transmission cost

and subscription IMS networks directly. In The TQoD and QoHR scenarios, the originating IMS forwards voice packets to the subscription IMS through the NRH IMS in the default cases. The Voice Transmission Cost with different p is shown in Fig. 7. Note that to reduce the traffic loading, the NRH IMS can skip the voice traffic by revising the *Session Description Protocol* (SDP) fields.

5 Conclusions

This paper proposes four ENUM-based NP scenarios (i.e., OQoD, TQoD, QoHR and Redirect) based on the 3GPP IMS architecture. The paper then analyzes these scenarios in terms of the routing independence, the extra call setup cost and the voice transmission path. Among these NP scenarios, the OQoD scenario is the scenario with the highest degree of independence. In the OQoD scenario, the originating network forwards the signaling messages to the subscription network without passing through the NRH network. If the percentage of the ported MSISDNs is over the threshold (e.g., 40%), the extra cost of the OQoD scenario is less than that of the other scenarios. Otherwise, the redirect scenario has the lowest extra cost. The voice transmission paths of OQoD and redirect scenarios are the same and the shortest.

References

1. Lee, S.-W., Kim, D.J., Park, M.-C.: Demand for number portability in the Korean mobile telecommunications market: contingent valuation approach. In: Proceedings of the 37th Annual Hawaii International Conference on System Sciences. IEEE (2004)
2. Rudinsky, J.: Private enum based number portability administrative system evaluation. In: International Conference on Ultra Modern Telecommunications & Workshops, ICUMT 2009, pp. 1–7. IEEE (2009)

3. ITU-T: The International Public Telecommunication Number Plan. Recommendation E.164 (2015)
4. de Oliveira, R.G., Sigrist, P., Higashino, W.A., Becker, C.O., Pagani, C.E., Silva, J.: An Application Server Approach for Number Portability in IMS Networks
5. Geum, G., Kim, N., Ji, Y., Ahn, T.: A study on implementation issues of number portability in IMS networks. In: 2011 13th International Conference on Advanced Communication Technology (ICACT), pp. 1080–1083. IEEE (2011)
6. IP Multimedia Subsystem (IMS): Stage 2. 3GPP. TS 23.228 (2015)
7. Telephone Number Mapping. https://en.wikipedia.org/wiki/Telephone_number_mapping
8. RFC 3404: Dynamic Delegation Discovery System (DDDS) Part Four: The Uniform Resource Identifiers (URI) Resolution Application. IETF (2002)
9. RFC 2961: E.164 number and DNS. IETF (2000)
10. RFC 6116: The E.164 to Uniform Resource Identifiers (URI) Dynamic Delegation Discovery System (DDDS) Application (ENUM). IETF (2011)
11. RFC 3261: SIP: Session Initiation Protocol. IETF (2002)
12. IP Multimedia Call Control Protocol Based on Session Initiation Protocol (SIP) and Session Description Protocol (SDP): Stage 3. 3GPP. TS 24.229 (2015)
13. RFC 4769: IANA Registration for an Enumservice Containing Public Switched Telephone Network (PSTN) Signaling Information. IETF (2006)
14. RFC 3966: The tel URI for Telephone Numbers. IETF (2004)
15. RFC 4694: Number Portability Parameters for the "tel" URI. IETF (2006)
16. Lin, Y.B., Chlamtac, I., Yu, H.C.: Mobile number portability. IEEE Netw. **17**(5), 8–16 (2003)
17. Support of Mobile Number Portability (MNP): Technical realization; Stage 2. 3GPP. TS 23.066 (2015)
18. RFC 3482: Number Portability in the Global Switched Telephone Network (GSTN): An Overview. IETF (2003)

Game-Based Uplink Co-tier Interference Control in LTE Smallcell Networks

Chih-Cheng Tseng[1]([⊠]), Fang-Chang Kuo[1], Hwang-Cheng Wang[1], Kuo-Chang Ting[2], and Shih-Han Lo[1]

[1] National Ilan University, Yilan, Taiwan
{tsengcc,kfc,hcwang}@niu.edu.tw,
linda050829@gmail.com
[2] Minghsin University of Science and Technology, Xinfeng, Taiwan
kcting82@gmail.com

Abstract. As the advancements of communication technologies and the demands for high-speed mobile data in indoor environments, deploying smallcell is recognized as one of the feasible solutions to improve the indoor signal quality and, hence, provide high-speed data transmission. However, uplink co-tier interference between smallcells deteriorates the system performance. To solve this problem, this paper adopts the Stackelberg game in which Leader and Followers bargain the uplink transmit power by a two-way pricing mechanism to meet the uplink co-tier interference constraints of Leader and Followers. Simulation results show, by controlling the uplink co-tier interference, the two-way pricing mechanism outperforms the one-way pricing mechanism not only in the power conservation but also in the sum-capacity.

Keywords: Stackelberg game · Two-way pricing mechanism · Smallcell networks · Uplink co-tier interference · LTE

1 Introduction

Due to the widely deployment of 4G LTE/LTE-A mobile communication networks, aside from the mobile data services, more and more real-time multimedia applications are requested by the mobile users. Although the original application scenarios for wireless mobile communication were aimed for outdoor users, an interesting finding in [1] indicates that nearly 70% of data transmissions and 50% of mobile voices are originated from indoor users. In general, the penetration loss caused by outer wall and inner wall are regarded as −20 dB and −5 dB, respectively [2]. As a consequence, it is impossible to provide high data rate to support indoor real-time multimedia applications under such a poor radio signal quality environment.

Recently, due to the flexibility and convenience in deploying smallcell base station (SBS), smallcell has been regarded as one of the feasible solutions to improve indoor

This research was supported in part by the Ministry of Science and Technology of Taiwan under the grant numbers. 104-2221-E-197-007, 104-2221-E-197-009, 104-2221-E-197-016.

© ICST Institute for Computer Sciences, Social Informatics and Telecommunications Engineering 2017
J.-H. Lee and S. Pack (Eds.): QShine 2016, LNICST 199, pp. 344–354, 2017.
DOI: 10.1007/978-3-319-60717-7_34

radio signal quality and support high-speed data transmission. However, unlike the WiFi APs that are operated in the unlicensed band, SBSs are operated in the licensed based. Different SBSs can either operate in the same frequency band (i.e., co-channel mode) or in un-overlapped sub-bands (i.e., dedicated channel mode). In addition, the access mode of an SBS includes open subscribe group (OSG), close subscriber group (CSG), and hybrid modes [3]. In the OSG mode, SBS can be accessed by any user equipment (UE) that is within the coverage of the SBS. In the CSG mode, only authorized UE that is within the coverage of the SBS can do so. In the hybrid mode, the frequency band of an SBS is partitioned into two sub-bands, one of which is for OSG mode and the other one is for CSG mode.

However, as SBSs are widely deployed and operated in the co-channel and CSG modes, interference between them, i.e. co-tier interference, becomes a major problem to deteriorate the system performance. As illustrated in Fig. 1, when UE-f_1 is uplink transmission to SBS-F_1 (i.e., the red solid line in Fig. 1), the radio signal interferes SBS-F_2 in receiving the uplink transmission from UE-f_2 (i.e., the red dashed line in Fig. 1). We call this as the uplink co-tier interference. Similarly, when SBS-F_2 is downlink transmission to UE-f_2 (i.e., the blue solid line in Fig. 1), the radio signal interferes UE-f_1 in receiving the downlink transmission from SBS-F_1 (i.e., the blue dashed line in Fig. 1). This paper mainly focuses on controlling the uplink transmit power of UE in the smallcell networks so that the uplink co-tier interference is mitigated.

Fig. 1. Co-tier interference in the smallcell network. (Color figure online)

The rest of this paper is organized as follows: The system model is introduced in Sect. 2. In Sect. 3, the Stackelberg game with two-way pricing mechanism is proposed. The simulated parameter values and simulation results are demonstrated in Sect. 4. Section 5 concludes the paper.

2 System Model

In the past years, due to its inception, game theory has been applied to study problems in wired and wireless communication networks [4–6]. To control the uplink co-tier interference in the smallcell networks, this paper first employs the concepts of Stackelberg game to classify all SBSs in the network into Leader and Followers. Then, under the premise that the tolerable uplink co-tier interference constraints of Leader and Followers are not violated, a bargaining procedure together with a two-way pricing mechanism are proposed to find the uplink transmit power of Leader and Followers by adaptively adjusting pricing strategies of Leader and Followers. We consider $(N + 1)$ smallcells that are installed in an indoor environment, e.g., shopping mall or office. Each smallcell consists of one SBS and one UE. All the SBSs are operated in the co-channel and CSG modes. To fit the Stackelberg game, among the $(N + 1)$ small-cells, one is randomly selected as the Leader. The SBS and UE of the Leader smallcell are represented as SBS-L and UE-l, respectively. The rest of N smallcells are regarded as Followers. The SBS and UE of the ith Follower smallcell are represented as SBS-F_i and UE-f_i, respectively, where $i = 1, 2, 3, ..., N$. In addition, among the Follower SBSs, one is randomly selected as the delegate of the Followers and is represented as SBS-F. The path loss from UE-x to SBS-Y, $g^{x,Y}$ is based on the model in [7] and is given as follows:

$$g^{x,Y} = 10^{((38.46 + 20 \log_{10} d_{x,Y} + X_\sigma)/10)} \tag{1}$$

where x can be $l, f_1, f_2, ..., f_N$, Y can be $L, F_1, F_2, ..., F_N$, $d_{x,y}$ is the distance between UE-x and SBS-Y in meter, and X_σ is the log normal shadowing with zero mean and standard deviation σ. The log normal shadowing X_σ is assumed to be an independent and identically distributed (i.i.d.) random variable. To focus our study on the uplink co-tier interference, the interference between macrocell and smallcell, i.e., cross-tier interference, is ignored.

Based on the above descriptions, the system model is depicted in Fig. 2. As mentioned earlier, there are $(N + 1)$ smallcells in this system model. One is selected as Leader and the rests are Followers. Each smallcell contains one SBS and one UE. All smallcells are connected by the backhaul network. In this figure, when a UE is uplink to its corresponding SBS (i.e., the solid line), it also interferes the other SBSs simultaneously (i.e., the dash line).

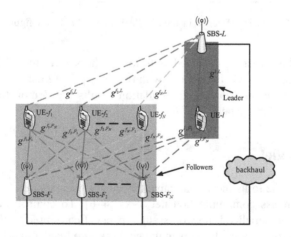

Fig. 2. The system model for a network with $(N + 1)$ smallcells.

3   Game-Based Uplink Co-tier Interference Control

3.1   Stackelberg Game with Two-Way Pricing Mechanism

Inspired by [8], Stackelberg game [9] is used to mitigate the uplink co-tier interference in smallcell networks. Simply speaking, Stackelberg game is a strategy- based game. In this game, utility functions for Leader and Followers are defined in advanced. Then, both Leader and Followers propose a strategy that maximizes its own utility individually. In particularly, Leader has the priority to first propose a strategy that favors itself to Follower. Based on the strategy proposed by Leader, each Follower updates its strategy to maintain its maximal utility and response the updated strategy to Leader. Next, Leader and Followers take turn to update their strategies until their utilities cannot be further improved. When this condition is met, we say the Stackelberg game achieves the Stackelberg Equilibrium (SE) point.

To incorporate the two-way pricing mechanism into the utility functions of Leader and Followers, we first let Q_L and Q_F be the maximal tolerable co-tier interference of Leader and each Follower, respectively. When Leader is interfered by Followers, it proposes a pricing strategy β and charges the Followers based on this pricing strategy. Similarly, when Follower SBS-F_i is interfered by Leader and other Followers, it proposes a pricing strategy α_i. Among the unit price α_i, $i = 1, 2, 3, \ldots, N$. the highest one is selected as the pricing strategy of all Followers, represented as α, and is used to charge the interferers. With this two-way pricing mechanism, as the total amount of co-tier interference approach to Q_L (or Q_F), Leader (or Followers) increases the unit price β (or α) to push the interferers to lower the uplink transmit power.

Let the total co-tier interference from Followers perceived at Leader be I_L (in mW). Based on Fig. 2, I_L can be derived as follows:

$$I_L = \sum_{i=1}^{N} \frac{p^{f_i}}{g^{f_i,L}} \leq Q_L, \tag{2}$$

where p^{f_i} is the uplink transmit power of UE-f_i. From Fig. 2, different from the SBS-L, the interferers of SBS-F_i includes UE-l and all other UE-f_j ($j \neq i$). Let the aggregated co-tier interference be p^{f_i} (in mW) and is obtained by

$$I_{F_i} = \frac{p_i^l}{g^{l,F_i}} + \sum_{j=1, j \neq i}^{N} \frac{p^{f_j}}{g^{f_j,F_i}} \leq Q_F, \tag{3}$$

where p_i^l is the uplink transmit power of UE-l that SBS-F_i suggested. Next, the SINR for SBS-L to receive signal from UE-l can be represented as

$$SINR\_L(p^l, \boldsymbol{p}^f) = \frac{p^l/g^{l,L}}{\sum\limits_{i=1}^{N} \frac{p^{f_i}}{g^{f_i,L}} + \eta}, \tag{4}$$

where p^l is the actual uplink transit power of UE-l, $\boldsymbol{p}^f = [p^{f1}, p^{f2}, \ldots, p^{fN}]$ is a vector of the uplink transmit power of all UEs, η is the power of thermal noise. Based on (4) and the concept of two-way pricing, the utility function of SBS-L is defined as follows:

$$U^L(p^l, \boldsymbol{p}^f, \alpha, \beta) = \lambda B \log_2(1 + SINR\_L(p^l, \boldsymbol{p}^f)) + \sum_{i=1}^{N} \beta \frac{p^{f_i}}{g^{f_i,L}} - \sum_{i=1}^{N} \alpha \frac{p^l}{g^{l,F_i}}, \quad (5)$$

where λ is a capacity transformation gain and is a system parameter, B is the system bandwidth. The meanings of the three terms on the right-hand side of (5) are explained in the follows. In the first term, the Shannon capacity of SBS-L is transferred into utility by λ. The second term is the reward obtained by charging all UE-f_i. The third term is the payoff paid to the FUEs. Again, based on Fig. 2, SINR for SBS-F_i to receive signal from UE-f_i can be expressed as follows:

$$SINR\_F_i(p^l, \boldsymbol{p}^f) = \frac{p^{f_i}/g^{f_i,F_i}}{\sum\limits_{j=1,j\neq1}^{N} \frac{p^{f_j}}{g^{f_j,F_i}} + \frac{p^l}{g^{l,F_i}} + \eta}. \quad (6)$$

Hence, the utility function of SBS-F_i is obtained as follows:

$$U^{F_i}(p^l, \boldsymbol{p}^f, \alpha, \beta) = \lambda B \log_2(1 + SINR\_F_i(p^l, \boldsymbol{p}^f)) - \beta \frac{p^{f_i}}{g^{f_i,L}} + \alpha \frac{p^l}{g^{l,F_i}}. \quad (7)$$

3.2   Finding the Stackelberg Equilibrium (SE) Point

By combining Stackelberg game and two-way pricing mechanism, our objective is to find the pricing strategies α and β and the corresponding uplink transmit power p^l and $\boldsymbol{p}^f$ that maximize utilities of Leader and Followers without violating the maximal tolerable co-tier interference limits Q_L and Q_F. Hence, the whole problem is modelled as the optimization problem below:

$$\max U^L(p^l, \boldsymbol{p}^f, \alpha, \beta) \text{ and } U^{F_i}(p^l, \boldsymbol{p}^f, \alpha, \beta)$$
$$\text{subject to} \quad (8)$$
$$0 \leq p^l \leq 200, I_L \leq Q_L, \text{ and } 0 \leq p^{f_i} \leq 200, I_{F_i} \leq Q_F, i = 1, 2, \ldots, N.$$

Our approach to solve the solution of (8) is to find the SE point of the Stackelberg game with two-way pricing mechanism. First, to satisfy the Karush-Kuhn-Tucker (KKT) condition, a Lagrange multiplier is introduced to (5). Then, taking the partial derivative of (5) with respect to p^{f_i} and let the results to be zero, the optimal uplink transmit power of UE-f_i, p^{f_i} with respect to the pricing strategy β proposed by Leader is derived as follows:

$$
p^{f_i} = \left(\frac{\lambda B}{\beta / g^{f_i,L}} - \frac{\sum\limits_{j=1,j\neq 1}^{N} \frac{p_{\max}^{f}}{g^{f_j,F_i}} + \frac{p^l}{g^{l,F_i}} + \eta}{1/g^{f_i,F_i}} \right)^+ ,
\tag{9}
$$

where $p_{\max}^{f}$ is the maximum uplink transmit power of Follower UE. Similarly, to find the optimal transmit power of UE-l with respect to the pricing strategy proposed by SBS-F_i, α_i, a Lagrange multiplier is introduced to (7). Then, taking the partial derivative of (7) with respect to p^l and let the results to be zero, the optimal uplink transmit power of UE-l with respect to the pricing strategy α_i proposed by SBS-F_i, p_i^l is derived as follows:

$$
p_i^l = \left(\frac{\lambda B}{\sum\limits_{i=1}^{N} \frac{\alpha_i}{g^{l,f_i}}} - \frac{\sum\limits_{i=1}^{N} p^{f_i}/g^{f_i,L} + \eta}{(1/g^{l,L})} \right)^+ .
\tag{10}
$$

3.3 Bargaining Procedure for Two-Way Pricing Mechanism

Following, a bargaining procedure is introduced for Leader and Followers in a distributed manner to find the pricing strategies α and β and the corresponding uplink transmit power p^l and p^f without violating the maximal tolerable co-tier interference limits Q_L and Q_F. All information required for the bargaining procedures are exchanged through the backhaul network. The detail bargaining procedures are stated as below:

Step 0: The upper and lower bounds of the price strategy proposed by SBS-L are β^H and β^L whose initial values are β_0^H and β_0^L, respectively. The upper and lower bounds of the price strategy proposed by SBS-F_i, α_i, are α_i^H and α_i^L whose initial values are α_0^H and α_0^L respectively. $p^l = 200$ mW.

Step 1: $\beta^H = \beta_0^H$ and $\beta^L = \beta_0^L$.

Step 2: SBS-L sends $\beta = (\beta^H + \beta^L)/2$ and p^l to each SBS-F_i.

Step 3: After receiving β and p^l each SBS-F_i calculates p^{f_i} based on (9) and sends it to SBS-L and all other follower SBSs.

Step 4: Based on the received p^{f_i}, SBS-L adjusts its pricing strategy β as follows:
If $I_L > Q_L + \varepsilon_L$, $\beta = \beta$ and go to **Step 2**.
If $I < Q_L - \varepsilon_L$, $\beta^H = \beta$ and go to **Step 2**.

Step 5: $\alpha_i^H = \alpha_0^H$ and $\alpha_i^L = \alpha_0^L$.

Step 6: Each SBS-F_i sends its pricing strategy $\alpha_i = (\alpha_i^H + \alpha_i^L)/2$ to SBS-L.

Step 7: With α_i and p^f, SBS-L calculates p_i^l based on (10) and sends it back to SBS-F_i.

Step 8: Based on the updated follows: p_i^l each SBS-F_i adjusts its pricing strategy α_i as follows:

If $I_{F_i} > Q_F + \varepsilon_F$, SBS-$F_i$ checks if $p_i^l = 0$ mW. If true, send the updated $p^{f_i} = p^{f_i} - 1$ mW to SBS-L and go to **Step 5**. Otherwise, $\alpha_i^L = \alpha_i$ and go to **Step 6**.

If $I_{F_i} < Q_F - \varepsilon_F$, $\alpha_i^H = \alpha_i$ and go to **Step 6**. Otherwise, each SBS-F_i sends p_i^l to SBS-F.

Step 9: SBS-F sends $p^{l^*} = \min_i p_i^l$ and $\alpha = \max_i \alpha_i$ to SBS-L. If $|p^{l^*} - p^l| > \omega$, $p^l = p^{l^*}$ and go to **Step 1**. Otherwise, $p^l = p^{l^*}$ and stop the procedures.

In fact, if only **Step 0–Step 4** are considered, it is regarded as the one-way pricing mechanism. In other words, in the one-way pricing mechanism, the Leader power cannot be dynamically adapted. In our simulation, the uplink transmit power p^l is fixed at 200 mW for the one-way pricing mechanism.

4   Simulation Results

The simulation is coded by Matlab. In our simulation, the $(N + 1)$ SBSs are uniformly distributed within square area with size 40 m $\times$ 40 m. For each SBS, a UE is randomly deployed between the distance 0.2 m and 10 m to it. During the simulation, each SBS takes turn to be the Leader. Based on the proposed bargaining procedure, Leader and Followers update their pricing strategies β and α alternatively. Then, the corresponding uplink transmit power p^l and p^f are updated accordingly. The simulation is executed 100 times and the detail simulation parameter values are listed in Table 1. The transmit powers and capacities of Leader and Followers for two-way pricing mechanism are collected, analyzed, and compared to that for one-way pricing mechanism as shown in Figs. 3 and 4, respectively. In the one-way pricing mechanism, Q_F is assumed infinite. However, Q_F is assumed to be -40 dBm for the two-way pricing mechanism. The capacity is calculated based on the equation:

$$capacity = \min(90\,\text{Mbps}, B\log_2(1 + SINR)), \tag{11}$$

where 90 Mbps is the maximum achievable capacity when the most aggressive MSC in [10] is used together with the parameter values listed in Table 1. The SINR in (11) is taken from either (4) or (6) if the calculated capacity is for Leader of Followers, respectively. In Figs. 3 and 4, the red line represents the simulation results for Leader, while the blue line represents the simulation results for Followers. The circle represents

Table 1. Simulated parameter values.

Parameter	Value	Parameter	Value
$p_{\max}^f$	200 mW	λ	5×10^{-8} bps^{-1}
σ	4	$\varepsilon_L, \varepsilon_F$	10^{-8} mW
B	20 MHz	α_0^H, β_0^H	10^{15} mW^{-1}
η	-101 dBm	α_0^L, β_0^L	0 mW^{-1}
N	3	Q_L	$-100, -95, ..., 20$ dBm
ω	10^{-3} mW	Q_F	-40 dBm

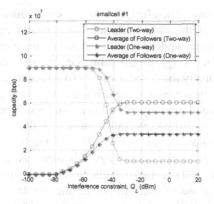

Fig. 3. Comparison of the capacities of Leader and Followers between two-way and one-way pricing mechanisms. (Color figure online)

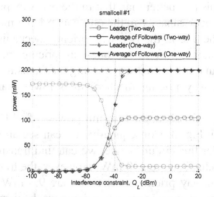

Fig. 4. Comparison of the transmit power between two-way and one-way pricing mechanisms. (Color figure online)

the simulation results for the two-way pricing mechanism, while the asterisk represents the simulation results for the one-way pricing mechanism. In addition, the simulation results demonstrated in Figs. 3 and 4 are obtained when the smallcell number 1 is selected as the Leader.

First, when $Q_L < -80$ dBm, which means Leader can only tolerate very limited uplink co-tier interference, Leader increases its pricing strategy β to restrain Followers from uplink transmission regardless what pricing mechanism is employed. Hence, the average uplink transmit power of Followers in Fig. 3 is zero. As a consequence, the average capacity of Followers is also zero in Fig. 4. However, different from 200 mW, the uplink transmit powers of UE-l in the one-way pricing mechanism, we can see the uplink transmit powers of UE-l reduces to 170 mw for the two-way pricing mechanism as shown in Fig. 3. The reason is, in the two-way pricing mechanism, the pricing strategy α will be increased in order to satisfy (3). Consequently, the uplink transmit power of UE-l is reduced. Therefore, when $Q_L <-80$ dBm, the two-way pricing mechanism saves 15% of the uplink transmit power with compared to that in the one-way pricing mechanism while the Leader capacity remains unchanged.

Next, when -80 dBm $\leq Q_L <- 30$ dBm, i.e., the tolerable uplink co-tier interference of Leader is gradually increased, Leader starts to reduce its pricing strategy β to encourage Followers to increase their uplink transmit powers. Thus, we can see the average transmit powers and capacity of Followers in Figs. 3 and 4 are increased as Q_L increases. However, as the uplink transmit power of Follower increases, the co- tier interference between Followers are increased accordingly. In the two-way pricing mechanism, to satisfy (3), the pricing strategy α is increased to push Leader to reduce its uplink transmit power. This also results in the reduction of SINR of Leader. However, due to the increase of transmit power and the decrease of the co-tier interference from Leader, the SINR of Follower is improved. Hence, this is the reason why the transmit power and capacity of Leader decreased, while that of Follower increased in Figs. 3 and 4, respectively. On the contrary, due to the transmit power of Leader is fixed at 200 mW for the one-way pricing mechanism, the SINR of Leader in the one-way pricing mechanism is better than that in the two-way pricing mechanism. That is the reason why the Leader capacity in the one-way pricing mechanism does not drop so much compared to the one in the two-way pricing mechanism. Meanwhile, due to the higher Leader transmit power in the one-way pricing mechanism, the SINR of Follower is worse than that in the two-way pricing mechanism. Therefore, the capacity of Follower in the one-way pricing mechanism is lower than that in the two-way pricing mechanism.

Finally, when $Q_L \geq -30$ dBm, the transmit powers of all UEs cannot be increased anymore as illustrated in Fig. 3. Consequently, we can see all the capacities in Fig. 4 remain unchanged. Under this circumstance, we can find transmit power of all UEs in the one-way pricing mechanism are 200 mW. However, the transmit powers of Leader and Follower in the two-way pricing mechanism are 9.4 mW and 105 mW, respectively. In other words, the proposed two-way pricing mechanism conserves the transmit powers of Leader and Follower by 95.3% and 47.5%, respectively.

As we mentioned earlier, the results demonstrated in Figs. 3 and 4 are obtained when smallcell number 1 is selected as the Leader. It is hence important to know if different results may be obtained if other smallcell is selected as Leader. In addition, it is also important to compare the sum-capacity achieved by the one-way and two- way pricing mechanisms. Figure 5 shows the obtained sum-capacities for one-way and two-way pricing mechanisms when different smallcell is selected as Leader. According to the discussions for Figs. 3 and 4 above, the sum-capacities in Fig. 5 are obtained for the four values of Q_L, -80 dBm, -50 dBm, -40 dBm, and 0 dBm, respectively. When $Q_L = -80$ dBm, since all Followers are forbidden to transmit, the sum-capacity for one-way and two-way pricing mechanisms are the same. When $Q_L = -50$ dBm and $Q_L = -40$ dBm, the capacities of Followers are quickly increasing. Besides, the capacities of Followers for the two-way pricing mechanism are higher than that for the one-way pricing mechanism. Hence, the sum-capacities of two-way pricing mechanisms are higher than that of one-way pricing mechanism. Since the capacities of Followers achieve the maximal and stable values when $Q_L \geq -30$ dBm, the sum-capacities for the two-way pricing mechanism at $Q_L = 0$ dBm remain higher than

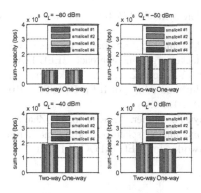

Fig. 5. The sum-capacity between two-way and one-way pricing mechanisms when different smallcell is selected as Leader.

that for the one-way pricing mechanism. In addition, for the four different values of Q_L, it is obviously that the selection of Leader impacts the sum-capacities very limited. In other words, selecting Leader is not an issue when the smallcells are uniformly distributed over the considered area.

5 Conclusions

By partitioning the smallcells into Leader and Followers and bargaining the pricing strategies between Leader and Followers, Stackelberg game with two-way pricing mechanism provides a feasible approach to control the uplink co-tier interference and achieves a higher sum-capacity that that achieved by using one-way pricing mechanism. In addition, simulation results also show that two-way pricing mechanism performs better power consumption. Specifically, up to 95.3% and 47.5% of the power conservations for the transmit powers of Leader and Follower are achieved when $Q_L \geq -30$ dBm.

References

1. Chandrasekhar, V., Andrews, J.G., Gatherer, A.: Femtocell networks: a survey. IEEE Commun. Mag. **46**(9), 59–67 (2008)
2. Xia, P., Chandrasekhar, V., Andrews, J.G.: Open vs. closed access femtocells in the uplink. IEEE Trans. Wirel. Commun. **9**(12), 3798–3809 (2010)
3. Altman, E., Boulogne, T., El-Azouzi, R.: A survey on networking games in telecommunications. Comput. Oper. Res. **33**(2), 286–311 (2006)
4. Felegyhazi, M., Hubaux, J.-P.: Game theory in wireless networks: a tutorial. EPFL Technical report: LCA-REPORT-2006-002 (2006)
5. Saad, W., Han, Z., Basar, T., Debbah, M., Hjorungnes, A.: Network formation games among relay stations in next generation wireless networks. IEEE Trans. Commun. **59**(9), 2528–2542 (2011)

6. https://ledoyle.files.wordpress.com/2013/01/example-technical-document-with-path-loss-details.pdf
7. Kang, X., Zhang, R., Motani, M.: Price-based resource allocation for spectrum-sharing femtocell networks: a Stackelberg game approach. IEEE JSAC **30**(3), 538–549 (2012)
8. Razaviyayn, M., Morin, Y., Luo, Z.-Q.: A Stackelberg game approach to distributed spectrum management. In: Proceedings of IEEE ICASSP 2010, Dallas, USA, March 2010
9. 3GPP TR 36.814 V9.0.0 (2010-03)
10. Lopez-Perez, D., Ladanyi, A., Juttner, A., Rivano, H., Zhang, J.: Optimization method for the joint allocation of modulation schemes, coding rates, resource blocks and power in self-organizing LTE networks. In: IEEE INFOCOM (2011)

Resource Allocation Scheme for LTE Uplink Transmission Based on Logical Channel Groups

Fang-Chang Kuo[1(✉)], Chih-Cheng Tseng[1], Kuo-Chang Ting[2],
and Hwang-Cheng Wang[1]

[1] National Ilan University, Yilan, Taiwan
kfc@niu.edu.tw
[2] Minghsin University of Science and Technology, Xinfeng, Taiwan

Abstract. It is still a difficult problem to allocate wireless resources for uplink transmission in LTE system. The main goals of previous researches aim at maximizing system throughput or fairness among UEs. However, the real requirements of UEs are not considered. The result is that Resource Blocks (RB) allocated by eNB are usually wasted and the requirements of UEs are not satisfied. We presented an AAG-2 scheduling scheme, which can ensure the QoS of GBR bearers, while at the same time efficiently distributes RBs to non-GBR bearers so as to improve resource utilization. However, in order to facilitate the management for many bearers, 3GPP suggested divide bearers into four Logical Channel Groups (LCG), rather than only two kinds of bearers mentioned above. So far, 3GPP has not specified how to map between LCG and bearers of different QoS Class Identifiers (QCIs), but left it to the operator for customization. As a result, it is an important issue about how to group bearers and how to guarantee QoS, while make good use of free RB. In this paper, we propose a new-version of AAG-2, named AAG-LCG, where bearers are classified into four LCGs with different priority levels. Especially, with the proposed scheme, eNB can efficiently allocate RBs to meet the QoS requirements of different LCG bearers, while also maintain sound overall system performance.

Keywords: AAG-LCG · Scheduling · Resource allocation

1 Introduction

For the LTE system, the importance of uplink resource allocation/scheduling in ensuring the Quality of Service (QoS) of guaranteed bit rate (GBR) bearers has led to the development of numerous resource allocation schemes. The criteria used in such schemes include maximizing system throughput [1, 2] or fairness [3, 4], or minimizing power consumption [5, 6]. However, the real requirements of UEs are neglected in these schemes. The result is that Resource Blocks (RB) allocated by eNB are usually wasted and the requirements of UEs are not satisfied. In our opinion, one of the most important objectives of resource allocation work is to meet the data rate granted by Radio Access Control (RAC), rather than maximizing system throughput or fairness. In [7, 8], we presented a scheme, named AAG-2 (Allocate As Granted-2), and show that it

© ICST Institute for Computer Sciences, Social Informatics and Telecommunications Engineering 2017
J.-H. Lee and S. Pack (Eds.): QShine 2016, LNICST 199, pp. 355–364, 2017.
DOI: 10.1007/978-3-319-60717-7_35

always provides GBR bearers with sufficient throughput (which is granted by RAC) and short delay, while at the same time achieves high resource utilization by efficiently providing RBs to non-GBR bearers. However, 3GPP has suggested divide bearers into four Logical Channel Groups (LCG) to alleviate signaling load induced by Buffer Status Reports (BSR) [9]. It raises new topics concerning how to divide bearers of different QCIs into four LCGs and how to allocate suitable resource to these LCGs. Based on AAG-2, in this paper, we present a new-version, named AAG-LCG, where eNB efficiently allocates RBs to meet the QoS requirements of different LCG bearers, while also maintains overall system performance.

This paper is organized as follows. The AAG-2 is described in Sect. 2 and the new version AAG-LCG is described in Sect. 3. The function of AAG-LCG is verified by comparing the performance with that of AAG-2 in Sect. 4. Finally, the conclusion and future works are drawn in Sect. 5.

2 Previous Work: AAG-2 Scheme

It could be quite normal for a UE to establish both GBR and non-GBR bearers at the same time. Because the QoS of non-GBR bearers is not guaranteed, they can be scheduled only if there are sufficient resources. The eNB may allocate RBs to all UEs according to priority sequence, so as to meet the requirement of all GBR bearers, and then allocate the rest of RBs to UEs which need to transmit non-GBR traffic. With this approach, however, the RBs allocated to a UE could often be discontinuous, which is not allowed for LTE uplink transmission.

To solve this problem, we proposed an AAG-2 scheme. It can allocate continuous RBs to meet the requirements of GBR bearers, and efficiently allocate the remaining RBs to transmit non-GBR traffic [7, 8]. The steps of AAG-2 are as follows:

(a) allocating RBs to meet the requirement of GBR and non-GBR traffic of high priority UEs,
(b) allocating the remaining RBs to meet the requirement of GBR traffic for the other UEs.

The scheme is briefly summarized as follows. Let's consider an eNB serving K UEs. For a UE_m, the total granted bit rate of the admitted h GBR bearers is expressed as $R_{m,GBR}^{grant} = \sum_{j=1}^{h} R_{m,j,GBR}^{grant}$. The $R_{m,j,GBR}^{grant}$ is the granted data rate of the j-th GBR bearer. Besides, we use $B_{m,MIX}^{grant} = B_{m,GBR}^{grant} + B_{m,AMBR}^{grant}$ to stand for the total data rate that is requested by both GBR bearers and Aggregate Maximum Bit Rate (AMBR) bearers. The $R_{m,AMBR}^{grant}$ is the AMBR of all non-GBR bearers of UE_m. Then we convert data rates to the number of bits to be sent in a Transmission Time Interval (TTI, 1 ms). That is to say, $B_{m,GBR}^{grant} = R_{m,GBR}^{grant} \times 10^{-3}$ and $B_{m,MIX}^{grant} = R_{m,MIX}^{grant} \times 10^{-3}$ with unit bits/TTI.

Let $\bar{B}_m(n)$ denote the average number of bits per TTI that has been sent. It is defined based on Exponentially Weighted Moving Average (EWMA) as $\bar{B}_m(n) = (1-\alpha)\bar{B}_m(n-1) + \alpha B_m(n)$. For the n-th TTI, if the eNB intends to meet the requirement of UE_m, it should plan to allocate RBs for UE_m to transmit the following number of bits

$$B_m^{plan}(n) = \min\left\{\max\left[\frac{B_m^{grant} - (1-\alpha)\bar{B}_m(n-1)}{\alpha}, 0\right], L_m(n-1)\right\}. \quad (1)$$

The $L_m(n-1)$, which is obtained through BSRs, is the total queue length of UE_m. This term is used to prevent wasting RBs when there are not so much data waiting in the buffer of UE_m. Because a UE may not transmit BSR in every TTI, the eNB may predict the value of BSR by subtracting the number of bits that has been scheduled for transmission. Whenever the eNB receives a new BSR, the total queue length is then updated. For the sake of ensuring the throughput of every UE, AAG allocates RBs to UEs based on the descending order of

$$P_m(n) = \frac{B_m^{grant} - \bar{B}_m(n-1)}{B_m^{grant}}. \quad (2)$$

This term, named priority metric, also indicates the current shortage ratio corresponding to the average data rate. UEs with higher priority metric is scheduled earlier.

The basic idea of AAG-2 is allocating RBs to firstly meet $B_{m,MIX}^{grant}$ for the UEs ranked in the top $x\%$ high priority, and then allocating the remaining RBs to meet $B_{m,GBR}^{grant}$ of the other UEs. The method for allocating RBs in each TTI is selecting free RBs with higher channel quality just like the AAG scheme described in [7, 8]. It is not easy to choose a fix value for x. If it is too small, more RBs are wasted by high priority UEs, and less non-GBR traffic is transmitted. On the contrary, with too large x, some high priority UEs may not get enough RBs to guarantee the quality of their GBR bearers. To prevent this problem, AAG-2 adjusts the value of x dynamically. For the n-th TTI we define the average satisfaction ratio associated with the GBR traffic as

$$S_{GBR}(n) = \frac{1}{K}\sum_{m=1}^{K} s_{GBR,m}(n-1). \quad (3)$$

The $s_{GBR,m}(n-1)$ is set to 1 if the queue length of the corresponding GBR predicted by eNB is 0, otherwise it is set to 0. At first, x is set to zero and then adjusted dynamically as follows:

$$x(n) = \begin{cases} \max(0, \min(100, x(n-1) + \Delta x_{raise})), & \text{if } S_{GBR}(n) \geq S_{th} \\ \max(0, \min(100, x(n-1) - \Delta x_{fall})), & \text{if } S_{GBR}(n) < S_{th}, \end{cases} \quad (4)$$

where S_{th} is a threshold for the average satisfaction ratio, while Δx_{raise} and Δx_{fall} are the step sizes for increasing and decreasing the value of x.

The performance of AAG-2 would be compared with the new version proposed in this paper in Sect. 4.

3 Proposed New Version: AAG-LCG Scheme

3.1 Motivation

As specified in 3GPP specification [9], a UE notifies eNB with "how many data is pending for uplink transmission" through different kinds of BSR. 3GPP has defined nine QoS Class Identifier (QCI) to classify bearers of different characteristics. A UE could establish many bearers especially when it acts as a WiFi access point. If BSR messages are sent in a per-bearer mode, these messages could be a heavy burden of PUCCH (Physical Uplink Control Channel). As a result, in order to facilitate the management for many bearers, 3GPP suggested divide bearers into four LCGs, LCG 0–LCG 3. Then, BSRs are reported per-LCG, rather than per-bearer. That means, for a UE, the queue lengths of all bearers of the same LCG are added together and then reported. So far, 3GPP only designates signaling channels to LCG 0, while hasn't specified how to map the other QCI bearers to the other LCGs, but left it to the operator for customization. As a result, it is an important issue about how to group bearers and how to ensure the corresponding data rate so as to guarantee QoS.

3.2 The Operation of AAG-LCG

Because the QoS of non-GBR traffic is not guaranteed, in this paper, we suggest divide GBR bearers into two groups, GBR1 and GBR2. As a result, bearers are mapped to four LCGs as illustrated in Fig. 1, where the priority of GBR1 is higher than that of GBR2. The operator can decide which QCIs are treated as LCG1 and which are regarded as LCG2. For example, operator may treat the bears with QCI = 5, whose typical service is non-conventional video, as LCG2.

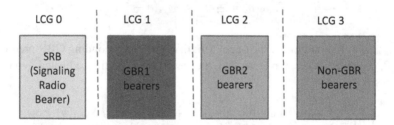

Fig. 1. The mapping between LCGs and bearers of different QCIs

In order to provide differential QoS to bearers of different LCGs, it is necessary to design a new scheme which can deal with the four LCGs. As a result, in this paper, we propose a new version AAG-LCG. For convenience, signaling traffic is excluded in the following discussion because it has been classified as LCG 0 with highest priority. Besides, in order to clearly express the corresponding characteristics of different LCGs, we use GBR1, GBR2, and non-GBR to stand for LCG 1, LCG 2, and LCG 3, respectively. The design principle is described as follows based on Fig. 1.

If the throughput of all GBR1 bearers reaches a threshold, eNB can allocate RBs for GBR2 bearers. If both GBR1 and GBR2 reach their respective thresholds, eNB can allocate RBs for non-GBR. As a result, we define two kinds of satisfactory degrees for GBR1 and GBR2, respectively. For GBR1,

$$S_{GBR1}(n) = \frac{1}{K}\sum_{m=1}^{K} s_{GBR1,m}(n-1),\tag{5}$$

where K is the number of UEs under service, while

$$s_{GBR1,m}(n-1) = \begin{cases} 0, & if\ L_{m,GBR1} \neq 0 \\ 1, & if\ L_{m,GBR1} = 0 \end{cases}\tag{6}$$

is the satisfactory degree corresponding to the UE_m. And $L_{m,GBR1}$ is the predicted queue length corresponding to the GBR1 of the UE_m.

The satisfactory degree of GBR2 is also defined in the similar way as follows.

$$S_{GBR2}(n) = \frac{1}{K}\sum_{m=1}^{K} s_{GBR2,m}(n-1)\tag{7}$$

$$s_{GBR2,m}(n-1) = \begin{cases} 0, & if\ L_{m,GBR2} \neq 0 \\ 1, & if\ L_{m,GBR2} = 0 \end{cases}.\tag{8}$$

We should keep in mind that the RBs allocated to a UE must be contiguous. That means, if the eNB want to allocate RBs for a UE to transmit its GBR1, GBR2, and non-GBR traffic, these RBs should be contiguous and had better to be allocated at a time. The same is for allocating the requirement for GBR1 and GBR2.

In order to keep the RBs allocated for a specific UE contiguous, we adopt an approach illustrated in Fig. 2. The objective is to meet the requirements of GBR1 and GBR2 traffic for the UEs with priority metric ranked in the top $x_1\%$, and also meet the requirements of GBR1, GBR2, and non-GBR traffic for the $x_2\%$ of them with higher priority. It is not good to set fix values for $x_1\%$ and $x_2\%$. With too small values, eNB may waste too many RBs, and less low-priority traffic is served. On the contrary, if $x_1\%$ and $x_2\%$ are too large, high-priority UEs may occupy too many resources, and the RBs for the low-priority UEs would be insufficient. Thus, we dynamically adjust the value of x as the following.

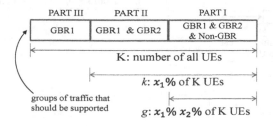

Fig. 2. Illustration for how many UEs should be supported with different groups

$$x_1 = \begin{cases} \max\left(0, \min\left(100, x_1 + \Delta x_{raise}\right)\right) & \text{if } S_{GBR1}(n) \geq S_{th1} \\ \max\left(0, \min\left(100, x_1 - \Delta x_{fall}\right)\right) & \text{if } S_{GBR1}(n) < S_{th1} \end{cases} \quad (9)$$

$$x_2 = \begin{cases} \max\left(0, \min\left(100, x_2 + \Delta x_{raise}\right)\right) & \text{if } S_{GBR2}(n) \geq S_{th2} \\ \max\left(0, \min\left(100, x_2 - \Delta x_{fall}\right)\right) & \text{if } S_{GBR2}(n) < S_{th2} \end{cases} \quad (10)$$

3.3 Flow Chart for Resource Allocation

The principle of AAG-LCG is described with the help of the flow chart shown in Fig. 3. For the allocation work of each TTI, eNB updates the values of parameters and

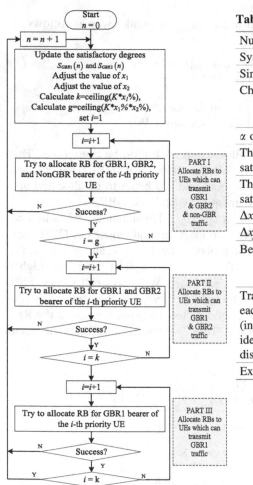

Fig. 3. Flow chart of AAG-LCG

Table 1. Parameters of simulation environment

Number of users	10, 20, 30, 35, 40, 50
System bandwidth	20 MHz
Simulation duration	20 s
Channel quality	MCS index = 28 (TBS index = 26) for all RBs
α of EWMA	0.01
Threshold of average satisfaction ratio S_{th1}	90%
Threshold of average satisfaction ratio S_{th2}	90%
Δx_{raise}	10
Δx_{fall}	1
Bearers of each UE	one GBR1 bearer; one GBR2 bearer one non-GBR bearer
Traffic pattern of each bearer (independent and identically distributed)	Near Real Time Video (NRTV), Truncated Pareto distribution, average data rate: 640 Kbps
Extra ratio	15%

variables at first. Then the PART I of the flow chart shows the steps that try to allocate RBs to the UEs which are entitled to transmit GBR1, GBR2 and non-GBR traffic. These are the g UEs as shown in Fig. 2. Then, PART II tries to allocate for the next $(k\text{-}g)$ UEs. The last PART III deals with the rest UEs.

4 Performance Evaluation

4.1 Simulation Environment

We will compare the performance between AAG-2 and AAG-LCG based on the simulation parameters listed in Table 1. In order to clearly observe the difference, we set all RBs with the same channel quality. However, when we average the data rate of a variable bit rate traffic patterns based on EWMA, the obtained values would vary over time. For example, whenever a big burst appears, the EWMA value at that instant would be higher than the long-term mean data rate of the pattern. The larger the burst is, the larger the instant EWMA value is obtained. Thus, B_m^{grant} in (1) and (2) should be set a little bit higher than the long term mean data rate. In this paper, we set $B_m^{grant} =$ (long term mean data rate) $\times$ (1 + extra ratio). The suitable value for the extra ratio depends on how smooth the input traffic pattern is. With too small extra ratio, the corresponding bearer would get insufficient RBs, and lots of the traffic would be blocked. On the contrary, with too large extra ratio, the eNB would allocate too many RBs for the bearer, thus less bearers can be accommodated. We set the extra ratio as 15% in this paper.

The parameters for AAG-2 are almost the same with that for AAG-LCG. For AAG-2, however, there is only one threshold value S_{th}, which is set as 90%, the same as the values of the two thresholds for AAG-LCG. Besides, the GBR traffic for AAG-2 is the combination of GBR1 and GBR2 traffic used for AAG-LCG because there is only one group of GBR traffic for the AAG-2. For a UE, when the number of LCGs of traffic (volumes/data rate) is changed, not only the B_m^{grant} in (1) and (2) should be changed, but also the $\bar{B}_m(n-1)$ should be changed to the same as B_m^{grant} at the same time. Otherwise, the instantaneous transmission rate would be unstable.

4.2 Numerical Results

Let's take a glance at Fig. 4. The utilization of RBs is 90% when the eNB is loaded with 50 UEs. According to the slope of the curve, the utilization would exceed 100% if there are 60 UEs. However, overloading is not allowed by the RAC. As a result, the maximum number of UEs is set as 50 UEs for the simulation scenario.

Figure 5 shows the throughput comparison between the AAG-2 and AAG-LCG. The throughput of GBR increases linearly to the load (the number of UEs). When there are 50 UEs, the throughput of non-GBR approaches zero for both schemes. For the AAG-LCG scheme, the throughput of GBR1 and GBR2 coincides and increases linearly with the number of UEs. That means the throughput of GBR1 and GBR2 traffic is ensured with high priority.

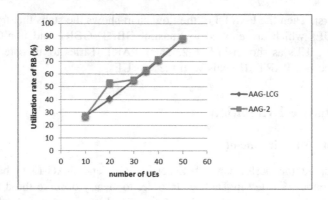

Fig. 4. Comparing the utilization for different schemes.

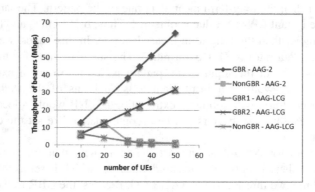

Fig. 5. Comparing the throughput of different LCGs for different schemes

For the AAG-2 scheme, when there is no more than 20 UEs, the throughput of non-GBR traffic keeps increasing linearly with the number of UEs. However, it decreases dramatically when there are more than 30 UEs because almost all of the RBs are allocated for GBR traffic.

For the AAG-LCG scheme, the throughput of non-GBR traffic is worse than that with AAG-2 scheme; it always decreases linearly with the increase of the number of UEs. So far, it seems that the AAG-LCG scheme does not differentiate the QoS of GBR1 and GBR2 traffic. However, let's observe the QoS in terms of packet delay shown in Fig. 5. For the AAG-LCG scheme, the delay of high priority GBR1 is always shorter than that of GBR2. While the delay of GBR bearer for AAG-2 is between them. That means the AAG-LCG scheme does differentiate the QoS of GBR1 and GBR2 traffic in terms of delay.

As for the delay of non-GBR traffic with AAG-LCG scheme, even though it is as short as 9 ms when the eNB is light loaded with 10 UEs, it diverges when the load increases. As a result, it is not shown in the figure. The delay of non-GBR traffic with AAG-2 scheme is better, it is as short as 30 ms when the eNB is light loaded with 20

UEs. However, when there are 30 UEs, because most of the RBs are occupied by GBR traffic, the delay of non-GBR traffic diverse and is not shown in the figure.

Let's return to Fig. 4, which illustrates the utilization of RBs. The two curves of AAG-2 and AAG-LCG almost coincide except when there are 20 UEs. The reason is that AAG-2 transmits more non-GBR traffic when there are 20 UEs as shown in Fig. 4.

The figures illustrated above reveal that the AAG-LCG scheme can divide the user traffic into GBR1, GBR2, and non-GBR traffic with different QoS in terms of throughput or delay. It meets the requirement that bears can be divided into four LCGs and scheduled with different QoS (Fig. 6).

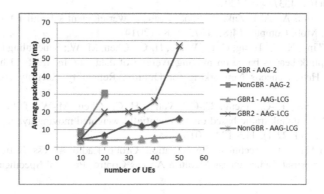

Fig. 6. Comparing the average delay of different LCGs for different schemes

5   Conclusion and Future Works

The 3GPP has suggested divide bearers into four LCGs to alleviate the signaling load of BSR. In this paper, based on the specification, we present an AAG-LCG scheme. This scheme classifies user traffic bearers into different LCGs according to the specification. Simulation results reveal that AAG-LCG can provide bearers of different LCGs with different QoS in terms of throughput and/or delay. Because there is always tradeoff between the QoS of GBR (including GBR1 and GBR2) traffic and RB utilization (and also the QoS of non-GBR traffic), the future work is investigating how to adjust the parameters so as to balance these performance metrics.

Acknowledgments.. This paper is supported by Ministry of Science and Technology of Taiwan under grant no. 104-2221-E-197-007, 104-2221-E-197-009, 104-2221-E-197-016. The authors also would like to thank Shing-Jye Huang, who helped the simulation work.

References

1. de Temino, L.R., Berardinelli, G., Frattasi, S., Mogensen, P.: Channel-aware scheduling algorithms for SC-FDMA in LTE uplink. In: IEEE 19th International Symposium on Personal, Indoor and Mobile Radio Communications, PIMRC (2008)

2. Liu, F., She, X., Chen, L., Otsuka, H.: Improved recursive maximum expansion scheduling algorithms for uplink single carrier FDMA system. In: IEEE 71st Vehicular Technology Conference (VTC 2010-Spring), pp. 1–5 (2010)
3. Lee, S.-B., Pefkianakis, I., Meyerson, A., Xu, S., Lu, S.: Proportional fair frequency-domain packet scheduling for 3GPP LTE uplink. In: IEEE INFOCOM (2009)
4. Calabrese, F.D., Michaelsen, P.H., Rosa, C., Anas, M., Castellanos, C.U., Villa, D.L., et al.: Search-tree based uplink channel aware packet scheduling for UTRAN LTE. In: IEEE Vehicular Technology Conference, VTC Spring, pp. 1949–1953 (2008)
5. Kaddour, F., Vivier, E., Mroueh, L., Pischella, M., Martins, P.: Green opportunistic and efficient resource block allocation algorithm for LTE uplink networks. IEEE Trans. Veh. Technol. 64(10), 4537–4550 (2015)
6. Kalil, M., Shami, A., Al-Dweik, A.: QoS-aware power-efficient scheduler for LTE uplink. IEEE Trans. Mob. Comput. 14(8), 1672–1685 (2014)
7. Kuo, F.-C., Ting, K.-C., Tseng, C.-C., Wang, H.-C., Chen, M.-W.: Scheduling both GBR and non-GBR uplink bearers based on moving average of data rate. In: IEEE 11th International Conference Heterogeneous Networking for Quality, Reliability, Security and Robustness (2015)
8. Kuo, F.-C., Ting, K.-C., Tseng, C.-C., Wang, H.-C., Chen, M.-W.: Differentiating and scheduling LTE uplink traffic based on exponentially weighted moving average of data rate. Mob. Netw. Appl. 22(1), 113–124 (2016)
9. 3GPP TS36.321, R13: Technical Specification Group Radio Access Network; Evolved Universal Terrestrial Radio Access Medium Access Control Protocol Specification (2015)

Time Detection Based Hybrid Clustering Strategy for JP-CoMP in LTE-A

Fengfei Song[✉], Liqiang Zhao, Kai Liang, and Cheng Guo

State Key Laboratory of Integrated Service Networks, Xidian University,
Xidian 710071, Shaanxi, China
Song.fengfei@hotmail.com

Abstract. Coordinated multipoint (CoMP) has been applied as a key technology to enhance the coverage of cell and mitigate the intercell interference (ICI) in LTE-A. Traditional fundamental research of cell clustering for CoMP concentrates on both static and dynamic clustering. However, in the high data demands and heavy ICI scenario, both the static and dynamic clustering cannot ensure good Quality of Service (QoS) for User Equipments (UEs). Hence, in this paper, we formulate the problem to maximize cell-edge throughput and analysis the system complexity, and the time detection based hybrid clustering strategy for JP (Joint Processing)-CoMP is proposed to solve this problem. Based on LTE system level platform, simulation results show that the proposed scheme has better performance than static clustering even gets close to dynamic clustering with less complexity.

Keywords: JP-CoMP · Hybrid clustering · Time detection · ICI · LTE-A

1 Introduction

Demands for mobile communications services and high data rates are increasing rapidly, which require better performance of wireless mobile communication service. Frequency reuse is an effective solution to meet the high data rate. The long-term evolution-advanced (LTE-A) system adopts Orthogonal Frequency Division Multiple Access (OFDMA), which can enhance the spectral efficiency as far as possible. Meanwhile, OFDMA can better eliminate the intra-cell interference with the cost of greater ICI. To mitigate the ICI, the 3rd Generation Partnership Project (3GPP) proposed CoMP and Inter-Cell Interference Coordination (ICIC) in LTE-A. Fundamental research has proved that CoMP is an advanced wireless mechanism to mitigate ICI, enhance the spectral efficiency and cell edge data rates [1].

The most basic principle of CoMP is to utilize multiple transmit and receive antennas from several different Transport Points (TPs). By making use of co-channel interference among different coordinated cells in coordinated downlink transmission, CoMP can effectively improve the interference environment to

© ICST Institute for Computer Sciences, Social Informatics and Telecommunications Engineering 2017
J.-H. Lee and S. Pack (Eds.): QShine 2016, LNICST 199, pp. 365–373, 2017.
DOI: 10.1007/978-3-319-60717-7_36

enhance the signal quality as well as to improve spectrum efficiency and increase the coverage area [2]. During the evaluation of CoMP, in Release 11, different kind of CoMP schemes have been put forward under a tight backhaul between eNBs, such as Coordinated Scheduling and Coordinated Beamforming (CS/CB) and JP [3]. The latter promises larger throughput and spectral efficiency than CS/CB by changing the interference signal into useful signal.

CoMP may require additional signal overhead on the air interface and backhaul. Therefore, only a limited number of TPs can participate in cooperation to meet the limited capacity backhaul demands. User selection should be done to indicate which TPs should form cooperation clusters [4]. Multi-trans points form a cluster which jointly serves a group of UEs in CoMP, the key of clustering for JP-CoMP is designing proper scheduling scheme to suppress the ICI.

In general, clustering can be categorized into static and dynamic clustering. Static clustering is designed based on geographical criteria as the position of TPs and the surrounding of cells, and the cooperative TPs will keep constant over time [4,5]. Therefore, it requires little signal overhead and less complexity. In addition, there are many strengths of static cluster such as fairly simple clustering algorithms, low complexity and relatively stable system. However, due to the irregular movement of UEs and the fast change of the interference environment, it cannot provide best serving performance to each UE in actual application. In the case of dynamic clustering, the system continuously adapts the clustering strategy to meet the fast change of UE locations and radio frequency (RF) conditions [4–6]. Because of its stronger sensitivity and adaptability to channel changes, dynamic clustering can guarantee the system performance keeps in the optimal state. But with the fast change of cluster structure, leading to high information sharing and heavily backhaul delay among cooperative TPs [7], meanwhile, the complexity of the system increased comparing to the static clustering.

In this paper, we propose a time detection based hybrid clustering strategy, for the purpose of maximizing the throughput of cell edge and minimizing the system complexity. Basing on the LTE system level platform, the performance gain is evaluated in terms of cell-edge and average throughput, system complexity and spectral efficiency.

The rest of the paper is organized as follows. In Sect. 2, we state a centralized cluster with JP-CoMP model for time detection based hybrid clustering, and the detail description of proposed scheme is given in Sect. 3. The simulation results and discussion are provided in Sect. 4 and followed by conclusions in Sect. 5.

2   System Model

To illustrate the system models for CoMP in downlink transmission, a centralized cluster with JP-CoMP model [4,7] is considered in this paper, as show in Fig. 1. A central unit (CU) performs all preprocessing for a cluster of cooperating cells. In other words, the CU collects the UEs' CSI firstly. Secondly the clustering strategy and coordinated scheduling to optimize network performance in coordination area are processed. Finally, those signal will be quantized and transmitted to each TP.

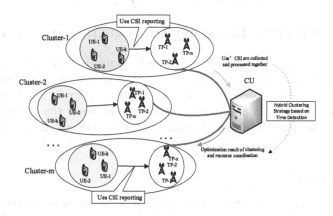

Fig. 1. System model

Each eNB serves three hexagonal cells through three high transmission power Remote Radio Heads (RRHs) that each cover one cell area. Following 3GPP standards, we considered the homogeneous network consisting of 7 eNBs that each one has three sectors, thereby making a total number of 21 sectors. The path loss between UEs and TPs is given by [5].

$$PL = 130.5 + 37.6 \lg(\frac{d}{km})[dB] \tag{1}$$

The antenna loss is affected by many factors, such as the antenna azimuth of TPs and UE, maximum attenuation. We consider the 20 dB as the maximum attenuation, and the antenna model is:

$$AL(\theta) = \min(12|\frac{\theta}{65}|^2, 20)[dB] \tag{2}$$

Assume that there are M UEs and N cells. The signal to interference plus noise ratio (SINR) of the mth UE in the Kth cluster [5] can be expressed as:

$$SINR_m^K = \frac{P \cdot \sum\limits_{k \in K} \lambda_m^k}{P \cdot \sum\limits_{k \in \{N \backslash K\}} \lambda_m^k + \sigma^2}[dB] \tag{3}$$

where λ_m^k represents the path gain of the UE m served from the coordinated cell k. P is the transmission power of the RRH and σ^2 is the noise power the UE m has received.

The received power of UE m^k is given by:

$$Pr_m^k = P - PL_m^k - AL(\theta_m^k)[dB] \tag{4}$$

In addition, the throughput of the mth UE in the Kth cluster can be expressed as:

$$TP_m^K = B \cdot \log(1 + SINR_m^K)[bps] \qquad (5)$$

3   Time Detection Based Hybrid Clustering Strategy

As mentioned in previous sections, the mechanism of static clustering cannot provide best serving performance for UEs. In the meanwhile, the dynamic clustering may cause heavy backhaul delay and high complexity. Therefore, we aim at maximizing the cell edge throughput and minimizing the system complexity and the time detection based hybrid clustering strategy is proposed in this paper.

3.1   Basic Idea

Time detection means in every major cycle, and for those base stations (BSs), whose channel state have no significant change, and the coordinated cluster of those BSs will not change obviously. In other words, their coordinated cluster will appear repeatedly or with high probability in one period. Therefore in next major cycle, those clusters appearing repeatedly or with high probability will use static clustering, and dynamic clustering will be used to those variable structure clusters. This is mentioned as hybrid clustering and specific introduction will be given in the next section.

3.2   The Proposed Solution

We consider a major cycle L consists of nT (T represent one Transmit Time Interval (TTI)), and set a experienced threshold value $SINR_{th}$ to distinguish the edge and center UEs.

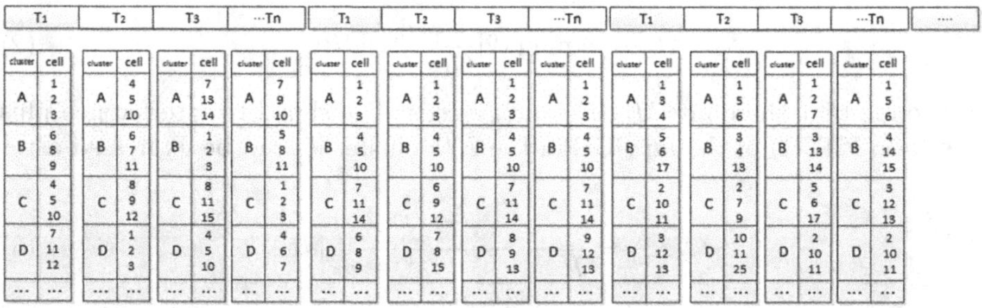

Fig. 2. Cluster structure instructions for time detection based hybrid clustering strategy

Figure 2 is an example for the time detection based hybrid clustering, and the proposed scheme works as following steps:

- *step*1. Dividing the edge and center UEs:
  - if $SINR_m^K < SINR_{th}$, the UE m is considered as cell edge user;
  - else if $SINR_m^K \geq SINR_{th}$, the UE m is considered as center user.
- *step*2. Dynamic clustering for cycle L_1. And storage the clustering information $C_1 = \{C_{11}, C_{12}, C_{13}, \ldots, C_{1i}\}$ [1].
- *step*3. Divide cluster information C_1 into three types[2]:
  - fixed structure cluster $F_1 = \{F_{11}, F_{12}, F_{13}, \ldots, F_{1i}\}$
  - high frequency cluster $H_1 = \{H_{11}, H_{12}, H_{13}, \ldots, H_{1j}\}$
  - variable structure cluster $V_1 = \{V_{11}, V_{12}, V_{13}, \ldots, V_{1k}\}$.
- *step*4. Clustering in cycle L_2.
  - if $F_1 \neq \emptyset$ or $H_1 \neq \emptyset$, using hybrid clustering. Static clustering[3] for those cells of F_1 and H_1, dynamic clustering for the rest cells of V_1.
  - else if using dynamic clustering for all cells.
- *step*5. Loop *step*2 to get clustering information C_2 and classified to get the results of F_2, H_2, V_2.
- *step*6. Simplified dynamic clustering of L_3.
  - the member cells of F_2 and H_2 give priority to the members of the same cluster when doing dynamic clustering in cycle L_3
- *step*7. End.

3.3   Analyzation and Discussion

First in each cycle L_n, each UE reports its CSI to the serving eNB in every TTI. Then CU can make the best resource allocation scheme and optimizing clustering strategy for coordinated cells according to CSI. In addition, in *step*4, static cluster is used to those cells belonging to F_i and H_j to reduce the cost of computation, and dynamic clustering is used to adapt the fast changing of wireless channel from BS to UEs. Moreover, the structure of F_i and H_j may have changed through serval cycle because of the change of wireless channel environment due to UEs random motion. So every few cycles one global dynamic clustering operation is necessary. In our scheme, the operation of dynamic clustering is used every three cycles. Finally, the *step*6 can not only reduce the complexity for the dynamic clustering in our architecture, but also balance the changes of wireless environment.

Taking advantages of dynamic clustering and static clustering, the proposed strategy makes clustering decision aiming at optimizing the system performance and minimizing the system complexity based on channel conditions in the previous and current slots.

---

[1] Such as clusters of (1,2,3), (4,5,10),...,(7,11,12) constitute C_{1i} in Fig. 2.

[2] As shown in Fig. 2, the fixed structure such as cell 1, 2, 3 is integrated a cluster (1,2,3) in each TTI of cycle L_1. The cluster (4,5,10) which appears frequently in most of TTI of cycle L_1 represents the high frequency cluster. Moreover the cluster structure changes obviously refers to variable structure cluster, such as clusters (6,8,9), (7,11,12) and (6,7,11).

[3] On the basis of the fixed structure of F_1 and H_1, (1,2,3) and (4,5,10) is processed as static cluster, and the cells of V_1 clustering in the mechanism of dynamic clustering for cycle L_2 in Fig. 2.

4   Simulation Results

According to Release 11 [8], some simulation parameters are used in the LTE system level simulator. First, we simulate 7 eNBs with 21 sectors using 2.14 GHz as the LTE frequency and 20 MHz as the bandwidth, the inter site distance (ISD) is considered as 500 m in the urban area. Besides, there are 20 UEs randomly distributed in one cell, the total of UE is 420, and they irregularly moving with the rate of 5 km/h. The full buffer traffic model is considered in our simulation. Some simulation parameters are listed in Table 1. Figure 3 shows SINR and the assignment of eNBs.

Table 1. Model parameters

Parameters	Value
Cell layout	7 eNBs/21 sectors (cells)
UE number	20 UEs/cell, total 420 UEs
ISD	500 m
Carrier frequency	2.14 GHz
Bandwidth	20 MHz
UEs rate	5/3.6 m/s
Resource block	100 RBs/cell
Scheduler	Round-robin
Traffic model	Full buffer
Channel model	ITU Pedestrian B channel
Simulation time	50 TTI

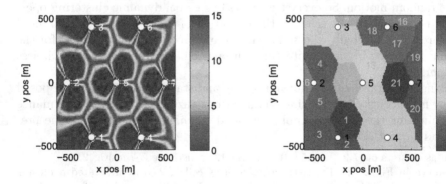

Fig. 3. SINR for different area, the assignment of eNBs and sectors

To verify the performance of the proposed scheme, we simulate Non-CoMP, Static-cluster and Dynamic clustering with different optimization criteria for comparison.

Figure 4 shows the evaluation of UEs throughput, and the cumulative density functions (CDF) is plotted in the Fig. 5. The corresponding simulation value of mean throughput, cell-edge throughput and peak throughput for four schemes are listed in Table 2. As shown in Fig. 4, the throughput of cell-edge UEs sharply increase after taking the operation of JP-CoMP. In addition, the mean and peak throughput also get improvement. What's more, the cell-edge throughput of hybrid clustering is better than static clustering and close to dynamic clustering.

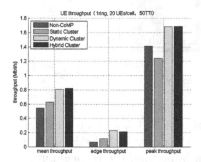

Fig. 4. UEs throughput   Fig. 5. UEs throughput CDF

Table 2. The UEs throughput (Mbit/s)

Throughput	Non-CoMP	Static	Dynamic	Hybrid
Edge	0.07(0)	0.12(↑71.4%)	0.23(↑228.6%)	0.21(↑200.0%)
Mean	0.54(0)	0.63(↑16.7%)	0.81(↑50.0%)	0.82(↑51.9%)
Peak	1.41(0)	1.24(↓12.1%)	1.68(↑19.1%)	1.69(↑19.9%)

In the previous introduction, we expect to reduce the complexity to cut the system overhead. By recording the simulation runtime and normalized processing, the evaluation of normalized complexity compared to dynamic cluster is shown in the Fig. 6. We can easily know that the complexity of our scheme is slightly higher than static clustering, but slightly lower than dynamic clustering. The algorithm complexity of hybrid clustering is between static clustering and dynamic clustering. Hence, the proposed clustering algorithm can not only enhance the cell-edge throughput but also reduce the complexity. It can be a very practical scheme for limited overhead JP-CoMP system.

The Figs. 7 and 8 show the average coordinated cell throughput and the average spectral efficiency of Non-CoMP, static clustering, dynamic clustering and hybrid clustering. And the simulation values of cell throughput are 10.88, 12.61, 16.17, 16.38 (Mb/s), compared with Non-CoMP, increasing by 15.9%, 48.6% and 50.5%. In addition, the spectral efficiency are 0.67, 1.05, 1.13, 1.14

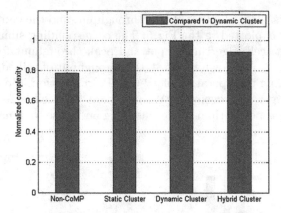

Fig. 6. Normalized complexity.

(bit/cu), and increasing by nearly 49.2%, 68.6% and 70.1% matching to Non-CoMP, respectively. In short, it clearly shows that the proposed hybrid clustering strategy performs as good as dynamic cluster in improving the throughput for UEs.

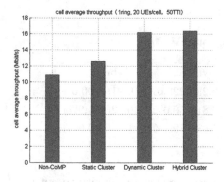

Fig. 7. Cell average throughput

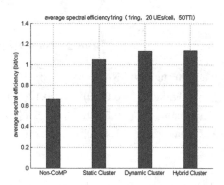

Fig. 8. Average spectral efficiency

5   Conclusion

In this paper, we investigate the homogeneous network CoMP architecture, and propose a time detection based hybrid clustering strategy for JP-CoMP. The simulation results show that our scheme can not only enhance the cell-edge throughput and spectral efficiency but also reduce the system complexity compared to non-CoMP, static and dynamic clustering based on LTE system level simulator. Hence, it can be more suitable to the limited overhead CoMP system.

Acknowledgement. This work was supported in part by National Natural Science Foundation of China (61372070), Natural Science Basic Research Plan in Shaanxi Province of China (2015JM6324), Ningbo Natural Science Foundation (2015A610117), National Science and Technology Major Project of the Ministry of Science and Technology of China (2015zx03002006-003), and the 111 Project (B08038).

References

1. Muqaibel, A.H., Jadallah, A.N.: Practical performance evaluation of coordinated multi-point (CoMP) networks. In: Proceedings of the 8th IEEE GCC Conference and Exhibition (GCCCE), Muscat, pp. 1–6. IEEE Press (2015)
2. Ali, M.S., Synthia, M.: Performance analysis of JT-CoMP transmission in heterogeneous network over unreliable backhaul. In: International Conference on Electrical Engineering and Information Communication Technology (ICEEICT), Dhaka, pp. 1–5. IEEE Press (2015)
3. Cui, Q., Wang, H., Hu, P., Tao, X., Zhang, P., Hamalainen, J., Xia, L.: Evolution of limited-feedback CoMP systems from 4G to 5G: CoMP features and limited-feedback approaches. IEEE Veh. Technol. Mag. **9**(3), 94–103 (2014). IEEE Press
4. Weber, R., Garavaglia, A., Schulist, M., Brueck, S., Dekorsy, A.: Self-organizing adaptive clustering for cooperative multipoint transmission. In: 73rd Vehicular Technology Conference (VTC Spring), Yokohama, pp. 1–5. IEEE Press (2011)
5. Marsch, P., Fettweis, G.: Static clustering for cooperative multi-point (CoMP) in mobile communications. In: 2011 IEEE International Conference on Communications (ICC), Kyoto, pp. 1–6. IEEE Press (2011)
6. Irmer, R., et al.: Coordinated multipoint: concepts, performance, and field trial results. IEEE Commun. Mag. **49**(2), 102–111 (2011)
7. Lee, H.J., Won, S.H., Kim, Y., Lee, J.: Centralized resource coordination scheme for Inter-enB CoMP with non-ideal backhaul. In: Globecom Workshops (GC Wkshps), Austin, TX, pp. 827–832. IEEE Press (2014)
8. 3GPP TR 36.819: Coordinated multi-point operation for LTE physical layer aspects (2011)

SNCC 2016

A Cross-Layer Protocol with High Reliability and Low Delay for Underwater Acoustic Sensor Networks

Ning Sun[1], Huizhu Shi[1], Guangjie Han[1(✉)], Yongxia Jin[1], and Lei Shu[2]

[1] College of Internet of Things Engineering, Hohai University, Changzhou, China
sunn2001@hotmail.com, graphite_123@126.com, hanguangjie@gmail.com, jinyx@hhu.edu.cn
[2] Guangdong University of Petrochemical Technology, Maoming, China
lei.shu@ieee.org

Abstract. A cross-layer protocol is proposed to deal with the problems of high latency, low bandwidth and high bit-error-rate (BER) in underwater acoustic sensor networks (UASNs). Nodes are organized as clusters based on depth and the nodes with same depth belong to same cluster and cluster head (CH) is chosen by the CH in high-level depth. At network layer, nodes in different depths send packet to their CH hop by hop and CH transmits the aggregated data to the one-depth higher CH till the data arrives at sink node in surface; At MAC layer, a CSMA/CA-based MAC protocol is used in each cluster while CHs use a pre-defined schedule to allocate the channel; At physical layer, nodes change the transmission power and frequency to decrease channel collision and energy consumption in a self-adaptive way. According to the simulation results, it brings benefits in improving transmission reliability and decreasing transmission delay.

Keywords: Underwater acoustic sensor networks · UASN · Cross-layer · Reliability · Low delay

1 Introduction

Underwater wireless sensor networks (UWSNs) [1] refers to the network in which the underwater sensor nodes with low energy consumption and shorter communication distance are deployed to the underwater area and the network are established in a self-organizing way. UWSNs often subject to the following challenges:

The work is supported by "Qing Lan Project", "the National Natural Science Foundation of China under Grant 61572172", "the Fundamental Research Funds for the Central Universities, No. 2016B10714".

© ICST Institute for Computer Sciences, Social Informatics and Telecommunications Engineering 2017
J.-H. Lee and S. Pack (Eds.): QShine 2016, LNICST 199, pp. 377–386, 2017.
DOI: 10.1007/978-3-319-60717-7_37

(1) Acoustic communication is generally adopted in UWSNs due to its physical characteristics. However, bandwidth achievable in underwater acoustic signals is strictly limited;
(2) Underwater channel attenuation is serious and the attenuation is variable;
(3) Due to the flow of water currents, drift may cause the sensor node's communication connection not reliable, and high BERs and temporary communication interruptions may occur;
(4) Node battery energy is limited and it is difficult to replaced [2].

Traditional wireless sensor network protocol uses a layered architecture, therefore when designing the network, each layer is designed to be independent of each other. Although the method of layered protocol makes the design simple, but it cannot guarantee the optimal design of the entire network. By using adaptive cross-layer protocol in sensor networks and considering the network protocol stack as a whole, levels that do not adjacent to each other can logically achieve more balanced performance [3].

In this paper, a novel cross-layer protocol is proposed to deal with the problems of high BER and high latency in UASNs. Based on depth in water, the nodes are organized as different clusters. The nodes in same depth organizes a cluster. The first-depth CH is chosen by sink node in water surface and then it designates the second-depth CH and CHs are chosen by this way in turn. At network layer, nodes in different depths send packet to their CH hop by hop and CH transmits the aggregated data to the one-depth higher CH till the data arrives at sink node in surface; At MAC layer, a CSMA/CA-based MAC protocol is conducted in each cluster while CHs use a pre-defined schedule to allocate the channel; At physical layer, nodes change the transmission power and frequency to decrease channel collision and energy consumption in a self-adaptive way. The proposed cross-layer protocol integrating the physical layer, MAC layer and network layer optimizes network performance in terms of reliability and latency.

The paper is organized as followings: In Sect. 2, we discuss several related works. In Sect. 3, we present the proposed cross-layer protocol in details. In Sect. 4, some simulations are conducted and the results are discussed. In the end, we draw the conclusion in Sect. 5.

2   Related Works

In recent years, cross-layer protocols for UASNs continue to be presented [4–7]. [5] proposes an underwater cross-layer protocol, assessing different power and frequency allocation scheme with the minimal energy consumption. The method uses DACAP protocol in MAC layer, and the functions of MAC layer and physical layer are closely coupled. And it uses FBR protocols in routing layer, which determines the routing protocols used in different standards, and then uses different power levels. But it needs to send RTS, CTS packet to exchange information in FBR protocol, that easily lead to excessive delays in underwater wireless sensor networks. At the same time, when the network is sparse, it has to repeatedly expand the size of the arc to find the next hop nodes [6].

[7] proposes a centralized cross-layer scheduling protocol for underwater wireless sensor networks, analyzing the relationship between transmission power and distance and frequency in underwater single link. Cluster heads collect and estimate the delay and distance information of each node by broadcasting beacon form. In the MAC layer, scheduling each link to reduce conflicts, by considering the characteristics of the delay of underwater link; In the physical layer, sensor nodes reduce energy consumption by adaptively changing the transmission frequency and transmission power. However, this method is only applicable to a centralized network, and when the network nodes is more, further consideration of energy-saving strategies is needed.

3 The Cross-Layer Protocol for UASNs

3.1 Network Model

Supposing that sensor nodes are deployed in a small-scale marine area, the marine areas can be represented by a cube model. With base station deployed in the middle of the horizontal plane, nodes underwater are deployed at different levels. In addition, different levels of sensor nodes carry different depth information. And we only analyze three-layer model, which is shown in Fig. 1. The nodes with the same depth of information can be divided into a cluster.

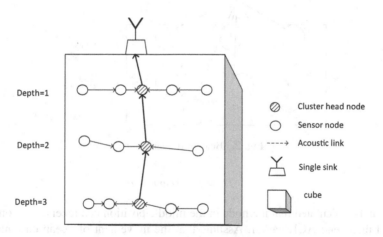

Fig. 1. Network model

3.2 Algorithm for Cluster Head Election

Sink node transmits a beacon message to elect the header of cluster in which the depth equals one (depth = 1). After receiving the beacon, the corresponding sensor nodes send an ACK message to the sink node in a competition period T1, using CSMA mechanism. Sink node records the ACK information received from the first record, and selects the head node of cluster in which the depth equals one (depth = 1). At the end of the competition period T1, the appointment message will be sent to the corresponding cluster head node and the election of cluster head in the first cluster is completed.

(1) The beacon sent by sink node includes message that the value of depth (Depth = 1), the position of the sink node, and the time permitted for ACK.
(2) Normal sensor nodes sends an ACK message to the sink node in a competition period T1, using CSMA mechanism. If some nodes failed to send ACK on time, they will abandon sending ACK. So it can avoid conflict with the appointment message from sink node.
(3) Once receive appointment messages, CH whose depth value equals one will broadcast the message that itself has been the cluster head node, with the maximum level of power. Other normal nodes in the cluster will record the ID and position of CH once they receive the message from the CH. Then, the CH continues to transmit a beacon message to elect the CH in which the depth equals two (depth = 2). And so on, CH of each depth and the propagation route between CHs have been formed.
(4) As is shown in Fig. 2, The formula of the relationship between the propagation loss and the distance in UASNs is:

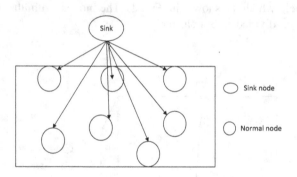

Fig. 2. Beacon transmission

$$TL = n \cdot 10 \lg r + \alpha r \tag{1}$$

It can be calculated that the node in the middle position can receive beacon earlier and then send ACK earlier. Assume that the movement of ocean currents cause the absolute position of the nodes to changes, but the relative position is substantially unchanged. As a result, frequent re-election of cluster node is not a must.

(5) Taking the energy of cluster into consideration, sink node can send reset massage after a long time. Waiting for all nodes have stopped transmission, the next round of initialization will be launched.
(6) Take underwater model of three-layer depth as an example, sink grasps the deep information of sensor networks in advance. Transmission slots of each cluster head are ruled in beacon messages while the route between clusters is formed as soon as the cluster head is elected. When the information collection in the cluster

is ended, CH in the bottom of the slot allocation will send information it has collected to the CH which is in superior depth, uploading the data to another after the data fusion.

3.3   The Cross-Layer Mechanism

3.3.1   Initialization

The goal of initialization is to realize the partition of clusters, the election of cluster head nodes, and the formation of routing path from nodes to sink node.

(1) *Divided clusters*

First, we need to establish the marine cube model. The base station is deployed in the middle of level, and assuming that the movement of ocean currents cause the absolute position of the nodes to changes, but the relative position substantially unchanged.

Sink node transmits a beacon (beacon) message to elect the header of cluster in which the depth equals one (depth = 1). After receiving the beacon, the corresponding sensor nodes sends an ACK message to the sink node in a competition cycle T1, using CSMA mechanism. Sink node records the ACK information received from the first record, and selects the head node of cluster in which the depth equals one (depth = 1). At the end of the competition period T1, the appointment message will be sent to the corresponding cluster head node and the election of cluster head node in the first cluster is completed.

The cluster head node who receives appointment messages will broadcast the message that itself has been the cluster head node, with the maximum level of power. Other normal nodes in the cluster will record the ID and position of the cluster head node once they received the message from the cluster head node. Then, the cluster head node whose depth equals one will transmit a beacon message to elect the header node of cluster in which the depth equals two (depth = 2). And so on, the cluster head node of each depth and the propagation route between cluster head nodes has been formed.

Normal nodes in the cluster who received the broadcast message from the cluster head node can obtain transmission power level Pr based on received signal strength (RSSI) and then can calculate the path loss according the formula:

$$\text{Ploss} = \text{PAP} - \text{sent} - \text{Pr}. \tag{2}$$

Also, they can estimate the distance between themselves and cluster head node according to the formula:

$$d = g(\text{Ploss}, f). \tag{3}$$

If the $d < d_{\text{onedrop}}$, the node is determined within the range of own-hop of head node in a cluster, and it then transmits ACK message to the cluster head node. A star topology has been formed around the cluster head node and is shown in Fig. 3.

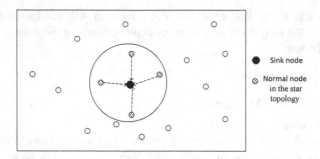

Fig. 3. Star topology

(2) *Distance estimation in the star topology*

Once received the broadcast message from the cluster head node, Normal nodes in the cluster can obtain transmission power level Pr based on received signal strength (RSSI) and then can calculate the path loss according the formula 2.

Also, they can estimate the distance between themselves and cluster head node according to the formula 3.

And preparing for power control, they can estimate both distance and optimal communication threshold $R_{threshold}$ witch can determine the optimum power to neighboring nodes successful communication.

(3) *Delay estimation in the star topology*

According to the agreement of [7], in star topology, sensor nodes in the one hop range of the cluster head node using CSMA mechanism to send ACK information to CH. Once CH receives ACK, it can estimate value of the propagation delay *tp* according to the propagation time difference [8]. The propagation time difference is shown in Fig. 4.

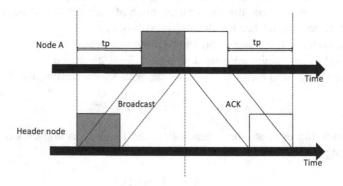

Fig. 4. Delay estimation

3.3.2 Communication Phase

(1) *Collision Avoidance between clusters*

As shown in Figs. 5 and 6, different clusters will be divided into different communication slots in the election when chose the cluster head node. First, sink node transmit time schedule by beacon transmission, and the time schedule will be transmitted to other normal nodes in the cluster and the cluster head node whose depth value is bigger than one by broadcast. In T1 slot, the sensor node whose depth equals one (depth = 1) will send an ACK message to the sink node. The T3 slot is for cluster internal information collection.

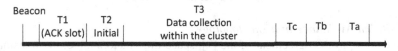

Fig. 5. Room graph slot

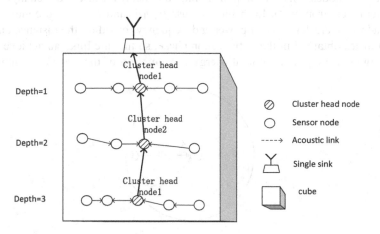

Fig. 6. Routing process

Take the underwater model with three depths for example, in Ta slot, CH3 will send the fusion date to CH2 with maximum level of power. in the slot *Tb*, CH2 fuses date, and then sends the date to CH 1. in *Tc* slot, CH1 will send the fusion date to the sink node with maximum level of power.`

(2) *Collision Avoidance within clusters*

As shown in Fig. 5, in T3 slot, data is transmitted within the cluster. As shown in Fig. 7, the nodes in the hop range of cluster head nodes only receive data and do not transmit data in the period T3-1; the nodes in the hop range of cluster head nodes communicate with the cluster head node in the period T3-2; and in the period Ta/Tb/Tc, other normal nodes in the cluster go to sleep, the cluster head node sends date to the sink node in assigned time period.

As shown in Fig. 8, normal nodes in the cluster send RTS to node A, and nodes around reply CTS that contains location information and residual energy. Then node A chooses node B who has short distance. Therefore, conflict within the cluster can be effectively avoided. Then node A sends data that contains the ID of node B to node B.

Fig. 7. Cluster head timeslot

(3) *Collision Avoidance in a star topology*

According to the agreement of the [7], space-time factors affect the transmission power between the two nodes. And node adjust the power based on spatial factors, adjust the delay according to the time factor (spatial factors include the distance between nodes, time factors including the delays caused by changes in the external environment). Each link can use *fopt(d)* and *Popt(d)* to control of their head to the cluster channel power and frequency, based on the distance and delay estimates obtained in the initialization phase, so that the link can achieve optimal energy consumption, the total energy consumption of the system is minimized.

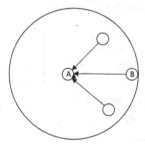

Fig. 8. Normal nodes send CTSs.

In underwater environment, the link propagation delay from point to point is longer, so the delay from each cluster to head node is not the same. Therefore, in order to avoid conflicts, it can make full use of system resources in time. through reasonable scheduling. As is shown in Fig. 9, when the cluster head node broadcasts a scheduling package, the delay of the package arrives at the node A and node A is Ta and Tb. If $2tB > 2tA + TdataA$, although the nodes A and B send signals to the cluster head in the same time, signals will arrive cluster head without conflict. The data transfer time *Tdata* can be calculated according to the transmission data packet length *Ddata*:

$$Tdata = Ddata/Rate. \qquad (4)$$

and Rate is the transmission rate.

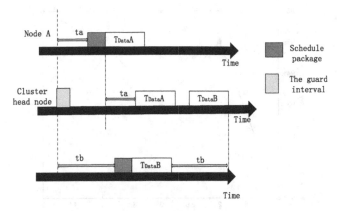

Fig. 9. MAC schedule.

4 Performance Evaluation

In this part, we simulate this protocol in MATLAB to evaluate the performances in terms of transmission reliability and delay. Simulation scenario is similar to the topology shown in Fig. 1. The underwater acoustic sensor network is deployed on the bottom of a shallow water volume of $100*100*600$ m^3. Sink node is fixed at the center of a horizontal plane. The generation of data follows the Poisson distribution, and wave frequency is set to 5–25 kHz, the control packet length is set to 30bits, the packet length is set to 1024bits, and the threshold level is set to SNR = 20 dB.

When the depth of the network topology is 1, 2, 3, 4, 5, the success rate of transmission and propagation delays are calculated. Simulation results are shown in Figs. 10 and 11.

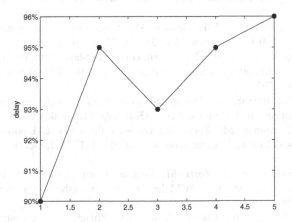

Fig. 10. The relationship between delay and layers

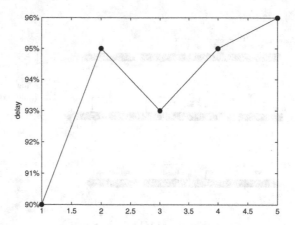

Fig. 11. The relationship between success rate and layers

5 Conclusion

A new method of cross-layer communication is proposed to deal with the high-latency, low-bandwidth and high-BER in UASNs, using cluster-based routing protocol. At MAC layer, it solves the collision between clusters and within cluster. At physical layer, nodes self-adaptively change transmission power and transmitting frequency to decrease energy. According to the simulation results, the proposed protocol achieves benefits in optimizing network performance.

References

1. Davis, A., Chang, H.: Underwater wireless sensor networks. In: 2012 IEEE Oceans, pp. 1–5 (2012)
2. Han, G.J., Jiang, J.F., Wan, L.T., Guizani, M.: Routing protocols for underwater wireless sensor networks. J. IEEE Commun. Mag. **53**(11), 72–78 (2015)
3. Han, G.J., Dong, Y.H., Guo, H., Shu, L., Wu, D.P.: Cross-layer optimized routing in wireless sensor networks with duty-cycle and energy harvesting. J. Wirel. Commun. Mob. Comput. **15**(16), 1957–1981 (2015)
4. Langendoen, K., Reijers, N.: Distributed localization in wireless sensor networks: a quantitative comparison. J. Comput. Netw. **43**(4), 499–518 (2003)
5. Jornet, J.M., Stojanovic, M., Zorzi, M.: On joint frequency and power allocation in a cross-layer protocol for underwater acoustic networks. J. IEEE J. Oceanic Eng. **35**(4), 936–947 (2010)
6. Jornet, J.M., Stojanovic, M., Zorzi, M.: Focused beam routing protocol for underwater acoustic networks. In: the Third ACM International Workshop on Underwater Networks, pp. 75–82 (2008)
7. Huang, C.B., Zheng, X.W., Gao, L., Yang, G.S., Zheng, J.C.: A centralized cross-layer scheduling protocol in UWSNs. J. Transducer Microsyst. Technol. **33**(10), 121–124 (2014)
8. Chen, Y.J., Wang, H.L.: Ordered CSMA: a collision-free MAC protocol for underwater acoustic networks. In: 2007 IEEE OCEANS, pp. 1–6 (2007)

An Optimization Technique of Spatial Reuse for Communication in Smart City Environment

Cong Ran, Qing-guo Xiong, Wen-xiang Li[✉], and Xia Wei

School of Information Science and Engineering,
Wuhan University of Science and Technology, Wuhan 430081, China
liwx2006@hotmail.com

Abstract. In the application scenario of smart city, there exist many portable mobile devices that communicate in Wi-Fi technique, so communication conflicts among them are unavoidable and lead to low network performance and high energy consumption. To address this problem, this paper studies the optimization method of spatial reuse based on dynamic control of transmit power. Considering the metric of spatial reuse factor, this paper explores how to select the proper transmission radius and power to decrease the adverse effects from the hidden terminals and the exposed terminals. By setting the frame control field in the MAC layer frame according to the received signal strength, the method can adaptively adjust the transmission power of the communication nodes pair to maintain the reception power in the appropriate range. Through the simulation experiment in NS-2, the feasibility and effect of the optimization method for spatial reuse and energy saving are verified.

Keywords: Smart city · Power control · Communication conflict · Spatial reuse

1 Introduction

In the wireless network for smart city environment, many Wi-Fi based smart devices share a common wireless channel and operate independently; thus, communication collisions among them may happen frequently, these will affect effective utilization of precious resource of space and time [1]. Moreover, as these devices have limited energy supply, unnecessary energy consumption will shorten the effective network lifetime [2]. To address these problems, a optimization method for spatial-reuse based on adaptive power control is proposed. This method can achieve the dynamic adjustment of transmit power and communication radius based on the received signal strength. Thus, wireless nodes in the network can avoid the problems such as the low ratio of spatial utilization caused by the exposed terminals and communication collision caused by the hidden terminals, and yield improved network availability and less energy consumption.

The rest of this paper is organized as follows. Section 2 analyzes the effect of power control and the influence of propagation radius on spatial reuse. Section 3

© ICST Institute for Computer Sciences, Social Informatics and Telecommunications Engineering 2017
J.-H. Lee and S. Pack (Eds.): QShine 2016, LNICST 199, pp. 387–395, 2017.
DOI: 10.1007/978-3-319-60717-7_38

proposes the method for implement spatial reuse based on power control. Section 4 conducts the simulation evaluation for the proposed method. Last, Sect. 5 gives the conclusions.

2   The Analysis on Optimal Spatial Reuse

2.1   The Effect of Power Control

Generally the two-ray ground reflection model [3] is applied to describe the characteristics of channel fading in the smart city environments. In this model, the total received signal strength is the superposition of the direct signal strength and the reflected signal strength. Thus, the reception power of this model is

$$P_r = P_t G_t G_r \frac{h_t^2 h_r^2}{d^4} \tag{1}$$

In (1), P_t and P_r are the transmission power and reception power respectively, G_t and G_r are the gains of transmitting antenna and receiving antenna respectively, h_t and h_r are the heights of transmitting antenna and receiving antenna respectively, and d is the propagation distance.

As can be seen from (1), when P_r is constant, P_t is directly proportional to d^4, indicating that even minor increase of distance between the communication nodes can result in the significant increase of P_t. If the constant P_t is used, it will be impossible for the communication to get adapted to the influence of change in propagation distance. Thus, the multi-level power adjustment technique can reduce the energy consumption and improve the network performance:

(1) when the communication distance is shortened, both communication sides can reduce P_t to save energy consumption and reduce interference against other nodes.
(2) when the communication distance is lengthened, both communication sides can increase P_t to keep the communication connection stable, and avoid such processes as route reselection and reconnection as a result of the excessively low signal strength.

2.2   The Influence of Propagation Radius on Spatial Reuse

The RTS/CTS mechanism in IEEE 802.11 [4] can overcome the hidden and exposed terminal problems to a certain extent, but the mechanism is not effective and cannot guarantee QoS when nodes can move freely. When a connection is established between a pair of nodes through the RTS/CTS interaction, the DATA/ACK packet communication can be carried out. Other nodes newly entering the communication range may be ignorant of the RTS/CTS interaction happened just now and send their own data, thus, giving rise to communication collision. This is known as the invading terminal problem, which essentially refers to the hidden and exposed terminal problems occurring randomly during the dynamic movement of nodes. According to (1), for a certain P_t, P_r

is set to be equal to the minimum power required for correctly receiving packets, which is labeled as RXThresh with default value of 3.652×10^{-10}W. The corresponding communication radius R_t represents the maximum communication radius needed for correctly receiving packets in the absence of interference.

We assume that the interference exists in the channel, the communication is going on between nodes A and B, the transmission power of the interfering node C is P_{ti}, the P_i is the interfering signal power received by node A from node C, the gains and heights of all antennas are identical, the SNR threshold is label as SNR_THRESH, the distance between nodes A and C is r, and that between nodes A and B is d. It can be derived that, to correctly receive packets between nodes A and B, the SNR must satisfy (2).

$$SNR = P_r/P_i = P_t r^4 / P_{ti} d^4 \geq SNR\_THRESH \tag{2}$$

If $P_{ti} = P_t$, $r \geq \sqrt[4]{4SNR\_THRESH} \cdot d$ can be derived, so $r_{th} = \sqrt[4]{4SNR\_THRESH} \cdot d$ is set as the critical radius of the interfering signal, and other nodes beyond this radius will not interfere against A. If the relative distance d between nodes is given, r_{th} can also be determined. If different values of P_t are used for the nodes, there will be different values of R_t accordingly [5]. According to the correlation between r and R_t, two conditions as shown in Fig. 1 are concluded as follows.

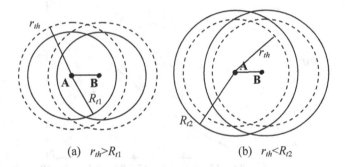

(a) $r_{th} > R_{t1}$ (b) $r_{th} < R_{t2}$

Fig. 1. Interference coverage under different conditions

(1) Figure 1(a) corresponds to the hidden terminal problem [6]. When the communication radius is smaller than the interference range, i.e., $R_{t1} < r_{th}$, the nodes inside the two dashed circles and outside the two solid circles may affect the normal communication between nodes A and B.

(2) Figure 1(b) corresponds to the exposed terminal problem. When the communication radius is larger than the interference range, i.e., $R_{t2} > r_{th}$, the nodes inside the two solid circles and outside the two dashed circles are covered by communication signals, but in fact these nodes will not affect the normal communication between nodes A and B.

For the sake of simplicity, only the case of single-hop links is considered, and the Spatial Reuse factor (*SRI*) is defined as the ratio of the total area that may generate interference against communication to the total area covered by the signals of both communication sides, i.e., the ratio of the total area of the two dashed circles to the total area of the two solid circles in Fig. 1. It represents the efficiency of spatial reuse. When d/Rt is set as a variable and SNR_THRESH = 10, the expression of *SRI* can be written as

$$SRI = \frac{13.4247(d/R_t)^2}{6.28 + (d/R_t)\sqrt{1 - (d/R_t)^2/4} - 2\arccos[(d/R_t)/2]} \tag{3}$$

The curve of *SRI* [7] is drawn in Fig. 2. As can be seen from Fig. 2, to achieve the best level of spatial reuse (i.e., the point on the curve where *SRI* is 1), $d = 0.56R_t$ is required. At this point, both the hidden and exposed terminal problems do not exist, and the optimal reception power is $P_{rop} = 10*$RXThresh. The curve where *SRI* > 1 corresponds to the hidden terminal problem, and that where *SRI* < 1 corresponds to the exposed terminal problem. The communication radius can be changed to achieve the optimum state by adaptive power control, thus to make the optimal utilization of the wireless channel and avoid channel collision.

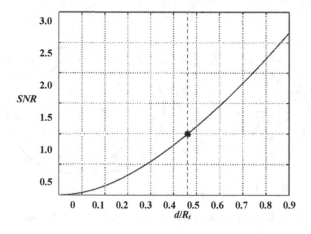

Fig. 2. SRI change with d/R_t

3   The Implementation of the Optimal Spatial Reuse

3.1   The Interference-Aware Setting of Reception Power Range

Given that small-scale fading effect exists in the wireless channel and the P_r of each packet changes randomly, it is difficult to accurately control P_t in reality. Considering that we try to achieve $P_r = P_{rop}$, and generally $P_{ti} \neq P_t$ in actual situations, the value of P_{rop} depends on the specific situations.

(1) When $P_{ti} < P_t$, strong communication signals between nodes lead to the exposed terminal problem, and the channel may not be fully utilized, but the communication without interference can be realized as no hidden terminal problem exists.

(2) When $P_{ti} > P_t$, there are stronger interference signals; at this moment, the exposed terminal problem disappears while the hidden terminal problem exists, and the communication interference may be generated.

One feasible solution is to limit P_r within a proper range to generate less interference to other communications and achieve the optimal spatial reuse. According to (2), when $P_{ti} = kP_t$ ($0 < k < 5$), we assume the interference is tolerable, and the optimal reception power is $P_{rop} = 10\ k*$RXThresh. Thus, the desired reception power range is set as (4).

$$P_r \in \begin{cases} [10k \times RXThresh, 10RXThresh] & 0 < k \leq 1 \\ [10RXThresh, 10k \times RXThresh] & 1 < k < 5 \end{cases} \tag{4}$$

When P_{ti} is very strong (corresponding to $k \geq 5$), it is impossible and unnecessary to adjust transmission power for continuing communication. In such case, the "Wait-to-Restore" mechanism can be employed, and the relevant steps include:

(1) suspend the communication and saving the communication state;

(2) set the timer according to the NAV field from the received interfering packet;

(3) enter the sleep state and wait until the communication of interference nodes finishes;

(4) after the waking up of relevant nodes, complete the paused transmission and reception of the remaining packets.

3.2   The Interaction Mechanism Between Nodes

Power control is realized by the feedback mechanism. Based on the IEEE 802.11 protocol, the corresponding "power adjustment information piggyback" function is added to the MAC layer, and P_t is modified synchronously at both communication sides. The specific conditions are as follows:

(1) When the sender transmits DATA packet to the receiver, the receiver judges if it is necessary to adjust P_t according to the P_r from the obtained packets. The receiver sets the instruction requiring the sender to carry out power control in the frame control field of ACK packets, and sends the ACK packets with the modified P_t.

(2) When the receiver replies to the sender with an ACK packet, the sender acts as the feedback provider who will judge whether it is necessary to adjust P_t according to the P_r of the received ACK packet. It sets the instruction requiring the receiver to carry out power control in the frame control field of the next DATA packet, and sends the DATA packet with the modified P_t.

3.3   The Trigger Mode of Power Control

Since the signal strength of packets can objectively reflect the communication links' quality, it can be used as a reference for power control. As the actual P_r may be different from the theoretical value derived from (1) due to the small-scale fading effect, it is necessary to consider the macroscopic statistical characteristics of small-scale fading and use the statistical average of the recently received packets to represent the effective P_r value. Therefore, the feedback provider maintains a queue of PrRec[N], stores the P_r values of N recently received packets [8]. Further the feedback provider designates two counters, i.e., *LoCnt* and *HiCnt*, to represent the number of packets when P_r is below the lower limit (10*RXThresh) and above the upper limit (50*RXThresh) respectively. Besides, two dynamic count ranges for *LoCnt* and *HiCnt*, i.e., R_L and R_H, are initialized with N respectively.

When a packet is received, the range that this packet's P_r falls into is judged, and the corresponding counter is updated if necessary. The relevant rules to be observed are:

(1) When the counter value exceeds the threshold ($0.5*R_L$ or $0.5*R_H$), the new transmission power and the frame control field of feedback packet are set.
(2) When the counter value is between the threshold and 0.2 N, the binary exponential back-off process is used to reduce the length of the count range to reflect new states.
(3) When the counter value is below 0.2 N, the length of the count range is increased linearly until the range restores to N.

Figure 3 shows the detailed process on how a newly received packet is processed.

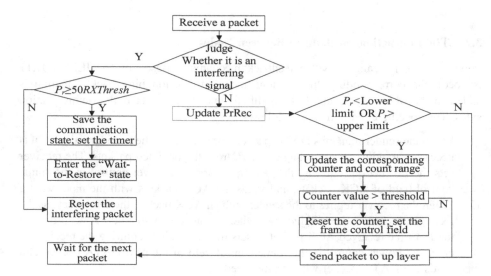

Fig. 3. The packet processing process

3.4   The Calculation of New Transmission Power

For setting the frame control field, we take P_r of the latest M packets from RrRec [N] and the previous transmit power P_{t0} as the reference for calculating new transmission power. Considering $d \propto \sqrt{4P_t/P_r}$, we define the equivalent distance d_e for this M packets as

$$d_e \propto \frac{1}{M} \sum_{s=1}^{M} \sqrt[4]{\frac{P_{t0}}{(P_r)_s}} \tag{5}$$

According to (1), we obtain the new optimal transmit power P_{tn} in (6).

$$P_{tn} = 10RXThresh(\sqrt[4]{P_{t0}} \frac{1}{M} \sum_{s=1}^{M} \frac{1}{\sqrt[4]{P_{rs}}})^4 \tag{6}$$

4   Numerical Evaluation

4.1   The Settings of Simulation

The network performance is analyzed among three schemes with the simulation experiment in NS-2 [9], the schemes include: the scheme that transmits by default transmission power of 0.2818 W without power control (NoPC), the scheme using the 10 preset power levels for multi-level power control (SimPC) [10], and our proposed scheme using the adaptive power control for spatial reuse optimization (AdpPC).

The nodes movement scenario is set as follows: 36 nodes move randomly at the speed of 5 m/s in a 1200 m*1200 m area. There are five traffic scenarios of different traffic volumes, i.e., 3, 6, 9, 12 and 15 traffic flows respectively for each scenario. Each flow uses the constant bit rate (CBR) sources and the transmitting rate is 1000 packets per second. The duration of each flow is 25 s and the total simulation time lasts for 100 s. For different schemes, the following four performance indexes are calculated: (1) *AvePt* – the average transmit power; (2) *RtOh* – the routing overhead, i.e., the ratio of the number of total routing packets to the number of total received packets; (3) *PDR* – the packet arrival ratio; (4) *ThrPt* – the network throughput measured in Mega Byte.

4.2   Simulation Results and Analysis

The results of simulation are shown in Fig. 4. As can be seen from Fig. 4(a), SimPC achieves the best energy-saving effect as it can use extremely low P_t when the communication distance is short. The energy-saving effect achieved by AdpPC is also obvious, although slightly inferior to SimPC, for this scheme can restrict the increase of P_t by confining P_r of the packets below the upper limit. According to Figs. 4(b) and (c), AdpPC achieves the lowest *RtOh*, the highest *PDR*, and the least collision arising from hidden terminals. Following it is SimPC which can also control P_t to a certain degree to reduce communication interference. As the communication traffic volume increases, there is more severe communication collision, which will increase *RtOh* and reduce *PDR*. From Fig. 4(d), it can be seen that AdpPC prevails over other schemes. It achieves the optimal network performance by appropriately adjusting the communication radius to eliminate collision and making the best use of the limited space.

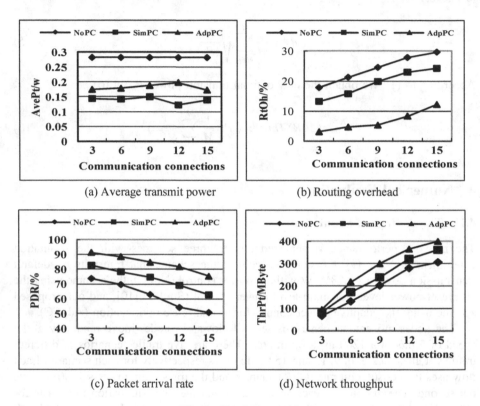

(a) Average transmit power   (b) Routing overhead

(c) Packet arrival rate   (d) Network throughput

Fig. 4. Simulation results

5   Conclusion

In the proposed method, the channel condition is obtained based on the signal strength of the received packets, so the data sender can get accurate guidance to use appropriate power for communication and effectively utilize space and energy. The topic to be explored in future include the following. In-depth analytical work needs to be conducted on spatial reuse in the case of complex topology structures. Besides, the proposed method can also be used in conjunction with other optimization techniques for spatial reuse, such as dual-channel, directional antennas and cognitive access.

Acknowledgement. Supported by the Scientific Research Foundation for Returned Overseas Chinese Scholars of State Education Ministry (the 50th, 2015).

References

1. Zhu, C., Leung, V.C.M., Shu, L., Ngai, E.C.-H.: Green internet of things for smart world. IEEE Access. **3**, 2151–2162 (2015)
2. Zhu, C., Yang, L.T., Shu, L., Leung, V.C.M., Hara, T., Nishio, S.: Insights of top-k query in duty-cycled wireless sensor networks. IEEE Trans. Ind. Electron. **62**(2), 1317–1328 (2015)
3. Zhu, C.-S., Shu, L., Hara, T., Wang, L., Nishio, S., Yang, L.T.: A survey on communication and data management issues in mobile sensor networks. Wirel. Commun. Mob. Comput. **14** (1), 19–36 (2014)
4. Mattbew, S.: Gast: 802.11 Wireless Networks – The Definitive Guide. O'Reilly, Sebastopol (2005)
5. Zhu, C., Yang, L.T., Shu, L., Leung, V.C.M., Rodrigues, J.J.P.C., Wang, L.: Sleep scheduling for geographic routing in duty-cycled mobile sensor networks. IEEE Trans. Ind. Electron. **61**(11), 6346–6355 (2014)
6. Santi, P.: Topology Control in Wireless Ad Hoc and Sensor Networks. Wiley, Hoboken (2005)
7. Ye, F.J., Yi, S., Sikdar, B.: Improving spatial reuse of IEEE 802.11 based Ad hoc networks. In: IEEE GLOBECOM, pp. 1013–1017. IEEE (2003)
8. Klemm, F., Ye, Z., Krishnamurthy, S.: Improving TCP performance in ad hoc networks using signal strength based link management. Ad Hoc Netw. J. **4**(3), 123–129 (2004)
9. The CMU Monarch Project Group. The CMU Monarch Project's Wireless and Mobility Extension for ns [EB/OL] (2012-01-12) [2012-08-06]
10. Agarwal, S.: Distributed power control in ad hoc wireless networks. In: Personal, Indoor and Mobile Radio Communications, vol. 2, no. 6, pp. 59–66 (2001)

Efficient Beacon Collision Avoidance Mechanism Using Neighbor Tables at MAC Layer

Ke Wang, Wei Chen$^{(\boxtimes)}$, Junna Zhou, and Yang Zhang

School of Computer Science and Technology,
China University of Mining and Technology, Xuzhou, China
chenw@cumt.edu.cn

Abstract. NLC-BOP algorithm is proposed for the beacon collision problem in IEEE802.15.4. Beacon collision is divided into direct conflict and indirect conflict and NLC-BOP algorithm is used to solve these two kinds of beacon collision problems. NLC-BOP algorithm based on BOP uses neighbor tables to solve beacon collision. The coordinator establishes 1 hop and 2 hop neighbor tables at MAC layer and allocates the beacon transmitting order for other coordinators at the same time. Finally, the size of the BOPL can be estimated and we make assumption and processing for the coordinator of death and isolation. The simulation results indicate that new algorithm compared with the original algorithm greatly reduces energy consumption, packet loss rate. In the case of guaranteeing delay, it improves the throughput.

Keywords: IEEE802.15.4 · MAC · Beacon collision · Neighbor tables

1 Introduction

There are beacon mode and non-beacon mode of MAC layer in IEEE802.15.4. In the non-beacon mode, nodes are always active in the network. However, in the beacon mode, coordinators periodically transmit beacon frame and make nodes synchronization. A personal area network (PAN) is composed of multiple nodes and the coordinator transmits a packet to another coordinator through direct links or multiple hops. If the node is not succeed to access the channel, the node will discard the packet and then a new packet is generated in the next superframe [1]. Beacon collision will be caused when multiple devices almost join piconet at the same time. Each device selects its own beacon slot in order to avoid collision. Choosing improper beacon slot leads to repeated collision and then increases time overhead achieving devices synchronism. When the device is not able to avoid repeated collision, it is difficult for the device to join piconet, even in deadlocks [2].

In IEEE802.11, using RTS (request to send) and CTS (clear to send) avoids beacon collision. There are no RTS/CTS in IEEE802.15.4. In order to overcome the problem, TG4b groups provide two beacon scheduling techniques: superframe duration scheduling (SDS) and beacon only period (BOP). [3, 4] allows the network to dynamically modify the BOP length for better adapting the dynamic network. The

© ICST Institute for Computer Sciences, Social Informatics and Telecommunications Engineering 2017
J.-H. Lee and S. Pack (Eds.): QShine 2016, LNICST 199, pp. 396–405, 2017.
DOI: 10.1007/978-3-319-60717-7_39

results also show the throughput ratio of the dynamic BOPL is better than BOP. There is much technology to solve the beacon collision through multiple channels. [5] presents a fixed channel management mechanism which divides network into several sub network. Each sub network occupies a channel and using BOP beacon scheduling technique in the internal of sub network. [6] proposes a receiver tracking contention (RTC) scheme, which achieves high throughput by allowing the receivers to assist for channel contention. In RTC, link is the basic unit for channel access contention. Specifically, transmitter is used to contend for the channel and receiver is used to announce the potential collision. [7] presents VFA, namely virtual frame aggregation, to achieve high coordination efficiency by amortizing the overhead over multiple transmissions. [8] aims at mitigating the so-called Funneling Effect for S-MAC, particularly by improving the throughput and fairness of S-MAC.

There never will be beacon collision in a single star topology of the IEEE802.15.4. But there is more or less beacon conflict in mesh network [9]. In multihop mesh network, each node periodically transmits its beacon and then monitors whether there are others or their activities by checking beacon. As a result, losing beacon message cause low efficiency and high cost [10, 11]. When multiple nodes send a beacon to the same place at almost the same time, there will be continuous collision which blocks the normal operation of the network. Nodes can not join the piconet. When the beacon information contains key information, such as network and time parameters, the topology of the network will be destroyed [12].

Researchers have proposed a variety of methods to solve the beacon collision problem. An adaptive beacon scheduling with power control in cluster-tree network is presented [13]. The scheduling mechanism assumes that LR-WPANS (low-rate wireless personal networks area technology) technology can support environmental monitoring applications in IEEE 802.15.4 standard. Node clustering is a very effective method to manage topology in wireless sensor networks, which can reduce the beacon collision and improve the network lifetime [14]. The author improve the above method by allocating the accurate beacon sequence values and superframe values for coordinator cluster, coordinators PAN and device nodes and determining the exact time of the PAN and coordinator nodes beacon transmission. Game theoretical models are used in the wireless medium access control [15]. To avoid the beacon collision, every coordinator decides its time to send beacon frame according its transmission probability and power level. A new beacon slot technique (TBoPS) is presented in cluster tree topology [16]. In order to avoid the beacon collision in the large-scale IEEE 802.15.4 cluster tree Zig Bee network, a beacon scheduling using utilization-aware hybrid is presented [17]. This method can improve the scheduling performance of the target network by better using the transmission medium and avoid the inter-clusters collision. Simple time conversion scheme is presented based on IEEE 802.15.4 [18, 19]. SDS and BOP basic beacon scheduling mechanisms are analyzed [20].

In the article, NLC-BOP algorithm is proposed to avoid beacon collision without using multichannel. Analyzing nature of the direct and indirect conflict, NLC-BOP tries its best to use neighbor tables to avoid occurrence of beacon collision. The remaining part of the paper is organized as follows. The details of our algorithm are described in Sect. 2, where we propose a beacon collision improvement method. The simulation results of experiments and performance evaluation are presented in Sect. 3. We conclude our algorithm in the last section.

2 NLC-BOP Algorithm

In view of the two kinds of conflict, this paper puts forward the NLC-BOP (Neighbor List Control–Beacon Only Period) algorithm which adopts coordinator neighbor table to solve beacon conflict based on the BOP. NLC - BOP algorithm includes three parts. The first part is set up the coordinator neighbor list and beacon order allocation and the second part chooses BOPL length. The third part processes the dead or isolated coordinators.

2.1 Neighbor Table Establishment and Order Allocation

To simplify the narrative language, we set the following variables. 1 hop coordinator neighbor table, 2 hops coordinator neighbor table, beacon order which a coordinator sends in BOP.

Steps:

(1) PAN coordinator establishes the main network and the order is 1.
(2) After a new coordinator joins the network, the first broadcast around the hello beacon. Once A coordinator receives the hello beacon, the address of the new coordinator joins one, and then putting one in beacon A to broadcast.
(3) If the new coordinator continues receiving the beacon frames from around B, it first looks at whether address of the beacon B in their two. If in two, the address is removed from the two and added to one. If not in the two, it adds the address to the one directly. At the same time processing the one of beacon B one, it adds the address which does not exist in one to two.
(4) If there will be other coordinators around the new coordinator, it will perform step 3 repeatedly. The new coordinator argues that it has received all beacon frames which sent by other coordinators after t seconds.
(5) New coordinators view their own one and two and choose a minimum order that has not yet appeared as the value of the order.
(6) The new coordinator sends beacon frames with its beacon order; around 1 hop coordinator perfects its own one after receiving beacon frames and transmits the information to the peripheral coordinators at the same time in order to make some coordinators perfect the two of themselves.
(7) Network building repeats steps 2 to 6 until the entire network is steady.

Now analyzing t value of the above 4 steps. We assume that there is no beacon conflict or missing during building tables. Communication range of nodes is r, the density of nodes deploy is ρ and receiving a beacon frame average every θ seconds.

So the number of node is *num* as (1) within the scope of the new communication coordinator.

$$num = \rho \pi r^2 \tag{1}$$

The minimum value of t is $t_{\min}$, such as (2) formula (2).

$$t_{\min} = num * \theta \tag{2}$$

Due to the assumptions, there is no beacon conflict and missing during building tables, so the actual value of t is much larger than $t_{\min}$. According to the (1) and (2), we get $t \propto \rho$ and $t \propto r^2$. So deployment and power control of the nappropriate nodes will lead t increasing sharply and it is harmful for the establishment of the neighbor tables.

2.2 BOPL Length Estimation

How to estimate the BOPL approximation and as far as possible to expand the length of the CAP are an important purpose of NLC-BOP. In Fig. 4, this article assumes that beacon length is the fixed symbols λ, the time slot between the beacons is the SIFS and 12 symbols are default. So sending a beacon frame need to consume $12 + \lambda$ symbols in BOP phase.

Running after a period of time on the Internet, NLC-BOP will assign a beacon order for each coordinator, so there is a maximum of order in this network. Assuming the value is μ.

According to the assumption of values, we can get the minimum value $BOPL_{\min}$ of BOPL that network requires, as shown in the (3).

$$BOPL_{\min} = \mu * (12 + \lambda) \tag{3}$$

And the size of a time slot cycle is *SlotLength*, as shown in the (4).

$$SlotLength = aBaseSlotDuration * 2^{SO} \tag{4}$$

Assuming that the *SO* of network is α, the default value of aBaseSlotDuration is 60. So we rewrite the (4) and get the (5).

$$SlotLength = 60 * 2^{\alpha} \tag{5}$$

According to the (3) and (5), we obtain n time slots at least which meet the needs of the BOPL.

$$n = \left\lceil \frac{BOPL_{\min}}{SlotLength} \right\rceil \tag{6}$$

Through the (6) we infer that the network may occur the following two situations. The first situation: After allocating BOPL, the rest number of symbols is $(aNumSuperframeSlots - n) * 2^{SO} = (16 - n) * 2^{\alpha}$, it still meet the minimum aMin-CAPLength of CAP and the default value is 440 which indicates that the network is normal and do not need to adjust. The second situation: If excessive nodes are deployed densely or at the PHY layer use improper RF power, it will lead to the nodes increase sharply in the neighbor table which needs more beacon order. By (3), BOPL will increase sharply. So after the assignment BOPL, the rest of the activity time slot can't meet the minimum of CAP. At this time we can take measures to increase the value of the SO to expand the network activity time, adjust the duty ratio, control the RF power and reduce the communication range. These measures are not in consideration of this paper, the concreteness can reference literature [3, 5], etc.

According to the Fig. 1 and (6), NLC-BOP selects BOPL whose unit is time slot. So the starting point of CAP should be placed at the beginning of a time slot rather than in the middle. As shown in Fig. 1, the starting of CAP is the point between the end of the second time slot and the start of third time slot. The purpose of NLC-BOP is to make it easier to coordinate each coordinator data transmission. At the same time set aside some time in preparation for later adding new coordinator at any time.

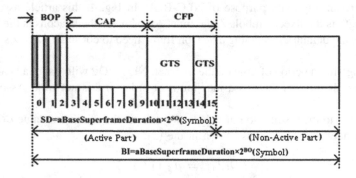

Fig. 1. Starting CAP based on NLC-BOP

According to Fig. 1 and combing the (4) with (6), we conclude how to calculate the values of the BOP, as shown in (7). We assume the node sending beacon order is *order*.

$$postBeaconDelay = N * SlotLength - [order * \lambda + (order - 1) * 12] \tag{7}$$

2.3   Coordinator Death or Isolation

NLC-BOP adds the neighbor tables based on IEEE802.15.4 and modifies the beacon frames. Def_macCAPStarting and def_macSendingBeaconOrder are added to the MAC_PIB, def_phyEnergyMultiple is added to PHY_PIB.

The data structure of the neighbor tables of 1 hop and 2 hop as shown in Table 1. NLC-BOP algorithm process is made the 1 hop neighbor table be loaded to BeaconPayload of beacon frames and is sent out with beacon frames.

Table 1. Neighbour list

Address of nodes	SendingBeaconOrder

A Flag is added to the beacon frames. But in the Flag, the previous two used to distinguish the hello beacon and beacon of death respectively, after six record beacon order of detail drawing 6 in Fig. 4. Specific is shown in Table 2.

Table 2. Structure of flag

Bit:0 1	1	2–7
IsHello	IsDeath	SendingBeaconOrder

According to Ho - j [3], we know that it is enough to use that distribute 16 orders for the network with 40 nodes. SendingBeaconOrder accounts for a total of 6 bits, 64 orders can be allocated which can meet the network that is not serious dense. According to IsHelloand and IsDeath of Table 2, we distinguish these frames: normal beacon frames, hello beacon frames, death beacon frames and beacon frames with sequence. Details as shown in Table 3.

Table 3. Four kind of beacon frame

IsHello 1	IsDeath	Type of frame
0	**0**	Normal beacon frames
1	**0**	Hello beacon frames
0 g	**1**	Death beacon frames
1	**1**	Beacon frames with sequence

3 Simulation Experiment and Analysis

The whole network simulation parameters are shown in Table 4. There are three graphs, respectively, the conflict rate chart, the average energy consumption graph, as well as three cases of effective throughput rate chart. Among them, the simulation

Table 4. Parameter of simulation experiment

Simulation parameters	Parameter values
Network size (m2)	500 × 500
Simulation time (s)	1000
Number of nodes	100
Topological structure	Reticular
Routing protocol	AODV
Packet size (B)	70
Queue length	30
Sending power (mW)	300
Receiving power (mW)	300
Initial energy (J)	1000

analysis of the effective throughput graph can obtain the relationship between the time interval T and BO, SO at the case of that SO was 3 and BO were 3, 4, and 5.

3.1 Conflict Rate Analysis

From Fig. 2, the network in about 100 s, the original algorithm beacon collision immediately increased significantly, while the new algorithm has also increased with slow speed. In 200 s, the highest point which the collision rate of the new algorithm reached only is the half of the conflict rate of the original algorithm. After 200 s to 250 s, the new algorithm has been assigned to the network to send a beacon sequence, resulting in a conflict rate of 300 s after the decline has been reduced, until the maximum simulation time of 1000 s, almost down to 1 points or less. And the original algorithm is still maintained a high rate of conflict, until the end of the simulation is also in a high position. Although the conflict rate of the original algorithm is not more than 20%, but the ratio of the conflict rate, that is, the ratio of the rate of conflict equals that original algorithm conflict rate divides conflict rate of the new algorithm. The result is that the conflict rate ratio was 100%, and finally up to more than 1600%. It can be concluded that the new algorithm can effectively reduce the beacon collision.

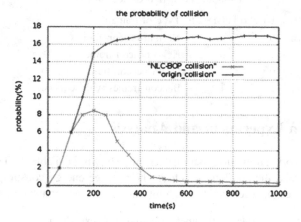

Fig. 2. Probability of collision

3.2 Energy Consumption Analysis

The average energy consumption of the original algorithm in the whole simulation for 1000 s is always stable, and it is in a linear trend. In the first 250 s of simulation, the new algorithm is faster than the original algorithm because of the need to establish the neighbor table and the allocation order. However, between 250 s to 400 s, the speed of energy consumption has eased. In 400 s time, the energy consumption of the algorithm has reached a balance, after the conflict rate of the new algorithm is much smaller than the original algorithm, so the energy consumption continues to decline, as shown in Fig. 3 in 400 s, the trend to maintain a slow rise.

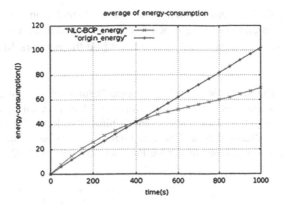

Fig. 3. Average of energy consumption

3.3 Goodput

Figure 4 shows the relationship between the different BO, SO and the sending data packet interval time with new algorithm. The effective throughput rate is directly related to the transmission data packet rate of the whole network simulation node. If the packet is sent too short or too fast at a time, it will cause the buffer queue of the node to be filled quickly, and then the packet will be discarded.

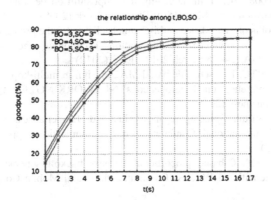

Fig. 4. Relationship among t, BO and SO

4 Conclusion

The paper proposes NLC-BOP algorithm based on IEEE802.15.4 protocol to solve the beacon collision which leads the performance of entire network to drop in the mesh network. At the beginning of the establishment of the network, the coordinators in the MAC layer build 1 hop and 2 hop neighbor tables and allocate the beacon order for the coordinators to avoid the emergence of beacon collision. Then, it estimates the size of

BOPL and deal with dead and isolated coordinators. Simulation results show that the NLC-BOP algorithm can solve the beacon collision problem and make the collision rate of the entire network significantly decrease, while the network life cycle is greatly extended.

Acknowledgment. The work is supported by National Natural Science Foundation and Shanxi Provincial People's Government Jointly Funded Project of China for Coal Base and Low Carbon (No. U1510115), the Qing Lan Project, the China Postdoctoral Science Foundation (No. 2013T60574), the National Natural Science Foundation of China (Grant No. 51404258), and the Natural Science Foundation of Jiangsu Province (no. BK20140202).

References

1. Buratti, C.: Performance analysis of IEEE 802.15.4 beacon-enabled mode. IEEE Trans. Veh. Technol. **59**(4), 2031–2045 (2010)
2. Vishnevsky, V.M., et al.: Study of beaconing in multihop wireless PAN with distributed control. IEEE Trans. Mob. Comput. **7**(1), 113–126 (2008)
3. Jeon, H.I., Kim, Y.: BOP (beacon-only period) and beacon scheduling for MEU (mesh-enabled USN) devices. In: 9th International Conference on Advanced Communication Technology: Toward Network Innovation Beyond Evolution, vols. 1–32007, pp. 1139-1142. IEEE, New York (2007)
4. Kim, E.J., Choi, H.H.: EBBS: energy-efficient BOP-based beacon transmission scheduling for WSNs. In: 2008 IEEE 19th International Symposium on Personal, Indoor and Mobile Radio Communications, pp. 810–815. IEEE, New York (2008)
5. Sahraoui, M.: Collisions avoidance multi-channel scheme for the protocol IEEE802.15.4. In: 2012 International Conference on Information Technology and e-Services (ICITeS), Piscataway, NJ, USA, 24–26 March 2012. IEEE (2012)
6. Dong, X., et al.: RTC: link schedule based MAC design in multi-hop wireless network. In: International Conference on Heterogeneous NETWORKING for Quality, Reliability, Security and Robustness (2015)
7. Dong, X., et al.: Virtual frame aggregation: clustered channel access in wireless networks. In: 2015 IEEE International Conference on Communications, pp. 3497–3502. IEEE, New York (2015)
8. Zhu, C., et al.: SMAC-based proportional fairness backoff scheme in wireless sensor networks. In: International Wireless Communications and Mobile Computing Conference (2010)
9. Woon-Yong, L., et al.: Distributed fast beacon scheduling for mesh networks. In: 2011 IEEE 8th International Conference on Mobile Ad-Hoc and Sensor Systems, 17–22 October 2011. IEEE Computer Society, Los Alamitos (2011)
10. Lee, J., Rhee, E.: Efficient beacon collision detection/avoidance mechanism in WLAN-based mesh networks. In: Gan, B., Gan, Y., Yu, Y. (eds.) Advances in Applied Materials and Electronics Engineering, pp. 501–504. Trans Tech Publications Ltd., Stafa-Zurich (2013)
11. Sanchez, J.A., Marin-Perez, R., Ruiz, P.M.: Beacon-less geographic multicast routing in a real-world wireless sensor network testbed. Wirel. Netw. **18**(5), 565–578 (2012)
12. Park, T.R., et al.: Stochastic beacon transmission in wireless sensor networks: IEEE 802.15.4 case. In: 2007 4th IEEE Consumer Communications and Networking Conference, vols. 1–32007, pp. 844–849. IEEE, New York (2007)

13. Cho, J., An, S.: An adaptive beacon scheduling mechanism using power control in cluster-tree WPANs. Wirel. Pers. Commun. **50**(2), 143–160 (2009)

14. Lee, B.H., Al Rasyid, M.U.H., Wu, H.K.: Analysis of superframe adjustment and beacon transmission for IEEE 802.15.4 cluster tree networks. EURASIP J. Wirel. Commun. Netw. **2012**(1), 219 (2012)

15. Kwon, Y.H., Rhee, B.H.: Bayesian game-theoretic approach based on 802.11 p MAC protocol to alleviate beacon collision under urban VANETs. Int. J. Automot. Technol. **17**(1), 183–191 (2016)

16. Nefzi, B., et al.: TBoPS: a tree based distributed beacon only period scheduling mechanism for IEEE 802.15.4. In: 2012 IEEE 8th International Conference on Distributed Computing in Sensor Systems (DCOSS), pp. 341–346 (2012)

17. Han, J., Lee, D., Lee, C.: Utilization-aware hybrid beacon scheduling in cluster-tree ZigBee networks. IEICE Trans. Inf. Syst. **E98D**(9), 1657–1666 (2015)

18. Wong, C.M., Chang, C.F., Lee, B.H.: A simple time shift scheme for beacon broadcasting based on cluster-tree IEEE 802.15.4 low-rate WPANs. Wirel. Pers. Commun. **72**(4), 2837–2848 (2013)

19. Kim, E.J., Youm, S., Choi, H.H.: Energy-efficient BOP-based beacon transmission scheduling in wireless sensor networks. IEICE Trans. Commun. **E91B**(11), 3469–3479 (2008)

20. Villaverde, B.C., et al.: Experimental evaluation of beacon scheduling mechanisms for multihop IEEE 802.15.4 wireless sensor networks. In: 2010 Fourth International Conference on Sensor Technologies and Applications (SENSORCOMM), pp. 226–231 (2008)

21. Lee, M., Zheng, J., Liu, Y., Shao, H.-R., Dai, H., Zhang, J., Jeon, H.: Combined beacon scheduling, proposal to IEEE 802.15.4b, September 2004

Industrial Wireless Sensor Network-Oriented Energy-Efficient Secure AODV Protocol

Weidong Fang[1], Chuanlei Zhang[2], Wei He[1(✉)], Wei Chen[3],
and Fengying Ma[4]

[1] Key Laboratory of Wireless Sensor Network and Communication,
Shanghai Institute of Micro-system and Information Technology,
Chinese Academy of Sciences, Shanghai 201800, China
{weidong.fang,hewei}@mail.sim.ac.cn
[2] School of Computer Science and Information Engineering,
Tianjin University of Science and Technology, Tianjin 300222, China
a17647@gmail.com
[3] School of Computer Science and Technology,
China University of Mining and Technology, Xuzhou 221116, China
chenw@cumt.edu.cn
[4] School of Electrical Engineering and Automation,
Qilu University Technology, Jinan 250353, China
mafengy@163.com

Abstract. As a traditional routing protocol, the Ad hoc On-demand Distance Vector routing (AODV) protocol has been applied in many Industrial fields. Meanwhile, researches on AODV have very in-depth, whether in improving performance, or enhancing security. Unfortunately, there are few researches on joint energy efficiency and security. In this article, we propose an Energy-efficient Secure AODV Protocol (E-SAODV) in Industrial Wireless Sensor Network (IWSN). In E-SAODV, the low complexity verification and the Delayed Transmitting Mechanism (DTM) is proposed and applied. The mechanism involve two parts: the polynomial of the Cyclic Redundancy Check 4 (CRC-4) that substitutes the shortest key of RSA digital signature in SAODV guarantees the integrity of data verification, and reduces storage space, computation and energy consumption. DTM is implemented to separate the check code and valid data, and to achieves tamper-proof. The simulation results show that comprehensive performance of proposed E-SAODV is a trade-off the energy efficiency and security, and better than AODV and SAODV, and could meet the requirement of the throughput in the industrial scene.

Keywords: Industrial Wireless Sensor Network · Security · AODV · Energy efficiency

1 Introduction

As the emergence and development of Wireless Sensor Network (WSN) [1], Cloud Computing [2], Big Data [3] and intelligent terminal, Industrial Wireless Sensor Network (IWSN) [4] has become networking technologies to lead the trends in technology

© ICST Institute for Computer Sciences, Social Informatics and Telecommunications Engineering 2017
J.-H. Lee and S. Pack (Eds.): QShine 2016, LNICST 199, pp. 406–415, 2017.
DOI: 10.1007/978-3-319-60717-7_40

development. IWSN is an interdisciplinary research, which involves automation, computer and communications. The requirements of IWSN mainly focused on the following fields: Localization [5], Optimization of Production Process [6], Equipment Monitoring and Maintenance [7] and so on.

Unfortunately, the particularity of the industrial environment makes application of IWSN have to consider some adverse factors: wireless signal multipath caused by reflection and scattering of large-scale equipment and metal pipes, interference to wireless communications caused by electromagnetic noise, which generated by the motor and equipment operation. Especially, in industrial production process, the key point of IWSN application is secure transmission of production process parameters. This is due to that network information security is facing a growing challenge. The possibility that control systems of industrial facilities are damaged by network intrusion does exist. Perhaps, this loss of risk may be too large to measure.

The promotion of open network technologies improve industrial data rate of transmission, and reduce the integration of information technology on the one hand. It also makes network security become more challenging. The information security in IWSN mainly involves information sensing security and network transmission security. Meanwhile, the low-power technology has been one of the hot topics [8]. In this paper, an Energy-efficient Secure AODV protocol is proposed to meet these requirements of defense attack and low-power in IWSN. The rest of this paper is organized as follows: in Sect. 2 a brief review of AODV and its evolution are given. The preliminary knowledge and analysis are represented in Sect. 3. The E-SAODV protocol is proposed, and simulation results and analyses of the proposed protocol are presented in Sect. 4. Finally, some concluding remarks are provided in Sect. 5.

2   Related Works

As a traditional routing protocol, AODV protocol has been a hot topic. At presented, research on AODV is divided into two categories: one is focus on enhancing its security; the other is improving its performances, such as reliability, transmission performance under dynamic topology, and so on.

2.1   Security Enhancement

As we all know, the design of AODV protocol does not take account for security. To meet different application requirements, various security schemes have been researched. These schemes mainly detect, defense or mitigate some specific attacks. In recent years, the studies have focused primarily on sinkhole attack, blackhole attack and Sybil attack.

Gandhewar and Patel proposed a mechanism for detection and prevention of Sinkhole Attack on the context of AODV protocol [9]. This mechanism of detection & prevention considered the behavior of sinkhole attack and AODV working, which mainly consist of four phases as Initialization Phase, Storage Phase, Investigation Phase, and Resumption Phase. The mechanism could improve the performance of

AODV under sinkhole attack. Tomar and Chaurasia put forward the mechanism of detection and isolation of sinkhole attack [10]. The key point of this mechanism is that a threshold value of sequence number was assumed based on average sequence number of packet to successfully received/transmitted by the destination and source node. Xiong et al. adopted the FP-Growth (Frequent Pattern Garwth) according to the AODV route table information, gave s rank sequence method for detecting black hole attack in ad hoc network [11].

As above mention, almost all of secure schemes and secure protocols in AODV only detected and defended/mitigated against the special attack. Unfortunately, these secure techniques seemed seldom to consider energy consumption.

2.2 Performance Improvement

AODV is a distance vector routing protocol [12]. It supports intermediate nodes reply, make source node quickly obtain routing, and effectively reducing the number of broadcast. Since nodes only store on-demand routing, the scheme reduces the memory requirements and unnecessary duplication. However, because of periodically broadcast packets, a certain energy consumption and network bandwidth have to be considered. Due to the existing of stale routing, AODV requires a relatively long latency to establish routes. Currently, performance improvements of AODV mainly involve in the following areas: Energy efficiency, improving throughput, load balancing and so on, especially, in the industrial scene.

Jain and Suryavanshi proposed a new maximum energy Local Route Repair (LRR) approach with multicast AODV routing protocol [13]. These schemes included two processes: establishing path and forwarding packets from source node to destination node. Joshi and Kaur aimed at improving the Infrastructure based AODV (I-AODV) routing by considering V2V (Vehicle to Vehicle) and V2I (Vehicle to Infrastructure) communication. I-AODV facilitated communication among vehicles through RSUs (Road-Side Units) and broadcasted in nature. They discussed prediction based multicasting which aided in reducing delay and improves other performance metrics, and applied multicasting to solve the purpose of proper utilization of resources as well as prediction technique helped in improving localization overhead [14].

From above analysis, enhancing security and improving performance have been research in AODV. Unfortunately, the joint works of above two aspects are seldom researched. Therefore, we will propose an Energy-Efficient Secure AODV Protocol (E-SAODV) in the following sections.

3 Preliminary Knowledge and Analysis

3.1 AODV

AODV is a source driven routing protocol [12], it could realize dynamic, bootable and multiple hops routing between mobile nodes, which are useful to establish and maintain the Ad hoc network. Because of the similarity between the Ad Hoc network and the wireless sensor network, the AODV protocol could also be used in the wireless sensor network. AODV protocol allows the mobile nodes to get the routing quickly and respond to link disruption and the network topology changes regularly. AODV protocol is non-cyclic, which avoid the Bellman-Ford "infinite computing" problem and could converge rapidly when the network topology changes. AODV will notify the affected nodes to avoid using the broken links when the link is destroyed. The AODV protocol involves two phases: route discovery and route maintenance.

3.2 Secure AODV

SAODV (Secure AODV) is an extension of the AODV routing protocol, used to protect routing discovery and provide security features, such as integrity, authentication and non-repudiation. SAODV assumes that each node has got the signing secret key pair from the asymmetric encryption algorithm. Moreover, every node could verify the relations between address and public key of the other nodes. SAODV needs key management mechanism and there are two mechanisms used to ensure the safety of AODV messages:

- Digital signatures: make sure that the message has not been tampered with.
- Hash chain: ensure the safety of variable hop in the message.

Authentication could be performed in the form of point to point for the immutable information, but that is not available for the variable information. It really doesn't matter which node initiate or forward routing error message, but instead adjacent nodes notifying the other nodes that could not be routed to a destination. Therefore, any node (initiate and forward routing error message) sign for *RERR* packet with a digital signature, any adjacent nodes received *RERR* packet verify the signature.

1. SAODV Hash chain
   Hash chain is used to detect the integrity of *RREQ* and *RREP* messages hop. By running the one-way Hash function to form the Hash chain. Every time one node initializes a *RREQ* or *RREP* messages, it performs the following operations:
   (1) Generate a random number (seed).
   (2) Set the maximum hop count *Max_Hop_Count* as the survival time *TTL*.
   (3) Set Hash as the seed value.
   (4) Set up the Hash function to be used
   (5) Calculate *Top_Hash* through the seed and *Max_Hop_Count*

   In which, *H* is a Hash function. *hi (x)* is the result running function h i times based on parameter *x*. Whenever a node receives message of *RREQ* or *RREP*, it performs the following operations to verify the hop. Hash function *h* is used to calculate Hash value *Max_Hop_Count* minus the value after Hash operations *Hop_Count* times, verifying whether the result is equal to the top of the Hash value.
   The node calculates new Hash value using Hash function before broadcasting *RREQ* or forwarding *RREP* again.

2. SAODV Digital Signature
   SAODV used asymmetric encryption, such as RSA for digital signature certification. The node used the only private key signature information first, and then uses

the public key that all nodes have to decrypt while the node receives encrypted signature. The demonstration is given below to illustrate RSA digital signature process.

(1) Choose two large prime numbers first, such as $p = 13$, $q = 11$;
(2) Calculate $n = p * q = 143$, $z = (p - 1) * (q - 1) = 120$;
(3) Choose a random private key $d = 19$ that co-prime of z;
(4) Assume e as the public key, require $e * d$ mod $z = 1$, choose $e = 139$.

3.3 Performance Analysis

As there is no security mechanism, AODV may be attacked by malicious nodes, compromised nodes and selfish nodes.

1. Message tampering attacks
   An attacker could change the content of the routing messages, for instance, while forwarding RREQ, an attacker could reduce the hop count to increase the probability chosen for routing, so that it could analyze the communication between source node and destination node. One aim of this attack is to increase the destination sequence number to make the other nodes believe that the routing is the latest. The simulation results show that, in some scenarios, an attacker could discard 75% of packets by manipulating the destination sequence number.
2. Message discarding attacks
   The attacker and selfish nodes could selectively discard (or all) the routing and data information. Because all mobile nodes could be used as terminal nodes or routing nodes, so this attack will lead the network paralyzed completely with the increase in the number of discarded messages.
3. Message replay (wormhole) attacks
   The attacker could make a retransmission of the eavesdropped message in different positions. One of the replay attacks is a wormhole attack. Wormhole attacker could uses private channel to transfer RREQ directly to the destination node. Because wormholes attackers may not increase jump number, which will prevent other routing from being found. Wormhole attack could be combined with information discarding attack to prevent destination nodes to receive packets.

SAODV ensures the safety of AODV by adding encryption arithmetic (Hash chain and digital signature).

4 Energy-Efficient Secure AODV Protocol

The use of RSA digital signature in SAODV is to guarantee the data is not tampered, and the use of Cyclic Redundancy Check (CRC) could also achieve this goal. CRC is a kind of error detection code, which usually used for detecting the unexpectedly data change in storage devices or Internet. Data uses CRC algorithm to get a check code, this code attached at the back of the original data is transferred with the original data, then the receiver reuses the same CRC algorithm to check whether the data been tampered with. Popular representation is that appends a piece of data behind the original data and make sure that could be divided exactly by specific values.

The shortest key of RSA digital signature is for 1024 - bit, the polynomial of CRC-4 is 5 bit; In addition, the computational complexity of CRC is much lower than that of RSA digital signature. So, we propose an Energy-efficient secure AODV protocol, which could effectively reduce the storage space and energy consumption of SAODV protocol, increase energy efficiency by using CRC instead of RSA digital signature to test whether the data has been changed.

4.1 Theoretical Derivation

1. Principal Algorithm

   Any binary strings could be written as a polynomial with coefficients of 0 or 1, for example: code '1101' could be written as polynomial '$x^3 + x^2 + x^0$'. Accordingly, polynomial '$x^4 + x^1 + x^0$' could be written as code '10011'.

The length of raw data is K, the polynomial of original data is set to $m(x)$, the length of check code for R, then the polynomial $g(x)$ is generated with $R + 1$ bits:

The division of formula (6) is die second division, that is, the highest power of the divisor and dividend is aligned, doing exclusive or calculation; In which, move $m(x)$ left to R places to get $M(x)$ times x^R, so as to empty out CRC check code for R places; $r(x)$ is the remainder that is CRC check code.

Attach the gotten CRC check code at the back of the next original data and then make a transmission together, the receiver divide the data by $g(x)$, and it represents the data has not been tampered with when there is no remainder.

2. CRC Tamper-proof Mechanisms

   Generally, the error caused by natural factors such as interference or harass could use the CRC mechanism detect the data which has been altered effectively, though if data is artificially manipulated and the CRC is changed at the same time by malicious nodes, it could not be detected whether the data has been tampered with the mechanism of CRC.

In order to defend the tamper attack, we would like to generate pseudorandom polynomials. Usually the polynomial generated by CRC is a kind of fixed form, so that malicious nodes could tampered with the data and CRC easily at the same time, while if we use pseudorandom polynomials, it could reduce the possibility of tampering with the data and CRC. The transmitter and the receiver only need to make an appointment about the sequence of the using of the polynomial generate by pseudorandom in advance. In addition, we could use broadcast authentication protocol μTESLA to release the secret key later, the transmitting of CRC latency once, and let the data and the corresponding CRC transmit separately, reduce the possibility of malicious nodes tampering with the data and CRC at the same time. The transmitter uses the generated polynomial $G(x)_i$ to calculate $R(x)_i$ when it transmits data $M(x)_i$, and transmit the last calculated $R(x)_{i-1}$. The receiver could receive the $R(x)_i$ and check the authenticity of the data using the generated polynomial $G(x)_i$ on a single latency.

3. Low Complexity Verification and Delayed Transmitting Mechanism
   In a sense, the entire points of using RSA digital signature and CRC are both to guarantee the data not to be tampered. Although CRC is sample, and its security strength is not as RAS, Compared with RAS digital signature (1024 bytes), CRC (4 bytes) has certain advantages in computation and transmitted energy consumption, especially for resource-constrained nodes. Then, how to guarantee the integrity of CRC becomes critical issue. In this sub-section, we give the low complexity verification and delayed transmitting mechanism to solve above problem, and use checksum for CRC code to guarantee its integrity to a certain extent.

4.2 Simulation and Analysis

Simulation analysis is performed using Network Simulator (NS-2), which most known tool for simulation of network scenarios and topologies. We simulated AODV, SAODV and E-SAODV agreement, made a comparison in terms of energy consumption, throughput and BPUE (Bits Per-Unit of Energy). BPUE is a multi-parameter joint evaluation metrics based on the transmission distance and modulation level [15]. The simulation parameters are shown in Table 1:

Table 1. Simulation parameters

Parameter	Value
Number of nodes	50
Initial energy of nodes (J)	2
Simulation area (m^2)	1000 * 1000
Node movement speed (m/s)	0
Simulation time (s)	800
Transmission range (m)	250
Antenna type	Omni antenna
Mobility model	Random way point

The energy consumption of the three kinds of agreement is compared in Fig. 1. It could be seen from the diagram that the AODV protocol has the largest energy consumption, the network energy consumption tends to be constant at about 700 s, which means that most of the nodes are energy depletion, network stops working; SAODV agreement has the minimum energy consumption, SAODV and E-SAODV deal is still in a rising state in the 800 s, which means that the nodes have residual energy, the network could continue working.

The throughput of the three kinds of agreement is compared in Fig. 2. It could be seen from the diagram that the throughput of AODV protocol is biggest at about 700 s, and the throughput is no longer up due to stopping working of network; The throughput of SAODV agreement is the minimum.

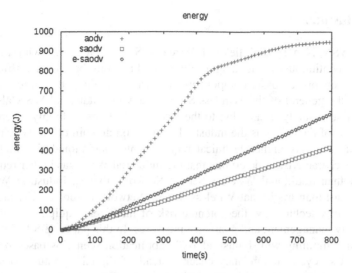

Fig. 1. Energy consumption of AODV, SAODV and E-SAODV protocols

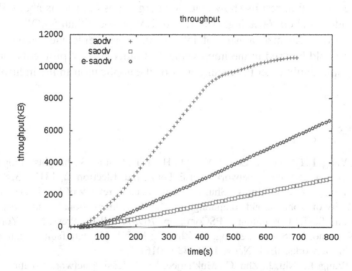

Fig. 2. Throughput of AODV, SAODV and E-SAODV protocols

As AODV protocol has no security mechanism, the operating speed is the fastest and the energy consumption and throughput of it is the largest; Instead, SAODV agreement joins the security mechanism, more complicated than the E-SAODV agreement, therefore it has the minimum energy consumption and throughput. The energy consumption and throughput of E-SAODV agreement is between AODV and SAODV protocol. It could be concluded from the Figs. 1 and 2: E-SAODV agreement is to reduce energy consumption by average of 35% in terms of SAODV when they have the same throughput.

5   Conclusions

Industrial WSN is a special field of Wireless Sensor Network, with the internal architecture continuously extending in different directions based on instrumentation and private network as basic components, its own technology therefore may be different from the general of the Wireless Sensor Network. Industrial WSN also gives a higher request to safety in addition to the technical features of highly heterogeneous, huge amounts of data. This is the industrial application domain of the Wireless Sensor Network, usually has higher technical requirements, operational risk and financial return, these characteristics determine that the Industrial WSN has higher requirements on security than traditional Wireless Sensor Network, that is, Industrial WSN has a higher standard than traditional Wireless Sensor Network in the security architecture, network security technology, the potential risk of intelligent equipment, privacy protection, safety management and guarantee measures. In this paper, E-SAODV protocol is proposed combining with Industrial WSN application scenarios based on SAODV agreement. Use cyclic redundancy check instead of digital signature to reduce the complexity of agreement and improve the energy efficiency of the agreement, the tamper-proof of information is guaranteed by latency strategy of CRC in information domain. The simulation results show that the energy consumption is about 35% lower and BPUE index is about 60% higher in E-SAODV protocol than SAODV agreement. At the same time, the mechanisms of increasing energy efficiency and information tamper-proof could be used in the improvement of other AODV protocols. Finally, the better throughput could meet the requirement of the application in the industrial scene.

References

1. Zhu, C., Yang, L.T., Shu, L., Leung, V.C.M., Hara, T., Nishio, S.: Insights of top-k query in duty-cycled wireless sensor networks. IEEE Trans. Ind. Electron. **2**, 1317–1328 (2015)
2. Zhu, C., Leung, V.C.M., Hu, X., Shu, L., Yang, L.T.: A review of key issues that concern the feasibility of mobile cloud computing. In: The IEEE International Conference on Cyber, Physical and Social Computing (CPSCom), pp. 769–776. IEEE Press, New York (2013)
3. Wang, K., Shao, Y., Shu, L., Zhang, Y., Zhu, C.: Mobile big data fault-tolerant processing for eHealth networks. IEEE Netw. **1**, 36–42 (2016)
4. Shu, L., Wang, L., Niu, J., Zhu, C., Mukherjee, M.: Releasing network isolation problem in group-based industrial wireless sensor networks. IEEE Syst. J. **10**, 1–11 (2015)
5. Luis, P., Francisco, A., Lorenzo, F., Oscar, R.: Performance of global-appearance descriptors in map building and localization using omni-directional vision. Sens. (Basel) **2**, 3033–3064 (2014)
6. Liu, T., Gao, X., Wang, L.: Study on multi-objective optimization of oil production process. In: The 11th World Congress on Intelligent Control and Automation, pp. 1824–1829 (2014)
7. Moyne, J., Yedatore, M., Iskandar, J., Hawkins, P., Scoville, J.: Chamber matching across multiple dimensions utilizing predictive maintenance, equipment health monitoring, virtual metrology and run-to-run control. In: The 25th Annual SEMI on Advanced Semiconductor Manufacturing Conference, pp. 86–91 (2014)

8. Dujovne, D., Watteyne, T., Vilajosana, X., Thubert, P.: 6TiSCH: deterministic IP-enabled industrial internet (of things). IEEE Commun. Mag. **12**, 36–41 (2014)
9. Gandhewar, N., Patel, R.: Detection and prevention of sinkhole attack on AODV protocol in mobile ad hoc network. In: The Fourth International Conference on Computational Intelligence and Communication Networks, pp. 714–718 (2012)
10. Tomar, S.P.S., Chaurasia, B.K.: Detection and isolation of sinkhole attack from AODV routing protocol in MANET. In: The International Conference on the Computational Intelligence and Communication Networks, pp. 799–802 (2014)
11. Xiong, K., Yin, M., Li, W., Jiang, H.: A rank sequence method for detecting black hole attack in ad hoc network. In: The International Conference on Intelligent Computing and Wireless Sensor Network, pp. 155–159 (2015)
12. Perkins, C.E., Royer, E.M.: Ad-hoc on-demand distance vector routing. In: The Second Workshop on Mobile Computing Systems and Applications, pp. 90–100. IEEE Press, New York (1999)
13. Jain, P., Suryavanshi, A.: Energy efficient local route repair multicast AODV routing schemes in wireless ad hoc network. In: The International Conference on Advanced Communication Control and Computing Technologies, pp. 1168–1173 (2014)
14. Joshi, A., Kaur, R.: A novel multi-cast routing protocol for VANET. In: The IEEE International Advance Computing Conference, pp. 41–45. IEEE Press, New York (2015)
15. Fang, W., Shi, Z., Shan, L., Li, F., Xiong, Y.: A multi-parameter joint evaluation scheme in energy consumption for wireless sensor networks. Chin. High Technol. Lett. **8–9**, 753–759 (2015)

Adaptive Genetic Algorithm to Optimize the Parameters of Evaluation Function of Dots-and-Boxes

Fangming Bi, Yunchen Wang, and Wei Chen[✉]

School of Computer Science and Technology,
China University of Mining and Technology,
Xuzhou City 221116, Jiangsu Province, China
{bfm,wyc,chenw}@cumt.edu.cn

Abstract. Designed an evaluation function with parameters, and used genetic algorithm to optimize the parameters. This paper considers the objective function's variation trends in searching point and the information is added to the fitness function to guide the searching. Simultaneously adaptive genetic algorithm enables crossover probability and mutation probability automatically resized according to the individual's fitness. These measures have greatly improved the convergence rate of the algorithm. Sparring algorithm is introduced to guide the training, using gradient training programs to save training time. Experiments show skills in playing Dots-and-Boxes are greatly improved after its evaluation function parameters are optimized.

Keywords: Adaptive genetic algorithm · Evaluation function · Game

1 Introduction

Machine game is an important branch of artificial intelligence research and has been hailed as drosophila in the field. Computer Game System can be divided into four parts: situation represents, action set, the evaluation function and game tree search. Search algorithm is the basic method to solve the problems in artificial intelligence. Minimax theorem proposed by Von Neumann and Boerl in the 1920s is the mathematical basis for searching algorithm. Alpha-beta pruning algorithm which began in the 1950s is a big step forward in the search efficiency. PVS (Principal Variation Search, also known as NegaScout) search algorithm in 1980 has higher search efficiency than alpha-beta search algorithm when the game tree is strong orderly [1]. MTD(f) algorithm appeared in 1994, always with an empty window detection approaching true value, complete search with the help of "Transposition Table", is slightly better than the PVS search. Both are the current mainstream method. Most game trees are so large that unable to

F. Bi—Fund Project: National Natural Science Foundation and Shanxi Provincial People's Government Jointly Funded Project of China for Coal Base and Low Carbon (No. U1510115), the Qing Lan Project, the China Postdoctoral Science Foundation (No. 2013T60574).

© ICST Institute for Computer Sciences, Social Informatics and Telecommunications Engineering 2017
J.-H. Lee and S. Pack (Eds.): QShine 2016, LNICST 199, pp. 416–425, 2017.
DOI: 10.1007/978-3-319-60717-7_41

complete the search. Conventional measure is to search for a certain depth, then the leaf node is approximately evaluated by evaluation function. The quality of the evaluation function directly affects the development of the situation [2]. If search engine is the game system's eyes, the evaluation function would be the system's brain. Evaluation function generally must contain elements of five aspects, that is fixed pawn value, pawn position value, pawn flexibility value, threats and protect value, dynamic adjustment value, and the value of each aspect is composed of a number of parameters. Combination of the above parameters in the evaluation function is often dependent on the programmer's own knowledge and experience which makes it difficult to achieve the optimal. Some scholars have introduced genetic algorithm into the evaluation function, trying to learn the dynamic relation between the pieces, but the effect is not very satisfactory. In this paper we take the dots-and-boxes as example, design an evaluation function, use adaptive genetic algorithm [3] to optimize evaluation function parameters. In order to enhance the local searching ability of genetic algorithms, knowledge of problem domain is added to the fitness function [4]. Our study has been organized as followings: Sect. 2 specify the challenges for genetic algorithm to be applied to optimization of evaluate function parameters and gives the scheme of genetic algorithm that we used in this paper and describes the adaptive genetic algorithm; Sect. 3 describes the experimental strategies and presents the experimental results; Sect. 4 is the conclusion of this paper.

2 Solutions of Genetic Algorithm Applied to Optimization of Evaluate Function Parameters

2.1 Challenges for Genetic Algorithm to Use in Game

The genetic algorithm was proposed by professor Holland at the University of Michigan in American in 1969 and formed a type of simulated evolutionary algorithm after summarized by Dejong, Goldberg et al. In recent years, Genetic Algorithm as an important part of the intelligent computing (neural networks, fuzzy processing and evolutionary computation), has been a focus of research and made very good results in the field of application such as more extreme value function optimization problems, combinatorial optimization problems, scheduling problems and so on.

Traditional hill-climbing algorithm finds the optimal solution by comparing with neighboring nodes, and is restricted by ranges of initial samples and single direction searching, and is easy to fall into local optimum [5].

Simulated annealing is a stochastic optimization algorithm based on the Monte-Carlo iterative solution strategies. It attempts to simulate the high temperature object annealing process to find the global optimal solution or the approximate global optimal solution. It can avoid local minima, but the fatal flaw is too slow, running too long [6].

Ant colony algorithm (ACO) converges on the optimization path through pheromone accumulation and renewal. It has the ability of parallel processing and global searching and the characteristic of positive feedback. But the convergence speed of ACO is lower at the beginning for there is only little pheromone difference on the path at that time.

Genetic Algorithm has a high degree of parallel, weak dependence on initial value and the quick global searching ability. Its robustness is also significantly better than the previous two algorithms. But it has such disadvantages as premature convergence, low convergence speed and so on. To used in game, these disadvantages will be amplified in particular as the fitness of the generation depends on the game result. With the increase of the degree of evolution, it will take more rounds to fight it out. In view of its weakness, in this paper, the first-order differential information of adjacent two generations of the objective function was added into the fitness function to strengthen the search ability and prevent premature. The adoption of the adaptive genetic algorithm greatly improved the convergence speed. So it is most likely to succeed in Dots-and-Boxes.

2.2   Parameter Selection and Coding Scheme of the Evaluation Function

Dots-and-Boxes starting with an empty grid of dots, players take turns, adding a single vertical or horizontal line between two adjacent dots. A player who completes the fourth side of a 1×1 box earns one point and takes another turn. The game ends when no more lines can be placed. The winner of the game is the player with the most points.

The design of evaluation function of Dots-and-Boxes typically rely on several theorems [7], introduced as following.

Theorem 1. Regardless of the initial size of the board, there is always the following equation holds:

$$Dots + Doublecrosses = Turns$$

where Dots is the number of point of the initial board, Doublecrosses is the number of doublecross in the whole play and Turns is the total number of rounds to go through in the whole play.

Theorem 2. If total number of the board nodes is odd, then the Upper Hand side must form an odd number of Long Chain in order to win, and the After Hand side must form an even number Long Chain for win, and vice versa.

Theorem 2 is known as Long-Chain Theorem, and it is an important basis for the design of the evaluation function. Take 4×4 chessboard as example, according to Long-Chain Theorem, the Upper Hand side must form an odd number of Long Chain in order to win. Suppose that after the Upper Hand moves, it forms the situation (there are two Long-Chains marked as a, b) as shown in Fig. 1(a). So, no matter what strategy the After Hand to take, the final chain will be captured by the Upper Hand who is in a dominant position. However, relying solely on the Long-Chain theorem can not guarantee the accuracy of evaluation function. For example, suppose after the Upper Hand moves, it forms the situation as shown in Fig. 1(b) where there are also two long chains (marked as a, b), but the opponent simply select the edge numbered 1 in the Fig. 1(b), then the situation reverses, and the Upper Hand are in absolute disadvantage.

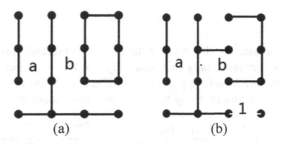

Fig. 1. An even number of Long-Chain case

The above analysis shows that the valuation depends on the combination of a variety of board elements and is sensitive to the parity of the number of board elements. So, we design the following evaluation function.

$$v(r_1, r_2, r_3 \ldots r_n) = \sum_{i=1}^{N} A_{i1}^{r_i} A_{i2}^{|1-r_i|} \tag{1}$$

where $r_i = n_i \bmod 2$, n_i represents the number of the i-th type of board elements in the current chess game; A_{i1}, A_{i2} is the parameter of the i-th type of chess-type; N is the number of types of different board elements. In this article, we select some main board elements as Long-Chain, Short-Chain, DoubleCross, boxes with Freedom Degree of 3 and 4, so N equals 5.

Encode each parameter A_{ij} with 6 bit binary code, a total of 60 bits constitute a set of chromosomes string.

2.3 Calculation of the Fitness Function and Population Selection

Fitness is a main indicator that describes the individual performance and genetic algorithm select the fittest individuals based on it. Selection of the fitness function determines the algorithm optimization orientation and has a great impact on the convergence of the algorithm and the convergence rate.

We use the following method to design objective function. Let each individual play with an existing game algorithm (sparring algorithm), then determine the value of the objective function according to the number of rounds per game takes. If we win, the fewer the number of rounds is, the greater the function of the value should be; if the other side wins, then the more the number of rounds is, the greater the value of the function should be. Therefore, the objective function is designed as follows.

$$f(x) = \begin{cases} 60 + \frac{(60-x)^2}{k} & \text{we wins} \\ x & \text{the other side wins} \\ 60 & \text{draw} \end{cases} \tag{2}$$

where x is the number of rounds of a game, k is adjustable coefficient that represents the importance of the number of rounds to fitness when we wins. Here take k = 6. The fitness function is mapped directly from the objective function, namely:

$$\text{fit}(x) = f(x) \tag{3}$$

In order to fully considering the trend of the objective function, preventing the preferred chromosome hovering only in a relatively flat area in genetic process which would cause "premature", and we put the first difference of the objective function of adjacent generations to join in, using the following new fitness function [4]:

$$\text{fit}(x)' = \varepsilon \cdot \frac{\text{fit}(x) - \text{fit}_{min}}{\text{fit}_{max} - \text{fit}_{min}} + (1 - \varepsilon) \cdot \frac{\nabla f(x) - \nabla f_{min}}{\nabla f_{max} - \nabla f_{min}} \tag{4}$$

where weights $\varepsilon \in [0, 1]$ called the control factor, to reflect the importance of values of the fitness function and the rate of change of the function in solving this problem. $\text{fit}(x)$ is the original fitness function. fit_{min} and fit_{max} denote respectively the minimum and maximum value of individual fitness in the current generation of the population. ∇fit_{min} and ∇fit_{max} are defined as:

$$\nabla f(x) = f(x^p) - f(x^c) \tag{5}$$

$$\nabla f_{min} = \min\{f(v_1^p) - f(v_1^c), \ldots, f(v_n^p) - f(v_n^c)\} \tag{6}$$

$$\nabla f_{max} = \max\{f(v_1^p) - f(v_1^c), \ldots, f(v_n^p) - f(v_n^c)\} \tag{7}$$

where x^p, x^c denote the parent and offspring chromosomes respectively, n represents the size of the population.

2.4   Crossover and Mutation Operation

There are many crossover methods, single-point crossover, multi-point cross, sequence cross, cycle cross, etc. For convenience, we use single-point crossover, randomly select one of the binary bits in the chromosome as a cross point, then cross the two parameters of the parent individuals to form the sub's parameters [8]. Each parameter's cross rate is p_c.

Each parameter is mutated at variation rate p_m. Because of the use of the binary string representation, here just flip 0–1 for the gene according to the gene mutation rate. Mutation is a local random search, in conjunction with the selection/crossover to ensure the effectiveness of the genetic algorithm and maintain the diversity of the population at the same time, to prevent the emergence of non-mature convergence.

Here choosing to operate each parameter in the chromosome is due to that a chromosome contains many parameters. If directly operate the entire chromosome, some parameters may not get enough crossover and mutation which makes the convergence time become longer and the effect is not ideal.

2.5   Adaptive Genetic Algorithm

The convergence of the genetic algorithm is affected by crossover rate p_c and mutation rate p_m. The larger the cross rate, the faster the rate of new individuals to produce. But if the crossover rate is too large, it is not conducive to the protection of chromosome structure of the current high fitness individuals. But if the crossover rate is too low, the individual evolution is too slow and the search process is stalled. For the mutation rate, if it is too low, it's not conducive to generate new individuals and easy to fall into local optimum search; If it is too high, the genetic algorithm can easily degenerate into a random search algorithm. Since there is no fixed way to determine p_c and p_m, the optimization can only be optimized through continuous experiment and this process is very fussy. To this end, we introduce adaptive genetic algorithm which can automatically adjust with individual fitness [9, 10]. Here are the formulas of p_c and p_m:

$$p_c = \begin{cases} p_{c1} - \frac{(p_{c1}-p_{c2})(f'-f_{avg})}{f_{max}-f_{avg}} & f' \geq f_{avg} \\ p_{c1} & f' < f_{avg} \end{cases} \tag{8}$$

$$p_m = \begin{cases} p_{m1} - \frac{(p_{m1}-p_{m2})(f_{max}-f)}{f_{max}-f_{avg}} & f \geq f_{avg} \\ p_{m1} & f < f_{avg} \end{cases} \tag{9}$$

where $p_{c1} = 0.9$, $p_{c2} = 0.6$, $p_{m1} = 0.1$, $p_{m2} = 0.001$. f_{max} is the group's largest fitness value. f_{avg} is the average fitness value of each generation of the population. f' is the greater fitness value of the two individuals to cross. f is the fitness value to the mutation individual. Expression analysis shows that when it is closer to the maximum fitness value, the value of p_c and p_m is smaller, and this reduces the possibility of good genes being destroyed and ensure the convergence of the algorithm.

3 Experimental Testing and Results

3.1 Experimental Strategies

Adaptive genetic algorithm requires a lot of training to get a better race result, time is the key factor that must be considered. In this paper, we take gradient training method to achieve the purpose that takes less time to achieve better results. It specifically includes three aspects, gradually increase the search depth of the game algorithm; gradually increase the intensity of sparring algorithm and choosing an efficient game tree search algorithm.

Search depth has an enormous influence on the time, in the beginning, due to evaluation function parameters have not been effectively optimized, even if searching a great depth the estimates are still not accurate. Therefore, the time cost is too high. However, when the function parameters are effectively optimized, if the search depth is still not corresponding increase, chess will not be able to better enhanced, genetic algorithms will think this is because of the current individual's gene is not good, so it continue evolution and then convergence time will increase.

Sparring algorithm will also affect the accuracy of the training results and time. If sparring algorithm is too strong in the beginning, choice to the genetic algorithm tend to be simplify. If sparring algorithm is always weak, it's not conducive to choose the best individual. If always use the same kind of sparring algorithm, it's easy to fall into local optimum. In this paper, the different stages of the training use different intensity of sparring algorithm and in the training process, the evaluation function is interspersed with random parameters to prevent the search into the local optimum.

The strength of sparring algorithm is reflected in two aspects - the accuracy of the evaluation function and the depth of the search. At the start of training, we use the evaluation function designed according to our own experience. After the training reaches a certain stage, we use the evaluation that is consistent with the sparring algorithm, and at this time, we use the depth of search to distinguish the skill in playing chess. In the early, middle, late stage of the training, take 2, 5, 7 as the search depth of the genetic algorithm, and 2, 8, 10 as the sparring algorithm's. Now, we need choosing an efficient search algorithm.

In 1978, Stockman proposed SSS* algorithm and proved that it is a correct minimax algorithm and that it never explores a node that alpha-beta ignore. Moreover, for practical distributions of tip value assignments SSS* will explore strictly fewer game tree nodes than Alpha-Beta. However, SSS* algorithm has disadvantages of big storage requirement and the need to maintain the OPEN table [11, 12].

Paper [13] proposed that by reformulating the algorithm, SSS* can be expressed simply and intuitively as a series of calls to Alpha-Beta, yielding a new algorithm called AB-SSS*. AB-SSS* visits the same interior and leaf nodes in the same order as SSS* and resolves the problems mentioned above with SSS*. AB-SSS* has been implemented in high-performance game-playing programs for checkers, Othello and chess. In this paper, we using AB-SSS* as the searching algorithm.

3.2   The Experimental Results

Train the evaluation function optimized by adaptive genetic algorithm that has an improved fitness function with gradient training experiment. Champions of 50th generation, 100th generation, 150th generation, 200th generation, 250th generation, 300th generation formed a group to carry out round robin of successively hand. One is awarded 3 points for a win, 1 for a draw and 0 for a lose. Finally, the case is shown in Fig. 2.

It can be found by the line chart that for the evaluation function optimized by improved genetic algorithm and gradient training, the more generations to train, the

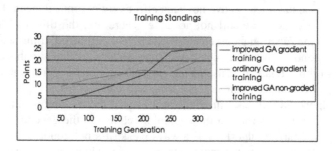

Fig. 2. Training standings

stronger the chess is and more obvious the effect is. However the differences between evaluation functions optimized by ordinary genetic algorithm gradient training and improved genetic algorithm non-graded training respectively is relatively small between generations. This shows that the improved genetic algorithm has faster convergence rate.

It was found that after the program is iterated to 300 generations, the optimized parameters are substantially no longer change. The parameter values at this time are shown in Table 1.

Table 1. Training results.

Parameter	A_{11}	A_{12}	A_{21}	A_{22}	A_{31}	A_{32}	A_{41}	A_{42}	A_{51}	A_{52}
Value	53	7	27	19	12	15	11	9	5	8

Experiment results show that game algorithm with evaluation function using the above parameter combination has greater possibilities to win compared with sparring algorithm.

In order to verify the gradient training method we proposed can reduce the training time and ensure the accuracy, our experiment take 8 as the search depth of both genetic algorithm and training algorithm in the training in different stages and using the same evaluation function. Due to the time cost is too high, we only train 50 generation. The results are shown in Table 2 and Fig. 3.

Table 2. Trainning time.

Generation	Time consumption (min)	
	Gradient training	Non-gradient training
10–20	10	50
20–30	23	66
30–40	21	80
40–50	25	103

Running time ratio

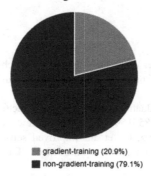

■ gradient-training (20.9%)
■ non-gradient-training (79.1%)

Fig. 3. Running time ratio

In the Table 2 and the Fig. 3 we find that the time gap of two is obvious. Then we used the same evaluation function of the same generation of both gradient training and non-gradient training to play with each other for 50 rounds. Winning statistics are shown in Table 3.

Table 3. Winning statistics.

Generation	Win (rounds)	
	Gradient training	Non-gradient training
10–20	27	23
20–30	24	26
30–40	25	25
40–50	23	27

In the Table 3 we find that increment of the search depth dose not bring obvious advantages. It validates our strategy to a certain extent.

4   Conclusion

There are precocious and other defects for classical genetic algorithm. In this paper, we introduced a new method of calculating the fitness function that considers the objective function's trends in search point, and the trend information is added to the fitness function to guide search. Simultaneously adaptive genetic algorithm enables crossover probability p_c and mutation probability p_m automatically resized according to the individual's fitness. These measures have greatly improved the speed of convergence of the algorithm. The genetic algorithm is introduced to optimize the evaluate function parameters which avoids manually adjust parameters in the traditional way and ensures the accuracy and objectivity of the parameters. Experiments show skill in playing Dots-and-Boxes greatly improved after its evaluation function parameters optimized. This also provides a new way of thinking for development of high-level game algorithm.

References

1. Hongkun, Q., Peng, Z., Yajie, W., et al.: Analysis of search algorithm in computer game of Amazons. In: 26th Chinese Control and Decision Conference, pp. 3947–3950. IEEE Press, New York (2014)
2. Duan, Z.: An improved evaluation function for Connect6. In: 24th Chinese Control and Decision Conference, pp. 1685–1690. IEEE Press, New York (2012)
3. Wei, X.-K., Shao, W., Zhang, C., et al.: Improved self-adaptive genetic algorithm with quantum scheme for electromagnetic optimization. IET Microw. Antennas Propag. **8**, 965–972 (2014)

4. He, X., Liang, J.: The objective function using genetic algorithms gradient. J. Softw. **12**, 981–985 (2001). (in Chinese)
5. Luo, B., Zheng, J., Yang, P.: GA-based directional climbing. Comput. Eng. Appl. **44**, 92–95 (2008). (in Chinese)
6. Qi, J.-Y.: Application of improved simulated annealing algorithm in facility layout design. In: 29th Chinese Control Conference, pp. 5224–5227. IEEE Press, New York (2010)
7. Li, S., Li, D., Yuan, X.: Research and implementation of dots-and-boxes. J. Softw. **7**, 256–262 (2012)
8. Deng, X.: Application of adaptive genetic algorithm in inversion analysis of permeability coefficients. In: Second International Conference on Genetic and Evolutionary Computing, WGEC 2008, pp. 61–65. IEEE Press, New York (2014)
9. Huang, Y.-P., Chang, Y.-T., Sandnes, F.-E.: Using fuzzy adaptive genetic algorithm for function optimization. In: Annual Meeting of the North American on Fuzzy Information Processing Society, NAFIPS 2006, pp. 484–489. IEEE Press, New York (2006)
10. Yanhong, P.: Wind power fitness function calculation based on niche genetic algorithm. In: International Conference on Sustainable Power Generation and Supply, pp. 1–5. IEEE Press, New York (2012)
11. Stockman, G.C.: A minimax algorithm better than alpha-beta? Artif. Intell. **12**, 179–196 (1978)
12. Ibaraki, T.: Generalization of alpha-beta and SSS* search procedures. Artif. Intell. **29**, 73–117 (1986)
13. Plaat, A., Schaeffer, J., Pijls, W., de Bruin, A.: SSS* = alphabet + TT. Technical report TR-CS_94-17, Department of Computing Science, University of Alberta, Edmonton, AB, Canada (1994)

A Design of the Event Trigger for Android Application

Ting Hu, Zhuo Ning, and Zhixin Sun$^{(\boxtimes)}$

Key Laboratory of Broadband Wireless Communication and Sensor Network
Technology, Nanjing University of Posts and Telecommunications,
Nanjing, China
sunzx@njupt.edu.cn

Abstract. The exploding of Android malware makes security analysis more important and urgently calls for automation in its analysis. Often automation analysis includes static and dynamic methods. And an important work of the dynamic analysis is gathering accurate behavior information of Android apps. However, traditional methods, which are used to inject random events to exercise the user interface, can not capture the behavior triggered by the event. To overcome the above shortcomings, this paper designs a framework of the Android malware detection based on cloud and focuses on how to design an Event Trigger to trigger more behaviors. This method can enlarge the dynamic analysis scope to find more information of malicious behaviors.

Keywords: Android malware · Dynamic analysis · Event Trigger

1 Introduction

In recent years, smart phone sales have grown tremendously. Until the first quarter of 2015, according to the report from Gartner, worldwide sales of smart phones to end users have reached 336 million [1]. Among various platforms, Google's smart phone platform, Android, has captured more than 75% of the total market-share. In another word, it is the most popular operating system at present. Unfortunately this explosive growth also has drawn the attention of cyber criminals who try to trick the user into installing malicious software on the device.

Android terminal stores a lot of personal information, such as contacts, messages, social network access, browsing history and banking credentials, so it has become a prime target for malicious attacks. Android malwares such as premium rate SMS Trojans, spyware, botnet, aggressive adware and privilege escalation attack have reported exponential rise from the Google Play store and well known third-party market places. According to the statistics from Kasper sky, the number of malicious Android applications topped the 10 million mark in January 2014 [2]. These malicious applications pose a great security risk to mobile phone owners and solving the security issue of Android has become a hot topic in the field of information security.

Given the enormous growth of Android malware, security researchers and vendors must analyze more and more applications (apps) in a given period of time to understand the purpose of the software and to develop countermeasures accordingly. Through the

© ICST Institute for Computer Sciences, Social Informatics and Telecommunications Engineering 2017
J.-H. Lee and S. Pack (Eds.): QShine 2016, LNICST 199, pp. 426–434, 2017.
DOI: 10.1007/978-3-319-60717-7_42

efforts of researchers, Android security has made much progress both in static and dynamic analysis [3]. The classical approach to automated analysis of suspicious applications is static analysis. Static analysis investigates software properties that can only be investigated by inspecting the downloaded app and its source code [4]. A typical example of it is signature based detection similar to the common approach of antivirus [5]. However, malware usually uses obfuscation techniques to puzzle static analysis [6, 7]. Thus dynamic analysis does not inspect the source code, but rather executes it within a controlled environment, often called sandbox to get a more accurate result. By monitoring and logging every relevant operation of the execution (such as sending SMS messages, reading data from storage, and connecting to remote servers), an analysis report is automatically generated. Dynamic analysis can combat obfuscation techniques rather well, but it is thwarted by runtime detection methods. Therefore, combing the static and the dynamic usually makes sense in practice.

A big problem of dynamic analysis is how to trigger malicious behaviors as many as it can, especially for those one which could not be triggered just by installing the application. And some behaviors can not be triggered except for particular interaction. Generally, for each Activity, Monkey [8] is used to inject random UI events to exercise the user interface. Furthermore, some behaviors of Android apps are triggered by events, such as the arrival of new SMS and location change, which sometimes could not be triggered by random event streams. Our Event Trigger can inject in-time fake events at the most appropriate execution time, which can enlarge the scope for analyzing Android apps and make the report more accurate.

Last but not least, static analysis, dynamic analysis and other processes of our research require a large amount of computing resource. Therefore, we deploy the core solution on the cloud to provide the parallel service for a large number of smart phones.

2 Background

In order to automatically install the application and simulate the user operation in the actual equipment or simulator, most of the detection schemes used automatic control scripts. For instance, TaintDroid [9], DroidBox [10], AppPlayground [11], PuppetDroid [12], Andrubis [13] and Mobile-Sandbox [14] used the MonkeyRunner provided by Android SDK, which could generate enough random User Interface (UI) events to ensure a large number of interactive behaviors are triggered. However, the event frequency of different applications varies considerably, and the random UI events can not target the application's vulnerability. DroidTrace solved the problem in a different way. It triggered different dynamic loading behaviors by physical modification. Firstly, it found the function which loaded other functions dynamically; then inserted the trigger code into these functions to generate forward execution path; finally packaged this app as a new application [15]. In this way, DroidTrace can trigger targeted behaviors, but it was not a real-time solution. Both of the above two methods can not trigger behaviors which can only be triggered by particular events. For example, if the user moved to a new place, the location will be changed, and such location change event cannot be achieved by both DroidTrace and automatic control script. Another example of the event trigger is receiving short messages and calls. All these events could trigger some malicious behaviors of application, such as leaking the location change or the received new SMS.

To overcome the above shortcomings, an event trigger is explored. It injects recurrent fake events, including the arrival of new SMS, calls and location changing, to trigger the malicious behaviors as many as possible during the execution. Compared with the ordinary, it can perform in-time event injection at the most appropriate time, for not only callbacks listed in the Manifest but also API callbacks that invoked at runtime. At the same time, it provides more behavior analysis information for the developers or users to promote the accuracy.

Currently, there is a tendency to malware detection service from the host terminal to the cloud. Cloud computing is the development product of distributed computing, parallel computing and utility computing. It congregates large numbers of computation resources and provides on-demand IT services to the remote Internet users. Wang et al. [16] provided a new android multimedia framework based on Gstreamer. It can greatly improve the multimedia processing ability in terms of efficiency, compatibility, feasibility and universality. Cloud resources and their loads possess dynamic characteristics. Zuo et al. [17] proposed a scheduling method called interlacing peak which can balance loads and improve the effects of resource allocation and utilization effectively. Meanwhile they proposed a Self adaptive threshold based Dynamically Weighted load evaluation Method (termed SDWM) [18]. It evaluates the load state of the resource through a dynamically weighted evaluation method. For task-scheduling problems in cloud computing, a multi-objective optimization method is also proposed [19]. In this paper, we deploy the core solution on the cloud to provide the parallel service.

The paper is organized as the following. The second section discusses the implement of it in details, including the process design, the communication architecture and the function module. In the third section a security detection architecture based on cloud is designed accordingly.

3 Event Trigger Implementation

3.1 Process of the Event Trigger

The Event Trigger runs in the sandbox when faking events, while its specific process is shown in Fig. 1.

Step 1: Firstly, the application manifest file (AndroidManifest.xml) will be analyzed to extract API list of registered callback functions, which are predefined event functions;

Step 2: Running an application in the sandbox and notifying the Event Trigger to inject related events when a callback function is registered through the API;

Step 3: The Event Trigger injects related fake events, and then the hardware device will detect the occurrence of the event and notify the application to update the latest information.

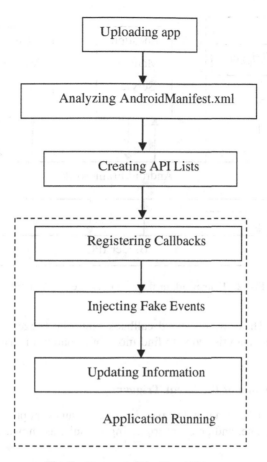

Fig. 1. Process of the Event Trigger

3.2 Communication Architecture of the Event Trigger

The class that implements the service in the Android framework layer is ManagerService. ServiceManager is another class dedicated to the management of system services. And it is responsible for the registration and management of all system services. Both of them communicate via the Binder protocol. When the application calls for a system service, it needs to invoke the service through the service agent and then sends a request to the system server process via the inter process communication, then the process is responsible to return the results. The entire communication architecture is shown in Fig. 2. For example, the Event Trigger will automatically inject fake location change events when the corresponding callbacks are registered through the LocationManager._requestLocationUpdates() API. Then the location change monitoring request is delegated to LocationManagerService via the Binder protocol, which will notify LocationManagerService immediately to fake a location change event. Finally, the hardware will detect an event occurred and notice the application to update the

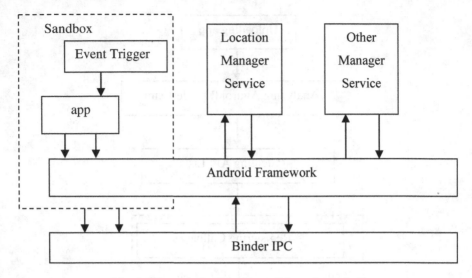

Fig. 2. Framework of the Event Trigger in Android

latest information. Thus, the registered callback could be triggered for execution to enlarge the dynamic analysis scope to find more information of malicious behavior.

3.3   Function Module of the Event Trigger

The Event Trigger includes a manifest parsing module, an event pre-triggering module, an event faking module, and an event triggering module, as shown in Fig. 3.

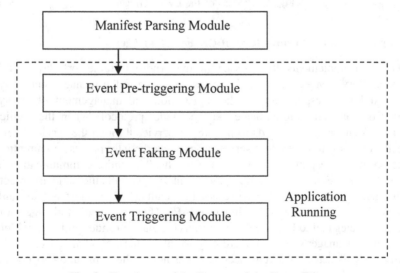

Fig. 3. Function module diagram of the Event Trigger

Manifest Parsing Module, which parses the application manifest file (AndroidManifest.xml) to extract API list of registered callback functions, namely the predefined some event functions.

Event Pre-triggering Module, which will send a request to the Event Faking Module to inject corresponding false events when an application wants to use a system service, the callbacks of which will be registered through the API, that is, some of the predefined event functions will soon be called.

Event Faking Module, which could perform in-time event injection when received the request information for fake events. The fake events include not only callbacks listed in the Manifest but also API callbacks that invoked at runtime.

Event Triggering Module, which could trigger fake events and the hardware will sniff an event occurred and notice the application to update the latest information. Thus, the registered callback could be triggered for execution to enlarge the dynamic analysis scope to find more information of malicious behavior.

The fake events include location change, the arrival of new SMS, receiving calls, etc. in the Event Faking Module. Take the location change injection as an example, the whole process of which is running in the process of the sandbox. The Event Faking Module could firstly fake current geographic coordinates (Android simulator in sandbox cannot automatically position coordinates) when received the request information for location injection from the Event Pre-triggering Module. Secondly, a series of location information initialization: location initialization, interface initialization, search module initialization, data initialization and so on, are prepared for the location change. Then run the thread to set the coordinate information of the location change. Finally, destroy the geographic coordinate information after the location change event is triggered and wait for the next trigger.

4   The Security Detection Architecture for Android Application

In this paper, we intend to develop an Android malware detection system, which includes the client and the server with a synergy framework based on cloud.

The Client. Prototype system installs itself as the Android app on the user's smart phone to detect the specific software. Users can upload the Android APK file to the cloud manually.

The Cloud. The static analysis and the dynamic analysis of our research require a large amount of computing resource. Therefore, we deploy the core solution on the cloud to provide the parallel service for a large number of smart phones. We suggest that each end host run a lightweight process to acquire executables entering a system, send them into the network for analysis, and then run or quarantine them based on a threat report returned by the network service. The system monitors the dangerous functions. When sufficient evidences are found, the request/response manager will upload the suspicious applications. The cloud server is responsible to detect the vulnerability and maliciousness of the uploaded app. After the completion of detection, it will return back the evaluation information. Finally, the App manager will determine the next steps to be taken. The Event Trigger runs in the sandbox when faking events. The architecture of the synergy framework is shown in Fig. 4.

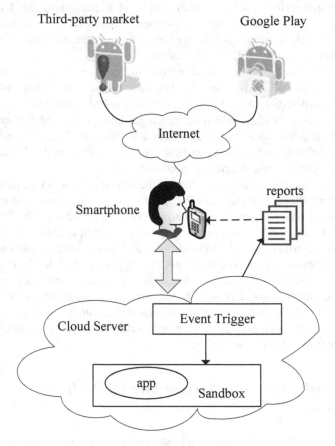

Fig. 4. Deployment of the security synergy detection framework.

This paper uses open source cloud computing platform Eucalyptus established by Santa Barbara universities to achieve specific architecture [20]. And we use virtual machine nodes in the cloud to implement parallel distributed detection with dynamic and static analysis. Meanwhile, the enclosed environment in virtual machine nodes is used to construct the corresponding event triggers to monitor dynamic behavior in the sandbox. The distributed Propagation of Information with Feedback (PIF) protocol algorithm is used to formally describe the procedure of dynamic analysis and analysis report return.

Our experiment results show that in many cases we can: detect the existence of trigger-based behavior, find the conditions that trigger such hidden behavior, and find inputs that satisfy those conditions and advance its performance.

5 Conclusion

In this paper, we propose an Event Trigger which can automatically trigger the application event behaviors. Compared with existing event injection techniques, our technique could perform in-time event injection at the most appropriate time, for not only callbacks listed in the Manifest but also API callbacks that invoked at runtime. With the help of runtime injected events, the scope of the dynamic analysis is enlarged, and the accuracy is also promoted.

Though many techniques are introduced to drive the application execution, it is worth noting that our Event Trigger could not guarantee a complete coverage over all possible behaviors. Generally it is a difficult problem for all dynamic analysis work. This paper tries to design a better behavior approximation for analyzing Android apps, and leaves the coverage problem as our future work.

Acknowledgments. This paper was supported by the National Natural Science Foundation of China (Nos. 61170276, 61373135) and the Key University Science Research Project of Jiangsu Province (Grant No. 12KJA520003).

References

1. Gartner, Inc.: Gartner Says Emerging Markets Drove Worldwide Smartphone Sales to 19 Percent Growth in First Quarter of 2015. http://www.gartner.com/newsroom/id/3061917
2. Kaspersky, Lab.: Number-of-the-week-list-of-malicious-Android-apps-hits-10-million (2014). http://www.kaspersky.com/about/news/virus/2014/Number-of-the-week-list-of-malicious-Android-apps-hits-10-millon
3. Enck, W.: Defending users against smartphone apps: techniques and future directions. In: Jajodia, S., Mazumdar, C. (eds.) ICISS 2011. LNCS, vol. 7093, pp. 49–70. Springer, Heidelberg (2011). doi:10.1007/978-3-642-25560-1_3
4. Application Exerciser Monkey. http://developer.android.com/tools/help/monkey
5. Schmeelk, S., Yang J., Aho, A.: Android malware static analysis techniques. In: 10th Annual Cyber and Information Security Research Conference, pp. 1–2. ACM, New York (2015)
6. Batyuk, L., Hernich, M.: Using static analysis for automatic assessment and mitigation of unwanted and malicious activities within Android applications. In: Malicious and Unwanted Software (MALWARE), pp. 66–72. IEEE, Fajardo (2011)
7. Moser, A., Kruegel, C., Kirda, E.: Limits of static analysis for malware detection. In: Proceedings of the 23rd Annual Computer Security Applications Conference (2007)
8. Willems, C., Freiling, F.C.: Reverse code engineering—state of the art and countermeasures. it-Inf. Technol. 53–63 (2011)
9. Enck, W., Gilbert, P., Chun, B.-G., Cox, L. P., Jung, J., McDaniel, P., Sheth, A.N.: TaintDroid: an information-flow tracking system for realtime privacy monitoring on smartphones. In: Proceedings of the USENIX Symposium on Operating Systems Design and Implementation (OSDI), October 2010
10. Dynamic analysis of Android apps. https://github.com/pjlantz/droidbox
11. Rastogi, V., Chen, Y., Enck, W.: Appsplayground: automatic security analysis of smartphone applications. In: Proceedings of the Third ACM Conference on Data and Application Security and Privacy, CODASPY 2013. ACM, New York (2013)

12. Gianazza, A., Maggi, F., Fattori, A., Cavallaro, L., Zanero, S.: PuppetDroid: a user-centric UI exerciser for automatic dynamic analysis of similar android applications. CoRR, vol. abs/1402.4826, 2014

13. Lindorfer, M., Neugschwandtner, M., Weichselbaum, L., Fratantonio, Y., van der Veen, V., Platzer, C.: Andrubis-1,000,000 apps later: a view on current Android malware behaviors. In: Proceedings of the 3rd International Workshop on Building Analysis Datasets and Gathering Experience Returns for Security, BADGERS (2014)

14. Spreitzenbarth, M., Schreck, T., Echtler, F., Arp, D., Hoffmann, J.: Mobile-Sandbox: combining static and dynamic analysis with machine-learning techniques. Int. J. Inf. Secur. **14**(2), 141–153 (2015). Springer, Berlin

15. Zheng, M., Sun, M., Lui, J.C.S.: DroidTrace: a ptrace based Android dynamic analysis system with forward execution capability. In: Wireless Communications and Mobile Computing Conference (IWCMC), pp. 128–133. IEEE Press, Nicosia (2014)

16. Wang, H., Hao, F., Zhu, C., Rodrigues, J.J.P.C., Yang, L.T.: An android multimedia framework based on Gstreamer. In: Rodrigues, J.J.P.C., Zhou, L., Chen, M., Kailas, A. (eds.) GreeNets 2011. LNICSSITE, vol. 51, pp. 51–62. Springer, Heidelberg (2012). doi:10.1007/978-3-642-33368-2_5

17. Zuo, L., Shu, L., Dong, S., Zhu, C., Han, G.: A multi-queue interlacing peak scheduling method based on tasks classification in cloud computing. IEEE Syst. J. (2016)

18. Zuo, L., Shu, L., Dong, S., Zhu, C., Zhou, Z.: Dynamic weighted load evaluation model based on self-adaptive threshold in cloud computing. ACM Mob. Netw. Appl. 1–15 (2016)

19. Zuo, L., Shu, L., Dong, S., Zhu, C., Hara, T.: A multi-objective optimization scheduling method based on the ant colony algorithm in cloud computing. IEEE Access **3**, 2687–2699 (2015)

20. HPE Helion Eucalyptus. https://github.com/eucalyptus

Cloud Resource Combinatorial Double Auction Algorithm Based on Genetic Algorithm and Simulated Annealing

Bing Hu[1], Lin Yao[1], Yong Chen[2], and Zinxin Sun[1(✉)]

[1] Key Laboratory of Broadband Wireless Communication and Sensor Network Technology, Nanjing University of Posts and Telecommunications, Nanjing, China
`sunzx@njupt.edu.cn`
[2] Nanjing LongYuan Microelectronic Company Limited, Nanjing, China
`andychenyin@163.com`

Abstract. In this paper, on the basis of the analysis of common market model and some economic theories in the cloud computing resource management process, we propose a cloud resource management model based on combinatorial double auction. In order to solve the winner determination problem (WDP) in the combinatorial double auction, a cloud resource combinatorial double auction algorithm based on genetic algorithm and simulated annealing algorithm is proposed. Simulation results reveal that the algorithm combines genetic algorithm with simulated annealing algorithm (SAGA) outperforms genetic algorithm on fitness value and stability, and as the number of bidders increase, the solution have higher fitness value can be obtained.

Keywords: Cloud computing resource · Combinatorial double auction · Genetic algorithm (GA) · Simulated annealing (SA)

1 Introduction

Cloud computing is the mainstream way to provide web services. Based on the internet platform, it is primarily using virtualization technology to provide customers with a flexible, dynamic web services. Many researchers predicted that "the core competition of cloud computing in the future is in cloud datacenter" [1]. Cloud datacenter is a concentration place used for containing the computing equipment resources, and provides energy and maintenance for the computing equipment. It can be constructed separately, located within other buildings or distributed in multiple systems that in different geographical locations. Cloud resources together to serve multiple customers through a multi-tenant pattern. Although the resources exist in distributed sharing way in the physical, it is presented to users in the form of a single overall in the logical eventually [2]. The resource scheduling technology for cloud datacenter is the core of the cloud computing applications, and the key technology for cloud computing to realize

© ICST Institute for Computer Sciences, Social Informatics and Telecommunications Engineering 2017
J.-H. Lee and S. Pack (Eds.): QShine 2016, LNICST 199, pp. 435–445, 2017.
DOI: 10.1007/978-3-319-60717-7_43

large-scale applications, improve system performance and reduce energy consumption.

Cloud computing can conveniently on-demand access to a common set of configurable computing resource (such as, network, servers, storage device, application program and service). These resources can be quickly provided and released, while minimizing management cost or the interference of service provider. For the users, the management of computing resources is transparent. Users obtain the service they needed by paying to the resource providers without purchasing, maintaining and managing the infrastructure. Consequently, it is crucial to select appropriate providers based on the users requirement to complete the allocation of resource.

The researches of grid computing and distribution computing are worth cloud resource scheduling algorithm using for reference. According to the scheduling characteristics of cloud computing, many different scheduling strategies have been proposed. Resource scheduling problem is a NP-hard problem. A number of heuristic algorithms have been proposed to achieve a linear optimal. With an aim towards the biodiversity of resources and tasks in cloud computing, Zuo *et al.* propose a resource cost model and an improved ant colony optimization algorithm to solve the multi-objective optimization-scheduling problem [3]. Based on the diversity of tasks and the dynamic factors of resources, a multiqueue interlacing peak scheduling method is proposed to balance loads and improve the effects of resource allocation and utilization effectively in [4]. In order to accurately reflect the resource states, a self-adaptive threshold based dynamically weighted load evaluation method, which is evaluates the load state of the resource through a dynamically weighted evaluation method, is presented in [5]. However, since cloud computing services have many QoS constraints, practical scheduling scheme of cloud computing system is very few.

According to the economic characteristics of cloud computing, a cloud resource management model based on the economics is designed in [6]. And auction model is widely used in the cloud computing environment, because it is easy to realize and the required price information is smaller. Auctions can be categorized into single-side auctions, double-side auctions and combinatorial auctions according to the number of providers and users and the amount of resources. Combinatorial double auction is a combination of combinatorial auction and double auction. In the combinatorial double auction, both sides submit bids for multiple items. Compared with other auction mechanism, combinatorial double auctions solve the problem that bidder and auctioneer have unequal status, at the same time, reduce the auction times and improve the trade efficiency [7].

The key problem in combinatorial double auction is the winner determination problem (WDP). The process for solving combinatorial double problem not only involve the process of two-player game, but also result in large number of feasible solutions since the uncertainty of combination. If we simply adopt the method of exhaustion, the efficiency is very low. Moreover, it has been proved that the combinatorial double problem is a NP-hard problem. Xia et al. [8] reduce a general combinatorial double auction to a combinatorial single-sided auction, which is a multi-dimensional knapsack problem. Hsieh and Liao [9] take advantages of the surplus of combinatorial double auctions to reward winners based on the surplus of auctions, and proposed a computationally efficient approximate algorithm to tackle the complexity issue in combinatorial double auctions. In this paper, we propose a combinatorial double auction model based on genetic algorithm and simulated annealing algorithm, combined with the advantages of the two algorithms to solve the cloud resources allocation problem based on combinatorial double auction.

The organization of this paper is as follows. A cloud resource management model based on combinatorial double auction is proposed in Sect. 2. In Sect. 3, the algorithm of combinatorial double auction for cloud resources based on SAGA is elaborated. Section 4 presents the simulation results. Finally, conclusions are presented in Sect. 5.

2   Cloud Resource Management Model Based on Combinatorial Double Auction

The cloud resource management model based on combinatorial double auction is described in Fig. 1. This model is consisted of cloud resource consumer, cloud resource service agent, auctioneer, and cloud resource provider. Cloud Resource Provider (CRP) and Cloud Resource Consumer (CRC) are two main members in the market-oriented cloud resource management. Generally, CRC regards the Cloud Resource Agent (CRA) as its representative to complete all the work. Auctioneer formulates auction rules, CRC and CRP use different strategies to achieve their respective purposes under the precondition of abiding by the rules.

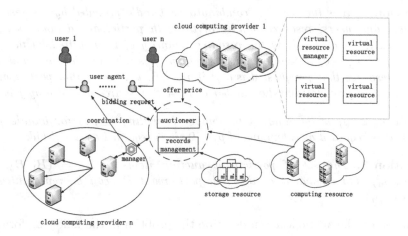

Fig. 1. Cloud resource management model based on combinatorial double auction.

The main auction steps in the cloud resource management are as follows.

(1) CRP provides price for the auctioneer.
(2) CRA submits a bid to the auctioneer.
(3) Auctioneer decides allocation policy according to the corresponding strategies.
(4) The CRP and the CRA who complete the assignment can coordinate with the requests related to the performance via Service Level Agreements (SLA).
(5) If coordination is successful, the auction is over, else, the auctioneer will choose other CRP, until there is no CRP can complete or a CRP is selected to complete a secondary assignment of CRA.

3   Cloud Resource Combinatorial Double Auction Algorithm Based on SAGA

3.1   Problem Description

In the process of the auction, buyers and sellers provide their own combinatorial bid document for the auctioneer, the bid document contains the number of the goods that they need and the price or the bid price of the goods. The auctioneer integrates the bid document, under the premise of ensuring that the number of each goods that buyer needs is not exceeding the number that seller provides, selecting an appropriate allocation scheme to maximize the social surplus.

Assuming that in the process of the auction there are m bidders and k types of different cloud resources (including CPU, memory, hard disk, bandwidth and so on) are auctioned by n auctioneers. Then the total number of participants in the auction is N, $N = m + n$.

Definition 1. **a** *is the resource combinatorial bundle provided by the resource providers and users, resource bundle of the j-th participant denote as* $\mathbf{a}_j = (a_{1j}, \cdots, a_{ij}, \cdots, a_{kj})$. a_{ij} *is the resource quantity of i submitted by the participant j, if $a_{ij} > 0$, it denotes that participant j is a buyer and the number of the i-th resource that j requested is a_{ij}; if $a_{ij} < 0$, it denotes that participant j is the resource provider and the number of the i-th resource provided by j is a_{ij}.*

Definition 2. p_j *is the amount the bidder is willing to pay for bundle j, if $p_j > 0$, it is regarded as a buy bid; if $p_j < 0$, it is regarded as a sell bid.*

Definition 3. *The set of participant auction items is* $B = (B_1, B_2, \cdots, B_i, \cdots, B_n)$, *bid document of the j-th participant B_j can be represented as* $B_j = (\mathbf{a}_j, p_j)$.

Therefore, the auctioneer can describe the problem in the following form:

$$\max \sum_{j=1}^{N} p_j x_j \tag{1}$$

$$s.t. \sum_{i=1}^{N} a_{ij}x_j \leq 0, \ \forall i \in I \tag{2}$$

$$X = [x_1, \cdots, x_n], \ x_i \in \{0,1\}, \ \forall j \in \{1, \cdots, N\} \tag{3}$$

where x_j stands for the results of allocation, if $x_j = 1$, it denotes that the j-th bids win the bid; if $x_j = 0$, it denotes that the j-th bids lose the bid. Formula (1) is the objective function, formula (2) is the constraint function, and formula (3) simplifies the problem into 0-1 programming problem. The objective of the model is to maximize social surplus while satisfying the constraint that the resource number of the winning buyer does not exceed the number supplied by the winning seller, i.e. supply is greater than demand. So the problem is the 0-1 programming problem, but also a NP-hard problem.

3.2   Algorithm Description

Currently, genetic algorithm (GA) is still one of the best methods to solve the winner determination problem (WDP). GA has good performance in global search, it can find out all the solutions in the solution space in a short time, while without falling into a rapid decline snare of local optimal solution, and distributed computing can be carried out conveniently to speed up the solution by using its intrinsic parallelism. Simulated annealing algorithm (SA) is a stochastic searching optimization algorithm based on Mente Carlo iterative solution strategy. Its starting point is the similarity between the annealing process of solid material and the general combinatorial optimization problem. Starting from an initial temperature, with the decreasing of temperature, the optimal solution is searched in solution space combined with the probabilistic jumping property, i.e. the local optimal solution can jump out probabilistically and tend to global optimal eventually.

GA converge to the optimal solution of the problem with probability 1. However, in practical application, the poor ability of searching the local optimal and prematurity phenomenon will be came out in GA. SA is a stochastic algorithm, which can avoid the problem falling into a local optimal solution. But its control ability to the whole search domain is rather poor so that the global optimal solution is not always found out. Hence, a combination of genetic algorithm and simulated annealing algorithm is proposed in this paper. Take advantages of the strong global search capability of genetic algorithm and strong local search capability of simulated annealing algorithm, during each genetic process, simulated annealing method is used for each individual.

Firstly, the algorithm obtains an initial population randomly, and then searches the global optimal solution via an improved genetic algorithm, if a more optimal solution is not found through genetic algorithm, local optimal search is performed by simulated annealing algorithm. When the initial temperature of the simulated annealing algorithm reduced to zero, genetic algorithm is used for global search again. Iterate this process until satisfy the end condition.

Algorithm 1. Cloud resources combinatorial double auction algorithm based on SAGA

1: Initialize the variables of GA and SA
2: create an initial population randomly
3:     for i from 1 to generation number
4:         for j from 1 to population size
5:             select parents
6:             create new_solutions with applying crossover and mutation on parents
7:             Δt = fitness(parents) - fitness(new_solutions)
8:             if $\Delta t < 0$
9:                 new_solutions accept to new generation
10:            else
11:                if $\exp(\Delta t/T) > \text{rand}(0 \sim 1)$
12:                    new_solutions accept to new generation
13:                else
14:                    parents go to new generation
15:                end if
16:            end if
17:        end for
18:        decrease T
19:        if the stop conditions are satisfied stop the algorithm
20: end for

First of all, the specific content of the genetic algorithm and simulated annealing algorithm is defined.

(1) Chromosome coding

Assuming that the number of people participated the auction is N and the chromosome X to be solved is represented by a binary string with length N, where $X = [x_1, \cdots, x_n]$, $x_i \in \{0, 1\}$, $\forall j \in \{1, \cdots, N\}$, x_j represents the allocation results, if $x_j = 1$, it denotes that the j-th bids win the bid; if $x_j = 0$, it denotes that the j-th bids lose the bid. For example, assume $X = 10110110...01$, it means participants 1, 3, 4 and so on win the bid, others lose the bid.

(2) Fitness function

Fitness function is the only standard for judging the quality of the solution. In this paper, the value of the objective function serves as the fitness function, i.e.

$f(X) = \sum_{j=1}^{N} p_j x_j$, $x_j \in \{0, 1\}$ represents the size of the obtained social surplus

when the current chromosome is $X = [x_1, \cdots, x_n]$, $x_i \in \{0, 1\}$. The greater the value of $f(X)$ is, the closer the X get to the optimal solution.

(3) Parents selection

In this paper, parents selection is selected by calculating the proportion of fitness value of each individual in the total fitness value of all the individuals.

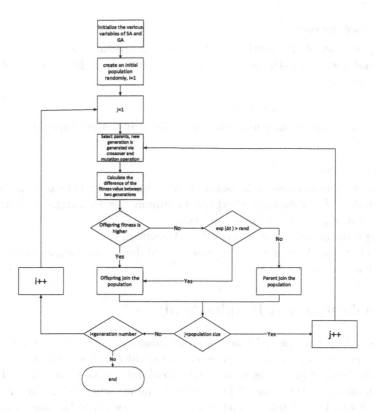

Fig. 2. Flow chart for cloud resources combinatorial double auction algorithm based on SAGA.

The larger the proportion is, the greater possibility of the individual is selected. So, the probability that the current group $P = [X_1, \cdots, X_N]$ is selected can be expressed as

$$p(X_j) = \frac{X_j}{\sum\limits_{i=1}^{N} X_i} \tag{4}$$

(4) Crossover

Nonuniform arithmetic crossover is adopted in crossover operation. Suppose that the individuals who are going to cross are X_1^s and X_2^s respectively, then two new individuals are generated via a crossover.

$$\begin{cases} X_1^{s+1} = \alpha X_2^s + (1 - \alpha)X_1^s \\ X_2^{s+1} = \alpha X_1^s + (1 - \alpha)X_2^s \end{cases} \tag{5}$$

$$\alpha = e^{(-\alpha_0 S/s)} \tag{6}$$

where α_0 is the crossover coefficient, S represents the maximum iteration number of genetic algorithm, s represents the number of the current iteration.

(5) Mutation operation

This paper adopts the method of the mutation position invert, that is, change the original gene 1 to 0 in a probabilistic manner, and the original gene 0 is mutated into 1.

(6) Simulated annealing algorithm

After the crossover and mutation operation, simulated annealing algorithm is performed.

(7) End condition

When the fitness value of the optimal individual reached the optimal solution or the number of iterations reached the maximum iteration number, output the optimal solution, and the iteration is over.

The specific algorithm is described in Algorithm 1.

Flow chart for cloud resources combinatorial double auction algorithm based on SAGA is shown in Fig. 2.

4   Simulations and Results Analysis

Since CloudSim was the most advanced simulator among the simulation environments, and it had great properties such as scaling well and having a low simulation overhead [10], in this paper, the CloudSim toolkits was selected as the experimental simulation tool. Before the test, the parameters involved in SAGA need to be set. Table 1 lists the parameters value needed in the algorithm.

Table 1. Main parameters of algorithm

Parameter name	Parameter value
Population size	200
Chromosome number	16
Crossover probability	0.5
Mutation probability	0.05
Population genetic number	20
Changes on temperature T	$T = T * 0.9$

Suppose there are three kinds of resources A, B and C in the auction. Each buyer and seller offer their bid documents, which including the resource number and price, to the auctioneer. Combinatorial resource bundles for buyer and seller are listed in Table 2. The total number of participants is 16, the number of users is 6, and the remaining is providers.

Table 2. The sample of combinatorial resource bundle

Number	1	2	3	Price	Number	1	2	3	Price
1	0	3	3	104	2	4	3	3	136
3	3	3	4	144	4	2	0	1	33
5	4	3	2	124	6	1	5	1	93
9	−2	−3	−1	−80	10	−1	−3	0	−36
11	−2	−2	0	−38	12	0	−1	−3	−70
13	−3	−3	−1	−93	14	−2	0	−3	−71
15	0	−3	−3	−76	16	−3	−1	−1	−54

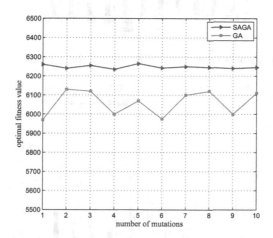

Fig. 3. The convergence of fitness value of the optimal solution for the SAGA and GA.

In order to judge the performance of SAGA algorithm, SAGA algorithm and general GA was compared to observe their convergence. Suppose there are 400 bidders in the simulation experiments. After 10 mutations, Fig. 3 shows the convergence of fitness value of the optimal solution for the genetic algorithm (GA) and genetic algorithm mixed with simulated annealing algorithm (SAGA). We can observe that SAGA has higher fitness value than GA, and the difference among every fitness values of SAGA is smaller than that of GA. Hence SAGA has better stability.

Then optimization results and computing time are compared between SAGA and GA under different number of participants. 10 groups of test samples with different number of bid documents are selected in the test process. Their fitness value and computing time is presented in Figs. 4 and 5 respectively. Although the computing time of SAGA is longer than that of GA with the number of bidders increase, SAGA can obtain the solution with a higher fitness value.

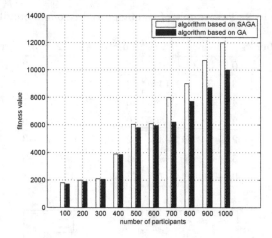

Fig. 4. Fitness value under different number of participants.

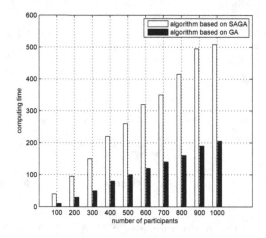

Fig. 5. Computing time under different number of participants.

5   Conclusion

The purpose of cloud computing is to realize collaborative work and resource sharing, while the heterogeneity and dynamic of various resources in the cloud computing and diversity of user requirements make the resource management abnormal complexity under the environment of cloud computing. However, due to the economic characteristics of cloud computing itself, the allocation algorithm based on economic model become a research hotspot in the cloud computing resource allocation. In this paper, we propose a cloud market model based on combinatorial double auction, and in order to solve the winner determination problem in the combinatorial double auction, a cloud resource combinatorial double auction algorithm based on SAGA is presented. The simulation results clearly illustrated that the proposed method has higher fitness value and stability than that of GA, and the proposed method can obtain the solution with a higher fitness value as the bidders increase.

Acknowledgement. This paper was supported by the National Natural Science Foundation of China (Nos. 61170276, 61373135); Project for Production Study and Research of Jiangsu Province (Grant No. BY2013011); Science and Technology Enterprises Innovation Fund Project of Jiangsu Province (Grant No. BC2013027); Key University Science Research Project of Jiangsu Province (Grant No.12KJA520003); Natural Science Foundation of Jiangsu Province of China (Grant No. BK20140883).

References

1. Barroso, L.A., Clidaras, J., Holzle, U.: The datacenter as a computer: an introduction to the design of warehouse-scale machines. Synth. Lect. Comput. Archit. **8**(3), 1–154 (2013)
2. Armbrust, M., Fox, A., Griffith, R., Joseph, A.D.: A view of cloud computing. Commun. ACM **53**(4), 50–58 (2010)
3. Zuo, L., Shu, L., Dong, S., et al.: A multi-objective optimization scheduling method based on the ant colony algorithm in cloud computing. IEEE Access **3**, 2687–2699 (2015)
4. Zuo, L., Dong, S., Shu, L., et al.: A multiqueue interlacing peak scheduling method based on tasks classification in cloud computing. IEEE Syst. J. **PP**(99), 1–13 (2016)
5. Zuo, L., Shu, L., Dong, S., et al.: Dynamically weighted load evaluation method based on self-adaptive threshold in cloud computing. Mob. Netw. Appl. 1–15 (2016)
6. Buyya, R., Yeo, C.S., Venugopal, S.: Market-oriented cloud computing: vision, hype, and reality for delivering it services as computing utilities. In: 10th IEEE International Conference on High Performance Computing and Communications (HPCC), pp. 5–13 (2008)
7. Samimi, P., Teimouri, Y., Mukhtar, M.: A combinatorial double auction resource allocation model in cloud computing. Inf. Sci. (2014)
8. Xia, M., Stallaert, J., Whinston, A.B.: Solving the combinatorial double auction problem. Eur. J. Oper. Res. **164**(1), 239–251 (2005)
9. Hsieh, F.S., Liao, C.S.: Schemes to reward winners in combinatorial double auctions based on optimization of surplus. Electron. Commer. Res. Appl. **14**(6), 405–417 (2015)
10. Son, J., Dastjerdi, A.V., Calheiros, R.N.: CloudSimSDN: modeling and Simulation of software-defined cloud data centers. In: 2015 15th IEEE/ACM International Symposium on Cluster, Cloud and Grid Computing (CCGrid), pp. 475–484 (2015)

Improving ELM-Based Time Series Classification by Diversified Shapelets Selection

Qifa Sun[1], Qiuyan Yan[1,2(✉)], Xinming Yan[1], Wei Chen[1],
and Wenxiang Li[3]

[1] School of Computer Science and Technology,
China University of Mining Technology, Xuzhou 221116, China
sunqifa@live.com, {yanqy,yanxm,chenw}@cumt.edu.cn
[2] School of Safty Engineering, China University of Mining Technology,
Xuzhou 221116, China
[3] School of Information Science and Engineering,
Wuhan University of Science and Technology, Wuhan 430081, China
liwx2006@hotmail.com

Abstract. ELM is an efficient neural network which has extremely fast learning capacity and good generalization capability. However, ELM fails to measure up the task of time series classification because it hard to extract the features and characters of time series data. Especially, many time series has trend features which cannot be abstracted by ELM thus lead to accuracy decreasing. Although through selection good features can improve the interpretability and accuracy of ELM, canonical methods either fails to select the most representative and interpretative features, or determine the number of features parameterized. In this paper, we propose a novel method by selection diversified top-k shapelets to improve the interpretability and accuracy of ELM. There are three contributions of this paper: First, we put forward a trend feature symbolization method to extract the trend information of time series; Second, the trend feature symbolic expressions are mapped into a shapelet candidates set and a diversified top-k shapelets selection method, named as **Div-TopkShapelets,** are proposed to find the most k distinguish shapelets; Last, we proposed an iterate ELM method, named as **DivShapELM**, automatically determining the best shapelets number and getting the optimum ELM classifier. The experimental results show that our proposed methods significantly improves the effectiveness and interpretability of ELM.

Keywords: Extreme Learning Machine · Time series classification · Shapelets · Diversified query

1 Introduction

Extreme Learning Machine (ELM for short), based on single-hidden layer feedforward neural networks (SLFNs), was proposed for addressing the slow speed of traditional neural networks. ELM has the extremely fast learning capability and good generalization capability through assign the weights connecting inputs to hidden nodes randomly. The weights between hidden nodes and outputs are learned in a single step,

© ICST Institute for Computer Sciences, Social Informatics and Telecommunications Engineering 2017
J.-H. Lee and S. Pack (Eds.): QShine 2016, LNICST 199, pp. 446–456, 2017.
DOI: 10.1007/978-3-319-60717-7_44

which essentially amounts to learning a linear model. In terms of these superiorities, a plethora of methods on ELM optimizing and applying have been designed [1–3].

In spite of so many advantages, there still are some shortcomings of ELM. As we all known, the black-box character of neural networks prevent ELM measuring up to time series data classification by itself. The characters of noisy and high-dimensional increase the complexity and decrease the performance of canonical ELM classifiers. Meanwhile, many time series data has the trend characters, and the problem of trend analysis in time series has attracted significant recently. However, ELM classifiers cannot focus on the trend character, whereas lead to performance decreasing. A possible solution to resolve this issue is to improve the interpretability of ELM by feature selection. A set of good features not only can remove the noises and reduce the dimension of time series, but also can express trend character better.

In this paper, we tackle these issues by a diversified representative and interpretative feature selection–based framework, and the selected feature named shapelets. Shapelet was introduced by Ye and Keogh [4] as a primitive for time series data mining, which is supervised segments of time series that are highly descriptive of the target variable [5]. As a popular data analysis technique, shapelets-transformation classification methods have achieved a high momentum in terms of research focus [6–8] and widely applied in Landcover Classification [9], lung cancer predicting [10], and sensor-based human activity recognition [11].

There are two challenges in applying shapelets extraction method in ELM. First, the original shapelets candidates set are so huge and there are many redundant shapelets which decreasing the accuracy and efficiency of classification. Second, current proposed shapelets selection schemes all fail to extract trend behavior from time series. In order to address these two issues, in this paper, we propose a novel shapelets selection method to adapting ELM to time series data classification. First, a trend feature symbolization method is proposed to extract the trend features in time series. Second, combined with trend symbol expressions, we calculate all the shapelet candidates and get rid of all the similar and redundant shapelets in candidates based on diversity graph. Third, we use the shapelets transformed data to iteratively training ELM and get the optimal classifier. The experimental results show that the proposed approach significantly improves the effectiveness and efficiency of ELM and most time series classifiers.

The rest of this paper is organized as follows. Section 2 brief introduce the conceptions of ELM and shapelets. Section 3 elaborate the proposed method. Experimental analysis is reported in Sect. 4. Finally, Sect. 5 concludes this paper.

2 Related Works

In this section, we will introduce some basic conceptions about ELM and shapelets which are used in this paper.

2.1 ELM

Extreme Learning Machine (ELM) is a generalized single hidden-layer feedforward network. In ELM, the hidden layer node parameter is mathematically calculated instead of being iteratively tuned; thus, it provides good generalization performance at thousands of times faster speed than traditional popular learning algorithms for feedforward neural networks.

Suppose there are N arbitrary distinct training instances $(x_i, t_i) \in R^N \times R^M$, where x_i is one $N \times 1$ input vector and t_i is one $M \times 1$ input vector. If a SLFNs with L hidden nodes can approximate these N samples with zero error, it then implies that there exist β_i, a_i and b_i, such that:

$$f_L(x_j) = \sum_{i=1}^{L} \beta_i G(a_i, b_i, x_j) = t_j, \ j = 1 \ldots \ldots N \tag{1}$$

Where $a_i = [a_{i1}, a_{i2}, \ldots, a_{in}]^T$ and $b_i = [b_{i1}, b_{i2}, \ldots, b_{in}]^T$ denote the weight and bias of the ith hidden layer node, $\beta_i = [\beta_{i1}, \beta_{i2}, \ldots, \beta_{im}]^T$ is the weight vector connecting the ith hidden node to the output nodes. Then Eq. (1) can be written compactly as:

$$H\beta = T \tag{2}$$

Where

$$H(a_1, \ldots \ldots a_L, b_1, \ldots \ldots b_L, x_1, \ldots \ldots x_N)$$
$$= \begin{pmatrix} G(a_1, b_1, x_1) & \cdots & G(a_L, b_L, x_1) \\ \vdots & \ddots & \vdots \\ G(a_1, b_1, x_N) & \cdots & G(a_L, b_L, x_N) \end{pmatrix}$$

$$\beta = \begin{bmatrix} \beta_1^T \\ \cdots \\ \cdots \\ \beta_L^T \end{bmatrix}_{L \times M} \quad \text{and} \ T = \begin{bmatrix} t_1^T \\ \cdots \\ \cdots \\ t_N^T \end{bmatrix}_{N \times m}$$

Here, $G(a_i, b_i, x_j)$ denotes the activation function which is used to calculate the output of the ith hidden node for the jth training instance. In ELM, many nonlinear activation functions can be used, including sigmoid, sine, hardlimit and radial basis functions. H is called hidden layer output matrix of the network, where with respect to inputs $x_1, x_2 \ldots x_N$ and its jth row represents the output vector of the hidden layer with respect to input x_j.

ELM assigned values to parameters a_i and b_i randomly according to any continuous samplings distribution. Equation (2) then becomes a linear system and the output weight β are estimates as:

$$\widehat{\beta} = H^{\dagger}T, \tag{3}$$

where $H^{\dagger}$ is the Moore-Penrose generalized inverse of the hidden layer output matrix H. $H^{\dagger} = (H^T H)^{-1} H^T$ if $H^T H$ is nonsingular or $H^{\dagger} = (H^T H)^{-1}$ if HH^T is nonsingular. Here, $\widehat{\beta}$ is the minimum-norm least squares solution of Eq. (2).

2.2 Shapelets

Shapelets are discriminative patterns in time series that best predict the target variable when their distances to the respective time series are used as features for a classifier. The original shapelets-based classifier embeds the shapelets discovery algorithm in a decision tree method, and information gain is adopted to assess the quality of candidate shapelets [4]. Shapelets transformed classification method was proposed to separate the processing of shapelets selection and classification [8]. In this category, distances of time series to shapelets can be viewed as new classification predictors. It has been shown by various researchers that shapelets-derived predictors boost the classification accuracy [6]. In addition, shapelets also provide interpretive features that help domain experts to understand the differences between the target classes.

Research challenges of the shapelets technology include that shapelets candidates selection is time consuming and large quantities of redundant shapelets decreases the accuracy of classification. Some works tried to relieve this issue by introducing clustering [7] or pruning method [12, 13] to reduce the redundancy. But the research issue is still an open question.

3 Proposed Method

In this section, we give the similar shapelets conception, diversified top-k shapelets conception and using diversity graph based on the similar shapelets to get the diversified top-k shapelets results. We detailed four parts of our work (1) a trend feature symbolization algorithm, (2) a mapping algorithm transform the trend symbolic expression to shapelets candidates, (3) a method of extraction diversified top-k shapelets, and (4) transforming the data based on diversified top-k shapelets and classification using ELM. The following contents will discuss above three contribution separately.

3.1 Trend Feature Symbolization

In this section, we proposed a trend feature symbolization method, which express the subsequence as a tuple list, named as TFSAList, and each tuple contains two elements: the gradient k and the feature symbol u. The detailed algorithm of find TFSAList is shown in Algorithm 1.

```
Algorithm 1 CreateTFSAList
Input: Dataset: D
          An instance in D: T_id
          The number of instance in D: N
          The number of subsequence in each T_id: num
          The angle threshold: γ
          Trend feature tuple: TT
Output: TFSAList of D
1:  i=0
2:  For id = 1 to N
3:     L= T_id.length / num
4:     S_1←T_id [0, L-1]
5:     K_1=gradient (S_1)
       i= i+1
6:     TT [i].U= L
7:     TT [i].K= K_1
8:     For j = 2 to T_id.length-L+1
7:        S_2=←T [j, j+L-1]
8:        K_2=gradient (S_2)
9:        If (|K_1-K_2|>γ)
10:           i=i+1
11:           TT [i].U = TT [i-1].U+1
12:           TT [i].K = K_2
13:           j = TT [i].U
14:           S_1←T [j, j+L-1]
15:           K_1 = gradient (S_1)
16:        Else
17:           K_1 = (K_1+K_2) /2
18:           TT [i].U = TT [i].U +1
19:     End For
20:     TFSAList [id] ←Symbolization (TT)
21:  End For
22:  Return TFSAList
```

3.2   Map Trend Symbolic Expression to Shapelets

In this section, we map the trend symbolic expressions (TFSAList) generated in Algorithm 1 to shapelet candidates. The detailed procedure is shown in Algorithm 2.

```
Algorithm 2 MaptrendToshap
input: trend symbolic expression list TFSAList
       data set: D
output: shapelets candidiates
1: for i=1 to TFSAList. Length
2:   score[i] = GenerateScore (TFSAList[i])
3: end for
4: TFSA_sort=Sort (TFSAList, Score)
5: subsequence_set= Map (TFSA_sort, D)
6: for i=1 to subsequence_set.size
7:    info=CallInfoGain (Subsequence_set[i])
8:    shapeletsCandidates. Add (Subsequence_set[i], Info)
9: end for
```

3.3 Extraction Diversified Top-k Shapelets

Diversified query aims to find the objects which are relevant to query according to scores, however, are not similar to others. Considerable works have focused on the diversify top-k query, but they almost applied on a typical circumstance. In our work, we hope to find a general method to find diversified top-k shapelets, so we got the idea from [11] and acquire diversified top-k shapelets based on diversity graph. In algorithm 3, the diversified top-k shapelets selection method, named as **DivTopkShapelets** is elaborated.

```
Algorithm 3 DivTopkShapelets
input:  shapelets candidates: ShapeletsCandidates
        diversified number: k
output: top k number of diversified shapelets: kShapelets
1: shapGraph=genGraph (ShapeletsCandidates)
2: kShapelets = ∅, n =V(Graph).size
3: kShapelets.add (v1)
4: while (|kShapelets|<k)
5:    for i=2 to n
6:       if (Graph[i] ∩kShapelets = ∅)
7:          kShapelets.add (vi)
8:       end if
9:    end for
10: return kShapelets
```

3.4   Diversified Top-k Shapelets Based ELM Classification

After getting diversified top-k shapelets, we can use these optimal shapelets to transform testing datasets. Actually, each shapelet equal to a special feature, every time series T can be transformed an instance have k number of features by calculating the distance between time series T and every shapelet. Meanwhile, in order to get the best classification accuracy and also to get rid of the independence on the parameter k, we set k in an interval $[1,\kappa]$ which means the iterate times to model ELM classifier. Then we use the ELM to learning the transformed dataset and evaluate every diversified top-k shapelets candidate. The typical k value with the largest prediction accuracy is selected. In this paper, we refer to the proposed ELM classification method as **Div-ShapELM**. DivShapELM is a general method to improve the ELM learning accuracy by select diversified and trend features of time series.

4   Experiments

In this section, we study the performance of **DivTopkShapelets** and **DivShapELM** by evaluating its efficiency and effectiveness. The algorithms are coded in C++. All experiments are conducted on a 2.0-GHz HP PC with 1G memory running Window XP and using Weka framework with Java. The UCR time series datasets [15] were used in our experiments.

4.1   Accuracy Comparison

In this section, we verified the accuracy improvement for DivTopkShapelets and DivShapELM separately. Firstly, in Sect. 4.1.1, we select two similar works: ClusterShapelet and ShapeletSelection, to compare with DivTopkShapelets. We hope to find whether DivTopkShapelets can select more representative and representative shapelets than compared methods. Secondly, in Sect. 4.1.2, we compared the accuracy of DivShapELM with state-of-the-art ELM to clarify if our proposed method can improve the effectiveness of ELM.

4.1.1   Accuracy Comparison with ClusterShapelet and ShapeletSelection

In Table 1, we compared the relative accuracy of DivTopkShapelets between ClusterShapelet on six different classifier and on fifteen datasets. The 'average' column means average relative accuracy on six different classifier on one typical dataset. From Table 1 we can draw the conclusion that DivTopkShapelets can enhance the accuracy on all these six classifiers and the most is 10.80% accuracy improved on Naïve Bayes. Especially, DivTopkShapelets overhead ClusterShapelet 30.87% on ECGFiveDays dataset.

In Table 2, we compared the relative accuracy between DivTopkShapelets and ShapeletSelection. We can see that compared with ShapeletSelection, DivTopk-Shapelets can enhance the accuracy on all these six classifiers and improved the average accuracy on ten datasets. On Adiac dataset, DivTopkShapelets has the best improvement, the accuracy improved 20.80%. For classifiers, DivTopkShapelets

Table 1. Relative accuracy between DivTopkShapelets algorithm and ClusterShapelet algorithm

Data	C4.5	1NN	Naïve Bayes	Bayesian network	Random forest	Rotation forest	Average
Adiac	14.07	17.90	17.90	11.76	21.48	21.48	17.43
Beef	−3.33	−3.33	13.33	−16.67	3.33	−3.33	−1.67
ChlorineConcentra	−1.02	−2.84	−8.46	−1.74	−3.67	−2.06	−3.30
Coffee	10.71	0.00	0.00	3.57	3.57	3.57	3.57%
DiatomSizeReducti	0.98	6.86	−3.59	0.33	−4.58	−6.86	−1.14
ECG200	18.00	4.00	9.00	3.00	12.00	7.00	8.83%
ECGFiveDays	**48.43**	28.11	25.0	24.62	**29.85**	**29.15**	**30.87**
FaceFour	2.93	27.60	29.04	12.20	14.33	18.08	17.36
Gun_Point	2.67	9.33	6.67	8.00	6.00	6.67	6.56
MedicalImages	2.63	1.58	−0.26	−4.74	5.00	1.45	0.94
MoteStrain	3.19	19.49	**31.79**	9.35	6.79	11.42	13.67
RobotSurface	25.62	**37.44**	26.96	**30.12**	20.13	25.12	27.57
SyntheticControl	4.67	5.00	18.33	20.00	7.33	5.67	10.17
Trace	7.00	−2.00	−5.00	0.00	4.00	−2.00	0.33
TwoLeadECG	18.00	8.96	1.23	5.36	10.89	−2.46	6.99
Average improved	10.30	10.54	**10.80**	7.01	9.10	7.53	10.00
Data sets improved	13	12	11	12	13	10	12

enhance the average accuracy most on 1NN classifier, the value improve 6.06% and on the Robot Surface dataset, the DivTopkShapelets enhance 1NN classifier 32.61% on accuracy.

4.1.2   Accuracy Comparison Between DivShapELM and ELM

As shown in Table 3, DivShapELM has obvious advantages than state-of-art ELM on 12 out of 15 datasets. Especially, On ECGFiveDays Dataset, DivShapELM has the accuracy of 90.57%, better then ELM 32.7%. So by introduction the conception of diversified top-k shapelets, we can get the most representative attributes of dataset and also can get rid of the redundant, which can obviously improve the accuracy of ELM and also can enhance the explainable of selected features.

4.2   Time Cost Comparison

DivShapELM has three extra pre-procedures: shapelets candidate selection, diversified shapelets selection time and data transform time. Once the transformed data got, the rest procedure is a usual classification process. Table 4 give the extra time and classification time of DivShapELM and ELM. The time cost of diversified shapelets selection are varied with dataset, but which can be conducted in an offline manner. Apparently, DivShapELM has the less classification time than ELM apparently on 13 out of 15 datasets.

Table 2. Relative accuracy between DivTopkShapelets and ShapeletSelection

Data	C4.5	1NN	Naïve Bayes	Bayesian network	Random forest	Rotation forest	Average
Adiac	16.62	21.23	**17.14**	**16.37**	**26.09**	**23.02**	**20.08**
Beef	−3.33	3.33	16.67	0.00	3.33	10.00	5.00
ChlorineConcentration	0.10	14.24	−10.70	−0.65	13.54	0.78	2.89
Coffee	−3.57	7.14	0.00	0.00	−7.14	7.14	0.59
DiatomSizeReduc	5.56	9.15	−6.86	−4.90	−16.34	−5.89	−3.21
ECG200	4.00	−6.00	2.00	3.00	5.00	0.00	1.33
ECGFiveDays	−0.46	−0.23	−1.28	−0.58	−0.35	0.70	−0.37
FaceFour	3.41	0.00	1.13	−7.95	−1.13	9.09	0.76
Gun_Point	0.67	−2.00	−1.34	−0.67	−3.33	−0.67	−1.22
MedicalImages	1.84	8.55	0.53	−4.08	15.00	5.92	4.63
MoteStrain	−4.63	1.77	−5.11	−5.59	−6.15	−1.03	−3.46
RobotSurface	**16.97**	**32.61**	5.99	8.49	12.64	11.32	14.67
SyntheticControl	3.00	1.67	−0.67	0.67	−1.00	0.00	0.61
Trace	6.00	0.00	−4.00	2.00	0.00	−2.00	0.33
TwoLeadECG	−3.07	−0.52	0.88	−0.35	−6.05	−2.46	−1.93
Average improved	2.87	**6.06**	0.96	0.38	2.27	3.73	2.71
Data sets improved	10	11	8	7	7	10	10

Table 3. Accuracy comparison between DivShapELM and ELM

Data	DivShapELM	ELM
Adiac	**58.70**	41.05
Beef	**67.88**	55.42
ChlorineConcentration	50.30	**59.77**
Coffee	**95.44**	90.60
DiatomSizeReduction	82.76	**88.95**
ECG200	**90.12**	67.15
ECGFiveDays	**90.57**	57.87
FaceFour	**87.34**	80.12
Gun_Point	**95.43**	88.65
MedicalImages	51.23	**62.00**
MoteStrain	**84.70**	66.19
SonyAIBORobotSurface	**94.16**	74.55
SyntheticControl	**97.63**	85.40
Trace	**93.17**	90.77
TwoLeadECG	**94.23**	78.12

Table 4. Run time of DivShapELM and ELM

Data	Candidate selection (s)	Diversified shapelets selection (s)	Data transform (s)	DivShapELM (s)	ELM (s)
Adiac	1277	2.09	0.811	**0.04992**	0.13728
Beef	1026	251.894	0.702	0.0156	0.0156
ChlorineConcentration	2636	3.136	7.363	**0.01716**	0.05148
Coffee	337	234.422	0.436	0.04368	0.00936
DiatomSizeReduction	95	476.331	2.294	**0.02652**	0.0312
ECG200	216	0.905	0.14	**0.0156**	0.02496
ECGFiveDays	84	0.858	0.717	**0.02184**	0.02652
FaceFour	634	66.94	0.671	**0.02184**	0.06864
Gun_Point	151	3.167	0.218	**0.0312**	0.09048
MedicalImages	732	0.219	0.514	**0.00468**	0.05304
MoteStrain	30	0.687	0.483	**0.03276**	0.04368
SonyAIBORobotSurface	28	0.39	0.249	0.01404	0.00624
SyntheticControl	340	0.343	0.25	**0.04368**	0.07488
Trace	1168	268.165	1.201	**0.01716**	0.1638
TwoLeadECG	25	0.265	0.546	**0.039**	0.1017

5   Conclusion

In order to improve the interpretable and representable of ELM, we proposed a novel method to select distinct and optimal features through selecting k number shapelets of time series dataset, meanwhile, the selected shapelets can express the trend information as well. We verified the effectiveness and efficiency of ELM and other 6 classifies on 15 datasets. The experiments results that DivTopkShapelets can improve the effectiveness and efficiency on almost all of the classifiers on almost datasets. The DivShapELM method also has outstanding accuracy than state-of-the-art ELM method.

Acknowledgement. Supported by the Natural Science Foundation of Jiangsu Province of China (BK20140192). National Natural Science Foundation and Shanxi Provincial People's Government Jointly Funded Project of China for Coal Base and Low Carbon (No. U1510115), the Qing Lan Project, the China Postdoctoral Science Foundation (No. 2013T60574).

References

1. Huang, G.-B., Zhu, Q.-Y., Siew, C.-K.: Extreme learning machine: a new learning scheme of feedforward neural networks. In: Proceedings of International Joint Conference on Neural Networks (IJCNN 2004), pp. 985–990 (2004)
2. Huang, G.-B., Zhu, Q.-Y., Siew, C.-K.: Extreme learning machine: theory and applications. Neurocomputing **70**, 489–501 (2004)

3. Huang, G.-B., Zhu, Q.-Y., Mao, K.Z., Siew, C.-K., Saratchandran, P., Sundararajan, N.: Can threshold networks be trained directly. IEEE Trans. Circuits Syst. II **53**(3), 187–191 (2006)

4. Ye. L., Keogh, E.: Time series shapelets: a new primitive for data mining. In: Proceedings of 15th ACM SIGKDD International Conference on Knowledge Discovery and Data Mining, pp. 947–956. ACM (2009)

5. Ye, L., Keogh, E.: Time series shapelets: a novel technique that allows accurate, interpretable and fast classification. Data Min. Knowl. Disc. **22**(1–2), 149–182 (2011)

6. Mueen, A., Keogh, E., Young, N.: Logical-shapelets: an expressive primitive for time series classification. In: Proceedings of 17th ACM SIGKDD International Conference on Knowledge Discovery and Data Mining, pp. 1154–1162. ACM (2011)

7. Rakthanmanon, T., Keogh, E.: Fast shapelets: a scalable algorithm for discovering time series shapelets. In: Proceedings of 13th SIAM Conference on Data Mining (SDM) (2013)

8. Lines, J., Davis, L.M., Hills, J., et al.: A shapelet transform for time series classification. In: Proceedings of 18th ACM SIGKDD International Conference on Knowledge Discovery and Data Mining, pp. 289–297. ACM (2012)

9. Hills, J., Lines, J., Baranauskas, E., et al.: Classification of time series by shapelet transformation. Data Min. Knowl. Disc. **28**(4), 851–881 (2014)

10. Zakaria, J., Mueen, A., Keogh, E.: Clustering time series using unsupervised-shapelets. In: 2012 IEEE 12th International Conference on Data Mining (ICDM), pp. 785–794. IEEE (2012)

11. Xing, Z., Pei, J., Philip, S.Y., et al.: Extracting interpretable features for early classification on time series. In: SDM, vol. 11, pp. 247–258 (2011)

12. Chang, K.W., Deka, B., Hwu, W.M.W., et al.: Efficient pattern-based time series classification on GPU. In: 2012 IEEE 12th International Conference on Data Mining (ICDM), pp. 131–140. IEEE (2012)

13. Yuan, J.D., Wang, Z.H., Han, M.: Shapelet pruning and shapelet coverage for time series classification. J. Softw. **26**(9), 2311–2325 (2015). (in Chinese)

14. Qin, L., Yu, J.X., Chang, L.: Diversifying top-k results. Proc. VLDB Endow. **5**(11), 1124–1135 (2012)

15. Chen, Y., Keogh, E., Hu, B., Begum, N., Bagnall, A., Mueen, A., Batista, G.: The UCR Time Series Classification Archive. [DB/OL] (2015). http://www.cs.ucr.edu/~eamonn/time_series_data/

Research on Energy Control Policy in Low-Power Consumption Wireless Image Sensor Networks

Yinbo Xie[1(✉)], Jianfeng Yang[1], Chengcheng Guo[1], and Wei Hu[2]

[1] Electronic Information School, Wuhan University, Road LuoJia,
Wuhan 430072, China
{xyb,yjf,netccg}@whu.edu.cn
[2] College of Computer Science and Technology,
Wuhan University of Science and Technology, Wuhan, China
huwei@wust.edu.cn

Abstract. With its low power consumption characteristics, a new type network named wireless sensor image networks (WISN) combined the traditional wireless sensor networks (WSN) and the latest image sensing technology have been attracting attention. This paper presents a kind of wireless image sensor networks energy optimization methodology which was based on the routing nodes buffer state schedule. According to the running mechanism of routing nodes in wireless sensor networks, when a sensor node transfers data to another node, the energy consumption will happen mainly during transit between the routing nodes, each routing node will analysis and storage the state transition in its buffer, this state transition was usually caused by sending and receiving operation. Also, the node can dynamically adjust their energy consumption count and service values compared to the other nodes, also these nodes can determine itself whether to be a critical path node or not. During the data transmission in the network, the nodes can be scheduled to be used as the routing node with regarding of each energy level, and finally the network can sustain longest.

Keywords: Wireless Image Sensor Networks · Low Power Consumption · Energy control strategy · Reliability · Performance analysis

1 Introduction

The low-power consumption WISN (Wireless Image Sensor networks) is a kind of particular WSN (Wireless Sensor networks), which consists of sensor nodes equipped with an image sensor or sensors [1, 2], using traditional low-power wireless sensor networks such as IEEE 802.15.4 protocol to communicate between nodes inside. Because the image sensor nodes usually need to be set up in remote areas or the harsh environment with lack of power supply, the energy consumption control method becomes particular serious to the WISN with high energy consumption image sensors. In addition to reduce the energy consumption of the every sensor node itself, it is more important to control that of the whole network, and the consumption during transit from the sensor node to sink node will be the key point [3].

© ICST Institute for Computer Sciences, Social Informatics and Telecommunications Engineering 2017
J.-H. Lee and S. Pack (Eds.): QShine 2016, LNICST 199, pp. 457–465, 2017.
DOI: 10.1007/978-3-319-60717-7_45

However, to the best of our knowledge, the theoretical analysis and research works regarding the problem of energy consumption in WISN are relatively lacking, Some research using the traditional WSN energy control strategy to improve the network life cycle in WISN always ignore the following observations:

1. Because of the high energy consumption of image sensor, so there exists function difference between the routing nodes in WISN and the same nodes in traditional WSN.
2. With the traditional energy consumption control method, when a large number of data packet from the same sensor node need to be transmitted, it will be easier to make effective path failure because the cluster head died for battery drain.
3. There may be exists data dependence between packet arrived in the sink node one after the other, the multiple packets from the same sensor node can be restored to the original image.

By self-configuration between the mobile routing nodes, [4–6] proposed a very clever sleep scheduling method based on mobile cloud computing to solve the energy balance problem inside cloud. However, the deployment of mobile nodes is limited and restricted by the environment in many cases.

Because of bandwidth limitations in WISN, an image data need to be divided into appropriate package which can be sent by consequent time slots, and the all or essential parts of divided data can be regrouped and restored to the original image in the sink node. Under the condition of a fixed image size and wireless transmission rate, the nodes will transmit the image packets as quickly as possible to reduce the energy consumption. When a packet from an image sensor node has arrived in a cluster or cloud, which was composed of routing nodes, the energy consumption mostly happened the transmission consumption between routing nodes. In WSN, the routing nodes can be configured into buffer mode and non-buffer mode [7]. According to one hop transmission, the buffer mode can hold more packet waiting to send, on the contrary, the non-buffer mode is easier to set up an end to end immediate transmission.

Even in the non-buffer mode, the source sensor nodes and sink nodes still need to work with buffer used to storage temp data. Because the buffer is so small that the intermediate routing node need to send the data to the next hop before the new image data arrive in [8], benefit from transmitting only small amounts of data packets, this kind of non-buffer structure is very effective in the traditional small data quantity, low-energy consumption, low latency WSN [9], however, there exist large number of correlative image packets in WISN, once interference in the link lead to the transmission failed, too much energy will be consumed in the data retransmission process, and it will be large number of packet data were congested or lost in one or some routing nodes, so, to the end, the sink node can only obtain parts of image data, and the final image from sensor node will not be assembled.

In the buffer mode, all nodes have to maintain their buffer, although the existence of the buffer unit increases the energy consumption of the single nodes, as far as higher energy consumption in data transmission is concerned, it is tolerable to set up some efficient buffer unit for holding packets to forward. At the same time, more forwarding data are transferred into the node buffer to queue, the block loss probability in the nodes is reduced, less retransmission improve the life cycle of the whole network.

As to routing nodes, the state change of buffer unit is responding to the process of data transmission. After validation, data into the node's buffer means some kind of packet from a sensor node or the other routing node has been received, on the other hand, data out from the node's buffer means a packet has been delivered successfully, in order to reduce the energy consumption in network transmission, we present a method base on buffer state change in the routing nodes with queue theory.

The remaining parts of the paper are organized as follows. The WISN network model base on routing cloud architecture and the definition of the state space are described in Sect. 2, according to the model discussed in Sects. 2 and 3 analyzes the energy optimization policy based on three buffer allocation ways and presents the energy formulation and constraint. Evaluation about energy consumption in these three buffer allocation ways are shown in Sects. 4 and 5 concludes this paper.

2 Network Model and State Space

For the sake of argument, we consider a single layer or multilayer area as a sensor routing cloud or cluster which is made up of large number routing nodes with buffer units, as shown in Fig. 1, generally, we could always separate this kind small cloud or cluster structure from a larger and more complex WISN. When an image packet from an image sensor node has been broadcasting into the sensor routing cloud, the transmission energy consumption is the key point to the whole cloud energy consumption [10], that is to say, the change in buffer state reflects its energy consumption in a single routing node inside the cloud, the whole changes in buffer state of all nodes reflect the energy consumption trend of the cloud.

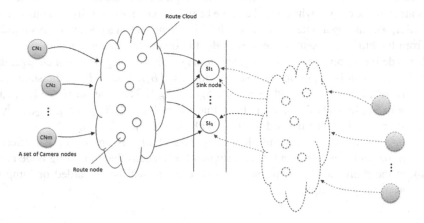

Fig. 1. A WISN system model based on sensor routing cloud

2.1 Network Model

Because of the higher energy consumption of image sensor, slightly different from homogeneous nodes in traditional WSN, there exist the function difference between the sensor nodes and routing nodes in WISN, when a node in WISN work as a routing node, we are just to say it act as a routing node, obviously, it may also work as a sensor node when it is equipped with image sensor. To discuss the state transition process, we present an abstract routing nodes cloud mode, at the same time, we consider a wireless image sensor networks consisting of m image sensor nodes, n routing nodes, and q sink nodes, as shown in Fig. 1, so we define some sets as: m image sensor nodes represented by set CN with $CN = \{cn_1, cn_2, ..., cn_m\}$, n routing nodes represented by set $RN = \{rn_1, rn_2, ..., rn_n\}$, and q sink nodes represented by set $SI = \{si_1, si_2, ..., si_q\}$.

After acquiring image data, CN split the image data into a series of packets, then push them one by one to the routing cloud RN from the side near to them, then the packets is transferred to SI in the other side. When all the packets from an image sensor node have been delivered to the sink node, the image data can be recombined.

When there are many packets from different image sensor nodes reach the same routing node, they have to queue in the buffer of the current routing node, and be delivered to the next hop according to their arrived order and priority. To achieve buffer occupancy for temporary data storage at the routing nodes, we develop a semi-Markov decision process (SMDP) based buffer allocation policy [11]. We have made the following assumptions base on SMDP theory, first of all, the process to deliver packet between routing nodes is independent, and follows Poisson distribution with mean arrival rate λ, with mean forwarding rate μ. Secondly, the time duration for all buffer state is identically distributed [12]. Thirdly, the mean holding time at different buffer states is small compared to data arrival time. The last the buffer is finite, and error sending and receiving communication protocol data do not cause the state transition in the buffer.

Without losing its generality, we define a set L with $L = \{l_{c1}, l_{c2}, ..., l_{cm}\}$, for the size of image data in CN, moreover, we consider CN work in periodic wake, and their buffer work as a FIFO (First In and First Out) with v segments, to each segment, there exist two states: full or empty, when a packet have been received successfully and pushed into the buffer, we can say a state changed, on the other hand, when a packet has been pulled out from the buffer and sent to the next node, the other state change occurs.

If we define a transition from a segment to a neighboring segment as a change, then the buffer size can be represent by a set B with $B = \{B_{r1}, B_{r2}, ..., B_{rm}\}$, the state space can be represent by a set S with $S = \{S_{r1}, S_{r2}, ..., S_{rm}\}$. Take the ith ($i \in \{1,2,...,n\}$) node, for example, its buffer size can be defined a set B_{ri} with $B_{ri} = \{b_{i,1}, b_{i,2}, ..., b_{i,v}\}$, and its state space can be defined a set S_{ri} with $S_{ri} = \{s_{i,1}, s_{i,2}, ..., s_{i,v}\}$.

Among above: $s_{i,1}$ means the ith routing node buffer is empty, or the effective length of the packet is less than that of a segment, $s_{i,v}$ means the ith routing node buffer is full, at the moment, one more packet next received will be discarded or jump the queue on priority principle.

2.2   State Space

Definition: A transition from state s_j to state s_{j+1} ($j < v-1$) occurs with probability $p_{i,s_j \to s_{j+1}}$, when the data is stored into the buffer of rn_i node, while a state transition from state s_j to state s_k (k < j and j, k < v) occurs with probability $p_{i,s_j \to s_k}$, when the data is delivered to a next routing node in RN or a sink node in SI.

So whether data from a routing node is stored into the buffer or is loaded from the buffer for sending may be consider as two actions in an action space.

According to this, let A with $A = \{A_1, A_2,..., A_n\}$ as an action set, and A_i with $A_i = \{0,1,...,m\}(i \in \{0,1,...,n\})$ is used to represent all possible transition states set in the buffer of the ith routing node.

Then an action $a_i \in A_i(s_j) \subseteq A_i \subseteq A$ can have following values:

$$a_i = j\,(\exists\,\text{packet has been stored into the buffer of } cn_i \text{ from } cn_i\, j \in \{0, 1, \ldots, m\}) \quad (1)$$

When the ith node has not received any data from any sensor node, we can describe the action with $a_i = 0(a_i \in A_i)$, however, if we have assumed half duplex communication between the nodes, an action $a_i = 0$ does not imply that the same buffer state is maintained due to equal number of data arrivals and departures.

Based on the assumptions above, the state transition probabiilities along with $\tau_{i,s_j}(a_i)$ which is the expected time in current state s_j when action a_i is taken in routing node r_i, describe the dynamics character of the system. The state transition probability can be given by:

$$p_{i,s_j \to s_k}(a_i) = \begin{cases} 1 - \frac{1}{\lambda} - \frac{1}{\mu} & \begin{array}{l} j = k, a_i = 0,\, i \in \{1, 2, \ldots, n\}, \\ j \in \{1, \ldots, v-1\} \end{array} \\ \frac{1}{\lambda} & \begin{array}{l} k = j + 1,\, a_i \in \{1, 2, \ldots, m\}, \\ i \in \{1, 2, \ldots, n\};\, j \in \{0, 2, \ldots, v-1\} \end{array} \\ \frac{1}{\mu} & \begin{array}{l} k = j - 1,\, a_i \in \{1, 2, \ldots, m\}, \\ i \in \{1, 2, \ldots, n\};\, j \in \{0, 2, \ldots, v+1\} \end{array} \\ 0 & other \end{cases}$$

$$= \begin{pmatrix} 1 - p_{i,s_0 \to s_1} & p_{i,s_0 \to s_1} & 0 & 0 \\ p_{i,s_1 \to s_1} & 1 - p_{i,s_1 \to s_0} - p_{i,s_1 \to s_2} & \cdots & 0 \\ \cdots & & \cdots & \cdots \\ \cdots & & & \end{pmatrix}$$

$$= \begin{pmatrix} 1 - \frac{1}{\lambda} & \frac{1}{\lambda} & 0 & 0 \\ \frac{1}{\mu} & 1 - \frac{1}{\lambda} - \frac{1}{\mu} & \cdots & 0 \\ \cdots & \cdots & \cdots & \cdots \\ \cdots & \cdots & & \end{pmatrix}. \quad (2)$$

3 Energy Formulation and Constraints

RN working in the dormant state has extreme low energy consumption, so the key point to the energy consumption is data receiving, data holding and data sending, which can be showed by the state change in the buffer. When an action a_i ($a_i \in A_i$) is taken, incurs a mean consumption $\bar{E}_{i,s_j}(a_i)$ to the ith routing node changing its buffer state from state s_j to the other state.

$$\bar{E}_{i,s_j}(a_i) = \bar{E}_{\text{Hold}}(a_i) + \bar{E}_{\text{Trans}}(a_i) + \Delta\bar{E}_{\text{Trans}}(a_i). \tag{3}$$

In (3), $\bar{E}_{\text{Hold}}$ is the fixed energy consumption to hold the buffer state in the ith node, and $\bar{E}_{\text{Trans}}$ is the energy consumption of buffer state change caused by data sending or data receiving, and $\Delta\bar{E}_{\text{Trans}}$ is the energy consumption because of retransmission.

According to the Semi-Markov decision framework, so $\bar{E}_{i,s_j}(a_i)$ can be obtained as:

$$\bar{E}_{i,s_j}(a_i) = \sum_{s_k} p_{i,s_j \to s_k}(a_i)(\bar{E}_{s_j}(a_i) + (1+\delta)\bar{e}_{s_j \to s_k}(a_i)\tau_{i,s_j}(a_i))). \tag{4}$$

In (4), δ is the retransmission factor, $\bar{e}_{s_j \to s_k}$ is the energy consumption from state s_j to state s_k for action a_i in the ith routing node.

If $\varepsilon_{i,s_j}(a_i)$ is marked as the nonnegative decision variable, the optimal energy consumption problem in the whole RN networks is a NP problem, which can be formulated as the following linear program.

Minimize:

$$\sum_i \sum_{s_j \in S} \sum_{a_i \in A(s_j)} \bar{E}_{i,s_j}(a_i)\varepsilon_{i,s_j}(a_i). \tag{5}$$

Subject to:

$$\sum_i \sum_{s_j \in S} \sum_{a_i \in A(s_j)} \tau_{i,s_j}(a_i)\varepsilon_{i,s_j}(a_i) = 1 \ , \boxplus \varepsilon_{i,s_j}(a_i) \geq 0 \ . \tag{6}$$

$$\sum_{a_i \in A(s_j)} \varepsilon_{i,s_j}(a_i) - \sum_{s_j \in S} \sum_{a_i \in A(s_j)} p_{i,s_j \to s_k}(a_i)\varepsilon_{i,s_j}(a_i) = 0 \quad (\forall i, \ s_k \in S). \tag{7}$$

$$\sum_x b_{i,x} \leq \max(L) \leq n \times \sum_x b_{i,x} \quad (\forall i, \ \exists a_x, \ x \in \{0, 1, \ldots, m\}). \tag{8}$$

The first constrain in (5) represents the balance equations, the second constrain in (6) is given to guarantees that the sum of the steady state probabilities is one. The last in (7) ensures that the individual contribution of a routing sensor in a buffer is limited by between maximum and minimum value of segment.

4   Performance Evaluation and Result

A. Parameter and Environment

Referenced the specifications given in [2, 13] about the node composition and network topology in a typical WISN, we built a test environment base on IEEE 802.15.4 with 3 image sensor nodes, 6 routing nodes and 1 sink node. We can get images and their arrival time from 3 image nodes in the sink node per several minutes.

To test the difference in energy consumption under the condition of different packet workload, we set two kinds of typical node parameters in the image sensor nodes to compare, One is 320 × 240 resolution, JPEG image format, 3 KB image size, 80 Byte packet length, and 36 segments, the other is 640 × 480 resolution, JPEG image format, 17 KB image size, 80 Byte packet length, and 216 segments.

B. Result and Analysis

To transmit an image with same size, the energy consumption in the nodes of RN under the condition of using optimal energy optimization policy, non-buffered policy, and buffered node policy, respectively will shows difference.

In Fig. 2, the mean energy consumption of the routing nodes with three different node structure has been compared with different arrival rate λ and transmission rate μ, we can see clearly that the routing nodes with buffer policy presented in the paper shows the lowest energy consumption, which mean there will be a longer network lifetime to the RN when the energy optimal control method is considered, in addition, when data forwarding rate is lower than the data arrival rate, the energy consumption was increased to some extent.

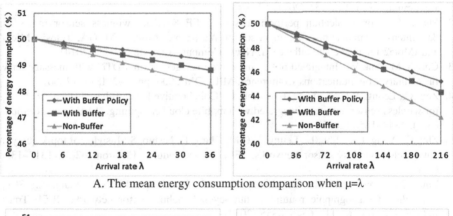

A. The mean energy consumption comparison when μ=λ

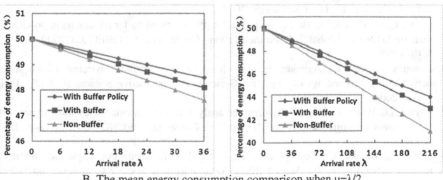

B. The mean energy consumption comparison when μ=λ/2

Fig. 2. Comparison of energy consumption with three different buffer policies in routing nodes

Especially, if some interference lead to the decrease of channel transmission performance, the energy consumption of the routing nodes is increased, it will play a positive role in reduced the energy consumption of RN to improve the ability to receive data of the sink node.

5 Conclusion

With increasing service rate, more image packet are pushed into the routing cloud or cluster made up of sensor routing nodes in the unit time, compare to the traditional WISN without buffer or non-optimized buffer in the sensor nodes, it has better energy saving effect to increase the network life cycle by using the energy consumption control policy base on node buffer allocation. The paper is supported by the nature science of foundation of Liaoning province (L2013433).

References

1. Oliveira, L., Rodrigues, J.: Wireless sensor networks: a survey on environmental monitoring. J. Commun. **6**(2), 143–151 (2011)
2. Pham, C.: Communication performances of IEEE 802.15.4 wireless sensor motes for data-intensive applications: a comparison of WaspMote, Arduino MEGA, TelosB, MicaZ and iMote2 for image surveillance. J. Netw. Comput. Appl. **46**, 48–59 (2014)
3. Chuah, M., Ma, W.: Integrated buffer and route management in a DTN with message ferry. In: Military Communications Conference, MILCOM 2006, pp. 1–7. IEEE (2006)
4. Zhu, C., Leung, V.C.M., Yang, L.T., Shu, L.: Collaborative location-based sleep scheduling for wireless sensor networks integrated with mobile cloud computing. IEEE Trans. Comput. **64**(7), 1844–1856 (2015)
5. Zhu, C., Yang, L.T., Shu, L., Leung, V.C.M., Hara, T., Nishio, S.: Insights of top-k query in duty-cycled wireless sensor networks. IEEE Trans. Industr. Electron. **62**(2), 1317–1328 (2015)
6. Zhu, C., Yang, L.T., Shu, L., Leung, V.C.M., Rodrigues, J.J.P.C., Wang, L.: Sleep scheduling for geographic routing in duty-cycled mobile sensor networks. IEEE Trans. Industr. Electron. **61**(11), 6346–6355 (2014)
7. Li, Y., Qian, M., Jin, D., Su, L., Zeng, L.: Adaptive optimal buffer management policies for realistic DTN. In: Global Telecommunications Conference, GLOBECOM 2009, pp. 1–5. IEEE (2009)
8. Downes, I., Rad, L., Aghajan, H.: Development of a mote for wireless image sensor networks. In: Proceedings of Cognitive Systems with Interactive Sensors (COGIS), Paris, March 2006
9. Niyato, D., Wang, P., Teo, J.: Performance analysis of the vehicular delay tolerant network. In: Wireless Communications and Networking Conference, WCNC 2009, pp. 1–5. IEEE (2009)
10. Krifa, A., Baraka, C., Spyropoulos, T.: Optimal buffer management policies for delay tolerant networks. In: 5th Annual IEEE Communications Society Conference on Sensor, Mesh and Ad Hoc Communications and Networks, SECON 2008, pp. 260–268. IEEE (2008)

11. Yap, D.F.W., Tiong, S.K., Koh, J., Andito, D.P., Lim, K.C., Yeo, W.K.: Link performance enhancement for image transmission with FEC in wireless sensor networks. J. Appl. Sci. **12** (14), 1465–1473 (2012)
12. Yu, W., Sahinoglu, Z., Vetro, A.: Energy efficient JPEG 2000 image transmission over wireless sensor networks. In: IEEE Global Telecommunications Conference (GLOBECOM), vol. 5, pp. 2738–2743 (2004)
13. Zhou, R., Liu, L., Yin, S., Luo, A., Chen, X., Wei, S.: A VLSI design of sensor node for wireless image sensor networks. Circuits Syst. 149–152 (2010)

Short Papers

Efficient Authentication for Tiered Internet of Things Networks

Chi-Yuan Chen[✉]

Department of Computer Science and Information Engineering,
National Ilan University, Yilan, Taiwan
chiyuan.chen@ieee.org

Abstract. Tiered Internet of Things (IoT) and Wireless Sensor Networks (WSN) are popular for efficient resource management. In order to reduce the communication overhead for unnecessary sensed data and avoid obtaining a false result, we propose to use aggregate signature to deal with the authentication problem.

Keywords: Authentication · Internet of Things · Wireless Sensor Network

1 Introduction

The flat structure of networks is usually difficult for resource management. Thus, a middle tier as shown in the Fig. 1 is introduced to ease the management difficulty. Moreover, the sensors are cheap and therefore resource-limited [1]. It is impossible for sensors to keep all the sensed data in their local memory. They need to offload their sensed data for saving memory space. However, not all the sensed data are required by the network owner. Therefore, the simple solution that sensors simply send back to the network owner all the sensed data for each time period is also impractical. A middle tier for temporarily storing the sensed data collected from sensors is becoming necessary.

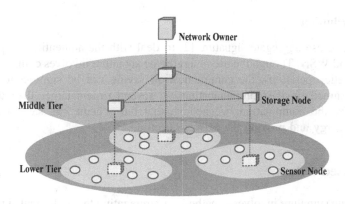

Fig. 1. Tiered Internet of Things (IoT) and Wireless Sensor Networks (WSN).

© ICST Institute for Computer Sciences, Social Informatics and Telecommunications Engineering 2017
J.-H. Lee and S. Pack (Eds.): QShine 2016, LNICST 199, pp. 469–472, 2017.
DOI: 10.1007/978-3-319-60717-7_46

One can know from the above description that the only necessary requirement for the middle tier is the large storage space. Therefore, such a middle tier is also called *storage node*. The benefits of placing storage nodes in the network have been proven in [5].

The introduction of the storage node also redefines how the network owner acquires the sensed data. In particular, with the storage node, the network owner issues queries to the storage node to retrieve the part of sensed data it wants. The storage reports to the network owner the queried data. From the above statement, one can know that the benefit implied by the storage node is that the communication overhead for unnecessary sensed data between the storage node and network owner can be saved.

1.1 Security Risk

The placement of storage node also incurs new security challenge. Because sensors could be compromised, their compromises imply a large security risk, which means that all the sensed data and all the query results will be maliciously manipulated. In this paper, our concern is the authenticity of the query result. For example, in the presence of compromised sensors, the network owner issues a range query and then will obtain a false result.

A straightforward method to this problem is to attach a cryptographic hash to each individual sensed data. However, it also incurs a downside, which is that the communication overhead is also doubled. As the communication overhead is the main concern of the design of a network protocol, such method is unacceptable.

The existing methods conduct different approach to solve this problem. An encoding approach is used in [4]. Crosscheck is used in [6, 8]. Both these two also simply use conventional hash operation. In [3], a neighborhood chain, which is the hash of the consecutive sensed data, is used to guarantee the authenticity but still with the drawback of overwhelming communication burden. In [7], an aggregation tree is constructed before the network is deployed in order to aggregate the individual hashes. However, the method in [7] assumes too much information about the network topology.

1.2 Contribution

We propose to use aggregate signature [2] to deal with the authentication problem in tiered IoT and WSN. Though the use of aggregate signature involves complicated finite field arithmetic operations, the communication saving can be significant. Since the energy consumed by the communications is several orders larger than the energy consumed by the computation, we believe that our scheme can save a significant portion of energy and prolong the network lifetime.

2 Proposed Scheme

The aggregate signature involves a method for aggregating the traditional signatures. In particular, the use of traditional signature is to attach a signature to each individual data. However, in the bilinear setting, the aggregate signature is that each sensor also generates a signature for each individual data. However, to aggregate the signatures into one, each sensor performs multiplication operation on their generated signatures and the signatures sent from the neighboring sensors. Specifically, when a sensor has a tuple $\langle a, \sigma_a \rangle$, where a denotes the sensed data and σ_a is the corresponding signature, if it also receives a tuple $\langle b, \sigma_b \rangle$ from the neighboring, then it generally sends out the message $\langle a, b, \sigma_a \cdot \sigma_b \rangle$. The storage node in possession of the public keys and the claimed sensed data is therefore able to verify the legitimacy of the received signature $\sigma_a \cdot \sigma_b$ by the method in [2].

Despite the simplicity of the proposed scheme, it actually suggests the role change of which entity being needed to verify the legitimacy of the signature. In particular, in the traditional use of the signature, the storage node acts as only a relay that forwards the message from sensors to the network owner. However, in our proposed scheme, since the network owner no longer has the entire sensed data, it is unable to generate the corresponding hash so as to make sure whether the sensed data is authentic. It turns out that the storage node needs to check the legitimacy of received signatures regularly.

Thus, the whole picture of the proposed scheme is that, from ordinary sensor point of view, it generates and aggregates the signatures as mentioned above. From the storage node point of view, for each time period, it verifies the legitimacy of the received signature. Once at the end of the time period, the storage node does not report to the network owner that the signature is problematic, it implicitly implies that the received data is authentic. This gives an additional overhead on the storage node. However, as mentioned above, one can save more energy in our scheme than in existing schemes.

3 Performance Evaluation

The primary evaluation metric used in this paper is the communication overhead due to its important role in affecting the network lifetime. It is obvious that the communication overhead O_{comm}^T of the traditional method, which generates signatures for each individual data, can be computed as

$$O_{comm}^T = \sum_{i=1}^{N} L(\ell_d n_d + \ell_s n_s), \tag{1}$$

where L is the average number of hops between sensors and storage node, N is the total number of sensors, ℓ_d is the number of bits for representing sensed data, n_d is the number of sensed data of each sensor, ℓ_s is the number of bits for representing signature, and n_s is the number of signature. The corresponding computation overhead O_{comp}^T is therefore:

$$O_{comp}^T = \ell_s O_{ts}, \tag{2}$$

where O_{ts} is the number of operations used in generating traditional signature.

On the other hand, the communication overhead O_{comm}^A of our proposed aggregate signature scheme, which generates and aggregates signatures, can be computed as

$$O^A_{comm} = \sum_{i=1}^{N} L(\ell_d n_d + \ell_s),$$ (3)

where N is the total number of sensors, ℓ_d is the number of bits for representing sensed data, n_d is the number of sensed data of each sensor, and ℓ_s is the number of bits for representing signature. We particularly note that the n_s is equal to 1 in O^A_{comm} because all of the signatures is aggregated into one for each sensor. The corresponding computation overhead O^A_{comp} is therefore:

$$O^A_{comp} = \ell_s O_{as},$$ (4)

where O_{as} is the number of operations used in generating aggregate signature. In essence, O_{as} can be approximately computed as

$$O_{as} = O_{ts} + O_m,$$ (5)

where O_m is the energy consumed by the multiplication operation.

4 Conclusion

In this paper, we utilize aggregate signature to reduce the authentication overhead in tiered IoT and WSN. We also provide a simple performance evaluation for our proposed approach. Though the use of aggregate signature involves a slightly computation overhead, the communication overhead can be reduced to prolong the network lifetime.

References

1. Chen, C.-Y., Chao, H.-C.: A survey of key distribution in wireless sensor networks. Secur. Commun. Netw. **7**(12), 2495–2508 (2014)
2. Boneh, D., Gentry, C., Lynn, B., Shacham, H.: Aggregate and veriably encrypted signatures from bilinear maps. In: Annual International Conference on the Theory and Applications of Cryptographic Techniques (Eurocrypt) (2003)
3. Chen, F., Liu, A.X.: SafeQ: secure and efficient query processing in sensor networks. In: IEEE International Conference on Computer Communications (INFOCOM) (2010)
4. Sheng, B., Li, Q.: Verifiable privacy-preserving range query in twotiered sensor networks. In: IEEE International Conference on Computer Communications (INFOCOM) (2008)
5. Sheng, B., Li, Q., Mao, W.: Data storage placement in sensor networks. In: ACM International Symposium on Mobile Ad Hoc Networking and Computing (MobiHoc) (2006)
6. Shi, J., Zhang, R., Zhang, Y.: Secure range queries in tiered sensor networks. In: IEEE International Conference on Computer Communications (INFOCOM) (2009)
7. Yu, C.-M., Tsou, Y.-T., Lu, C.-S., Kuo, S.-Y.: Practical and secure multidimensional query framework in tiered sensor networks. IEEE Trans. Inf. Forensics Secur. **6**(2), 241–255 (2011)
8. Zhang, R., Shi, J., Zhang, Y.: Secure multidimensional range queries in sensor networks. In: ACM International Symposium on Mobile Ad Hoc Networking and Computing (MobiHoc) (2009)

Intelligence Cloud-Based Image Recognition Service

Wei-shuo Li[✉] and Jung-yang Kao

Information and Communications Research Laboratories,
Industrial Technology Research Institute, ITRI, 195, Sec. 4, Chung Hsing Road,
Chutung, Hsinchu, Taiwan, R.O.C.
{ansonli,Yang_Kao}@itri.org.tw

Abstract. Cloud-based vision service provide a opportunity of intelligence and programming support to meet different needs of embedded applications. To reduce the complexity of cloud-based computation, we proposed a method can be by performing Hamming distance. This approach relates in general to a method for feature description, in which a feature patch is described by using a binary string. Our method can achieve near-optimal precision and reduce the bandwidth and computation time.

Keywords: Cloud service · Image recognition · Feature descriptor

1 Cloud-Based Vision Service

The emergence of widespread mobile devices has created vast new opportunities for intelligent applications. When consider the on-device recognition process, for example, the mobile device has the ability to recognize 1,000 images without connecting to the Internet. However, there are applications that need to recognize more than million images. The solution for this is the cloud-based image recognition service [1,2]. All the recognitions will be done in the cloud. Cloud recognition service allows mobile device to work with million of target images stored in the cloud, and provides for a high accuracy recognition rate and very quick response characteristics. This make it very usable to build a conveniently interactive application. Therefore, cloud-based vision can accomplish this with a small memory, near-real time, and low power consumption embedded device [3].

Intelligent vision has been widely used in various application fields of image processing. In general, these applications include a basic process, that is, to extract the features of each image and further compares the extracted feature with a reference feature of the database to locate the best matching target [4]. However, when a large quantity of features is extracted from the images, the required comparison time will be greatly increased. Besides, if the features carry a large volume of data, more bandwidth will be required for transmitting relevant feature description. Therefore, it has become one of the prominent tasks for

© ICST Institute for Computer Sciences, Social Informatics and Telecommunications Engineering 2017
J.-H. Lee and S. Pack (Eds.): QShine 2016, LNICST 199, pp. 473–477, 2017.
DOI: 10.1007/978-3-319-60717-7_47

the industries to provide a method for feature description and a feature descriptor using the same capable of expediting feature comparison and reducing the required data volume.

Our key contribution is proposing a descriptor that transforms the input feature space into binary signature such that Hamming distance in the resulting space is closely with similarity measures.

2   Similarity-Preserve Transformation

For clarity, we use SIFT feature as our example, however, our method is applicable to a variety feature descriptor [5,6]. When a keypoint has been detected, we then need describe it by a patch that collecting the nearby pixels. For example, the SIFT algorithm includes (1) take a 16×16 window around detected interest point, (2) divide into a 4×4 grid of cells (3) compute 8 bins angle histogram in each cell. Thus, a SIFT descriptor form a 128 dimension histogram, each bin has 8 bits, and is of 1024 bits size.

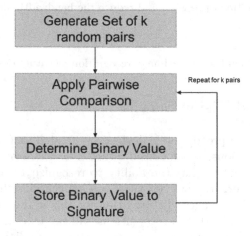

Fig. 1. Flow chart

SIFT need compute the cosine similarity of two histograms to decide a pair of descriptor is similar or not. Our main idea is two similar signatures will preserve similar pairwise relations, thus any descriptor can be represented by binary string of pairwise comparison. From this viewpoint, the original similarity can be approximated by Hamming distance. The key problem is how to choice an appropriate set of pairwise relations. For SIFT, there are $\binom{128}{2}$ pairwise relations, and this information obviously too large. We propose a random projection method, that is, randomly project the original feature space ($[0,1]^d$) to a k-dimension $\{0,1\}^k$ space, and we expect $k < d$, see Fig. 1. Now, the question remains how to determine the value of k to approximately preserve the similarity.

2.1   The Comparative Reason

We shall first consider the question of the probability that random k-projection can preserve similarity. Note that original space, for SIFT, is of size $2^{1024} \gg \binom{128}{2}$, but the feature point is generally sparse, that is, far small than $\binom{128}{2}$ key points(image are typically describe by thousands of keypoints). Thus, we can reasonably assume the pairwise relations can fully distinct two different patches. First, we analysis the probability that similarity is unchanged of a random k-projection method. Denote by S the event fo two descriptors successful matching, and $\delta_H(x, y)$ the Hamming distance. We match a pair of descriptors (x, y) if their hamming distance $\leq h$ with signature size n.

Let k the number of bits select uniformly and randomly from n pairwise relations.

$$Pr(S) = 1 - Pr(\delta_H(x, y) > h)$$

$$= 1 - \left(\frac{\binom{n-h}{k-h}}{\binom{n}{k}} \right)^2$$

$$\geq 1 - \left(\frac{\binom{n-h}{k}}{\binom{n}{k}} \right)^2, \tag{1}$$

using $h = cn, c < 1/2$, and $\binom{n}{k} \leq \left(\frac{en}{k} \right)^k$, the probability $Pr(S)$ is given by

$$Pr(S) \geq 1 - \left(1 - \frac{h}{n} \right)^{2k}$$

$$\geq 1 - e^{-\frac{2hk}{n}}$$

$$= 1 - \frac{1}{n} \rightarrow 1, \text{ if } k = \frac{1}{c} \log n^2. \tag{2}$$

Equation 2 tell us that we need select larger k, i.e., more bits, as h is deceasing. Since the event S is a tail event, the probability admit a threshold phenomenon, see [7] for more detail. To be more precisely, the behavior of k can be obtained by estimating $Pr(\delta_H(x, y) = h)$, and we can derive additional information of k around the threshold.

We know

$$Pr(\delta_H(x, y) = h) = 0 \text{ for } h > n - k, \tag{3}$$

and

$$Pr(\delta_H(x, y) = h) = Pr(\delta_H(x, y) > h) - Pr(\delta_H(x, y) > h + 1)$$

$$= \left(\frac{\binom{n-h}{k}}{\binom{n}{k}} \right)^2 - \left(\frac{\binom{n-h-1}{k}}{\binom{n}{k}} \right)^2$$

$$= \frac{\binom{n-h}{k}}{\binom{n}{k}} \cdot \left(1 + \frac{k}{n-h} \right) \cdot \frac{\binom{n-h}{k}}{\binom{n}{k}} \cdot \left(1 - \frac{k}{n-h} \right)$$

$$= \frac{\binom{n-h}{k}}{\binom{n}{k}} \cdot \left(1 - \frac{k^2}{(n-h)^2}\right)$$

$$= \left(1 - \frac{k^2}{(n-h)^2}\right) \prod_{i=0}^{k-1} \left(1 - \frac{h}{n-i}\right). \tag{4}$$

This function tell us about the influence of k in the distribution around the threshold.

Table 1. Precision of the random projection method.

# of bits	Precision
128	100%
64	100%
32	93%
16	86%
14	50%
13	30%
12	21%
8	14%

For SIFT 128-bins histogram, choose $k = \frac{1}{c} \cdot \log \binom{128}{2}^2 \approx 32$ for carefully selected c. In practice, $k = 32$ is enough to tackle the recognition problems. In Table 1 we choose 1000 images and run SIFT description process. Then we randomly select difference k compared bits of the 128 bins of SIFT histogram.

Our method is faster than original descriptor. The random projection method only need to perform 32-bits XOR, and is suitable for hardware design. In the case of SIFT, our method is bandwidth-efficient than original descriptor, and we can reduce original SIFT bandwidth to 1/32.

3   Conclusions

The main contribution of our paper is a similarity-preserve transform that transforms the input feature space into binary signature. This paper is directed to a method for cloud-based feature matching service and a feature descriptor using a binary string to describe a feature patch obtained by a feature extraction algorithm. The generated binary string may be used to expedite feature comparison to a near-real time cloud manner. Moreover, since the binary string only requires a small amount of data volume, the required bandwidth may be greatly reduced.

We have shown that (1) our method is similarity-preserve (2)the bandwidth performs comparably to the original SIFT descriptors, (3) computing power degrades gracefully as the number of patch is increased. Moreover, our approach is applicable to a variety of feature description methods.

References

1. Buyya, R., et al.: Cloud computing and emerging IT platforms: vision, hype, and reality for delivering computing as the 5th utility. Future Gener. Comput. Syst. **25**, 599–616 (2009)
2. Foster, I.: Globus online: accelerating and democratizing science through cloud-based services. IEEE Internet Comput. **3**, 70–73 (2011)
3. Soyata, T., et al.: Cloud-vision: real-time face recognition using a mobile-cloudlet-cloud acceleration architecture. In: IEEE Symposium on Computers and Communications (ISCC). IEEE (2012)
4. Bhat, D., Nayar, S.: Ordinal measures for visual correspondence. In: Computer Vision and Pattern Recognition, 2 (1996)
5. Lowe, D.G.: Distinctive image features from scale-invariant keypoints. Int. J. Comput. Vis. **60**, 91–110 (2004)
6. Bay, H., Ess, A., Tuytelaars, T., Van Gool, L.: Speeded-up robust features (surf). Comput. Vis. Image Underst. **110**(3), 346–359 (2008)
7. Bollobás, B.: Random Graph. Academic Press, London (1985)

Inter-correlation of Resource-/Flow-Level Visibility for APM Over OF@TEIN SDN-Enabled Multi-site Cloud

Muhammad Usman[✉], Aris Cahyadi Risdianto, Jungsu Han,
and JongWon Kim

Networked Computing Systems Laboratory (NetCS), EECS, GIST,
Gwangju, South Korea
{usman, aris, jshan, jongwon}@nm.gist.ac.kr

Abstract. Cloud computing and SDN technologies have potential to bring advanced capabilities to data centers and inter-connecting networks by maximizing resources utilization. However, SDN/Cloud composition also brings monitoring and visibility challenges, for operators to diagnose p+vResources (server, network and storage), flows and cloud based applications for end-to-end performance management, because legacy tools lack adequate visibility support for such kind of dynamic environments. In this paper, by developing and integrating open source tools, we present a unified visibility solution to inter-correlate Resource-/Flow-level visibility over OF@TEIN to assist cloud-based APM (Application Performance Management). Furthermore, a verification environment has been setup, to show the feasibility of our inter-correlation approach.

Keywords: SDN · Cloud · Visibility · Visualization · DevOps automation

1 Introduction

Unlike traditional network-focused testbeds, Future Internet testbeds should provide experimental networking facility without the limitations of number of simultaneous users with varying resources requirements, number of supported services, types of applications and most importantly in the deployed network topology. Thanks, to the open and programmable nature of emerging SDN (Software-Defined Networking) paradigm that encouraged the construction and operation of SDN-enabled testbeds over international Research & Education networks. In 2012, we launched OF@TEIN project [1], aligned with Future Internet testbed projects like GENI and FIRE to build an SDN-enabled Multi-site Cloud testbed over TEIN (Trans-Eurasia Information Network). As of now, OF@TEIN connects 10 international sites spread across 9 countries (i.e. Korea, Malaysia, Thailand, Indonesia, India, Vietnam, Pakistan, Taiwan and Philippines) as shown in Fig. 1.

This SDN/Cloud integration over multiple international sites with diverse networks, and heterogeneous hardware/software compositions at OF@TEIN provides diverse resource combinations for developers. However, SDN/Cloud integrated environment at

© ICST Institute for Computer Sciences, Social Informatics and Telecommunications Engineering 2017
J.-H. Lee and S. Pack (Eds.): QShine 2016, LNICST 199, pp. 478–484, 2017.
DOI: 10.1007/978-3-319-60717-7_48

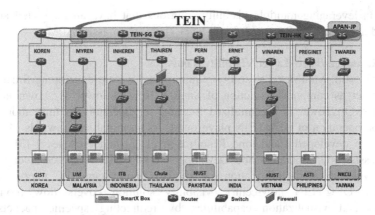

Fig. 1. OF@TEIN SDN-enabled multi-site cloud physical infrastructure

OF@TEIN also brings new challenges for operators like operational complexity and lack of visibility. Furthermore, OF@TEIN developer's also face APM issues; but they don't really know, where exactly problem is happening (i.e. application, p+vBox (physical/virtual), overlay/underlay network). As a result, it becomes quite challenging to provide a highly available and sustainable environment to OF@TEIN developers.

So, in order to deal with visibility challenges associated with cloud-based APM, we need further troubleshooting in multiple-levels of visibility (e.g. Resource-/Flow-/Service-level), to enable the operators with minimum efforts, to identify root cause of application performance degradation. Thus, to address the visibility challenges, in this paper, we focus on the inter-level correlation of Resource-level [2] and Flow-level [3] visibility, to provide adequate actionable information for APM to ease the job of operators. Furthermore, in our initial prototype, we verified the usability of operational data captured from multiple systems and identified missing data elements which can help to further optimize overall performance of OF@TEIN playground.

The rest of the paper is organized as follows. In Sect. 2, we discuss Multi-level Visibility requirements and related visibility solutions. In Sect. 3, we present our initial design and implementation details of Inter-level Correlator. In Sect. 4, we discuss verification environment. In Sect. 5, we conclude the paper.

2 Multi-level Visibility and Related Work

2.1 Multi-level Visibility Requirements and Support Tools

2.1.1 Multi-level Visibility Requirements

The OF@TEIN Multi-level Visibility framework should provide an innovative solution that should bridge Cloud, SDN and physical/virtual infrastructure for end-to-end visibility for automated troubleshooting. Furthermore, this, Multi-level visibility with centralized access must assure integration of independent and isolated operation data, captured from multiple visibility levels, from multiple sources. Thus, in this paper, we focused on leveraging multiple visibility solutions that have an integrated and synchronized awareness of Resource-/Flow-level visibility to assist APM.

2.1.2   Resource-/Flow-Level Visibility Tools

In order to fulfill Multi-level visibility requirements, we are developing SmartX Visibility Center as component solution of SmartX DevOpsTower as shown in Fig. 2. SmartX DevOpsTower is a centralized location for operators to fully monitor and control the operation of OF@TEIN playground. As an initial step towards Multi-level visibility we developed standalone Resource-level [2] and Flow-level [3] visibility tools to assist both Operators and Developers. OF@TEIN Resource-level visibility tools provide detailed information of p+vBox and status of inter-connecting links/paths. OF@TEIN flow-centric visibility solution covers flow monitoring, inspection and visualization capabilities by redirecting specific packets from OpenFlow-enabled switches to SmartX Visibility Server for further analysis.

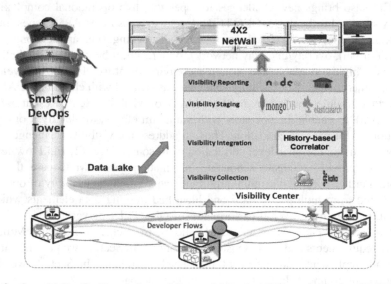

Fig. 2. SmartX DevOpsTower for enabling multi-level visibility support for OF@TEIN

2.2   Related Work

There are few, unified visibility solutions available that uses different approaches to collect, transform and inter-correlate visibility data. Gigamon Visibility Fabric [4] and ThousandEyes [5] are well-known visibility solutions that can process, inspect and filter data packets from internal and external networks by correlating metrics to optimize performance. Unfortunately, both Gigamon Visibility Fabric and ThousandEyes are commercial products and require dedicated hardware and specific software licenses which makes the Multi-level visibility solution too expensive to be implemented in open networking environment. ONUG (Open Networking User Group) [6] also focused its effort on what is needed to deliver an open network state collection, correlation and analytics service to the enterprise market without providing any details to how to achieve this task. Furthermore, most studies related to multi source data correlation, mainly focuses on security related aspects [7–9], typically for anomalies detection problem, instead of multi-level visibility aspect of the system.

3 Inter-level Correlation: Design and Implementation

3.1 Inter-level Correlation: Design

By leveraging available visibility tools, we are designing Inter-level Correlator for OF@TEIN to integrate resource and flow information at one place. The initial design of Inter-level Correlator is shown in Fig. 3. In the initial design, we focused on operational data verification, and defining keys for inter-level correlation. We defined five tuple (source/destination instance ip, source/destination TCP/UDP ports and protocol type), timestamp and OpenDaylight Controller IP as correlation-key. Based on correlation-key, Inter-level Correlator filters and extracts flows information from Data Lake and calculates critical flow stats. Then, Inter-level Correlator extracts Open-DayLight Configurations from Data Lake for finding associated Operation/Developer Flows, SDN topology information and related performance statistics. Followed by, instance configurations and performance data filtering based on UUID (Universally Unique Identifier) search-key from Data Lake. After that, Inter-level Correlator determines pBox where instance is deployed and extracts CPU, Memory and Disk performance data from Data Lake. Finally, this unified Resource-/Flow-level data is stored in Inter-level Data Lake and visualized.

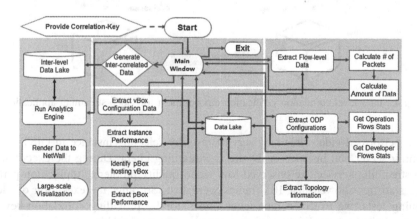

Fig. 3. Initial design of Inter-level correlator for OF@TEIN

3.2 Implementation of Inter-level Correlation

In this paper we focused on inter-level correlation of Resource-/Flow-level visibility for two hyper-convergent SmartX Boxes.

Inter-level Correlator: We implemented Inter-level Correlator by using Java. We also, extensively used OpenDayLight REST API's for extracting SDN Topology/Configurations information and OpenStack Nova REST API's for extracting instance configurations.

Inter-level Data Storage: For storing Inter-level Correlation data generated by Inter-level Correlator we used Elasticsearch [10] which is distributed, scalable and real-time search engine using index-based approach for data storage and retrieval.

Inter-level Data Visualization: Finally, this unified Inter-level Visibility data is visualized by using Kibana [10] Visualization Engine (by creating relevant visualizations and searches) over SAGE-enabled [2] NetWall.

4   Inter-level Correlation: Verification

To verify our unified visibility approach, we created verification environment with two OpenStack instances in two regions (GIST and ID). Followed by, assigning specific Operator and Developer Controller's to manage the SDN topology. Our simplified, verification environment is shown in Fig. 4.

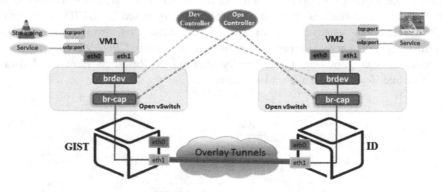

Fig. 4. Inter-level correlation verification environment for video streaming application

We performed video streaming service tests by selecting instance in GIST site as streaming server and instance in ID site as streaming client. During the execution of video streaming service, we observed low video quality problem. Application performance statistics showed that 105 frames were lost. So, after the execution of video streaming tests, we executed Inter-level Correlator by providing correlation-key for inter-correlating captured data, to figure out root cause of problem.

Inter-level Correlator, linked and filtered flows data, from multi sites. Inter-Correlator output shows, that numbers of packets were dropped in tunnel (e.g. number of packets captured from operator bridge brcap in GIST site was 1,999 but numbers of packets received in ID site operator bridge brcap were only 1,356). Then, Inter-level Correlator analyzed SDN topology over the period of time, but there were no changes, also no changes were recorded in Operation/Developer flows. Further, Inter-level Correlator filtered vBox configurations without any changes and pBox performance stats were also satisfactory. So, the problem found to be in tunnel network. In Fig. 5, some of simplified visualizations generated by Inter-level Correlator execution are shown. Similarly we also performed streaming tests by setting wrong configurations in brdev (Developer Bridge) in client site. Again Inter-level Correlator was able to identify that packets received up to brcap but cannot reach to OpenStack instance and there were some changes in brdev configurations over the period of time. Further, Inter-level Correlator has capabilities to figure out application problems due to p+vBox performance issues.

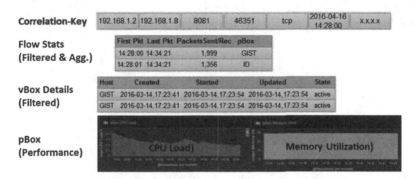

Fig. 5. Results of inter-level correlator execution

5   Conclusion and Future Work

In this paper, we have shown an early effort for inter-correlating Resource-/Flow-level visibility to assist cloud-based APM. In, the future, we are planning to extend our work towards multi-level visibility.

Acknowledgment. This work was supported in part by Institute for Information & communications Technology Promotion (IITP) grant funded by the Korea government (MSIP) (No. R7117-16-0218, Development of Automated SaaS Compatibility Techniques over Hybrid/Multisite Clouds). This work was also supported in part by Institute for Information & communications Technology Promotion (IITP) grant funded by the Korea government (MSIP) (No. B190-15-2012, Global SDN/NFV Open-Source Software Core Module/Function Development).

References

1. Risdianto, A.C., Kim, J.: Prototyping media distribution experiments over OF@TEIN SDN-enabled testbed. APANNRW **38**, 12–18 (2014). Nantou
2. Usman, M., Risdianto, A.C., Kim, J.: Resource monitoring and visualization for OF@TEIN SDN-enabled multi-site cloud. In: ICOIN, Kota Kinablu, pp. 427–429 (2016)

3. Risdianto, A.C., Kim, J.: Flow-centric visibility tools for OF@TEIN OpenFlow-based SDN testbed. In: CFI, Seoul, pp. 46–50 (2015)
4. Gigamon unified visibility fabric. https://www.gigamon.com/best-practices
5. ThousandEyes. https://www.thousandeyes.com/
6. Network State Collection, Correlation and Analytics Product/RFI Requirements. White paper, Open Networking User Group (2015)
7. Pierazzi, F., Casolari, S., Colajanni, M., Marchetti, M.: Exploratory security analytics for anomaly detection. J. Comput. Secur. **56**, 28–49 (2015)
8. Jagadeesan, L., Bride, A.M., Gurbani, V.K., Yang, J.: Cognitive security: security analytics and autonomics for virtualized networks. In: IPTComm, Chicago, pp. 43–50 (2015)
9. Cao, P., Badger, E.C., Kalbarczyk, Z.T., Iyer, R.K., Withers, A., Slagell, A,J.: Towards an unified security testbed and security analytics framework. In: HostSoS, Illinois, pp. 24–25 (2015)
10. ELK Stack. https://www.elastic.co/webinars/introduction-elk-stack

A Novel DMM Architecture Based on NDN

Zhiwei Yan[1,2(✉)], Jong-Hyouk Lee[3], Guanggang Geng[1,2],
Xiaodong Lee[1,2], and Yong-Jin Park[4]

[1] China Internet Network Information Center, Beijing, China
{yan, gengguanggang, xl}@cnnic.cn
[2] National Engineering Laboratory for Naming and Addressing,
Beijing 100190, People's Republic of China
[3] Department of Computer Software Engineering, Sangmyung University,
Seoul 110-743, Republic of Korea
jonghyouk@smu.ac.kr
[4] Department of Communications and Computer Engineering,
School of Fundamental Science, Waseda University, Tokyo 169-8555, Japan
yjp@ieee.org

Abstract. The unprecedented expansion of mobile Internet traffic has resulted
in the development of distributed mobility management architecture. In this
paper, based on Named Data Networking (NDN), traditional mobility support
services are distributed among multiple anchor points in the IPv6 core network,
to overcome some of the major limitations of centralized IP mobility management solutions.

Keywords: MIPv6 · PMIPv6 · DMM · NDN

1 Introduction

Mobility management which provides wireless devices with connectivity service to
Internet becomes major marketable goods as mobile computing is frequent and pop-
ularized. The Mobile IPv6 (MIPv6) proposed by IETF allows Mobile Nodes (MNs) to
be reachable, regardless of its current location [1]. When the MN moves to other
subnet, it acquires address in the new location and performs home registration with its
Home Agent (HA), which enables the MN to keep its active communications. In order
to cut down the signaling overhead by network-based mobility management manner
and avoid the host-based mobility stack in the MN, the Network-based Local Mobility
Management (NetLMM) functional architecture is defined in RFC 4831 [2]. According
to this architecture, the Proxy Mobile IPv6 (PMIPv6) [3] was developed. Being different from MIPv6, PMIPv6 introduces two important entities, Local Mobility Anchor
(LMA) and Mobility Access Gateway (MAG), which manage all mobility related
signaling so that the MN is freed from the mobility management task.

In the future mobile Internet, MIP/PMIP will be the basic protocols to support the
mobility management. However, how to effectively address the scalability issue caused
by the large-scale mobile terminals and traffic is vital to promote the all-IP based
mobile Internet. According to the current protocol specifications, the single serving

© ICST Institute for Computer Sciences, Social Informatics and Telecommunications Engineering 2017
J.-H. Lee and S. Pack (Eds.): QShine 2016, LNICST 199, pp. 485–491, 2017.
DOI: 10.1007/978-3-319-60717-7_49

point (HA or LMA) is deployed to manage all the binding states and transmit the traffic for the MN. Then the key point to guarantee the scalability of MIP/PMIP is to distribute the HA/LMA function to multiple equal entities. In order to address architectural limitations of the centralized mobility management, the IETF has established the Distributed Mobility Management (DMM) working group aiming at distributing mobile Internet traffic in an optimal way while not relying on centrally deployed mobility anchors [4]. Although there are many studies about the distributed extensions of the MIPv6 and PMIPv6, most of them remedy or optimize the MIPv6 and PMIPv6 based on the extensions of the basic protocols and cannot satisfy the farsighted requirements of MIPv6 and PMIPv6 in the distributed mobile Internet. In this paper, we use the idea of Name Data Networking (NDN) to support the distributed extensions of both MIPv6 and PMIPv6.

2   Proposed Architecture

2.1   Why Can NDN Help?

In order to effectively solve the problems of the current Internet caused by the location-based communication model and make the Internet more suitable for the future applications, the concept of Information-Centric Networking (ICN) [5] was proposed and the Named Data Networking (NDN) [6] is one of the most important representatives among the ICN proposals. In NDN, the communication is consumer- initiated and a consumer retrieves an individual content object by sending an Interest packet which specifies the name of the desired content object. The NDN changes the communication model in the TCP/IP network and it is shown in Fig. 1.

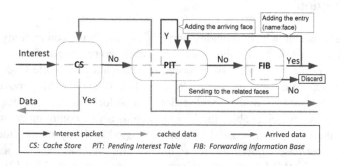

Fig. 1. NDN communication model

Requests (Interest packets) for some content are forwarded toward a publisher location. A NDN router maintains a Pending Interest Table (PIT) for forwarded requests, which enables request aggregation; that is, a NDN router would normally not forward a second request for a specific content when it has recently sent a request for that particular content. The PIT maintains state for all Interest packets and maps them to the network interfaces from which the corresponding requests have been received. Data packet is then routed back on the reverse path using this state. NDN supports in-network caching: contents received by a NDN router (in response to requests) can be cached in the Content Store (CS) so that subsequent received requests for the same object can be answered from that cache. If the Interest packet cannot be consumed by the CS and has no match entry in the PIT, the router will send it out according to the Forwarding Information Base (FIB), which is maintained as the IP routing table.

NDN adopts the distributed routing algorithm to retrieve the named data, and pays no attention to its location. This kind of scheme can always fetch the data from the most optimized location and be suited in the dynamic environment. Although NDN is well designed for the content-centric Internet, its large deployment will be a long way. Then we can make use of its advantages if it can be overlapped with the IP protocols. In which, the NDN is used as a signaling layer to manage the binding states dynamically to support the distributed MIPv6 and PMIPv6.

2.2 Basic Architecture

Multiple HA/LMA entities are deployed in the core network as shown in Fig. 2.

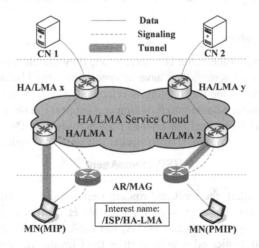

Fig. 2. Distributed mobility management architecture

They share a common name, which is stored in the Domain Name System (DNS) or policy store as basic information of the MIP/PMIP service [7, 8]. For the deployment flexibility, we also design the mobility management protocols with both network-based manner and host-based manner, which are described in the following subsections.

2.3   Host-Based Case

(A) Binding Update

When the MN receives the new Router Advertisement (RA) message from the new access network, it will configure a new Care-of Address (CoA) and initiate the binding update. MN sends out the Interest packet with the name as

/ISP/HomeAgent

The routers will route this signaling message to the domain of the identified Internet Service Provider (ISP) and then the routers in the ISP's domain will find the FIB to match the *HomeAgent* label. Then the nearest (or the best) HA will receive the Interest packet finally. In order to make this work, the Interest packet has to be extended to identify that this packet is used as a binding update message and then the HA can parse it accordingly. Of course, the necessary information in MIPv6 has to be included, for example, CoA and Home address (HoA) are the mandatory information.

Besides, all the HAs in the same HA service set (or cloud) have to announce their existence as the NDN content publisher does. Then the routers can maintain the FIB entry corresponding to the optimized HA according to the actual location and network condition. Because our solution is overlapped on the IP protocol, the HA also has an available IPv6 address to transmit IP traffic to and from the MN. Then the HA which received the Interest packet will response with a Data packet to acknowledge the location update.

(B) State Synchronization

For the multiple HAs in the same HA service set, they should function equally in a distributed manner. In this way, they have to synchronize the binding state if the new binding is established or the old binding is refreshed. We also use the NDN routing scheme herein because the name-based routing can support the multicast in nature. For example, when the HA received the Interest packet from the MN and established the binding state, it will send a new Interest packet out with the content name as

/ISP/HomeAgent

In this Interest packet, the multicast routing requirement should be flagged. Then the router will send this message to all the possible HA entities according to all the recorded FIB entries. In this Interest packet, the HoA and CoA are also mandatory information. More sophisticated scheme such as the ChronoSync [9] can be well used here for the state synchronization.

(C) Packet Transmission

For the packet sent from MN to the Corresponding Node (CN), it can be directly transmitted to the CN with the HoA and CN's address as the source and destination addresses, respectively. All the HAs have to announce the same IPv6 prefix containing the served HoA set to attract the packets for the related MN. In this way, the packet sent from CN to the MN will arrive at the nearest HA due to the routing protocol of the bypassed routers. Then the HA entity will check its binding update table to locate the entry of the related HoA. If there is positive match, the HA will replace the destination address with the related CoA and attach the HoA for example in the Type 2 routing header [1]. In this way, the packet can arrive at the MN finally. If there is no positive match, the HA will send an Interest packet with the flagged multicast requirement, which contains the HoA of the MN. The other HAs will recognize that this Interest is used to fetch the corresponded CoA. And then the first HA who knows the CoA will response with a Data packet including the CoA. If the HA cannot learn the CoA within a reasonable period, the packet will be discarded because it will conclude that the MN has not established the available binding.

2.4   Network-Based Case

(A) Binding Update

When the MN attaches to the new access network, the MAG will trigger the location update. It sends out the Interest packet with the name as

/ISP/LocalMobilityAnchor

The routers will route this signaling message to the domain of the identified ISP and then the routers in the ISP's domain will find the FIB to match the *LocalMobilityAnchor* label. Then the nearest (or the best) LMA will receive the Interest finally. In order to make this work, the Interest packet has to be extended to identify that this Interest is used as a proxy binding update message and then the LMA can parse it accordingly. Of course, the necessary information in PMIPv6 has to be included, for example, MN's identification and the address of MAG are the mandatory information.

Besides, all the LMAs in the same LMA service set (or cloud) have to announce their existence as the NDN content publisher does. Then the routers can maintain the FIB entry corresponding to the optimized LMA according to the actual location and network condition. Because our solution is overlapped on the IP protocol, the LMA also has an available IPv6 address to transmit IP traffic to and from the MN. Besides, the LMAs have to maintain a common IPv6 prefix (which is shorter than 64bits). Then the LMA which received the Interest packet will response with a Data packet to acknowledge the location update. In the Data packet, the allocated Home Network Prefix (HNP) is contained.

(B) State Synchronization

For the multiple LMAs in the same LMA service set, they should function equally in a distributed manner. In this way, they have to synchronize the binding state if the new binding is established or the old binding is refreshed. We also use the NDN routing scheme herein because the name-based routing can support the multicast in nature. For example, when the LMA received the Interest from the MAG and established the binding state, it will send a new Interest packet out with the content name as

/ISP/LocalMobilityAnchor

In this Interest packet, the multicast routing requirement should be flagged. Then the router will send this message to all the possible LMA entities according to all the recorded FIB entries. In this Interest packet, the MN's HNP and the current serving MAG's address are also mandatory information. More sophisticated scheme such as the ChronoSync [9] can be well used here for the state synchronization.

(C) Packet Transmission

For the packet sent from MN to the CN, it can be directly transmitted to the CN with the HoA (configured by the HNP) and CN' address as the source and destination addresses, respectively. All the LMAs have to announce same IPv6 prefix containing the served HNP set to attract the packets to the related MN. In this way, the packet sent from CN to the MN will arrive at the nearest LMA due to the routing protocol of the bypassed routers. Then the LMA entity will check its binding update table to locate the entity of the related HNP. If there is positive match, the LMA will replace the destination address with the related MAG's address and attach the original destination address for example in the Type 2 routing header [1]. In this way, the packet can arrive at the MN finally. If there is no positive match, the LMA will send an Interest packet with the flagged multicast requirement, which contains the source address of the MN. Then the other LMA will recognize that this Interest is used to fetch the corresponded MAG's address. And then the first LMA who knows the MAG's address will response with a Data packet including the MAG's address. If the LMA cannot learn the MAG's address within a reasonable period, the packet will be discarded because it will conclude that the MN has not established the available binding.

2.5   Conclusions

This paper proposes the DMM architecture in all-IP mobile network with the NDN-based control plane. Accordingly, the name-based routing solution in NDN facilitates the DMM requirements to distribute the anchor point and optimize the packet transmission path in the mobile environments. As our future work, the performance of the proposed architecture will be studied and evaluated.

Acknowledgments. This paper was supported by the National Natural Science Foundation of China under Grant No. 61303242. The work of Yong-Jin Park was supported by the JSPS KAKENHI under Grant No. 26330119.

References

1. Perkins, C., Johnson, D., Arkko, J.: Mobility support in IPv6. IETF RFC 6275, July 2011
2. Kempf, J.: Goals for network-based localized mobility management (netlmm). IETF RFC 4831, April 2007
3. Gundavelli, S., Leung, K., Devarapalli, V., Chowdhury, K., Patil, B.: Proxy mobile IPv6. IETF RFC 5213, August 2008

4. Chan, H. (ed.): Requirements of distributed mobility management. IETF RFC 7333, August 2014
5. Ahlgren, B., Dannewitz, C., Imbrenda, C., Kutscher, D., Ohlman, B.: A Survey of information-centric networking (Draft). In: Proceedings of Dagstuhl Seminar, February 2011
6. Jacobson, V., et al.: Networking named content. In: Proceedings of ACM CoNEXT, Rome, Italy, December 2009
7. Giaretta, G., Kempf, J., Devarapalli, V.: Mobile IPv6 bootstrapping in split scenario. IETF RFC5026, October 2007
8. Korhonen, J., Devarapalli, V.: Local mobility anchor (LMA) discovery for proxy mobile IPv6. IETF RFC 6097, February 2011
9. Zhu, Z., Afanasyev, A.: Let's ChronoSync: decentralized dataset state synchronization in named data networking. In: Proceedings of IEEE ICNP, Göttingen, Germany, October 2013

Pulse-Coupled Oscillator Desynchronization (PCO-D) Based Resource Allocation for Multi-hop Networks

Ji-Young Jung and Jung-Ryun Lee[(✉)]

School of the Electrical Engineering, Chung-Ang University,
Seoul 156-756, Republic of Korea
{jiyoung, jrlee}@cau.ac.kr

Abstract. In recent years, because of the increasing number of network nodes and the rapidly changing network environment, several studies have attempted to extend biologically inspired algorithms to distributed resource-allocation schemes. In this paper, we present an algorithm representative of the class of bio-inspired resource allocation algorithm and propose a new distributed resource-allocation algorithm for fair sharing in multi-hop networks. Through simulation, we show that the proposed algorithm works well in a multi-hop network environment, with all nodes in the multi-hop network evenly sharing resources with their two-hop neighbors in a non-overlapping way.

Keywords: Bio-inspired · Multi-hop network · Pulse-coupled oscillator desynchronization · Distributed · Resource allocation

1 Introduction

In multi-hop network environments, nodes are needed to access the communication medium in a distributed way for stable, fair and efficient resource allocation. A number of studies have been conducted with the goal of applying biologically-inspired (bio-inspired) algorithms to a various resource allocation problems. Bio-inspired algorithms are modeled on the simple and distributed heuristic behavior of organisms on Earth without the aid of a central coordinator. Previous researches attempt at developing bio-inspired algorithms have shown that these algorithms have excellent characteristics such as convergence, scalability, adaptability, and stability [1]. A resource allocation algorithm based on bio-inspired algorithms can therefore be expected to be able to cope with multi-hop networks.

The PCO based desynchronization algorithm (PCO-D), that is proposed by Pagliari et al. in 2010 [2], is a representative of the class of bio-inspired resource allocation algorithms. PCO-D comprises elements that, when interconnected, pulse in sequential order, with constant intervals between each other; the interconnected oscillators are thus evenly spaced around a phase ring. Let us assume that, in a set of N nodes, each node pulses with period of T. Let $\phi_i(t) \in [0, 1]$ denote the phase of node i at time t, where phases 0 and 1 are identical and $0 \leq i \leq N - 1$. Upon reaching $\phi_i(t) = 1$, node i "pulses" to indicate the termination of its cycle to the other nodes. Upon pulsing, the

© ICST Institute for Computer Sciences, Social Informatics and Telecommunications Engineering 2017
J.-H. Lee and S. Pack (Eds.): QShine 2016, LNICST 199, pp. 492–495, 2017.
DOI: 10.1007/978-3-319-60717-7_50

node resets its phase to $\phi_i(t^+) = 0$. In the PCO-D, as show in Fig. 1(a), when node i pulses, node j whose phase is located within the range moves towards its desired phase position $1 - 1/N$ as follows:

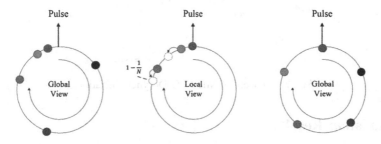

Fig. 1. Concept of PCO-Desynchronization.

$$\phi_j(t_i^+) = (1 - \alpha)\phi_j(t_i) + \alpha\left(1 - \frac{1}{N}\right)$$ (1)

where $\alpha \in [0, 1]$ is a scaling parameter that determines how much the phase of node j moves from its current value toward $1 - 1/N$.

All the nodes observe their neighbor's pulsing phases, and use this information to change their phase according to (1). Therefore, all the oscillators are evenly spaced around the phase ring, as shown in Fig. 1(b). Node i occupies the time division multiple access (TDMA) slots beginning at its pulsing phase, and ending at its next-phase neighbor j pulsing phase. In this way, all the nodes occupy non-overlapping time slots, covering T evenly.

2 Design of a Multi-hop Pulse-Coupled Oscillator Based Desynchronization (MH-PCO-D)

We propose the MH-PCO-D algorithm to allocate resources fairly between two-hop neighbors contending for medium access. Let N_2^j be the number of two-hop neighbors of node j. In the proposed MH-PCO-D, and as shown in Fig. 2, when node i pulses, node j, the node with the highest phase among its two-hop neighbor nodes, moves toward its desired phase position, as follows:

$$\phi_j(t_i^+) = (1 - \alpha)\phi_j(t_i) + \alpha\left(1 - \frac{1}{N_2^j}\right)$$ (2)

where $\alpha \in [0, 1]$ is a scaling parameter that determines how much the phase of node j moves from its current value toward $1 - 1/N_2^j$.

Node j occupies the TDMA slots beginning at the pulsing phase of its previous-phase neighbor i, and ending at its own pulsing phase.

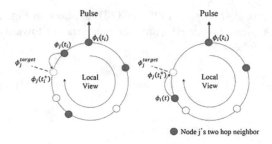

Fig. 2. Concept of MH-PCO-Desynchronization.

3   Simulation Results

To evaluate the performance of the proposed MH-PCO-D algorithm in multi-hop networks, a linear topology is used, as shown in Fig. 3. The period T is set to 1, and the scale parameter α is set to 0.5. We assume that all nodes observe their two-hop neighbor's pulsing phase, and use this information to change its phase forwards or backwards, according to (2).

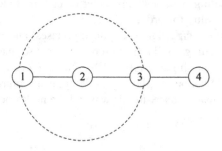

Fig. 3. A linear topology

Simulation results show that in this multi-hop environment there are two different desynchronized configurations, reachable from the various initial pulsing phase configurations, as shown in Fig. 4(a), (b). We define "node pair" as being a set of two nodes separated by more than two hops. In a multi-hop environment, two nodes forming a node pair (e.g., (1, 4) in our case) are not affected by the pulsing phases of each other. Thus, if the initial pulsing phases of two nodes are adjacent, the two pulsing phases will be coupled as in an oscillator, as shown in Fig. 4(b).

Figure 4(a) and (b) shows the pulsing phase of each node as the round progresses, when no node pair (a node pair) exist. Because the amount of requested resources exceeds (no exceeds) the amount of resources occupied by the nodes, when node i pulses, the phase of node j moves away from (toward to) the phase of node i according to (3), for all nodes i and j. As a result, the pulsing phase of each node does not converge. All the nodes will therefore occupy non-overlapping time slots that cover T, but not evenly at every round.

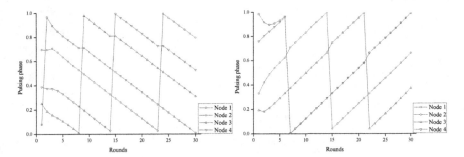

Fig. 4. Two desynchronization configurations

4 Conclusions

In this paper, we proposed the MH-PCO-D algorithm capable of solving the allocation problem in multi-hop networks, without collisions. Through simulation, we confirmed that, with this algorithm, all the nodes in a linear topology will occupy non-overlapping TDMA slots, even though not evenly. The results of our study will contribute to motivate research on distributed fair resource allocation algorithm in multi-hop network environments.

References

1. Mahale, R.A., Chavan, S.D.: A survey: evolutionary and swarm based bio-inspired optimization algorithms. Int. J. Sci. Res. Publ. 2(12), 1–6 (2012)
2. Pagliari, R., Hong, Y.W.P., Scaglione, A.: Bio-inspired algorithms for decentralized round-robin and proportional fair scheduling. IEEE J. Sel. Areas Commun. 28, 564–575 (2010)

Author Index

Printed in the United States
by Bookmasters

Printed in the United States
By Bookmasters